THE

WISDEN

COLLECTOR'S GUIDE

THE *WISDEN* WOODCUT

'Robert Henry Harling, who died on July 1, 2008, aged 98, was the typographer responsible for the redesign of *Wisden* to mark the 75th edition in 1938. It was Harling who suggested to the then publishers, Whitaker's that they should commission the artist Eric Ravilious, who he knew loved cricket, to produce something appropriate. The engraving that resulted adorns the almanack's cover to this day. Harling wrote fifty years later that it "remains an ideal graphic introduction to one of England's most durable publications." He himself complemented the engraving by setting the word WISDEN in Playbill, a chunky, heavily serified typeface he had designed the same year, redolent of Victorian theatre and the Wild West. This also endures.

He had no other known connection with cricket – his sports journalist son Nicholas recalls only one family visit to a Test – but he packed almost everything else into his life. He edited *House and Garden* magazine for 36 years, until he was well into his eighties, was typographical consultant and architectural correspondent for the *Sunday Times*, wrote several well-regarded novels set in and around Fleet Street, including *The Paper Palace*, took part in the Dunkirk evacuations, became a close friend of Ian Fleming, and, in the words of a former employee, had an encyclopaedic knowledge of the sex lives of dowager duchesses.'

Obituary – *Wisden* **2009**

'Ravilious, Eric William, was presumed dead after a Coastal command plane in which he was travelling [he was an official war artist] disappeared on a flight from Iceland in September 1942. He was 39, and famous as a water-colour landscape artist and wood-engraver. Amongst his work is the colophon that has appeared on the front cover of *Wisden* since 1938.'

Supplementary Obituary (51 years late) – *Wisden* **1994**

THE
WISDEN
COLLECTOR'S GUIDE

JONATHAN RICE

AND

ANDREW RENSHAW

FOREWORD

BY

SIR TIM RICE

Published in the UK in 2011 by
John Wisden & Co
An imprint of Bloomsbury Publishing Plc
36 Soho Square, London W1D 3QY
www.wisden.com
www.bloomsbury.com

ISBN 978 14081 2673 8

Permission to reproduce Sir Tim Rice's 2008 article
'What a catch: how wise I was to buy those *Wisdens*' by kind permission of the *Daily Telegraph*
Cover photograph © John Wisden & Co
Inside photographs © John Wisden & Co except on page 281 © Getty Images
Commissioned by Charlotte Atyeo
Designed by Peter Ward

Typeset in 9¼ on 10 Minion by Saxon Graphics Ltd, Derby
Printed and bound in the UK by Martins the Printers

CONTENTS

AUTHORS' NOTE

VII

FOREWORD BY SIR TIM RICE

IX

PART ONE

THE HISTORY OF THE ALMANACK

1

PART TWO

THE ALMANACKS 1864–2010

9

WISDEN CRICKETERS' ALMANACK AUSTRALIA

302

PART THREE

A GUIDE FOR COLLECTORS

311

COLLECTING WISDEN	312	MIND THE LANGUAGE	329
BUYING WISDEN	312	A HISTORY OF WISDEN	331
BOOK DEALERS	313	PUBLISHERS	331
AUCTIONS	316	OWNERS SINCE 1985	331
REPRINTS	317	COMPILERS AND EDITORS	331
DUST JACKETS	319	PRINTERS	332
PHOTOGRAPHIC PLATES	322	PRINT RUNS	333
INSERTS IN WISDEN	322	COVER PRICES	334
REBINDS	323	ILLUSTRATIONS	336
RESTORING WISDEN	324	SECOND EDITIONS	336
SIGNED COPIES	327	STYLE OF FRONT COVER OF	
MY UNCLE'S WISDENS	328	LIMP EDITIONS	337

STYLE OF LETTERING ON SPINE
OF LIMP EDITIONS 337

STYLE OF BRASSES ON FRONT
COVER OF CLOTH BOARD
EDITIONS 338

STYLE OF BRASSES ON SPINE
OF CLOTH BOARD EDITIONS 338

COVER DESIGNS 339

COLOUR OF LIMP COVERS 339

COLOURING OF LIMP COVER
AND DUST JACKET SPINE
TEXT FROM 1965–78 340

COLOURING OF DUST JACKET
COVERS FROM 1965–78 340

LEATHERBOUND LIMITED
EDITIONS 341

LARGE FORMAT EDITIONS 341

FACSIMILE EDITIONS 341

WISDEN ANTHOLOGIES 341

WISDEN INDEXES 342

WISDEN AUSTRALIA 342

WISDEN INDIA 342

WISDEN RUGBY FOOTBALL
ALMANACKS 343

CONDITION TIMELINE 343

PRICES/AUCTION TIMELINE 348

PAGINATION GUIDE 351

PRICES 355

AUTHORS' NOTE

Cricket followers have always had a strong streak of collector-mania running through them. We have to know everything about the game and its heroes, and ideally to possess memorabilia which remind us of our noble game. It may be wrong to describe these desires as an obsession, but there is certainly an element of the all-consuming passion about it. And cricket, with its rich and varied literature, provides its fans with plenty of affordable, and some not so affordable, items for the collection.

No sport has as vast a literature as cricket, and the centrepiece of any collector's cricket library is *Wisden Cricketers' Almanack*. From the very beginning, *Wisden* gained for itself a reputation for fine writing, impartiality and accuracy that enabled it to see off its early rivals and establish itself as the one true authority on cricket all over the world. It is not for nothing that the fat book in the yellow covers is known as 'The Cricketers' Bible', a nickname that dates back the best part of a century. After only seven editions, in 1870, *Wisden* listed the special features that could be found in the earlier numbers, an indication that the Almanack was already highly collectable.

This guide has been produced to help cricket fans build their own collection of *Wisdens*, not only by giving details of every *Wisden* so far published, but also by giving tips on how to find, buy, restore and protect *Wisdens*, so that they build into a collection that will not only be read and re-read, but will also be likely to appreciate in value rather more quickly than most other investments. This is not an index to *Wisden*, nor a price guide, but it is a dip into the treasures that *Wisden* contains, to whet the appetite for all those who have not yet completed their collection, and to refresh the palate of those fortunate enough to possess a set, but who may not yet have found the time to read all their volumes.

One of the joys of *Wisden* is the single-mindedness of the editors through the years. For them all, it is cricket first, the rest of life second. After the first few editions, which included such unlikely items as the rules of knur and spell and the winners of classic horse races, as the Almanack found its feet, it is only during the war years that they allow some aspects of what was going on around them to impinge on their world. Even then it is only to record the actions of the cricketers involved in battle, or to apologise for late publication because a German bomber scored a direct hit on the Wisden works.

As an example of this clear focus only on what happens on the cricket field, we quote from *Wisden* 1935, Essex v Worcestershire at Chelmsford: "On Whit-Monday morning, Nichol, the Worcestershire batsman, was found dead in bed – a sad event that marred the enjoyment of the match but did not prevent Worcestershire gaining first innings lead." This single-minded focus on the important issues is what distinguishes the successful collector as much as the successful editor or cricketer. We have deviated a little from this custom by listing some of the events going on beyond the cricket field: it is strange to think, from a distance of 140 years, that a few weeks after W.G. Grace became the first man to score 2,000 runs in a season, Stanley found David Livingstone at Ujiji; or that Bonnie and Clyde met their deaths, rather more gorily, two days after the Worcestershire scorecard recorded: 'M. Nichol (died during match)'.

In the preparation of this book, we have had a great deal of help from a number of people. In alphabetical order, we would like to thank Derek Barnard, Bill Furmedge (whose original idea this was), David Jenkins, Mark Jukes, John McKenzie, David Rayvern Allen, Sir Tim Rice, Chris Ridler, Dominic Roberts and Christopher Saunders, not forgetting Adam Chadwick, Curator of the M.C.C. and his Library team. At our publishers, Bloomsbury, we have been nudged and guided with great expertise by Christopher Lane, Jill Coleman, Charlotte Atyeo and Becky Senior, whose help we gratefully acknowledge. However, any mistakes must remain our responsibility.

Jonathan Rice and Andrew Renshaw
April 2011

FOREWORD
BY
SIR TIM RICE

Over the decades I have sunk money into a variety of schemes and objects, few of which have proved the financial bonanza I had hoped, or been told, they would be, but in 1973 I made a very untypical sound investment. I purchased a set of books for £750.

The books in question were *Wisden Cricketers' Almanacks* – a complete run from the first edition in 1864 through to the 110th. Since then I have added a further 38 editions to my shelves and eagerly await the arrival of each new version of the yellow-sheathed masterpiece every April. It is impossible to say how much a full set of original *Wisdens* would fetch today but I have noted with quiet satisfaction that, in May 2007, a run from 1864 to 1999 sold for £120,000 (plus commission). Around the same time an 1896 edition (the 23rd in the series) made £9,400 on its own. Even taking into account some years of manic inflation since the purchase, I suspect the most voracious hedge-fund manager would be quite relaxed about my investment.

However, my *Wisdens* are the one feature of my library, indeed of my entire house, that I would not part with until every other money-raising avenue had been fully exploited. I would rather flog the dog or dispose of my Peter Blake portrait of the Everly Brothers. Ever since I first leafed through a *Wisden* belonging to Michael Dunning (a fellow nine-year-old inmate of the fifth form) in the extremely damp summer of 1954, I have been hooked on this peerless publication.

What a book! It told the tale of England winning the Ashes with even more insight than Patrick Pringle's *The Boys' Book of Cricket*. It had page after page of statistics and records; it contained stories of cricket in places I had never heard of, from Amritsar to Ashby-de-la-Zouch; it was as majestic to hold as a Bible and exuded the same authority. It taught me history, geography and mathematics. Even the advertisements were riveting. It smelt good. It had a photograph of England's triumphant skipper waving to the crowd while enjoying a post-victory climactic fag.

Not every *Wisden* since has meant quite so much to me as the 1954 tome but, as I explore the sequence both forward and backward in time, I quickly see that this is no ordinary sporting annual – indeed, no ordinary publication by any literary standards. I gaze at my rows of *Wisdens* and know that, whichever season I choose to revisit, I shall soon be reminded not merely of the cricket of the time, but of the time itself. Nothing has yet prevented *Wisden's* springtime unveiling; not war, not the General Strike, not even Health and Safety (but they're working on it).

My two runners-up to 1954 are probably the 1916 and 2006 editions. The 1916 volume, with no first-class cricket to report, is a rare and valuable one because of wartime paper shortages, and because it includes obituaries of W.G. Grace and Victor Trumper alongside a list of tributes to cricketers killed in the Great War. The 2006 *Wisden* recalls the Ashes battle of 2005 in a myriad gripping ways. Enough said.

Wisden has not always moved immediately with the times, but it has absorbed and reflected the changes in cricket over the years, whether gradual or frantic. As book publishing embraces the digital world, *Wisden* is now available as a fully searchable e-book for purchase from its website. However, online versions, crucial though they will be to shelfless cricket-lovers, don't sound like such a good investment as the one I made back in 1973. I think I'll stick to the traditional format of pages bound together within covers, the whole shebang wrapped by the unmistakeable golden sleeve.

This foreword is adapted from an article originally published in the Daily Telegraph.

PART ONE

THE HISTORY
OF THE *ALMANACK*

John Wisden. This portrait of him at 26, taken from the lithograph by John Corbet Anderson,
appeared in the 1913 Jubilee edition of the Almanack which he founded in 1864.

John Wisden's cricketing career was summed up in the 1913 edition of his *Almanack* thus:

Born September 5, 1826; Died April 5, 1884.

Wisden played his first match for Sussex, against Kent at Brighton, in July, 1845, and his last, against the M.C.C. and Ground at Brighton, in August, 1863. After 1863 he did not take part in first-class cricket. He made his first appearance at Lord's in 1846. His first Gentlemen v. Players' match was in 1848, and his last in 1859. He and James Dean founded in 1852 the United All-England Eleven, whose famous matches with the All-England Eleven began in 1857. In conjunction with George Parr, Wisden took an England Eleven to Canada and the United States in 1859 – two years before the first England team, with H. H. Stephenson as captain, went to Australia.

John Wisden, at 5ft 4in and weighing in at seven stone, had hardly the build for a fast bowler, and yet he was one of the very best of his era. Quite probably 'fast' in early Victorian times was the equivalent of an Underwood or a Kumble of more recent years, but Wisden was nevertheless a much feared bowler. He took all ten South wickets when playing for North at Lord's in 1850, and was as famous as a sportsman could be in that era. Sir Spencer Ponsonby-Fane, writing in that same 1913 edition, considered that 'Jack' Wisden:

… was a very fine and accurate bowler, perfect length, but with little work, except what the ground gave it. He was a fast medium, but I think he was classed as a fast bowler – and played on that side in the match, Fast v. Slow. He was a delightful bowler to play against, but required very careful watching, for he was apt to send in occasionally a very fast shooter, then so fatal on Lord's Ground.

He noted that Wisden also liked to distinguish himself from his playing contemporaries – 'I believe he was the first of the players to play in a straw hat, instead of the white topper worn by the older players. He was a good field, and an excellent bat, which was rather exceptional for a bowler at that time, when bowlers were not expected to be very able performers with the bat.' He was also 'a genial, pleasant, and respectable fellow in every way, liked and respected by every one with whom he came in contact,' although in Wisden's own *Almanack* they would say that, wouldn't they, even thirty years after his death.

Wisden's great memorial is not his place in the record books (though that is indelible) but in the *Almanack* that bears his name. In 1864, a 116-page volume was published in London, and was put on sale for a shilling. *John Wisden's Cricketer's Almanack* (note the position of the apostrophe then; it changed to *Cricketers'* in 1869) was hardly big enough to qualify as a book, but it proved to be the first edition of an annual publishing and sporting phenomenon that has lasted for a century and a half.

Wisden was not an original thinker, but he was commercially very astute and, just as importantly, a lucky man. The idea of a cricketer's almanack was not a new one – his former business and cricketing partner Fred Lillywhite had been involved in the publication of *The Young Cricketer's Guide* since 1849 – but John Wisden was not bothered about whether the idea was his own – the only question was, would it work? Lillywhite Brothers & Co. used their *Guide* as much as a promotional tool for their own business –

'dealers in foreign cigars, tobacco etc. (unrivalled shag, highly recommended at 6s. 6d.) and sports equipment' – as a commercial venture in its own right, and no doubt Wisden thought he could do the same. An injury had decided him to retire from professional cricket at the end of the 1863 season, so he had more time to concentrate on his own burgeoning business, which had grown from an early partnership with George Parr in the ownership of a sports ground in Leamington into a tobacconist's and sports equipment store in Leicester Square (close to where Lillywhites is today, still a sports equipment store but long since divorced from the influence of tobacco). One of the results of his extra spare time was *Wisden's Cricketer's Almanack*.

In 1864, the world was in a state of change. Perhaps it always is, but the 1860s were a particularly turbulent decade. America was in the throes of its Civil War, Japan was emerging from its cocoon of two and a half centuries of isolation in a particularly violent way, Brazil was fighting Paraguay and the British Empire was defending itself aggressively across two continents. Cricket in England was changing too. Wisden had been an integral part of the revolution that transformed cricket from an amateur and bucolic pastime to a town-based professional entertainment, but, as the All-England teams crumbled in an overdose of internal strife, the county clubs were just beginning to establish themselves. Cricket was about to become a truly national sport, mixing professional and amateur players in the same team, appealing to all strata of English society, and it was Wisden's good luck that he chose this moment to launch his *Almanack*.

An even greater stroke of luck, for him and for all those connected with cricket, was the emergence in the mid-1860s of the man many still consider the greatest cricketer who ever lived – W.G. Grace. Grace, born in 1848, played his first major matches in 1864, and went on to dominate English – and indeed the world's – cricket until the turn of the century. He transformed batting, he was tireless in his bowling. In his youth he was a magnificent fielder, especially at point, and even in his late middle age he was a shrewd and ruthless captain. Above all, he was news. The general public wanted to read about him and about his cricket. *Wisden's Cricketers' Almanack* was there to fulfil that need.

Of course, it would take a very good publication to keep its readers interested over a century and a half. *Wisden* launched with the cautious statement from its editors (W.H. Crockford and W.H. Knight – the shrewd Jack Wisden did not interfere with detailed editorial matters) that:

> We have taken great pains to collect a certain amount of information, which we trust will prove interesting to all those that take pleasure in this glorious pastime. Should the present work meet with but moderate success, it is intended next year to present our readers with a variety of other matches, which the confined nature of an Almanack precludes us from doing this year.

This first edition had a great deal of non-cricketing material in it, details of the Wars of the Roses and 'the winners of the Derby, Oaks and St. Leger; Rules of Bowls, Quoits, and Knur and Spell, and other interesting information.' We are even informed that tea 'was introduced into England by Lords Arlington and Ossory in 1666. It was not till nearly a century later that the middle classes of London and Edinburgh began to use tea daily.' The editor of the *Almanack* a century and a half later would kill for the space to meander down such interesting byways. We must assume that the editors were hedging their bets: they just did not know if a book entirely devoted to cricket would work, but a book about cricket and knur and spell and the art of taking tea daintily, on the other hand ...

Despite competition from Fred Lillywhite's publication (which lasted from 1849 to 1866) and from 1865, from John Lillywhite's *Cricketers' Companion*, the first few editions did meet with more than the moderate success wished for. In 1865, *Wisden* was confident enough to increase the size from 116 pages to 164 pages, an increase of over 40 per cent in extent, and all for the same price. In 1866, the *Almanack* was 200 pages long. This was worth a shilling of anybody's money. However, the rarity of copies of the first few editions seems to imply that print runs, and therefore sales, were not massive.

As the seasons passed, *Wisden* slowly increased its sales and began to establish its position as the pre-eminent cricket publication, but it was by no means a smooth ride. James Lillywhite began publication in 1872 of his *Cricketers' Annual*, so that between 1872 and 1885 (when John Lillywhite's annual ceased publication) there were three annuals for the cricketing public to choose from.

Wisden's editorial team set about creating a structure of regular features which became familiar to readers over the years, and gave a sense of authority and reliability to the publication. It also helped to set it apart from the competition. Some of the features of the *Almanack* which we know and trust today, however, had a very long gestation period. 'Births And Deaths Of Cricketers' appeared in the 1867 edition for the first time, but full obituaries, now one of the most widely read sections of *Wisden*, did not make an appearance until 1892, the second edition under the editorship of Sydney Pardon.

The original policy was not to comment at all on the matches, but merely to record the scores, on the basis that the editors preferred 'leaving the cricketer to form his own opinion with regard to the merits of the men, since a great many of our readers are at least equal, if not superior, to ourselves in arriving at a right judgment of the play.' Perhaps Wisden was wary of upsetting his former team-mates, for in recording the scores of the great professional Elevens, the editors 'abstained from making any remarks concerning the individual play of any man, since, where all are so good, it would, perhaps, be invidious to single out any one as being superior to those with whom he has so often played with varied success.' Wisden, remembered by contemporaries for his 'unfailing good temper' and his 'genial disposition' was clearly not a man to court controversy by suggesting in a publication that bore his name that one player was not as good as another. Today's editor is fortunately made of sterner stuff: he would have a very thin tome to present to the world if comment was excluded.

By 1870, the *Almanack* was sufficiently sure of itself to change the strict 'No Comment' policy. For the first time, match reports as well as match scores were included. This meant that *Wisden* was 28 pages fatter than the year before, though still only 152 pages, but the comment was mild and uncontroversial: the Varsity match report, for instance, mentioned that 'Mr. Pauncefote stayed whilst 6 wickets went. This gentleman played an innings of 33 runs so correctly and well as to elicit the commendations of all good judges on the ground.'

For the rest of the Victorian age (with the notable exception of 1886, when *Wisden* appeared very late in the year, because of the 'indisposition' of the then editor George West), *Wisden* expanded its sales steadily. In 1880, the Cricket Reporting Agency was founded, and from then on, for 85 years until 1965, when it merged with the Press Association, the editor of *Wisden* was a senior member of the CRA team. Under the leadership of Charles Pardon and his brother Sydney, from 1887 onwards, the *Almanack* began to take the shape we know today. They brought in some brilliant people to the team, like the statistician F. S. Ashley-Cooper, but the Pardon brothers, most especially Sydney, who edited the *Almanack* from 1891 to 1925, gave *Wisden* its voice.

In 1889, Charles Pardon had the inspired idea of selecting 'Six Great Bowlers Of The Year', and so popular was this article that he reprised his idea in 1890 with 'Nine Great Batsmen Of The Year' and, in 1891, his brother continued the theme with 'Five Great Wicket-Keepers'. The Wicket-Keepers were only five in number, probably because there just were not any more than five Great Wicket-Keepers to write about, but this number seemed to work. Also, because three distinct groups of players had been featured in the first three articles, there had been nobody who might have been selected twice, and when, in 1892, the subject was 'Five Great Bowlers', Pardon chose five different names from three years previously. A precedent was set. It was not until 1898 that the phrase 'Five Cricketers Of The Year' was first used, but since that time the choice of the selected five, a personal choice of the editor which he does not delegate, has been a major talking point each year. We can usually pick four of the five before they are announced, but there always seems to be an editorial wild card – think of Phil Bainbridge in 1986, Nigel Briers in 1993 or Claire Taylor in 2009 among recent examples. And how could Wes Hall, Jacques Kallis and Jeff Thomson have missed out?

By 2010 there were over 200 pages of comment and reviews, which are the heart of what makes each year's *Wisden* unique, but it was not until 1901 that Sydney Pardon introduced 'Some Notes By The Editor.' In his very first Notes, he launched into a tirade (a polite tirade, but a tirade nevertheless) against the scourge of throwing, and from this moment *Wisden* began to take sides on the major issues of the day. He particularly deplored Arthur Mold's action (despite having chosen him as one of 'Five Great Bowlers' in 1892), and eventually had the satisfaction of seeing the Laws changed to clarify the position on unfair bowling, the first major campaign that the *Almanack* had been involved in, and thus ended up on the winning side.

For the first century or so of its existence, *Wisden's* views tended to be on the side of the cricket establishment. On the issue of payments for amateurs, a big talking point from the Golden Age at the turn of the century and onwards, *Wisden* generally deplored the idea of gentlemen taking payment for playing, and thereby perhaps keeping a professional cricketer out of the side. However, the editors were more than happy to turn a blind eye to W.G. Grace, who, they admitted, was a law unto himself.

The Great War presented a new set of problems for *Wisden*, those of scarcity and rationing. However, throughout the war years, there was a determination to keep cricket, and cricket reporting, going. Even as the toll of lives on the battlefields became ever more appalling, articles about schools cricket and, most significantly, how to bring back first-class cricket as soon as possible after the war, dominated the pages that were not devoted to Deaths in the War. The 1916 edition is only 299 pages long, but it is now perhaps the most sought after of all, because it features the obituaries of two of the great cricketers – W.G. Grace and Victor Trumper – not to mention A.E. Stoddart and Sir Spencer Ponsonby-Fane among other cricketing names who died outside the war. From the battlefield, that year's *Wisden* also includes the obituary of one of the more surprising schoolboy cricketers: Rupert Brooke, the poet.

The enthusiasm of Sydney Pardon, as well as his editorial flair, meant that *Wisden* held a fine reputation when the war finally ended, and he made sure that *Wisden* was there to ride the crest of the wave of popularity that cricket enjoyed in the early 1920s. Pardon remained strong in his likes and dislikes (he liked MCC and Lord Harris, but disliked 'unseemly barracking' and the two-day county cricket experiment of 1919, for example) and, by the time he died in November 1925, still in harness, *Wisden* was an integral part of the cricketing summer. Many collectors were already pushing up the prices of the first editions.

Bodyline presented a difficult case for *Wisden*. Stewart Caine, the editor of *Wisden* at the time, and a long-time associate of the Pardon brothers, died in April 1933, as the England cricketers were making their way home from Australia, and, although he added a few lines to his notes for the 1933 edition, they were written largely on the basis of newspaper reports from Australia. His view was that 'the ball to which such strong exception is being taken in Australia is … dropped short and is alleged in certain quarters to be aimed at the batsman rather than at the wicket. It may at once he said that, if the intention is to hit the batsman and so demoralise him, the practice is altogether wrong – calculated, as it must be, to introduce an element of pronounced danger and altogether against the spirit of the game of cricket. Upon this point practically everybody will agree. No one wants such an element introduced. That English bowlers, to dispose of their opponents, would of themselves pursue such methods or that Jardine would acquiesce in such a course is inconceivable.' To him it seemed that the Australians must be either exaggerating or misunderstanding the issue.

His successor, Sydney Southerton, was presented with the biggest hot potato to affect cricket in a generation. A tour review carrying his initials seemed to take the line of least resistance, perhaps hoping that he would not revive bitter memories. 'Suffice it to say here that a method of bowling was evolved – mainly with the idea of curbing the scoring propensities of Bradman – which met with almost general condemnation among Australian cricketers and spectators and which, when something of the real truth was ultimately known in this country, caused people at home – many of them famous in the game – to wonder if the winning of the rubber was, after all, worth this strife.' He later wrote a more prominent article on the subject in which he appears to take it more seriously, admitting he was wrong in his initial suppositions.

In 1937, *Wisden* ceased to be an independent publisher in its own right, and ownership of the *Almanack* passed to J. Whitaker and Sons, who already published *Whitaker's Almanack*, the biggest-selling general annual compendium, which still contained many of the hallmarks of a true almanac that *Wisden* had long since lost. Wilfrid Brookes continued as editor, but the influence of Whitaker's was quickly felt. In 1938, many changes to the layout were made: the woodcut made its first appearance on the cover, the counties were arranged in alphabetical order rather than in the order in which they had finished in the previous year's Championship, a full index was provided and more illustrations were included. Sales jumped by more than 50 per cent.

From 1944, *Wisden* was published by Sporting Handbooks Ltd, a joint venture between Whitaker's and John Wisden & Co., and it remained under this imprint for 35 editions. The same year the Wisden company had been acquired by the Co-Operative Wholesale Society, shortly after a German bomb hit the Wisden factory in Mortlake.

Hubert Preston was appointed editor as the new owners moved in, and his first offering was a mere 343 pages, less than half the size of the 1940 edition. Paper restrictions meant that only 7,000 copies could be printed. Preston, ably assisted by his son Norman, was not discouraged. When the war ended, English cricket enjoyed a few seasons of massive popularity, and *Wisden* celebrated the return of first-class cricket, rejoicing in the performances of great players such as Bedser, Compton, Edrich, Hutton, Bradman, Miller, Morris and many others. By 1949, with wartime printing restrictions eased, sales topped 30,000, around four times the annual sale in the mid-1930s.

When Norman Preston took over from his father in June 1951, post-war county cricket had settled comfortably back into something of a rut, but in many ways the 1950s saw *Wisden* in its pomp.

The cricket was not of the highest quality during much of that decade, with increasingly slow over-rates and dreary batting, but *Wisden's* take on the situation was shrewd, readable and rather more against dangerous bowling than it had been two decades earlier. The Editor sympathised, for example, with the West Indian batsmen who had been subjected to a barrage of bumpers in Australia in 1951-52. 'In its origin cricket was never meant to be played that way. No matter what the issue involved, the game is greater than the individuals. It is a sad thought that sometimes this truth is submerged in the quest for victory.' West Indies took their revenge in due course.

Preston also lamented the increasing slowness of play: 'Watching some modern batsmen at the wicket one gains the impression they are shouldering the burdens and troubles of the whole world. They certainly give little indication of enjoyment.'

By the end of the 1950s, Preston was appalled by much of what was happening on the cricket fields of the world: 'It would seem that the time is ripe for a complete overhaul of our ideas in regard to pitches, batsmanship and the general conduct of the game.' So *Wisden* tended to approve the changes that came into cricket in the 1960s – the ending of the distinction between amateurs and professionals, the beginnings of limited-overs cricket. It also reported on apartheid in sport and the isolation of South Africa, as well as the age-old problems such as the lbw law, throwing, time-wasting and the decline in sportsmanship, county finances and public interest in cricket, without necessarily proposing any solutions which were practical rather than theoretical.

When Norman Preston died in 1980 (like several of his predecessors still in harness), the editorship passed to John Woodcock, one of the great cricket reporters of his generation, and we can see a subtle change in the mindset of *Wisden*, from a leisured occupation of the moral high ground to a more pragmatic, though equally principled, view on the issues of the day. *Wisden* began to take sides: compare the somewhat equivocal views put forward by Norman Preston on the Packer affair with the forthright views of Graeme Wright on Shoaib Akhtar's bowling action or Jagmohan Dalmiya's administrative skills in the early 2000s. Woodcock brought more immediacy to the *Almanack*, and his successors, distinguished cricket journalists to a man, have followed his lead. Matthew Engel made some bold but successful decisions to reorganise the book, and Tim de Lisle shocked traditionalists by putting a photograph on the dust jacket, but somehow *Wisden* retains its traditional charm.

Wisden has grown massively as cricket has expanded around the world: where once there were three or four Test-playing countries meeting each other sporadically, and seventeen counties disputing one competition each summer, now there are ten Test-playing nations, three different formats of the game and eighteen counties fighting among themselves for three, four or sometimes more pieces of silverware. And *Wisden* has always reported cricket overseas, cricket at the universities, cricket in schools, club and league cricket and, since 1938, women's cricket. It now also finds room for book reviews, website reviews, ICC meetings, curious occurrences, cricket charities, the upcoming season's fixtures, cricket in the media, umpiring and, of course, the Laws. It is published in four different formats (leatherbound, clothbound and paperbound in standard size, and clothbound in large size; you can also have a traditional dust cover for an extra £3.00) and finds its way into every cricket library every year. It crashes into the bestselling charts every spring: it remains a publishing phenomenon.

The ownership of John Wisden & Co. – the sports goods manufacturer as well as the *Almanack* publisher – changed several times in the latter part of the twentieth century, but the *Almanack* maintained its shape, its popularity and its quality throughout. In 1961, the Co-Operative Wholesale Society allowed Wisden to merge with two other sports goods firms – Surridge and Ives, and Gray-Nicolls – to create a new independent firm, Tonbridge Sports Industries, which was bought in 1970 by Grays of Cambridge. In 1979, the publication of *Wisden* passed to Macdonald and Jane's, then a part of Robert Maxwell's empire. It did not take the *Wisden* editorial and production team long to realise that this was not the best place to be. By 1985, the John Wisden imprint was back on the spine of *Wisden* – this being owned in part by Grays and in part by the printers, McCorquodale. In 1993, J. Paul Getty, the American millionaire who had been introduced to cricket by Mick Jagger, bought *Wisden* and allowed it to continue to flourish, but after his death there was some uncertainty about the company's future, despite record sales being achieved by the 2006 edition in the wake of England's Ashes success in 2005. Then in 2008, John Wisden and Co. was bought by the Bloomsbury Publishing Group.

And so *Wisden* marches strongly on towards its sesquicentennial edition, with thousands of collectors in its thrall. Spring just isn't spring without that fat yellow book by the bedside.

PART TWO
THE ALMANACKS
FROM 1864 TO 2010

1864

WISDEN 1864

1st EDITION
EDITOR: W.H. Crockford and W.H. Knight
PAGES: 116
PRICE: Limp 1/-
REPRINT:
1. Billing & Sons 1960 (1864-78 in set, limp, 150 limit)
2. Lowe & Brydone 1974 (1864-78 in set, limp, 150 limit)
3. Wisden 1991 (1864-78 in boxed set, cloth, 1,000 limit)

THE WORLD AT LARGE

• Abraham Lincoln re-elected as President of the United States
• British warships bombard Shimonoseki, Japan
• General Ulysses S. Grant appointed commander of Union forces in USA
• General Sherman's troops march through Georgia 'from Atlanta to the sea'
• Opening of the Clifton Suspension Bridge
• The first fish and chip shop opens in London

CRICKET HEADLINES 1863

Yorkshire CCC formed

Second team to Australia 1863-64, under George Parr

First cricket club formed in Transvaal

TO THE READER

'In offering our first edition of the CRICKETER'S ALMANACK to the patrons of the "Noble Game", we have taken great pains to collect a certain amount of information, which we trust will prove interesting to all those that take pleasure in this glorious pastime. Should the present work meet with but moderate success, it is intended next year to present our readers with a variety of other matches, which the confined nature of an Almanack precludes us from doing this year. JOHN WISDEN & Co.'

FEATURE ARTICLES

'The Laws of Cricket, as revised by the Marylebone Club; the first appearance at Lord's and number of runs obtained by Many Cricketing Celebrities; Scores of 100 and upwards, from 1850 to 1863; Extraordinary Matches; All the Matches played between the Gentlemen and Players, and the All England and United Elevens, with full and accurate Scores taken from authentic sources; together with The Dates of the University Rowing Matches, the winners of the Derby, Oaks and St. Leger; Rules of Bowls, Quoits, and Knur and Spell, and other interesting information.'

MATCH REPORTS

The Gentlemen and Players
'We have taken great pains and been at considerable expense, in collection for the information of our readers, the matches which have been annually played between the Gentlemen and Players. We have begun with the first match, thinking it would prove an agreeable reading for our subscribers to see the doings of the past distinguished cricketers who in their day stood pre-eminent in the "Noble Game". We of course make no comments upon the matches, leaving the cricketer to form his own opinion with regards to the merits of the men, since a great many of our readers are at least equal, if not superior, to ourselves in arriving at a right judgment of the play.'

The Two Elevens
'We have great pleasure in presenting to our readers a full and correct account of all the matches that have been played between these distinguished Elevens. We can vouch for the

accuracy of the scores, since they have been taken from well-authenticated sources. With regard to these matches, we have abstained from making any remarks concerning the individual play of any man, since, where all are so good, it would, perhaps, be invidious to single out anyone as being superior to those with whom he has so often played with varied success.'

MISCELLANEOUS

'The graces of the modern tea-table were quite unknown to the country folk, although that favourite beverage, brought by the Dutch to Europe, was introduced into England by Lords Arlington and Ossory in 1666. It was not until nearly a century later that the middle classes of London and Edinburgh began to use tea daily. In the latter city, in the reigns of the Georges, tea was taken at four o'clock, and the meal was thence called "four hours".'

This first edition contains full scorecards of the Gentlemen v Players matches since 1806 and of the games between the All England and United England elevens from 1857. Under 'extraordinary matches' there is the scorecard of the game in 1855 between the 2ⁿᵈ Royal Surrey Militia and Shillinglee, Sussex, when the militia were dismissed for 0 in their first innings. From the outset, Wisden was both a book of record and also rejoiced in the off-beat and quirky.

1865

WISDEN 1865

2nd EDITION
EDITOR: W.H. Crockford and W.H. Knight
PAGES: 164
PRICE: Limp 1/-
REPRINT:
1. Billing & Sons 1960 (1864-78 in set, limp, 150 limit)
2. Lowe & Brydone 1974 (1864-78 in set, limp, 150 limit)
3. Wisden 1991 (1864-78 in boxed set, cloth, 1,000 limit)

THE WORLD AT LARGE

- American Civil War ends
- President Lincoln assassinated
- Salvation Army formed
- *Alice in Wonderland* published
- Matterhorn climbed for the first time
- Speed limit introduced in Britain: 2mph in towns and 4mph elsewhere

CRICKET HEADLINES 1864

W.G. Grace plays his first major game

Overarm bowling legalised

Middlesex CCC and Lancashire CCC formed

TO THE READER

'John Wisden and Co return their most sincere thanks to the Cricketing public for the support given by them to this little work. Induced by the flattering patronage of many of the most distinguished Cricketers of the day, they have ventured upon the publication of a second number, trusting that its contents will win for it the same generous support as for its predecessor.'

FEATURE ARTICLES

'Calendar of the Births and Deaths of nearly all the celebrated players who have appeared before the public; The Laws of Cricket, as revised by the Marylebone Club; all the matches played Between the Universities of Cambridge and Oxford since their commencement; the Matches played by the Marylebone Cricket Club, the counties of Buckinghamshire, Cambridgeshire, Hampshire, Kent, Middlesex, Nottinghamshire, Surrey, Sussex and Yorkshire in 1864; The Doings of the Twelve in Australia, and other interesting information.'

MATCH REPORTS

Oxford v Cambridge

'In our first number of the Cricketer's Almanack, these matches were ready for the press; but owing to the observations of one of our friends we did not publish them, though we were well aware that they would have been as interesting to the reader as those recorded. In this number we therefore submit them for the perusal of our friends, because we are quite certain that our work will be incomplete if these matches are not published together with those of the two Elevens and those of the Gentlemen and Players.'

Eton v Harrow

'On the 8th and 9th of July the Annual match between the Etonians and the Harrovians was played at Lord's. The company was far more numerous than on any previous occasion, there being about nine thousand spectators present … Two marquees stood in opposite ends of the ground, the one being appropriated to the supply of the more substantial necessities of life, while the other was well stored with strawberries, ices, and cooling beverages. Both were at times crowded with customers.'

The scores of the University matches from 1827 are given, and with the coverage of domestic cricket and the tour to Australia, Wisden is already getting into its stride. The publishers hope readers 'will find the Almanack, from its size, a readier reference and a more convenient companion than larger volumes of greater pretensions' – a shot across the bows of the competition in the form of John Lillywhite's Cricketers' Companion which made its debut this year.

1866

WISDEN 1866

3rd EDITION
EDITOR: W.H. Crockford and W.H. Knight
PAGES: 200
PRICE: Limp 1/-
REPRINT:
1. Billing & Sons 1960 (1864-78 in set, limp, 150 limit)
2. Lowe & Brydone 1974 (1864-78 in set, limp, 150 limit)
3. Wisden 1991 (1864-78 in boxed set, cloth, 1,000 limit)

THE WORLD AT LARGE

• Unsuccessful assassination attempts on Otto von Bismarck and Tsar Alexander II
• Austro-Prussian War (The Seven Weeks War)
• SS Great Eastern successfully lays transatlantic cable
• Alfred Nobel invents dynamite
• Beatrix Potter and H.G. Wells born

CRICKET HEADLINES 1865

Unofficial county champions: Nottinghamshire

Practice nets first used at Lord's

Worcestershire CCC formed

V.E. Walker, for Middlesex against Lancashire, and G. Wootton, of All England against Yorkshire, both take all ten wickets in an innings

FEATURE ARTICLES

'Calendar of the Births and Deaths of nearly all the celebrated players who have appeared before the public; The Laws of Cricket, as revised by the Marylebone Club; the Matches played by the Marylebone Cricket Club, the counties of Buckinghamshire, Cambridgeshire, Hampshire, Kent, Middlesex, Nottinghamshire, Surrey, Sussex and Yorkshire in 1865; also the matches played in 1865 by the All England, United All England, and United South Of England Elevens.'

TO THE READER

'JOHN WISDEN AND CO. have again to thank the Cricketing Public for the encouragement given to the Almanack, and they beg respectfully to offer the third number for the perusal of their friends, trusting that it will be received with as much favour as its predecessors.

J.W. and Co. have this year published the matches of the three All England Elevens, feeling certain, from the great favour with which these celebrated Elevens are received in all parts of the country, their doings will be read with interest.

J.W. and Co. have carefully avoided making any remarks upon the play or players, as the purport of this little work is to record the scores of the matches published as a book of reference.'

MISCELLANEOUS

From the Calendar section:
    March 1866
    10th Sat. Prince of Wales married 1863. James Street, of Surrey b. 1840
    11th Sun. 4th Sunday in Lent. Sir Rowland Hill retires from the General Post Office 1864
    12th Mon. Bartholomew Good, of Lincolnshire and Notts, d. 1848 *aetat.* 36
    13th Tues. Henry Sampson, of Yorkshire, b. 1813
    14th Wed. Fly fishing begins. Geo. Fremantle of Hants, b. 1806

1867

WISDEN 1867

4th EDITION
EDITOR: W.H. Crockford and W.H. Knight
PAGES: 164
PRICE: Limp 1/-
REPRINT:
1. Billing & Sons 1960 (1864-78 in set, limp, 150 limit)
2. Lowe & Brydone 1974 (1864-78 in set, limp, 150 limit)
3. Wisden 1991 (1864-78 in boxed set, cloth, 1,000 limit)

THE WORLD AT LARGE

• First volume of *Das Kapital* published
• Emperor Maximilian of Mexico executed by firing squad
• Queensberry Rules for boxing published
• Garibaldi's troops march on Rome
• Russia sells Alaska to United States for $7 million

CRICKET HEADLINES 1866

Unofficial county champions: Middlesex

Oxford win the University match by 12 runs

TO THE READER

'JOHN WISDEN & Co. very respectfully offer to the Cricketing Public their fourth number of the Almanack, and have again to thank their numerous friends for the kind support they have received during the past three years.

In consequence of the great increase in the number of matches played during the past season, J.W. & Co. have most reluctantly been compelled to limit the Eleven v. Twenty-two Matches to the Results only, though they are aware that many of their friends are very much interested in them; but, having added the Results of many other Clubs, they trust the Work, as a whole, will give general satisfaction.'

FEATURE ARTICLES

'Calendar of the Births and Deaths of nearly all the celebrated players who have appeared before the public; The Laws of Cricket, as revised by the Marylebone Club; the Matches played by the Marylebone Cricket Club, the counties of Buckinghamshire, Cambridgeshire, Essex, Hampshire, Kent, Lancashire, Middlesex, Nottinghamshire, Surrey, Sussex and Yorkshire in 1866; also the matches of the following clubs: All England, United All England, and United South Of England Elevens. Anomalies, Butterflies, Cambridge University, Civil Service, Free Foresters, Gravesend and Milton, Incogniti, I Zingari, Kennington Park, Longsight, Oxford University, Quidnuncs, Royal Artillery, Southgate and Upper Tooting.'

MATCH REPORTS

All England Eleven

'John Wisden and Co. would have gladly given the Scores of these twenty-two matches, knowing the interest that is taken in them; but in consequence of the great number played during the past season (in all 69), they are compelled to give the Results only. Had they given the scores in full, this little work would have been so increased in size as to render necessary an addition in price.'

MISCELLANEOUS

'The Scorers of 1000 (or more) runs in 1866.
W.G. Grace Esq: Runs Scored 2168; Matches played in 33; Innings played out 40; Times not out 7; Highest innings 224*

C.F. Buller Esq.: Runs Scored 1647; Matches played in 39; Innings played out 54; Times not out 6; Highest innings 196

Henry Jupp: Runs Scored 1605; Matches played in 40; Innings played out 68; Times not out 8; Highest innings 165'

Although from the first edition the Almanack carried a two-page 'List of Articles kept by J. Wisden and Co', the first full-page advertisement appears in this edition with a line drawing of the company's patent Catapulta (pictured), an early form of bowling machine. Despite the reduction in pagination from the previous year, coverage of club cricket is expanded, but at the expense of the scorecards of the three England Eleven matches – All England, United All England and United South of England, which played all around the country, often against opposition of up to 22 players.

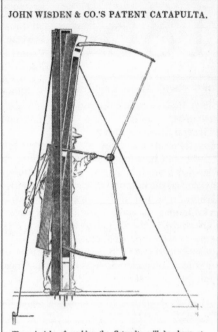

JOHN WISDEN & CO.'S PATENT CATAPULTA.

The principle of working the Catapulta will be shown at
2, New Coventry Street, Leicester Square, London, W.

1868

WISDEN 1868

5th EDITION
EDITOR: W.H. Crockford and W.H. Knight
PAGES: 116
PRICE: Limp 1/-
REPRINT:
1. Billing & Sons 1960 (1864-78 in set, limp, 150 limit)
2. Lowe & Brydone 1974 (1864-78 in set, limp, 150 limit)
3. Wisden 1991 (1864-78 in boxed set, cloth, 1,000 limit)

THE WORLD AT LARGE

• First Trades Union Congress held in Manchester
• General Ulysses S. Grant elected President of USA
• Last public hanging in Britain
• World's first traffic lights installed at the junction of Great George Street and Bridge Street in London
• Overthrow of the Shogunate and restoration of imperial authority under Emperor Meiji in Japan
• 33 die in Abergele rail disaster, Wales

CRICKET HEADLINES 1867

Culmination of a long period of rivalry and ill-feeling between professionals of North and South, and of the two 'All England' elevens: these two great matches abandoned this year

MCC sends a team to Paris

Sussex dismiss Kent (batting one man short) for 18 at Gravesend

TO THE READER

'In consequence of the great increase in the number of matches played during the past season, W. & M. have most reluctantly been again compelled to limit the Eleven v. Twenty-two Matches to the Results only, though they are aware that many of their friends are very much interested in them; but, having added the Results of some other Clubs, they trust the Work, as a whole, will give general satisfaction.'

FEATURE ARTICLES

'Calendar of the Births and Deaths of nearly all the celebrated players who have appeared before the public; The Laws of Cricket, as revised by the Marylebone Club; the Matches played by the Marylebone Cricket Club, the counties of Cambridgeshire, Kent, Lancashire, Middlesex, Norfolk, Nottinghamshire, Surrey, Sussex and Yorkshire in 1867; also the results of the following clubs: All England, United All England, and United South Of England Elevens. Cambridge University, Incogniti, Islington Albion, I Zingari, Oxford University and Southgate.'

MATCH REPORTS

[*Wisden continued its policy of not commenting on the matches, but merely giving the scores. One of the scorecards printed under 'Extra Matches' was a twelve-a-side match, 'One Leg vs. One Arm', played at Islington on April 22 and 23. The match was left drawn with One Arm needing 20 more runs to win, with two wickets in hand.*]

The Almanack is, just for this year, 'published and sold by Wisden and Maynard' – hence the reference to W. & M. in 'To the Reader'. Unfortunately, the calendar pages for April, May and August show the year as 1867, the compositor having forgotten to update the standing type from the 1867 Almanack. The 1991 reprint by John Wisden & Co contains a printer's erratum slip explaining: 'No, there is not an error in this facsimile reprint of the Almanack; the error was made when the Almanack was originally printed in 1868 … We did check with the Library at Lord's that their copy also showed the incorrect years. In the circumstances, as this facsimile is published as an exact copy of the original Almanack, we have not corrected the errors contained in the original.'

1869

6th EDITION
EDITOR: W.H. Crockford and W.H. Knight
PAGES: 124
PRICE: Limp 1/-
REPRINT:
1. Billing & Sons 1960 (1864-78 in set, limp, 150 limit)
2. Lowe & Brydone 1974 (1864-78 in set, limp, 150 limit)
3. Wisden 1991 (1864-78 in boxed set, cloth, 1,000 limit)

THE WORLD AT LARGE

• American Transcontinental Railroad completed in Promontory, Utah
• First Sainsbury's store opens in Drury Lane, London
• Suez Canal opens
• End of transportation to Australia as a sentence for British criminals

CRICKET HEADLINES 1868

Unofficial county champions: Nottinghamshire

Australian aborigine team visits England

W.G. Grace scores a century in each innings for South of the Thames vs. North of the Thames at Canterbury, the first time this feat has been achieved since 1817

E.F.S. Tylecote scores 404* for Classical v Modern at Clifton College

TO THE READER

'WISDEN AND Co. very respectfully offer to the Cricketing Public their sixth edition of the Almanack, and have again to thank their numerous friends for the kind support they have received during the past five years. In consequence of the great increase in the number of matches played during the past season, W. & Co. have most reluctantly been again compelled to limit the Eleven v. Twenty-two Matches to the Results only, though they are aware that many of their friends are very much interested in them; but, having added the Results of some other Clubs, they trust the Work, as a whole, will give general satisfaction."

FEATURE ARTICLES

'Calendar of the Births and Deaths of nearly all the celebrated players who have appeared before the public; The Laws of Cricket, as revised by the Marylebone Club; the Matches played by the Marylebone Cricket Club, the counties of Cambridgeshire, Kent, Lancashire, Middlesex, Norfolk, Nottinghamshire, Surrey, Sussex and Yorkshire in 1868; also the results of the following clubs: Marylebone, I Zingari, Incogniti, Australian Aboriginals, All England, United All England, and United South Of England Elevens.'

Individual Innings of 200 or More Runs, by W.H. Knight

"'404 runs by one man!'" "Of course that is the largest innings yet hit?" – and "Pray, whose is the second highest innings?" – and "Third highest?" – and "Next?" and "Next?" Such – when Mr. Tylecote's great innings became generally known last season – were the oft repeated enquiries respecting the great scores made of those who are supposed to be well posted in these matters …

So when last year's hot, heavy and enormous run-getting season had become part and parcel of cricket history, I thought the said history would be a trifle more complete if these innings of 200 runs were gathered together and published in a form handy for reference. I have collected them, and trust the accompanying list of such innings, with the few "Notes by the way" that precede them, will be found interesting to the readers of "The Cricketer's Almanack".'

Knight's 'Notes by the way', which cover three pages, is the first article to appear in Wisden. *The Almanack reverts after one year to being 'published and sold by Wisden and Co'.*

17

1870

WISDEN 1870

7th EDITION
EDITOR: W.H. Knight
PAGES: 152
PRICE: Limp 1/-
REPRINT:
1. Billing & Sons 1960 (1864-78 in set, limp, 150 limit)
2. Lowe & Brydone 1974 (1864-78 in set, limp, 150 limit)
3. Wisden 1991 (1864-78 in boxed set, cloth, 1,000 limit)

THE WORLD AT LARGE

• First international football match between England and Scotland
• Franco-Prussian War. Emperor Napoleon III deposed
• Siege of Paris begins
• Unification of Italy completed: Rome becomes the capital of the new country
• Death of Charles Dickens

CRICKET HEADLINES 1869

Unofficial county champions: Nottinghamshire and Yorkshire

Emmett (T.), of Yorkshire, takes 16 wickets for 38 runs in the match against Cambridgeshire

W.G. Grace scores nine centuries and G.F. Grace five during the summer

TO THE READER

'In this, the Seventh Edition of the Almanack, an endeavour has been made to render the little Annual more complete as a work of reference on the past season's cricket. Hitherto the Batsman has monopolised all attention by the batting scores only finding a place in the book. This year, the Compiler has tried to do justice to the Bowler, by recording, wherever they were attainable, the bowling summaries to each match, thus bringing "The Ball and The Bowler" into equality with "The Bat and The Batsman" and thereby more equitably telling "The Story of Cricket" in 1869.'

FEATURE ARTICLES

For the first time, Wisden features comments on the playing skills of the cricketers whose feats it recorded.
The Marylebone Club was given three pages of prose before the scorecards
Reports of all matches were included
Articles on each of the counties whose matches are recorded (**Surrey, Nottinghamshire, Kent, Yorkshire, Sussex, Lancashire, Middlesex and Hampshire**)
The Kent Bowler from 1851 to 1869-70, Edgar Willsher
The Three Yorkshire Batsmen of 1869: Roger Iddison, Rowbotham, Ephraim Lockwood

MATCH REPORTS

Cambridge v Oxford, *at Lord's, June 21 and 22*
'The Grand Stand was fully occupied; the Pavilion (seats and roof) crowded with Past and Present of both Universities; and altogether about 8000 of the cream of English society thronged the ground. At 11.25 they resumed play. A splendid one-hand catch by Mr. Absolom, and a clever stump out by Mr. Richardson, got rid of the steady player, Mr. Gibbon, and the dashing free-hitter, Mr. Evetts; but Mr. Pauncefote stayed whilst 6 wickets went. This gentleman played an innings of 33 runs so correctly and well as to elicit the commendations of all good judges on the ground.'
The Canterbury week, *August 9th, 10th, 11th, 12th*
'The week of all weeks in the cricketing season is this, annually held in August on the St. Lawrence ground at Canterbury. As a Cricket County gathering of all classes, from Peer to Peasant, it never had an equal, and as a Cricket week played out by the most eminent Amateurs and Professionals in the country, it is far away beyond rivalry …'

THE BATTING, after the first day, thoroughly mastered the bowling, as many as 1678 runs having been scored during the 5 days and few hours' cricket. Mr. W. Grace's 96 and 127 were capital antidotes to his 0 on the Monday. His 127 was the highest individual score of the week. His 96, made in one hour and 35 minutes, was hit from some of the best bowling in England, and was a grand display of fine judgement in placing the ball, clean, powerful hitting, and rapid scoring.'

M.C.C. and Ground v The South Of England
Played at Lord's, May 17 and 18

'About 3000 visitors present on Monday and 300 on Tuesday (weather queer that day). Wickets smooth, but dead. Hearne was out for 8 from a capital catch at point by Griffith, who stopped the ball (very hot) with one hand and caught it with the other.'

COUNTY REVIEW

KENT

'The present Kent County Club was formed in 1859. In its earlier seasons the club played their home matches in various parts of the county. In 1864 Notts v Kent was played on the new, prettily surrounded, but not very good Crystal Palace ground; subsequently the little, but good old ground at Gravesend was the home of the K.C.C., and last season the Crystal Palace ground was again selected to play the county's home matches on. But this roving, homeless position is one unbefitting a cricketing county like Kent.'

For the first time, the book is called John Wisden's Cricketers' Almanack *(pictured) rather than* Cricketer's Almanack, *with the apostrophe making the cricketers plural rather than singular as it had appeared in the first six editions. On the page inside the cover is a summary of 'the contents of previous numbers'.*

Entered at Stationers' Hall.

SEVENTH EDITION.

JOHN WISDEN'S
Cricketers' Almanack for 1870:
A RECORD
OF
THE FULL SCORES AND BOWLING SUMMARIES
OF THE
PRINCIPAL MATCHES PLAYED IN 1869.
WITH
OTHER INFORMATION USEFUL AND INTERESTING
TO CRICKETERS.

LONDON:
PUBLISHED AND SOLD BY JOHN WISDEN AND CO.,
AT THEIR
CRICKETING AND BRITISH SPORTS DEPÔT,
2, New Coventry Street, Haymarket, W.

One Shilling.]   1870.   [Post free 13 Stamps

W. H. CROCKFORD, GREENWICH.

1871

- German Empire formed:
Wiiliam I of Prussia proclaimed
Emperor of Germany
- Scotland beat England in the
first ever rugby union
international
- Queen Victoria opens the Royal
Albert Hall
- Henry Morton Stanley finds Dr.
David Livingstone at Ujiji
- Trades unions legalised

WISDEN 1871

8th Edition
Editor: W.H. Knight
Pages: 152
Price: Limp 1/-
Reprint:
1. Billing & Sons 1960 (1864-78 in set, limp, 150 limit)
2. Lowe & Brydone 1974 (1864-78 in set, limp, 150 limit)
3. Wisden 1991 (1864-78 in boxed set, cloth, 1,000 limit)

CRICKET HEADLINES 1870

Unofficial county champions: Yorkshire

Heavy roller first used at Lord's: improvement in quality of
wickets begins

W.G. Grace scores 215 for Gentlemen v Players at The
Oval, the first double-century in this fixture

Cobden's Match, Oxford v Cambridge: Cobden wins the
game for Cambridge by 2 runs with a hat-trick.

Derbyshire CCC formed; Kent CCC re-formed

INTRODUCTION

'The compiler's earnest thanks are here proffered to SECRETARIES of CLUBS, PROFESSIONALS
and other Cricketers, for the valued information with which they so readily assisted his
endeavours to render this edition a full and faithful record of the Principal Matches
Played in 1870.'

FEATURE ARTICLES

'Marylebone Cricket Club in 1870
At a Special General Meeting of the Members of M.C.C., held in the Pavilion on the 4th of
May, the Hon. F. Ponsonby proposed, Mr. F. N. Micklethwait seconded, and (after discussion)
it was duly carried, that Law IX should read as follows: The Bowler shall deliver the ball with
one foot on the ground behind the bowling crease, and within the return crease, and shall
bowl one over before he change wickets, which he shall be permitted to do twice in the same
innings, and no bowler shall bowl more than two overs in succession.
A proposition to add to Law xliv the words "Or any agreed number" was not carried.'
Statistical lists now include:
'All Individual Innings of 200 Runs Yet Hit
Individual Innings of three Figures hit in 1870
Two Three Figure Scores in One innings in 1870
Twenty-Eight of the Largest Innings Played by The Elevens in 1870
Single wicket Matches in 1870
Closely Contested Matches in 1870'

MATCH REPORTS

North v. South Of England (Return), *at Canterbury, August 8th, 9th, 10th*
'The Northerners were all ready for play early on the Monday, but owing to missing the train,
Jupp and Southerton had not arrived, and it was 12.45 ere the match and the week's cricket
was commenced. On the Tuesday the North Eleven (and Jupp not out) were out in the field

for action at 11.20, but consequent on a misunderstanding by Mr. Ottaway, the other not out of the preceding evening, as to the time set for resumption of play, he had not arrived, and it was 11.40 ere play began that day. On the Wednesday they commenced at 11.50, but when time was called at 10 minutes to 7, the match was unfinished, the South having 4 wickets to fall and 55 runs to score to win. The time lost on the two days being ample for one side to have obtained the wickets or the other to have made the runs, and thus have finished what in all probability would have been one of the closest contested, as it certainly was the best played, match of the season.'

Cambridge v Oxford, *played at Lord's, June 27 and 28*

'When Mr. Ottaway left, the innings was at 160 for 5 wickets, and the time 10 past 7; so 20 minutes remained for 5 wickets to make the 19 runs then required to win. But a catch at slip and an "lbw" speedily got rid of Mr. Townshend and Mr. Francis, making 7 wickets down for 175 runs, or 4 to win – an apparently easy task. But then (in an indifferent light for batting), Mr. Cobden bowled his now famously effective last over:-

From the 1st ball a single was made (3 to win with 3 wickets to fall)
From the 2nd ball, Mr. Butler was superbly caught out at mid off
The 3rd ball bowled Mr. Belcher
The 4th ball bowled Mr. Stewart

And so, accompanied by excitement unparalleled, did the 8th, 9th and 10th wickets fall with the score 176, Cambridge after all winning this "match of matches" by 2 runs.'

COUNTY REVIEW

GLOUCESTERSHIRE

'This county played a brief but brilliant cricket season in 1870, winning every match the Eleven played. There was no county club then in existence, the matches being arranged by, and played under, the management of Mr. W.G. Grace; however there is very little doubt but that in 1871 a County Cricket Club for Gloucestershire will be established on a firm basis.'

MISCELLANEOUS

'The sad deplorable accident that ended in the untimely death of poor George Summers will distressingly assist in rendering the past season at Lord's a memorable one to all classes of cricketers, by whom the unassuming manners, excellent conduct, and great cricketing abilities of Summers were held in high esteem; and it must be some consolation to his relatives and friends to know that no professional cricketer ever left us who in life was more highly respected, and whose death was so deeply deplored, than George Summers.'

[The Nottinghamshire batsman Summers, 25, was hit on the head by a short delivery in the match against MCC at Lord's. He died four days later. The next batsman, Richard Daft, went to the wicket with a towel wrapped round his head for protection. There was criticism of the pitch, but the match report in Wisden *notes 'the wickets were excellent'.]*

1872

9th EDITION
EDITOR: W.H. Knight
PAGES: 172
PRICE: 1/-
REPRINT:
1. Billing & Sons 1960 (1864-78 in set, limp, 150 limit)
2. Lowe & Brydone 1974 (1864-78 in set, limp, 150 limit)
3. Wisden 1991 (1864-78 in boxed set, cloth, 1,000 limit)

THE WORLD AT LARGE

• First ever F.A. Cup Final, at Kennington Oval. Wanderers beat Royal Engineers 1-0
• The *Mary Celeste* is discovered drifting without a crew off the Azores
• James Whistler exhibits *The Artist's Mother (Mrs. George Washington Whistler, or Arrangement in Grey and Black No. 3)*
• President Grant re-elected: his main opponent Horace Greeley dies during the election campaign
• Secret ballot introduced in Britain

CRICKET HEADLINES 1871

Unofficial county champions: Nottinghamshire

W.G. Grace scores 2,739 runs at an average of 78.25, when every stroke was run out. This was the first time any batsman had made 2,000 runs in a season, and the feat was not equalled by another batsman until 1893

S.E. Butler of Oxford takes all ten Cambridge wickets for 38 runs at Lord's

Lancashire dismissed for 25 by Derbyshire at Old Trafford, still the county's lowest score

Gloucestershire CCC formed

INTRODUCTION

'John Wisden & Co. thankfully acknowledge the annual increasing support awarded to the "Cricketers' Almanack". *[A mere 15 words.]*

OBITUARIES

[For the first time, obituaries were printed in Wisden. *They appear on page 71 surrounded by a heavy rule.]*

Mr. James Henry Dark
'Mr. Dark's connection with Lord's Grounds commenced when he was a boy of (about) 10 years old … In 1836 Mr. Dark became proprietor of Lord's Ground; in 1864 (or 65) he disposed of his interest therein to THE MARYLEBONE CLUB, and to the honour of the deceased it should be known that, when more lucrative offers were made him for the ground for building purposes, he rejected them all, in order that – so far as he could aid in keeping it so – Lord's Ground should be Lord's *Cricket* Ground for ever. Mr. Dark was of tempestuous temper, but …'

Stephen Slatter
'"Steevie" was engaged on Lord's Ground for 44 years. It is curious that after being in Mr. Dark's employ for so long a period, the same year should see the death of both MASTER and MAN.'

MATCH REPORTS

Summary of the Week's Cricket at Canterbury
'1718 runs scored; 106 wickets down
Average per day: 286 runs and 18 wickets
Of the 106 wickets down, 39 were "bowled", 37 were caught, 15 were stumped, 11 were "c and b", 3 were run out and 1 hit wicket. And it may be of interest to some to know that so many as 45 of the 106 wickets fell to slow bowling, 25 of the 45 slow wickets being due to the bowling of Mr. Rose.'

H.H. Stephenson's Match

North v South, *played at THE OVAL July 31, and August 1 and 2*

'The weather was bright throughout, and the company present so numerous that the attendance averaged 6000 per day, and those present the three days witnessed Mr. Grace out from the first ball bowled in the match, and subsequently play the largest innings ever scored by a cricketer on The Oval, his two innings forming the sensational contrast of 0 and 268.'

COUNTY REVIEW

Sussex in 1871

'The Sussex season, '71, was the more interesting from the fact that it was the last the club could play on the old ground by the sea, inasmuch as that "eligible plot of land" made so famous by cricketers and cricket, was required for more of "those magnificent mansions facing the sea" for which "The Queen of Watering Places" is so celebrated.'

MISCELLANEOUS

[From the Marylebone Cricket Club report]

'June was nippingly cold, and July was wet and windy, but there are two sides to all tales told, and if the greater portion of the three months up at Lord's in 1871 was unseasonably stormy and showery (and it *was* so), sunshine at other times beamed brilliantly on the famous old turf, most opportunely so at the North v. South; at the Oxford v. Cambridge; and at the Eton v. Harrow matches, and those three attractive contests collectively drew to Lord's audiences more numerous than had ever before been attracted there to three matches in one season.'

1873

THE WORLD AT LARGE

- The Alexandra Palace destroyed by fire just two weeks after its opening
- The Jesse James gang carries out its first train robbery near Des Moines, Iowa.
- The QWERTY keyboard invented
- *Around The World in Eighty Days* by Jules Verne is published

WISDEN 1873

10th EDITION
EDITOR: W.H. Knight
PAGES: 208
PRICE: 1/-
REPRINT:
1. Billing & Sons 1960 (1864-78 in set, limp, 150 limit)
2. Lowe & Brydone 1974 (1864-78 in set, limp, 150 limit)
3. Wisden 1991 (1864-78 in boxed set, cloth, 1,000 limit)

CRICKET HEADLINES 1872

Unofficial county champions: Nottinghamshire

Counties meet to set qualifications for county players

James Lillywhite takes all ten wickets for North v South at Canterbury

Ross Mackenzie, at Toronto, throws the cricket ball a record 140 yards and 9 inches

MCC and Ground dismissed for 16 by Surrey at Lord's, the lowest innings total in a major match since 1839

W. G Grace scores 2,571 runs in 57 completed innings

INTRODUCTION

'John Wisden & Co., in again thankfully acknowledging the annual increasing support awarded to the "Cricketers' Almanack," beg to inform the cricketing community that, notwithstanding THE CRICKET AT PRINCE'S and THE VISIT OF THE TWELVE TO CANADA AND AMERICA necessitated an enlargement by 36 pages of this year's edition, their little record of THE FULL SCORES &c., of the season's important matches, *is not increased in price*.'

FEATURE ARTICLES

Qualifications for a County Cricketer
'A meeting of representatives of the leading counties was held … for the purpose of determining what shall be the future qualifications for a county player. It may be stated that early in the season the committee of the Surrey County Cricket Club, at whose instance the meeting was convened, communicated with the Marylebone Club with a view of securing the services of that body in endeavouring to remove the laxity which has of late existed relative to the qualifications that constitute a county player.'

OBITUARIES

Deaths of Cricketers in 1872
'Mr. R. Baggallay, Mr. Benjamin Dark, Thomas Heath (of Notts), Mr. Lighton, Mr. Butler Parr (Notts), Mr. G.F. Parry, Major Wolfe, R.A., Lord Harris *(late President of the Kent County Club)*.' *[Only the list is given: no details.]*

COUNTY REVIEW:

Yorkshire in 1872
'The match at Prince's against Notts, and at Sheffield against Surrey, were gallant and close fights that brought defeat, but entailed no disgrace on the Yorkshiremen.

So many defeats were not pleasant; but the fact that Yorkshire had no "foreigners" in their ranks, but always fairly fought out their fights with true sons of their Shire, is a credit to them.'

North v. South, *at Canterbury, August 6th, 7th, 8th*
'The South commenced the batting with Jupp and R. Humphery, the North bowlers at starting being J. C. Shaw and Lockwood. (Here it is as well to state that all hits to the seated visitors counted 4 and were not run out, hence so very many 4's were made.) … A stirring Kentish cheer notified Mr. Thornton's walk to the wickets and I hope he will do 50, exclaimed one of the many admirers of hard hitting present; but the 50 did not come off, for when, by a brace of 4's and a 2 (all leg-hits and all from J. C. Shaw), Mr. Thornton had made 10 runs in 5 minutes, Shaw bowled him.'

All the Twenty wickets
Mr. C. Absolon – an old liberal supporter of Metropolitan cricket and cricketers – was the grey haired hero of this very successful bowling feat, i.e. – having a hand in the downfall of all the twenty wickets; he bowled 10, two hit wicket, six were caught from his bowling, and he caught out the remaining two. The match made famous by this bowling of Mr. Absolon's was Wood Green v United Willesden, played at Wood Green, July 21, 1872 … Summing up Mr. Absolon's bowling in 1872, *Bell's Life* of the second of November last states: "Mr. Absolon is entitled to seven hats for taking three wickets in consecutive balls on seven different occasions. *B.L.* also states that Mr. Absolon scored 1109 runs and took 519 wickets last season!!!'

1874

WISDEN 1874

11th EDITION
EDITOR: W.H. Knight
PAGES: 180
PRICE: 1/-
REPRINT:
1. Billing & Sons 1960 (1864-78 in set, limp, 150 limit)
2. Lowe & Brydone 1974 (1864-78 in set, limp, 150 limit)
3. Wisden 1991 (1864-78 in boxed set, cloth, 1,000 limit)

THE WORLD AT LARGE

• Disraeli succeeds Gladstone as Prime Minister
• 'Sphairistike', an early form of lawn tennis, patented by Walter Clopton Wingfield
• The Factory Act establishes a 56-hour working week, and prohibits children being used as chimney sweeps
• Death of the original Siamese twins, Chang and Eng Bunker, aged 62

CRICKET HEADLINES 1873

Unofficial county champions: Gloucestershire and Nottinghamshire

Sussex dismissed for 19 by Nottinghamshire at Hove, still their lowest first-class total

W.G. Grace completes the first double of 1,000 runs and 100 wickets in a season (2,139 runs and 106 wickets)

Adelaide Oval opened

Leicestershire CCC formed

INTRODUCTION

'John Wisden & Co., in again thankfully acknowledging the annual increasing support awarded to the "Cricketers' Almanack," hope for a continuance of that support to the edition for 1874.'

FEATURE ARTICLES

The Counties – Qualifications for a County Cricketer

'This, we believe (we are not sure) was the last of the meetings in 1873 on this subject, and we *suppose* that the above five regulations are the laws that explain what really does constitute a County Cricketer; anyhow, the practical result of all these meetings, discussions, divisions, rules and regulations was that in 1873
Mr. G. STRACHAN played for Surrey against his native county Gloucestershire
SOUTHERTON played for Surrey against his native county Sussex
T. PALMER played for Surrey against his native county Kent …'

COUNTY REVIEW

Marylebone Cricket Club

'With a view to promote county cricket, and to establish a new and interesting series of matches at Lord's Ground, the committee, in the course of winter, offered a challenge cup competition. Regulations were drawn up and sent to the counties. The project was favourably received by some and declined by others. Five acceptances were received in the first instance, ties were drawn, and the prospect of an interesting season was afforded. For various reasons two of the five accepting counties withdrew from the competition, and finally, as the liberal views of the committee did not meet with general support, or were otherwise misrepresented, the original idea was abandoned …
In justice to themselves the committee must repeat that the challenge cup matches were only projected with a view to promote county cricket. The fact that all expenses would be borne by the M. C. C., and that the matches would be played on a neutral ground, afforded a reasonable belief that such contests would be viewed with interest by cricketers in general.'

Middlesex C.C.C.
'Old TOM HEARNE was not up to his big hitting form of 1872; nevertheless he made double figures in six innings out of eight, a proof that "there is lots of hitting in the old boy yet".'

The Gentlemen v. The Players of England, *played at Lord's, June 30 and July 1*
'When Mr. Grace had made 65 runs, he was caught at point by Carpenter from a NO BALL bowled by J.C. Shaw; barring this bit of luck his truly "great" innings was a splendid sample of how to time, hit and place the ball. His 163 was made by the following hits:- one 7, a straight drive to the Nursery ground wall; a five (four for an overthrow), thirteen 4's (including some superb cuts), six 3's, 17 2's and 47 singles.'

Lancashire v Surrey, *played at Old Trafford, June 19 and 20.*
'A most decisive victory this of Lancashire's, whose Eleven won by an innings and 117 runs, their two bowlers being unchanged throughout Surrey's two innings. Richard Humphrey, with 11 and 25 was highest Surrey scorer in both innings. The Lancashire men fielded well, Mr. Hornby especially well; they gave no extra in either innings.'

Lancashire bowling unchanged throughout both matches.
'To Watson and William McIntyre it is due to record that they were the only Lancashire bowlers tried in *both* Lancashire v Surrey matches played in 1873. In those two matches they bowled as follows:-

		Overs	Mdns	Runs	Wkts.
At Old Trafford	McIntyre bowled	46.3	19 for	70 and	11
	Watson "	45	15 "	79 "	8
On the Oval	McIntyre "	40	17 "	52 "	11
	Watson "	39	15 "	49 "	8'

98 and 90 not out in One Match
'Mr. G. Podmore made 98 and 90 not out in Residents v Visitors match at Eastbourne last autumn.'

1875

12th EDITION
EDITOR: W.H. Knight
PAGES: 212 and 214
PRICE: 1/-
REPRINT:
1. Billing & Sons 1960 (1864-78 in set, limp, 150 limit)
2. Lowe & Brydone 1974 (1864-78 in set, limp, 150 limit)
3. Wisden 1991 (1864-78 in boxed set, cloth, 1,000 limit)

THE WORLD AT LARGE

• Captain Matthew Webb becomes the first person to swim the English Channel
• U.S. Congress passes Civil Rights Act, prohibiting racial discrimination
• The first Kentucky Derby is run
• Britain buys the Khedive's shares in the Suez Canal

CRICKET HEADLINES 1874

Unofficial county champions: Gloucestershire

W.G. Grace performs the double again

Alfred Shaw takes all ten wickets for MCC against The North at Lord's

INTRODUCTION

'John Wisden & Co., in again thankfully acknowledging the annual increasing support awarded to "The Cricketers' Almanack," hope for a continuance of that support to the edition for 1875.'

FEATURE ARTICLES

The Largest Innings and the Smallest Innings Scored in 1874

'A Side out for 2 (Leg Byes). Nether Stowey v Bishop's Lydiard. From *Bell's Life* of Sept. 19 Old *Bell* did not state when or where this innings was brought off, nor did it state in what part of England "Nether Stowey" or "Bishop's Lydiard" is situated; what *B.L.* did state is: "The smallest score of the season was recently played between Nether Stowey and Bishop's Lydiard. It will be seen that not one of the Nether Stowey batsmen obtained a run in the second innings … (Small as the total of this innings is, it is not the smallest on record, as there are others of only 2 runs and "a few" the total of which are 0.' *[Nether Stowey and Bishop's Lydiard are in Somerset.]*

The Three English Twelves who have Visited Australia

'Mr. W.G. Grace's team … played 15 matches, winning 10, losing 3 and leaving 2 unfinished; a fairly successful tour, considering the undoubted improvement made by Australian cricketers since the visit of Parr's team, and the generally admitted fact that Mr. Grace's team did not nearly represent the full cricketing strength of the old country.'

OBITUARIES

Roger Kynaston Esq

'For many years Hon. Sec., and subsequently, Treasurer, to M.C.C. A popular and efficient Hon. Sec. A courteous and esteemed gentleman.'

John Lillywhite

'John Lillywhite was buried Oct. 31, in Highgate Cemetery, his remains being laid in the grave where rest his Father, his Mother, and his Wife.'

COUNTY REVIEW

Surrey in 1874

'All other bat work for Surrey seems dwarfed into comparative nothingness by the batting deeds of Jupp, whose splendid double *not out* of 43 and 109 in the match against Yorkshire;

whose 154 and 144 in the Sussex matches; whose 900 out of the 3,215 runs made by 28 batsmen for Surrey last season, and whose fine average of 45 runs per innings for his County, stand so pre-eminently in front of all others that the probability is the Surrey season of 1874 will in future be thought and spoken of throughout the county as JUPP'S YEAR.'

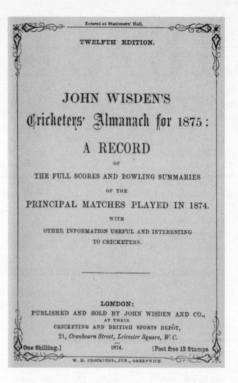

MATCH REPORTS

12 of M.C.C. and G. v 16 Amateurs Who Had Never Played At Lord's *played at Lord's, May 28*
'This match was one of the novelties of the M.C.C. season of 1874. It failed to create the faintest interest in cricketing circles; brought to light no wonder in the "Amateur" line, and was not proceeded with after the one day's cricket.'

Gloucestershire v. Yorkshire, The Return, *played at Clifton, August 14, 15, 16.*
'Although stormy weather marred the attendances, the pleasure, and the wickets so carefully prepared for this match, it did not mar the hitting of the three brothers, who contributed 259 of the 303 runs from the bat scored for Gloucestershire; Mr. W.G. Grace making 127 runs, Mr. G.F. Grace 81 and Dr. E.M. Grace 51.'

MISCELLANEOUS

The Marylebone Club
'The committee have had under their consideration the advisability of continuing the publication of the work known as *Cricket Scores and Biographies*. An occasion has occurred of purchasing the valuable MSS of Mr. Haygarth, which presents an unbroken record of the game up to the present time. The expense of publication will be considerable, and the committee have not thought proper at present to fully commit themselves to it … A continuous history of cricket should be preserved, if nowhere else, in the Pavilion at Lord's.'

The American Baseball Players in England
'Twenty-two baseball players from America visited England at the back end of the cricket season, 1874, their mission – it was semi-officially stated – being to give the English a practical insight into the workings of baseball … They were a finely-framed, powerful set of men, and, although baseball did not take the popular fancy here, the splendid long-distance throwing and truly magnificent out-fielding of the Americans at once won the full and heartily-expressed admiration of Englishmen, who frankly and freely acknowledged the Americans' superiority to the generality of English fielders.'

This edition (pictured) was published in late 1874 – as opposed to earlier editions which came out at the beginning of the year – in what is believed to be a small print run, which sold out. A second issue was also published, with different pagination. One issue was of 214 pages, the other 212. Today, it is the rarest Wisden of all, followed in scarcity by the first edition in 1864.

1876

WISDEN 1876

13ʰ EDITION
EDITOR: W.H. Knight
PAGES: 224
PRICE: 1/-
REPRINT:
1. Billing & Sons 1960 (1864-78 in set, limp, 150 limit)
2. Lowe & Brydone 1974 (1864-78 in set, limp, 150 limit)
3. Wisden 1991 (1864-78 in boxed set, cloth, 1,000 limit)

THE WORLD AT LARGE

• Alexander Graham Bell speaks the first words over the telephone – "Mr. Watson, come here. I want to see you."
• Battle of Little Big Horn – General Custer and troops of the U.S. Seventh Cavalry are wiped out by Sioux warriors led by Sitting Bull
• Parliament ratifies the Merchant Shipping Act, prohibiting overloading of vessels and introducing the Plimsoll line to the hull of all British ships
• Bayreuth's *Festspielhaus* opens with a complete performance of Wagner's *Ring Cycle*

CRICKET HEADLINES 1875

Unofficial County Champions: Nottinghamshire

Alfred Shaw of Nottinghamshire takes 7 for 7 against MCC at Lord's

The North v South match at Lord's finishes in a day, with the South winning by ten wickets and James Southerton taking 16 wickets for 52 runs

Lord Harris is President, Secretary and Captain of Kent CCC

INTRODUCTION

'John Wisden & Co., in again thankfully acknowledging the annual increasing support awarded to "The Cricketers' Almanack," hope for a continuance of that support to the edition for 1876.'

FEATURE ARTICLES

Great Scoring by a Clifton Collegian

'Mr. R.E. Bush was first man in both innings; his 80 runs (out of 116 from the bat!) were made by two 6's, one 5, four 4's, six 3's, five 2's and 19 singles. His 228 *not out* comprised seven 6's, six 5's, nine 4's, twenty-one 3's, nine 2's and 39 singles … Between the falls of the 4ᵗʰ and 5ᵗʰ wickets Mr. F. Bryant (who made 107) and Mr. R.E. Bush put on 252 runs! The rest of their side made only 10 runs between them, consequently there was no "double". Just fancy an innings of 379 runs with no double figure score in it. If *this* be not "a cricket curiosity", what is?'

The Largest Innings Ever Scored (full particulars)

'724 runs for 8 wickets. Royal Engineers v I Zingari, played at Chatham, August 20 and 21, 1875 When "time" was called on that Saturday evening, and the stumps finally drawn, there had been 10 1/2 hours' cricket played, 1,224 balls bowled by I Zingari, and 724 runs (including 55 extras) scored, and 8 wickets lost, by R.E.'

OBITUARIES

Edward Hayward Budd Esq

'M.C.C., Middlesex, Gentlemen of England. One of the most accomplished Cricketers and Athletes of his time. "Mr. Budd's career as a batsman, bowler, wicket-keeper, single wicket player, and field, has been most brilliant, his average altogether being one of the highest on record." – *Scores and Biographies*.'

Mr. William Davey
'Mr. Davey was Assistant Secretary to the Kent County Cricket Club, and, for many years, one of the most active, efficient, obliging, and courteous officials connected with the Canterbury Cricket Week.'

George Street
'George Street was thirteen years Ground Keeper on the Surrey Ground. During his management "Wickets on The Oval" were famed all over cricketing England for their truth, excellence and easy run-getting qualities.'

COUNTY REVIEW

Middlesex in 1875
'The Committee consisted of sixteen Gentlemen of the County.
Middlesex cricketers failed to win a match in 1875. Of the seven matches played by the County eleven, five ended in defeat and two were drawn battles, one, v. Yorkshire, against them, the other, v Notts, in their favour, foul weather alone snatching from Middlesex an almost certain victory over Notts, the crack county of the season.'

MATCH REPORTS

Nottinghamshire v Surrey, *played on the Trent Bridge Ground, June 10, 11 and 12*
'"Rain until after dinner; Notts began at 3.30: all out at 5.15; ground low." Such was the verbatim report sent to the compiler of this book respecting the first day's cricket in this match. On that day the good bowling of Southerton and Street got the Notts eleven out for 49 runs, and the good bowling of Alfred Shaw and Martin McIntyre got rid of Jupp's, Richard Humphrey's and Potter's wickets for 11 runs, including 4 extras; that is to say thirteen county wickets had that day fallen for 60 runs (56 from the bat); then a storm stopped play.'

Lancashire v Yorkshire, *played at Old Trafford, June 24, 25, 26*
'Mr. A.N. Hornby and Barlow accomplished a big thing in batting in this match. They commenced Lancashire's second innings, their side requiring 146 to win; they made the runs *without either losing his wicket*, and so Lancashire won by ten wickets. The bowlers against them were Hill, Emmett, Clayton, Ulyett and Lockwood, but the two batsmen beat the five bowlers so decisively that they made 148 runs from 72 overs (less two balls) and left their sticks up unconquered, thus accomplishing a batting feat unequalled in the history of county cricket.'

MISCELLANEOUS

A Great Catch by Fox of Westminster School
'In T.A. Mantle's annual, played last September on the Westminster school ground, Fox was fielding at deep square leg, the batsman gave a leg ball a frightful smack; Fox ran quite thirty yards to the ball, leapt up, and dashing out his hand when running at top speed, caught the ball in grand style; three lusty ringing cheers greeted the fine catch, which Flanagan the M.C.C. man (playing in the match) subsequently said was, in his opinion, nearly as good as Webbe's in the Universities' match at Lord's.'

1877

WISDEN 1877

14th EDITION
EDITOR: W.H. Knight
PAGES: 248
PRICE: 1/-
REPRINT:
1. Billing & Sons 1960 (1864-78 in set, limp, 150 limit)
2. Lowe & Brydone 1974 (1864-78 in set, limp, 150 limit)
3. Wisden 1991 (1864-78 in boxed set, cloth, 1,000 limit)

THE WORLD AT LARGE

• Queen Victoria proclaimed Empress of India
• Transvaal annexed to British Empire
• First Test Match, Australia v England at Melbourne
• First Wimbledon lawn tennis tournament
• Oxford v Cambridge Boat Race ends in a dead heat

CRICKET HEADLINES 1876

Unofficial County Champions: Gloucestershire

W.G. Grace scores the first-ever first-class triple centuries: 344 for M.C.C. v Kent, in Canterbury Week, and 318* for Gloucestershire v Yorkshire

Between those two innings he makes 177 against Notts, a total of 839 runs in a week.

He finishes the summer with 2,622 runs and 129 wickets

W. Mycroft takes 17 wickets for 103 runs for Derbyshire v Hampshire

INTRODUCTION

'John Wisden & Co., in again thankfully acknowledging the annual increasing support awarded to "The Cricketers' Almanack," hope for a continuance of that support to the edition for 1877.'

FEATURE ARTICLES

The Four English Twelves to Australia
Statistical features include
  Matches of 1,000 runs hit in 1876
  A truly 'Great' bit of Batting by Mr. W.G. Grace
  A few large innings hit by sides in 1876
  Individual innings of three figures hit in 1876

OBITUARIES

Mr. N. Felix (Mr. Nicholas Wonostrocht) [sic]
'An accomplished Cricketer, Artist, Musician and Gentleman. "Was a left handed batsman and possessed the most brilliant cut to the off (from the shoulder) ever seen. His drives and forward play were also very good." – Scores and Biographies.'

Samuel Biddulph
'A real good wicket-keeper, a hard hitter and a "straight" man. He served M.C.C. faithfully and well for twelve years.'

COUNTY REVIEW

Surrey in 1876
'The alterations on the ground consist of a well conceived utilisation of the space between The Pavilion and The Hut, by the erection, and enclosure, of rows of seats, which (when

finished by the laying down of an asphalte footing, and the putting up a sun and rain shade) will be a polite, and remunerative bid for the patronage of the Ladies. At the other end of the Ground – down by the gasometers – is "The Skating Rink", the exterior of which is an eyesore, so very ugly is it.'

MATCH REPORTS

North v. South, (Tom Hearne's match), *played at Lord's, Whit Monday, Tuesday, and Wednesday, June 5, 6, 7*
'Wednesday was a bright breezy day; the wickets continued to play surprisingly well, the attendance was good, and as the South had lost 3 wickets and were only 90 runs on, the prospect of a good match and an enjoyable day's cricket was anticipated and realised. Play was renewed at 5 past 12, and when, in Hill's first over Lord Harris drove one ball very finely to the off for 4, and the succeeding ball to the on for 3, the applause told that the lungs of lookers-on were all right, and that good cricket would on that day meet with a warm welcome.'

The County of Kent v. The Gentlemen of M.C.C., *played at Canterbury, August 10, 11 and 12 1876*
'The day was intensely hot, and so was the hitting of the M.C.C. two – Mr. W. Grace and Mr. Crutchley – who resumed their innings at noon, and were not parted until late in the afternoon when they had increased the score by 227 runs! as Mr. Crutchley went to wickets with the score at 203, and was out for 84 with it at 430. There were then 5 wickets down at an average of 86 runs per wicket, and Mr. Grace as full of fine hitting as he had been at any phase of this great display, and he kept on hitting, scoring, and fagging the field until near the end, for he was not out until 546 runs had been scored, and play finally ceased when the score was at 557, nine wickets having then fallen. Then time was up for the Canterbury Week of 1876; and this stupendous run-getting match was drawn; 19 different bowlers having bowled therein; 1999 balls bowled; 1099 runs from the bat, and 75 extra scored, and 31 wickets having fallen. Mr. W. Grace commenced M.C.C.'s second innings; he was 6 hours and 20 minutes at wickets, and had scored 344 runs out of the 540 booked, when he was caught out at mid-off.'

MISCELLANEOUS

[From the Almanack]
April, 1877
Th 12 Snow, lightning, thunder, frost, '76
F   13 Snowstorm, *very cold*, 1876
S   14 Heavy snowst. destructive gale, '76
S   15 *Second Sunday After Easter*
M   16 Mutiny at Spithead, 1797
Tu 17 London in a fog, 1876

1878

WISDEN 1878

15th EDITION
EDITOR: W.H. Knight
PAGES: 250
PRICE: 1/-
REPRINT:
1. Billing & Sons 1960 (1864-78 in set, limp, 150 limit)
2. Lowe & Brydone 1974 (1864-78 in set, limp, 150 limit)
3. Wisden 1991 (1864-78 in boxed set, cloth, 1,000 limit)

THE WORLD AT LARGE

• A 287 carat diamond discovered at Kimberly, South Africa.
• Gilbert and Sullivan's *H.M.S. Pinafore* opens in London
• Thomas Edison patents his phonograph and produces first successful incandescent electric light
• Over 640 people die when the pleasure boat *Princess Alice* collides with the *Bywell Castle* in the Thames.
• First floodlit football and rugby matches are played at Bramall Lane, Sheffield

CRICKET HEADLINES 1877

Unofficial County Champions: Gloucestershire

W.G. Grace takes 17 wickets for 89 runs, for Gloucestershire v Nottinghamshire at Cheltenham

Fred Morley takes 7 wickets for 6 runs for MCC and Ground as Oxford University are dismissed for 12 – the lowest first-class total on record. He then takes 6 wickets for 8 in the second innings – 13 wickets for 14 runs in a day.

In Australia, the first Test Match is played: Australia win by 45 runs

INTRODUCTION

'John Wisden & Co., in again thankfully acknowledging the annual increasing support awarded to "The Cricketers' Almanack," hope for a continuance of that support to the edition for 1878.'

FEATURE ARTICLES

Emmett's Match in 1878
'Tom Emmett is one of the most popular cricketers that ever put on flannel for his Shire, and cricketing Yorkshiremen will doubtless flock in thousands to the three-days' match which the Yorkshire C.C.C. have decided to play next July in compliment to Emmett.'
Southerton's Match in 1878
George Parr's Match in 1878
[These three features, previewing benefit matches to be held in 1878, may be considered proto-Five Cricketers of the Year articles, lauding famous cricketers.]
The Four English Twelves In Australia
[Although the twelve players who toured under James Lillywhite in 1876–77 are listed, there are no match reports or scorecards of the tour.]
The Three Gentlemen v Players of England Matches in 1877

OBITUARIES

Thomas Barker
'A good cricketer who played his first match for Notts in 1821, and who was for several seasons engaged at Lord's by M.C.C. As a good bowler, steady bat, fearless and excellent umpire, and entertaining companion, there was no man in his time better known or respected than old Tom Barker.'
The Hon. Frederick Cavendish
'Was a member of M.C.C. since 1820.'

Lancashire in 1877

'The fresh professionals tried last season were five in number, the two most promising being F. Blake who, with time, is likely to become a useful batsman for his county; and R. Pilling, a fair bat and promising wicket-keeper, who shaped like training on to the true P form of Pinder, Pooley, Phillips and Plumb. With all this promising young blood ripe and ready to battle on the cricket field for the honour of the Red Rose of Lancaster, there are justifiable hopes of a successful cricketing season in '78 for the Shire, whose eleven, it is to be hoped, will next season be found testing their skill against the famous West-Countrymen.'

The Three Gentlemen v Players of England Matches of 1877

'As to the nine days' cricket the batting and fielding will long retain a bright spot in the memories of those who witnessed the play, and when beardless and hearty youngsters of the present day have grown grey and feeble, they will have many a tale to tell the cricketers of the future how, in one of the 1877 matches, Mr. W.G. Grace was bowled out for a one hit (a 3) innings; how perfect was the cricket played by young Arthur Shrewsbury for his 78; how Mr. I.D. Walker in one match went twice to the wickets, received but one ball in that match, and that ball bowled him; how unsurpassably splendid Mr. J.M. Cotterill hit for his 59 and 92, and what a grand 7, all run out, he made at Lord's; how daringly Mr. A.N. Hornby hit, and how daringly he ran for his 144 (the largest innings hit in the three matches); – with what care, patience, skill, and success Mr. W.W. Read played for his 72; how very finely Mr. G.F. Grace hit for his 134, and his brother, Mr. W.G. did ditto for his 41; how Ulyett made 53 and 118 in one match; how Mr. A.J. Webbe caught out 6 of them in one innings; how the Hon. A. Lyttelton, as stumper, captured 5 of them in another innings, and 8 in that match.'

Bats v Broomsticks

'The abrupt and early termination of the match on the third day was the cause of a fill-up-the-time match being arranged for the Gloucestershire Eleven with broomsticks, to play the Eleven of Cheltenham with bats. The Broomsticks made a first innings of 290 runs; of these runs, Dr. E.M. Grace made 105 and Midwinter 58. The Batsmen had lost two wickets and scored 50 runs, when time was up.'

From the report on Canterbury Week:

'An epilogue usually finishes up the dramatic performances of "The Week". In the epilogue spoken in the theatre on the conclusion of the 1877 performances Lord Harris had to utter his indignant protest against all "obstructives", cricketing or otherwise, and thus his lordship spoke:

    "Hold! I protest, for here I represent
    All – M.C.C., I Zingari and Kent
    Ne'er shall such trivial, childish schemes be found
    To desecrate our famed St. Lawrence Ground.
    There, let Kent's white horse banner be unfurled
    Against All England – aye, 'gainst all the World.'

This is the last edition in which the almanack (annual calendar) section is included in its day-by-day format. In 1879 just a calendar appeared; the calendar was then included in every edition to 1941. In 1994, a monthly review reappeared as 'Chronicle of 1993' in the 'Miscellaneous' section where it continues to this day. From 2004, 'The Almanack' became the final section of each edition, listing fixtures, dates, anniversaries etc.

1879

WISDEN 1879

16th EDITION
EDITOR: W.H. Knight
PAGES: 246
PRICE: 1/-
REPRINT: Willows 1991 (1,000 limit)

THE WORLD AT LARGE

- Battles of Isandlwana and Rorke's Drift. Six months later, Zulu Wars end with defeat of Cetshwayo's armies at Ulundi
- Tay Bridge Disaster: 75 people killed when the bridge collapses as a train passes over it
- *A Doll's House* by Henrik Ibsen published
- Gladstone's Midlothian campaign

CRICKET HEADLINES 1878

Unofficial County Champions: Undecided / Middlesex

Visit of first Australian team to England, under D.W. Gregory. They play no Test matches

Edward Barratt of Surrey takes all ten Australian wickets for 43 runs while playing for Eleven English Professionals

Fred Morley takes 7 wickets for 9 runs for Notts v Kent at Town Malling, and Tom Emmett of Yorkshire achieves the same analysis against Sussex at Hove

INTRODUCTION

'John Wisden & Co., in again thankfully acknowledging the annual increasing support awarded to "The Cricketers' Almanack," hope for a continuance of that support to the edition for 1879.'

FEATURE ARTICLES

The Australians in England

'On the 20th of May the Australians got into cricketing harness, and from then up to the 17th of September they were hard at work, railing it by night and match playing by day nearly all over cricketing England, busily finishing up their last eight cricketing days in the old country by playing on a Monday and Tuesday in Scarborough in the far north, on the Wednesday and Thursday at Prince's in London, on the Friday and Saturday at Glasgow in Scotland, and on the following Monday and Tuesday at Sunderland, whereat they were entertained at a banquet, presided over by the Mayor of Sunderland.'

The Marylebone Club in 1878
The Counties in 1878
Largest scores and individual innings of three figures in 1878

OBITUARIES

John George Davey (M.C.C. Professional)

'J.G. Davey (of Sussex) was a fairly good wicket-keeper, one of the most painstaking and efficient scorers that ever correctly chronicled the progress of a match in the M.C.C. scoring books, and a worthily respected man. Davey was in his 32nd year when his long sufferings from consumption were ended by death.'

Mr. C.J. Ottaway

'Mr. Ottaway was one of the most scientific batsmen that ever played cricket, and an accomplished gentleman.'

Mr. W.P. Mynn

'Mr. Walter Mynn was one of the County Eleven in Kent's palmiest cricketing days.'

Mr. I.D. Burnett   Julius Caesar   W. Jupp

Middlesex in 1878

'Middlesex in 1878 was as fortunate in County v County contests as Middlesex was unfortunate in 1877; for, in '77, Middlesex did not win a match; and in '78 Middlesex did not lose one when pitted against County Elevens. The only defeat suffered in '78 by the Middlesex Eleven was from the now famous Australians, and even that defeat was brightened up by the brilliancy of The Hon. E. Lyttelton's 113 for the County, an innings that is not only the largest made against the Colonials, but is pre-eminently the finest hitting display made in 1878 by any batsman.'

The Thames Calamity Fund Match. North v South, *played on The Oval, September 17, 18, 19 [The 'Thames Calamity' occurred on September 3, 1878, when two boats collided on the Thames, and 640 lives were lost.]*

'Two really splendid sides were selected willing and ready to play for so praiseworthy an object, and albeit the season was old for cricket, London was out of town, the weather was uncomfortably cold for lookers on, and the batting of one side collapsed in curiously brief form, there were fairly large attendances of spectators on the first two days, and the satisfactory end was attained of £258 being sent in aid of The Thames Calamity Fund.'

The Australians v Leicestershire (11-a-side), *played at Leicester, July 15, 16, 17*

'The Australian cricket was wound up in sensational form by Charles Bannerman. At one o'clock on the third day Charles Bannerman and Murdoch began the Australians' second innings, 209 being the number of runs required to win. Bannerman began in ominously successful form by making three 4's from the first over. At two o'clock they left for luncheon, Charles Bannerman having then made 58, not out. At three o'clock they went at it again, Bannerman characteristically resuming his innings with two 4's and a 2 … At seven minutes past four Bannerman had made his 100 (and mightily was he cheered thereon); and when, at a quarter to 5, the score stood at 201, Bannerman was thrown out for 133.'

For the first time, there are advertisements other than for John Wisden & Co, which extends its own publicity. The Sporting Life and The Sportsman each have a full page. Kaye's Worsdell's Pills 'purify the blood, cleanse from disease, remove obstructions, improve digestion, establish health: may be taken with perfect safety by old and young. Sold everywhere'. The back cover is an illustrated advertisement for Eno's Fruit Salt (pictured): 'The present system of living – partaking of too rich foods, as pastry, saccharine, and fatty substances, alcoholic drinks, and an ill-sufficient amount of exercise – frequently deranges the liver.'

The contents list of the previous Almanacks now moves from the inside cover to the last page of text.

1880

WISDEN 1880

17th EDITION
EDITOR: George H. West
PAGES: 236
PRICE: 1/-
REPRINT: Willows
1. 1987 (500 limit)
2. 2004 (250 limit)

THE WORLD AT LARGE

• Ned Kelly hanged for murder
• Gladstone defeats Disraeli in the general election to become Prime Minister again
• British troops win the Battle of Kandahar on the North-West Frontier between India and Afghanistan
• James Garfield elected President of USA
• First Boer War begins
• Transvaal declared a republic

CRICKET HEADLINES 1879

Unofficial County Champions: Lancashire and Nottinghamshire

Derbyshire all out for 16 v Notts at Trent Bridge, Fred Morley taking 7 wickets for 7 runs

Spofforth's hat-trick destroys England's batting in the only 'Test' of Lord Harris's tour. Australia win the match by ten wickets

W.G. Grace's Testimonial match yields him £1,458

INTRODUCTION

'John Wisden & Co., in again thankfully acknowledging the annual increasing support awarded to "The Cricketers' Almanack" hope for a continuance of that support to the edition for 1880.'

FEATURE ARTICLES

Cricket Match On The Ice By Moonlight
'About the time Lord Harris's team were playing one of their matches under the bright and burning sun of an Australian summer, an English team were playing their game in the dear old country at home under the bright and brilliant beauty of the new year's full moon.'

Daft's Team in Canada and America
'They played twelve matches, winning nine, and having three drawn … Full details of their various encounters have been given below. We will, however, content ourselves with giving a marvellous item of bowling:

	Matches	Overs	Runs	Wickets	Runs per Wicket
A. Shaw	12	544	426	178	2.70

Beyond mentioning that the team were on most amiable terms throughout, that they were well satisfied, and that the captain, after defraying expenses, had a satisfactory balance in hand, which was assuredly well deserved, we leave our readers to glean the particulars for themselves from the subjoined reports.'

Lord Harris's English team in Australia

OBITUARIES

Death of Mr. W.H. Knight
'We sincerely regret to announce the death of this gentleman, who for years has been identified with the cricketing press. For some time he reported "the national game" for a daily paper, but in recent years he was the compiler of "Wisden's Cricketers' Almanack", and for accuracy had scarcely an equal. Long a martyr to a painful disease, he passed away on August the 16th last, to the great grief of his many friends, and especially of professional cricketers, but, probably, to none more so than the proprietors of this Almanack, who have lost in him a painstaking and conscientious compiler.'

T. Burgoyne Esq

'This gentleman, the Treasurer of the Marylebone Cricket Club, was born on December 30th, 1805. Elected Treasurer in May, 1866, he filled this important post to the satisfaction of all with whom he was connected.'

George Griffith

'George Griffith, well known for his batting powers, which obtained for him the *soubriquet* of "Lion-hitter of the South" was born at Ripley, Surrey, on December 20th, 1833. Poor Griffith, who had been for a time suffering from some aberration of the mind, was found hanging to the post of his bedstead on May 3rd.'

COUNTY REVIEW

Surrey in 1879

'The attendances … were probably hardly so numerous; but this is an outcry that was heard all over the country. Among the contests we are glad to note one for the benefit of that truly deserving cricketer – James Southerton. Originally played for Sussex for his batting, he soon developed a wonderful degree of ability as a slow bowler, and of late years adopted Surrey as his county under the residential qualification. *[Southerton was 51 years old in 1879.]*

MATCH REPORTS

Lord Harris's Eleven v The Australian Eleven, played on the East Melbourne Ground, January 2, 3, 4

'Lord Harris stayed well, but when Mr. Royle had made three single's, Spofforth's bowling captured three wickets with three successive balls – the victims being Mr. Royle, Mr. Mackinnon and Emmett, seven wickets being then down for 26 runs. Mr. Absolom was next man in; he forthwith played his old, old game of knocking the ball all over the ground, and with Lord Harris, increased the score to 89, when Garrett bowled his lordship for 33 – a good innings.'

Over Thirty v Under Thirty, played at Lord's, July 22, 23

'It is admitted beyond all dispute that Mr. W.G. Grace is the greatest cricketer "the world e'er saw". Whatever may be the prejudices of those whose memories carry them back to the heroes of the last generation, even they give way and yield the palm to the Gloucestershire captain … Mr. W.G. Grace compensated in great measure for his poor batting by showing some excellent bowling. When only a single had been made, he induced the Hon. A. Lyttelton to return him the ball, while with an additional 5 runs, he caused his brother Mr. G.F. Grace to lodge it in the hands of the wicket-keeper.'

MISCELLANEOUS

Presentation to Mr. W.G. Grace

'Lord Charles Russell, who had been asked as one of the oldest members of the Marylebone Club to say a few words on the occasion, said "he was not satisfied with the amount". He thought £1,400 was an odd sum to present to any one, and he pledged his word it would be £1,500 before they were done with it. He was an old cricketer, and the enjoyment he had had in the cricket field for many years past was in seeing Mr. Grace play cricket. He looked upon cricket as the sport of the people, from the prince to the peasant, and he was delighted to see that it was increasing in popularity year by year, and that in some respects also it was being better played.'

Wisden *has a new editor, but the book's early reputation for accuracy owed much to the 'painstaking and conscientious' work mentioned in W.H. Knight's obituary, which appears at the front of the book. The advertisements grow in number, with more remedies, such as Page Woodcock's Wind Pills; a reappearance of the 'newly invented Catapulta' ('the most effective substitute for the Professional Bowler'); Ransomes' lawn mowers (illustrated); and the first advertisement for* Wisden's *printer since its inception, W.H. Crockford ('Special facilities for printing works on Cricket and other Sports').*

1881

WISDEN 1881

18th Edition
Editor: George H. West
Pages: 240
Price: 1/-
Reprint: Willows
1. 1985 (500 limit)
2. 2004 (limit 250)

THE WORLD AT LARGE

• Natural History Museum opens in Kensington
• Death of Disraeli
• Tsar Alexander II assassinated in St. Petersburg
• President Garfield assassinated in Washington
• The Wild West is really wild: Billy The Kid is shot dead by Pat Garrett, and the Earps and the Clantons shoot it out at the Gunfight at OK Corral

CRICKET HEADLINES 1880

Unofficial County Champions: Nottinghamshire

Murdoch's Australians tour and play the first Test match on English soil – at the Oval. England win by 5 wickets

Fred Morley takes 7 wickets for 9 runs for the second time – this time against Surrey, who are all out for 16

Death of Fred Grace, W.G.'s younger brother, and of James Southerton, the first two Test cricketers to die

FEATURE ARTICLES

The Marylebone Club in 1880

'For the greater convenience and comfort of the members, and for the better protection of those in charge of the entrance gates and Pavilion, the committee have thought it advisable to supply a voucher of membership to each member, in accordance with the plan now almost universally adopted in clubs of a similar character. This voucher will have to be produced at the members' entrance gate, and also at the Pavilion.'

Individual innings of Three Figures in 1880
The Universities in 1880
The Counties in 1880
The Australian Matches

OBITUARIES

Gloucestershire county review

'This notice would indeed be incomplete were mention omitted of the very sad loss the county, and indeed the whole cricketing world, sustained by the death of Mr. G.F. Grace. A brilliant field, a splendid batsman, at times a very successful bowler, and one of the most genial and popular men that ever appeared in the cricket field, his early demise will long be deplored, and his memory cherished by all who were acquainted with him, and it will be very difficult to fill the void his death has created.'

Surrey county review

'The greatest misfortune of all was that when death claimed James Southerton on the 16th of June, and thereby deprived Surrey of the services of one of the most successful bowlers that ever appeared in the ranks of the County Eleven, and one of the most straightforward, popular, intelligent, respectful and deserving cricketers that ever put on flannels.'

COUNTY REVIEW

Sussex in 1880

'Sussex is to be congratulated on the improved condition of affairs, and may well be proud of the gallant fight the eleven made with the Australians. The generosity of the Earl of Sheffield in engaging the services of W. Mycroft to instruct the young players of the county has given an impetus to cricket in Sussex that has already borne excellent results, and will possibly be the means of again raising the county to the proud position it once held.'

MATCH REPORTS

England v Australia, played at Kennington Oval, September 6, 7, 8

'The compiler much regrets that the limited space allotted to the Australians' matches precludes the possibility of giving a lengthened account of this famous contest. He must therefore rest content to put on record the following facts anent the match: That in the history of the game no contest has created such world-wide interest; that the attendance on the first and second days were the largest ever seen at a cricket match; that 20,814 persons passed through the turnstiles on the Monday; 19,863 on the Tuesday, and 3,751 on the Wednesday; that fine weather favoured the match from start to finish; that the wickets were faultless; … that universal regret was felt at the unavoidable absence of Mr. Spofforth; and that England won the match by 5 wickets.'

Surrey v Nottinghamshire, played at Kennington Oval, July 26, 27, 28

'Wind and sun, following on the rain of the previous day, had caused the wickets to be in a very bad state, when Surrey began that memorable innings in which a good county eleven were dismissed for the extraordinarily small total of 16. Taking into consideration the calibre of the Surrey team it is probable that the bowling success of Morley and Shaw, in this match, stands unsurpassed in the history of the game. Morley was almost unplayable, as his wonderful analysis will tell.'

Instead of the customary John Wisden & Co introduction hoping for continued support, there was a page of advertisements for 'John Wisden and Co.'s Special Outfits for Members of Cricket Clubs, For Cash Only … On receipt of remittance, Gentlemen may rely upon having them the same day, if in Town, and the following if in the Country.' A new advertiser was Dr. J. Collis Browne's Chlorodyne: 'There has never been a remedy so vastly beneficial to suffering humanity …'

1882

WISDEN 1882

19th Edition
Editor: George H. West
Pages: 224
Price: 1/-
Reprint: Willows
1. 1988 (500 limit)
2. 2004 (250 limit)

THE WORLD AT LARGE

• Failed assassination attempt on Queen Victoria at Windsor
• Anglo-Egyptian War breaks out. British forces occupy Suez Canal
• Problems in Ireland: Charles Stewart Parnell released from prison by Prime Minister Gladstone, but four days later the Chief Secretary for Ireland and his under-secretary are murdered in Dublin by militant republicans
• A second Married Women's Property Act comes into law, allowing British married women to own property in their own right for the first time

CRICKET HEADLINES 1881

Unofficial County Champions: Lancashire

W.N. Roe scores 415* in a Cambridge inter-college match, the highest score in any organised match to date

FEATURE ARTICLES

The Highest Individual Score Recorded
'For two or three minutes Roe played carelessly, but being warned of his so doing, he settled down to careful play. Shortly after this he gave his first chance. He, however, went on hitting very finely, and at 6.30 had made 415, not out; Mr. W.N. Roe thereby has beaten E.F. Tylecote's record of 404, not out. Roe was batting for four hours 55 minutes and ran no less than 708 runs ... Previous to Roe coming to Cambridge (in October 1879) he was at the Clergy Orphan School, Canterbury, where he did great things in 1878, scoring once 266, not out ... Since his arrival here he has several times scored largely in college matches, but when being tried for his Blue, he has been unsuccessful.'
Individual Innings of Three Figures in 1881

OBITUARIES

[No detail, beyond a list of those who died in the past year]
Bathurst, Sir. F. (Hants)
Chatterton, George (York)
Dean, James, senior (Sussex)
Earp, Thomas (Essex)
Fillery, Richard (Sussex)
Fitzgerald, Mr. R. A. (many years Secretary of M.C.C.)
Frere, Mr. H. (Hants)
Hone, Mr. N.
Halliwell, Mr. R. Bossett (Middlesex and M. C. C.)
Howitt, George (Nottinghamshire and Middlesex)
King, Mr. George (Sussex)
Meade, George (Sussex)
Wilkinson, Mr. E. O. H.
Wilson, Mr. C. W. (Surrey)
Webster, Charles (York)

Lancashire in 1881

'Champion of the Counties in 1881! A title most justly earned by a series of brilliant successes almost unparalleled in the history of County Cricket. Undefeated by a single County, Lancashire won no less than six matches by an innings, with plenty of runs to spare; one by ten wickets; one by eight wickets; one by 216 runs; and one by 50 runs; and as to the three drawn games, there was not the remotest chance of either of them ending in defeat, had they been played out … But the summaries do not tell how much of the magnificent success of Lancashire was due to the untiring energy of Mr. Hornby, to the splendid fielding of the eleven, or to the unflagging exertions of every man in the team.'

Hampshire

'It is sincerely to be regretted that the earnest efforts of Mr. Bencraft in the cause of his county's cricket should have met with no success. Hampshire was twice defeated by Sussex, twice by Somersetshire, and of the two matches with M.C.C., one was a defeat and the other a draw.'

Cambridge University v England: *played on the University Ground, Cambridge, May 9, 10, 11*

'Had time permitted, there is no manner of doubt the university would have won an easy victory, as 283 runs were required to win, with only three wickets to fall … The result of the match, therefore, was highly creditable to the Cantabs. Of those who greatly distinguished themselves, three were brothers, Messrs. G.B., J.E.K., and C.T. Studd … and their performances sum up thiswise: Mr. G.B. Studd scored 117, his principal hits being three 5's, eleven 4's and six 3's

Mr. J.E.K. Studd made 83 runs, including one 6, one 5, four 4's and five 3's

Mr. C.T. Studd put together 49, and bowled 40 overs and 2 balls (23 maidens) for 34 runs and 5 wickets.'

Nottinghamshire v Gloucestershire: *played on the Trent Bridge Ground, July 28, 29, 30*

'This match was productive of some large scoring, 878 runs being made for the loss of 30 wickets, giving an average of 29 runs per wicket. Notts went in first, and succeeded in scoring 249. Mills and Shore hit freely and Gunn and Butler played well, but Attewell's 46 not out was certainly the best innings. Gloucestershire, on going in, scored 155, of which number Dr. W.G. Grace made 51, but should have been caught when he made 11. The southern county had to follow on, and the Nottingham bowling was severely punished. Dr. W.G. Grace went in with the score at 82 and stayed until it reached 440. He was then out l.b.w. for a splendid innings of 182, for which he was deservedly applauded on retiring. This is the highest score ever made in a county match on the Trent Bridge ground.'

[From the Marylebone Cricket Club report]

'Pearce spared no pains to render the old ground as true, firm, and green as ever, and on the opening day of the season the wickets left nothing to be desired. The burning sun and drying winds in May, however, materially discounted the care and labour he had bestowed, destroying the beautifully fresh appearance of the turf and rendering it in places scant of herbage.'

1883

- Death of Karl Marx
- Brooklyn Bridge, New York, opens for traffic
- Channel swimmer Matthew Webb dies trying to swim across the Niagara River
- Eruption of Krakatoa, a volcano between Java and Sumatra, kills almost 40,000 people
- The last surviving quagga, a zebra-like animal, dies in Amsterdam Zoo

WISDEN 1883

20th EDITION
EDITOR: George H. West
PAGES: 304
PRICE: 1/-
REPRINT: Willows
1. 1988 (500 limit)
2. 2004 (250 limit)

CRICKET HEADLINES 1882

Unofficial County Champions: Nottinghamshire and Lancashire

The touring Australians win the only Test match of the summer, by 7 runs.

W. Barnes (266) and W. Midwinter (187) put on 454 for the third wicket for MCC and G in a two-day match v Leicestershire

G. Nash takes four wickets in four balls for Lancashire against Somerset

E. Peate (Yorkshire) takes 214 wickets in the season

FEATURE ARTICLES

The Australians in England 1882

'The third team of cricketers from Australia sailed from Melbourne for England in the Peninsular and Oriental Company's steamer *Assam* on March 16th, 1882, and after a very pleasant though not particularly speedy voyage, the vessel anchored at Plymouth at 10.30 on the morning of Wednesday, May 3rd. The manager of the team, Mr. C.W. Beal, of the New South Wales Cricket Association, accompanied by Messrs. Murdoch, Bonnor and Garrett, left the ship and proceeded by train to London. On arriving at Paddington, they at once drove to the quarters secured for them at the Tavistock Hotel, Covent Garden, by Mr. Henry Perkins, Secretary of the Marylebone Cricket Club, who had been acting as their agent. The other members of the team came round to London in the steamer, and joined their companions about twelve hours after.'

Alfred Shaw's Eleven in America, New Zealand and Australia, 1881-82

OBITUARIES

Adams, W. (Surrey)
Earle, Mr. J.H. (Essex)
Kingscote, Mr. R.H. (President of M.C.C. in 1827)
Letby, R. (Yorks)
Lillywhite, James, Sen. (Sussex)
Mills, R. (Kent)
Pauncefote, Mr. Bernard (Oxford University and Middlesex)
Sclater, Mr. A.W.B. (Sussex) (accidentally shot himself)

Kent in 1882

'The five leading batsmen of Kent had higher averages than the five leading batsmen of Notts, and yet the bowling of the southern county was so deplorably weak that, while Notts won nine and lost only two matches, Kent won only two and lost eight. Wootton and G.G. Hearne had the largest share of the bowling, but their wickets cost respectively 18.30 and 26.18 each. Mr. Foord-Kelcey came next to Wootton and G.G. Hearne in point of number of overs bowled and his excellent trundling against Yorkshire, at Gravesend, and against Surrey, at Maidstone, enabled him to come out a the end of the season with an average of 15.11, though his bowling in the other four matches in which he took part was very expensive.'

England v Australia, *at Kennington Oval, August 28 and 29*
'At 114 Jones was run out in a way which gave great dissatisfaction to Murdoch and other Australians. Murdoch played a ball to leg, for which Lyttelton ran. The ball was returned, and Jones having completed the first run, and thinking wrongly, but very naturally, that the ball was dead, went out of his ground. Grace put his wicket down, and the umpire gave him out. Several of the team spoke angrily of Grace's action, but the compiler was informed that after the excitement had cooled down a prominent member of Australian eleven admitted that he should have done the same thing had he been in Grace's place. There was a good deal of truth in what a gentleman in the pavilion remarked, amidst some laughter, that Jones ought to thank the champion for teaching him something … Read joined Lucas, but amid intense excitement he was clean bowled without a run being added. Barnes took Read's place and scored a 2, and 3 byes made the total 75, or 10 to win. After being in a long time for 5 Lucas played the next ball into his wicket, and directly Studd joined Barnes the latter was easily caught off his glove without the total being altered. Peate, the last man, came in, but after hitting Boyle to square-leg for 2 he was bowled, and Australia had defeated England by 7 runs.'

Yorkshire v I Zingari, *played at Scarborough, September 4,5,6*
'By far the most extraordinary thing in the whole match was that NO ANALYSIS OF THE I ZINGARI BOWLING WAS KEPT! *The Field* says "most of the eleven tried their luck with the ball, Mr. Evans doing the lion's share, though, perhaps, the best bowling shown was Mr. Studd's towards the finish, when he gave up lobs." That is all the compiler could learn with regard to the bowling in a part of the match which Yorkshire won by an innings and 91 runs.'

The Largest Innings, 920. The Longest Partnership on Record, 605

Rickling Green Cricket Club v Orleans Club, played at Rickling Green, Friday, Saturday, August 4,5, 1882
[The full scorecard of the inevitably drawn game is given, showing Mr. G.F. Vernon of the Orleans Club made 259 and Mr. A.H. Trevor 338 as they took the score from 20 for 1 to 625 for 2. Rickling Green used nine bowlers, four of whom went for over 100 runs each. Rickling Green, batting first, had been all out for 94.]

The first advertisement to appear after the internal title page was for Thurston's Billiard Tables. 'Prize Medal, London, 1851. Honourable Mention, 1862. Prize Medal, Sydney, 1879, "First Award". Established 1814. By Appointment.' This advertisement appeared several times in subsequent years.

1884

WISDEN 1884

21st EDITION
EDITOR: George H. West
PAGES: 288
PRICE: 1/-
REPRINT: Willows
1. 1984 (500 limit)
2. 2004 (250 limit)

THE WORLD AT LARGE

• Four die in an earthquake in Colchester
• The International Meridian Conference in Washington D.C. establishes world time zones based on Greenwich Mean Time
• Grover Cleveland elected President of USA
• Mark Twain's *Adventures of Huckleberry Finn* published
• China declares war on France

CRICKET HEADLINES 1883

Unofficial County Champions: Nottinghamshire

E. Peate takes 8 wickets for 5 runs for Yorkshire against Surrey

W. Bates takes 14 wickets for 102 runs, including a hat-trick, for England against Australia at Melbourne, as Hon. Ivo Bligh's team win back the Ashes, and the urn is created

FEATURE ARTICLES

The Draft Amended Rules

'On Tuesday, July the 31st, 1883, the Marylebone Cricket Club issued the following draft Amended Rules, to be submitted to all the counties in England, the Cricket Associations of Victoria, New South Wales, Philadelphia and New York, and the universities of Oxford and Cambridge ... Lord Harris's notice of proposed amendment of Law X is as follows: The ball must be fairly bowled, not thrown or jerked, and if the umpire be of the opinion that the delivery is not absolutely fair he must call "no ball".'

[These Laws were adopted in 1884, and for the first time excluded the rules governing the settlement of bets.]

The Hon. Ivo Bligh's Team in Australia

'While taking part in the game called "Tug Of War" on board the *Peshawur* – the steamship which carried the English Cricketers to the Antipodes – the Hon. Ivo Bligh severely injured his right hand, and this mishap prevented his playing in either of the first six matches. This accident was not, unfortunately, the least serious one to befall a member of the team. On Monday, October 16th, the *Peshawur* came into violent collision with the barque *Glenroy*, a short distance from Colombo ... It was subsequently ascertained that Morley had sustained a severe injury to one of his ribs, and though, with admirable pluck, he bowled in several matches, the unfortunate accident compelled him to leave the field during the progress of the second game, and prevented his taking any part in the 3rd, 7th, 8th, 9th, 10th, 14th, 15th, and 17th contests.'

OBITUARIES

Boys, John James (Musician) (Hants, Kent, R.A.)
Brown, John (Notts) (One of the old Nottingham Town Eleven)
Denison, S. (Yorks)
Joel Joby (Many years bowler, & c., at Eton College)
Morse, Mr. Charles (I Zingari)
Randon, F. (Notts, Leicester, and M. C. C.)

46

Gloucestershire in 1883

'With two bowlers to start with and not a single effective one to back them up, the good averages of five or six of the batsmen were powerless to save the county from another disastrous season. Gloucestershire gained a most creditable victory over Lancashire in the last match they played, but the other two victories were over the weak county of Somersetshire. They were twice beaten by Surrey, and once each by Notts, Yorkshire, Middlesex and Lancashire, while of the three drawn games one was a moral victory for Middlesex, and their opponents had the best of the others.'

Australia v England, *played at Melbourne, Jan 19, 21, 22, 1883*

'Massie was clean bowled at 56 for a brilliant 43, and when Murdoch joined Bannerman the play became so exceedingly slow that half an hour was consumed in scoring ten runs. Bannerman was clean bowled at 72, and at 75 Horan was finely caught – right-handed very high up. Then at 78 Bates accomplished the 'hat-trick', dismissing McDonnell, Giffen, and Bonnor with successive balls. Blackham was bowled at 85, and Garrett shared the same fate at 104. With an addition of ten runs a yorker got rid of Palmer, and without any increase in the total Spofforth was bowled and the innings terminated at 5.15 for 114, Murdoch carrying his bat for 19, the result of a two and a half hour stay at the wickets.'

Lancashire v Surrey, *played at Manchester, July 12, 13, 14*

'There were some extraordinary changes in the aspect of the game during the three days this match occupied. On the Thursday, Lancashire, after scoring a first innings of 204 dismissed seven of their opponents for 46 runs, and a crushing defeat seemed in store for Surrey. On the Friday, Surrey, after following-on in a minority of 105 runs played an uphill game so pluckily and successfully, that at the conclusion of the day's play, Lancashire, with all their wickets to fall, had the heavy total of 184 to get to win, a by no means easy task … Some splendid hitting by Briggs and wonderfully defensive play by Barlow, ultimately enabled Lancashire to win the match by three wickets.'

Allen Hill's Benefit Match in 1884

'A splendid bowler in his day, and a thoroughly honest, straightforward, obliging, open-handed man is to have a benefit in the coming season, and the match selected is Yorkshire v Lancashire, to be played at Bramall Lane, Sheffield. Hill's first appearance in a match of importance was on September 9th, 1870, when he played for 22 Colts of Yorkshire v The United North Eleven of England. The late Mr. W.H. Knight, then editor of "Wisden's", wrote of him thus: "Hill (who bowled 5 of the XI) is a bowler who is sure to work his way to the front rank." Though perhaps one of the unluckiest of cricketers (for he seldom went through a season without some mishap), he thoroughly fulfilled his early promise, and has been one of the best, truest, and most effective of fast bowlers. Let us hope his reward, therefore, will be in proportion to his merits.'

1885

WISDEN 1885

22nd EDITION
EDITOR: George H. West
PAGES: 312
PRICE: 1/-
REPRINT: Willows 1983 (unnumbered)

THE WORLD AT LARGE

- General Gordon killed in the Siege of Khartoum
- Lord Salisbury's Conservatives take over from Gladstone's Liberals in a minority administration
- King Leopold II of Belgium proclaims the Congo Free State to be his personal possession
- Professional football is made legal in the U.K.
- The world famous elephant Jumbo, part of Barnum's Circus, is killed in a train crash

CRICKET HEADLINES 1884

Unofficial County Champions: Nottinghamshire

Alfred Shaw takes two hat-tricks in one innings for Nottinghamshire v Gloucestershire at Nottingham

G. Giffen scores a hundred and takes a hat-trick for the Australians against Lancashire

F.R. Spofforth takes 207 first-class wickets during the summer

Robert Percival throws the cricket ball 140 yards and 2 feet, a record that still stands

FEATURE ARTICLES

The Late Mr. John Wisden

'A splendid all-round cricketer in his day: a good bat, a fine field, and as a bowler unsurpassed. A quiet, unassuming and thoroughly upright man.

A fast friend and a generous employer. Beloved by his intimates and employés, and respected by all with whom he came in contact … In 1864 he issued the first number of the "Cricketers' Almanack," a very primitive production consisting of scores only, but which, thanks to the enthusiasm of subsequent editors, has now been accorded the title of "the most accurate and authentic record of the game" published.'

The Gentlemen of Philadelphia in England

'Personnel of the Team

William C. Lowry – Merion Club. Born June 11, 1860. Bowls slow left hand round arm, with a good break from the leg and a peculiar hang. On his day and wicket is very difficult. An active fielder, being the fastest runner and quickest thrower in the team. Is a poor bat.

William C. Morgan, jun – Germantown Club. Born January 31, 1865. Batsman in very correct style, with a stubborn defence, but can hit well to leg and has a good "cut". Is slow in the field.'

The Fourth Australian Team in England

'The compiler regrets that the length to which this book has already extended will not permit of his entering fully into the details of the play in a series of matches which have been the feature of the cricket season in England during the past year, and in taking this course he feels that no apology is necessary, inasmuch as an exhaustive account of the Australian's matches was published in book form immediately after the close of the season, whereas no other annual has appeared, or is likely to appear, in which so much space will be found devoted to the leading Counties, the Universities, the Gentlemen of Philadelphia, the M.C.C., and the great matches of 1884, as in the present number of the Almanack.'

OBITUARIES

Grimston, Hon. Robert
King, Rev. R.T.
Mantle, T.A. (Middx.)

Morley, F. (Notts.)
Mortlock, W. (Surrey)
Ward, Rev. A.R.
Westell, John
Wisden, John (Sussex)
[Grimston is the only MCC President to have died in office.]

Nottinghamshire in 1884

'Arthur Shrewsbury scored innings of 209, 127, 70 and 61, and with an aggregate of 681 runs and very fine average of 37.15 was at the top of the tree in all three important batting columns, and thereby considerably improved on his form of the previous year. But of all the Notts batsmen not one made so remarkable an advance as Scotton, who comes second on the list with the second highest aggregate of 567 and first-rate average of 31.9. Scotton's batting was consistently good throughout the season. Out of 22 innings he was not once dismissed without scoring, and on only three occasions failed to reach double figures. Considering that his average in 1883 for eight completed innings was only 12.3, his success in the past season has been wonderful, and his title to be ranked as the best left-handed batsman in England is indisputable.'

Australia v England, *played at Lord's, July 21, 22, 23*

'Next morning Steel commenced his remarkable innings, joining Ulyett, the overnight not out. At 120 Ulyett was bowled by a yorker for a good 32, and at 135 Harris was clean bowled. Barlow then came to Steel's aid and a complete mastery was obtained over the Australian bowling, 98 runs being put on before the professional was caught in the slips for an invaluable 38. Just previous to Read's dismissal Steel had completed his 100, and he was now joined by Lyttelton. Another long stand was made, 76 runs being put on before Lyttelton was bowled for a capital innings of 31. Only three runs were added, and Steel's magnificent innings came to a close. Steel had been at the wickets while 261 runs had been scored, and a hard chance to Boyle when he had made 48 was the only blemish on his innings. His 148 consisted of thirteen 4's, four 3's, eighteen 2's, and 48 singles, and was the highest score made against the Australians during the season.'

Nottinghamshire v Gloucestershire, *played at Nottingham, July 31, August 1*

'These counties met on most unequal terms, as Notts had won every county match in which they had engaged during the season, while Gloucestershire, in addition to having been beaten in every contest, lost the services of the brothers Grace, who were absent in consequence of the death of their mother. Under such circumstances, a ten wickets' victory for Notts was not a matter for surprise ... Shaw and Attewell bowled throughout both innings of Gloucestershire, and the former not only accomplished the "hat-trick" in *both* innings, but in the first he followed up the feat by taking three wickets in four balls later on.'

[Shaw's figures in the first innings were 41–24–29–8, and in the second innings 38–23–36–6.]

John Wisden is accorded a full-page obituary, inside a heavy black border, immediately after the contents page. Note that the Almanack now has a reputation as 'the most accurate and authentic record of the game'.

1886

WISDEN 1886

23rd EDITION
EDITOR: George H. West
PAGES: 384
PRICE: Limp 1/-
REPRINT: Willows
1. 1985 (500 limit)
2. 2005 (250 limit)

THE WORLD AT LARGE

• Lord Salisbury resigns in January, but regains the premiership in a General Election in July
• Gold is discovered in the Witwatersrand, prompting a gold rush to Transvaal
• Rodin's *The Kiss* first displayed: Robert Louis Stevenson's *The Strange Case Of Dr. Jekyll and Mr. Hyde* and Thomas Hardy's *The Mayor of Casterbridge* published

CRICKET HEADLINES 1885

Unofficial County Champions: Nottinghamshire

W.E. Roller scores a double hundred and performs the hat-trick as Surrey beat Sussex – a unique achievement in cricket

The first five Test series takes place in Australia in 1884-85: England win three Tests, and Australia two

PREFACE

'In issuing the twenty-third edition of their Cricketers' Almanack, Messrs. John Wisden & Co. desire to express their regret at the delay which has occurred in its publication – a circumstance due to the long-continued indisposition of the Compiler.'

FEATURE ARTICLES

Shaw's Team in Australia, 1884-85

'At Adelaide they were met by the leading members of the South Australian Cricketing Association Committee, who conducted them to the city, where the Mayor accorded them an official reception of a very cordial character, remarking that he was sure their visit would be a very pleasant one. Similar kindly greetings were extended to them wherever they went, but from the moment the members of Murdoch's team landed from the *Mirzapore,* prior to the commencement of the third match, it became evident they were animated by a feeling of bitter hostility towards Shaw and his party. As a commencement, the Victoria contingent of the team declined to play for their Colony against the Englishmen, urging as an excuse their want of practice, while it afterwards transpired that Murdoch's eleven had endeavoured to arrange a match with New South Wales on the same days as those fixed for the contest between Shaw's team and Victoria. Next, Murdoch and A. Bannerman refused to take part in the match New South Wales v. Shaw's Eleven, and after the South Australian Cricket Association had succeeded in bringing about a meeting between Shaw's team and Murdoch's eleven at Adelaide, each side receiving 450 pounds, the climax of the quarrel was reached when Murdoch's men declined to play for Combined Australia against the Englishmen on New Year's Day. This unpatriotic conduct was severely condemned by the public and press of Australia.'

The Georgetown Cricket Club

Mr. E.J. Sanders' Team In the United States and Canada

OBITUARIES

Blackman, William (Sussex)
Blore, Rev. Edward William (Eton and Cambridge)
Dudley, Earl of (Oxford University and M.C.C.)

Juniper, John (Sussex)
Luck, William Henry (Umpire)
McIntyre, Martin (Notts)
Oscroft, John (Notts)
O'Shaughnessy, Edward (Kent and M.C.C.)
Sims, Rev. Herbert Marsh (Cambridge University)
Walker, John (Cambridge and Middlesex)
Wilder, Emond (President of the Cricketers' Fund)
Willsher, Edgar (Kent)

ROWLANDS' ODONTO

Is the best, purest, and most fragrant preparation for the teeth. Health depends in a great measure upon the soundness of the teeth, and their freedom from decay; and all dentists allow that neither washes nor pastes can possibly be as efficacious for polishing the teeth and keeping them sound and white as a pure and non-gritty tooth-powder; such ROWLANDS' ODONTO has always proved itself to be. 2s. 9d.

ROWLANDS' MACASSAR OIL

Preserves, strengthens, and beautifies the hair; it contains no lead or mineral ingredients, and can now be also had in a golden colour, which is especially suited for fair or golden-haired children and persons. Sizes, 3/6; 7/; 10/6, equal to four small.

ROWLANDS' KALYDOR

Is a most cooling, healing, and refreshing wash for the face, hands, and arms, and is perfectly free from any mineral or metallic admixtures; it disperses freckles, tan, redness, pimples, sunburn, prickly heat, &c. 4s. 6d.

Ask any Chemist or Hairdresser for Rowlands' Articles, of 20, Hatton Garden, London, and avoid spurious, worthless imitations under the same or similar names.

COUNTY REVIEW

Sussex in 1885

'Death removed Mr. William Blackman and John Juniper, and business kept Mr. H. Whitfield away from all but one of the matches, and Sussex therefore lost the services of three cricketers who had contributed largely to the successes of the previous season. These losses, however, did not wholly account for the decadence of Sussex cricket in 1885. The batting and bowling generally was not nearly up to the standard of 1884. In that year eight batsmen secured averages of 20 or upwards, in place of only three in 1885, and in bowling, five out of the six regular bowlers in 1884 each obtained a large number of wickets at an average of less than 19 runs, while in 1885 not one except Juniper took any at a less average cost than 21.17. Juniper played in the first six matches, and bowled with much success, 22 wickets falling to him at an average of 13.3.'

MATCH REPORTS

Surrey v Sussex – A Record. *Played at Kennington Oval, June 29, 30, July 1*

'The last Surrey wicket was not obtained until three-quarters of an hour after luncheon on the Tuesday, occupying in all eight hours and three-quarters in compiling. Mr. Roller, who had made 131 on the Monday, was the ninth man out with the total at 585, having been in while 418 runs were put on. Like Mr. Read, he made his long and splendid score apparently without a mistake, and the figures of his 204 – the highest innings scored by him during the season – were seventeen 4's, seventeen 3's, twenty-seven 2's and thirty-one singles … Sussex, whose bowling and fielding had been thoroughly worn out, started their batting at 3.55, and were dismissed in just over three hours for 168, their last wicket falling within a few minutes of time. The first two or three batsmen did fairly well, and indeed 130 went up with only four out, but then came a series of disasters. Mr. Roller was put on to bowl, and after being hit for several overs, he performed the "hat trick" by getting J. Hide caught at point off the last ball of one over and bowling Humphreys and Mr. Brann with the first two balls of his following over.'

Advertisements now include full pages for 'J. Davenport, Cricket, Lawn Tennis and Football Maker' and Rowlands' Articles, including 'Odonto – Is the best, purest, and most fragrant preparation for the teeth' (pictured) and 'Kalydor – Is a most cooling, healing, and refreshing wash for the face, hands, and arms; it disperses freckles, tan, redness, pimples, sunburn, prickly heat, &c. 4s 6d.'

1887

WISDEN 1887

24th EDITION
EDITOR: Charles F. Pardon
PAGES: 348
PRICE: Limp 1/-
REPRINT: Willows
1. 1989 (500 limit)
2. 2004 (250 limit)

THE WORLD AT LARGE

• Arthur Conan Doyle's first Sherlock Holmes story, *A Study In Scarlet,* published
• The first book of Esperanto grammar is published in Poland by the language's inventor, Dr. Ludovic Zamenhof
• Lottie Dod, aged 15, wins the women's singles at Wimbledon
• The year of Queen Victoria's Golden Jubilee, celebrating her 50 years on the throne

CRICKET HEADLINES 1886

Unofficial County Champions: Nottinghamshire

England win all three Tests against the touring Australians

A.E. Stoddart makes 485* for Hampstead against the Stoics, the highest individual score yet recorded in an organised match

W.G. Grace takes all ten wickets for M.C.C. against Oxford University, and scores a hundred in the same game

PREFACE

'… The Almanack has unfortunately suffered during the last few years from irregularities in time of publication; but, as I am assured of every assistance from the proprietors, I can promise the numerous subscribers that they will receive it regularly in future. Messrs. Wisden requested me to undertake to tell the story of the chief play of 1886, and that task I have been able to accomplish owing to the assistance promptly and generously rendered to me by Mr. Sydney H. Pardon, Mr. Edgar S. Pardon, Mr. C. Stewart Caine and other writers upon, and reporters of, cricket who have now been associated with me for several years … I hope next year to devote more space to the less important counties, several of which, besides those given, are making capital progress … Charles F. Pardon.'

FEATURE ARTICLES

The Australians in England
'The causes of the non-success of our last opponents were the limited amount of high-class batting, the partial failure of Spofforth's bowling, the uncertainty of the fielding, a lack of enthusiasm and cohesion in the team, and the absence of the necessary amount of authority and experience on the part of the captain. W. L. Murdoch, who was chief in the field of the three teams of 1880, 1882, and 1884, may not have exhibited all the qualities which go to make up that rare and valuable being, an ideal captain – but he certainly had a larger experience and a stronger will than the gentleman who, with the best of intentions, and the greatest sincerity of purpose, led the team of 1886. It is exceedingly doubtful whether even an ideal captain would have pulled the team through its engagements, unless, indeed, he had been backed up by that confidence and energy which we see so seldom in any teams but those that meet with early and brilliant successes.'

The Tour of the Parsees
'From a cricket point of view the tour of the Parsees was a failure, and we have not thought it worth while to print any of the scores. In arranging the fixtures, the powers of the players had been much overrated, and in the whole series of matches, the Parsees only gained one victory. Despite their ill-success, however, they thoroughly enjoyed the trip, and returned home with the pleasantest remembrances of English cricket and English hospitality.'

The County Qualification
The Highest Individual Innings on Record

CRICKETERS' ALMANACK FOR 1887.

TWENTY-FOURTH EDITION.

JOHN WISDEN'S

CRICKETERS' ALMANACK

FOR 1887.

CONTAINING THE

FULL SCORES, BOWLING ANALYSES & DESCRIPTIONS

OF THE

AUSTRALIAN AND OTHER PRINCIPAL MATCHES

PLAYED IN 1886,

WITH

COUNTY AND GENERAL AVERAGES

AND OTHER INFORMATION USEFUL AND INTERESTING

TO CRICKETERS.

Edited by

CHARLES F. PARDON.

London:

PUBLISHED AND SOLD BY JOHN WISDEN AND CO.,

AT THEIR

CRICKETING AND BRITISH SPORTS DEPÔT,

21, Cranbourn Street, near Leicester Square, London, W.C.

AND OF ALL BOOKSELLERS AND AT ALL BOOKSTALLS.

One Shilling.]   [Post Free 1s. 3d.

Entered at Stationers' Hall.

COUNTY REVIEW

Essex in 1886

'Essex achieved a fair amount of success last season, and their record in the twelve matches played of five won, six lost and one drawn, is distinctly creditable, considering that one-half of these contests were against first-class counties. They twice scored innings of over 200 against Derbyshire, and made the second highest total hit against Lancashire. The smallest total for which they were dismissed was 33 in the return match with Surrey. The Essex Club have made considerable progress of late years, and may now fairly rank as one of the best of the second-class counties. Their new county ground at Leyton, which is a very attractive one, was acquired at considerable expense, and will no doubt go a long way to improve their position in the cricket world.'

MATCH REPORTS

Australians v Surrey, *played at Kennington Oval, May 20, 21, 22*

'The first day was rendered additionally important by the visit of the Prince of Wales to the ground. This was the first time that His Royal Highness, who is the ground landlord of Kennington Oval, had attended a cricket match on the ground, and the Australians naturally considered it a great compliment that he should make his visit on the occasion of their first appearance in London.'

Eton v Harrow, *played at Lord's, July 10, 11*

'Eton went in first and made 265, but this performance, good as it was, sunk into insignificance when compared to what followed. Harrow's innings began at five-and-twenty minutes past four, and when seven o'clock came 219 runs had been scored with only one wicket down – an unparalleled achievement in the long series of matches between the two schools.'

[Despite a partnership of 235 for the second wicket, Eton fought back, and Harrow only narrowly secured victory, by three wickets.]

Charles Pardon takes over as editor and so begins his family's long connection with Wisden. *This is the first time an editor's name appears on the cover (pictured). Apart from the apology in the previous edition for delays caused by the 'indisposition' of George H. West, there is no mention of him. West died in 1896 and a brief obituary appears in* Wisden *1897.*

1888

WISDEN 1888

25th EDITION
EDITOR: Charles F. Pardon
PAGES: 412
PRICE: Limp 1/-
REPRINT: Willows
1. 1989 (500 limit)
2. 2005 (250 limit)

THE WORLD AT LARGE

- Vincent van Gogh cuts off half of his left ear
- The Football League is formed. The first matches take place on 8 September, between the twelve member clubs
- Kaiser Wilhelm II of Germany succeeds to the throne
- Benjamin Harrison beats incumbent Grover Cleveland in the US presidential election

CRICKET HEADLINES 1887

Unofficial County Champions: Surrey

England win both Test matches in Australia

M.C.C. celebrates its centenary with festival matches at Lord's

PREFACE

'The present issue of Wisden's Almanack is the twenty-fifth, and while all the old features have been retained, several new ones have been added.

It will be seen that additional space has been given to County Cricket, as not only have the leading clubs been exhaustively treated, but most of the minor counties have had their claims recognised to the utmost of my power.'

FEATURE ARTICLES

The Forthcoming Season and the Classification of Counties, by the editor

'A question that during the autumn has aroused some attention has been the division, for purposes of what I have just called statistical comparison, of counties into first-class and second-class. It is not desired that in matters of legislation, or where the common interests of county clubs are involved, there should be any line of demarcation established between, say, Surrey and Hampshire. When, however, the point under discussion is not legislative, but refers to tables of results and averages, it is clear that some distinction must be made between the leading teams and those of less ability.'

Shaw and Shrewsbury's Team in Australia, 1886-87

'The team taken out to Australia in the autumn of 1886 was one of the strongest that ever left England for the Colonies. It consisted of A. Shrewsbury, W. Barnes, W. Gunn, W. Scotton, W. Flowers, M. Sherwin and A. Shaw (Notts), R. G. Barlow and J. Briggs (Lancashire), G.A. Lohmann and M. Read (Surrey), W. Bates (Yorkshire), and James Lillywhite (Sussex). The team took part in twenty-nine matches, of which ten were of first-class importance. Of these ten first-class matches the Englishmen won six, lost two, and left two unfinished. They lost two matches out of three with New South Wales, but on the other hand they beat two combination teams (one of them a very powerful side), gained two victories over the Melbourne Club's Australian team, and won their return match with Victoria. It is understood that the tour did not yield much profit, but the cricket shown was very fine indeed, not a single defeat being sustained on a hard wicket.'

Formation of a County Cricket Council

The L.B.W. Discussion

Elphinstone, Sir Robert D.H. (In Harrow eleven, 1859, 1860)

Lindow, Mr. H.W. (played in the famous match, Rugby School v M.C.C., described in *Tom Brown's Schooldays*)

Welch, Mr. J.B. (a regular frequenter of Lord's)

Romilly, Mr. Charles (M.C.C.)

COUNTY REVIEW

[Wisden *now distinguishes between the 'Counties' (Surrey, Lancashire, Nottinghamshire, Middlesex, Yorkshire, Sussex, Kent, Gloucestershire and Derbyshire) and the 'Minor Counties' (Leicestershire, Essex, Somersetshire, Warwickshire, Northamptonshire, Cheshire and Hampshire]*

Derbyshire in 1887

'Circumstances generally seemed to conspire against Derbyshire last summer, and for the second year in succession not a single victory rewarded the efforts of the eleven in engagements with their great rivals. For several years the bad luck of Derbyshire had been notorious, but their misfortunes reached a climax in 1887. Through lack of funds the engagements with Kent – the only first-class county matches in which the result was not to some extent a foregone conclusion – had to be abandoned … and, to complete a tale of misfortune, the example of Shacklock in abandoning Derbyshire for a more prosperous county was followed by Frank Sugg, while, in addition, Mr. L.C. Docker discovered he had no qualification to play for the side.'

MATCH REPORTS

Shaw's Team v. Australia, *played at Sydney, January 28, 29, 31*

'The great match, and also the most conspicuous triumph of the tour, the Englishmen winning by 13 runs, after being dismissed in their first innings for a total of 45. When stumps were drawn on the Saturday they did not seem to have even a remote chance of success, being only some 20 odd runs to the good with three wickets to fall in their second innings. On the Monday, however, they played up in splendid style, and gained a victory that might fairly be compared to the seven runs win of Australia over England at Kennington Oval in 1882. Briggs, Flowers, and Sherwin batted so well that Australia had to go in with 111 to get to win. With the wicket in very fair order this seemed an easy task, and defeat was not thought of, but Barnes bowled so finely, and was so ably supported by Lohmann that the total only reached 97. Barring one mistake the English fielding was magnificent. Except that Giffen was still too ill to appear, the Australian team was almost a representative one, though Palmer and Horan should have been played in preference to Midwinter and McShane.'

MISCELLANEOUS

Mr. C.A. Absolon

'Though in his 70th year, Mr. C.A. Absolon, the veteran cricketer, showed no decline of energy in 1887. He scored 1,070 runs, with an average of 16.30 per innings, and took no fewer than 222 wickets. Three times he did the "hat trick"; once he took four wickets in four balls, and once five wickets in ten balls.'

Charles Pardon greatly expanded the Almanack – as he explains in the Preface – and ordered the contents fully for the first time so that regular readers could find their way around this increasingly thick volume with comparative ease. He also included editorial comment on the state of the game for the first time, in his four-page article 'The Forthcoming Season and the Classification of Counties'.

1889

WISDEN 1889

26th EDITION
EDITOR: Charles F. Pardon
PAGES: 420
PRICE: Limp 1/-
REPRINT: Willows
1. 1990 (500 limit)
2. 2005 (250 limit)

THE WORLD AT LARGE

• A strike by London's dockers in August and September cripples the capital's trade
• The Eiffel Tower is completed after three years' construction
• The last bareknuckle boxing match – John L Sullivan defeats Jake Kilrain after 75 rounds lasting over two hours in 100° heat in Mississippi
• Cleveland Street scandal – stories of a male brothel in London frequented by nobility and royalty titillate the public

CRICKET HEADLINES 1888

Unofficial County Champions: Surrey

England win both Tests of the summer against Australia

Charles Turner takes 283 first-class wickets at 11.68 runs apiece while touring with Australia (314 wickets in all matches)

George Lohmann also takes over 200 wickets, as he will in each of the next two seasons

W.W. Read scores 338 for Surrey against Oxford University

PREFACE

'Wisden's Almanack has now reached its twenty-sixth year, and, without losing any of the old features, we have been able to make the book even more comprehensive than before, and to signalise the extraordinary success that bowlers achieved in 1888 by giving new portraits, specially photographed by Hawkins of Brighton, of six of the most prominent and skilful of their number.'

FEATURE ARTICLES

County Cricket, by the editor
'I ought, perhaps, to repeat my conviction that county cricket is the very best sort of cricket, and that competition, whatever can be said against it by well-intentioned theorists, is an altogether admirable thing for the game. Competition means keen feeling on the part of all the players, and hearty interest on the part of the local public. This interest takes the practical shape of subscriptions and gate-money for the county club, and as cricket is a public game, with heavy expenses, gate-money is a first necessity of existence.'

A Few Jottings, by Robert Thoms
'The past season has undoubtedly been a bowler's one, for the grounds on many occasions were so treacherous through rain that most of the leading bowlers could do a nice little bit of conjuring with the batsmen. Cricket, like other events of life, alters according to its surroundings, and the goodness of the wickets during the last twenty years has brought forth not only more forcing batting, but also deep out-fielding, with bowling that partakes more of the art of trying to get the batsman caught than, as of yore, going for the sticks.'

SIX GREAT BOWLERS OF THE YEAR

G.A. Lohmann

'George Alfred Lohmann was born at Kensington, June 5, 1865, and first played for Surrey in 1884. He is by general consent admitted to be one of the best bowlers and most accomplished all-round cricketers ever seen, and he fairly challenged comparison with Turner by what he did during the season of 1888. Lohmann and Turner are, indeed, very much alike. They bowl with remarkable skill and judgment; their batting and fielding are invaluable to their side, and they both have that peculiar electrical quality of rising to a great occasion. It has often enough been said of cricketers of proved skill, when they have failed, that the match has been too big for them, but certainly no match was ever too big for George Lohmann or Charles Turner.'

**J. Briggs   J.J. Ferris   R. Peel
C.T.B. Turner   S.M.J. Woods**

OBITUARIES INCLUDE

Dallas, Lieut.-Col. G.F. (Harrow Eleven, 1843)
Baker, Mr. W. De Chair (A founder of the Canterbury Week)
Shaw, J. C. (Notts)
Fox, Mr. H. (Somersetshire). Lost in the Caucasus
Sewell, Thomas, Sen. (Surrey)
Dawson, E. (Yorkshire)

COUNTY REVIEW

Yorkshire in 1888

'Bearing especially in mind that the county started the year as badly as can be, the executive must be heartily congratulated upon the fact that the team came out practically only inferior to Surrey among the eight important counties. The position of second place among the crack counties was, it will be remembered, very keenly contested towards the end of the season, and when all the results were made up it was found that Yorkshire and Kent tied for that honour, just ahead of Gloucestershire.'

MATCH REPORTS

Lancashire v Surrey, *played at Manchester, August 2*
A start was made punctually at noon, and at half past six the match was all over … Just at half-past six Lohmann bowled Pilling, the innings finishing for 63, and the match resulting in favour of Surrey by an innings and 25 runs. This memorable match – the only first-class county engagement, we believe, which was ever played out in a day – attracted nearly ten thousand people. In the second innings Lohmann's five wickets cost 38, but his figures for the entire game – 13 wickets for 51 runs – were exceptionally fine.'

England v Australia, *played at Kennington Oval, August 13, 14*
'The crowd followed the game with great attention, and applauded heartily the few good things that the Australians did, while they naturally and very properly rewarded with the cheers so dear to public men, the magnificent all-round cricket of the winners. We have praised the Colonial team for what they did at Lord's, but the confidence and the abounding energy were this time on the side of England, and it was worth going miles to see how freely and with what skill our representatives acquitted themselves.'

Charles Pardon introduces the forerunner to the Five Cricketers of the Year with his selection of six bowlers – complete with a photograph (pictured): 'Our portraits are from fresh negatives taken by the well-known Brighton firm of E. Hawkins and Co., who have made cricket photography their speciality, and whose reputation will certainly not suffer by the present specimen of their ability.' The appearance of a two-page section entitled 'Some Cricket Records' signals the beginning of a more ordered editorial policy towards the statistical side of the game.

1890

WISDEN 1890

- 27th Edition
- Editor: Charles F. Pardon
- Pages: 376
- Price: Limp 1/-
- Reprint: Willows
- 1. 1990 (500 limit)
- 2. 2007 (250 limit)

THE WORLD AT LARGE

- The Forth Bridge, the longest in Britain, is opened
- Kaiser Wilhelm II forces Bismarck to resign as Chancellor: Punch prints Tenniel's celebrated cartoon, *Dropping The Pilot*
- Death of Vincent van Gogh at his own hand after a short period in which he produced many of his greatest works
- The Meiji Constitution comes into effect in Japan, and the first elected Diet (Parliament) is convened

CRICKET HEADLINES 1889

Unofficial County Champions: Surrey, Lancashire and Nottinghamshire

New Lord's pavilion completed

5-ball overs introduced

A team led by C.A. Smith tours South Africa and plays what subsequently are declared to be the first Test matches between England and South Africa; England win both games

PREFACE

'It may be taken for granted that *Wisden's Cricketers Almanack* needs little nowadays of either introduction to the public or apology for its existence ... Every effort has been made to render *Wisden* complete, accurate and readable, and I hope the novelty will be appreciated of collecting a mass of expert opinion upon current topics.'

FEATURE ARTICLES

Bowling, by George Lohmann
'I think it is necessary for a bowler to understand at least the theory of batting, as he is then able to find out the batsman's weak points, and bowl accordingly. You cannot lay down any hard and fast rule to break through all defences, for what one man has great difficulty in playing another will score from. The wickets are in such good order nowadays that in dry weather it is no easy matter to get really first-class batsmen out.'

Some Questions of the Day
The System of Appointing Umpires: 'We can all remember when the counties did as clubs generally do now – appointed their own umpires in all matches. I do not think there was much downright dishonesty under the old plan. There was some, no doubt, but the real objections were that the county umpire got to regard himself as a member of the team – and a pretty useful twelfth man he sometimes was – and, further, no man could forget he had to look for his living to the county that employed him. The plan was emphatically open to suspicion, and I suppose no one would wish to go back to it.'

The Reforms of 1889

NINE GREAT BATSMEN OF THE YEAR

A. Shrewsbury

'At the age of nineteen ... [Shrewsbury] appeared in the Nottingham county eleven, and a year later he was chosen for Players against Gentlemen. Finely as he played on many occasions it was not until after his visit to Australia in the winter of 1881-2 that he took his present position at the head of professional batsmen. Just before he went to the Colonies his health was so delicate as to cause considerable anxiety, but a winter in the warmer climate of Australia did wonders for him; and his batting during the last few years, as all cricket readers are well aware, has been some of the most remarkable in the history of the game. Indeed, on performances he can claim superiority over all English batsmen save and except Mr. W. G. Grace. In the season of 1887 his batting average in first-class matches was 78, which, curiously enough, just tied the highest average that Mr. Grace had ever obtained.'

R. Abel   W. Barnes   W. Gunn   L. Hall   R. Henderson   J.M. Read   F.H. Sugg   A. Ward

---

OBITUARIES INCLUDE

Cropper, William (Derbyshire). Killed at Football
Ridley, Bob (known as Bob the Bellman at Canterbury)
Jupp, Henry (Surrey)
Absolom, Mr. C. A. (Cambridge University and Kent). Accidentally killed in Port of Spain, West Indies
Joy, Jonathan (Yorkshire)
Papillon, Rev. John (Played in First University Match)

COUNTY REVIEW

Kent in 1889

'Last summer, in addition of course to the Canterbury Week, there were two matches at Maidstone, and one match each at Gravesend, Blackheath, and Beckenham. The peculiarities of the Maidstone ground have been commented upon very often, and the slope is so considerable there that no amount of care or cultivation would make Mote Park a really fit place for a big match. Still the difficulties of the ground are small compared with those encountered at Beckenham on the occasion of the return match with Nottinghamshire. The Kent Committee should certainly put pressure upon local committees to see that suitable wickets are prepared.'

MATCH REPORTS

The English Team in South Africa

'In all, they took part in nineteen matches, winning thirteen, losing four, and leaving two unfinished. All the beatings were sustained in the early part of the trip, and it is no libel to say that for a time generous hospitality had a bad effect upon the cricket ... However, as soon as the men settled down to the serious business of their tour they did even better than might have been expected from the composition of the side, and went on from victory to victory. It was never intended, or considered necessary, to take out a representative English team for a first trip to the Cape, and certain laments which were indulged in at home when the news of the early defeats came to hand were found to be quite uncalled for. The heroes of the trip were undoubtedly Abel and Briggs, the former with the bat and Briggs with the ball literally doing marvels.'

MISCELLANEOUS

'On Tuesday, December 10, a private meeting of representatives of the eight first-class counties – Surrey, Notts, Lancashire, Kent, Middlesex, Gloucestershire, Yorkshire and Sussex – was held at Lord's to discuss the method of deciding the county championship, and it was agreed that in future drawn games should be ignored altogether, and only wins and losses counted ... In future, therefore, county competitions will be estimated by wins and losses alone, the defeats being deducted from the victories.'

The 1889 innovation of featuring six bowlers with a photograph was clearly a success. 'Encouraged by the many kind things that were said about the portraits we published last year, we determined to issue something of the same kind with the Almanack for 1890.' So now we have nine great batsmen of the year – plus 'a mass of expert opinion', as the editor tells us in the Preface.

59

1891

WISDEN 1891

28th Edition
Editor: Sydney H. Pardon
Pages: 420
Price: Limp 1/-
Reprint: Willows
1. 1991 (500 limit)
2. 2007 (250 limit)

THE WORLD AT LARGE

• London-Paris telephone system opens
• The Carnegie Hall opens in New York, with Tchaikovsky as guest conductor
• The first penalty kick is awarded in football: John Heath of Wolverhampton Wanderers scores against Accrington Stanley
• Canada's Prime Minister, Sir John MacDonald, dies in office aged 76
• The first motor car is sold, by Armand Peugeot for Ffr 3,500

CRICKET HEADLINES 1890

County Champions: Surrey

England win the series against Australia by two matches to nil, with the Manchester Test being abandoned without a ball being bowled

In South Africa, the Currie Cup tournament is established

PREFACE

'The death in April last of my brother, Mr. Charles F. Pardon, left *Wisden's Almanack* without an editor, and the task devolved upon me of filling the vacant position.'

FEATURE ARTICLES

Cambridge Memories, by A.G. Steel
'As I was one of the unvanquished 1878 team I am naturally open to the charge of prejudice; I shall risk that, however, and say that in my opinion that was the best side that Cambridge has turned out in my recollection. It played eight matches, and won everyone, including a defeat of Gregory's Australian team by an innings and 72 runs … Alfred and Edward Lyttelton were then at their very best; in fact, the latter's success that one season was phenomenal. Always a good batsman, the office of captain had no sooner become his than he played as he never did before, or since. He went to the very top of the tree, and the close of the season's record showed his to be the highest amateur average – viz. 29.25, the champion running a very close second.'

The Australians In England, 1890
'The one serious mistake in making up the side was the selection of K. E. Burn. The Tasmanian player had on many occasions – and notably against Mr. Vernon's English Eleven in the season of 1887-8 – proved himself a capable batsman, but it was as a wicket-keeper, not as a batsman, that he was chosen, and only when he had accepted the terms offered him and joined the ship at Adelaide was the discovery made that he had never kept wicket in his life. How this ludicrous blunder arose we are quite unable to say, but fortunately for the team the consequences were less serious than they might have been.'

The English Team in India

FIVE GREAT WICKET-KEEPERS

M. Sherwin
'For the last ten years he has, among English professional wicket-keepers, fairly divided honours with Pilling. Always in the best of spirits, and never discouraged, however much the game may be going against his side, Sherwin is one of the cheeriest and pluckiest of cricketers.

In point of style behind the wicket he is more demonstrative than his Lancashire rival, but, though the applause and laughter of the spectators may occasionally cause him to go a little too far, he has certainly never done anything to really lay him open to censure. For a man of his great bulk he is wonderfully quick on his feet, and at times brings off extraordinary catches. Apart from his wicket-keeping, he is by no means a bad bat, and he has on many occasions scored well for Notts when runs have been sadly needed.'

J.M. Blackham   G. MacGregor   R. Pilling   H. Wood

OBITUARIES INCLUDE

Charles F. Pardon
'When Mr. Pardon first became associated with it, the Almanack had reached a critical stage of its existence, an unfortunate delay in the production of the volume for 1886 – a delay for which we were in no way responsible – having to some extent injured its influence. However, Mr. Pardon set to work with characteristic energy to make up the lost ground, and the best proof of his success was found in the largely-increased favour extended to the Almanack by the public during the years of his editorship.'

Iddison, Roger (Yorkshire)
Midwinter, W. (Gloucestershire and Australia)

COUNTY REVIEW

Gloucestershire:
'Not the least noteworthy fact in connection with the season's work was the great amount of success achieved by Mr. E.M. Grace – now the oldest cricketer taking part in first-class matches. His record in county contests – 512 runs, with an average of 20.12 – is one of which many a younger batsman might feel proud, but when it is remembered Mr. Grace reached the zenith of his fame twenty-seven years ago, his achievements are little short of marvellous.'

MATCH REPORTS

England v Australia, *played at Lord's, Jul 21, 22, 23, 1890*
'The England team was an immensely strong one, and yet not quite so powerful as that originally chosen by the M.C.C. committee, the places intended for Mr. Stoddart and Briggs being given to Maurice Read and Barnes. Mr. Stoddart preferred playing for Middlesex against Kent at Tonbridge, and Briggs very properly resigned his place when he found that he had not sufficiently recovered from a strain to enable him to bowl. The eleven, if not quite the best in the country, still formed a splendid combination, and, as it happened, the batting can best be judged from the fact that the three last men on the order were Lohmann, Mr. McGregor and Attewell. It was a great compliment to Mr. McGregor to select him as wicket-keeper for England against Australia, but no one disputed that the distinction had been fairly earned by his achievements for Cambridge. It may be said at once that, though he missed one or two difficult chances, he kept wicket magnificently all through the match, fairly dividing honours with Blackham. In the whole course of the game neither wicket-keeper gave away a single bye.'

Sydney Pardon takes on the editor's role from his brother, Charles, who was only 40 when he died. The four editions he edited had seen Wisden *expanded and given a shape that we recognise today. Sydney is left with the problem that has tested every editor since, as he explains in his Preface: 'With an ever-increasing list of matches it becomes more and more difficult each succeeding year to do justice, within the space at command, to the season's cricket ...'*

Scorecards and reports of inter-colonial matches in Australia are given for the first time.

1892

WISDEN 1892

29th EDITION
EDITOR: Sydney Pardon
PAGES: 412
PRICE: Limp 1/-
REPRINT: Willows
1. 1992 (500 limit)
2. 2008 (250 limit)

THE WORLD AT LARGE

• Death of Prince Albert Victor, Duke of Clarence, second in line to the throne, aged 28
• After a general election in July, Gladstone finally becomes Prime minister again in August
• Grover Cleveland defeats President Harrison in the U.S. election, to become the only man to serve two non-consecutive terms as President
• The first performance of The Nutcracker Suite by the Imperial Ballet in St. Petersburg. Despite Tchaikovsky's music, it is not a success

CRICKET HEADLINES 1891

County Champions: Surrey

Somerset admitted to the County Championship

PREFACE

'A full record of a year's cricket makes, as time goes on, such increased demands upon the space available that it is always difficult to introduce new matter, but as far as possible I shall always endeavour to present some novel features ... Some little difficulty was experienced in choosing the subject for the photograph which is now an essential feature of Wisden ...'

FEATURE ARTICLES

Meeting of County Secretaries
'Mr. E. M. GRACE said he had been asked by the umpires named to bring their memorial before the meeting of county secretaries, and he was entirely in favour of the increase asked for ... He (Mr. Grace) did not know whether any of the gentlemen present had officiated as umpires, but if they did so they would probably find it was extremely hard and tiring work ... If umpires were properly paid for their duties there was much less chance of having inferior men, and there would be no inducement for an umpire to give a man out leg-before-wicket when he was not out. Mr. Grace concluded by moving that in future umpires be paid £6.'
The Development of Cricket, by Hon. R.H. Lyttelton
The Bibliography of Cricket, by Alfred J. Gaston
The English Team in America

FIVE GREAT BOWLERS

J.W. Sharpe
'Bowling always above medium pace, [Sharpe] has a beautifully easy action, and can, with the least possible indication of what he is going to do, put down an extra fast ball. This peculiar gift, for a gift it may fairly be called, has been the means of getting him many a wicket. For a bowler of his pace he has a remarkable break from the off, and of the players now before the public perhaps no one, except Mr. Woods, can bowl so good a yorker. As a bat and field,

Sharpe is unfortunately handicapped by the fact that he has only one eye, but despite this great deprivation, he has many a time made a useful score for Surrey.'
W. Attewell   J.T. Hearne   F. Martin   A.W. Mold

[For the first time, a full obituary section is included]
George Parr
'George Parr (Notts) died June 23. As he was born at Radcliffe-on-Trent on May 22, 1826, he had, at the time of his death, completed his sixty-fifth year. Readers of Wisden's Almanack will not need to be told that George Parr for many years occupied an undisputed position as the best bat in England, succeeding Fuller Pilch in that enviable distinction … His career as a public player was a very long one, commencing in 1844 and not coming to an end until 1871. He lived all his life in his native village, and the attendance at his funeral there showed the respect in which he was held. With the wreaths on his coffin was placed a branch from the tree at the Trent Bridge ground which has for a generation past been known as George Parr's Tree.'
Richard Pilling
'Richard Pilling, the greatest English wicket-keeper of his day, died on March 28. He was born on July 5, 1855, and was thus in his thirty-sixth year … Succeeding Mr. Jackson in the county team, he was the regular wicket-keeper for Lancashire from his match in 1877 down to the end of the season of 1889, and, no doubt, but for the unfortunate failure of his health, would have retained the post for several years longer. Unhappily in the winter of 1889-90 he caught a severe cold while taking part in a football match. An attack of influenza and inflammation of the lungs followed, and from this he never recovered.'
Edward Barratt   Joseph Hunter   Edward Lumb

Somersetshire
'With the close of his brilliant career at Cambridge University it was feared that Mr. Woods would be lost to Somersetshire after the past season, but happily his return to Australia has been delayed for at least another year. Sooner or later, however, Somersetshire will have to take the field without the famous Cantab, and it behoves the executive in the meantime to discover fresh bowling talent.'

Victoria v South Australia, *played at Melbourne, January 1,2,3,5*
'In this match South Australia beat Victoria by an innings and 62 runs. The victory was mainly the work of George Giffen, who has never displayed in a more conspicuous light his pre-eminent qualities as an all-round cricketer. He played an innings of 237, and took in all twelve Victorian wickets – five for 89 runs and seven for 103. His magnificent display dwarfed everything else in the game, but several other players showed good batting, notably Trott with a second innings of 81 for Victoria. Phillips again bowled well, taking in an innings of 472, six wickets for 91 runs.'
Somersetshire v Surrey, *played at Taunton, August 13, 14, 15*
'From every point of view this game, so far as Somersetshire were concerned, was a great success, the home team having the distinction, subsequently shared by Middlesex, of beating the famous Surrey eleven in the county championship competition. The attendances were larger than at any previous match on the Taunton ground, fine weather prevailed throughout, and the contest, which was played on a good wicket, produced a remarkable finish, Surrey being only beaten a minute before time.'

For collectors of cricket books, the bibliography compiled by Alfred Gaston is of immense importance. This is the earliest attempt at a definitive list, and it is continued two years later. Ultimately, in 1977, came 'Padwick's Bibliography'.

1893

WISDEN 1893

30th EDITION
EDITOR: Sydney Pardon
PAGES: 448
PRICE: Limp 1/-
REPRINT: Willows
1. 1992 (500 limit)
2. 2008 (250 limit)

THE WORLD AT LARGE

• The Independent Labour Party holds its first meeting, under the chairmanship of Keir Hardie
• New Zealand becomes the first country to give women the vote
• European colonial powers are rampant: France gains control over Laos, Dahomey and Ivory Coast, and establishes French Guiana in South America. Britain annexes part of Afghanistan into British India
• Wall Street market collapse in June triggers recession that will last four years
• Statue of Eros is put up in Piccadilly Circus

CRICKET HEADLINES 1892

County Champions: Surrey

English teams tour both Australia and South Africa in 1891-2, playing tests in both countries: England win the only Test in South Africa, but lose the Ashes to a revitalised Australia

PREFACE

'As a friend of mine – not wont to be demonstrative – assured me the other day that he had no pleasanter evenings in the whole year than when the appearance of Wisden enabled him to fight the battles of the cricket season over again, I am fortified in the belief that the Almanack fulfils its mission and preserves in a readable and attractive form a record of all that is essential in connection with our glorious game. Lest there should seem to be any suspicion of vanity or egotism in my saying this, I may point to the ever-increasing favour with which Wisden is received, and to a constantly-growing circulation.'

FEATURE ARTICLES

Hints from the Press Box, by C. Stewart Caine
'At Lord's the arrangements for Press men are far from adequate, and, I imagine, it is only the uniform courtesy which one experiences from everyone connected with the headquarters of cricket that has prevented strong representations being made to the M.C.C. The accommodation is far too rough and limited, and indeed quite unworthy of Lord's Cricket Ground.'

English Team in South Africa
'In batting Chatterton, the Derbyshire professional, quite distanced his colleagues, and throughout the tour he played consistently good cricket. In thirty-one innings he scored 955 runs, and had the splendid average of 41.12. Mr. George Brann, Mr. W. L. Murdoch, and Alec Hearne also did themselves justice, and Wood, the Surrey wicket keeper, aided by a big not-out innings of 134, came out fourth on the list. Mr. Walter Read had – for him – an indifferent record, and there is little doubt that the anxieties connected with the tour affected his cricket. Financially the trip was a failure, but, apart from an unpleasant incident at the close, the cricketers were cordially received.'

A Few Words on Fielding, by George Lohmann
Lord Sheffield's Team in Australia
Cricket In India

64

L.C.H. Palairet

'He has been re-elected captain at Oxford for 1893, and given a continuance of good health, there can be little doubt that even greater distinction awaits him in the cricket world. He has almost every good quality as a batsman, combining strong defence with fine hitting, and playing always in beautiful style. Indeed, among the young cricketers of the day there is no one better worth looking at. His father, an enthusiastic supporter of the game, spared no pains in securing him the best coaching, and we believe we are correct in saying that he owes a good deal to the valuable practice he obtained against Attewell and Martin.'

H.T. Hewett   W.W. Read   S.W. Scott   A.E. Stoddart

OBITUARIES INCLUDE

M.P. Bowden

'M.P. Bowden, whose death had some time before been incorrectly announced, died in South Africa in February. Born on November 1st, 1865, Mr. Bowden was educated at Dulwich College, and made his first appearance in the Surrey eleven in the season of 1883. His batting that year, especially in the Bank Holiday match against Notts at the Oval, showed enormous promise, and raised hopes which were never quite realised.'

Cardinal Manning

'It may seem a little strange to include Cardinal Manning's name in a cricket obituary, but inasmuch as he played for Harrow against Winchester at Lord's in 1825, in the first match that ever took place between the two schools, his claim cannot be disputed.'

COUNTY REVIEW

Middlesex

'Unquestionably the feature of the season was the exceptionally fine batting of Mr. Stanley Scott, who surpassed all his previous performances for the county. In the first few matches he displayed form that was altogether surprising, and had there been an England team to be picked against the Australians, he would have been practically certain of a place. Against Gloucestershire at Lord's he achieved the rare distinction of laying an innings of over 200 in first-class cricket, and though the feat was also accomplished by Shrewsbury and Mr. Hewett, it was certainly most remarkable in the case of the Middlesex amateur, then in his thirty-ninth year.'

MATCH REPORTS

Lord Sheffield's Team v Combined Australia, *played at Sydney, January 29, 30, February 1,2,3*

'On the fourth day the weather was unsettled and rain considerably affected the wicket. Everything went wrong with the Englishmen who made several bad mistakes in the field. The Australians' innings closed for 391, and the Englishmen, wanting 230 to win, had to go in when the ground was in a very treacherous state. Abel, Bean, and Grace were got rid of for 11 runs, and only a downfall of rain prevented further disasters … George Giffen and Turner, however bowled wonderfully well, and despite the very fine batting of Stoddart, the innings was finished off for 156, Australia winning the game by 72 runs, and so gaining the rubber in the Test matches. Bannerman's innings of 91 had much to do with the victory. Invaluable as it was, however, it would in a match of less interest have thoroughly tired out the spectators. The New South Wales batsman was actually at the wicket seven hours and twenty-eight minutes. Out of 204 balls bowled at him by Attewell he only scored from five. At the finish of the game, there was a scene of almost indescribable enthusiasm.'

The editor in his Preface refers, once again, to the pressure on space, pointing out 'the modest price of a shilling'. It is remarkable that after 30 editions, Wisden is still the same price as when it started, but now with almost four times the pagination.

1894

WISDEN 1894

31ˢᵗ EDITION
EDITOR: Sydney Pardon
PAGES: 488
PRICE: Limp 1/-
REPRINT: Willows
1. 1992 (500 limit)
2. 2008 (250 limit)

THE WORLD AT LARGE

- William Gladstone resigns and Lord Rosebery becomes Prime Minister in a minority Liberal government
- Captain Alfred Dreyfus of the French Army is arrested and convicted of treason
- Michael Marks and Thomas Spencer begin trading together from a market stall in Leeds
- President Sadi Carnot of France is assassinated
- Tsar Alexander III of Russia dies and is succeeded by his son, Nicholas II
- Blackpool Tower is opened

CRICKET HEADLINES 1893

County Champions: Yorkshire

England win back the Ashes as they win one Test, with two drawn, against the touring Australians

Frank Shacklock takes four wickets in four balls for Nottinghamshire against Somerset

Nottinghamshire's Charles Wright is given out 'handled the ball' against Gloucestershire

W.H. Brain stumps three Somerset players in successive balls to give Townsend a hat-trick, at Cheltenham

PREFACE

'*Wisden* is received every year with such increasing favour by the cricket public, and is on all hands so kindly spoken of, that in bringing out a fresh volume I am absolved from the need of saying very much. In the fact that the circulation has for the last seven years steadily gone up there is tangible evidence that the book serves its purpose.'

FEATURE ARTICLES

The Follow-On

'Up till within a comparatively recent period it was generally regarded as a distinct advantage to gain a lead of 80 or more runs on the first innings, and so compel the opposing side to go in for the second time; but there has gradually come about a marked change of opinion on this point, captains having found that on the carefully-prepared wickets to which we are accustomed at the present day there is considerable risk in having to bowl and field through two innings in succession … Thinking that a free discussion on this point would be of interest to the readers of *Wisden's Almanack,* I communicated with a large number of prominent players and other first-rate authorities, whose various views may be found on the following pages.'

The Australians In England

'Commencing their tour on May 8 at Sheffield Park, the Australians played two matches a week for eighteen weeks, no holiday being permitted, except when the men were set free by the fact of a game finishing in two days. The point has often been argued whether or not it is well to keep a travelling team at such constant tension, but inasmuch as they had fourteen players available, the Australians entered upon a heavy programme with better chances of carrying it through successfully than had fallen to the lot of any of their predecessors in this country.'

Cricket Bibliography (continued from Wisden for 1892), by Alfred J. Gaston

George Lohmann in First-Class Cricket

F.S. Jackson

'The end of the season of 1892 certainly left him in a far higher position than he had occupied before, but had it then been necessary to put the full strength of England into the field, no one would have thought of giving him a place. All the more remarkable, therefore, was his extraordinary development last season as a batsman … His first big match at Cambridge, where he was again captain, showed he was in splendid form, and he went on playing with such conspicuous success that when it became known that the M.C.C. Committee had chosen him for England in the first of the three representative matches against Australia, satisfaction was expressed on all hands. How abundantly he justified his selection need not here be stated. No one who was so fortunate as to be at Lord's on the 17th of July will ever forget the batting shown by him and Arthur Shrewsbury.'

G. Giffen   A. Hearne   G.H.S. Trott   E. Wainwright

Canon Cazenove

'Canon Cazenove, who died in August while playing lawn tennis, performed an extraordinary bowling feat at Oxford on the 5th and 6th of May, 1853. Playing for the Undergraduates of Oxford against Oxfordshire, he obtained no fewer than sixteen wickets, securing all the ten in the first innings of the county, and six in the second. Five of the ten wickets were taken in one over, the umpire inadvertently allowing an extra ball.'

W. Scotton

'William Scotton (Notts), who died by his own hand on the 9th of July, was born on January 15th, 1856, and was thus in his thirty-eighth year. For some time previous to his tragic end he had been in a very low, depressed condition, the fact that he had lost his place in the Notts eleven having, so it was stated at the inquest, preyed very seriously upon his mind.'

Yorkshire

'Naturally, the success of the eleven aroused enthusiasm all over the county; indeed, we might fairly say, all over the North of England, for not only had the South been robbed of the championship for the first time for several years, but there were other aspects of the Yorkshire victory calculated to render it popular. In the first place, the success was due not to one or two players of exceptional ability, but was shared by the whole team, and, with many people there was additional cause for rejoicing in the recollection that the side which did such great things was, almost to a man, Yorkshire born.'

Oxford v Cambridge, *played at Lord's, July 3,4*

'Nine wickets were down for 95, and then on Wilson, the last man, joining Brain, an incident occurred which is likely to be talked about for a good many years to come. Three runs were added, making the score 98, or 84 short of Cambridge's total, and Oxford thus required only 5 runs to save the follow-on. The two batsmen were then seen to consult together between the wickets, and it was at once evident to those who had grasped the situation that the Dark Blues were going to throw away a wicket in order that their side might go in again.'

1895

WISDEN 1895

32nd EDITION
EDITOR: Sydney Pardon
PAGES: 478
PRICE: Limp 1/-
REPRINT: Willows
1. 1992 (500 limit)
2. 2008 (250 limit)

THE WORLD AT LARGE

• Conservatives win the general election. Lord Salisbury becomes Prime Minister again
• Oscar Wilde loses his libel case against the Marquess of Queensberry. He is arrested and tried for sodomy and gross indecency and sentenced to two years in Reading Gaol
• The Jameson Raid – an attempt to disrupt the Boer government in Transvaal – proves a spectacular failure
• Sino-Japanese War ends: China cedes Taiwan to Japan
• Freud publishes his first work on psychoanalysis
• Death of Lord Randolph Churchill

CRICKET HEADLINES 1894

County Champions: Surrey

Tom Richardson of Surrey takes all ten Essex wickets for 45 runs

Lancashire's Arthur Mold takes 207 wickets in the season, but murmurings about his action increase

PREFACE

'… in view of the very proper promotion of Warwickshire, Derbyshire, Essex, and Leicestershire, I was bound to give increased attention to the doings of those counties … Thinking … that Throwing in first-class matches was again becoming prevalent, I asked the opinion on the subject of a number of the best-known amateurs, and some of them, it will be found, feel strongly that the evil needs to be grappled with … Mr. Frederick Tempest of Morley has sent me some statistics of Robert Peel's career in the cricket field – specially interesting in the year of the Yorkshire player's benefit – and I had been promised to again have Mr. C.B. Fry's estimate of the Public School cricket of the season. However, that famous athlete failed me and it was too late to get a substitute for him.'

FEATURE ARTICLES

Cricketers – Past and Present, by An Old Cambridge Captain
'In weighing the difference between past and present players much is said about the improved state of the grounds. While this is quite true, still such grounds as Fenner's at Cambridge, the Canterbury ground, the Oval, etc., etc., were both true and good. They had not, indeed, the advantage of the mowing machine, but they were well kept and sheep-eaten, and the ball travelled truly. What the over-hand balls would have done on those wickets I cannot say. On Lord's they would probably have broken our heads! Then (as now) Lord's was the finest ground in the world for scoring runs upon. There is something in the soil that makes the ball travel very fast.'
Throwing in First-Class Cricket
Robert Peel In The Cricket Field
The South African Team In England

C.B. Fry

'We would not put Mr. Fry as a batsman in the same class with such a player as Mr. MacLaren, but he has any amount of pluck and resolution, and, inasmuch as he played three innings of over a hundred in first-class matches, he has a distinct claim to a place among the prominent batsmen of 1894. Mr. Fry is a brilliant field, but for his bowling we cannot express admiration. In point of fairness of delivery it is by no means so bad now as it was when he first appeared in the Oxford eleven, but it still leaves a great deal to be desired.'

T.W. Hayward

'Thomas Hayward was born at Cambridge on the 19th of March, 1871. He is a striking instance of hereditary talent for the game, being a son of Daniel Hayward and a nephew of the famous Thomas Hayward who, thirty odd years ago, was by common consent the first professional batsman in England. Inasmuch as he was only five years old at the time of Hayward's death, the subject of our sketch could scarcely have seen his uncle play, but curiously enough he shares with him the distinction of having a beautiful style of batting.'

W. Brockwell   J.T. Brown   A.C. MacLaren

OBITUARIES INCLUDE

J. Selby

'... died on the 11th of March ... It is to be feared that in his later days he was anything but successful or prosperous. Indeed it is probable that the stroke of paralysis which ended his life in his forty-fifth year was partially due to a criminal charge brought against him in Nottingham of which he was acquitted.'

Sir Gerald Portal   Lord Charles Russell

COUNTY REVIEW

Nottinghamshire

'The season of 1894 was one of continuous disaster for Notts, the eleven proving even less successful than in the previous year and falling from the sixth to the seventh position among the nine leading counties. The decline of the county that for so long stood pre-eminent is in every way to be deplored, but it must be said at once that there was a good deal of excuse for failure, the loss of Arthur Shrewsbury's services during the whole of the season being sufficient in itself to discourage and dishearten the team.'

MATCH REPORTS

Surrey v Essex, *played at Kennington Oval, June 18, 19, 20*

'Having regard to the respective strength of the sides, there was nothing surprising in the fact of Surrey beating Essex, but it was scarcely to be expected that they would win by such an enormous margin as an innings and 261 runs. The Surrey men gave a remarkable display of batting, but beyond everything else the feature of the game was the bowling of Richardson, who, in the first innings of Essex, took all ten wickets, a feat that had not been performed in first-class matches since 1890.'

South Africans v Gloucestershire, *played at Bristol, June 28, 29, 30*

'On the occasion of their meeting W.G. Grace for the second time, the South Africans received striking evidence of the great cricketer's powers, both with bat and ball. After taking nine wickets *[the other batsman was c W.G. Grace b E.M. Grace]* he played, as will be seen from the score below, a not-out innings of 129. In the second innings of the South Africans, Halliwell and Frank Hearne gave a fine display, but Gloucestershire won the match very comfortably by five wickets.'

For the first time, the batting and bowling averages of amateurs and professionals are combined, rather than listed separately as before.

1896

WISDEN 1896

- 33rd EDITION
- EDITOR: Sydney Pardon
- PAGES: 524
- PRICE: Limp 1/- cloth 2/-
REPRINT: Willows
- 1. 1993 (limit 500)
- 2. 2011 (limit 250)

THE WORLD AT LARGE

- Cecil Rhodes resigns as Prime Minister of the Cape Colony in the aftermath of the Jameson Raid
- A Kent man is the first driver in the world to be fined for speeding in his motor car: Mrs. Bridget Driscoll becomes the first person in the world to die in an automobile accident, when she was run down outside the Crystal Palace
- The Anglo-Zanzibar War lasts for 45 minutes on 27 August. Britain wins
- The first modern Olympic Games are held in Athens
- William McKinley elected President of the U.S.A.
- Gold discovered in the Klondike

CRICKET HEADLINES 1895

County Champions: Surrey

The enlarged county championship now includes Derbyshire, Essex, Hampshire, Leicestershire and Warwickshire

W.G. Grace returns to his greatest form at the age of 47 by scoring 1,016 runs in May, hitting his 100th hundred in the process

Archie MacLaren scores 424 for Lancashire against Somerset at Taunton

A.E. Stoddart's team retains the Ashes in Australia, by three Tests to two

Tom Richardson takes a then record 290 wickets in the season

PREFACE

'In one respect, however, the reports of matches, extreme condensation has for some time past been absolutely necessary. So many first-class matches are played nowadays that to give the descriptions at the old length would be quite impossible. In every other direction, *Wisden* yearly expands.'

FEATURE ARTICLES

Personal Recollections of W.G. Grace
'Lord Harris writes: "I do not know whether it is fancy, but I shall always believe that W.G.'s later style of batting is quite different from what it was between '70 and '80. Now he plays the regulation back and forward strokes, but at that time he seemed to me to play every good length straight ball just in front of the popping crease, meeting it with a perfectly straight bat every time, but a kind of half stroke, only possible when great experience of the bowling, a very clear eye, and great confidence are combined. Remembering how many straight balls he used to place on the on side in those days, and the improbability therefore of the full face of the bat being given to the ball at the moment of impact, his extraordinary accuracy of eye can perhaps be realised."'

Mr. Stoddart's Team in Australia
'It is perfectly safe to say that since the visit of George Parr's eleven in 1863-64 no tour of English cricketers in Australia has been from every point of view more brilliantly successful than that of Mr. Stoddart's team … They had abundant reasons for satisfaction, inasmuch as in the series of contests with All Australia they had won the rubber by three matches to two … Never, probably, have five matches excited more widespread interest.'

Special feature on W.G. Grace
'No one interested in cricket will need to be told that Mr. Grace last summer played with all the brilliancy and success of his youth. In one respect, indeed, he surpassed all he had ever done before, scoring in the first month of the season a thousand runs in first-class matches

– a feat quite without parallel in the history of English cricket. As everyone knows, in the course of the month of May he made, on the Gloucestershire county ground at Ashley Down, Bristol, his hundredth hundred in first-class matches, this special circumstance being the origin of the national testimonial which was afterwards taken up with such enthusiasm in all parts of the country, and in many places far beyond the limits of the United Kingdom.'

Mr. R.S. Lucas' Team in West Indies

MR. W. G. GRACE.

E. HAWKINS & COMPY.   PRESTON STREET, BRIGHTON.

G. Freeman

'George Freeman, the famous Yorkshire cricketer, died at Thirsk on November 18th, in his fifty-second year. He was by general consent the finest fast bowler of his generation. His career was short, but quite dazzling in its brilliancy … [He] remained unapproachable so long as he devoted himself to the game. A profitable business as an auctioneer, however, soon drew him away from the cricket field, and after playing for Yorkshire, if we remember rightly, from 1867 to 1871 inclusive, he practically retired, his powers being almost unimpaired.'

Earl of Bessborough   Dr. H. Grace   Rev. J. Pycroft

COUNTY REVIEW

Warwickshire

'Considering that only in the previous year had Warwickshire been promoted to the first class, this state of things was eminently satisfactory, and should encourage the cricketers from the Midland county to even greater exertions in the future. So far, the hard work of the executive in trying to get together a good eleven at all points, has been attended with highly successful results.'

MATCH REPORTS

English Team v Australia, *played at Melbourne, March 1, 2, 4, 5, 6*

'As was only natural, with the record standing at two victories each, the fifth and last of the test matches excited enormous interest. Indeed, it may be questioned whether any previous game in the Colonies had ever aroused such intense and widespread excitement … The position was desperate, but at this point Albert Ward and Brown made the stand which, if they are never to do anything more, will suffice to keep their names famous in the history of English and Australian cricket. By wonderful batting – Ward's patient defence being scarcely less remarkable than Brown's brilliant hitting – they put on 210 runs together.'

For the first time, Wisden *is published in a cloth-bound (hardback) edition as well as limp-bound. The cloth-bound book costs twice as much (two shillings) and collectors to this day will find they must pay much more if they wish to acquire original hardbacks – but for the determined (and wealthy), it is the ultimate dream. This edition, which contains* Wisden's *first full-page portrait (pictured), is one of the hardest to find in hardback.*

1897

WISDEN 1897

34th EDITION
EDITOR: Sydney H. Pardon
PAGES: 528
PRICE: Limp 1/-   cloth 2/-
REPRINT: Willows
1. 1994 (limit 500)
2. 2011 (limit 250)

THE WORLD AT LARGE

• Queen Victoria's Diamond Jubilee celebrations
• George Smith, a London taxi driver, earns Britain's first conviction for drunk driving
• United States annexes the Hawaiian Islands
• Bram Stoker's *Dracula* is published
• Englishman Bob Fitzsimmons knocks out James J. Corbett to gain the heavyweight championship of the world

CRICKET HEADLINES 1896

County Champions: Yorkshire

England retain the Ashes in a three-match series with the touring Australians, despite England's professionals threatening to strike before the final Test

England win all three Tests in South Africa

J.T. Hearne and Tom Richardson take 253 and 246 wickets respectively during the summer

K.S. Ranjitsinhji scores 2,780 runs in the season, breaking W.G. Grace's record of 2,739, set in 1871

SOME CURRENT TOPICS, BY THE EDITOR

'Nothing in connection with cricket has for some years past caused so much excitement as the so-called strike of the professionals, on the eve of the England and Australian match at the Oval. Happily the storm subsided almost as soon as it was raised, the players quickly withdrawing for the position which, without thoroughly weighing the consequences, they had taken up. I thought at the time, and I think still, that the players were right in principle, but that their action was ill-judged and inopportune.'

FEATURE ARTICLES

Lord Hawke's Team in South Africa
'At one time it was feared that the disturbances in the Transvaal would seriously affect the tour, but such happily was not the case. The finances no doubt suffered in consequence, but we understand there was no loss. As was the case with the previous teams, the Englishmen were received with great cordiality and had a thoroughly enjoyable trip.'
The Batsmen of 1,000 Runs, by A.J. Gaston

FIVE CRICKETERS OF THE SEASON

S.E. Gregory
'During the tour in Australia of Mr. Stoddart's team, in the Colonial season of 1894-95, he took his place once for all among the great batsmen of Australia … After these fine performances no one was surprised at the splendid cricket he showed in this country last season. On all wickets – fast and slow – he was clearly the best bat in the Australian eleven, his position at the head of the averages being only the fitting reward of work that was both brilliant and consistent. For a short man, Gregory bats in very finished style, and if his extraordinary facility for taking balls off the middle stump and sending them to square leg occasionally loses him his wicket, it earns him a lot of runs and has a demoralising effect upon even the most skilful and self-possessed of bowlers.'
A.F.A. Lilley   K.S. Ranjitsinhji   T. Richardson   H. Trumble

F.P. Fenner

'F.P. Fenner's death, on the 22nd of May, destroyed one of the few remaining links between the cricket of the present day and the generation of Mynn and Fuller Pilch. Born at Cambridge on the 1st of March, 1811, Mr. Fenner had reached a ripe old age. In his day he was a capital cricketer, taking his part with no little distinction in big matches, but his fame rests not so much upon what he did in the field, as on the fact that he laid out the beautiful ground at Cambridge, which, though now the property of the University, is nearly always spoken of by old cricketers as Fenner's.'

Rev. E.L. Fellowes   H.H. Stephenson

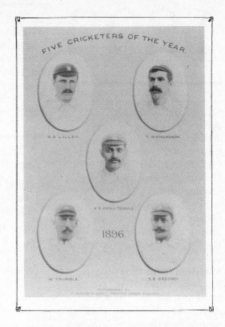

Derbyshire

'Far and away in front of everything else that occurred last season in connection with Derbyshire cricket, was the marvellous form displayed by William Storer. The famous professional not only filled his accustomed position behind the wicket in a style fully worthy of his great reputation, but made a vast improvement as a batsman, and frequently succeeded as a change bowler when his more trusted companions had failed.'

English Team v South Africa, *played at Port Elizabeth, February 13, 14, 15*
'The South Africans, without A. B. Tancred, Innes, Richards, and Rowe, were completely outplayed, the English team winning by 288 runs. The batsmen seemed quite helpless before the skilful bowling of Lohmann, whose analysis in the second innings was extraordinary. *[His figures were 9.4-5-7-8, after taking 7 for 38 in the first innings.]*

England v Australia, *played at Kennington Oval, August 10, 11, 12*
'It was anybody's game on the third morning, everything depending on the condition of the ground. It was freely predicted that the wicket would improve, but such was far from being the case, the pitch being perhaps more difficult than ever. England's innings was finished off for 84, the Australians being left with 111 to get to win. This task they commenced shortly before half-past twelve, the excitement being of course at a very high pitch. In the second over, before a run had been scored, Darling was bowled, and then the Australians went from bad to worse, the climax being reached when the seventh wicket fell at 14. All this time, Hearne and Peel had bowled in wonderful form, the latter having been put on in place of Richardson directly Darling was out. The ninth wicket was lost at 25, and the Englishmen had the game in their hands, but McKibbin, by some plucky hitting, delayed the end, the total having reached 44 when Abel caught him most brilliantly at slip with one hand. Thus amidst great enthusiasm, England won the match by 66 runs.'

This is the first edition containing the Five Cricketers of the Year as they are called in the title of the photograph (pictured), although the accompanying article is headed 'Five Cricketers of the Season'.

1898

WISDEN 1898

35th EDITION
EDITOR: Sydney Pardon
PAGES: 546
PRICE: Limp 1/-   cloth 2/-
REPRINT: Willows
1. 1995 (limit 500)
2. 2011 (limit 250)

THE WORLD AT LARGE

- China and Britain sign agreement to lease the New Territories of Hong Kong to Britain for 99 years
- A U.S. warship blows up in Havana Harbour, precipitating the Spanish-American War
- Treaty of Paris, signed in December, ends the war and cedes Puerto Rico, Guam and the Philippines to U.S., and grants Cuba its independence
- Battle of Omdurman – Lord Kitchener's troops wipe out the Dervish army, and go on to capture Khartoum
- Emile Zola publishes *J'Accuse,* a letter in which he accuses the French Government of anti-Semitism in the Dreyfus case

CRICKET HEADLINES 1897

County Champions: Lancashire

Abel and Brockwell put on a record 379 for Surrey's first wicket against Hampshire, four weeks after Brown and Tunnicliffe put on 378 for Yorkshire's first wicket against Sussex

Tom Richardson takes 273 wickets at 14.45 apiece

A NOTE BY THE EDITOR

Throwing : 'In reviewing in last year's *Wisden* the tour of the Australian team of 1896, I ventured to condemn as unfair the bowling of both Jones and McKibbin. I had no wish to say anything disagreeable, but while closely watching all the matches played in London by the team, I was so struck by the deplorable change that had come over the methods of Australian bowlers, that I did not see how the question could be ignored. The criticism has, I think, been more than justified by subsequent events.'

FEATURE ARTICLES

The Oldest Living Cricketer – Mr. Herbert Jenner-Fust
'Even so recently as 1880, when he was over 74 years of age, he made a final appearance in the cricket field, captaining his village of Hill against Rockhampton. Considering his advanced age his play on this occasion was remarkable. He bowled, so Mr. Norman tells us, at one end throughout, and when not bowling kept wicket. He did not, however, venture to run for himself, and through the over-eagerness of his substitute lost his wicket after scoring eleven. In various ways he got ten wickets, besides helping to run two men out, and he had the satisfaction of seeing his side win the game. Altogether a worthy close to his long career. It is recorded that in this, his last match, he used a bat which had been made in 1829 and presented to him in 1831 by Benjamin Aislabie then secretary of the Marylebone Club.'
Cricket in the West Indies and America, by P.F. Warner
Richardson's Bowling in First-Class Cricket
Briggs and Wainwright In the Cricket Field
The Philadelphians in England

G.L. Jessop

'We have heard him say that, with bowling that keeps at all low, he is apt to be very soon out. Taking such liberties as he does and trying to score so continually from good-length balls, this can be readily understood. Having regard to all he has done, no good judge of cricket would wish him to be other than he is. A batsman who can in half an hour win an apparently lost game is a prize for any eleven. As everyone knows, however, Mr. Jessop is a great deal more than a mere batsman. Even if he lost his power to get runs his bowling and fielding would ensure him a prominent place in first class cricket. There is scarcely another amateur fast bowler who can keep up an end so long without tiring, and at cover-point he can hold his own with almost anyone. He is altogether a most brilliant and remarkable cricketer.'

F.G. Bull   W.R. Cuttell   N.F. Druce   J.R. Mason

William Martingell

'... died September 29th, at Eton Wick. This famous old cricketer, one of the last of the Mynn and Fuller Pilch era was born at Nutfield, in Surrey, on the 20th August 1818, and was thus within a few weeks of completing his 79th year ... In his day he was one of the best bowlers in England. Forming his style under the old law, he delivered the ball a little below the shoulder and depended like the late Frank Silcock – a younger bowler of the same school – on his bias from the leg-side.'

Earl of Sefton   Frank Silcock   H.F. Ward

Hampshire

'Of the first six matches four were lost, and the middle of July was reached before the run of ill-luck was broken by a victory over Somerset at Portsmouth. The promise of better things held out by this success and by a splendid struggle with Surrey was not for a time fulfilled, but of their doings in August, the county have every reason to be proud. Playing throughout the month with only one break, eight matches were engaged in, three being won, four drawn and only one lost.'

Sussex v Essex, *played at Brighton, July 29, 30, 31*

'A beautifully firm and true wicket had been prepared and after three full days' cricket under delightful conditions the result was a draw. In the course of the game 1074 runs were scored for the loss of only twenty-five wickets, a striking testimony to the excellence of the Brighton ground. Essex, who decided to play without their regular wicket-keeper, Russell, won the toss and made a splendid start running up a total of 475 ... Sussex at their first attempt were dismissed ... for 219 and following on in a minority of 256, were in a position of considerable anxiety. A failure or two at the start might have proved fatal, but such was far from proving the case, and by scoring 389 for five wickets, Sussex not only saved the game, but left off with little the worst of the position.'

P.F. Warner writes an article on tours in which he took part in West Indies and America. Unfortunately, on the title page there is a misprint and his initials appear as W.P.

1899

WISDEN 1899

36th EDITION
EDITOR: Sydney H. Pardon
PAGES: 578
PRICE: Limp 1/-   cloth 2/-
REPRINT: Willows
1. 1995 (limit 500)
2. 2011 (limit 250)

THE WORLD AT LARGE

• The second Boer War begins in South Africa: Boer armies lay siege to Mafeking and Ladysmith
• Marconi transmits a radio signal across the English Channel
• The Mahdist war in Sudan ends in decisive Anglo-Egyptian victory
• Scott Joplin publishes his *Maple Leaf Rag* which sells more than one million copies in sheet music form
• Aspirin is patented and put on sale by Bayer
• The paperclip is invented in Norway

CRICKET HEADLINES 1898

County Champions: Yorkshire

Brown (300) and Tunnicliffe (243) put on 554 for the first wicket for Yorkshire against Derbyshire

Australia regain the Ashes, winning 4-1 at home in 1897-98

Board of Control set up to administer Test matches played in England

Tom Hayward hits 315* for Surrey v Lancashire

A NOTE BY THE EDITOR

Throwing

'The no-balling of Mr. Fry was only a case of long-delayed justice. As a matter of fact he ought never, after his caricature of bowling in the M.C.C. and Oxford match at Lord's in 1892, to have been allowed to bowl at all.'

FEATURE ARTICLES

High Scoring and the Law of Leg-Before-Wicket

'Mr. E.M. Grace sends me the following ... "No one can speak more feelingly about l.b.w. than I, for in more than fifty innings the ball has hit me full on the right hand and nowhere else. How's that umpire? Out l.b.w. Then again, in our local matches the ball has only to hit me on the leg. How's that – nine times out of ten it is given out ... At our country matches the umpire is almost always the best player for his side generally giving two or three out of opponents and two or three in for his own side".'

Mr. R.A.H. Mitchell and Eton Cricket
The Highest Score on Record
The Bowlers of 100 Wickets, by A.J. Gaston

FIVE GREAT PLAYERS OF THE SEASON

A.E. Trott

'As a bowler Albert Trott is a true Australian, commanding as he does every variety of pace and device ... He says that in bowling his curly ball he owes much to the practice he obtained as a pitcher at baseball. As a pitcher is allowed to throw as hard as he can at sixteen yards, it says a good deal for Trott that, despite his experience of base-ball, his bowling action should be unimpeachably fair. Born on the 6th of January, 1873, he is just now in the very prime of his cricket, and as he seems to have definitely thrown in his lot with Middlesex he is likely to play a very important part on our cricket grounds for a good many seasons to come.'

W.H. Lockwood   W. Rhodes   W. Storer   C.L. Townsend

E.S. Pardon

'Mr. Edgar Searles Pardon died on the 16th of July, in his 39th year. From the time he left school till within about a month of his death. Mr. Pardon was constantly engaged in the task of reporting cricket matches and it is no exaggeration to say that he was a familiar figure on nearly every county ground. He was in peculiarly close touch with the Australians, travelling all over England with David Gregory's team in 1878 and being present at every England and Australia match in this country. His association with Wisden's Almanack commenced in 1886 and during recent years he had taken a very large share in the preparation of the annual. He was buried at Highgate Cemetery on July 20.'

John Platts

'John Platts, the well-known Derbyshire cricketer – one of the best all round players possessed by the county in its early days – died on the 6th of August. He was in his 50th year having been born on the 6th of December, 1848. A tragic interest attached to the start of Platts' career as a cricketer, as it was a ball bowled by him in the M.C.C. and Notts match at Lord's in 1870 that caused the death of George Summers. At that time a very fast bowler, Platts afterwards lessened his pace and the catastrophe made such a painful impression upon him, that it is said he never in subsequent years could play, with any pleasure, at Lord's ground.'

G. Ulyett

'George Ulyett died on Saturday evening, June 18th. He was only in his forty-seventh year, his last season in the Yorkshire eleven being 1893. His health had been failing for some time, but the immediate cause of death was an acute attack of pneumonia, contracted at Bramall Lane during the Yorkshire and Kent match. Yorkshire has always been rich in first-rate cricketers, but a finer player than Ulyett the county has never produced. He was for years the best bat in the team, and even if he had not been able to get a run he would have been worth his place for his bowling and fielding.'

I.D. Walker

'To an even greater extent than in 1897 – there being no visiting team of any kind in England – the County Championship dominated the season's cricket. It cannot be said, however, that the struggle was by any means so close as in the previous year. Yorkshire took the lead at the start, and met with no check until the middle of July. In August, after suffering defeat at the hands of both Surrey and Middlesex, they were in momentary danger of losing the position for which they had fought so hard, but in the end they came out first with a good deal in hand.'

Derbyshire v Yorkshire, played at Chesterfield, *August 18, 19, 20*

'This game will live long in the memories of those who were fortunate enough to witness it, for Brown and Tunnicliffe, commencing Yorkshire's innings on the Thursday, were not parted for five hours and five minutes, their stand lasting until Friday and producing the unprecedented number of 554. Needless to say, this remarkable achievement completely eclipsed all previous records in important cricket not only for the first, but for any wicket. Tunnicliffe was out first and Brown, having reached his 300, knocked his wicket down. Subsequently the other batsmen threw away their wickets in the most sportsmanlike fashion.'

Sydney Pardon starts his Preface: 'My first duty in bringing forward the thirty-sixth edition of Wisden *is to refer to the loss the book has sustained in the death of my brother, Mr. Edgar S. Pardon. For twelve years he had worked in producing the Almanack and of late he had practically divided with me the duties of Editor. His interest in* Wisden *was extremely keen and his last task was to prepare some of the following pages. I take this opportunity of thanking many cricketers for their kind expressions of sympathy at his death.'*

1900

WISDEN 1900

37th EDITION
EDITOR: Sydney H. Pardon
PAGES: 646
PRICE: Limp 1/-   cloth 2/-
REPRINT: Willows 1996 (500 limit, in two formats)

THE WORLD AT LARGE

• The Conservative Party, under Lord Salisbury, wins the 'khaki' General Election at the end of the year. Two Labour candidates are elected for the first time, as is Winston Churchill
• King Umberto of Italy is assassinated, and succeeded by his son, Victor Emmanuel III
• Britain wins the gold medal for cricket at the Paris Olympics – the only time cricket has been an Olympic sport
• Mafeking is relieved after a seven month siege, to scenes of great rejoicing throughout Britain
• The Boxer Rebellion in China: a multinational force eventually breaks through to the foreign legation in Peking (Beijing) and lifts a 55-day siege

CRICKET HEADLINES 1899

County Champions: Surrey

A.E.J. Collins hits 628* in a Clifton College house match

The touring Australians under Joe Darling retain the Ashes

K.S. Ranjitsinhji becomes the first man to make 3,000 runs in a season, scoring 3,159 at an average of 63.18

Victor Trumper becomes the first touring Australian to hit a triple-century, 300* against Sussex

Bobby Abel hits 357* for Surrey against Somerset, and R.M. Poore hits 304 for Hampshire, also against Somerset

PREFACE

'The portraits this year are those of Darling, Noble, Major Poore, Clement Hill and A.O. Jones. No apology is needed, I am sure, after such a season, for giving three places to the Australians.'

FEATURE ARTICLES

E.M. Grace in the Cricket Field
'As a batsman, E.M. Grace may fairly be described as the great revolutionist. When he came before the public, batting was a very orthodox science indeed, the pull with which we are now almost too familiar being regarded as little less than a sin. E.M. Grace changed all that.'
[According to the statistics in this article, in all cricket, first-class and lower grades, E.M. Grace scored 72,482 runs and took 10,006 wickets.]
Suggested Reforms, by (1) Lord Harris and (2) A.G. Steel
'Why should so many old lovers of the game be agitating themselves about the future? Simply because cricket, as played under its present conditions, is in the very direst peril of degenerating from the finest of all summer games into an exhibition of dullness and weariness. Cricket to maintain its hold on the national character must be eager, quick and full of action. To-day it is the reverse.' *[by A.G. Steel, writing after a summer in which Ranjitsinhji scored seven centuries for Sussex! See Match Reports.]*
Bibliography of Cricket by A.J. Gaston
'A Charming Treatise, on Cricket, by Mr. J.M. Barrie, the popular novelist, was issued for private circulation during the past year.' *[Gaston updates his list which appeared in 1892 and 1894.]*
The Highest Individual Score On Record

C. Hill

'Of his [Hill's] special characteristics as a batsman it is not necessary to say very much, his style being now so familiar to all followers of the game in this country. No left-handed player has ever depended so much upon skill and so little upon mere punishing power in front of the wicket. Of course he can drive an over-pitched ball when he is so disposed, but for most of his runs he relies upon his wonderful facility in scoring on the leg side. The way in which on a hard wicket he can turn straight balls to leg must be seen to be believed.'

J. Darling   A.O. Jones   M.A. Noble   Major R.M. Poore

OBITUARIES INCLUDE

W. Barnes

'Once in the course of conversation at Lord's he said that some careful batsmen – he was referring especially to Mr. A. P. Lucas – were content to play just the same strict game when they had made a hundred runs as when they first went to the wickets, but that he himself always wanted to do something more than that. It may be that by acting on this principle he sometimes cut his innings short, but the spectators at Lord's, Trent Bridge, and elsewhere reaped the benefit in nearly always seeing a bright attractive display when he was in form.'

G. Davidson   E. Mills

COUNTY REVIEW

Hampshire

'Major Poore and Captain Wynyard had always to be reckoned with when in the eleven, and had they been able to play throughout the summer the county would have undoubtedly held a higher position in the struggle for the Championship … In the previous summer Poore had proved himself a great acquisition to English cricket and for two months last season he was perhaps the most prominent man playing. Between the 12th of June and the 12th of August he scored 1,399 runs in 16 innings, with an average of 116.58. No one has ever approached such figures as these.'

MATCH REPORTS

England v Australia, Second Test Match, *played at Lord's, June 15, 16, 17*
'In their different styles Hill and Trumper, who curiously enough made exactly the same score, played magnificent cricket. Trumper's innings was by far the more brilliant of the two, but inasmuch as Hill went in while there was still a chance of an even game, and had to play the English bowling at its best, it is only right to say that the left-handed batsman had the greater share in the ultimate success of his side.'

Sussex v Essex, *played at Brighton, August 17, 18, 19*
'At the close of the second day's play, Sussex seemed in danger of defeat as, after following on against a balance of 125, they lost Fry's and P.H. Latham's wickets for 35 runs. On the Saturday, however, Ranjitsinhji played a magnificent innings and put defeat out of the question. He scored his 161 in less than three hours.'

MISCELLANEOUS [PAGE 498]

'At a meeting summoned at Lord Hawke's instigation to consider the subject of benefits to professional players, the following resolution was unanimously passed: "That this meeting is strongly of the opinion that the Counties should reserve direct control over the investment and disposal of all benefit monies".'

1901

WISDEN 1901

- 38th EDITION
- EDITOR: Sydney H. Pardon
- PAGES: 632
- PRICE: Limp 1/-   cloth 2/-
- REPRINT: Willows 1996 (500 limit, in two formats)

THE WORLD AT LARGE

- Queen Victoria dies on January 22, succeeded by her son who takes the title Edward VII
- Australia becomes one country on January 1 under the Commonwealth Of Australia Constitution Act
- President McKinley is shot and dies eight days later. Theodore Roosevelt becomes the youngest ever U.S. President at 42
- Nobel Prizes first awarded
- Elgar's *Pomp and Circumstance March* ('Land of Hope and Glory') is performed for the first time

CRICKET HEADLINES 1900

County Champions: Yorkshire

The six-ball over becomes standard in England

Ranji again tops 3,000 runs for the season – 3,065 at 87.57

Tom Hayward scores 1,000 runs before June

Gilbert Jessop scores 2,000 runs and takes 100 wickets; Albert Trott scores 1,000 runs and takes 200 wickets for the second season in a row

SOME NOTES BY THE EDITOR

'I had intended to write at considerable length on the subject of unfair bowling and the no-balling of Mold and Tyler by James Phillips, but before I had started on my task the announcement appeared that at the meeting of the county captains at Lord's, on December 10, an agreement had been made to take united action in the season of 1901, for the purpose of ridding English cricket of all throwing and dubious bowling … A throw may be difficult to define in words, but to the eye of a practical and unbiased cricketer it is, I think, very obvious. James Phillips holds to the opinion that when a bowler strikes one at first sight as being a thrower, the odds are a hundred to one that he is not bowling fairly. In support of his opinion there is the fact that no bowler with an unimpeachable fair action has ever been accused of throwing.'

FEATURE ARTICLES

Fielding in 1900, by D.L.A. Jephson
'Taken as a whole the fielding has been bad, thoroughly bad. Men stand in the field to day like so many little mounds of earth, A timid, though euphonious paraphrase of Clods of Dirt; a definition given by an old cricketer, of many latter day fieldsmen, or waxen figures in a third-rate tailor's shop. The energy, the life, the ever-watchfulness of ten years ago is gone, and in their place are lethargy, laziness, and a wonderful yearning for rest.'
The West Indian Cricket Team, by P.F. Warner

MR. R.E. FOSTER AND FOUR YORKSHIREMEN

T.L. Taylor
'As a batsman, Mr. Taylor has many fine qualities, not the least of them being a remarkable power of getting runs on slow and difficult wickets. On this he gave convincing evidence last summer against Surrey at the Oval and Sussex at Brighton. His style is neat and finished to a degree and his driving clean and powerful. As a wicket-keeper he is much above the average, but he probably does not regret that when playing for Yorkshire he is able to give all his attention to batting without having his hands knocked about behind the stumps. As regards

other sports than cricket, he is fond of hockey and golf, but is no lover of football. He played the Rugby game once or twice while he was at Uppingham but was so much hacked that he quickly decided to give it up.'

R.E. Foster   S. Haigh   G.H. Hirst   J. Tunnicliffe

OBITUARIES INCLUDE

F.W. Milligan
'Born at Aldershot, March 19, 1870, died whilst with Colonel Plumer's force, (endeavouring to relieve Mafeking), March 31, 1900. An excellent all-round player, a splendid field, fast bowler, and hard hitter.'

R.C. Tinley
'His fame, however, rested not upon his fielding or batting, but upon his remarkable skill as a lob bowler. His success during a number of seasons for the All England eleven against local twenty-twos was extraordinary, and he took an immense number of wickets when he went out to Australia in 1863 with George Parr's famous team. Alfred Shaw, who came out as a colt for Notts while Tinley was still a member of the county eleven, thinks that he never saw so good a lob bowler.'

W. Bates   R. Daft   J.J. Ferris   E. Peate

COUNTY REVIEW

The Leading Counties in 1900
'The Championship in 1900 was from first to last simply a race between Yorkshire and Lancashire, no other county being in the running for first place. For a long time the two elevens remained on even terms. Their matches with each other could not be played out, and at the beginning of the last week in July both were unbeaten. Then, however, Lancashire sustained an unexpected defeat at the hands of Gloucestershire, and as it turned out this one reverse would have been sufficient to put them out of court, Yorkshire to the end of the season enjoying a career of uninterrupted success in county matches.'

MATCH REPORTS

Oxford University v Sussex, *played at Oxford, May 24, 25, 26*
'This match was played on the Christ Church Ground, at which, unlike the University Ground in the Parks, a charge can be made for admission. Rain restricted the first day's play to an hour and twenty minutes, and the wicket never recovered. A hard fought game ended in victory for Oxford by eleven runs. Bosanquet clearly won the match for his side, taking in the two innings fifteen wickets for 65 runs. In the second innings of Sussex he took at a cost of 31 runs the first nine wickets that fell. Fry did not play for Sussex, and Ranjitsinhji was greatly handicapped by lameness.'

MISCELLANEOUS

The advertisement placed by John Wisden & Co. for their cricket goods includes: 'Testimonials Just Received: "Dear Sirs, I return the Bat as I promised you I would if I scored a century with it. I have made over 1,000 runs with the bat … I shall be much obliged if you will make me two more like it. Yours truly, W.G. Grace."'

Notes by the Editor appear as such for the first time, although headed 'Some Notes by the Editor'. It is a section to which many readers turn first, to read the often trenchant views. Although the Five Cricketers of the Year format had become established, this year the five are headed 'Mr. R.E. Foster and Four Yorkshiremen'. The editor explains in the Preface how near Yorkshire came to having a clean sweep: 'I should have liked to have a portrait of Lord Hawke, the captain of the eleven that played twenty-eight county matches without once suffering defeat, but I could only have put him in the centre of the picture and Mr. Foster's claims to the place of honour were paramount.' Lord Hawke gets his turn in 1909.

1902

WISDEN 1902

39th EDITION
EDITOR: Sydney H. Pardon
PAGES: 702
PRICE: Limp 1/-   cloth 2/-
REPRINT: Willows 1997 (500 limit, in two formats)

THE WORLD AT LARGE

- The Second Boer War ends
- Lord Salisbury retires and is succeeded by his nephew Arthur Balfour, prompting the saying, 'Bob's your uncle'
- Edward VII is crowned
- 25 people are killed and over 500 injured when a stand collapses during a Scotland v England football match at Ibrox Stadium in Glasgow
- King Alfonso XIII of Spain is crowned upon reaching the age of 16
- Publication of *The Tale of Peter Rabbit* by Beatrix Potter

CRICKET HEADLINES 1901

County Champions: Yorkshire

C.B. Fry scores six hundreds in successive innings, and thirteen in the season, then a record

Bobby Abel scores 3,309 runs in the season, then the record aggregate. Fry and J.T. Tyldesley also score over 3,000.

Two players, Straw of Worcestershire and Whiteside of Leicestershire, are given out 'obstructing the field', the last time this happens for 50 years

Nottinghamshire all out 13, v Yorkshire

John Tunnicliffe takes 70 catches in the season

NOTES BY THE EDITOR

[The editor returns to the subject of throwing, and supports the umpire James Phillips:] '… As to his action in no-balling Mold sixteen times at Old Trafford last July, I can say nothing, as I was not present at the match, but with regard to the agitation that was got up on Mold's behalf I have a very strong opinion indeed. To read some of the comments that appeared one might have supposed that nobody except Phillips had ever called Mold's fairness in question. The fact that the Lancashire fast bowler had been condemned as unfair by the county captains by a majority of eleven to one, at their meeting in December, 1900, was systematically ignored. … The mowing machine, the hose, and the heavy roller have in combination made the task of the modern batsman sufficiently easy, and in the opinion of many good judges of the game he did not need the further help that has lately been accorded him. The question of the preparation of wicket is urgent, as we do not wish to be driven to the necessity of deciding our three-day matches on the first innings.'

FEATURE ARTICLES

Leg Break Bowling in 1901, by D.L.A. Jephson
'When the annals of our game come to be chronicled in some great book, the extraordinary growth of this leg-break bowling, or "tosh" as we were wont to call it, will find a prominent place in the year of grace 1901'
Mr. C.B. Fry in First-Class Cricket

FIVE CRICKETERS OF THE YEAR

C.P. McGahey
'At one time there was a fear that bad health would put a stop to his career in the cricket field, indications of lung disease causing him anxiety, but a trip to Australia during the winter of 1897-98 did him a lot of good, and since then he has been strong and quite capable of bearing the fatigue of county cricket – no light matter in these days of almost incessant play from the

beginning of May to the end of August. Even now McGahey is not quite so straight and fine a player as Perrin, but while falling a little short of the front rank of batsmen, he is a most valuable man on a side, and consistently heavy run-getter. By nature he is essentially a hitter, but of late years he has gained very largely in defence.'

L.C. Braund   F. Mitchell   W.G. Quaife   J.T. Tyldesley

OBITUARIES INCLUDE

G.A. Lohmann

'For a bowler who nearly always had to go on first, whatever side he played for, he got too many runs, and, as everyone knows, he was one of the most brilliant and untiring of fieldsmen. If he had not been able to bowl at all, his batting and fielding would have entitled him to a place in any eleven. He made the position of cover-slip more important than it had ever been before his day, constantly bringing off catches that ordinary men would not even have tried for. In this part of the game he, perhaps, reached his highest point in the England and Australia match at the Oval in 1888. The catch with which he got rid of Alec Bannerman in the first innings of Australia approached the miraculous. It was said at the time that Bannerman talked of nothing else for the rest of the day. Still, it is upon his bowling that his fame will mainly rest.'

R. Carpenter   J. Jackson

COUNTY REVIEW

Warwickshire

'Warwickshire had an excellent season on 1901, and though the bowling does not come out very well in the averages, it is safe to say that the team, when Field was well and in form, were as strong all round as at any time since the county gained promotion to the front rank … The great strength of Warwickshire cricket lay in their batting. W.G. Quaife and Kinneir – both at the top of their form all through the season – stood ahead of all their colleagues, but there were many other good run-getters on the side.'

MATCH REPORTS

London County v M.C.C. and Ground, *played at Crystal Palace, August 8, 9, 10*

'Some remarkable scoring was witnessed in this match, three full days' cricket producing 1134 runs for the loss of 20 wickets. London County scored 309 for six wickets on the first afternoon, their veteran captain making his first and only hundred in first-class cricket during the season, and Walker, the Surrey amateur, compiling 209 not out. While the pair were together they added 281 in less than three hours. Grace was dismissed at 332, having played faultlessly for three hours and fifty minutes … It will be noticed that the bowling was absurdly weak on both sides.'

Yorkshire v Rest of England, *played at Lord's, September 12, 13, 14*

'The feature of the game was the astounding batting of Jessop, who has never hit in more wonderful form. At the end of the first afternoon, he was not out 176, and on the following morning he carried his score to 233. His innings – the highest he has ever played in a first-class match – lasted two hours and a half.'

MISCELLANEOUS

[Cambridgeshire batting averages include the first mention of Jack Hobbs in Wisden*]*

'Mr. J. Hobbs junr. Innings 4; Runs 35; Most In Innings 30; Times Not Out 0; Average 8.75'

1903

WISDEN 1903

40th EDITION
EDITOR: Sydney H. Pardon
PAGES: 714
PRICE: Limp 1/-   cloth 2/-
REPRINT: Willows 1997 (500 limit, in two formats)

THE WORLD AT LARGE

- First transatlantic radio transmission between U.S. and Britain
- The first Tour de France cycle race takes place
- The first teddy bears are put on sale and become an immediate sensation
- Royal family of Serbia assassinated
- The Wright brothers achieve the first true powered aircraft flight, at Kittyhawk in North Carolina

CRICKET HEADLINES 1902

County Champions: Yorkshire

Joe Darling's Australians beat England 2-1 in the series in England, having beaten them 4-1 in Australia a few months earlier

Wilfred Rhodes takes more than 200 wickets for the third consecutive year

C.J. Eady scores 566 for Break-o'-Day v Wellington at Hobart

Monty Noble and Warwick Armstrong put on 428 for the Australians' sixth wicket against Sussex

Ranji and W. Newham put on 344 for Sussex's seventh wicket against Essex

NOTES BY THE EDITOR

'There seems to be a strong feeling in favour of playing Test games in this country out to a finish, irrespective of the time they occupy, and if our leading players are at one with the Australians in wishing the plan to be adopted there is not much use in raising objections. Personally, however, I am very doubtful of the wisdom of making cricket altogether independent of a time limit. Desirable as it is to see one side or the other victorious, the result at cricket is not everything.'

FEATURE ARTICLES

The Second-Class Counties and the Law of 'Leg Before Wicket'
'During the season of 1902 the Second-class Counties gave in their competition matches – at the request of the Marylebone Club – a trial to the suggested law of Leg-Before-Wicket, carried by a large, though insufficient, majority at the Annual Meeting of the M.C.C. at Lord's in May, 1901. The proposed law read: If with any part of his person (except the hand), which is between wicket and wicket, he intercept a ball which would hit his wicket, 'Leg-Before-Wicket'. Wishing to publish in Wisden the opinions of those who had subjected the proposed rule to the test of actual play I wrote to the various counties concerned … It will be seen that the proposed alteration … met with comparatively little favour.'
Mr. W.G. Grace's Hundreds, compiled by F.S. Ashley-Cooper

FIVE CRICKETERS OF THE YEAR

V.T. Trumper
'Against MacLaren's team in the Australian season of 1901-2 … he did not do himself justice, his cricket being affected by the fact that he was engaged a great deal in office work at night time. His performances in this country during the past season are fully described in the record of the Australian tour, and it will be sufficient to say here that he put into the shade everything that had ever before been done in England by Australian batsmen, scoring, despite the bad weather and wet wickets, 2,570 runs. Apart from his batting, Trumper is one of the finest of out-fields, and a very serviceable change bowler. Success has not in any way spoilt

84

him, and alike on English and Australian cricket fields he is deservedly one of the most popular of players.'

W.W. Armstrong   C.J. Burnup   J. Iremonger   J.J. Kelly

OBITUARIES INCLUDE

J. Briggs
'Though he rallied so wonderfully from his seizure at Leeds, during the Test match in 1899, as to bowl with nearly all his old skill and success through the season of 1900, it was known that his ailment – a form of epilepsy – admitted of no permanent cure, and was liable to recur at any time. He had another attack sooner than had been expected; was compelled to go back to Cheadle Asylum; and took no part in the cricket of 1901.'

Rev. W. Fellows
'For Westminster against Rugby, at Westminster, in 1852, he obtained nine wickets in the first innings and six in the second, but was on the losing side, Westminster making only 19 and 11, against Rugby's scores of 114 and 129. Although Mr. Fellows' bowling was effective, it was certainly expensive, as there were 15 byes in the first innings, and 27 in the second. Moreover, he bowled 30 wides, thereby giving away as many runs as Westminster made in their two innings combined.'

G. Strachan
'Mr. George Strachan, who thirty years ago was one of the finest all-round players in the world, died from fever in January, whilst in charge of one of the concentration camps in the Transvaal.'

COUNTY REVIEW

'There can be no disputing the fact that County Cricket in 1902 was quite overshadowed by the presence of the Australian Team. All through the season the Australian matches were being discussed by everybody, and the County Championship sank to a very modest position. Things would no doubt have been different had there been any real struggle for first honours, but the Yorkshire eleven, as in 1901, were so far ahead of all their rivals that there was never the slightest likelihood that they would lose their position.'

MATCH REPORTS

England v Australia, Fifth Test Match, *played at Melbourne, February 28, March 1, 3, 4*
'The Englishmen were left with 211 to get, and at the drawing of stumps they had scored 87 with three men out, all three wickets falling in the last few minutes. The prospects of victory would have been hopeful next morning if the ground had improved, but the pitch turned out very difficult, and no one except A.O. Jones could cope with Noble's bowling. The result was that the Australians won the game, and so left off with a record in the Test matches of four victories as against one defeat.'

England v Australia, Fifth Test Match, *played at Kennington Oval, 11, 12, 13 August*
'Australia having already won the rubber, the fifth and last of the Test matches had not at starting the same importance that would under other circumstances have attached to it, but it produced a never-to-be-forgotten struggle and a more exciting finish, if that were possible, than the one at Manchester. In face of great difficulties and disadvantages England won by one wicket after the odds had been fifty to one on Australia. Some truly wonderful hitting by Jessop made victory possible after all hope had seemed gone, and Hirst and Rhodes got their side home at the close.'

1904

WISDEN 1904

41st Edition
Editor: Sydney H. Pardon
Pages: 682
Price: Limp 1/-   cloth 2/-
Reprint: Willows 1998 (500 limit, in two formats)

THE WORLD AT LARGE

• Entente Cordiale signed between Britain and France
• J.M. Barrie's play, *Peter Pan* opens in London
• The Dogger Bank Incident: the Russian fleet mistakes British trawlers for the Japanese navy and opens fire, sinking one trawler

CRICKET HEADLINES 1903

County Champions: Middlesex

G.L. Jessop hits 286 out of 355 in less than three hours for Gloucestershire against Sussex

Yorkshire dismiss Worcestershire for 24 at Huddersfield

NOTES BY THE EDITOR

'It is difficult at the time of writing to tell what will be the ultimate upshot of the proposed county tournament on the "knock-out" principle, in which Mr. C.B. Fry has so keenly interested himself. If adopted in 1904 the tournament cannot be carried out on anything like the scale originally designed, Yorkshire, Lancashire and Surrey being so fully engaged as to leave themselves no room for extra fixtures. Moreover, Yorkshire, as I understand, does not favour the scheme at all, and Surrey, together with some other leading counties, has declared against it. As some of the first-class counties, however, approve of the competition, there seems to just a chance next season of a modest beginning.'

FEATURE ARTICLES

Schoolboys' Bowling, by F.R. Spofforth
'No one can ever think of being a first-class bowler without he really works hard and often and starts early, for this is the great secret, because it gives elasticity to the muscles without which it is almost impossible to excel, and this elasticity cannot be got without one starts quite young, and certainly not after twenty-one years of age. This is where the professional has the advantage.'
Play Back, by D.L.A. Jephson
Arthur Shrewsbury in First-Class Cricket

FIVE CRICKETERS OF THE YEAR

C. Blythe
'On slow wickets he breaks back very quickly, and is in Ranjitsinhji's opinion more difficult to play than Rhodes, the lower flight of the ball making it a hard matter to go out and drive him. Bowling, with a very easy action he can, despite the slightness of his physique, get through a good amount of work without tiring. As he is still under twenty-five the best of him may not have been seen, but even if he should only remain at his present standard of excellence he ought with ordinary luck to be a most valuable member of the Kent eleven for ten years to come. So far he is a bowler pure and simple, his batting counting for little or nothing.'
J. Gunn   A.E. Knight   W. Mead   P.F. Warner

OBITUARIES INCLUDE

A. Haygarth
'Although a very capable exponent of the game which he loved so much, he will always be chiefly known to fame as the compiler of the *Cricket Scores and Biographies.* In 1842, while

still at Harrow School, he commenced his labour of love, being but sixteen years of age at the time, and it says much for his enthusiasm for his work that to the day of his death [aged 77] his interest in the subject remained as great as ever.'

A. Shrewsbury

'There was such an easy grace of style and such a suggestion of mastery in everything he did that, whether he scored slowly or fast, his batting, to the true judge of cricket, was always a delight. Excepting of course W.G. Grace, it may be questioned if we have ever produced a more remarkable batsman. On sticky wickets he was, by universal consent, without an equal in his best seasons his defence being so strong and his patience so inexhaustible. Personally, Shrewsbury was a man of quiet, retiring disposition, and while very proud of the place he had won in the cricket-field, always modest when speaking of his own doings.'

R. Thoms

'No one had a more thorough knowledge of cricket, or could speak with greater authority about all the leading players of the last sixty years … He often talked about putting into book form his 60 years' experience of the cricket field, but whether he ever seriously commenced the task one cannot say.' *[Thoms wrote several articles for Wisden.]*

COUNTY REVIEW

The Leading Counties in 1903

'Never has County Cricket been so much affected by rain as in 1903. The summer was the wettest within the experience anyone now playing first-class cricket, worse even than 1879, and in nearly all parts of the country the game had to contend against overwhelming disadvantages. As was inevitable under such conditions, the various county clubs suffered severely in pocket, but, except in one or two quarters, public support, when the weather proved decently favourable, showed no great falling off. The altogether abnormal character of the season may be judged from the fact that six county matches had to be abandoned without a ball being bowled.'

MATCH REPORTS

Middlesex v Notts, *played at Lord's, June 11, 12, 13*

'So far Middlesex had been favoured with fine weather for their matches at Lord's, but their meeting with Notts was ruined. Rain had reduced the ground to such a state that not a ball could be bowled on the first two days. A start was made on the Saturday morning, but after an hour and a half's cricket rain set in and the match was promptly abandoned. Even while play was in progress the conditions were dismal in the extreme, the light being so bad that from the press box the figures on the scoring board could hardly be distinguished.'

Gentlemen v Players, *played at Lord's, July 6, 7, 8*

'For two days the Gentlemen were completely outplayed, following on 293 in arrear, and entering upon the concluding stage of the contest with one wicket down and 219 runs required to escape a single innings defeat. Some truly grand batting by Fry and MacLaren, however, not only saved the amateurs from being beaten, but left them with the honours of the match. These two famous cricketers came together at five minutes past one on the Wednesday with two wickets down for 191, and, on a pitch which had never been perfect, actually hit up 309 runs in rather less than three hours.'

MISCELLANEOUS

Meeting of County Secretaries:

'Mr. Mallett then spoke upon the proposed system of promotion by merit, put forward by the Minor Counties' Cricket Association. They had striven to make it as simple as possible, and their aim had been to protect as far as possible those first-class counties who might be in danger of relegation if the scheme were adopted.' *[The editor has harsh words to say about this idea in the next edition.]*

1905

WISDEN 1905

42nd Edition
Editor: Sydney H. Pardon
Pages: 746
Price: Limp 1/-   cloth 2/-
Reprint: Willows 1998 (500 limit, in two formats)

THE WORLD AT LARGE

• The Conservative party splits over tax reform, and Balfour resigns. The Liberal leader, Henry Campbell-Bannerman, takes over pending an election
• The first outward signs of revolution in Russia as sailors on the battleship Potemkin mutiny in Odessa, and a peaceful demonstration in St. Petersburg is fired upon by guards
• After the crushing naval defeat in the Battle of Tsushima, Russia agrees peace terms with Japan in the Treaty of Portsmouth (New Hampshire)
• Albert Einstein publishes *On the Electrodynamics of Moving Bodies*, outlining his theory of relativity

CRICKET HEADLINES 1904

County Champions: Lancashire

R.E. Foster scores 287 on debut for England against Australia at Sydney, and P.F. Warner leads the first MCC touring team to a 3-2 series victory

Percy Perrin hits 68 fours in his 343* for Essex against Derbyshire, but they still lose by nine wickets

A South African team tours England, but does not play any Tests

George Hirst scores 2,501 runs and takes 132 wickets in the season

NOTES BY THE EDITOR

'The promotion of Northamptonshire to a place among the first-class counties is to my mind a very good step and one calculated to increase the harmony of county cricket. If the second-class teams realize that if they show sufficiently marked superiority over their rivals promotion will follow as a matter of course, and we shall hear no more of proposals to adopt the system of the Football League. I have not a word to say against that body, but the system which answers very well with football would not do at all for cricket. The idea of a county with the traditions of Surrey or Notts being relegated to the second-class as the result of one bad season could not be entertained for a moment.'

FEATURE ARTICLES

On the Preparation of Wickets, by A.C. MacLaren
'With less perfect wickets to play upon, the game would not last so long, nor would it be robbed one bit of its science, which assuredly it will be if ever stumps are lengthened or widened and bats lessened.'

M.C.C. in Australia, Impressions of the Tour, by B.J.T. Bosanquet
'In future tours one would like to see the up-country matches omitted. They are no sort of trial, even for one's opponents, and cause slackness, if only from the fact that they can never be finished. They do more harm than good, and in future a team would do far better either to play only first-class matches or, if that would be too great a strain, take six weeks' holiday in the middle of the tour, and visit New Zealand and Tasmania, playing a few matches, which would pay well – "*pecunia omnia vincit*" – and be of far more interest than those matches in Australia.'
Robert Abel in First-class Cricket
The South Africans' Tour

B.J.T. Bosanquet

'Though he sends down more bad balls than any other front rank bowler, Bosanquet is now a distinct power in any eleven he plays for. On his good days he is more likely than any other bowler we have to get a strong side out cheaply on a perfect wicket. How he manages to bowl his off-break with apparently a leg-break action one cannot pretend to say. Even F.S. Jackson has confessed that he has not the least idea how it is done.'

E. A. Halliwell   J. Hallows   P.A. Perrin   R.H. Spooner

T. Emmett

'Tom Emmett died suddenly on June 30th, in his 63rd year. He had long ago dropped out of the public gaze, his connection with the Yorkshire eleven ending in 1888, but he had assuredly not been forgotten. There was never a more popular professional, his cheery nature, and the inexhaustible energy with which he played the game, making him a prime favourite wherever he went. His closing days were, unhappily, rather clouded, but on this point there is no need to dwell.'

W.J. Ford

'His longest measured hit was 143 yards 2 feet. He hit out of almost all the grounds upon which he played, including Lord's and the Aigburth ground at Liverpool. Playing once for M.C.C. and Ground v. Eastbourne, at the Saffrons, he hit J. Bray over the trees, the ball pitching 60 yards beyond them. On another occasion, when playing at Torquay, he hit a ball out of the ground (above the ordinary size), across a road, and so far into another field that it put up a brace of partridges.'

J.T. Brown   J. Cranston

Somerset

'Not much that is favourable can be said about Somerset's cricket in 1904. The county had a very poor season, winning only five of their county matches, losing eleven and drawing two. The best point about their play was that, unlike some of their rivals, they generally arrived at a definite result.'

Oxford v Cambridge, *played at Lord's, June 30, July 1, 2*

'In one respect the match was memorable, J.F. Marsh, with an innings of 172 not out, setting up a new record for these contests. It was a remarkable feat, but to enable him to beat R.E. Foster's score of 171 in 1900 much valuable time was sacrificed on the Saturday, and F.B. Wilson, the Cambridge captain, was sharply criticised for allowing the glory of an individual player to prejudice the chance of winning the game.'

1906

WISDEN 1906

43rd EDITION
EDITOR: Sydney H. Pardon
PAGES: 763
PRICE: Limp 1/-   cloth 2/4d
REPRINT: Willows 1999 (500 limit, in two formats)

THE WORLD AT LARGE

- Liberal Party wins the general election with a large majority
- Suffragettes (the word is coined in this year) disrupt the State Opening of Parliament
- In London, both the Bakerloo (in March) and Piccadilly (in December) underground lines are opened
- Rolls-Royce Ltd begins trading
- San Francisco earthquake on 18th April kills perhaps 3,000 people and destroys 28,000 buildings. Over half the population are left homeless

CRICKET HEADLINES 1905

County Champions: Yorkshire

England retain the Ashes, winning the series against Joe Darling's Australians 2-0: England captain F.S. Jackson wins all five tosses

George Hirst scores 341 for Yorkshire v Leicestershire: for the second successive year he scores over 2,000 runs and takes over 100 wickets

Warwick Armstrong scores 303* for the Australians against Somerset

A.H. Hornby scores 100 in 43 minutes for Lancashire against Somerset

NOTES BY THE EDITOR

'I hold strongly to the opinion that the toss, as an essential feature of cricket, should not be tampered with. Apart from all other considerations – such as the delightful uncertainty before a match begins as to which side will bat first – the toss for innings affords the best guarantee that wickets will in all cases be fairly and properly prepared. I would not for a moment suggest that in the case of out and home county matches the knowledge that the opposing team were going in first would in the ordinary way lead to any wrong-doing on the part of the ground-keepers. All the same there would be a danger which the law in its present shape prevents.'

FEATURE ARTICLES

The Australians in England 1905, by Sydney Pardon
'Though they only suffered three defeats, the general feeling of the Australians with regard to the tour of 1905 was one of disappointment. The reason for this is not far to seek. The plan, which in this country only dates from 1899, of having five Test Matches makes the cricket success dependent to a far greater degree than was the case in the early tours upon the result of the meetings with England, and the fact of Darling's side losing the rubber without winning one of the five matches, outweighed everything that was done in the other fixtures. There is no need to go over familiar ground and insist upon Jackson's extraordinary luck in winning the toss upon all five occasions. Even making the most liberal allowance for this good fortune, the play pointed to the superiority of England, and this, I believe, the Australians themselves admitted, though they naturally thought they would have got on far better if they had once or twice had the advantage of batting first.'
Thomas Hayward in First-class Cricket
Hundreds in Test Matches in England

FIVE CRICKETERS OF THE YEAR

L.G. Wright
'Curiously enough, Wright has with advancing years gone on improving and last summer found him better than ever – a far finer bat than he was in his young days. In another respect

his position in the cricket world at the present time is still more remarkable. As a rule the man of forty and upwards, even when capable of getting an unlimited number of runs, shows only too plainly in his fielding the effects of time, but Wright has as yet found no difficulty in getting down to the ball. He is almost as quick and sure as he was ten years ago, and is … almost the only English cricketer who gives the public any idea of what an extremely important position point was in E.M. Grace's great days.'

D. Denton   W. Lees   G.J. Thompson   J. Vine

W.G. Grace jnr.
'… eldest son of the greatest of cricketers, died suddenly at three o'clock on the morning of March 2nd, at East Cowes, after an operation for appendicitis. As he was born on July 6th, 1874, he was under thirty-one years of age at the time of his death. He was in the Clifton College XI. in 1891-92-93, being captain in his second year, and assisted Cambridge against Oxford in 1895 and 1896.'

R.A.H. Mitchell
'Mike was a deep student of all that goes to turn out a sure cricketer, that is to say a cricketer who leaves as little as possible to chance: he could turn the most unpromising material into something useful, and from promising material he produced many very perfect cricketers.' – Lord Harris

W.P. Pickering
'His career as a cricketer ended in 1852 as far as England was concerned, but in Canada, his new home, he played regularly until 1857, taking part in all the matches against The United States. It was chiefly through his efforts that George Parr's team visited Canada in 1859.'

COUNTY REVIEW

Surrey
'A Cambridgeshire man by birth and the best bat for that county in 1904, Hobbs had duly qualified by two years' residence and at the opening of the season it was known that a great deal was hoped of him. His early play exceeded all expectations and by the end of May he had firmly established his reputation, his scoring for three or four weeks being extraordinary.'

MATCH REPORTS

England v Australia, First Test Match, *played at Nottingham, May 29, 30, 31*
'The light grew worse and worse with every sign of on-coming rain, and the Englishmen had reason to fear that all their efforts would be thrown away and the match left drawn. For a quarter of an hour play went on in deep gloom, and then McLeod was out leg-before-wicket, England winning a memorable game by 213 runs. In bringing off the victory that MacLaren's hitting had first made possible, the Englishmen owed everything to Bosanquet. He took eight of the nine wickets that fell, completely demoralising the batsmen with his leg-breaks. He gained nothing from the condition of the ground, the pitch remaining firm and true to the end. In the first flush of his triumph his place in the England team seemed secure for the whole season, but he never reproduced his form, and dropped out of the eleven after the match at Leeds.'

The cricket records are for the first time subdivided into sections including Great Individual Scores; The Biggest Totals; The Highest Aggregates; Small Totals; Two Hundreds In One Match; Three Hundreds Or More In Succession; First Wicket Partnerships; Other Big Partnerships; Wicket-keeping Feats; Bowling Feats; Australian Teams In England (see also 'Small Totals') etc. The section is now 23 pages long, and ends with the statement that in all matches, E.M. Grace has scored 76,098 runs and taken 11,395 wickets, including 277 in 1904 and 303 in 1905 – when he was 63.

1907

WISDEN 1907

44th EDITION
EDITOR: Sydney H. Pardon
PAGES: 725
PRICE: Limp 1/-   cloth 2/4d
REPRINT: Willows 1999 (500 limit, in two formats)

THE WORLD AT LARGE

• Cunard Lines' *Mauretania* and *Lusitania* both complete their maiden voyages
• An exhibition of Cubist paintings by Georges Braque, Pablo Picasso and others causes a sensation in Paris
• Korea becomes a protectorate of Japan
• Rudyard Kipling wins the Nobel Prize for Literature
• Sweden's King Oskar II dies and is succeeded by his son, King Gustav V

CRICKET HEADLINES 1906

County Champions: Kent

Tom Hayward scores 3,518 runs in the season, a record that will stand for 41 years: he also scores four centuries in successive innings over two matches in six days

George Hirst scores 2,385 runs and takes 208 wickets – a unique 'double double'

P.F. Warner leads England to a crushing 4-1 series defeat against South Africa in South Africa

NOTES BY THE EDITOR

'One subject has come up for discussion since the end of the season. At the meeting of the Advisory Committee at Lord's on December 19th, a proposal was brought forward by Kent that in the case of a cricketer coming to this country to make a livelihood out of the game the period of qualification should be extended … The proposal was lost but only by a majority of one, there being seven votes in its favour and eight against … The question is a very delicate one and there is much to be said on both sides. No one I think wishes Australian or other Colonial players to be excluded absolutely from our county elevens but at the same time there is a very strong feeling that the free importation of ready-made players does not make for the good of county cricket.'

FEATURE ARTICLES

A Short History of Kent Cricket for the Past Thirty Years and More, by George Marsham
'In looking back over these past 30 years one fact stands out prominent, and that is that the success to which the county has at length attained is in a large degree due to the energy, the ability, the foresight, the thoughtfulness of one man. Though no doubt he would say that he has been loyally backed up by lovers of county cricket both in and out of the field, yet I have no hesitation in saying that to Lord Harris we chiefly owe the proud position in which the county now stands.'
The Tonbridge Nursery, by Capt. W. McCanlis
W.G. Grace in Gentlemen v Players Matches

FIVE CRICKETERS OF THE YEAR

A. Fielder
'Fielder had a good season for Kent in 1904, taking 84 wickets in county matches and at times doing excellent work. In 1905, however, he went back instead of forward and failed to retain a regular place in the Kent eleven … At the end of the season there was a general feeling that he had missed his opportunity and that he would not fulfil his previous promise. His brilliant success last summer came therefore as a genuine surprise. Bowling in a form he had never

approached before, he was undeniably first-rate. He began well and though an immense amount of work devolved upon him, he never looked back, being just as good in September as he had been in May.'

J. N. Crawford   E. G. Hayes   K.L. Hutchings   N. A. Knox

OBITUARIES INCLUDE

W.W. Read

'The turning point of his cricket life came in 1881, when an appointment as assistant secretary at The Oval enabled him to devote all his life to the game. From that year until his powers began to wane he was, as a batsman, the mainstay of the Surrey eleven. In the revival of Surrey cricket, which began in 1883, he and the late George Lohmann had the chief share. They, far more than anyone else, enabled Surrey, under Mr. John Shuter's captaincy, to recover in 1887, after an interval of twenty-three years, the first position among the counties.'

V.E. Walker

COUNTY REVIEW

Kent

'The colt, Woolley, deserves more than passing notice. It was unfortunate that he had to be left out of some matches after he had established himself in the team, but this was only an accident due to the super-abundance of capable players. Good as he already is, Woolley will no doubt, with increased physical strength, go far ahead of his first season's doings.'

MATCH REPORTS

Somerset v Yorkshire, *played at Bath, August 27, 28, 29*

'Yorkshire led on the first innings by 243 but, with plenty of time to spare, Ernest Smith let his own side bat a second time instead of making Somerset follow on. Having the match in hand he was, no doubt, actuated by a desire to let Hirst complete his 2,000 runs for the season. In this Hirst succeeded, he and Rhodes putting on 202 in an hour and a quarter. In making two separate hundreds in the match, Hirst rivalled Denton's achievement … earlier in the season … It was quite Hirst's match as apart from his batting, he took eleven wickets for 115 runs.

South Africa v England, *First Test Match played at Johannesburg, January 2, 3, 4*

'The first of the five test matches was the most remarkable of the series, the Englishmen being beaten by one wicket after they had seemed to have the game in their hands. South Africa had 284 to get in the last innings, and when the sixth wicket fell before lunch the score was only 134. White played wonderfully well, resisting the bowling for four hours and ten minutes, but despite all his efforts – he was out eighth at 226 – forty-five runs were still required when Sherwell, the last man, joined Nourse. Amid ever increasing excitement the runs were hit off, South Africa thus winning by one wicket.'

1908

WISDEN 1908

45th EDITION
EDITOR: Sydney H. Pardon
PAGES: 781
PRICE: Limp 1/-   cloth 2/4d
REPRINT: Willows 2000 (500 limit, in two formats)

THE WORLD AT LARGE

• Campbell-Bannerman resigns as Prime Minister in April on ill-health grounds, and dies two weeks later
• H.H. Asquith is the new Prime Minister: he appoints David Lloyd George as Chancellor and Winston Churchill as President of the Board of Trade
• Olympic Games held in London: Britain wins 56 gold medals
• Robert Baden-Powell establishes the Boy Scout movement
• William H Taft wins the U.S. presidential election
• China's dowager Empress Cixi dies, having been the power behind the throne for decades
• Donald Bradman born, August 27

CRICKET HEADLINES 1907

County Champions: Nottinghamshire

England, under R.E. Foster, wins the three Test series against South Africa 1-0

A.D. Nourse is given out 'handled the ball' when playing for the South Africans v Sussex, the last time that will happen in England for 58 years

A.E. Trott takes four wickets in four balls for Middlesex v Somerset in his benefit match at Lord's, and then takes a hat-trick later in the innings

Northamptonshire dismissed for 12 by Gloucestershire (Dennett 8 for 9, Jessop 2 for 3)

NOTES BY THE EDITOR

[On a proposed Triangular Tournament in 1909]
'The result of this arrangement, so far as English cricketers are concerned, would be that for six weeks of our comparatively short season no county with a representative in the England eleven could depend on having its full strength in ordinary engagements … I am far from making a fetish of the Championship, but such a complete upset of county cricket for a whole summer cannot be contemplated without some misgiving. There is the further objection that it is possible to have too much of a good thing. Even in an ordinary year our fixture list is too heavy, and there is a danger with two teams touring throughout the summer of cricket becoming a toil rather than a pleasure.'

FEATURE ARTICLES

South African Bowling, by R.E. Foster
'The interest in the attack of the South Africans is centred round four men - Schwarz, Vogler, Faulkner, and White. These men all bowled with a leg-break action, and could make the ball come in from the off. Though England can claim the 'proud originator' of this style of bowling in Bosanquet, it has been left to South Africa to improve it – I will not say perfect – as I am convinced that this style is capable of still further improvement, which in time will be brought nearly to perfection. Bosanquet taught Schwarz, and Schwarz taught the others, and the others are better than their mentors.'
John Tunnicliffe in First-Class Cricket

A. Hallam

'On the slow wickets of last summer he was by general consent ... the best of English bowlers. Far surpassing all his previous doings he bowled with consistent success in match after match and ... scarcely knew what it was to be mastered. Like his predecessors in the Notts eleven, Alfred Shaw and Attewell, Hallam places his chief reliance on accuracy of pitch. When the ground helps him he can make the ball turn either way but there is nothing startling about his break.'

R.O. Schwarz   F.A. Tarrant   A.E.E. Vogler   T. Wass

OBITUARIES INCLUDE

H.F. Boyle

'It is a very old story now to tell how Spofforth and Boyle on the 27th of May, 1878, dismissed the M.C.C. for totals of 33 and 19, and in one afternoon established for good and all the reputation of Australian cricket.'

E.W. Pooley

'Edward Pooley, the once famous Surrey wicket-keeper, died in Lambeth Infirmary on the 18th of July. He had for a long time been in very poor circumstances and was often compelled to seek the shelter of the workhouse. Born on the 13th of February, 1838, he was in his seventieth year. All through his cricket career it was generally supposed that he was born in 1843 and the real date of his birth was only made known by himself in his interview in "Old English Cricketers". It seems that when he determined to take up cricket professionally his father thought that he would have a better chance if he knocked a few years off his age.'

C. Absolon   C.W. Alcock   A. Shaw   Earl of Winterton

COUNTY REVIEW

'After an interval of twenty-one years Notts finished in an unchallenged position at the head of the counties, going right through the season unbeaten ... As regards the other counties there is no need in this place to say very much. Worcestershire did better than in any previous seasons, and Yorkshire, with limited resources in batting, fought on so pluckily in face of early disasters as to tie for second place.'

MATCH REPORTS

Northamptonshire v Kent, *played at Northampton, May 30, 31, June 1*

'Rain restricted cricket on the opening day to three hours and prevented anything being done on the Friday, but despite this serious loss of time Kent had won at half past four on the Saturday afternoon by an innings and 155 runs. This was mainly the work of Blythe who, bowling superbly, took all ten wickets in Northamptonshire's first innings, and had a record for the match of seventeen wickets for 48 runs ... Kent only just won in time, for no sooner had the players left the field than rain fell heavily.'

The editor explains in his Preface: 'In its general features the Almanack remains unchanged, but some sections grow bigger and bigger. The list of Births and Deaths of Cricketers is far more complete than before, over three hundred names having been added. For this improvement I have to thank Mr. F.S. Ashley-Cooper and, in a lesser degree, Mr. A.C. Denham of Huddersfield.'

1909

THE WORLD AT LARGE

- National old age pension scheme introduced
- Suffragettes who have gone on hunger strike in prison, are force fed
- Britain's Secret Service Bureau is established: it is the forerunner of MI5
- Union of South Africa formed
- U.S. Admiral Robert Peary claims to reach the North pole, but his claim is never proven
- Louis Blériot becomes the first person to fly across the English Channel

WISDEN 1909

46th Edition
Editor: Sydney H. Pardon
Pages: 771
Price: Limp 1/-   cloth 2/4d
Reprint: Willows 2000 (500 limit, in two formats)

CRICKET HEADLINES 1908

County Champions: Yorkshire

W.G. Grace plays his final first-class match

Monty Noble's Australian XI win back the Ashes down under, winning 4 and losing 1 of the five Tests

Northamptonshire dismissed for 15 by Yorkshire

NOTES BY THE EDITOR

[On the possibility of the county championship becoming a two-division affair]
'Speaking for myself, I think the aim should be to make cricket less rigid. Rather than run the risk of putting a famous county into the second rank on the strength of one bad season, I would abolish the present system of points altogether and let the order of merit be decided on the general play by the M.C.C., or by an independent committee appointed by the leading club. The great point is that the championship exists for cricket, not cricket for the championship. This is a truism that cannot too often be insisted on.'

FEATURE ARTICLES

Cricket in the Sixties and at the Present Day, by Alfred Lubbock
'I think Bob Carpenter, Tom Hayward, Richard Daft and one or two others were quite as good bats as any professionals of the present day, though I admit they didn't get quite so many hundreds as are now obtained. The simple reason for this is that now the wickets are so perfect that bumping balls, shooters, or bad kickers, are seldom seen. At Lord's, it was a common occurrence to have three shooters and the other ball out of an over of four bump right over the batsman or wicket-keeper's head.'
K.S. Ranjitsinhji in First-class Cricket

FIVE CRICKETERS OF THE YEAR

'Lord Hawke and Four Cricketers Of The Year
Lord Hawke
'The presentation to Lord Hawke at Leeds last July in celebration of the fact of his having in the previous summer completed twenty-five years service as captain of the Yorkshire Eleven, afforded a happy opportunity of giving his portrait in Wisden.'
J.B. Hobbs
'Few batsmen in recent years have jumped into fame more quickly than Hobbs.'

A. Marshal

'Marshal has not Jessop's ability to score in all directions from bowling of all kinds of length, but with his immense advantages of height and reach – he must stand nearly 6ft 3ins – he can certainly send the ball further. His fame will no doubt rest chiefly on his batting, but in every way he is a thorough cricketer. Place him where you will, there is no finer fieldsman to be found – he is about the safest catch in England – and though there has perhaps been a tendency to exaggerate his merits as a bowler, he commands a good variety of pace with plenty of spin.'

W. Brearley   J.T. Newstead

OBITUARIES INCLUDE

Rev. R. Lang

'His round-armed bowling at the commencement of his cricketing career was slow, but afterwards (about 1858) the pace was tremendous, being one of the fastest bowlers that has ever appeared, and with a break-back from the off. If he had only been a little straighter, he would have been excelled by none.'

H. Storer

'… brother of the well-known wicket-keeper, died in the first week of May of consumption at the early age of 38. He played for Derbyshire on a few occasions in 1895, his highest score being 35 against Leicestershire at Derby. As an Association footballer he gained much distinction, and played for Liverpool in two of the memorable English Cup semi-finals with Sheffield United.'

A. Blackman   S.M. Crosfield

COUNTY REVIEW

Derbyshire

'Perhaps the one man on the side who did himself complete justice was Joseph Humphries who, besides batting well at times, kept wicket magnificently throughout a disastrous season.'

Hampshire

'Financially, Hampshire as usual did badly, but they are facing a deficit of £1,000 with cherry [sic] optimism, perhaps born of the fact that with much the same set of players as were available a year before they raised their position from twelfth to eighth among the counties. Due largely to the young members of the team this improvement should be more than transitory.'

MATCH REPORTS

Australia v England, Second Test Match, *played at Melbourne, January 1, 2, 3; 4, 6, 7*

'On the sixth and last day the Englishmen began badly and when their eighth wicket fell with 73 runs still required, the match looked all over. However, Humphries and Barnes put on 34 together and then, to the astonishment of everyone concerned, Barnes and Fielder hit off the remaining 39 runs, and won the match. Barnes played with great judgment and coolness for his 38 not out. The last run was a desperately short one and if Hazlitt, throwing in from cover point, had managed to hit the wicket, the result would have been a tie.'

Sydney Pardon's Preface is almost triumphalist: 'Wisden *nowadays needs few words of introduction. Having survived other annuals which at one time dealt with cricket, it now has the field very much to itself but, though enjoying something like a monopoly, it is, I hope and believe, more comprehensive than ever.'*

1910

WISDEN 1910

47th EDITION
EDITOR: Sydney Pardon
PAGES: 749 pages
PRICE: Limp 1/-   cloth 2/4d
REPRINT: Willows 2001 (500 limit, in two formats)

THE WORLD AT LARGE

• King Edward VII dies: he is succeeded by his son, who becomes King George V
• Dr. Crippen murders his wife and attempts to flee to America. He becomes the first person to be caught thanks to a telegraph message. He is returned to Britain, tried and hanged
• Two general elections are held during the year: Asquith's Liberals retain power through the year
• Revolution in Portugal: King Manoel II is deposed and the country becomes a republic
• Charles Rolls, half of the Rolls Royce partnership, becomes the first Briton to die in an aircraft accident
• Halley's Comet makes its predicted return, 76 years after its previous passing

CRICKET HEADLINES 1909

County Champions: Kent

The visiting Australians retain the Ashes by two matches to one, their captain Monty Noble winning all five tosses

E.G. Arnold and W.B. Burns establish a then world fifth-wicket record stand of 393 for Worcestershire v Warwickshire; Woolley and Fielder add 235 for Kent's tenth wicket v Worcestershire, still the English record

C. Blythe takes 215 wickets in the season

Wilfred Rhodes scores 2,094 runs and takes 141 wickets during the summer

New South Wales v Victoria at Sydney yields a then record aggregate 1,911 runs for the loss of 34 wickets

NOTES BY THE EDITOR

'To this day the extraordinary blundering in connection with the team for the Test Match at Lord's – the game that was the beginning of England's troubles – remains unexplained. Lord Hawke was away from England at the time, the responsibility for the selection of the eleven resting entirely on C. B. Fry, H. D. G. Leveson Gower, and A. C. MacLaren. How these three gentlemen came to make such a muddle of the business no one has ever been able to understand.'

FEATURE ARTICLES

Modern Batting, by Lord Harris
'I regret to have to say so, but I do declare that in the little first-class cricket I see nowadays I have seen more bad batting this year than I can remember to have seen in any previous year; and I fear that a bad style is spreading, for I know from conversation with young cricketers that this style is not condemned by them; and I therefore venture in the interests of English cricket, and for the welfare of school cricketers, now while there is yet time, to raise one voice at any rate against it.'
George Herbert Hirst in First-Class Cricket

D.W. Carr

'He duly appeared for England at the Oval in August. As everyone will remember he started off in great form in that memorable game, getting rid of Gregory, Armstrong, and Noble very cheaply. He might have followed up these early successes more effectively, but MacLaren, with a sad lack of judgment, tired him out, letting him bowl for fully an hour and a half without a rest. After the Test Match, Mr. Carr did some capital work for Kent, especially on the last morning of the Canterbury Week.'

A.P. Day

'He is one of the chief hopes of England's batting in the near future. He has a fine commanding style with plenty of hitting, but his sovereign merit is the watchful defence which enables him to do well on all sorts of wickets. In view of what may be in store for him one could wish that he had specialized a little more in fielding.'

W. Bardsley   S.F. Barnes   V.S. Ransford

OBITUARIES INCLUDE

A. Craig

'Albert Craig, The Surrey Poet, died after a long illness at 8, Mayflower Road, Clapham, on July 8th in his sixtieth year. A Yorkshireman by birth and up-bringing, he started life as a Post Office Clerk in Huddersfield, but was still a young man when, discovering that verse-making was his forte, he decided to devote his time and energies to celebrating the doings of cricketers and footballers. He was a familiar and welcome figure on the chief grounds in all parts of the country, but especially those of Surrey and Kent. He was possessed of much humour and it was seldom indeed that anyone had the best of him in a battle of wits. His pleasantries, which were never ill-natured, served to beguile many a long wait occasioned by the weather.'

W.H. Benthall   Earl of Leicester   Earl of Sheffield

COUNTY REVIEW

Kent

'Owing to bad weather and the presence of the Australians the competition for the championship in 1909 proved rather less interesting than usual. When in the middle of June Kent lost both matches in the Tonbridge Week, they did not look to have much chance of repeating their triumph of three years before, but thenceforward they did not know what it was to be beaten, and some time before the county season ended their position at the head of the list was practically assured.'

MATCH REPORTS

England v Australia, Third Test Match, *played at Leeds, July 1, 2, 3*

'There seemed every promise of a fine finish on Saturday, but England's batting failed lamentably in the last innings … The task of getting 214 was not thought likely to be beyond England's powers, but the early play was far from encouraging. With the score at 17 Fry played a ball from Cotter on to his foot and into his wicket and, at 26, Tyldesley was caught and bowled … After the interval there came a doleful collapse. Cotter and Macartney bowled in great form and nothing could be done against them, the last seven wickets falling in less than an hour for 31 runs. To Macartney belonged the chief honours of the Australian victory. In the whole match he took eleven wickets, and only 85 runs were hit from him.'

1911

WISDEN 1911

48ᵗʰ EDITION
EDITOR: Sydney Pardon
PAGES: 767
PRICE: Limp 1/-   cloth 2/4d
REPRINT: Willows 2001 (500 limit, in two formats)

THE WORLD AT LARGE

• The Siege of Sidney Street: Latvian extremists shoot it out with the police in London's East End
• Coronation of King George V
• Members of the House of Commons vote to pay themselves salaries for the first time
• China declares itself a republic, ending millennia of Imperial rule. By the end of the year, Sun Yat-Sen is proclaimed president
• Irving Berlin's *Alexander's Ragtime Band* becomes a worldwide hit

CRICKET HEADLINES 1910

County Champions: Kent

The MCC team in South Africa loses the Test series by three matches to two

W.C. Smith (Surrey) takes 247 wickets in the season

G.A. Faulkner (South Africa) becomes only the second man to score a century and take five wickets in an innings of a Test match

NOTES BY THE EDITOR

'It is a long time since we have had, in the absence of Australian or South African visitors, such a thoroughly interesting season as that of 1910, but it is equally true that lamentations from the county committees on the score of poverty have seldom been so loud. Since the season ended one has heard little save complaints of diminished receipts and deplorable balance sheets.'

FEATURE ARTICLES

Our Young Cricketers, by P.F. Warner
'Hendren is but a year or two older than J.W. Hearne. Very quick on his feet he is an extremely powerful driver. He does not always play back quite straight, and occasionally he starts jumping in to hit a little too early in his innings, but he is full of strokes, and a most attractive bat to watch.'
Lord Hawke in the Cricket Field

FIVE CRICKETERS OF THE YEAR

A. Hartley
'Hartley is not a batsman to draw the crowd, his methods being the reverse of striking to the eye. His style is good and his bat straight, but he does nothing to astonish those who are looking on. Still there is reason to think that, having now fully established his position, he will let himself go a little more than he has done hitherto... He is understood to be ambitious of further distinction in the cricket field, but whether he will ever rise to Test Matches remains to be seen.'
W.C. Smith
'Given at last a full chance, he jumped to the top of the tree as incontestably the best right-handed slow bowler in England. The details of what he did will be found in other pages of *Wisden*. Sufficient to say that in first-class matches he took 247 wickets, only J. T. Hearne having a better average. It is a curious fact that Smith is the only great slow bowler Surrey have had since the days of James Southerton.'
H. K. Foster   C.B. Llewellyn   F.E. Woolley

H.M. King Edward VII
'As a small boy he received tuition at Windsor from F. Bell, of Cambridge, but it cannot be said that he ever showed much aptitude for the game. He played occasionally during his Oxford days, however, and, while he was staying at Madingley Hall, a special wicket was reserved for his use at Fenner's.'

H. Luff
'Mr. Henry ("Harry") Luff, proprietor of Wisden's Cricketers' Almanack and of the firm of Messrs. John Wisden & Co., of Cranbourn Street, died on July 18th. Born at Petersfield, in Hampshire, on January 26th, 1856, Mr. Luff was in his fifty-fifth year at the time of his death.'

G.E. Palmer
'Following his return to Australia after the unsuccessful tour of 1886, he had the misfortune to fracture his knee-cap and not much more was seen of him in first-class cricket. The latter part of life was the reverse of prosperous, but on this point there is need to dwell. He married a sister of Blackham, the great wicket-keeper.'

A. Woodcock
'After dropping out of county cricket he continued to play for the M.C.C., and, in a match against Lewes Priory on the Dripping Pan, Lewes, as recently as 1908, bowled a bail off the wicket 149 feet six inches, sending it over a fourteen feet bank and a wall on the boundary.'

H.J.H. Scott   M. Sherwin   J.Wells

Surrey
'Surrey had an eventful season in 1910, their play being marked by the sharpest contrasts of failure and success. In the end they finished second to Kent, the new method of reckoning points telling much in their favour. Under the old system their record in the Championship would have been nothing out of the common but, with seven defeats ignored, their sixteen victories gave them a very good percentage.'

South Africa v England, Fifth Test Match, *played at Cape Town, March 11, 12, 14, 15*
'The Englishmen finished their tour with a dazzling performance, winning the last Test Match by nine wickets. For this victory they had to thank Hobbs, Rhodes and Blythe. On England winning the toss, Hobbs and Rhodes scored 221 for the first wicket in rather less than two hours and forty minutes … Rhodes was overshadowed by his partner's brilliancy, but he scored his 79 without a mistake of any kind. Hobbs – out fifth at 327 – was unlucky in touching his stumps with his foot and dislodging a bail. He scored his 187 in three hours and three quarters, hitting in his superb innings twenty three 4's.'

United States v Canada
'This match, which it had been arranged should take place in Philadelphia on September 12th and 13th, was scratched by the Canadian Cricket Association as they were unable to get together a representative team. There was some friction over the selection, Ottawa, who expected at least three of their players to be asked, not being satisfied at having only one invited.'

Sydney Pardon writes in his Preface: 'Having now edited Wisden *for twenty years, I find it difficult to say anything fresh when bringing out a new issue … As regards the photographs I felt tempted to give five of the young men who came to the front during the season but changed my mind.' He also records: 'Mr. H. Luff, the proprietor of* Wisden, *died in July after a long illness from which there was never any hope of permanent recovery. I must not omit a tribute to his unvarying kindness. He gave me a perfectly free hand in conducting the Almanack, and our relations were always of the pleasantest nature.'*

1912

WISDEN 1912

49th Edition
Editor: Sydney Pardon
Pages: 787
Price: Limp 1/-   cloth 2/4d
Reprint: Willows 2001 (500 limit, in two formats)

THE WORLD AT LARGE

• A few days after the Norwegian Amundsen gets there, Robert Falcon Scott and his party reach the South Pole. They will all die on the return journey
• *Titanic* sinks after hitting an iceberg on its maiden voyage; over 1,500 passengers and crew die
• What is said to be the remains of an unknown type of proto-human are discovered near Piltdown in Sussex. The hoax was uncovered in 1953
• Japan's Meiji Emperor dies, and is succeeded by his mentally feeble son, the Taisho Emperor
• Woodrow Wilson defeats incumbent President Taft in the U.S. presidential election

CRICKET HEADLINES 1911

County Champions: Warwickshire

E.B. Alletson scores 189 in 90 minutes for Nottinghamshire v Sussex, the last 142 coming in 40 minutes. He hits 34 off one over from E.H. Killick

Rhodes and Tarrant both score over 2000 runs and take over 100 wickets during the season

Kent's F.H. Huish becomes the first wicket-keeper to trap 100 victims in a season

NOTES BY THE EDITOR

'Never in an English summer has there been so much sunshine as in 1911, and on the whole cricket flourished. Assuredly there was nothing to justify the attitude of the pessimists who, during the winter, had argued that the game was declining and could only be saved by drastic alterations in the rules. The methods of modern batsmen often make one wish that the change in the law of leg-before-wicket, brought forward by the M.C.C. in 1901, had obtained the requisite two-thirds majority at Lord's, but apart from this I can see nothing in modern cricket that needs the interference of the reformer.'

FEATURE ARTICLES

Mr. Archibald Campbell MacLaren in First-Class Cricket
The All-Indian Tour
Warwickshire in First-class Cricket, a Statistical Review, compiled by R.O. Edwards

FIVE MEMBERS OF THE M.C.C.'s TEAM IN AUSTRALIA

J.W. Hearne

'At first there was a difficulty about Hearne going to Australia. Some members of the Middlesex committee thought he was too young for such a heavy tour, but in the end they yielded to Mr. Warner's urgent request that he might be allowed to join the team. Up to the time I write he has done nothing as a bowler in Australia, but as a batsman he has met with wonderful success, making scores in the first two Test Matches of 79, 43, and 114. As he has done so much before completing his twenty-first year, Hearne's future as a cricketer, given a continuance of good health, seems assured.'

S.P. Kinneir
'It was thought that with his strong defence and extreme steadiness, he would be just the man for the Sydney and Melbourne wickets, and he soon received an invitation to join the M.C.C.'s team for Australia. The compliment was well deserved at the time, but I doubt whether Kinneir would have been asked if Mead had in the first half of the season obtained the big scores that he afterwards made. To take to Australia for the first time a man of 38 was obviously something of an experiment.'

F.R. Foster   C.P. Mead   H. Strudwick

OBITUARIES INCLUDE

E.M. Grace
'Mr. Edward Mills Grace died on May 20 after a long illness … But for the accident that his own brother proved greater than himself, E.M. Grace would have lived in cricket history as perhaps the most remarkable player the game has produced. Barring W.G., it would be hard indeed to name a man who was a stronger force on a side or a more remarkable match winner.'

H. Graham
'Graham did many brilliant things as a batsman but scarcely gave himself a fair chance. Had he ordered his life more carefully he might have had a much longer and more successful career in first-class cricket. His natural powers were great. He did not play with quite a straight bat but he was a splendid hitter with any amount of dash and vigour.'

W.L. Murdoch
'Present at the Test match between Australia and South Africa, he was seized with apoplexy during the luncheon interval and passed away later in the afternoon. Murdoch had a long career as a cricketer, but his fame will rest mainly on what he did for the Australian teams of 1880, 1882, and 1884. He captained the three elevens, and in all three he was incontestably the finest batsman.'

T. Sherman   H.B. Steel

COUNTY REVIEW

'The County Championship of 1911 was decided on a new points system of scoring – brought forward in the spring by Somerset – five points being allowed for a win outright, and in drawn matches three points being given to the side leading and one point ot the side behind on the first innings. Matches in which no result on the first innings was arrived were not counted. Playing in great form from the end of June, Warwickshire, for the first time in the county's history, won the Championship, finishing up with a fractionally better record than Kent.'

MATCH REPORTS

The first South African tour of Australia, 1910-1911
'From the South African point of view the tour was a disappointment, Australia winning four of the five Test matches. The vast superiority of the Australian batting was, from the first, freely admitted, but some people thought that the three bowlers who had done such wonderful things in England – Vogler, Schwarz, and Faulkner – would redress the balance and win the rubber for their side. Unfortunately for the South Africans, however, Vogler was in no form at all, and except on rare occasions, Schwarz and Faulkner had few terrors for the Australian batsmen. As Mr. P.F. Warner had predicted before the team, left home, the bowlers found the Sydney and Melbourne wickets very different indeed from the matting pitch at Johannesburg.'

The Cricket Records section is now indexed, and a list of England Test cricketers appears for the first time, compiled by F.S. Ashley-Cooper. There are now regular sections dealing with domestic cricket in Australia, South Africa and India, and frequent if not annual sections dealing with cricket in the West Indies and America.

1913

WISDEN 1913

50th EDITION
EDITOR: Sydney Pardon
PAGES: 849
PRICE: Limp 1/-   cloth 2/4d
REPRINT: Willows 2002 (500 limit, in two formats)

THE WORLD AT LARGE

• Suffragette Emily Davison throws herself in front of the King's horse at the Derby, and dies a few days later
• 439 miners die in the Senghenydd Colliery disaster
• The first performance of Nijinsky's ballet *The Rite of Spring*, with music by Stravinsky, causes riots among the audience
• The Ford Motor Co. introduces the first moving assembly line

CRICKET HEADLINES 1912

County Champions: Yorkshire

The Triangular Tournament is a failure: England win 4 of their 6 Tests to win the tournament, but the concept is not tried again

T.J. Matthews of Australia takes two hat-tricks for Australia against South Africa at Manchester

England win back the Ashes under J.W.H.T. Douglas in the 1911-12 season

NOTES BY THE EDITOR

'The Fates fought against the Triangular Tournament. Such a combination of adverse conditions could hardly have been imagined. To begin with, the Australians, who had been allowed to have everything their own way in choosing the time for the first trial of Sir Abe Bailey's ambitious scheme, quarrelled so bitterly among themselves that half their best players were left at home. In the second place the South Africans, so far from improving, fell a good way below their form of 1907 and, to crown everything, we had one of the most appalling summers ever known, even in England.'

JOHN WISDEN

[For this Jubilee edition of the Almanack (pictured), instead of the Five Cricketers of the Year, a photograph of John Wisden and recollections of him take pride of place.]
'Wisden had a perfect delivery … In round-arm bowling there was not, I imagine, the same power of manipulating the ball with the fingers, so as to make it break from the off, or come in from the leg, at pleasure, as can be done by the 'windmill' bowlers of the present day. On the other hand, what was a prominent feature of the bowling of the past, seems, so far as my observation goes, to have entirely disappeared. I do not believe that any one under the age of fifty has ever seen a real shooter.' – Sir Kenelm Digby

FEATURE ARTICLES

J.R. Mason and R.E. Foster in the Cricket Field

OBITUARIES INCLUDE

G.J. Bonnor
'Though he was last seen on an English cricket ground more than twenty years ago, George Bonnor had not in one sense outlived his fame, his doings being constantly recalled and talked about. He was, indeed, far too striking a personality to be forgotten in less than a generation. Australia has sent to England many finer batsmen, but no other hitter of such extraordinary power.'

E.B. Dwyer
'John Elicius Benedict Bernard Placid Quirk Carrington Dwyer – always referred to as E.B. Dwyer – died on October 19th at Crewe, where he had been engaged during the season. He was

born on May 3rd, 1876, at Sydney (N.S.W) … Dwyer was a great-grandson of Michael Dwyer, the Wicklow chieftain, who was one of the boldest leaders in the Irish insurrection of 1798. He held out for five years in the Wicklow mountains and was exiled in 1804 to Australia, where he died in 1826.'

T. Richardson
'Like a wise man, Richardson in his great days treated himself as a bowler pure and simple. He once scored 60 against Gloucestershire at The Oval, but he never took his batting seriously. His business was to get wickets … He was one of the pre-eminent cricketers of his generation.'
R.A. Duff   Andrew Lang   W. Storer

COUNTY REVIEW

Northamptonshire
'The explanation of Northamptonshire's brilliant season is not far to seek. It is to be found in the possession of very good well-varied bowling, and in the fact that the county put practically the same eleven into the field on all occasions.'

CRICKETERS' ALMANACK FOR 1913.

PRICE ONE SHILLING NET.
POST FREE, 1s. 4d.   CLOTH, 2s. 4d.

JUBILEE NUMBER
OF THE ALMANACK.

JOHN WISDEN'S
CRICKETERS' ALMANACK
FOR 1913.

FULL SCORES AND BOWLING ANALYSES
OF
ALL IMPORTANT MATCHES
PLAYED IN 1912.

SPECIAL PHOTOGRAPH OF JOHN WISDEN
WITH PERSONAL RECOLLECTIONS.

Edited by
SYDNEY H. PARDON.

LONDON : JOHN WISDEN AND CO.,
CRICKETING AND BRITISH SPORTS DEPÔT,
21 & 23, Cranbourn Street, nr. Leicester Square, London, W.C.
AND OF ALL BOOKSELLERS AND AT ALL BOOKSTALLS.
Entered at Stationers' Hall.

BALDING AND MANSELL, PRINTERS, LONDON AND WISBECH.

MATCH REPORTS

Australia v South Africa, *played at Lord's, July 15, 16, 17*
'Kelleway and Bardsley practically won the match for Australia. Playing wonderfully well on a wicket, which, though fast, was far indeed from being at all easy, they took the score from 86 to 256 in something under two hours. In all they put on 242 runs for the third wicket in three hours and a quarter. To look at, there was no possible comparison between the two, Bardsley's free style and brilliant all-round hitting putting Kelleway quite in the shade. Still, in his own quiet methodical way Kelleway played an exceptionally good innings. His patience was limitless, and his defence impregnable.'

MISCELLANEOUS

Presentation to S.E. Gregory
On the occasion of his fiftieth Test match appearance for Australia
'Sir George Reid, G.C.M.G., Agent-General for the Commonwealth of Australia, made the presentation … He went on to say that Gregory could feel proud of a record unapproached by any other cricketer, and, moreover, he was captain of the team in which he made his fiftieth appearance. Although not Australia's best team, owing to some incredible stupidity somewhere or other, it was a thoroughly good side.'

In a brief history of the 50 years of Wisden, *Sydney Pardon in his Preface hints at how difficult was the period it went through in the 1880s. He writes: 'Descriptions of matches first appeared in the book for 1870, being written up to the time of his death in 1879 by the compiler of the Almanack in those days, Mr. W.H. Knight. A few years later the Almanack fell upon evil days, the revival beginning when in 1887 my brother, Charles F. Pardon, became editor. Thenceforward the book increased rapidly both in size and circulation.'*

1914

WISDEN 1914

51st EDITION
EDITOR: Sydney Pardon
PAGES: 799
PRICE: Limp 1/-   cloth 2/4d
REPRINT: Willows 2002 (500 limit, in two formats)

THE WORLD AT LARGE

• Irish Home Rule Bill finally passed
• In June, Archduke Franz Ferdinand is assassinated in Sarajevo. Within a few weeks, the Great War has begun
• Trench warfare begins: major battles at the Marne and Ypres cause massive loss of life on both sides
• Death of Pope Pius X. He is succeeded by Cardinal della Chiesa, Archbishop of Bologna, who takes the title Benedict XV
• Passenger pigeon becomes extinct as the last known bird dies in Cincinnati Zoo

CRICKET HEADLINES 1913

County Champion: Kent

Tom Hayward scores his 100th century

Schofield Haigh takes his 2,000th wicket and retires at the end of the season

H. Dean takes 17 wickets for 91 runs for Lancashire against Yorkshire

Huish again snares 100 victims behind the stumps

Kent dismiss Warwickshire for 16

NOTES BY THE EDITOR

'The encouraging fact about our cricket is that we have so many men who while still quite young have reached the top of the tree – J.W. Hearne, Woolley, and Mead are the most striking examples – and so much new talent. I have no wish to take up the role of prophet, but looking back upon what happened last season, it will be disappointing indeed if, to mention only a few names, Lee of Notts, Kilner of Yorkshire, Jeeves of Warwickshire, Chester of Worcestershire, R.B. Lagden and D.J. Knight, do not do a great deal for us in the next few years.'
[Jeeves was killed in the Great War, and Chester lost an arm.]

FEATURE ARTICLES

Hayward's 100's
Schofield Haigh in First-class Cricket

FIVE CRICKETERS OF THE YEAR

Major W. Booth
G. Gunn
'When at his best George Gunn is a delightful bat to watch, but he carries to an extreme the practice of getting right in front of the wicket, often playing fast as well as medium pace and slow bowlers in this fashion. His easy style and quickness in judging the length of a ball suggest that, as a boy at Trent Bridge, he studied Arthur Shrewsbury's methods very carefully. No one at the present day in playing back seems to have more time to spare.'
J.W. Hitch   A.E. Relf   Hon. L.H. Tennyson

Hon. A. Lyttelton

'Such matchless brilliancy in every athletic game, such wise and unquestioned leadership among boys and elders alike, and this without neglect of the more serious side of school life, for our friend was among the ablest students of history, both at School and University. And then the personality of the hero of all this boyish achievement. Tall, vigorous, muscular, athletic grace characteristic of every movement, the merriest eye, the most engaging smile that ever gladdened the heart of a friend – were ever so many brilliant and attractive qualities blended in one youthful person?' – Earl of Darnley

W.H.B. Evans

'Mr. William Henry Brereton Evans, whose tragic death at Aldershot in August, when flying with Col. Cody, caused such a painful shock, was one of the best all-round amateur cricketers of his day. Indeed, if he had been able to keep up his cricket regularly after he left Oxford, it is quite likely that he would have had the distinction of playing for England. He was a batsman of very high class, and one of the best amateur fast bowlers seen in University cricket since Woods.'

T. Jayes

'Jayes was one of the men originally picked for the Test match between England and Australia at Lord's in 1909. At the last moment, however, it was decided to leave him out, and England, going into the field without a right-hand fast bowler, suffered defeat by nine wickets.'

E. Rodriguez

'Chevalier Epifanio Rodriguez, who died in London … aged 57, was a well-known M.C.C. and Emeriti cricketer. He was known facetiously as "the best cover-point in Spain".'

Lancashire

'The most unsuccessful season that Lancashire have had for many years ended in a domestic storm. While the last match – the return with Essex – was in progress at Old Trafford, Mr. A.H. Hornby, in an interview in the *Manchester Guardian*, expressed great dissatisfaction at the way in which the affairs of the club were being conducted, taking particular exception to the proposal, contemplated at that time, of reducing the fixture list in 1914. He raised various points, but as everything was afterwards amicably settled, it is hardly necessary now to go into details.' *[Details follow at great length.]*

V. Trumper's Benefit Match: New South Wales v Rest of Australia, *played at Sydney, Friday, Saturday, Monday, Tuesday, February 7, 8, 10, 11*

'Abundant testimony to Trumper's popularity was furnished by his benefit match, the receipts, including donations, amounting to nearly £3,000 – easily a record in Australia. Unfortunately a most interesting game had to be left drawn. Some splendid cricket was shown, Trumper himself being seen at his very best. On a rather difficult pitch he took nearly three hours to score his 126 not out, but he hit sixteen 4's. His only mistakes in this fine innings were two possible chances of being caught and bowled. In honour of Trumper, Noble reappeared in first-class cricket, batting with much of his old skill.'

Two Separate Hundreds in One Match

'In India, in February 1904, Mr. Lionel P. Collins, the Old Marlburian, three times made two separate hundreds in a match within a space of ten days, scoring quite without parallel in the history of the game. He made his runs whilst on tour with the Gurkha Brigade.'

1915

WISDEN 1915

52nd Edition
Editor: Sydney H. Pardon
Pages: 791
Price: Limp 1/6d   cloth 2/10d
Reprint: Willows 2002 (500 limit, in two formats)

THE WORLD AT LARGE

- Attack on the Dardanelles fails
- *Lusitania* sunk by German U-boat, killing 1,198 passengers and crew
- Nurse Edith Cavell executed by German firing squad
- D.W. Griffith's film *Birth Of A Nation* has its premiere in Los Angeles
- Rupert Brooke dies
- P.G. Wodehouse publishes his first *Blandings* novel
- British and German troops play football between the lines on Christmas Day

CRICKET HEADLINES 1914

County Champions: Surrey

The season is curtailed by the outbreak of war

England win the Test series in South Africa by four matches to nil, with one drawn

S.F. Barnes takes 49 wickets in the series, at under 11 runs each – still a record almost a century later

A. Drake (Yorkshire v Derbyshire) and S.G. Smith (Northants v Warwickshire) both take four wickets in four balls. The first three of Smith's victims are all caught by G.J. Thompson at slip. Drake also takes all ten wickets for 35 for Yorkshire v Somerset

J.W. Hearne and F.E. Woolley both score over 2,000 runs and take over 100 wickets

NOTES BY THE EDITOR

'Writing in the early days of the New Year it is impossible to take other than a gloomy view with regard to the immediate future of cricket. Never before has the game been in such a plight. One may take it for granted that, in any circumstances, county cricket, as we have known it for the last forty years or more, will be out of the question this season, but in the happy event of the War coming to an end at an earlier date than the experts expect, we are sure to see plenty of games of a less competitive character... I hope no attempt will be made to close the game down entirely.'

FIVE CRICKETERS OF THE YEAR

S. G. Smith
'From his good start Smith has seldom fallen away as a batsman, but in 1910 and 1911 his bowling was both expensive and ineffective. He was the first batsman who ever made a thousand runs for Northamptonshire and, in the same season – 1910 – he set up what was then another record for the county, playing an innings of 204 against Gloucestershire. In 1912 he regained all his skill with the ball and, thanks chiefly to the splendid work done by him and Thompson, Northamptonshire jumped into second place among the counties, finishing very little below Yorkshire.'

J.W.H.T. Douglas   P.G.H. Fender   H.T.W. Hardinge   D.J. Knight

OBITUARIES INCLUDE

A.E.J. Collins
'... who was killed in action on November 11, came suddenly into note by scoring 628 not out for Clarke's House v. North Town, in a Junior house match at Clifton College, in June, 1899, when only thirteen years old. During the six hours and fifty minutes he was in he hit a 6, four 5's, thirty-one 4's, thirty-three 3's, and 146 2's, carrying his bat through the innings, and

Clarke's, who scored 836, won by an innings and 688 runs. Collins also obtained eleven wickets in the match.'

A.O. Jones

'Always rather eager and impetuous, he had not quite the right temperament for Test match cricket. All through his career his fielding was even finer than his batting. Indeed it may be claimed for him that a better all-round fieldsman has never been seen. Unequalled in his favourite position in the slips – a sort of short third man – he was almost as brilliant in the deep field, and in the England v. Australia match at Birmingham in 1909 he made a catch at short-leg that has become historical.

A.G. Steel

'A.G. Steel as a man was always cheery and he never made an enemy. Nothing made him lose his temper, and many a young cricketer was helped by him, and there never existed anybody of whom he was jealous either among his professional brethren at the Bar or in the cricket field. In his later years his financial position was easy, and he gave up active work as a Barrister, but if he had stuck to it he might in Liverpool have made a good practice.' – Hon. R.H. Lyttelton

A.E. Trott

'Trott, Albert Edwin, shot himself at his lodgings, Denbigh Road, Willesden Green, on July the 30th. He had been very ill for some time without hope of recovery and, finding the monotony of life in hospital intolerable, he thought a pistol shot the best way out. His death, in his 42nd year, was indeed a tragedy.'

R.E. Foster   Field Marshal Earl Roberts

COUNTY REVIEW

'Following the declaration of War, county cricket struggled on gallantly for a month, but on the 31st of August it was cut short, the Surrey committee, at a special meeting, deciding unanimously to cancel their remaining fixtures with Sussex and Leicestershire. It was argued by a good many people that in taking this action Surrey voluntarily forfeited their position and that the County Championship remained in abeyance for the year. This view, however, received no official support.'

MATCH REPORTS

South Africa v England, Second Test Match, *played at Johannesburg, December 26, 27, 29, 30*
'The result was not quite so overwhelming as before, but the Englishmen won by an innings and 12 runs. It was Barnes's match. On no occasion during the tour was the great bowler seen to quite such advantage. He took seventeen wickets – eight for 56 and nine for 103 – proving quite irresistible on the last morning.'

The editor announces in the Preface: 'Owing to the heavy cost of production the proprietors have felt compelled to make a slight increase in the price of the book.' Wisden had maintained its price of one shilling from 1864 until now. An advertisement for back numbers puts the price of the 1914 edition at 20/-, representing a remarkable increase on the cover price just 12 months earlier.

Staff had rallied to the colours, as the editor notes: 'Mr. Ernest D. Allen, who for several years had assisted in the work, joined the Army during the first week of the War.' His death in France was recorded in Wisden 1916: 'Private Ernest Douglas Allen (Scots Guards) was shot through the head during a night attack at Cuinchy on January the 1st [1915].'

1916

WISDEN 1916

53rd EDITION
EDITOR: Sydney H. Pardon
PAGES: 299
PRICE: Limp 1/6d   cloth 2/10d
REPRINT: Willows
1. 1990 (1,000 limit)
2. 1997 (200 limit, denoted, uniquely, in Roman numerals)

THE WORLD AT LARGE

- Easter Rising in Ireland
- *HMS Hampshire* sinks: Lord Kitchener drowns
- First Battle of The Somme lasts from July to November: over 1 million soldiers die
- Lloyd George takes over as Prime Minister

First-class cricket is suspended through the war until 1919. The focus turns to obituaries as not only does Wisden *record the toll of war deaths, but four giants of the cricket scene die: W.G. Grace, Victor Trumper, Andrew Stoddart and Sir Spencer Ponsonby-Fane. Each is the subject of a special article, with full statistical records of the first three.*

PREFACE

'In the Preface to Wisden a twelvemonth back I wrote that the Almanack might in its next issue have to return to the slender proportions of fifty years ago. Though not reduced to quite such an extent it is, in comparison with its normal self, a very small volume. The question of coming out at all was seriously considered, but the proprietors decided not to break the continuity of over half-a-century. In the circumstances it was determined to dispense with the customary photographs … As regards the future the outlook is dark enough, but … there is every reason to hope that when peace comes cricket will quickly re-assert itself.'

FEATURE ARTICLES

W.G. Grace, A Tribute by Lord Harris

'He was originally a medium-paced bowler without peculiarity, meeting occasionally with considerable success, but in the seventies he adopted the delivery, slow with a leg break, by which he was known for the rest of his great career, and added to his otherwise extraordinary capacity as a cricketer. He must have been by nature a great bat and field, but he made himself, by ingenuity and assiduity, a successful bowler: and though I never knew anyone keener on having his innings, I am by no means sure he did not prefer the other department of the game; at any rate, it was very difficult to take him off once he had got hold of the ball. It was "Well, just one more over" or "I'll have him in another over or two," when one suggested a change.'

OBITUARIES INCLUDE

R.C. Brooke

'Sub-Lieut. Rupert C. Brooke (Royal Naval Division), born at Rugby on August 3, 1887, died at Lemnos of sunstroke on April 23. In 1906 he was in the Rugby Eleven, and although he was unsuccessful in the Marlborough match he headed the School's bowling averages with a record of nineteen wickets for 14.05 runs each. He had gained considerable reputation as a poet.'

Capt. C.H. Eyre

'He played for Harrow for three years (1900 to 1902) and for Cambridge the same period, being captain of each side during his last year, and it is worthy of mention that in his six great matches at Lord's – against Eton and Oxford – he was not once on the losing side. For this happy experience he himself was not largely responsible, as in the games with Eton he made only 68 runs in five innings and in the inter Universities' matches but 75 in six.'

W.G. Grace

'In no branch of sport has anyone ever enjoyed such an unquestioned supremacy as that of W.G. Grace in the cricket field. In his great days he stood alone, without a rival.'

Sir Spencer Ponsonby-Fane

'As a boy of fifteen he had played for the M.C.C. in 1839, although it was not until May 14th, 1840, that he was elected a member of the Club on the proposal of Mr. Aislabie, seconded by Lord Paget. His term of membership was without parallel in the history of the M.C.C., and during it he occupied almost every office possible, except the Presidency, which he declined several times ... Apart altogether from cricket, Sir Spencer's career was a noteworthy one. He entered the Foreign Office in 1840; was Private Secretary to Lord Palmerston, the Earl of Clarendon and Earl Granville; Attaché at Washington 1846-7; Comptroller of the Lord Chamberlain's Office until 1901; Gentleman Usher to the Sword; and Bath King of Arms since 1904. He also brought from Paris the treaty which ended the Crimean War.'

A.E. Stoddart

'Mr. Stoddart was one of the very few men who have represented their country at Rugby football as well as at cricket. Between 1886 and 1893 he took part in ten international Rugby matches, and would certainly have played in more but for the fact that in two of the intermediate seasons England, owing to a dispute with the other Unions, had no International matches. He appeared twice against Scotland, three times against Ireland, and four times against Wales, while in 1889 he played against the Maoris. A splendid runner, with plenty of pace and dodging ability, and not above jumping over an opponent on occasion, he was a great three-quarter – possessed of a very fine pair of hands – a brilliant kick, and a player full of resource.'

V.T. Trumper

'Of all the great Australian batsmen Victor Trumper was by general consent the best and most brilliant. No one else among the famous group, from Charles Bannerman thirty-nine years ago to Bardsley and Macartney at the present time, had quite such remarkable powers. To say this involves no depreciation of Clem Hill, Noble, or the late W. L. Murdoch. Trumper at the zenith of his fame challenged comparison with Ranjitsinhji. He was great under all conditions of weather and ground. He could play quite an orthodox game when he wished to, but it was his ability to make big scores when orthodox methods were unavailing that lifted him above his fellows.'

Viscount Alverstone   F.H. Bacon   Capt. F.O. Grenfell, V.C.   G.G. Napier   F.R. Reynolds

---

MATCH REPORTS

New South Wales v Victoria, *played at Sydney, January 23, 25, 26, 27*

'A very keen game ended in a win for Victoria by 16 runs. Ironmonger had a big share in the success, taking six wickets in the last innings for 73 runs. He kept such a length, either on the wicket or just outside the off-stump, the the batsmen could seldom hit him. Armstrong was steady at the other end, but his practice of bowling – as in England in 1905 – very wide of the leg stump, came in for sharp criticism, as being calculated to destroy public interest in cricket.'

A reduced print run, and the extra interest of the obituary for Grace, meant this edition was sold out 'in a few days' (Preface, 1917). Despite being the thinnest volume since the 224 pages of 1882, this edition (pictured) is a prized item and one of the most expensive for collectors today.

CRICKETERS' ALMANACK FOR 1916.

PRICE ONE SHILLING AND SIXPENCE NET.
POST FREE, 1s. 10d.   CLOTH, 2s. 10d.

FIFTY-THIRD EDITION.

JOHN WISDEN'S
CRICKETERS' ALMANACK
FOR 1916.

W. G. GRACE.
A TRIBUTE
BY LORD HARRIS.

FULL STATISTICS OF MR. GRACE'S CAREER
IN THE CRICKET FIELD.

Edited by
SYDNEY H. PARDON.

LONDON : JOHN WISDEN AND CO. LTD.,
CRICKETING AND BRITISH SPORTS DEPÔT,
Cranbourn Street, Leicester Square, London, W.C.
AND OF ALL BOOKSELLERS AND AT ALL BOOKSTALLS.
Copyright under Act, 1911.

BALDING AND MANSELL, PRINTERS, LONDON AND WISBECH.

1917

WISDEN 1917

54th EDITION
EDITOR: Sydney H Pardon
PAGES: 351
PRICE: Limp 1/6d   cloth 2/10d
REPRINT: Willows 1997 (500 limit, in two formats)

THE WORLD AT LARGE

- The Russian Revolution – Czar Nicholas abdicates and the Bolsheviks under Lenin take over by the end of the year
- The United States declares war on Germany
- The Battle of Passchendaele leaves over half a million dead and wounded
- The Balfour Declaration supports the idea of a Jewish homeland in Palestine
- T.S. Eliot's *Prufrock and Other Observations* published

PREFACE

'The fifty-fourth edition … is of necessity rather a mournful volume. Its chief feature is a record of the cricketers who have fallen in the War – the Roll of Honour, so far as the national game is concerned … Last year the wisdom of publishing Wisden in War time seemed very doubtful, but the experiment was more than justified, a small edition being sold out in a few days. As a natural result the proprietors had this year no hesitation in going on. At the time of writing the outlook for the game is as dark as possible, another blank season as regards first-class cricket being to all appearance certain. So far supporters of the various county clubs have for the most part been very loyal, but this year some further falling off in subscriptions is almost inevitable.'

FEATURE ARTICLES

A Great Bowling Feat

'I have been asked to draw attention to a feat by Frank Field, the Warwickshire fast bowler, which owing to the stoppage of the game by the War, has not been given the prominence among cricket records to which it is entitled... In the match between Worcestershire and Warwickshire, played at Dudley on June 1, 2, and 3, 1914, Field, in the second innings of Worcestershire, went on to bowl with the score of 85 for four wickets, and took the six outstanding wickets in eight overs and four balls, seven maidens, at a cost of only two runs. The score of the match published at the time credited Field with only six maiden overs, but the detailed analysis which has been sent to me shows that he bowled seven. In fact, the only scoring stroke made off him was a lucky two from the second ball in the second over before he had taken a wicket.'

P.F. Warner at Lord's and The Oval

OBITUARIES INCLUDE

Deaths in the War 1916:
A.C.P. Arnold

'At Cambridge he … did not receive his Blue until 1914 … For Hampshire he played several good innings that season, among them being 54 v. Kent and 69 v. Lancashire, both at Bournemouth, and 76 v. Somerset and 51 v. Warwickshire, both at Southampton. He would probably have developed into a cricketer of very high class.'

H.G. Bache

'He was a left-hand bat and a fair change bowler. At Association football he played for Cambridge University, West Bromwich Albion and the Corinthians, and also obtained his international cap.'

W. Booth

'In the 144 games in which he appeared for Yorkshire he scored 4,213 runs with an average of 22.65 and obtained 556 wickets for 18.89 runs each. Tall of stature, good-looking, and of engaging address, Booth was a very popular figure both on and off the cricket field.'

H.L.H. Du Boulay

'He was in the Cheltenham Eleven in 1913 and 1914... Of his last year at school Wisden said: "For a boy of his age he is a batsman far above the ordinary, and it is not too much to say that with average luck he might develop into a great cricketer".'

K.L. Hutchings

'Of all the cricketers who have fallen in the War he may fairly be described as the most famous … Hutchings was quite individual in his style of batting, recalling no predecessor. His driving power was tremendous, and when at his best he could score from good length balls with wonderful facility. It was said in 1906 that when he played for Kent against Yorkshire, even George Hirst – most fearless of fieldsmen at mid-off – went back several yards for him, so terrific being the force of his hitting.'

P. Jeeves

'… England losing a cricketer of whom very high hopes had been entertained.'

R. Sherwell

'He was left-handed as a batsman and had many strokes. He was the tenth son of his father, and one of his brothers is Mr. Percy Sherwell, a former South African captain.'

Other deaths in 1916:

H.T. Arnall-Thompson

'Whilst playing Shacklock's bowling in the Leicestershire v. M. C. C. and Ground match at Lord's in 1889, he had a painful and curious experience. The ball flew off the edge of his bat on to his eyebrow and rebounded to the bowler. Arnall-Thompson was momentarily stunned, and as the blood flowed freely suggested he should retire and finish his innings later. It was then gently broken to him that he was out, caught-and-bowled.'

Dr. A. Grace

'Dr. Alfred Grace, the last of the famous brotherhood, who was born at Downend on May 17, 1840, died in a nursing home in Bristol on May 24, and was buried at Chipping Sodbury. He never appeared at Lord's, but was a very useful cricketer, his usual post in the field being long-stop … Although he was not in the front rank of cricketers, he stood out as one of the finest horsemen in England, and for many years followed the Duke of Beaufort's hounds three or four times a week.'

COUNTY REVIEW

Warwickshire

'Mr. Ryder gives a very encouraging account of the conditions of the Warwickshire Club in war-time. Subscriptions were so well kept up as to cover the expenditure for 1916 – about £750 being received. The Club's bank balance remains untouched, and there is a sum of £1,400 in hand. The County suffered a grievous loss in the death in action of Percy Jeeves. J.H. Parsons, who enlisted as a trooper, has gained a commission. He has seen fighting in the Dardanelles and at Salonika.'

MATCH REPORTS

Marlborough v Rugby, *played at Marlborough, August 1, 2*
'Batting freely from the start, Rugby, despite a useful innings by McCarthy, met with so little success that they had seven men out for 135. At that point, however, Wright came in and hit with such vigour that the eighth wicket yielded 93 runs, the total in the end reaching 268. Wright's 94 included a 6 and sixteen 4's.'

A total of 107 pages were given over to deaths.

An advertisement for back numbers already has the price of the 1916 edition at 21 shillings (one guinea). Top price of 42 shillings is now for the years 1889, 1891, 1902 and 1904.

1918

WISDEN 1918

55th EDITION
EDITOR: Sydney H Pardon
PAGES: 339
PRICE: Limp 2/-   cloth 3/4d
REPRINT: Willows 1997 (500 limit, in two formats)

THE WORLD AT LARGE

- Communists move Russian capital from Petrograd to Moscow
- Russian Tsar and all his family executed at Ekaterinburg
- Second Battle of the Somme
- Royal Air Force founded
- Manfred von Richthofen, the 'Red Baron', dies in aerial combat
- Kaiser Wilhelm abdicates and escapes to Holland: The Great War ends on November 11
- Spanish flu outbreak kills an estimated 25 million people between August 1918 and mid-1919
- Women over the age of 30 win the right to vote in U.K.

NOTES BY THE EDITOR

'There can be no question that as regards the propriety of playing cricket in War time there was a great change of feeling last summer. People realised that with public boxing carried on to an extent never heard of before, and professional billiard matches played in the hottest weather, there was something illogical, not to say absurd, in placing a ban on cricket. The general result was highly satisfactory.'

SCHOOL BOWLERS OF THE YEAR

C.H. Gibson
'As a natural straightforward bowler, personally I think Gibson stood out by himself and for a boy with probably another year at school, he seems to be something quite out of the common.'
H.L. Calder *[see Wisden 1996, obituaries]*
J.E. d'E. Firth   G.A. Rotherham   G.T.S. Stevens

OBITUARIES INCLUDE

Deaths in the War in 1917 – The Roll of Honour:
C.Blythe
'Blythe had all the good gifts that pertain to the first-rate slow bowler, and a certain imaginative quality that was peculiarly his own … Blythe's spin was something quite out of the ordinary. On a sticky wicket or on a dry pitch ever so little crumbled he came off the ground in a way that beat the strongest defence. He had, too, far more pace than most people supposed. The ball that went with his arm often approached the speed of a fast bowler and had of course the advantage of being unsuspected.'
R.P. Lewis
'He had no pretensions as a batsman, and in the University match in 1894 he was very pleased that he managed to stay for a couple of overs, enabling Charles Fry to add seventeen runs and complete his hundred.'
J.E. Raphael
'The news that John Raphael was dead caused sorrow to a very wide circle of friends. Though he never gained quite the place as a batsman that his deeds as a school-boy had suggested, he was in the cricket field and still more in the world of Rugby football a distinct personality. Everything he did created more than ordinary interest, his popularity as a man, apart from his ability, counting for much.'

Deaths in the War 1914, 1915, 1916
Rear Admiral the Hon. H.L.A. Hood
'Was a very keen, if not very distinguished cricketer. When in command of a battleship he always endeavoured to secure good cricketers as the officers of his ward and gun-rooms.'

Other deaths in 1917:
F.E. Allan
'Frank Allan was the first of the long line of great Australian bowlers. There were good men before his day – Sam Cosstick and others – but he was the first to develop those special qualities that made Australian bowling – when the first team came to England in 1878 – the talk of the cricket world ... Allan, who bowled left-handed and batted right, had abundant spin, but his distinctive gift was a remarkable swerve, or as it was then called a curl in the air. Batsmen who met him for the first time were bewildered by the course of the ball.'
H.R.H. Prince Christian
'Very fond of the game.'
G.H.S. Trott
'Australia has produced greater cricketers than Harry Trott, but in his day he held a place in the front rank of the world's famous players. He was a first-rate bat, a fine field at point, and his leg breaks made him a very effective change bowler. Four times he came to England – first in 1888, again in 1890 and 1893, and, finally, in 1896, when he had the honour of captaining the team. As a leader in the field he perhaps gained even more distinction than as an all-round player. Ranjitsinhji considered him a better captain than Darling, and beyond that praise could hardly go.'

COUNTY REVIEW

Kent
'The ground at Canterbury was lent free of charge to the soldiers stationed in the neighbourhood, both for matches and practice, and despite a wet fortnight in August when several fixtures had to be scratched, 119 military and school matches were played during the season.'

MATCH REPORTS

English Army XI v. Australian Army XI, *played at Lord's, July 14*
'In the bright sunshine on the 14th of July, Lord's ground looked quite its old self. The public mustered in surprisingly large numbers, the pleasure felt in seeing even a one day match of general interest being very keen ... Two capital sides were got together, the English team being composed entirely of men who before the War had taken part in first-class cricket. Several of the Australian names were unfamiliar, but the presence of Macartney, Kelleway, Matthews and E.P. Barbour – an admirable batsman from New South Wales – lent distinction to the eleven.'

There is another price increase: in three years, the price has doubled. The photoplate returns after a two-year absence with portraits of the Five [public] School Bowlers of the Year. The editor says in the Preface: 'Again the chief feature of the book is the Roll of Honour – an appallingly long list.' The advertisement for back numbers makes it clear that cloth-bound copies from 1896 onwards cost a shilling more than limp-bound copies.

1919

WISDEN 1919

56th EDITION
EDITOR: Sydney H Pardon
PAGES: 327
PRICE: Limp 2/6d   cloth 4/4d
REPRINT: Willows 1997 (500 limit, in two formats)

THE WORLD AT LARGE

- Prohibition of alcohol enacted in the United States
- Treaty of Versailles signed by Germany and Allies
- Mussolini forms the Fascist Party in Italy
- Amritsar Massacre: British troops kill 379 Sikhs
- Alcock and Brown complete the first transatlantic flight
- President Woodrow Wilson partially paralysed by a stroke
- Lady Astor becomes the first woman MP to take her seat at Westminster

NOTES BY THE EDITOR

'The resumption of first-class matches was no sooner announced than all the faddists in Great Britain began to fill the newspapers with their ideas of what they were pleased to call reform or reconstruction. Some of the suggestions, such as the penalising of the batting side for every maiden over played, were too preposterous to be worth a moment's consideration. Still, even the most fatuous proposals found supporters. We were advised to play by the clock and, regardless of weather and wicket, to rule a batsman out unless runs came at a certain fixed rate per hour. Then followed a determined agitation to get the boundaries shortened.'

FIVE PUBLIC SCHOOL CRICKETERS OF THE YEAR

N.E. Partridge
"N.E. Partridge, of Malvern, certainly accomplished the most remarkable performances of any boy last year, and very few in any year have approached him … As a batsman he is essentially an attacking player, with the possession of almost every shot of the cricketer of potential fame; as a bowler his action is not particularly impressive, but he is sound and liable to defeat any one at any time.'

P.W. Adams   A.P.F. Chapman   A.C. Gore   L.P. Hedges

OBITUARIES INCLUDE

Deaths in the War in 1918 – The Roll of Honour:
['Again a terribly long list' – Preface]

F. Bennett-Goldney
'Died in American Hospital at Brest in July, aged 53, as result of a motor accident. Prominent in the Canterbury Week. M.P. For Canterbury since December, 1910. Mayor of Canterbury 1906-1911.'

L.G. Colbeck
'His name will live in cricket history by reason of the extraordinary innings he played in the University match of 1905. Going in for the second time against a balance of 101 runs Cambridge lost six wickets for 77, and looked to be a hopelessly beaten side. At this point Colbeck, in with the score at 11, was joined by McDonnell, and in the course of 85 minutes the two batsmen put on 143 runs together, completely pulling the match round.'

R.O. Schwartz
'Inasmuch as he always made the ball turn from the off and had no leg break Schwarz was not in the strict sense of the word a googly bowler, and was in this respect inferior to his colleagues Vogler and Faulkner. Still, when at his best, he was a truly formidable opponent, his accuracy of length in the season of 1907, in combination with such a big break, being extraordinary.'

G.W.E. Whitehead

'Among the many public school cricketers lost during the war perhaps none, except John Howell of Repton, had better prospects of winning distinction at the game than George Whitehead.'

Deaths in the War In 1917:
A.B. Cotter

'Albert Cotter was the successor to Ernest Jones as Australia's fast bowler, coming to England with the teams of 1905 and 1909. His first trip was not an unqualified success. It is true that in all matches he took 124 wickets for less than 20 runs apiece, but up to a certain point of the tour he had so little command over his length that his bowling was a quaint mixture of long hops and full pitches. Still, irregular as he was, his extreme pace often made him dangerous.'

Other Deaths In 1918:
George Tubow II, King of Tonga

'The last of the independent kings in the Pacific. Died April, aged 46. Very fond of cricket, gaining his love of the game while at school in Auckland. His subjects became so devoted to the game that it was necessary to prohibit it on six days of the week in order to avert famine, the plantations being entirely neglected for the cricket field.'

COUNTY REVIEW

Yorkshire

'Lord Hawke, who was re-elected President, said that Yorkshire would have a good side, with Sir A.W. White as captain, Hirst, Rhodes, Denton, Kilner and Dolphin being all ready to play. During the summer of 1918, the same plan was followed as in the previous year, the county players being freely utilised in assisting local clubs and taking part in charity matches.'

MATCH REPORTS

United Services Team v Capt. P.F. Warner's England XI

'The match at Dover between these teams on Friday and Saturday, September 13 and 14, was played on behalf of War Charities and realised a profit of about £47. Some capital cricket was shown, but there was not quite time to bring about a definite result, Capt. Warner's team, when stumps were finally drawn, wanting only 20 runs to win with seven wickets to fall. Warner himself and Philip Mead batted finely at the close. Special features of the game were the admirable bowling of Lieut. Marriott, who took seven wickets for 59 runs and eight for 69; and the smart wicket-keeping of Capt. Heath.'

There is yet another price increase. The editor apologises in his Preface for the late appearance of Wisden, *which usually came out in January. Writing in February, he explains: 'Not till the Armistice had been signed on the 11th of November did anyone know that, after four blank years, Cricket in 1919 would be something like its old self ... The fixtures, without which* Wisden *would be incomplete, were not arranged till the 6th of February, and even then the proposed tour of an Australian Service Team, now given up, remained in doubt. More than that, it was only on the previous day that the final decision – a most unhappy one in my opinion – was taken to restrict all county matches to two days.'*

1920

WISDEN 1920

57th EDITION
EDITOR: Sydney Pardon
PAGES: 727
PRICE: Limp 2/6d   cloth 4/4d
REPRINT: Willows 2003 (500 limit, in two formats)

THE WORLD AT LARGE

- First meeting of the League of Nations
- The Unknown Soldier is buried in Westminster Abbey
- Olympic Games held in Antwerp
- First female students admitted to Oxford University
- Bloody Sunday: IRA kill 12 British agents, after which British troops fire on a crowd at Croke Park and kill 14

CRICKET HEADLINES 1919

County Champions: Yorkshire

Two-day championship fixtures branded a failure

J.C. White takes 16 for 83 in a day for Somerset v Worcestershire

Andy Ducat scores 306* for Surrey v Oxford University

NOTES BY THE EDITOR

'Looking back on the events of the season it is quaint to think that we were asked to shorten the boundaries, to penalise the batting side for every maiden over played, to banish the left-handed batsman, and to limit to three, or at most four, the number of professionals in every county eleven. All these fatuous suggestions and others just as foolish were, it will be remembered, put forward quite seriously. Happily we shall not be worried by them again … I must not forget to mention the dinner given by Messrs. Wisden in September to the Australian Imperial Forces Team. Not since the M.C.C. dinner in 1914, to celebrate the Centenary of the present Lord's ground, had so many famous cricketers gathered together under one roof. Lord Harris took the chair and in all the speeches the one note was confidence in the future of cricket. To the compliments paid to *Wisden's Almanack* by P.F. Warner and F.S. Jackson I cannot – from motives of modesty – refer in detail, but I need hardly say they were keenly appreciated.'

FIVE BATSMEN OF THE YEAR

A. Ducat
'Ducat is a first rate bat, excellent in style with great power both in driving and pulling, and more than that he is painstaking to a degree. It is likely enough that for any other county than Surrey he would have earned an even bigger reputation than he now enjoys. In the nature of things he could not play on the same side as Hayward and Hobbs without being overshadowed. Ducat is hardly less distinguished at Association football than at cricket. He is a member of the Aston Villa team and has won his International cap.'

E.H. Hendren
'Hendren has abundant gifts, combining with his fine hitting great patience and self-control. He is very modern in his methods, using the pull and the hook at every opportunity. So sure is his eye, however, that he is not often at fault.'

P. Holmes   H. Sutcliffe   E. Tyldesley

OBITUARIES INCLUDE

Deaths in the War 1914–1919 – the Roll of Honour:
'Erratum. In *Wisden* for 1916 it was stated that 2nd Lieut. R.M. Chadwick (Rugby Eleven, 1902), died of wounds on May 12, 1915. Mr. Chadwick is happily alive and well. The mistake probably arose through some confusion of initials.'

Other deaths in 1919:

R.G. Barlow

'He stood first among the batsmen of the extremely steady or stonewalling school, and even if he had not been able to get a run he would for his bowling and fielding have been worth a place in almost any eleven. In batting he used forward play for purposes of defence to an extent unknown in these days, but his judgment of length was so perfect, and his eye so sure that bowlers found it a terribly hard job to bowl him out. In the ordinary way he was not a batsman one would have journeyed ten miles to see, but when he opened a Lancashire innings – as he did hundreds of times – with Mr. Hornby, he became a figure of extreme interest.'

W. Caffyn

'Many cricket memories were revived by the announcement that the veteran Surrey player, William Caffyn, died at his home, at Reigate, on Thursday, August 28. Born on Feb. 2, 1828, he had lived to the great age of 91. His fame rests mainly on the fact that he was the best all-round man in the Surrey eleven that, with the late F. P. Miller as captain, used to meet – and twice beat – the full strength of England at Kennington Oval.'

G. MacGregor

'Rest in peace, old friend. You were a great stumper – you were a great cricketer, and you saw in the grand old game more than a circus show on which men may find it worth while to spend sixpence – you saw in it, as C.B. Fry says, a physical fine art full of plot-interest, enlivened by difficulties, difficulties that through the long, long years you successfully overcame.' – D.L.A. Jephson

D.W. Gregory   E.A. Halliwell   F. Laver   H. Phillips   E. Wainwright   H. Wood

---

COUNTY REVIEW

Warwickshire

'With their impoverished bowling, Warwickshire did not look forward to a good season, but the record in the Championship was even worse than had been feared. Out of fourteen matches, the side won one, lost seven and drew six, the solitary victory being gained against Derbyshire.'

MATCH REPORTS

Surrey v Kent, *played at Kennington Oval, August 18, 19*

'Nothing quite equal to the cricket at the finish can be recalled. Surrey had 95 to get in less than three-quarters of an hour, and in thirty-two minutes, despite the disadvantage of bad light, Hobbs and Crawford hit off the runs.'

MISCELLANEOUS

Cricket in Australia: The Inter-State Matches;

'Quite the feature of the season was the bowling for Victoria of McDonald, who did wonders in the first innings of New South Wales at Sydney. *[His figures were 11-1-42-8.]* He is described as a fast bowler, but of nothing like the pace of Ernest Jones or Cotter. The experiment of bowling eight balls to the over was considered a great success.'

The editor writes in his Preface: 'After appearing for four years in a very attenuated form, Wisden's Almanack has returned to something like its normal size. First-class cricket was resumed in 1919 on a far larger scale than most people had dared to hope for in the first summer after the war. More than that the gloomy fears that the game would not retain its old popularity after such a long break proved utterly groundless. Despite the unhappy experiment of restricting all county matches to two days and the increased charge for admission at the gates, the season was one of great prosperity.'

1921

WISDEN 1921

58th EDITION
EDITOR: Sydney Pardon
PAGES: 795
PRICE: Limp 5/- cloth 8/-
REPRINT: Willows 2005 (500 limit, in two formats)

THE WORLD AT LARGE

- Crown Prince Hirohito of Japan makes an official visit to Britain
- Agatha Christie's first Hercule Poirot novel *The Mysterious Affair At Styles* is published
- Greece declares war on Turkey
- Irish Free State set up and the province of Northern Ireland is created as part of the United Kingdom
- Adolf Hitler becomes Fuehrer of the Nazi Party
- The Royal British Legion holds the first Poppy Day

CRICKET HEADLINES 1920

County Champions: Middlesex

Percy Holmes scores 302* for Yorkshire v Hampshire

Percy Chapman, a schoolboy Cricketer of the Year in 1919, scores a century on first-class debut for Cambridge University

Percy Fender hits the fastest-ever century, in 35 minutes for Surrey against Northamptonshire

P.H. Tarilton scores the first first-class triple hundred in West Indies, 304* for Barbados v Trinidad; and A.D. Nourse hits the first in South Africa – also 304*, for Natal v Transvaal

NOTES BY THE EDITOR

'A disappointing feature of our otherwise brilliant season was the extreme disparity between the strongest and the weakest counties … I should be the last to throw cold water on county cricket, but there is no getting away from the fact that since the scope of the Championship was so widely extended a lot of our so-called first-class cricket has been quite second-rate.'

P. F. WARNER

[In place of the Five Cricketers of the Year there is a portrait of Pelham Warner (pictured) and a single-page article by the editor.]
'When cricket came to its own again he was not the batsman he had been, but even in 1919, when the long hours of two-day matches did not suit him at all, he managed to add one to his splendid list of hundreds at Lord's, and last summer he was something like his old self. Still it was not his batting but his skill as a captain that made his final season memorable. But for his leadership Middlesex would never have gained in August the wonderful series of victories that culminated with the triumph over Surrey. His great asset as a captain in that month of strenuous matches, counting for even more than his judgment in changing the bowling and placing the field, was his sanguine spirit. He was full of encouragement and got the very best out of his men by making them believe in themselves.'
Modern Batting and the Law of Leg Before Wicket, by Hon. R.H. Lyttelton

OBITUARIES INCLUDE

J. Beaumont
'At his best Beaumont was a first-rate bowler, very accurate and apt even on the best wickets to get up to a nasty height. He was quite individual in style, walking up to the crease to deliver the ball. His action was high, and, without being exceptionally fast, he could keep up a fine pace for any reasonable length of time. A big, powerful man, Beaumont retained to the end of his life all his Yorkshire characteristics. Residence in London did not in the least affect his way of speaking.'

Galloway, 11th Earl (Randolph Henry Stewart)
'Born at Galloway House on October 14, 1836, died at Cumlodew, Newton Stewart, on February 7. He was a member of the Harrow elevens of 1853 and 1854, when he scored 4, 3, 8 and 12 v. Eton and 0, 17, 0 and 11 v. Winchester, and obtained 13 wickets against each school. He was contemporary with Mr. V.E. Walker, and his brother, Lord Garlies, later the 10th Earl, was also in the elevens. He had been a member of the M.C.C. since 1855.'

G.M. Kelson
'Mr. Kelson retired from first-class cricket so long ago that to the present generation he was not even a name, but in his day he held a prominent place, being at one time beyond question the best bat in the Kent eleven. Kent cricket in the '60's was in a very depressed condition, but Mr. Kelson took part in many a hard-fought game side by side with Willsher and George Bennett.'

Col. H.W. Renny-Tailyour
'He was an excellent all-round player, and could hit very hard, but was not seen in great matches as frequently as his skill entitled him. In 1873 and two following years, however, he assisted the Gentlemen against the Players at Prince's. In minor matches his scoring was very heavy. For Royal Engineers v. Civil Service at Chatham in 1880 he scored 331 not out (out of 498 made whilst in) in 330 minutes.'

J. Shuter   F. Townsend   A. Watson

COUNTY REVIEW

'With the restoration, after the ill-starred experiment in 1919, of three-day matches, the County Championship stood on its pre-war footing. Never has the competition excited such widespread interest, and never has the actual finish been more dramatic.'

MATCH REPORTS

Middlesex v Surrey, *played at Lord's, August 28, 30, 31*
'This was the match of the season. Middlesex and Lancashire were running neck and neck for the Championship, and as Lancashire on the same day had the simplest of tasks against Worcestershire, Middlesex knew that nothing less than an actual victory would be of real value to them. Never before has a county match proved such an attraction at Lord's. On the Saturday there must have been nearly 25,000 people on the ground, 20,700 paying for admission at the gates. A great fight was looked forward to, and as it happened all expectations were exceeded. It was a game never to be forgotten, Middlesex in the end winning by 55 runs, and so securing the Championship.'

The price of the Almanack doubled from 2/6d to 5/-. The cloth-bound version is now 8/-.

1922

WISDEN 1922

59th EDITION
EDITOR: Sydney Pardon
PAGES: 998
PRICE: Limp 5/-   cloth 8/-
REPRINT: Willows 2006 (500 limit, in two formats)

THE WORLD AT LARGE

- Stalin appointed General Secretary of the Soviet Communist Party
- Irish Civil War – Michael Collins assassinated
- The BBC begins radio broadcasts
- Lloyd George resigns as Prime Minister and Conservative leader Andrew Bonar Law takes over
- Mussolini's Fascist 'March on Rome'
- Publication of T.S. Eliot's *The Waste Land* and James Joyce's *Ulysses*

CRICKET HEADLINES 1921

County Champions: Middlesex

Glamorgan take part in the Championship for the first time

Warwick Armstrong's Australia win the Test series by 3-0

In Australia, during the 1920-21 season, Australia beat the touring Englishmen 5-0

C.G. Macartney scores 345 runs in a day for the Australians v Notts, a record until beaten by Brian Lara in 1994

Five bowlers take all ten wickets in an innings – a record for any season

NOTES BY THE EDITOR

'It seems to me that there is a good deal of misapprehension as to the real meaning and value of trial games. No sensible people, I take it, imagine that cricketers of the first rank would, in any literal sense, have to play for their places. That is an absurd idea, but there cannot surely be two opinions as to the desirability of giving the selected players a little preliminary work together. Even one game would be very helpful in accustoming men to unfamiliar positions in the field and giving the wicket-keeper a chance of studying bowlers to whom he may never have stood up before. The fact that thirty players appeared for England in the Test matches last summer is in itself proof that we had not a real eleven, but a series of scratch sides.'

FEATURE ARTICLES

The Australians In England 1921
'Given fine weather the Australians as a side had not a weak point of any kind. They could all get runs, even the last man being capable on occasion of hitting up twenty or thirty; their fielding was magnificent; and above all they possessed in Gregory and McDonald two very fast bowlers of the highest class. It was the fast bowling more than anything else that brought about our undoing. Never before have English batsmen been so demoralised by great pace.'

M.C.C. Team in Australia 1920-21
'The tour of the M.C.C.'s team in the winter of 1920-21 resulted, as everyone knows, in disaster, all the Test matches being easily won by Australia. Never before in the history of English or Australian trips since Test matches were first played had one side shown such an overwhelming superiority.'

Modern Batting, by C. Toppin

FIVE CRICKETERS OF THE YEAR

H. Ashton
'Quite remarkable was his success against the Australians. He played against them four times and came off in every match. At Cambridge he had to retire hurt with a score of 107 to his

credit and it was his partnership with Aubrey Faulkner that turned the fortunes of the memorable match at Eastbourne in which the Australians suffered their first defeat.'

C.G. Macartney
'Owing little or nothing to coaching he made himself a batsman by watching the big matches in Australia, and, of course, by persistent practice. A law to himself – a triumph to individualism – he is not a model to be copied. Young batsmen who tried to imitate him at all would in nineteen cases out of twenty fail, his success being so largely dependent on extraordinary quickness of eye, hand and foot.'

J.L. Bryan   J.M. Gregory   E.A. McDonald

OBITUARIES INCLUDE

E. Evans
'It was a thousand pities that Evans did not visit England while he was in his prime. If he had come over with the first team in 1878, or with the great side of 1882, there is every reason to think he would have justified the reputation he enjoyed at home. As it happened he delayed too long. When at last he came here, in 1886, his powers were obviously on the wane.'

H.T. Hewett
'After the season of 1893 he resigned the captaincy of the eleven and gave up county cricket. There is no doubt that he was largely influenced by an incident that occurred during the match with the Australians at Taunton. Owing to the wretched weather it was agreed in the morning to abandon play for the day, but late in the afternoon the players were gathered together and the game started. Some of Mr. Hewett's friends thought he made far too much of the matter, but he was very angry, considering that his authority had been unwarrantably overruled.'

H.M. Hyndman
'Mr. Hyndman, so well known as a Socialist leader, had some claim to be remembered for his powers in the cricket field. Whilst up at Cambridge he only just missed getting his blue in 1864.'

A. Mold
'He was one of the deadliest fast bowlers of his day, but right through his career the fairness of his delivery formed the subject of lively discussion.'

W. Gunn   S. Haigh   E. Lockwood   F. Martin

COUNTY REVIEW

Somerset
'The mainstay of the team, as in 1920, was J.C. White. Considering the character of the summer, the slow bowler was even better than before, taking 137 wickets in county matches for 15 1/2 runs each, as against 130 wickets for 14 1/2. Unfortunately he was not able to get anything like the support he deserved.'

MATCH REPORTS

England v Australia, Third Test Match, *played at Leeds, July 2, 4, 5*
'In order to strengthen the batting Brown was chosen as wicket keeper to the exclusion of Strudwick, and on the fast ground he did very well. There was great doubt up to the last moment as to the constitution of the England team ... It is not easy to understand why the selection committee gave a place to Ducat. No one, so it was said, felt more surprised than the Surrey batsman himself, and he failed rather dismally.'

1923

THE WORLD AT LARGE

- Howard Carter opens the tomb of Tutankhamun
- Wembley Stadium hosts its first Cup Final – Bolton Wanderers beat West Ham United by 2 goals to nil
- Bonar Law resigns as Prime Minister and is succeeded by Stanley Baldwin. Bonar Law dies later in the year
- Great Kanto Earthquake kills over 100,000 people in Tokyo and Yokohama
- U.S. President Warren Harding dies in office and is succeeded by Calvin Coolidge
- Munich Beer Hall Putsch – Hitler and the Nazi Party fail to overthrow the German government

WISDEN 1923

60th EDITION
EDITOR: Sydney H Pardon
PAGES: 974
PRICE: Limp 5/-   cloth 8/-
REPRINT: Willows 2006 (500 limit, in two formats)

CRICKET HEADLINES 1922

County Champions: Yorkshire

Tich Freeman takes 17 wickets for Kent v Sussex

Charlie Parker takes 206 wickets in the season, at 13 runs apiece; Alec Kennedy takes 205 at a little under 17, and also scores 1,000 runs

Frank Woolley scores 2,000 runs and takes 100 wickets for the second season in a row (he will repeat the feat in 1923)

Hampshire dismissed for 15 by Warwickshire: they follow on and win by 155 runs

NOTES BY THE EDITOR

'To some of us – I am in full accord with Mr. Ludford Docker, the Warwickshire president, in this matter – the recollection of England having lost eight Test matches in succession was a perpetual nightmare, but despondency affected only the old. It may have been due to the fact that Hobbs was back in the field, getting hundreds in his inimitable way, but I think English cricket as a whole was appreciably better than in 1921.'

FEATURE ARTICLES

Hendren at Lord's since the War

'Hendren's batting at Lord's in the four seasons since the War have been so marvellous that no apology is needed for setting out the figures in detail. For his record in such a number of innings in four successive years there can surely be no parallel in the history of Lord's. In 1920, when he reached his highest point, Hendren went in eighteen times and, with three not outs to help him, actually had an average of 100.'

J.T. Tyldesley and D. Denton in the Cricket Field, by Major R.O. Edwards O.B.E.
Lord Harris and Umpires' Decisions
Bibliography of Cricket, by A.J. Gaston
[Updated from 1892, 1894 and 1900.]

FIVE CRICKETERS OF THE YEAR

A.W. Carr

'Mr. Carr did not have a good season for Notts in 1920, but he won the Surrey match at the Oval with a splendid 105 not out and that made up for many disappointments. In 1921 he got on very much better and last summer, as everyone knows, his batting and fielding for the Gentlemen at Lord's gave him a higher place in English cricket than had ever been his before. His straight driving could almost have been described as the restoration of a lost art. Nothing quite so alarming to the bowlers had been seen since K.L. Hutchings was in his prime.'

A.P. Freeman   C.W.L. Parker   A.C. Russell   A. Sandham

OBITUARIES INCLUDE

W.N. Cobbold
'It is, of course, as an Association footballer that Mr. Cobbold will always be best remembered, for his fame at that game was deservedly great and he was known as "The Prince of Dribblers". He played for Charterhouse, Cambridge (4 times, 1883-6; captain in 1885 and 1886), Corinthians, England (9 times) and Old Carthusians. He also played lawn-tennis for his University.'

Lord Cobham (the Hon. C.G. Lyttelton)
'As he gave up cricket before he was twenty-five his deeds belonged to a distant past.'

J.H. Hargreaves
'who played occasionally for Hampshire as "J. Smith," died at Portsmouth on April 11 … His first match for Hampshire was in 1884, and his highest score for the county 72 not out v. Sussex at Southampton in 1889.'

H.V.H. Prichard
'He was well-known as a traveller and author, and during the war carried out responsible duties and was twice mentioned in despatches.'

R.D. Walker
'It seems strange that neither he nor any of the seven brothers ever married. A partial explanation of this is, I think, their wonderful attachment to each other. Never was there a more united family, and Russie was idolized up to the end of his long life by his numerous nephews and nieces – his five sisters were all married, but alas, there is no one to perpetuate the family name.'

COUNTY REVIEW

Glamorgan
'There was assuredly nothing in Glamorgan cricket last year to shake one's conviction as to the county's promotion to the first-class in 1921 having been altogether premature. Without in any way wishing to discourage ambition, one cannot get away from the patent fact that the Glamorgan team was first-class only in name.'

MATCH REPORTS

Warwickshire v Hampshire, *played at Birmingham, June 14, 15, 16*
'This was the sensational match of the whole season, at Birmingham or anywhere else, Hampshire actually winning by 155 runs after being out for a total of 15. That their astounding failure in the first innings was just one of the accidents of cricket, and not due in any way to the condition of the ground, was proved by their getting 521 when they followed on. The victory, taken as a whole, must surely be without precedent in first-class cricket. Hampshire looked in a hopeless position when the sixth wicket in their second innings went down at 186, but Shirley helped Brown to put on 85 runs and then, with Livsey after McIntyre had failed, the score was carried to 451. Brown batted splendidly for four hours and three-quarters and Livsey made his first hundred without a mistake.'

'There is one new feature in the Almanack,' *writes the editor in his Preface, 'a complete list of Oxford and Cambridge Blues from the first University match in 1827 to 1922.'*

1924

WISDEN 1924

61st EDITION
EDITOR: Sydney H Pardon
PAGES: 1015
PRICE: Limp 5/-   cloth 8/-
REPRINT: Willows 2006 (500 limit, in two formats)

THE WORLD AT LARGE

- Death of Lenin – Stalin begins his purges
- Ramsay MacDonald becomes Britain's first Labour Prime Minister
- Summer Olympics held in Paris; the Winter Olympics are held in Chamonix
- King George II of Greece deposed and a republic is declared
- Mallory and Irvine disappear almost at the summit of Everest. Did they get there?
- First performance of George Gershwin's *Rhapsody In Blue*

CRICKET HEADLINES 1923

County Champions: Yorkshire

England, under F.T. Mann, beat South Africa 2-1 in South Africa

W.H. Ponsford scores 429 for Victoria v Tasmania, a new world record

Victoria's total of 1,059 is the first time 1,000 runs have been scored in a first-class innings

Jack Hobbs scores his one hundredth hundred

Tate (219) and Parkin (209) both take over 200 wickets in the summer; Tate also scores over 1,000 runs

A West Indies team tours, without playing Test matches

NOTES BY THE EDITOR

'In looking back on the season of 1923 I am rather in doubt as to what should be said about it. Watching matches day after day at Lord's or the Oval, but nowhere else, I was on the whole disappointed. The dropped catches that left the Players nothing to hope for but a draw against the Gentlemen and the worse blunders committed by the England eleven in the Test Trial match in August had on me a depressing effect. Mistakes in the field now and then are inevitable but it was a new and painful experience to find two representative sides at Lord's so continually at fault. At both matches one had an uneasy feeling that if our best men went on like that the prospect of beating Australia in the near future, either away or at home, must be remote.'

FEATURE ARTICLES

England v South Africa, A Survey of the 34 Matches, by F.S. Ashley-Cooper
'The first game commenced at Port Elizabeth on March 2, 1889, and England won by eight wickets. The first over, a maiden to A.R. Innes, was bowled by Briggs, and the first scoring hit – a two, fifteen minutes from the start – was made by A.B. Tancred. The first nine overs, in which two wickets fell, were maidens – five by Briggs and four by Fothergill.'

FIVE BOWLERS OF THE YEAR

M.W. Tate
'Whether in him will be found the Test bowler of whom we are so badly in need remains to be seen, but many of the best judges are very hopeful about him. It is a great point in his favour that, thanks to his beautiful delivery, he can get through a lot of work without undue fatigue … Tate is a good, free-hitting batsman, capable at any time of getting his fifty runs, but one hopes that for the next few years, at least, the lure of long scores will not attract him. With heavy tasks ahead for English cricket his business is to take wickets.'
A.E.R. Gilligan   R. Kilner   G.G. Macaulay   C.H. Parkin

Rev. E.S. Carter

'His old colleague in the Oxford eleven, Lord Loreburn, when Lord Chancellor, presented him with a living and in the accompanying letter wrote: You broke my finger at Oxford but I bear no malice.'

Lord Loreburn

'Mr. Robert Threshie Reid, Ex-Lord Chancellor, familiarly known in the House of Commons for many years as "Bob" Reid, could spare no time for first-class cricket after starting his professional career, but he will be remembered as one of the best amateur wicket-keepers of his day.'

A.P. Lucas

'Mr. Lucas was in the truest sense of the word a classic batsman. A master of both back and forward play, he represented the strictest orthodoxy. No doubt if he had allowed himself a little licence he might have made more runs, but his method served him so well that right into middle age he kept up his form. It may fairly be said of him that no defensive batsman of any generation was better worth looking at. He played the ball so hard and his style was so irreproachable that one could watch him for hours without a moment of weariness.'

A.D. Taylor

'He was a well-known writer on the game and at the time of his death possessed the largest library on cricket which had ever been collected. Among his best-known books were *The Catalogue of Cricket Literature* – a model compilation and the standard work on the subject.'

Gloucestershire

'Of far more importance in its bearing on the future than the success of Dipper and Smith was the fine form shown by Hammond – checked in 1922 by the discovery that he was not properly qualified. Here we have in all likelihood one of the best professional batsmen of the future, irreproachable in style and not yet twenty-one years of age. Hammond has all the world before him and there is no telling how far he may go.'

Surrey v West Indies, *played at Kennington Oval, August 1, 2, 3*

'This match furnished the great triumph of the tour, the West Indies gaining a most brilliant victory by ten wickets. The match was really won at about a quarter past three on the first day. Surrey broke down hopelessly against the bowling of Francis and Browne, backed up as it was by splendid fielding, and nothing could compensate for a score of 87 on a hard wicket. Challenor as a batsman enjoyed the biggest of all his successes. Apart from a couple of hard chances towards the end of his innings, his 155 not out was a superb display, and when the West Indies went in to get 110, he and Tarilton hit off the runs together in just under seventy minutes. Jardine's 104 for Surrey was a masterpiece of defence.'

The editor begins his Preface: 'The only real difficulty in producing Wisden *in these days is to keep the book within reasonable limits, and so prevent it from becoming too cumbersome.'*

1925

WISDEN 1925

62nd EDITION
EDITOR: Sydney H Pardon
PAGES: 957
PRICE: Limp 5/-   cloth 8/-
REPRINT: Willows 2007 (500 limit, in two formats)

THE WORLD AT LARGE

• Benito Mussolini proclaims himself dictator of Italy
• Adolf Hitler publishes *Mein Kampf*
• Hindenburg elected President of Germany
• First double-decker buses introduced in London
• John Logie Baird constructs his first television transmitter
• Death of Queen Alexandra, King George V's mother

CRICKET HEADLINES 1924

County Champions: Yorkshire

England, led by A.E.R. Gilligan, beat South Africa 3-0 in the summer's Tests

South Africa all out for 30 in the Edgbaston Test

Charlie Parker takes two hat-tricks in the same innings for Gloucestershire v Middlesex

Tate, Parker and Parkin all take 200 wickets

NOTES BY THE EDITOR

'It was not surprising that some of the counties, driven to desperation by blank days, should have cast about for a means of escaping bankruptcy, but I am very glad that the new regulation as to covering the whole of the wicket, passed by the M.C.C. is permissive and not compulsory. After all, it may be many years before we have another summer so dismally wet as that of 1924. Avoiding what might have looked like panic legislation, the M.C.C. have asked the counties to do what seems to them best this year and report on their experiences at the end of the season.'

FEATURE ARTICLES

The Googly, by B.J.T. Bosanquet
'Somewhere about the year 1897 I was playing a game with a tennis ball, known as Twisti-Twosti. The object was to bounce the ball on a table so that your opponent sitting opposite could not catch it. It soon occurred to me that if one could pitch a ball which broke in a certain direction and with more or less the same delivery make the next ball go in the opposite direction, one would mystify one's opponent. After a little experimenting I managed to do this, and it was so successful that I practised the same thing with a soft ball at Stump-cricket. From this I progressed to a cricket ball, and about 1899 I had become a star turn for the luncheon interval during our matches at Oxford.'

FIVE CRICKETERS OF THE YEAR

H.W. Taylor
'It is no injustice to him to say that in this country last summer he fell far below the expectations of his friends. He made plenty of runs and played many a fine innings, but the responsibility of captaining a losing side proved rather too much for him, and in the Test Matches he did not do himself justice. He had not in any way lost his form, but circumstances were against him. Taylor's style is so good and his back play so exceptionally strong that one never while watching him has the least doubt as to his class as a batsman. Few players at the present day have so many scoring strokes in front of the wicket.'
R.H. Catterall   J.C.W. MacBryan   R.K. Tyldesley   W.W. Whysall

J.H. Board

'He had perhaps no special distinction of style, but his defence was sound, his hitting very hard, and his pluck unflinching. Board went only once to Australia, going out with Mr. Stoddart's second team in 1897-98. As wicket-keeper for that unsuccessful side he was simply the understudy to William Storer, and did not take part in any of the Test Matches.'

F.A. O'Keeffe

'A brilliant batsman and field as well as a very useful slow right-handed bowler, a great future seemed in store for him. He had performed splendidly in Australia before coming to England, and would, had he lived, have been qualified for Lancashire by residence last June. Our climate, unfortunately, did not suit him, and he was never in the best of health while in this country.'

G. B. Street

'The well-known Sussex wicket-keeper was killed at Portslade on April 24. He was riding a motor-cycle and, in endeavouring to avoid a lorry at a cross-roads, crashed into a wall and died immediately. Born at Charlwood, in Surrey, on December 6, 1889, he was in his thirty-fifth year at the time of his death.'

A.C. Bannerman   E.J. Diver   W.A. Humphreys   W.S. Lees   E. Robson   G. Wootton

Lancashire

'Not one fixture at Old Trafford escaped from the after effects of rain or serious interference by storms and heavy downpours. What this meant stands out clearly from the fact that every home fixture was interrupted more or less by the weather, with one exception, and then at Blackpool, early in August, the game could not be started until a quarter to two on the Saturday because the Essex team were delayed on their journey from Bristol.'

England v South Africa, First Test Match, *played at Birmingham, June 14, 16, 17*

'The sensation of the match came on the second day. England's innings soon ended for 438 and then in three quarters of an hour Gilligan and Tate rattled the South Africans out for 30 – the lowest total in any Test match in England. The lowest before this match – also, curiously enough, on the Edgbaston ground – was 36 by Australia in 1902. There was another record, Gilligan's figures of six wickets for 7 runs never having been equalled. He bowled very fast and with any amount of fire. Three times during the innings he took a wicket immediately after sending down a no ball. Tate, though he did not look quite so deadly, was also at the top of his form.'

This was Sydney Pardon's 35th edition as editor of Wisden – *and it was to prove his last.*

1926

WISDEN 1926

63rd EDITION
EDITOR: C. Stewart Caine
PAGES: 1031
PRICE: Limp 5/-   cloth 8/-
REPRINT: Willows 2007 (500 limit, in two formats)

THE WORLD AT LARGE

- The General Strike, 3 to 12 May: coalminers' strike lasts from May until October
- First British Grand Prix held at Brooklands
- Agatha Christie disappears from her home in Surrey and is found 11 days later in Harrogate
- A.A. Milne's *Winnie The Pooh* published
- Gertrude Ederle becomes the first woman to swim the English Channel

CRICKET HEADLINES 1925

County Champions: Yorkshire

England under Arthur Gilligan, lose the Test series in Australia by 4 matches to 1

Jack Hobbs scores 16 hundreds in the season, including four in successive innings: he passes W.G. Grace's total number of centuries

Charlie Parker takes 17 wickets for 56 runs for Gloucestershire v Essex

Five bowlers take over 200 wickets each

NOTES BY THE EDITOR

'A further point the authorities may well take into consideration is the provision of accommodation for the England players on the occasions of Test matches. Five years ago in a northern town a leading cricketer on the eve of one of these games was seen wandering about late in the evening in the search for a bed. Matters were better when the South Africans came here in 1924, but still the arrangements left something to be desired. Players chosen for England should be allowed to travel at a reasonable hour on the day preceding the match and on arrival should find themselves comfortably housed. Indeed the appointment of a special manager for such occasions might be taken into consideration. Possibly, too, some advantage would accrue if all the team stayed together for the period of the match.'

JACK HOBBS

'Hobbs playing such wonderful cricket and enjoying the distinction of heading W.G. Grace's list of centuries, the customary picture of "Five Cricketers of the Year" gives place to a full page portrait of the great Surrey batsman.'
'John Berry Hobbs surpassed himself in the summer of 1925. Never previously had he made 3,000 runs in one season or headed the batting averages, but he accomplished both those feats, his aggregate amounting to 3,024 and an average of 70.32 placing him above all his rivals ... Furthermore, whereas last summer the largest number of hundreds he had obtained in one season was eleven – his total in 1914 and again in 1920 – and the record for any batsman was thirteen – made by C.B. Fry in 1901 and equalled by Tom Hayward in 1906 and by Hendren in 1923 – he eclipsed those performances by reaching three figures on no fewer than sixteen occasions.'

OBITUARIES INCLUDE

W. Bruce
'Though in later years put quite in the shade by Clem Hill, Darling, Bardsley, and Ransford, Bruce has his place in cricket history as the first left-handed batsman sent to England with an Australian team. Free and attractive in style he was a brilliant hitter, but he lacked the defence of the great batsmen who followed him.'

R.O. Edwards

'He spent a considerable time in Africa, and years ago found solace during solitary days up country reading *Wisden* to which he frequently contributed. During the war he was gassed badly, and in a later expedition to Southern Russia he lost all his baggage which accompanied him on all his travels. Major Edwards never tired of retelling stories of first-class cricketers.'

Capt. R.St.L. Fowler

'Owing to his profession, he was not very well-known to the general cricket public, but he was the hero of a match which may, without exaggeration, be described as the most extraordinary ever played. The story of the Eton and Harrow match in 1910 has been told over and over again, but it can never grow stale.'

S.H. Pardon

'Despite his remarkable attainments in other directions, Sydney Pardon will be chiefly remembered for his writings upon cricket, and his long association with *Wisden's Almanack*. Keen and accurate, well-balanced in his conclusions, and gifted with a particularly graceful form of expression, he rapidly built up a name for himself. Steadily his reputation grew until at length all leading cricketers were glad to have his opinions upon the big questions of the day.'

T. Case   W. Hearne   A.N. Hornby

COUNTY REVIEW

Northamptonshire

'Up to the time of losing their last four matches, Northamptonshire fared uncommonly well and, as it was, a vast improvement upon their doings in any year since the war, raised them from sixteenth to eleventh place in the Championship. Playing two additional games, they gained nine victories as compared with two in 1924 – a notable advance even if the defeats increased from nine to twelve.'

MATCH REPORTS

Somerset v Surrey, played at Taunton, Saturday, Monday, Tuesday, August 15, 17, 18

'This was the match rendered forever memorable by the triumph of Hobbs who playing innings of 101 and 101, not out, equalled on the Monday morning W.G. Grace's aggregate of 126 centuries in first-class cricket, and on the Tuesday afternoon beat the "Grand Old Man's" record.'

MISCELLANEOUS

From the **Cricket Records** *section:*

'Seventeen Wickets In A Match:

In three consecutive innings for Gloucestershire in 1925 Parker took 26 wickets – 9 for 44 and 8 for 12 v. Essex and 9 for 118 v. Surrey. Both matches were played at Gloucester.

Playing for Gentlemen of England v. M.C.C., at Lord's in 1818, R. Holden took 19 wickets for 398 runs. One man was absent in the second innings of M.C.C., and the arrangement was that R. Holden should bowl throughout from both wickets.'

C. Stewart Caine, Wisden's new editor, writes in his Preface dated February, 1926: 'The sudden death in November last of Mr. Sydney Pardon broke an association with Wisden's Almanack which dated back to the issue of 1887. Succeeding to the editorship in 1890, Mr. Pardon had filled that post for 35 years. How ably he performed his duties the ever-increasing popularity of the Almanack has demonstrated beyond all question.'

Copies have an errata slip inserted on the page with the photoplate of Jack Hobbs: 'The portrait of Hobbs has been reproduced from a photograph by the Central News Agency.' The Willows reprint carries this slip.

1927

WISDEN 1927

64th EDITION
EDITOR: C. Stewart Caine
PAGES: 1043
PRICE: Limp 5/-   cloth 8/-
REPRINT: Willows 2007 (500 limit, in two formats)

THE WORLD AT LARGE

• The rugby union international between England and Wales becomes the first British sports event to be covered by a live broadcast
• First transatlantic telephone call from New York to London
• Kuomintang troops kill communist supporters in Shanghai, triggering a civil war that will last until 1949
• The Mississippi River basin floods, displacing three quarters of a million people
• Charles Lindbergh makes the first non-stop solo transatlantic flight
• *The Jazz Singer*, the first talking movie, opens in America

CRICKET HEADLINES 1926

County Champions: Lancashire

England regain the Ashes by defeating the visiting Australians at The Oval after four drawn games

Jack Hobbs scores 316* for Surrey v Middlesex at Lord's – the highest score on the ground until Gooch's 333 in 1990

Charlie Parker takes over 200 wickets – yet again

Essex v Somerset ends in a tie even though Essex had one more man to go in

NOTES BY THE EDITOR

'The Australians urge that, in future, Test Matches in this country shall not be restricted to three days, but that four days shall be allotted for the decision of those contests ... The probabilities ... appear to be rather in favour of the three-day limit being abolished, and if that course be taken no strong reason can be adduced in favour of four days as against five or six. The interference with county cricket would be the same in either case. That is to say, certain counties would find themselves in no fewer than ten Championship engagements without some of their leading players, the great annual Competition being consequently robbed of all real importance. In those circumstances, a return to the old system of three Test Matches might be suggested, but the representative games produce so much money that that plan is not at all likely to be adopted. The money question, in short, threatens to dominate the situation.'

FEATURE ARTICLES

Cricket Reform – *A letter to The Times by J.W. Trumble*
'Assuredly the secret of what is wrong with cricket lies in the wicket. Let us discard the binding soils and the heavy roller and get back to the old-time natural springy turf, and with batsman and bowler on equal terms matches will end in a reasonable time, and, instead of being tests of patience and endurance, they will bring out those qualities of initiative and resource and the ability to rise superior to surroundings which so characterized the play of many of our great cricketers of the past.'
Recollections of Mr. F.R. Spofforth

J. Mercer

'About five feet eleven inches in height Mercer is medium-pace, right hand, somewhat similar in type to Maurice Tate, but not quite so fast. Since leaving Sussex he has increased his pace. He can send down either an in-swinger or an out-swinger, and with a new ball his bowling requires watching closely. He keeps a good length, can get spin on, and does not mind being hit.'

G. Geary   H. Larwood   W.A. Oldfield   W.M. Woodfull

OBITUARIES INCLUDE

D.L.A. Jephson

'In 1900 he had an excellent all-round record, for, besides making 1,952 runs with an average of 41.53, he took sixty-six wickets for 23.40 runs each. In the Gentlemen v. Players match at Lord's in 1899 his lobs gained him an analysis of six for 21 – a splendid performance against a strong batting side. For Surrey he took five wickets for 12 runs against Derbyshire at Chesterfield in 1899, and performed the hat-trick v. Middlesex at the Oval in 1904.'

F.R. Spofforth

'In minor matches he naturally did many very remarkable things. Thus, in an up-country game in Australia, in 1881-2, he bowled down all twenty wickets of his opponents; for the Australian team of 1878 he took nine wickets in twenty balls against XVIII of Hastings, and for that of 1880, twelve in eighteen against XVIII of Burnley; while twice for Hampstead he obtained all ten wickets in an innings of Marlow on his opponents' ground – for 20 runs in 1893, and for fourteen a year later.'

A. Chevallier Tayler

'A well-known artist, he will be remembered by followers of the game on account of his series of drawings entitled *The Empire's Cricketers,* published in 1905.'

F.A. Iredale   E. Rutter   G.N. Wyatt

COUNTY REVIEW

The Leading Counties in 1926

'A most interesting struggle for first honours resulted in favour of Lancashire. So close was the fight that up to within ten days of the finish Yorkshire held the leading position. During those days, however, while Lancashire gained three victories, Yorkshire discounted two wins by losing first innings points to Surrey. In this way, the Championship, after a lapse of 22 years, passed once again into the hands of Lancashire.'

MATCH REPORTS

England v Australia, Fifth Test Match, *played at Kennington Oval, August 14, 16, 17, 18*

'England's eleven underwent no fewer than four changes from that which had met Australia three weeks earlier at Manchester. Chapman succeeded Carr in the captaincy, of the side, and Geary, Larwood and Rhodes displaced Ernest Tyldesley, Kilner and Root. The inclusion of Rhodes, a man nearly 49 years of age, naturally occasioned a good deal of surprise, but it was crowned with complete success, the bowling of the veteran Yorkshireman proving no small factor in determining the issue of the struggle. Chapman, too, despite lack of experience in leading a first-class team in the field, turned out a very happy nomination for the post of captain, the young amateur, for the most part, managing his bowling with excellent judgement, and in two or three things he did, showing distinct imagination.'

1928

WISDEN 1928

65th EDITION
EDITOR: C. Stewart Caine
PAGES: 1063
PRICE: Limp 5/-   cloth 8/-
REPRINT: Willows 2008 (500 limit, in two formats)

THE WORLD AT LARGE

• River Thames floods – 14 die
• Alexander Fleming discovers penicillin
• The summer Olympics are held in Amsterdam, the winter Olympics in St. Moritz
• The Royal Flying Doctor service in Australia begins
• Herbert Hoover wins the U.S. presidential election
• Mickey Mouse appears in a talking film for the first time – *Steamboat Willie*

CRICKET HEADLINES 1927

County Champions: Lancashire

New Zealanders tour England, without playing a Test

Philip Mead hits his 100th century, for Hampshire v Northamptonshire

C.K. Nayudu hits eleven 6s in an innings for Hindus v M.C.C.

Walter Hammond hits 1,000 runs in 22 days in May

NOTES BY THE EDITOR

'Yorkshire cricket circles were greatly perturbed by the announcement that, in succession to Major Lupton, Herbert Sutcliffe had been appointed captain of the county team. Objection was taken to this action by two different parties. Some people urged the undesirability of having a professional captain; others argued that, if the committee thought fit to choose a professional, the post should be given to Wilfred Rhodes rather than to Sutcliffe. Happily the trouble was eventually settled to the satisfaction of all concerned. Sutcliffe declined the honour and, an invitation being extended to Captain Worsley, that gentleman stepped into the breach.'

FEATURE ARTICLES

Oxford Memories, by Lord Harris
'In the match at Lord's that year my father-in-law having asked me to put something on Oxford for him, I was haggling about the odds with Charlie Thornton during lunch, standing out for 6 to 4. Cambridge had made a very good start on a dry wicket. It came on to rain and we went in to lunch. Just before the first ball was bowled when we resumed, Thornton ran down to me as I was fielding close to the rails and laid me the odds I asked for. The first ball got a wicket and we won in one innings.'

FIVE CRICKETERS OF THE YEAR

R.C. Blunt
'Roger Charles Blunt, the best all-round Cricketer of the New Zealand team, although born at Durham on November 3, 1900, can fairly claim to be a New Zealander, for he was taken out to that country when only six months old. He went to school at Christ's College, Christchurch, and was under T.C. Lowry's captaincy in the school eleven for two years. Originally he played as a slow leg break bowler, but when after two seasons tried as one of the opening pair of batsmen he, to a large extent, dropped his bowling. In 1925-26 he went to Australia as a member of the New Zealand team visiting that country. As there was no slow bowler in the side he again took up bowling and with such success that he obtained more wickets than anyone else in the course of the tour.'
C. Hallows   W.R. Hammond   D.R. Jardine   V.W.C. Jupp

H. Bagshaw

'… died at Crowden, near Glossop, on January 31, aged 65, and was buried in his umpire's coat and with a cricket ball in his hand.'

G. Giffen

'In matches between Australia and England he made 1,238 runs, and took 103 wickets, In 1922-3 the match at Adelaide between South Australia and Victoria was played for his benefit, and the resulting sum, £2,020, was vested in trustees. After being a Civil Servant in the General Post Office at Adelaide for 43 years, he retired on pension in March, 1925, thereafter finding the chief delight of his life, whilst health permitted, in coaching young boys in a purely honorary capacity.'

J.J. Lyons

'In May, 1893, at Lord's, Lyons played probably the most brilliant innings of his career. The Australians had to go in a second time against a powerful M.C.C. team 181 runs behind. Yet these were hit off before a wicket fell by Lyons and Alec Bannerman, and of this number Lyons obtained no fewer than 149. As such a terrific pace did he score that he completed his 100 in an hour, with the total at 124 … To this day people who saw that day's play describe his batting as the greatest display of fast-footed driving ever given at Lords'.

W. Attewell   The Earl of Darnley (Hon. Ivo Bligh)   D. Hunter

Leicestershire

'It was strange that in a season when rain so often affected pitches, the Leicestershire bowlers, with one notable exception, so far from following the example of the batsmen, should have rather deteriorated, and still more curious that Skelding, the fastest of several good-paced bowlers, taking for the first time in his career over 100 wickets in all Leicestershire matches, became the deadliest attacking force on the side.'

M.C.C. Team v. All-India (Indians) *played at Bombay, December 16, 17, 18*

'At the end of a drawn game, M.C.C. were badly placed, their lead with five men out in the second innings amounting to only 22. All-India lost seven wickets for 278, but then Mistri and Deodhar put on 88 by attractive cricket, and the home side eventually led by 75. Deodhar played a great game after giving a chance before reaching double figures.'

'In Honour Of Cricket'

'On Wednesday October 12, Sir Rowland Blades, Lord Mayor of London, gave a dinner at the Mansion House "In Honour Of Cricket". There gathered in response to the Lord Mayor's invitation a company of several hundred among whom, with comparatively few exceptions, was everybody of distinction in the cricket world.'

For the third year running, pagination hits a new high, and the editor admits in his Preface: 'The great trouble in producing Wisden *is that of keeping the book down to a reasonable size without sacrificing any of the regular features. In these days, when tours abroad of English cricketers, and visits of Dominions' players to this country are becoming so numerous, the task grows more and more difficult. The matter is one that must be grappled with in the near future, but no drastic changes have been attempted in the present issue.'*

Copies of this era are today often found in poor condition simply because of their size as the binding struggles to cope with the 1,000-plus pages.

1929

WISDEN 1929

66th EDITION
EDITOR: C. Stewart Caine
PAGES: 1015
PRICE: Limp 5/-   cloth 8/-
REPRINT: Willows 2008 (500 limit, in two formats)

THE WORLD AT LARGE

• General Election returns a hung parliament: eventually Ramsay MacDonald forms a minority Labour government
• St. Valentine's Day Massacre in Chicago
• First Academy Awards presented: *Wings* proves to be the only silent film ever to win Best Picture
• The Wall Street Crash: in a week more than $30bn is wiped from the value of stocks
• *Tintin* appears for the first time, in a Belgian children's comic

CRICKET HEADLINES 1928

County Champions: Lancashire

West Indies tour England but lose all three Tests

Patsy Hendren hits his 100th hundred

W.H. Ponsford scores 133, 437, 202, 38 and 336 in successive innings for Victoria

Walter Hammond takes 78 catches in the season, still a world record

Charlie Hallows scores 1,000 runs in May

Les Ames and George Duckworth both claim over 100 wicket-keeping victims

Tich Freeman takes 304 wickets in the summer: the only time any bowler has ever taken 300 wickets in a season

NOTES BY THE EDITOR

'The visit of a team from the West Indies was anticipated with considerable interest but proved a disappointment, the side being scarcely as well-equipped as that which came here in 1923. Experience showed only too clearly that the arrangement of Test matches between England and the West Indies was at least premature. Still, the games being treated seriously by the Selection Committee, furnished some useful practice for England's representative players.'

FEATURE ARTICLES

My Years At Cambridge, by G.H. Longman
'May I end on another personal note? The Rev. Hon. Edward Lyttelton wrote an article two years ago describing this match *(Oxford v Cambridge 1875),* and his last sentence was this: Has George Longman ever got over it? I will reply to that question, even at this distance of time, by telling him that considering the match only occurred 53 years ago, he must be patient, but that I am going on as well as can be expected.'

FIVE CRICKETERS OF THE YEAR

L.E.G. Ames
'Ames has a pretty style as a batsman and is not afraid to hit the ball full and hit it hard, and he may become the best wicket-keeper-batsman that England has ever had … He gets down very low when standing up – he has not yet had the practice of some other wicket-keepers in standing back to fast bowling – and keeps without fuss or attempt at spectacular effect. It has been said of him that he makes wicket-keeping look easy, which appears to be true; it is the greatest compliment which can be paid to a wicket-keeper.'
G. Duckworth   M. Leyland   S.J. Staples   J.C. White

A.J. Gaston

'So well-known in connection with cricket literature, records and curios, was … a zealous collector of cricket books, photographs and other things concerning the game, in the sale of which he had built up a considerable business.'

R. Kilner

'By his early death English cricket lost, not only a notable exponent of the game, but a man of rare charm. Few modern professionals commanded such a measure of esteem and kindly regard from his own immediate colleagues and his opponents in the cricket field as did Roy Kilner. He was modest to a degree concerning his own abilities, and generous in his estimate of those he played with and against.'

C.H.B. Marsham

'A hard worker and keen trier himself in the field, he inspired his men by fine example. As a captain, he secured unfailing support and unswerving loyalty from those under him, while a charming and courteous disposition endeared him to all opponents. His family have been associated with Kent cricket for about 150 years.'

J.S. Warden

'… one of the best all-round cricketers the Parsis ever had … For Jorah Bajan v. Customs, at Calcutta, in 1920, he took five wickets with the first five balls of the match. He was the author of *Knotty Cricket Problems Solved*.'

Kent

'Winning twelve and losing only one of their first twenty matches, Kent made a bold bid for the Championship until the month of July was well advanced, but then came such a striking change in the fortunes of the side that three games in succession ended in defeat. The team finished second in the competition, with a slightly better record than either Notts or Yorkshire, but after those three disasters they naturally, were never again really in the running for first honours.'

England v. West Indies, Third Test Match, *played at Kennington Oval, August 11, 13, 14*

'Glorious weather prevailing on Saturday, and the wicket being of a nice easy pace, the West Indies, on winning the toss, had every chance of doing themselves justice. Moreover, Challenor and Roach began the visitors' innings with a partnership which lasted seventy minutes and produced 91 runs. Roach batting in fine determined style, apart from a chance to Chapman when 34, and Challenor playing in a manner worthy of his high reputation, there existed for the moment promise of an interesting struggle but, once the opening stand had come to an end, the opposition to the England bowling proved so moderate that the last nine wickets went down for the addition of 147 runs.'

Stewart Caine starts to get to grips with the size of the book, as he explains in his Preface: 'In presenting the sixty-sixth edition of Wisden, *I have to announce that, in an endeavour to grapple with the ever-growing difficulty of keeping the book down to a reasonable size, many names have been eliminated from the list of Births and Deaths, and other economies of space practised. How necessary such action as this had become will be understood when it is mentioned, for instance, that, in the course of some twenty-five years, "Births and Deaths" has grown from 28 to 104 pages.'*

1930

WISDEN 1930

67th EDITION
EDITOR: C. Stewart Caine
PAGES: 1059
PRICE: Limp 5/-   cloth 8/-
REPRINT: Willows 2008 (500 limit, in two formats)

THE WORLD AT LARGE

• Gandhi's Salt March in protest against the British monopoly on salt
• Uruguay beats Argentina in the final of the inaugural football World Cup
• The R-101 airship crashes in France on its maiden voyage
• Amy Johnson becomes the first woman to fly solo from England to Australia
• *The Times* crossword is first published
• Deaths of Arthur Conan Doyle and D.H. Lawrence

CRICKET HEADLINES 1929

County Champions: Nottinghamshire

England beats South Africa by two Tests to nil, with three matches drawn

Les Ames claims 127 victims behind the stumps – still a world record

Don Bradman scores his first triple-century – 340* for New South Wales v Victoria

Frank Woolley hits his 100th century

NOTES BY THE EDITOR

'Another suggestion by the special sub-committee given a trial last season was one by which a batsman even if he "snicked" the ball, could, provided the ball pitched in a line between wicket and wicket, be out lbw. Over this experiment no … practical unanimity of approval prevailed. Batsmen generally, indeed, expressed their disapproval but a majority of umpires … came to the conclusion that the game had benefited by the regulation.'

FEATURE ARTICLES

Australian Tours and their Management, by Sir Frederick Toone
'During the last tour I was asked to give my definition of cricket, and as it roused considerable interest, and I believe was received with approval, I may be forgiven for including it in this, I fear somewhat sketchy, contribution to *Wisden's* immortal pages. It is a science, the study of a lifetime, in which you may exhaust yourself, but never your subject. It is a contest, a duel or melée, calling for courage, skill, strategy and self-control. It is a contest of temper, a trial of honour, a revealer of character. It affords a chance to play the man and act the gentleman. It means going into God's out-of-doors, getting close to nature, fresh air, exercise, a sweeping away of mental cobwebs, genuine recreation of the tired tissues.'

C.I. Thornton, by Lord Harris
'By way of chaff his friends used to ask him if he'd ever hit as far as Bonnor, who was a somewhat self-sufficient batsman, but it is recorded in Lillywhite's Annual of 1898 that, next to Mr. Fellowes' hit of 175 yards on the Christ Church ground at Oxford, the two next authenticated hits are 168 yards 2 feet and 162 yards – both by Thornton in practice at Brighton – measured at the time by that devoted cricketer, the Rev. James Pycroft, so he could treat our chaff with good humoured contempt.'

E.H. Bowley
'It is quite likely that he would have been an even better batsman but for the fact that so much depended on him in county matches. Repeatedly, if he failed, the batting broke down. Consequently in the earlier years after the war he had to exercise pronounced restraint. During the last three or four seasons, however, he played his natural game, attacking the bowling directly he went in, and this enterprise paid him. At his best he is a delightful cricketer to watch.'

H.G. Owen-Smith
'It would possibly be an exaggeration to say that he is a really great batsman -- his methods are, perhaps, a little too daring -- but as to his courage and refusal to be daunted by the odds against him no two opinions can be held. He drives, cuts and hits to leg very well indeed and is clearly a cricketer for whom the future holds unbounded possibilities.'

K.S. Duleepsinhji   R.W.V. Robins   R.E.S. Wyatt

A.H. Gregory
'Returning from the funeral of S.E Gregory he fell from a tramcar, and blood poisoning supervened as a result of injuries to arm. He was a member of the most famous of Australian cricket families, and, although perhaps better known as a graceful and well-informed writer on the game, was a sound batsman, a good field and a fair leg-break bowler.'

Jas. Lillywhite
'He was the last survivor of the team which, under his captaincy, went to Australia in the winter of 1876-77, and played what is now known as the first Test Match against Australia ... Of the twenty-two men who took part in that historic game there are now only three left, and they are all in Australia – Charles Bannerman, J. McCarthy Blackham, and Tom Garrett.'

Sir David Serjeant
'Born at Ramsey, Hunts., January 18, 1830, died at Camberwell, January 12, within a few days of entering upon his 100th year ... He was the author of *Australia: Its Cricket Bat, Its Kangaroo, Its Farming, Fruit and Flowers.*'

S.E. Gregory   A.A. Lilley   C.I. Thornton

The Leading Counties in 1929
'The struggle for the Championship, which for the first time since 1907 resulted in the success of Notts, was decided under conditions very different from those which governed the competition of 1928. Under the new regulations every county had to pay 28 matches – no more and no less... Furthermore, the Championship fixtures were contested under experimental laws which provided for the heightening and widening of the wicket and made it possible for a batsman, even if he had "snicked" the ball, to be out lbw.'

Australia v England, Third Test Match, *played at Melbourne, December 29, 31, January 1, 2, 3, 4, 5*
'When Australia went in a second time ... Bradman – nearly bowled by White when seven – assisted Woodfull to put on a valuable 58, and subsequently proceeded to make his first hundred in a Test match... Bradman batted over four hours, hit eleven 4's and brought off many splendid drives.'

1931

WISDEN 1931

68th Edition
Editor: C. Stewart Caine
Pages: 1067
Price: Limp 5/-   cloth 8/-
Reprint: Willows 2009 (500 limit, in two formats)

THE WORLD AT LARGE

• The pound sterling comes off the Gold Standard
• Highway Code published
• Construction of the Empire State Building completed
• Ramsay MacDonald's Labour government resigns, and is replaced by a National Government, also led by MacDonald
• The Mukden Incident: Japan incites trouble as a pretext to invade Manchuria

CRICKET HEADLINES 1930

County Champions: Lancashire

Don Bradman tours England for the first time, and sets all sorts of batting records

During the previous winter, Bradman scores 452*, the world record score.

Australia win back the Ashes, by two matches to one.

NOTES BY THE EDITOR

'What will be the fate of the battle for the championship? Interest in a competition must suffer when leading aspirants to first honours have to forego in a third or more of their engagements the services of some of their best men. The danger, no doubt, is not yet but it appears to be an inevitable outcome of modern developments and will have to be grappled with by the authorities. In what particular fashion those in control will approach the question it is impossible to say but I do trust that big monies resulting from tours in this country will not blind those with whom the power of action lies to the dangers threatening the future of county cricket.'

FEATURE ARTICLES

Lord's and the M.C.C.: Thirty Years of History, by Sir Francis Lacey
'The members of the professional staff used to be given a benefit match in rotation, subject to an agreement to retire on receipt and to the approval of the M.C.C. Committee with regard to the investment of the proceeds of the match. The fixture allotted was the Whitsuntide match at Lord's and the money taken fluctuated with the weather, the game more than once producing nothing.'
Wilfred Rhodes' Retirement

FIVE CRICKETERS OF THE YEAR

D.G. Bradman
'For a fast, true wicket his footwork, if not on quite such a high plane as that of Charles Macartney, is wonderfully good. When the ball is turning, however, there are limitations to Bradman's skill. As was observed by those who saw him on a turning wicket at Brisbane and on one nothing like so vicious at Old Trafford last summer, this young batsman still has something to learn in the matter of playing a correct offensive or defensive stroke with the conditions in favour of the bowler.'
C.V. Grimmett   B.H. Lyon   I.A.R. Peebles   M.J. Turnbull

OBITUARIES INCLUDE

Sir Arthur Conan Doyle
'Although never a famous cricketer, he could hit hard and bowl slows with a puzzling flight.'

Earl of Coventry
'A great lover of the game, he was also a hard slashing hitter and slow lob bowler, and had played for Worcestershire. Since 1856 he had been a member of the M.C.C. and in 1859, when twenty-one years of age, was the Club's President... At the time of his death he was Father of the House of Lords, having been a peer for the record period of 86 years and ten months.'

G.A. Faulkner
'... died of gas poisoning at the Faulkner School of Cricket, Ltd., on September 10, at the age of 48. During the South African War and whilst living in Cape Town, he received some coaching from Walter Richards, of Warwickshire, then engaged by Western Province, and later became not only one of the dominating figures in South African cricket but also one of the finest of all-round players.'

Dr. A.H. Grace
'Nephew of W.G., E.M., and G.F. Grace. His appearances for Gloucestershire were very few, although in good-class club cricket he was a free and successful bat, often going in without pads against all types of bowling and playing a dashing innings.'

Mrs. A.N. Grace
'Widow of W. G., died at Hawkhurst, Kent, on March 23, aged 76. Mrs. Grace possessed a rare fund of reminiscences of the game. Her memory will be cherished by many cricketers.'

J. Phillips
"... will be remembered more for his work as an umpire than for anything he accomplished as a player. To Phillips more than anyone else is due the credit for stamping out throwing in first-class cricket. Going out to Australia to act as umpire with A. E. Stoddart's team in 1897-98, he twice no-balled Ernest Jones, the fast bowler, whose delivery when visiting this country with Harry Trott's team in 1896 was condemned as unfair, and the courageous action of Phillips found many imitators.'

W.W. Whysall
'... who had reached the height of his fame last season, died in hospital at Nottingham on November 11. About a fortnight earlier he had fallen on a dance floor and injured his elbow. Septicaemia set in and, although a blood transfusion was performed, he passed away.'

C. Bannerman   **J.W.H.T. Douglas**   **J. Seymour**   **J.T. Tyldesley**

COUNTY REVIEW

Gloucestershire
'The secret of Gloucestershire's success last season is not directly indicated by the batting and bowling averages... We must look much deeper to discover where the strength of the side lay and I think it will be found in what was so happily described as their "spirit of fearless endeavour".'

MATCH REPORTS

Sussex v Northamptonshire, *played at Brighton, Wednesday, Thursday, Friday, May 7, 8, 9*
'To Duleepsinhji this match brought the great distinction of beating the Sussex record made by his uncle, K.S. Ranjitsinhji, at Taunton in 1901. Going in with one run on the board, Duleepsinhji scored 333 out of 520 and, when seventh out, was taking many risks. Batting for five hours and a half, he hit a 6 and thirty-four 4's, his stroke play all round the wicket being magnificent.'

MISCELLANEOUS

Cricket in India
'Owing to the unrest in India, the proposed visit of an M.C.C. team in 1930-1 was postponed and the Quadrangular Tournament in Bombay was abandoned.'

Stewart Caine reminds readers in his Preface: 'The present issue ... is the forty-fifth in the preparation of which I have been associated. Since the late Charles Pardon produced the Almanack of 1887 the book has trebled in size.'

1932

WISDEN 1932

69th EDITION
EDITOR: C. Stewart Caine
PAGES: 1035
PRICE: Limp 5/-   cloth 8/-
REPRINT: Willows 2009 (500 limit, in two formats)

THE WORLD AT LARGE

- Kidnapping and murder of Charles Lindbergh Jr.
- Sydney Harbour Bridge opens
- Manchuria becomes the Japanese puppet state Manchukuo
- Gandhi begins a hunger strike in prison in Pune
- Franklin D Roosevelt elected U.S. President
- The Dow Jones Industrial Average reaches its lowest point – 41.22 on 8 July

CRICKET HEADLINES 1931

County Champions: Yorkshire

England lose to South Africa in the only finished Test in their five match series during the 1930/31 season

England beat the touring New Zealanders by one Test to none, with two drawn

Tich Freeman again takes over 250 wickets, bringing his total for the past four seasons (1928-31) to 1,122

Herbert Sutcliffe scores over 3,000 runs, including 13 centuries

Ratcliffe (Cambridge) and the Nawab of Pataudi (Oxford) score the first double-hundreds in a Varsity match

NOTES BY THE EDITOR

'At the end of the forthcoming season we have to send a team out to Australia and it would be idle to suggest that the undertaking is being approached with great confidence … There remains the big question who shall captain the side. A year ago everything pointed to the probability of the post being offered to Jardine. The old Oxonian not only possesses the experience born of a tour in Australia but … showed last year that he has lost nothing of his qualities as an exceptionally sound watchful batsman. On the other hand he does not seem to have impressed people with his ability as a leader on the field.'

FEATURE ARTICLES

Fifty Years Of Yorkshire County, by Lord Hawke

'There followed in 1865 the strike of five of our professionals. The strike was not due to any friction with the County Club, but was mainly on the ground of a supposed grievance against Surrey. The professionals suspected Surrey of having instructed John Lillywhite to no-ball Edgar Willsher, who was a member of the All England Eleven of which our George Anderson and others were members. One result of this strike was that Yorkshire did not win a game in 1865 and arranged no matches in 1866. Another result was that all five professionals took the proper course in 1867, and ever since then, sixty-four years ago, complete harmony has existed between the Club and her players.'

FIVE CRICKETERS OF THE YEAR

H. Verity

'There is no doubt that in once again carrying off the Championship, Yorkshire owed a great deal to the fine work accomplished by their left-hand bowler. Verity does not yet suggest the ability to flight the ball which was such a marked characteristic of Rhodes' bowling, but he has fine finger spin and accuracy of length, while now and again he sends down a faster ball which goes with his arm.'

W.E. Bowes   C.S. Dempster   James Langridge   Nawab of Pataudi

Sir Murray Bissett

'At the time of his death he was Acting-Governor of Rhodesia. He captained Western Province for several seasons and when in 1898-99 Lord Hawke's team toured South Africa he played in two Test matches against them.'

J.J. Kotze

'It is doing him no injustice to say that he did not like being punished, and on more than one occasion he got a little disheartened when he had catches missed of him in the slips. The ball, however, always went at terrific speed to the fieldsmen, and it is likely that had it been possible for him to field to his own bowling his opinions on the catching of his colleagues would not have been quite so scathing.'

J.N. Pentelow

'He was a frequent contributor to *Cricket,* of which he was Editor and proprietor from January, 1912, *Lillywhite's Annual* and *The Cricketer* and to *Wisden.* Among his best-known publications are: *England v. Australia* (two editions); *Australian Team of 1899, Cricket's Guide to Cricketers, Who's Who In the Cricket World, Australian Cricket Teams in England* and *Historic Bats.'*

H.H. Duke of Schleswig-Holstein,

'In the Charterhouse XI of 1888, died in Berlin on April 27. He was a good average batsman.'

L.O.S. Poidevin   C.T. Studd   S.M.J. Woods

Warwickshire

'Warwickshire enjoyed, from a cricket point of view, the best season they had known since 1925. Only once after a disastrous encounter with Surrey at the beginning of June did the county know defeat and if five reverses in all had to be admitted, six victories were gained, the record thus comparing very favourably with that of 1930.'

England v New Zealand, First Test Match, *played at Lord's, June 27, 29, 30*

'Upon their doings in their first Test match in this country, the New Zealanders will always be able to look back with feelings of great satisfaction … For the performances of Dempster, Page and Blunt too high praise could not be given. Dempster had played very well overnight when he was not out 86 and both he and Page produced just the cricket the circumstances demanded … Altogether the stand realised 118 runs in ninety-five minutes and then Blunt and Page added 142 in an hour and three quarters.'

The editor writes in the Preface: 'I deeply regret to announce that this issue is the last to which Mr. F.S. Ashley-Cooper will be able to contribute. For more than thirty years that gentleman has been mainly responsible for Births and Deaths, Obituaries and Cricket Records, this last section of the Almanack under his watchful care growing from some ten pages to more than sixty. Everybody interested in the chronicles of the game is under a deep debt of gratitude to him. Ill health and failing sight have unhappily compelled his retirement from the labours he loved so well.' Ashley-Cooper died within a month of Caine writing the Preface.

1933

WISDEN 1933

70th Edition
Editor: C. Stewart Caine
Pages: 1031
Price: Limp 5/-   cloth 8/-
Reprint: Willows 2010 (500 limit, in two formats)

THE WORLD AT LARGE

- Adolf Hitler appointed Chancellor of Germany in January: by March he assumes full dictatorial powers
- Reichstag fire, February 27
- The Oxford Union approves the motion, "That this House will in no circumstances fight for its King and country."
- First modern 'sighting' of the Loch Ness Monster

CRICKET HEADLINES 1932

County Champions: Yorkshire

India lose only Test match on first full tour of England

Holmes and Sutcliffe put on 555 for Yorkshire's first wicket against Essex

Herbert Sutcliffe scores his 100th hundred in a season in which he makes 3,336 runs including 14 centuries

Hedley Verity takes 10 for 10 against Nottinghamshire

NOTES BY THE EDITOR:

'Twelve months ago in dealing with the sorry experience of most of the leading counties in 1931, I ventured the opinion that there could not be a third consecutive wet summer. I based that conclusion upon recollections covering a period of more than fifty years but precedent went by the board. May proved to be nearly the worst month from a cricket point of view that anyone could recall and the rains continued for some days into June. Up to that point the weather, in its interference with cricket, certainly beat all records.'

FEATURE ARTICLES:

The Umpire's Point Of View, Some Experiences and Suggestions, by Frank Chester
'At the time of writing, everyone seems to be discussing our bowling in Australia – the so-called leg theory bowling. If it is of the character described in the cables, I do not agree with it; it is sure to make cricket a good deal slower and may keep people away. It is said our bowlers are aiming to hit the leg stump, but to hit the wicket you do not pitch half way and there is a danger the practice may lessen interest in the game.'

FIVE CRICKETERS OF THE YEAR:

W. Voce
'He gained his place in the Notts eleven in 1927, taking part in nineteen matches for the county and obtaining 36 wickets. At that time he had moderated his pace and was definitely a spin bowler, and everybody who saw him thought at once that here was a young cricketer likely to take front rank and possibly to follow in the footsteps of Wilfred Rhodes and Colin Blythe in even more important cricket.'
W.E. Astill   F.R. Brown   A.S. Kennedy   C.K. Nayudu

OBITUARIES INCLUDE:

F.S. Ashley-Cooper
'To those associated in the production of *Wisden's Almanack* the passing of Ashley-Cooper is naturally felt as a personal loss. Year by year he had spared no endeavour to make the list of "Births and Deaths" as complete as possible, conducting an enormous correspondence on the subject and searching the columns of practically every paper he could obtain to bring

his information up to date and to eliminate any error. Equally zealous was he in his pursuit of any happening in the game of sufficient importance to be included in "Cricket Records". All this labour he performed with a measure of enthusiasm which never flagged even when the shadows were gathering and he knew his days were numbered.'

Lord Harris

'It is impossible to give an adequate idea of what an irreplaceable asset he was to our great game. He was the only one who had a close playing and watching experience of first-class cricket and also sixty-five years actual participation in the game. In 1862, at the age of eleven, he was practising at Lord's and, on the glorious Fourth of June, 1930, he batted in a Second Eleven Match at Eton.'

**J.McC. Blackham   F.C. Cobden
G.G. Hearne   W.H. Lockwood**

LORD HARRIS

COUNTY REVIEW:

Worcestershire

'The falling off in the abilities of Root at the age of 42 after so many strenuous seasons as he had gone through, could not be regarded as altogether surprising but it still quite upset the side, no one else being able to lure batsmen to their destruction or keep the runs down as Root had succeeded in doing for so many years.'

MATCH REPORTS:

Yorkshire v Notts, *played at Leeds, July 9, 11, 12*

'Verity in this match took – for the second time in his career – all ten wickets in an innings. Prior to lunch on the last day, Notts scored 38 without loss but on resuming, their ten wickets went down for 29 runs. Verity not only performed the "hat trick" in sending back Walker, Harris and Gunn, but got rid of Arthur Staples and Larwood with the last two balls of his next over, and then, disposing of Voce and Sam Staples with the third and fourth balls of his following over, brought the innings to a close.'

[Notts all out 67 in 47.4 overs: Verity 19.4 – 16 – 10 – 10, Macaulay 23 – 9 – 34 – 0]

MISCELLANEOUS:

Australian Tour In America

'D.G. Bradman secured remarkable batting figures, scoring 3,782 runs in 51 innings (14 times not out) giving an average of 102.21 with a highest of 260 against Western Ontario on July 4, which constitutes a Canadian record.'

For the first time, Wisden *has two photoplates – the traditional portraits of the Five Cricketers of the Year, plus a photograph of Lord Harris (pictured). From this edition up to and including the 1939 edition, the soft-bound editions included a bat-shaped bookmark attached to the spine. There is an errata slip in Births and Deaths because a line giving the date of W.R. Hammond's birth appeared in the details of the Marquis of Hamilton in the opposite column.*

145

1934

WISDEN 1934

71st EDITION
EDITOR: Sydney J. Southerton
PAGES: 1059
PRICE: Limp 5/-   cloth 8/-
REPRINT: Willows 2010 (500 limit, in two formats)

THE WORLD AT LARGE

• Death of President Hindenburg: Adolf Hitler takes the title Fuehrer, becoming head of state as well as head of government
• Bonnie and Clyde killed by police in Louisiana
• Donald Duck appears on screen for the first time
• Italy wins the 1934 football World Cup
• Stanley Matthews makes his England debut, scoring a goal as England beat Wales 4-0

CRICKET HEADLINES 1933

County Champions: Yorkshire

The 1932-33 M.C.C. tour of Australia creates a new word – 'bodyline' – and a crisis in Anglo-Australian relations

England win the three Test series at home against West Indies by two matches to nil

Walter Hammond scores 336* for England against New Zealand at Auckland, the record Test score

Hedley Verity takes 17 wickets in a day

NOTES BY THE EDITOR

'The M.C.C. afford an admirable example in setting their face resolutely against the preparation of the pitches at Lord's by the use of artificial aids. A bowler at Headquarters always has a reasonable chance and runs made there are thoroughly well earned. On most other grounds, however, the scales are weighted in favour of batsmen.'

FEATURE ARTICLES

The Bowling Controversy
P. Holmes (Yorkshire) 1913-1933

FIVE CRICKETERS OF THE YEAR

G.A. Headley
'George Alphonso Headley, born at Panama on May 30, 1909, is beyond all question the best batsman the West Indies have ever produced. Paying his first visit to England with the West Indies team last summer, he landed on these shores with a name already established. That the reputation which preceded him was in every way justified he quickly proceeded to demonstrate, and returned home with his fame considerably increased.'

M.S. Nichols
'In his contorted run up Nichols undeniably lacks the grace and rhythm of his predecessor, Buckenham, but nature has given him a more powerful frame and then, of course, his batting must also be thrown into the scale.'

A.H. Bakewell   L.F. Townsend   C.F. Walters

OBITUARIES INCLUDE

C.S. Caine
'The Editor of *Wisden* is an important personage. It is he who decides the policy of "the Cricketer's Bible" and cricketers the world over look to him to give a lead on all controversial problems. His is, therefore, no easy task, but *Wisden* has been fortunate in its editors, the

brothers C.F. and S.H. Pardon, and Mr. C. Stewart Caine. Mr. Stewart Caine filled the position in a manner worthy of the traditions of the past.' – P. F. Warner.

A.A. Jackson
'A native of Scotland, where he was born on September 5, 1909, he was hailed as a second Victor Trumper – a comparison made alike for his youthful success, elegant style and superb stroke play. Well set up, very active on his feet, and not afraid to jump in to the slow bowlers and hit the ball hard, he accomplished far more in big cricket than Trumper had done at his age.'

L.C.H. Palairet
'Palairet's cricket for Somerset will never be forgotten. His drives into the river and the churchyard at Taunton are still remembered by those who had the good fortune to see him in such form. He had almost every good quality as a batsman; combining strong defence with fine cutting and driving on either side of the wicket he always shaped in classic style.'

K.S. Ranjitsinhji
'He quickly became a great favourite with the public, a position he gained not only by his skill as a cricketer but in no small degree by a personality made additionally attractive by a modest demeanour and invariable courtesy which is a natural attribute of a Rajput. The disappointment at his failure, which was rare, was almost as great as the pleasure enjoyed from his success, even amongst the most enthusiastic supporters of his opponents.' – Sir Stanley Jackson

F.H. Sugg   W. Sugg

COUNTY REVIEW

Essex
'The reason for the Essex advance is not hard to find. For one thing, the prospects of the side were not prejudiced so severely as the year before by the lack of a regular captain. T.N. Pearce led the eleven for the first half of the season with tact, judgment, skill and no little personal success as a batsman. D.R. Wilcox, who took charge of Essex afterwards, was equally popular and just as good a leader.'

MATCH REPORTS

Australia v England, Third Test Match, *played at Adelaide, January 13, 14, 16, 17, 18, 19*
'Insulting remarks were hurled at Jardine, and when Larwood started to bowl his leg-theory he came in for his share of the storm of abuse. Not to put too fine a point on it, pandemonium reigned. A passage of words between Pelham Warner and Woodfull in the dressing-room increased the bitter feeling prevalent in the crowd, and the dispatch of the cablegram protesting against body-line bowling served no purpose in whatever endeavours were made to appease tempers already badly frayed by the various happenings.

Altogether the whole atmosphere was a disgrace to cricket. One must pay a tribute to Jardine. He did not shrink from the line of action he had taken up; he showed great pluck in often fielding near to the boundary where he became an easy target for offensive and sometimes filthy remarks; and above all he captained his team in this particular match like a genius. Much as they disliked the method of attack he controlled, all the leading Australian critics were unanimous in their praise of his skill as a leader.'

The new editor, Sydney Southerton, begins his Preface: 'The death in April last of Mr. C. Stewart Caine, my distinguished colleague and senior partner in business, severed a connection with Wisden's Almanack *that had existed for nearly fifty years, the last eight of which saw him as Editor.' Southerton faced a huge challenge with the reports of the 1932-33 'Bodyline' tour and its aftermath which he deals with in an article headed 'The Bowling Controversy'. Coverage of the Bodyline tour makes this a special edition for English collectors, although prices achieved for the same book appear to be lower in Australia.*

1935

WISDEN 1935

72nd Edition
Editor: Sydney J. Southerton
Pages: 1047
Price: Limp 5/-   cloth 8/-
Reprint: Willows 2010 (500 limit, in two formats)

THE WORLD AT LARGE

• Ramsay MacDonald retires as Prime Minister and is succeeded by Stanley Baldwin
• The driving test becomes compulsory
• Malcolm Campbell becomes the first man to drive a car at over 300mph (301.13mph), at Bonneville Flats, Utah
• Elvis Presley born (January 8)
• Death of T.E. Lawrence (Lawrence of Arabia) in a motorcycle accident
• Hitler announces German rearmament, in violation of the Treaty of Versailles

CRICKET HEADLINES 1934

County Champions: Lancashire

Australia regain the Ashes, winning the series by two matches to one, although under Bob Wyatt England beat Australia at Lord's for the only time in the 20th century

England win the series 2-0 on the first Test-playing tour by M.C.C. to India

Bradman scores a second Test triple-century at Leeds

Ernest Tyldesley scores his 100th hundred

Jack Hobbs retires

NOTES BY THE EDITOR

'I will quote and paraphrase a saying of a very famous Blackheath and England Rugby footballer, the late Arthur Budd. Asked one day if there was any difference between hard and rough play at Rugby he replied: "There is a very great difference, Sir, between hard and rough play, and a gentleman knows the difference." I would say in regard to this bowling which has caused such trouble that, "There is a great difference between fast bowling and direct attack bowling, and a cricketer knows the difference". There, I think, we can for the time leave it.'

FEATURE ARTICLES

The Hobbs Era, by Jack Hobbs
'In the last quarter of a century – and perhaps during a longer time – there has come about a great change for the better in the relations existing between amateurs and professionals. County committees have realised that both on and off the field their players are all members of the same team and professionals are not, as was largely the case some years ago, relegated to incommodious dressing-rooms with no amenities, while, as a general rule, amateurs and professionals now take their luncheon and tea together in the same room. The natural consequence of this, of course, has been a pronounced improvement in the bearing of professional cricketers off the field.'

Australian Cricket, by the Hon. Mr. Justice H.V. Evatt
'It is a great mistake to judge the Australian spectators by the reaction of some of them when many of their players were repeatedly hit in 1932-3 as a result of an entirely novel method of fast bowling. Unfortunately a section of the press exaggerates every trifle. It becomes an incident, then a dispute, and it ends in an international episode.'

Settlement of the Bowling Controversy

G.A.E. Paine
'Standing just over six feet in height, Paine bowls with an easy delivery and makes full use of his stature. In his early days with Warwickshire there were critics who questioned if he was spinning the ball as well as he might, but steady progress and increasing success lessened those doubts, which were dispelled finally last season, when, he set up a new bowling record for Warwickshire by taking 155 wickets in all matches for the county.'
S.J. McCabe   W.J. O'Reilly   W.H. Ponsford   C.I.J. Smith

OBITUARIES INCLUDE

W.H. Brain
'In 1893, when Somerset's second innings was finished with a hat-trick by C.L. Townsend, he accomplished the rare feat of stumping three men off consecutive balls.'
M. Nichol
'He failed to regain his real form, a long day in the field or an effort to put together a big innings being too exacting for his physical resources. Strangely enough during the Whitsuntide fixture of 1933, played at Leyton, he was taken ill at Stratford station and had to retire from the game, so that his death a year later while the Essex match was in progress came as a dramatic coincidence.'
W.J. Abel   T. Collins   A.W. Pullin (Old Ebor)   L.J. Tancred

COUNTY REVIEW

The Leading Counties in 1934
'Yorkshire, after three consecutive years as Champions, were second in the table for two weeks in May and two in July, but they never once led, and ultimately finished sixth – their lowest position since 1911 when Warwickshire carried off chief honours. Sussex ended up second for the third season in succession. A feature of the competition was the advance made by Derbyshire and Warwickshire. Derbyshire, indeed, possessed at one period an outside chance of finishing first, but no county near the top could wrest the honour from Lancashire.'

MATCH REPORTS

Nottinghamshire v Australians, *played at Nottingham, August 11, 13, 14*
'A match rendered unpleasant by the antagonistic attitude of the spectators towards the visitors ended in a draw. The Australians, encountering "direct attack" bowling for the first time during the tour, fared none too well … Voce placed five men on the leg-side, four of them close to the batsman, and of his eight victims, five fell to catches in this "leg trap" … The atmosphere grew increasingly hostile, and when the Australians took the field for the last innings, they were greeted by a storm of booing.'

MISCELLANEOUS:

From the report of the M.C.C. team in India
'In England batsmen have to play on such a variety of pitches changing from day to day that it was surprising that some of the team failed to come up to expectations under conditions new to them. But the heat, travelling, and constant social functions, always very pleasant, could be held responsible for anyone failing to do himself full justice.'

Within a month of publication, the editor, Sydney Southerton, was dead. In March 1935, he proposed the toast to 'Cricket' at a dinner at the Oval, 'sank down' and died. See 1936.

1936

WISDEN 1936

73rd EDITION
EDITOR: Wilfrid H. Brookes
PAGES: 1035
PRICE: Limp 5/-   cloth 8/-
REPRINT: Willows 2011 (500 limit, in two formats)

THE WORLD AT LARGE

• The Supermarine Spitfire has its maiden flight
• England defeat the All-Blacks for the first time, 13-0, thanks to two tries by debutant Prince Alexander Obolensky
• The Berlin Olympics – Jesse Owens wins 4 gold medals
• Abdication crisis: Edward VIII steps down in favour of his brother, who becomes King George VI
• Spanish Civil War begins

CRICKET HEADLINES 1935

County Champions: Yorkshire

South Africa tour and for the first time win a series in England

Andy Sandham and Walter Hammond score their 100th hundreds

Alf Gover takes four wickets in four balls for Surrey v Worcestershire

Freeman, Verity and Goddard each take over 200 wickets

NOTES BY THE EDITOR

'The compilers of *Wisden* are placed in a very difficult position. In the absence of official guidance it has been decided that until the definition of a first-class match is established for ever and ever, only the statistics of three-day matches at home and abroad will be accepted for inclusion in the first-class averages. Certain matches, those for instance between a touring side and a first-class county eleven to which it is not possible to allocate more than two days, are on a different footing, and in such cases an official ruling will be necessary.'

FEATURE ARTICLES

Trials of a County Secretary, by R.V. Ryder
'Yes, I remember it all very well. Not a single motor vehicle reached the scene of that cricket encounter *[the 1902 Edgbaston Test]*. Horse transport was the thing in those days. What quaint reading is afforded now by the perusal of this extract from the Warwickshire Committee Minutes of April 26, 1897: A member wrote suggesting that accommodation should be provided for horses as many members had to travel long distances.'
J.B. Hobbs – Twenty-Five Years of Triumph
Direct Attack and L.B.W.
Success of the L.B.W. Experiment

FIVE CRICKETERS OF THE YEAR

H.B. Cameron
'Horace Brakenridge Cameron, one of the finest wicket-keepers South Africa has produced and a courageous, hard-hitting batsman, died on November 2, 1935, shortly after his return home with the victorious team that toured England. Born at Port Elizabeth on July 5, 1905, he was in his 31st year when enteric fever proved fatal after only a few days' illness.'
A.W. Wellard
One of his finest performances was at Portsmouth in 1933. Somerset began the match by losing six wickets for 38 runs, but then Wellard, hitting four 6's and seven 4's, scored 77 out of 94; in the second innings he made 60 including two 6's and seven 4's. As he also took ten wickets for less than eleven runs apiece, his part in the defeat of Hampshire by 107 runs was very considerable.
E.R.T. Holmes   B. Mitchell   D. Smith

150

W. Brockwell
'A stylish and often brilliant batsman, strong in back play and a free hitter in front of the wicket, Brockwell also was a useful fast medium paced bowler and a smart fieldsman, notably at second slip where he succeeded George Lohmann – one of the surest catches ever seen in that position.'

Hon. F.S.G. Calthorpe
'Calthorpe had a lot to do with starting the Folkestone Cricket Festival. He enjoyed every minute of a game whether batting, bowling or fielding. Taking the joy of the cricket field to the golf links he became a scratch player with the Worplesdon Club, founded the Cricketers' Golf Society, and gave a cup for competition.'

R.W. Crockett
'Recognised by cricketers the world over as one of the finest umpires of his time, his quiet demeanour, unfailing good humour and strict impartiality endeared him to all players with whom he came in contact.'

C.P. McGahey
'His death was the result of an accident on Christmas Day when, slipping on a greasy pavement, he fell and damaged a finger. Septic poisoning ensued and proved fatal.'

S.J. Southerton
'His end came even more suddenly than that of each of his predecessors. Sydney H. Pardon collapsed in his office and died the next morning, November 20, 1925; Charles Stewart Caine, after fighting the trouble of a weak heart for many months, went to sleep in his chair at home and did not wake again; Southerton having proposed the toast of "Cricket" at the dinner of The Ferrets Club at the Oval, sank down and a few minutes later his life ebbed away. He had just seen the fruits of his labours in bringing out the seventy-second issue of Wisden and died in circumstances such as he might have wished. Surrounded by cricketers, many of them close friends and leading players, he surrendered his innings when in the full glow of success.'

H. Baldwin   H.B. Cameron   F. Mitchell

Leicestershire
'For Leicestershire, 1935 must be regarded as the most successful season in the history of the club. Not only did the side reveal a marked improvement on their achievements of recent years, but, by winning their last game, they set up a record for the highest number of victories by the county eleven in one season.'

Somerset v Essex, *played at Frome, May 18, 20, 21*
'A remarkable century by Gimblett, playing in his first match for Somerset, completely overshadowed everything else at Frome, where Essex were beaten by an innings and 49 runs. Full of confidence from the start of his innings, Gimblett, whose previous experience had largely been confined to club cricket at Watchet, reached three figures in sixty-three minutes, the fastest hundred of the season ... When Gimblett went in Somerset had lost six wickets for 107 runs; he attacked the bowling like a seasoned player and ninth out at 282 placed his side in what proved to be a winning position.'

The obituary of Sydney Southerton notes that he was the third editor to die in ten years. The new editor, Wilfrid Brookes, writes in his Preface that 'because of other heavy calls upon my time and energies, I must depend very considerably upon the help of my colleagues. Ungrudging assistance has been afforded by Mr. Hubert Preston, my partner in the Cricket Reporting Agency which has now been responsible for the production of 50 editions of the Almanack.'

1937

WISDEN 1937

74th EDITION
EDITOR: Wilfrid H. Brookes
PAGES: 1055
PRICE: Limp 5/-   cloth 8/-
REPRINT: Willows 2011 (500 limit, in two formats)

THE WORLD AT LARGE

• Coronation of King George VI
• Ex-King Edward, now the Duke of Windsor, marries Wallis Simpson
• *The Dandy* comic, featuring Desperate Dan and Korky The Cat, is first published
• Neville Chamberlain becomes Prime Minister on Stanley Baldwin's retirement in May
• The Japanese attack Nanking (Nanjing) and slaughter perhaps 300,000 civilians

CRICKET HEADLINES 1936

County Champions: Derbyshire

England beat the touring Indians by two Tests to none

Bradman hits two triple-hundreds during the Australian domestic season 1935/36, but still finishes second in the season's batting averages

Denis Compton makes his debut

Many greats of the English game retire – Mead, Ernest Tyldesley, J.W. Hearne, Freeman, Kennedy and Fender

NOTES BY THE EDITOR

'No doubt in due course competent successors to Hobbs and Sutcliffe will be discovered, but, although Barnett of Gloucestershire has played several noteworthy innings, a complete solution has still to be found for the problem facing England since Sutcliffe last played in a Test Match – against South Africa at Lord's in 1935. Much experimenting has been conducted in the hope of finding the best men available for this very important position. Since Sutcliffe was passed over, no fewer than eight players – D. Smith, A. H. Bakewell, R. E. S. Wyatt, A. Mitchell, H. Gimblett, A. Fagg, C. J. Barnett and T. S. Worthington – have been tried as opening batsmen in a Test Match, and we are little nearer overcoming the difficulty.'

FEATURE ARTICLES

A.P. Freeman in the Cricket Field
'Freeman's record is specially noteworthy because all but 29 of his wickets – his measure of success in 1914 – were taken after he had passed his 30th year. Nearly all his best work has been accomplished for Kent, and his bowling in the six seasons 1928-1933, when 1,673 wickets fell to him, was little short of astounding. As he continued to dismiss 200 or more batsmen in each season, his aggregate number of "victims" during the eight seasons ending 1935 was 2,090, no fewer than 1,754 in county matches.'
Recollections of Oxford Cricket, by H.D.G. Leveson Gower

FIVE CRICKETERS OF THE YEAR

A.R. Gover
'For many years Gover experienced some trouble over his run. He had a habit of overstepping the crease and being no-balled, but by assiduous practice he has almost eradicated those faults. He says he owes much to the excellent advice he received from Razor Smith and Strudwick. By constant practice during the winter months at Strudwick's indoor school he improved his run and delivery. Gover also pays tribute to Sandy Tait, the Surrey masseur, due to whose careful attention he has not missed a match during the last seven years on account of injury.'
C.J. Barnett   W.H. Copson   V.M. Merchant   T.S. Worthington

R. Abel
'If late in reaching his best, he was right at the top of the tree from 1895 to 1902, scoring over 2,000 runs in first-class matches in eight successive seasons. His highest aggregate of runs, 3,309, was obtained in 1901 and his average in these eight years of conspicuous ability ranged from 56 to 41. In 1903 his eyes troubled him again, and though playing in glasses helped him to some extent next year his first-class career then closed.'

B.J.T. Bosanquet
'In addition to cricket he represented Oxford University at Hammer Throwing in 1899 and 1900, and at Billiards in 1898 and 1900.'

H.M. King George V
'He habitually visited Lord's when Colonial teams were playing against England, and on such occasions the match was invariably interrupted in order that all the players and umpires could be presented to His Majesty in front of the pavilion, an informal ceremony which the spectators watched with keen interest marked by expression of loyalty.'

R.P. Northway
"… aged 27, was killed in a motor car accident when travelling with Bakewell, his Northamptonshire colleague, after the match with Derbyshire at Chesterfield, on August 25. It was the last engagement on their county's programme and the victims of the accident were Northamptonshire's opening batsmen.'

D.A.C. Page
'Captain of Gloucestershire, died in Cirencester Hospital on September 2 as the result of injuries received in a motor accident, which occurred when he was returning to his home, after leading his county to victory in an innings over Nottinghamshire, at Gloucester, on the last day of the County Championship season.'

G.H. Simpson-Hayward   E.G. Wynyard

COUNTY REVIEW

Derbyshire
'Friday, August 28, 1936, must be written down as the greatest day ever in the history of Derbyshire cricket. On that day Derbyshire became, beyond all shadow of doubt, Champion County; Yorkshire's desperate, if belated challenge had failed and there began a new era for the Midlanders.'

MATCH REPORTS

Nottinghamshire v Middlesex, *played at Nottingham, July 4, 6, 7*
'Drawn. Started on a slow pitch the match was ruined by rain which limited play on Monday to eighteen minutes and prevented a resumption until one o'clock on Tuesday … Allen had the curious experience of batting on all three days for 6 not out.'

1938

THE WORLD AT LARGE

- German troops occupy and annexe Austria
- Neville Chamberlain flies to Munich to meet Hitler, and flies back with his piece of paper and 'Peace in our time'
- Two days later, Germany annexes the Sudetenland of Czechoslovakia
- *Kristallnacht* – 'the night of broken glass' – in Germany sees an unleashing of lootings and burnings of Jewish businesses, synagogues and homes
- Italy retain the World Cup, beating Hungary in the final

WISDEN 1938

75th EDITION
EDITOR: Wilfrid H. Brookes
PAGES: 999
PRICE: Limp 5/-   cloth 7/6d
REPRINT: Willows 2011

CRICKET HEADLINES 1937

County Champions: Yorkshire

England beat the touring New Zealanders by one match to nil in a three Test series

England under G.O. Allen lose down under by three matches to two

E. Paynter (Lancashire v Sussex) and R.H. Moore (Hampshire v Warwickshire) both hit 300 in a day on 28th July

J.H. Parks scores 3,003 runs and takes 101 wickets, the only man in history to achieve this double

W.H. Copson becomes the first man to take five wickets in six balls, for Derbyshire v Warwickshire

NOTES BY THE EDITOR

'The counties, through the Advisory Committee, will decide their own future, but I fear the burden will eventually prove too heavy for more than one of their number. Because of that, the idea of amalgamations ought to be considered seriously. In both Rugby and Association football, combined county teams have been competing for years.'

FEATURE ARTICLES

Reflections, by E. Hendren
'Among the players with or against whom I have played, I shall never forget the famous W.G. I first played in a charity match with him and also for M.C.C. at Charlton, and very proud I was to be in the same side with him. In one of these games, I got a hundred and the Doctor 50 odd – he was past his best at that time – and I well remember him clapping me on the back and saying in that high-pitched voice of his: "You'll play for England one day, young 'un." I am glad he was right.'
Spin Bowling, by A.P. Freeman
Natural Wickets, by G.O. Allen
Bradman: An Australian View, by the Hon. Mr. Justice Herbert V. Evatt

FIVE CRICKETERS OF THE YEAR

L. Hutton
'Blessed with the right temperament for the big occasion, Hutton, given good health, should for many years serve Yorkshire as nobly as did Brown, Tunnicliffe, Holmes and Sutcliffe. In addition, he should furnish England with one of the opening batsmen so badly needed since the breaking of the Hobbs-Sutcliffe partnership. Eminently sound in defence, he plays the new ball extremely well and prefers to wear down the bowling rather than take risks.'
T.W.J. Goddard   J. Hardstaff jnr.   J.H. Parks   E. Paynter

G.W. Beldam

'In 1903 when Middlesex were Champions, Beldam closely followed P.F. Warner, their most consistent batsman, in aggregate and average. He maintained his form until 1907 when he dropped out of the side ... A pioneer in action photography, George Beldam produced, in conjunction with C.B. Fry, who wrote the descriptions, a remarkable book, *Great Batsmen, Their Methods at a Glance*.'

W. Brearley

'It was said at Old Trafford that when Walter Brearley hurried to the wicket the horse walked between the shafts ready to drag the heavy roller for use at the end of the innings.'

H.T. Gamlin

'... most famous as a Rugby full back, who died at Cheam, Surrey, on July 12, aged 59, played a few times for Somerset as a professional. In 1895 A.C. MacLaren, after making 424, the highest score by an Englishman in first-class cricket, was caught off Gamlin.'

Sir James Barrie   **G. Dennett**
E.A. McDonald   **W.N. Roe**

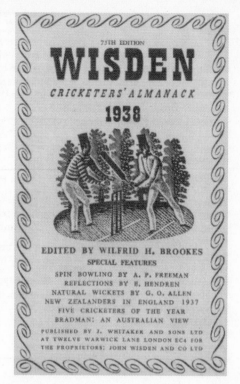

75TH EDITION

WISDEN

CRICKETERS' ALMANACK

1938

EDITED BY WILFRID H. BROOKES

SPECIAL FEATURES

SPIN BOWLING BY A. P. FREEMAN
REFLECTIONS BY E. HENDREN
NATURAL WICKETS BY G. O. ALLEN
NEW ZEALANDERS IN ENGLAND 1937
FIVE CRICKETERS OF THE YEAR
BRADMAN: AN AUSTRALIAN VIEW

PUBLISHED BY J. WHITAKER AND SONS LTD
AT TWELVE WARWICK LANE LONDON EC4 FOR
THE PROPRIETORS: JOHN WISDEN AND CO LTD

Middlesex v Surrey, *at Lord's, August 28, 30, 31*

'Middlesex lost two wickets for four runs, but Hendren, accorded a wonderful reception by 17,000 spectators upon the occasion of his last appearance in a Championship game, hit finely all-round ... *[He made 103]* Holmes, with a view to gaining use of the new ball, bowled an over that, consisting of deliveries tossed high or wide of the wicket, yielded 24 runs from byes and wides while a fieldsman in the deep made no effort to prevent the ball from reaching the boundary. Protests came from the crowd, but before the new ball could be brought into use, a successful appeal against the light ended the unhappy proceedings. As the sun shone, it was ridiculous to suggest that the light was unfit for cricket, but a farcical situation was ended by this pretence.'

Wisden, *published for the first time by J. Whitaker, undergoes a complete makeover. The now famous* Wisden *woodcut, designed by Eric Ravilious, first appeared on the cover of the limp edition (pictured) and the title page of the hardback, where it remains to this day. The limp edition was bound in linen cloth rather than paper. The old two-part division – which editor Wilfrid Brookes said had been called 'a quaint Victorian survival'– disappeared and a complete index was included. Illustrations were included in a 32-page section produced on better-quality paper. The counties were reviewed in alphabetical order rather than in their ranking in the previous year's Championship. Births and deaths and obituaries moved to the back of the book. Brookes writes in his Preface: 'Although new features have been introduced and the contents have been re-arranged, nothing, I hope, of real interest to lovers of cricket has been omitted. The major principles that have served the book so well in the past have been zealously guarded.'*

1939

WISDEN 1939

76th EDITION
EDITOR: Wilfrid H. Brookes
PAGES: 967
PRICE: Limp 5/-   Cloth 7/6d
REPRINT: Willows 2012

THE WORLD AT LARGE

• Britain pledges to support Poland should Germany invade
• King George VI, with Queen Elizabeth, visits Canada and the United States, the first reigning monarch to do so
• The Spanish Civil War ends and General Franco assumes power
• World War Two begins on 3 September
• The German battleship *Graf Spee* sunk by British forces in the Battle of the River Plate
• Nazi-Soviet Pact signed by von Ribbentrop on 23 August
• *The Wizard of Oz* and *Gone With The Wind* both open

CRICKET HEADLINES 1938

County Champions: Yorkshire

Len Hutton scores 364 for England against Australia at the Oval – the highest Test innings and the longest first-class innings to that time

Australia retain the Ashes, by sharing the series with England, one all

Don Bradman and Bill Edrich both score 1,000 runs before June

Arthur Fagg uniquely scores two double-centuries in one match, Kent v Essex

NOTES BY THE EDITOR

'Before the 1938 season was begun, the highest innings played by an Englishman in a home Test Match against Australia was 182 not out by C.P. Mead at the Oval in 1921. Last summer, no fewer that four different batsmen beat that record. Paynter made 216 not out at Nottingham, W.R. Hammond scored 240 in the Lord's Test and in the memorable Fifth Test at the Oval both Leyland (187) and Hutton (364) surpassed the figure reached by Mead seventeen years previously. The phenomenal innings of Hutton … may stand for all time.'

FEATURE ARTICLES

My Happy Cricket Life, by Frank Woolley
'Touching on another personal subject I have been asked if I can explain why I was dismissed so many times in the nineties. The statisticians inform me that I was out 35 times between 90 and 99... I can honestly say that with me it was never a question of the nervous nineties. Lots of times I was out through forcing the game. We were never allowed to play for averages in the Kent side... We always had to play the game and play for the team. It is a Kent tradition.'
Cricket at the Crossroads, by Don Bradman
Cricket Conundrums, by Arthur Gilligan

FIVE CRICKETERS OF THE YEAR

K. Farnes
'For a man of his speed, Farnes takes what is nowadays considered a short run – one of eleven paces – but he quickly gets into his stride and, when delivering the ball, is moving at a great pace. Perfectly proportioned, he is just under six feet five inches, and weighs 15 stone 6 pounds and, as he sends the ball down from well over eight feet, it is obvious that on a hard wicket his deliveries are liable to rise sharply.'
H.T. Bartlett   W.A. Brown   D.C.S. Compton   A. Wood

W. Bestwick

'The Derbyshire professional, died on May 3, aged 62. Of good height and heavy build, he brought all the force associated with his winter occupation as a miner into his right hand bowling so effectively and with such reserve of strength, that he continued in county cricket until his fiftieth year.'

Lord Hawke

'There can be few, if any whose services to cricket have more deserved acknowledgment and record in the pages of *Wisden* than the late Lord Hawke. What service he may have rendered to cricket and cricketers was for him a labour of love. He gained his greatest pleasure from playing cricket and doing what he believed to be best in the interests of the game.' – Sir Stanley Jackson

Dr. H.V. Hordern

'Medical studies limited his appearances in first-class cricket and he could not spare time to visit England with an Australian side but the cables of his doings against the team that went to Australia in the winter of 1911-12 caused a sensation. In the Test matches he took 32 wickets at an average cost of 24.37, an achievement little less remarkable than that of Sidney Barnes who, with 34 wickets at 22.88 apiece, was largely responsible for England winning four matches and the rubber.'

Maharajah of Patiala

'President of the Cricket Club of India, died on March 23, at the age of 46. At the opening of the Brabourne Stadium, Bombay, when Lord Tennyson's team played there in December 1937, the Maharaja expressed the hope that "the Stadium will become to India what Lord's ground is to England". That was typical of his keen interest in cricket when poor health compelled him to give up active participation in the game at which he was proficient as a free scoring batsman and keen field.'

**J.J. Kelly   G.H. Longman   P.A. McAlister   H.H. Massie   R.M. Poore   J. Sharp
H. Trumble   E.F.S. Tylecote**

The County Championship in 1938

'Though the issue remained in doubt until towards the close of the season, Yorkshire were beyond doubt the team of the year and deservedly gained their twentieth Championship … Middlesex, again runners-up, lacked players of calibre to replace those required for Test matches.'

England v Australia, (Fifth Test Match), *played at Kennington Oval, August 20, 22, 23, 24*

'This Test will always be remembered as Hutton's Match, and also for the calamity which befell Australia while their opponents were putting together a mammoth total of 903. First of all Fingleton strained a muscle and Bradman injured his ankle so badly that he retired from the match and did not play again during the tour. Before this accident, England had established a supremacy which left little doubt about the result; indeed, Hammond probably would not have closed the innings during the tea interval on the third day but for the mishap to the opposing captain.'

Wilfrid Brookes writes in his Preface: 'Since Wisden *for 1938 was published in a revised form, there have come from all parts of the world a large number of letters expressing strong approval of the changes introduced … An increase in sales of over seventy-five per cent forms an additional encouragement to those responsible for the production.'*

1940

WISDEN 1940

77th EDITION
EDITOR: Haddon Whitaker
PAGES: 875
PRICE: Limp 5/-   cloth 7/6d
REPRINT: Willows 2003 (500 limit, in two formats)

THE WORLD AT LARGE

- Fall of France
- Evacuation of Allied troops from Dunkirk
- Winston Churchill becomes Prime Minister
- Channel Islands occupied by Germany
- The Battle of Britain foils German invasion
- Food rationing introduced
- U.S. President Franklin D Roosevelt wins an unprecedented third term in office

CRICKET HEADLINES 1939

County Champions: Yorkshire

The West Indies tour England but lose to England in a three Test series

The outbreak of war curtails the season.

In the final innings of the county season, Hedley Verity takes 7 for 9 v Sussex

In South Africa, England have to abandon the Fifth 'timeless' Test to catch their ship home. They win the rubber 1-0 with four drawn matches.

NOTES ON THE 1939 SEASON

by R.C. Robertson-Glasgow

[Wilfrid Brookes had resigned as editor at the end of the 1939 season and publisher Haddon Whitaker co-ordinated this and the next three issues, handing over the notes to an established cricket writer.]

'It is true that throughout the season the rumble of war rolled louder and louder, that our guests the West Indies, excepting L.N. Constantine and E.A. Martindale, had to sail for home with seven matches unplayed, that in the County Championship several matches had to be abruptly cancelled; but, in a sense, it was a strangely happy season. There may have been more rain than is convenient to fast bowlers, thin shoes, or anxious secretaries; but, as is customary when great issues hang in the balance, men set themselves to a quiet but determined enjoyment. They turned to cricket as an old friend, who gives you a seat, a glass of beer, and something sane to talk about.'

FEATURE ARTICLES

Cricket in War-Time, by H.S. Altham

'There is a pleasant story of the Battle of Alma that shows how cricket was never far from some soldiers' minds; The Guards, Rifle Brigade and Black Watch were nearing the top of the rise when a round shot came bounding along and passed through the ranks which had "opened to avoid it in accordance with orders". Sir John Astley tells how "George Duff, a capital chap who was our best wicket-keeper, was just in front of me and I sang out 'Duff, you are keeping wicket, you ought to have stopped that one,' and of how he turned and smiling quietly said, 'No, sir, it had a bit too much pace on. You are a long stop, sir, so I left it to you.'"'

FIVE CRICKETERS OF THE YEAR

L. N. Constantine

'To the passionate love for the game which inspires so many of his countrymen, and to the lissomness of limb, the rapidity of vision and the elasticity of muscle which the climate of those islands engenders he adds qualities peculiarly his own, so that whether batting, bowling

or fielding he becomes the centre of all interest. So great has been his genius that his non-success with the bat in Test matches gives cause for wonderment.'
W.J. Edrich   W.W. Keeton   A.B. Sellers   D.V.P. Wright

OBITUARY INCLUDE

H.G. Deane
'He will always be remembered for his fine leadership of the young teams of 1927-28 and 1929, and there can be no doubt that his inspiration and careful team-building were chiefly responsible for the improvement in South African cricket of recent years.'

Sir Walter Lawrence
'An enthusiastic sportsman, who kept his own cricket field at Hyde Hall, Sir Walter in 1934 introduced his trophy and a 100 guineas order on a London store for the cricketer who hit the fastest hundred in a first-class match. It discouraged senseless stonewalling and was an inducement to enterprising players to try for the annual prize.'

A. Ward
'Albert Ward took his benefit in August 1902 when Yorkshire visited Lancashire. Over 24,000 people paid at the gates on the first day, and the total amount realised by the match was £1,739, although rain prevented play on the last day. Albert Ward was dismissed in an unusual way when Derbyshire were at Old Trafford in 1899. In playing a ball from Davidson he broke his bat; a piece of wood knocked off the leg bail and he was out for 72 hit wicket.'

T. W. Hayward   Hon. R.H. Lyttelton

COUNTY REVIEW

Gloucestershire
'Always ready to offer or accept a sporting challenge in the hope of providing an interesting finish, Gloucestershire set the fashion in the enterprising cricket which prevailed over most of the country. Their spirit of adventure made them second to none as an attraction. In addition their policy produced excellent playing results.'

MATCH REPORTS

South Africa v England, Fifth Test Match, *at Durban, March 3,4, 6, 7, 8, 9, 10, 11, 13, 14*
'When heavy rain prevented any more cricket after tea on the tenth day the South African Board of Control and the two captains went into conference before issuing a statement that the game had been abandoned because the England team had to catch the 8.05 p.m. train that night (Tuesday) from Durban in order to reach Cape Town in time to make the necessary arrangements for their departure on the *Athlone Castle* on Friday. The date of sailing for England could not be postponed.'

Haddon Whitaker from the publishers takes over as editor but sees his role as co-ordinator. He explains in the Preface: 'Wisden for 1940 remains unchanged in appearance. Future editions until the end of the war must conform with the smaller issues of the Great War ... At the end of last season Mr. Wilfrid H. Brookes resigned from the editorship, and from the Cricket Reporting Agency. In consequence I have taken on the responsibilities of co-ordinating the contributions from various sources and presenting them as a whole.' He dates it 'May, 1940' so the issue appeared later than normal.

1941

WISDEN 1941

78th Edition
Editor: Haddon Whitaker
Pages: 426
Price: Limp 5/- cloth 7/6d
Reprint: Willows 1999 (500 limit, in two formats)

THE WORLD AT LARGE

• Rommel begins his North Africa campaign
• Germany attacks the Soviet Union
• Japanese attack on Pearl Harbor brings United States into the war
• Orson Welles' masterpiece *Citizen Kane* has its premiere

CRICKET HEADLINES 1940

No first-class cricket is played in Britain

Vijay Hazare hits 316* for Maharashtra v Baroda, the first triple-century in India

Eric Rowan hits 306* for Transvaal v Natal, in a friendly but first-class match in Johannesburg

NOTES ON THE 1940 SEASON

by R.C. Robertson-Glasgow

'It is not easy to write notes on our First Class cricket season of 1940, because no competitive First Class cricket was played. Nearly all the County players were occupied in some form of National Service. The war was critical. Our ally France fell; and the British forces were evacuated from Dunkirk. There are those who still think that M.C.C. might have done more to encourage and foster the game. I cannot agree with this view. M.C.C. had given the County Clubs the opportunity to discuss the possibility of organised cricket, and nearly all the Counties in effect decided that such a thing would be impossible.'

FEATURE ARTICLES

Herbert Sutcliffe in First-Class Cricket

'Herbert Sutcliffe was born on November 25, 1894. In 1914 he played for Yorkshire 2nd eleven, scoring 249 runs and averaging 35.57 runs per innings. After serving in France as a commissioned officer, Sutcliffe was demobilised early in 1919, and immediately set to work to win a place in the Yorkshire team. In a match … between Yorkshire and Sixteen Colts, Sutcliffe opened the innings for the Colts, and retired after scoring 51 runs. He was included in Yorkshire's first match (v. M.C.C. at Lord's), scored 38 out of 120, and has been an essential part of the Yorkshire team ever since.'

Verity's Bowling, 1930-1939

OBITUARIES INCLUDE

Deaths in the War in 1940:

R.P. Nelson

'Robert Nelson's death is a tragedy. Having known him, you will appreciate what his loss means to this county. His own prowess allied to his patience with, and encouragement to, those under him worked wonders. At the end of 1937 the Northamptonshire side was a disorganised rabble. In two seasons he quietly and imperceptibly moulded them into a team which it was impossible to recognise as the same lot who had done duty before he took over the captaincy.'

P.T. Eckersley G.B. Legge G.G. Macaulay

Other deaths in 1940:

A.C. Bartholomew

'The oldest cricket Blue, passed away on March 29, some five weeks after completing his 94th year … He founded a cricket eleven and called them Guinea-pigs – because, he said, they had no tail.'

J.H.G. Devey
'If better known as a fine forward for Aston Villa and a director of the club for 33 years, John Devey was a very useful cricketer, doing good service in the Warwickshire Eleven from 1888 to 1907. A hard hitting batsman with plenty of strokes, he helped his County obtain promotion to the first class in 1895.'

M.A. Noble
'During his long career, Monty Noble showed exceptional ability in every detail of the game, and by many people was regarded as the greatest all-round cricketer produced by Australia. He excelled as a batsman, bowler, fieldsman and captain, notably in placing his field to block a batsman's favourite strokes ... Unable to continue a banking career when occupied so much with first-class cricket, Noble qualified in dentistry. As a lecturer on cricket he gained wide popularity in Australia, and his book, *Gilligan's Men,* gave graphic descriptions of events that happened in the 1924-25 season.' – Hubert Preston

F.G.J. Ford   M.K. Foster   W.P. Howell   T.R. McKibben   W. Wright

---

COUNTY REVIEW

Nottinghamshire
'In an effort to provide as much cricket as possible, Nottinghamshire played six matches, three with Royal Air Force teams and one each with Derbyshire, Leicestershire and the Notts and Derby Border League. Not only did these games show that leading county players now in the services retained their skill, but they brought to light some promising talent. Particularly noteworthy was the work as opening batsman of R.T. Simpson, a young policeman, of whom competent judges formed a high opinion ... The 1940 accounts showed a surplus of £43, but repairs and painting have not been done at Trent Bridge since the war began, and there is a bank overdraft of £525.'

MATCH REPORTS

Worcestershire v Warwickshire, *at Worcester, August 5*
'Worcestershire won by 91 runs. When an innings apiece was completed, each side batted for three-quarters of an hour. Among features of Worcestershire's batting was a polished display by Gibbons and a "hat-trick" by Mayer, who dismissed Gibbons, Perks and Singleton with following deliveries ... No charge for admission was made, but a ready sale of membership tickets for the Worcester Fighter Fund was popular among the crowd of some 2,000 ... Perks took seven wickets for the third time on consecutive days. On the Saturday he took seven for 68 runs for West Bromwich against Walsall, and on Sunday, in a charity match in Nottingham, seven men fell to him at a cost of 40 runs.'

This issue of Wisden *did not appear until December 1941, after the offices were hit in the Blitz, followed by a series of mishaps, as Haddon Whitaker explains in his Preface written in August 1941: 'First, the publishers' premises were completely destroyed by enemy action at the end of 1940, and a large part of the editorial material just being prepared for the printer was lost. Fortunately most of this was duplicated, but a small amount of interesting matter disappeared irretrievably. After this experience additional precautions were taken, and so when a further supply of editorial was charred beyond recognition in the printer's office safe, it could be replaced, although the re-compilation took some time. As a further blow the Public Schools section, entrusted to the post on the afternoon of the worst raid of the spring, did not reach its destination ... Finally, the printers, working under excessive pressure with a very much reduced staff, were unable through no fault of their own to provide their usual speedy service in production.'*

Wartime paper restrictions meant the print run was reduced from 8,000 to 3,200, with only 800 cloth-bound copies. As a result, the 1941 issue today attracts a premium.

In this edition, H.S. Altham first supplied a list of 'Some Dates In Cricket History', beginning a feature that is still a part of Wisden.

1942

WISDEN 1942

79th EDITION
EDITOR: Haddon Whitaker
PAGES: 391
PRICE: Limp 5/-   cloth 7/6d
REPRINT: Willows 1999 (500 limit, in two formats)

THE WORLD AT LARGE

- Fall of Singapore
- Malta awarded the George Cross
- Doolittle Raid on Tokyo
- Battle of Midway – U.S. naval victory stops the Japanese advance in the Pacific
- Germans halted at Stalingrad
- Rommel defeated at El Alamein
- Duke of Kent dies in an air crash

CRICKET HEADLINES 1941

53 matches played at Lord's during the summer, most of them one-day fixtures

In the 1940-41 season in Australia, Bradman plays only two matches, and makes only 18 runs in all, including two first-ball ducks

In the same season, Arthur Morris marks his first-class debut with a century in each innings

NOTES

by R.C. Robertson-Glasgow

'These one-day matches have given such good entertainment, where at one time little or none had been expected, that some critics have urged their retention as a regular process for the first-class County Championship in peace time. I do not agree with this view. Those who urge it most strongly would, I believe, be the earliest to tire of the experiment. The new clockwork monkey in the nursery, which waves its arms and waggles its head, delights for a few short hours or days. But the children soon return to the older, if more sedate toys, the tried companions in the familiar cupboard.'

FEATURE ARTICLES

County Championship Reviewed, by Hubert Preston

'In 1873 the Marylebone club offered a Champion County Cup for competition, all matches to be played at Lord's. The proposed tournament came to nothing because some acceptances of the invitation to play were withdrawn, but Kent and Sussex carried out their tie as arranged. Kent won by 52 runs in the only first-class county Cricket Cup-Tie. What became of the Cup seems an unsolved mystery.'

Hobbs hit 244 Hundreds in all Matches

'On his first appearance of the season, Jack Hobbs, at the age of 58, completed the Fathers' side against Kimbolton School, Huntingdonshire, and scored 116.'

W.R. Hammond in First-Class Cricket, by R.C. Robertson-Glasgow

OBITUARIES INCLUDE

Deaths in the War in 1941:

K. Farnes

'The Cambridge, Essex and England fast bowler was killed during the night of October 20, when the plane in which he was pilot crashed. His death at the age of 30 came as a great shock to countless friends and the whole world of cricket.'

G.J. Groves

'... died on February 18, as the result of a wound suffered through enemy action when at Newmarket on duty as a racing journalist. Born on October 19, 1868, in Nottingham, where his Yorkshire parents were on a visit, he had a county qualification which was discovered by a friend watching him make many runs for the Richmond club, and a recommendation obtained for him a trial when 30 years of age in the 1899 August Bank Holiday match at the Oval.'

D.F. Walker

Other deaths in 1941:

E.W. Dillon

'Very free in style, Dillon used his long reach to the best advantage. Going in to meet the ball, he drove straight and to the off with great power and placed his forcing strokes skilfully … Dillon took the highest honours in Rugby football. Developing into a splendid three-quarter when playing for Blackheath, he was capped against Scotland, Ireland and Wales in 1904 and next season against Wales.'

L.C. Eastman

'The Essex all-rounder, who was born at Enfield, died in Harefield Sanatorium on April 17, following an operation, at the age of 43. His end was hastened through a high-explosive bomb bursting close to him while he was performing his duties as an A.R.P. warden.'

R. Peel

'He scored 1,206 runs and took 128 wickets in all matches in 1896, the year before his remarkable career came to an end. Sent off the field by Lord Hawke during a game at Bramall Lane and suspended for the remainder of the 1897 season, he was not seen again in the Yorkshire team. He did, however, appear for an England XI against Joe Darling's Australian side at Truro two years later, taking five wickets. His benefit match at Bradford in 1894 realised £2,000.'

A. Sellers   A.J. Webbe

COUNTY REVIEW

Essex

'Apart from participating in the "Four Counties" match at Lord's, Essex played no first-class cricket. Nearly all their grounds were in prohibited areas, and the difficulty of raising teams decided the Committee to restrict their activities to fostering enthusiasm among the Schools.'

MATCH REPORTS

North v South Public Schools, *at Lord's, August 30. South won by 247 runs*

'Wilson, the North captain, was unfortunate in giving his rivals first innings. Deshon (Sherborne) completed his hundred before lunch, and his stand with Bailey realised 173 in an hour and fifty minutes. Their stroke play all round the wicket revealed marked skill in control and placing the ball. Bailey, bowling fast with accuracy and length, caused a complete collapse of the North batsmen. At one time he took three wickets in four balls.'

MISCELLANEOUS

'In May, 1941, the President of M.C.C., Mr. Stanley Christopherson, sent a letter to the Football Association expressing concern at the serious effect which the extension of the football season was having upon cricket, particularly upon games in the North of England and representative matches at Lord's.

Sir Pelham Warner told the Club Cricket Conference at their 1942 annual meeting that in July 1940 he was rung up by Mr. Ernest Bevin's secretary and asked to send a cricket team to the industrial North. After Dunkirk, men and women had been working extremely hard. Mr. Bevin *[Minister of Labour and National Service]* was anxious that some recreation should be provided for them.'

After the problems surrounding the 1941 edition, Haddon Whitaker breathes a sigh of relief in his Preface: 'Fortunately only small delay, due to the shortage of staff at printers and binders, has attended the production of this 79th annual issue of Wisden, *in contrast to the sustained efforts of the enemy to prevent publication of its predecessor.' He goes on to apologise to 'the many cricket lovers who were unable to obtain copies of last year's edition'. As well as the wartime paper restrictions, there was 'an actual shortage in the making of the supply of paper' which caused 'a serious shortage of copies'.*

1943

WISDEN 1943

80th EDITION
EDITOR: Haddon Whitaker
PAGES: 407
PRICE: Limp 6/6d   cloth 8/6d
REPRINT: Willows 2000 (500 limit, in two formats)

THE WORLD AT LARGE

• Allied invasions of Sicily and Italy: Italy surrenders
• Siege of Leningrad ends after 16 months: Germans retreat
• Churchill, Stalin and Roosevelt meet in Teheran
• Rodgers and Hammerstein's musical *Oklahoma!* opens on Broadway

CRICKET HEADLINES 1942

58 matches were played at Lord's, most of them one-day matches

Andrew Ducat dies while batting at Lord's for the Surrey Home Guard. The scorecard records 'not out 29'

NOTES ON SEASON 1942

by R.C. Robertson-Glasgow
'Every critic thinks that he alone is right; otherwise, why trouble to think at all? This confidence in personal judgement blossoms best in Sport, and in cricket comes to its full and redolent flower. A man may change his opinion about a Sten Gun or the Secretary of a Club; a woman may be converted to the tone of a wall-paper or the angle of feather; but no self-respecting follower of cricket will budge an inch from his view that A is the worst batsman who was ever invited, by mistake, to open the England innings, and that B is the best googly bowler who ever pined the afternoon away at deep long-leg. In short, no reasonable devotee is open to reason. It is too late to ask and too churlish to expect that this should be otherwise.'

FEATURE ARTICLES

Planning Post-War Cricket, by Norman Preston
'Many problems confronted the Counties, the chief being that of personnel. Few Counties could put a representative side into the field at short notice and no one was aware of the Government's plans for demobilisation and the control of man-power after the war. Certain grounds such as Kennington Oval, Old Trafford, and Bramall Lane, Sheffield, suffered severe damage from air raids, and some grounds which were requisitioned might not be free immediately hostilities ceased. Other obstacles were the possibilities of the continuation of travel and petrol restrictions, and the supply of equipments.'

OBITUARIES INCLUDE

Deaths in the War in 1942:
C.T. Ashton
'The triple Cambridge Blue and England Association football international was killed on active service on October 31 in a disaster which also caused the death of Squadron Leader R. de W.K. Winlaw, another Old Wykehamist and double Light Blue.'
R.J. Gregory
'Ross Gregory became one of the youngest cricketers to play in a Test, sharing in recent years with A.A. Jackson, S.J. McCabe and D.G. Bradman the distinction of playing for Australia before coming of age.'
H.R.H. Duke of Kent
'... life honorary member of Marylebone Cricket Club ...'

A.B.C. Langton
'... killed on active service in November, aged 30, was a member of the team which in 1935 gained the first triumph for South Africa in England, their victory by 157 runs at Lord's being the only definite result in the rubber. In that match he took six wickets for 89 – four for 31 in England's second innings, after helping Bruce Mitchell (164 not out) add 101 in two hours.'
R.G. Tindall   D.F. Walker   R. de W. K. Winlaw

Other deaths in 1942:
A. Dolphin
'Contemporary with Herbert Strudwick and E.J. Smith, Dolphin only once played for England – in the Fourth Test Match at Melbourne in February 1921, when Australia, captained by W.W. Armstrong, won the rubber with five victories over the team led by J.W.H.T. Douglas. During a career extending over 23 seasons, Dolphin held 488 catches and stumped 231 men.'
A. Ducat
'The sudden death at Lord's, on July 23, of Andrew Ducat, Surrey batsman of high talent and effective execution, England international Association footballer, captain of a cup-winning Aston Villa team, and in recent years cricket coach at Eton, came as a shock to countless friends and admirers. A man of delightful disposition, quiet and unassuming, he endeared himself to all who met him ... That Ducat should collapse and die, bat in hand, was the last thing anyone would have expected of such a well-set-up, vigorous, healthy-looking and careful-living man. Evidence of those in the field proved clearly that he expired directly after playing a stroke and as he prepared to receive another ball, for he was dead when carried to the pavilion.'
E.G. Arnold   Sir Jeremiah Colman   Rev. the Hon. Dr. E. Lyttelton   J. Stone

COUNTY REVIEW

Nottinghamshire
'The only county to carry through a programme during each year of the war, Nottinghamshire again showed a slight financial loss, due mainly to increased Income Tax and further reductions in members' subscriptions, but their officials felt that the position was not too serious. Playing cricket in the war entailed greater expense than if they had remained idle, but Mr. Brown, their enterprising Secretary, stated that the county considered the cost was worth while, for they kept the game alive and provided entertainment, as well as relaxation, for their followers.'

MATCH REPORTS

Army v Sir Pelham Warner's XI, *at Lord's, May 23, 25*
'Despite cold weather and rain the first big match of the season at Lord's drew nearly 7,000 people on Saturday and 9,000 on Monday. The Army were greatly indebted to two experienced left-handers in Leyland and Nichols for a stand of 90 after four wickets had gone for 61. Leyland withstood some very good bowling by Bedser and Clarke ... When Sellers declared leaving the opposition to make 191 in two and a quarter hours the game was sportingly carried on amidst continuous rain until it was given up at 6.15. The Red Cross received £170.'

MISCELLANEOUS

'Downend House, Downend, near Bristol, the birthplace of W.G. Grace, was sold on July 22. The buyer, Councillor H.F. Wren, who paid £1,200, expressed willingness to re-sell the house to any sportsmen who wished to form a "W.G." museum.'

In the Preface, Whitaker writes: 'The prices have had to be increased ... once again there will not be enough copies to go round – and I fear that of the 1944 edition, due a change in the working of the paper quota, there will be even fewer.' He adds: 'It has been found possible to include an abbreviated section of Cricket Records in response to the demands of those who have been unable to obtain copies of the 1939 and 1940 editions, the last in which this section appeared in full.'

1944

WISDEN 1944

81ˢᵗ EDITION
EDITOR: Hubert Preston
PAGES: 343
PRICE: Limp 6/6d   cloth 8/6d
REPRINT: Willows 2000 (500 limit, in two formats)

THE WORLD AT LARGE

- D-Day, 6ᵗʰ June: Allied troops invade Europe
- First V-1 and V-2 rocket attacks on Britain
- Attempt to assassinate Hitler by means of a bomb during a military planning meeting fails
- Paris liberated: Belgium and Netherlands also taken by Allies
- Blackout restrictions relaxed and Home Guard stood down
- Anne Frank and her family captured by the Gestapo
- Roosevelt wins a fourth term in office

CRICKET HEADLINES 1943

V.S. Hazare hits 309 for the Rest v Hindus in the final of the Pentangular Tournament in Bombay

MCC Select Committee formed to make proposals for post-war cricket

47 matches played at Lord's and 27 out-matches by MCC against schools

NOTES BY THE EDITOR

'When the question of war memorials is under discussion, nothing could prove more appropriate than the acquisition of the local cricket ground as perpetual reminder of what this greatest of games has done for the youth and manhood of Great Britain and her offspring in all parts of the world. Already Club Cricket Conference are concerned at the danger of many club enclosures being used as a help towards solving the housing problem; consequently an immediate move would seem advisable to secure such well-kept places as health resorts for the players and people of all ages.'

FEATURE ARTICLES

The Best Fast Bowler – Account of 'W.G.' Beard Incident, by Sir Stanley Jackson
Australians in English Club Cricket, by Bruce Andrew

OBITUARIES INCLUDE

Deaths in the War in 1943:
W.A.S. Clarke
  '... posthumously awarded the Victoria Cross, showed skill in all games at Uppingham. A useful bowler, he was in the School Second XI, and in 1935 took part at Lord's in two "under sixteen" games... A splendid soldier, he fell gloriously on St. George's Day, April 23, at Guiriat El Atach. After skilfully leading his platoon, he personally put guns out of action and though wounded, he advanced alone to within a few feet of the enemy before being killed. His grandfather, Colonel Sandys, was cousin of Field-Marshal Lord Roberts and General Sir W.M. Congreve, both of whom won the V.C., as also did their sons – a wonderful record of five V.C.s in one family.'
L.G.H. Hingley
  'He played for M.C.C. in the Rugby Centenary match. He arrived at the school late, and so did not appear in the photograph reproduced in 1942 Wisden; actually he went to the wicket within six hours of his return from a bombing raid on Dusseldorf.'

166

H. Verity

'Judged by any standard, Verity was a great bowler. Merely to watch him was to know that. The balance of the run up, the high ease of the left-handed action, the scrupulous length, the pensive variety, all proclaimed the master. He combined nature with art to a degree not equalled by any other English bowler of our time. He received a handsome legacy of skill and, by an application that verged on scientific research, turned it into a fortune.' – R.C. Robertson-Glasgow

Other deaths in 1943:
Lord Gainford

'… continued playing cricket until he was 74, when, as he wrote to Mr. Bulmer, secretary of Durham County C.C., "Inability to take a quick run forced me to give up the game".'

C.H. Parkin

'… earned the description cricket's chief comedian. Of medium height and rather slim, eccentric in character and in action, he brought every known device besides his own special jugglery into his right-arm bowling … Altogether in first-class cricket Parkin was credited with 1,060 wickets at an average cost of 17.49. As a batsman he was useful at times and showed good style, but his average of 11.47 denotes uncertainty to a high degree. Parkin told his early cricket life in a very vivacious book and, in conformity with his cricket gestures, was a conjurer of no mean ability.'

R.K. Tyldesley

'In 1930 his benefit match, when Surrey visited Old Trafford, realized £2,027, although it clashed with England versus Australia at Trent Bridge where Tyldesley was engaged. At different periods Dick Tyldesley shared in the Lancashire bowling honours with Cecil Parkin and E.A. McDonald, the Australian – and now all three are dead.'

Sir Russell Bencraft   F.L. Bowley   F.W. Tate   G.J. Thompson

---

COUNTY REVIEW

Yorkshire

'Yorkshire maintained their quest for young talent, and George Hirst, hale and hearty at the age of 71, visited every part of the county to coach promising players. Over four hundred passed through his hands, including a number of left-arm bowlers of merit.'

MATCH REPORTS

Sir Pelham Warner's XI v R.A.A.F, at Lord's, June 3

'Although beaten, the Australians made a good impression. In Miller they possessed a batsman of ability, graceful drives and crisp cuts bringing him 45 out of 53 in just over half an hour.'

England v The Dominions, at Lord's, August 2, 3

'England won by eight runs. A match remarkable for many changes of fortune and sensational incidents ended at a quarter to seven in a narrow victory for England, thanks to Robertson taking the last two wickets in the only over he bowled.'

Haddon Whitaker explains in a Publisher's Note how it had been 'advisable' that the co-ordination of the wartime issues should be dealt with by the publishers. 'That this policy was correct in the early war years is evidenced by Wisden's continued appearance despite the attentions of the enemy which certainly at the time seemed to be directed against its production.' But now there is a new editor, Hubert Preston, with whom the publishers 'look forward to many years of association' – a wish that was fulfilled. The new editor regretted that 'shortage of paper has again compelled the omission of "Cricket Records" – unchanged while the first-class game remains in abeyance.'

An advertisement is included for An Index to Wisden 1864 to 1943 compiled by Rex Pogson, which 'is being printed now for publication in the Autumn of 1944'. It has since become an intrinsic part of any Wisden collection.

1945

WISDEN 1945

82nd EDITION
EDITOR: Hubert Preston
PAGES: 367
PRICE: Limp 6/6d   cloth 8/6d
REPRINT: Willows 2000 (500 limit, in two formats)

THE WORLD AT LARGE

• Death of President Roosevelt
• Suicide of Hitler and surrender of Nazi Germany
• Atomic bombs are dropped on Hiroshima and Nagasaki
• Churchill and the Conservatives defeated by Attlee's Labour Party in General Election

CRICKET HEADLINES 1944

Three first-class triple-hundreds are scored during the winter of 1943-44, by Hazare and Merchant in India and by Worrell in West Indies

41 matches played at Lord's, despite flying-bombs

NOTES BY THE EDITOR

'Last summer some counties improved their programmes and expressed readiness to resume their places in the championship competition directly world conditions remove the paramount obstacle, or to engage in the emergency plan on a regional basis as decided by the special M.C.C. committee … Many prominent players have kept in practice with Service teams and several of high promise profited in the same way, so that confidence may be felt in the possibility of every county putting an eleven in the field. The urgent need will be for all to resume without worrying about getting together a team fully worthy of the county's strength – and, from what one hears, that is the general desire and resolution.'

FEATURE ARTICLES

Seeing Cricket After Four Years, by E.M. Wellings
'This one-day cricket has been good stuff for the casual Saturday afternoon spectator, and for the out-and-out enthusiast once a week under existing conditions, but it could hardly be expected to appeal as a regular dish. We should soon tire of seeing the skill of a Hammond, a Denis Compton or a Hutton being cast into the maelstrom of this hastily concocted game.'
Views and Values, by R.C. Robertson-Glasgow
Australian Survey, by A.G. Moyes
Cricketers of the Year, by A.S. Dixon

OBITUARIES INCLUDE

Deaths in the War in 1944:
F.G.H. Chalk
'For Uppingham, Oxford and Kent he batted and fielded so brilliantly that he became an attractive figure whenever he played.' *[See also obituaries, Wisden 1990.]*
E.M. Grace
'A grandson of the great hitter and lob bowler, Dr. E.M. Grace, "The Coroner," of Gloucestershire and England after whom he was christened, died of typhoid fever on March 14, the illness being caught when on active service in Italy. A useful cricketer, left-handed with both bat and ball … in build he resembled his illustrious grand-uncle W.G. Grace, and fielded finely close to the wicket – a characteristic of his grandfather as described in *The Cricketer*. He was aged 28.'
G.D. Kemp-Welch
'In February 1932 Kemp-Welch went to Jamaica with a team captained by Lord Tennyson, and … was associated with a record by an opponent, G. Headley scoring 344 not out, the highest individual innings played by a West Indies batsman. Kemp-Welch made 105 in the

same match and 186 in the return encounter with All Jamaica ... In 1934 he married Mrs. Richard Munro, daughter of Mr. Stanley Baldwin.'

M.J. Turnbull
'The news of his death came through while Glamorgan were fulfilling one of their war-time fixtures at Cardiff Arms Park, the scene of his first century and many subsequent triumphs. And, as the crowd stood in respectful silence, perhaps the more imaginative or sentimental among them may have pictured for a fleeting instant the well-known figure out there on the field, and derived some small measure of comfort. For Glamorgan were carrying on: and he would have wished that. – J.C.Clay'

Other deaths in 1944:
A.W. Lupton
'The unusual experience fell to him of captaining a county for the first time when 46 years of age, and he celebrated the notable choice of the Yorkshire club by leading them in 1925 to their fourth consecutive Championship. He retained the office for two more years and altogether scored 668 runs with an average of 10.27, but did not take a wicket.'

G.J.V. Weigall
'A stickler for orthodox batting, Gerry Weigall used to amuse and delight all comers in the Pavilion at Lord's with his portrayal of the correct follow through in the off-drive and of his stylish cut with a borrowed bat, stick or umbrella. Seldom did he miss a Kent match, and at Canterbury Gerry Weigall could be described as part of the Festival.'

Sir Julien Cahn   J.T. Hearne   C.E. Kellaway   A.C. MacLaren   J.W. Trumble   C.T.B. Turner

COUNTY REVIEW

Kent
'Except for the match at Lord's, where Kent and Surrey drew with Middlesex and Essex, the Kent club did not give its name to any fixture, but again the St. Lawrence ground at Canterbury was in constant use; always available for troops stationed in the district and war-time workers, the headquarters of Kent was the scene of 115 games during the season.'

MATCH REPORTS

Barbados v Trinidad, *at Bridgetown, February 12, 14, 15, 16*
'In the match, which saw the setting up of a new world record for a fourth-wicket partnership, only fifteen wickets fell while 1,210 runs were scored. J.B. Stollmeyer, Trinidad opening bat, played his highest innings; Gomez, brilliant in his cover-driving, helped him add 161 for the third wicket, and Jones took part in an eighth wicket stand of 105. Naturally, most enthusiasm was reserved for Worrell and Goddard. They came together in the late afternoon of the second day with the Barbados score 148 for three, and were undefeated, having put on 502 in 6 hours and 44 minutes, when Barbados declared at quarter to three on the fourth day. Worrell revelled in the fast bowling and drove it powerfully. When he passed Stollmeyer's 210 a Barbadian admirer rushed to the wicket and presented his countryman with a large white chicken.'

MISCELLANEOUS

'Mr. R.V. Ryder, who has given up the Secretaryship of Warwickshire after nearly fifty years' service to the club, wrote "Trials of a County Secretary" in 1936 *Wisden*. He took office when Warwickshire rose to first-class status in 1895. Only the late Mr. A.J. Lancaster, who was with Kent from 1885 to 1935, held the position of County Secretary for a longer period.'

An advertisement appears for Rex Pogson's Index to Wisden, *published at 15 shillings, with an example page. 'It answers immediately such diverse questions as: What teams have toured the Argentine? Did B.J.T. Bosanquet ever write in* Wisden *and on what? When did the Australians visit the U.S.A. to quote only three at random from the specimen page.'*

1946

WISDEN 1946

83rd EDITION
EDITOR: Hubert Preston
PAGES: 479
PRICE: Limp 6/6d   cloth 8/6d

THE WORLD AT LARGE

- League of Nations wound up and replaced by United Nations Organisation
- Winston Churchill delivers his 'Iron Curtain' speech in Fulton, Missouri
- Television licence introduced
- Juan Peron elected President of Argentina
- King Victor Emmanuel of Italy abdicates: one month later Italy is declared a republic

CRICKET HEADLINES 1945

First-class cricket resumes after the war, but there is no County Championship

England and Australia share the Victory Test series two games all, with one drawn

Eleven first-class matches were played during the summer: Len Hutton hit the most runs (782) but Keith Miller hit the most centuries (3)

The Australian Services tours India on its way home from England, and loses the representative 3 match series 1-0

NOTES BY THE EDITOR

'C.G. Pepper and Keith Miller emulated the giants of the past – not in the rate of scoring but in the carry of their big drives. In [the] Dominions match at Lord's, Miller on-drove a ball to the roof of the broadcasting box over the England dressing-room at a height said to exceed that of the record hit by Albert Trott which cleared the pavilion. That was one of seven 6's by Miller in a score of 185. Pepper hit six 6's while making 168 in two hours and a half at Scarborough against H.D.G. Leveson Gower's eleven. He revelled in straight drives, one of which off Hollies cleared the four-storied houses and landed the ball in Trafalgar Square.'

FEATURE ARTICLES

Cricket under The Japs, by E.W. Swanton
'With the Australian innings comes sensation. Captain Fizzer Pearson, of Sedbergh and Lincolnshire, the English fast bowler, is wearing BOOTS! No other cricketer has anything on his feet at all, the hot earth, the occasional flint being accepted as part of the game. The moral effect of these boots is tremendous. Captain Pearson bowls with shattering speed and ferocity, and as each fresh lamb arrives for the slaughter the stumps seem more vast, the bat even punier. One last defiant cheer from The Hill when their captain, Lieut.-Colonel E. E. Dunlop, comes in, another and bigger one from the English when his stumps go flying.'
Hundred Years of Surrey Cricket, by H.D.G. Leveson Gower
Edward Paynter, by R.C. Robertson-Glasgow

OBITUARIES INCLUDE

Deaths In The War in 1945:
J.G. Halliday

Supplementary Deaths in the War in 1940–1944:
K.C. Gandar-Dower
'In all, he represented Cambridge at six forms of sport: tennis, lawn tennis, Rugby fives, Eton fives, squash rackets and billiards. In fact, time hardly sufficed for their rival calls. He probably created a record when he played simultaneously in the Freshmen's Match and Freshmen's Tournament, with the connivance of the tennis but not the cricket authorities; he disappeared

to play off a round during the early part of his side's innings, with relays of cyclist friends to keep him informed as to the fall of wickets!'

C.P. Calvert   C.W. Walker

Other deaths in 1945:

C.J. Eady

'Of exceptional build, six feet three inches tall and weighing fifteen stone, he excelled in Tasmanian club cricket, but during his one visit to England in 1896 he failed to reveal his powers either as batsman or bowler … [He] was best known for his 566 scored out of 908 in less than eight hours for Break-o'-Day against Wellington in March 1902.'

P.A. Perrin

'While his batting was of a quality often described as faultless, one defect in his cricket hindered his progress to representative cricket. Often he was described as the best batsman who never played for England and the explanation was – inability to field with any spark of speed. Heavy on his feet, he could not move quickly to the ball, and this deficiency, though he would hold any catch within his long reach, prevented him from ever appearing in a Test match.'

E. Smith

'His free batting and fast bowling often proved valuable, as he made full use of his height and weight. A schoolmaster, he was a welcome member of the Yorkshire XI during vacations from 1888 to 1907, and in the absence of Lord Hawke, he occasionally captained the side.'

A.E. Dipper   C. Hill   E.M. Sprot   G.B. Studd

COUNTY REVIEW

Hampshire

'Nowhere in the United Kingdom did the turmoil of war cause more unrest than in Hampshire with its ports always used for essential work, and, until Germany surrendered, the county club were compelled to give up match play. Fortunately, the Southampton ground, apart from buildings, escaped injury, and, with many old players available, Hampshire arranged for 1945 a series of fixtures which proved both interesting and valuable in helping to get the county into active operation after a lapse of six seasons.'

MATCH REPORTS

England v Australia, Fifth Victory Match, *at Old Trafford, August 20, 21, 22*

'After six years of transport restrictions, the sight of dozens of special omnibuses labelled "Cricket Ground" was something remarkable with VJ Day less than a week behind … Rain halved the second day's cricket, but thousands of northerners showed their keenness for cricket by turning up first thing in the morning in the drenching rain. The weather turned fine a twelve o'clock … Hassett surprised many people by not having the wicket rolled between the innings. In any case the heavy roller was not available, as it was requisitioned during the war and used to lay out airfields in the Middle East.'

1947

WISDEN 1947

84th EDITION
EDITOR: Hubert Preston
PAGES: 747
PRICE: Limp 7/6d   cloth 9/6d

THE WORLD AT LARGE

- Britain nationalises its coal industry
- India and Pakistan gain independence from Britain.
- John Cobb sets world auto speed record at 394.2mph
- USAF pilot Captain Chuck Yeager breaks the sound barrier in level flight for the first time.
- Princess Elizabeth marries Lieutenant Philip Mountbatten

CRICKET HEADLINES 1946

County Champions: Yorkshire

England win the Test series against India 1-0, with two games drawn

Alec Bedser takes 11 wickets in each of his first two Tests

NOTES BY THE EDITOR

'Although handicapped by execrable weather, both wet and cold, the resumption of first class cricket showed in every way how ready players and public were to welcome their favourite pastime.'

FEATURE ARTICLES

South Africa and England, by R.C. Robertson-Glasgow
'We would do well to forget the Tests played in South Africa during 1938-39; not their social delights and friendships, but their cricket; that thirty-runs-an-hour crawl, and that grand climacteric of the ten-day Test when the homebound ship foreclosed on the battle between eight and a half whole Englishmen and seven and three-quarter South Africans still erect upon their legs.'

FIVE CRICKETERS OF THE YEAR

V. Mankad
'As chief agent in India's attack Mankad was called upon in first-class matches to bowl 1,160 overs, 380 in excess of any of his colleagues... In so doing he took 129 wickets, more than twice as many as the next most successful Indian bowlers, Hazare and Amarnath (56 each). As a batsman, accustomed at home to going in first, he was given no settled place but used rather as a utility man. In spite of so much bowling responsibility and the irregular batting position Mankad showed himself a very fine player... Mankad took part in the biggest stands of the tour for the first, fourth, sixth and eighth wickets.'
A.V. Bedser   L.B. Fishlock   T.P.B. Smith   C. Washbrook

OBITUARIES INCLUDE

A.E.E. Vogler.
'... whom R.E. Foster and many other great batsmen regarded as the best bowler in the world in the year 1907, died on August 10, aged 69 ... Scarcely any batsman claimed that he could detect differences in Vogler's delivery of either the googly or the leg-break. Vogler also mixed the off-break with a ball which came straight through at greater pace, and occasionally sent down a most deceptive slow yorker.'
J. Darling   J. Iddon   J.H. King   Sir Francis Lacey   J. Vine

Surrey v India *at Kennington Oval, May 11, 13, 14*
'A record-breaking last wicket stand between Sarwate and Banerjee featured India's first victory of the tour … Nine men were out for 205 when the last pair came together. They were not separated for three hours ten minutes, their partnership of 249 being the highest ever recorded for the last wicket stand in England. Never before in history had the nos. 10 and 11 in the batting order each scored a century in the same innings. Both Sarwate and Banerjee gave masterly displays.'

England v India (First Test Match) *at Lord's, June 22, 24, 25*
'Alec Bedser, one of the Surrey twins, accomplished probably the finest performance ever recorded by a bowler in his first Test Match. Using his height, six feet two inches, to the full extent and putting his weight behind every ball, Bedser maintained an admirable length at fast-medium pace, with swerve or spin which often turned the ball appreciably from the sodden turf.'

Yorkshire v Middlesex, *at Sheffield, August 17, 18, 20*
'A thunderstorm stopped play at quarter to five on Monday and, as the game went, the loss of time thus caused helped Middlesex to avoid defeat in a very exciting finish. When the fifth Middlesex wicket fell just before half past five, the time fixed for drawing stumps, Sellers claimed the extra half hour and set a field close in for Booth and Robinson, the slow spin bowlers. Sensation followed; Booth got Allen stumped and Harrington splendidly caught at slip next ball. Mann left in the following over without addition but Trapnell, the Cambridge Blue, held out with Sims for the last ten minutes.'

Yorkshire
'Yorkshire, Champion County from 1937 to 1939 and twelve times between the two wars, proved that the long break from first-class cricket in no way affected their ability by carrying off chief honours, just as they did after the First World War.'

Sussex
'Finishing last in the County Championship, Sussex experienced their worst season for fifty years; one has to look back to 1896 to find a parallel situation.'

North v South, *at Scarborough, September 11, 12, 13*
'The revival of this match, a regular feature for many years, proved popular, but unfavourable weather, particularly on the last day, when a piercing westerly wind made the conditions barely possible for cricket, affected attendances. Sellers appropriately led the winners, and he completed his 1,000 runs for the season, while Keeton raised his aggregate to over 2,000. Leyland concluded his first-class career by taking the last two South wickets, a return catch leaving him with the ball before going to President F.C. Whitaker's tent and receiving from H.D.G. Leveson Gower a cheque in appreciation of his association with many Scarborough Festivals.'

In his Preface, Hubert Preston writes: 'Many hindrances have contributed to another late appearance of Wisden. *Most troublesome was the abnormal winter with heavy snow blizzards which blocked railways, causing a shortage of coal with consequent curtailment of electric light and heat, to the detriment of printing facilities. This was the more regrettable because in covering the first full season of English cricket since 1939, the book returns practically to pre-war size.'*

1948

WISDEN 1948

85th EDITION
EDITOR: Hubert Preston
PAGES: 875
PRICE: Limp 9/6d   cloth 12/-

THE WORLD AT LARGE

- UK railway companies nationalised to form British Railways
- Mahatma Gandhi assassinated
- Independent state of Israel declared.
- MV *Empire Windrush* docks at Tilbury
- NHS launched in Britain
- Summer Olympics in London
- Muhammad Ali Jinnah, founder of Pakistan, dies
- Prince Charles born

CRICKET HEADLINES 1947

County Champions: Middlesex

South African tourists lose the Test series to England 3-0

Denis Compton and Bill Edrich rewrite the batting record books – Compton hits 18 centuries and scores 3,816 runs in the season, both still records

NOTES BY THE EDITOR

'In every way the season of 1947 bears favourable comparison with any year within living memory. This eulogistic remark applies equally to the cricket itself, personal performances in style and technique, quite apart from remarkable individual records.'

FEATURE ARTICLES

No Magic in Fast Bowling, by C.J. Kortright

'If England can find a real fast bowler who is willing to take a bit of advice from an old-timer, here is a wrinkle he might well remember. He should never forget to try bowling a fast yorker on the leg stump to a newly arrived batsman. It can be a deadly ball to face early in an innings; I have dismissed many top-class batsmen with it.'

FIVE CRICKETERS OF THE YEAR

N.W.D. Yardley

'His batsmanship is an admirable mingling of business and pleasure. He watches the ball carefully and hits it hard, and is therefore as welcome in a Festival as in a Test match. Much of his run-getting is to the on, where no contemporary plays the forcing stroke more neatly or convincingly.'

M.P. Donnelly   A. Melville   A.D. Nourse   J.D. Robertson

OBITUARIES INCLUDE

G. Challenor

'He excelled for the team which came in 1923, scoring 1,556 runs – more than twice as many as anyone else in the side obtained – average 51.86, with eight three-figure innings, the highest being 155 not out against Surrey at The Oval ... Generally he was regarded as reaching the standard set by the best English batsmen that season, only Hendren and Mead returning higher averages. He was elected to membership of M.C.C. as a special compliment, although unable to take part in the customary qualifying matches ... His admirable batting did much toward raising cricket in West Indies to Test match standard.'

Sir Stanley Jackson

'In the South African War Jackson served with the Royal Lancaster Regiment of Militia, and in the first Great War, 1914-18, he was Lieutenant-Colonel of a West Yorkshire Regiment battalion which he raised and commanded. He entered Parliament in 1915 and remained Unionist member for Howdenshire Division of Yorkshire until 1926. One day in the House of Commons dining room Mr. Winston Churchill, who had been his fag at Harrow, said, "Let me introduce you to Mr. Lloyd George." There came a quick exclamation, "I have been looking all my life for the man who gave Winston Churchill a hiding at school." When he wanted to make his maiden speech the debate went unfavourably, and he received a note from the Speaker: I have dropped you in the batting order; it's a sticky wicket. Then, at a better opportunity, he sent this hint: Get your pads on; you're next in.' – Hubert Preston

F.A. Mackinnon,

'The Mackinnon of Mackinnon (35th Chief of the Mackinnon Clan), the title to which Mr. Francis Alexander Mackinnon succeeded on the death of his father in 1903, passed away … on February 27. He would have been 99 years old on April 9. As it was he reached a greater age than attained by any other first-class cricketer.'

W.W. Armstrong   J. Hardstaff senior

MATCH REPORTS

England v South Africa, Third Test Match, *at Manchester, July 5, 7, 8, 9*

'England won by seven wickets … For being left to get only 129 in a possible two hours and a half England owed much to Edrich. To the end of the second South African innings he was on the field all the time except for half an hour, and, besides making his highest score in Test cricket, he sent down 57 overs of considerable speed for eight wickets … Apart from him and Wright, who was handicapped by his foot, England's bowlers looked ordinary. Washbrook again showed his intention of scoring quickly before the effects of the rolling wore off. In fifty-five minutes he punched his way to 40 out of 63, and his appreciation of the position soon afterwards became evident when Mann's left-arm leg-breaks began to turn nastily. Hutton and Compton found this to their cost, but Barnett hit merrily, and his winning stroke brought a Manchester Test to a definite conclusion for the first time for ten years.'

Middlesex (Champion County) v Rest of England, *at The Oval, September 13, 15, 16, 17*

'Middlesex won by nine wickets. The match provided further personal triumphs for Compton and Edrich, who concluded their remarkable season in superb style. Compton, despite a heavily strapped knee which restricted his freedom, played his highest innings in England and was only three short of the 249 he made for Holkar against Bombay in the Indian Championship final of 1944/45. Edrich followed Compton in beating Hayward's record aggregate.'

COUNTY REVIEW

Gloucestershire

'When, in their opening county fixture, Gloucestershire suffered a crushing reverse from Middlesex at Lord's, they gave no indication that they would participate in one of the closest fights for the Championship for many years. Their fielding was deplorable, the bowling unimpressive, and the loss of the run-getting powers of W.R. Hammond, who retired from first-class cricket upon returning from the M.C.C. Australian tour, appeared likely to prove irremediable.'

MISCELLANEOUS

'Cricket history has been made in Malaya, where a father and his sons, "The Augustins" have fielded an eleven during the past two years. The father is Mr. J.F. Augustin, headmaster of a government English school (the Ibrahim School) in Sungei Patani, Kedah … Of twelve matches played, the "all-Augustin" team have won eight and lost four.'

1949

WISDEN 1949

86th EDITION
EDITOR: Hubert Preston
PAGES: 943
PRICE: Limp 9/6d   cloth 12/-

THE WORLD AT LARGE

- NATO established
- People's Republic of China proclaimed by Mao Zedong
- Republic of Ireland becomes fully independent of U.K.
- USSR tests first nuclear bomb
- George Orwell's *1984* published
- First test flight of De Havilland Comet jet airliner

CRICKET HEADLINES 1948

County Champions: Glamorgan

The touring Australians beat England 4-0

Bradman is bowled second ball in his final Test innings, thereby ending with an average of 99.94

A few months later in Australia, Bradman hits his 100th hundred

NOTES BY THE EDITOR

'The triumph of Glamorgan reminds me of the time when St. Paul's School, "One and All", and other clubs were tenants at The Oval. My brother, who was at St. Paul's, took me for a "pick-up" game one August morning, and when we were settling down, Shepherd, the groundsman, came to us and said, "Now, boys, pull up your stumps, there's a match to-day." "What is it, Shepherd?" "Surrey Club and Ground v. Eighteen of Glamorgan." And from such a humble start about seventy years ago the Welsh county have become champions.'

FEATURE ARTICLES

Cricket and the British Commonwealth, by Rt Hon. Herbert V. Evatt
'In spite of the bare figures and the results, I am convinced that the difference between the Elevens of Australia and England was not considerable … Fortune always counts for much in these contests, and … in the long run, these things always even up. Who would dare to say that, in five years' time, the cricket supremacy within the British Commonwealth will not have passed to the West Indies? What a boon that would be, even if only to drive home the lesson that in cricket it is not an affair only of Lord's or The Oval or of Sydney or Melbourne.'
Sir Donald Bradman, by R.C. Robertson-Glasgow
W.G. Grace Centenary, by Hubert Preston
Glamorgan's March of Progress, by J.H. Morgan

FIVE CRICKETERS OF THE YEAR

R.R. Lindwall
'Putting power, rhythm and purpose into every stride of a sixteen-paced approach, this magnificent fair-haired athlete, five feet eleven inches tall and weighing nearly twelve stone, from the moment of starting his run-up indicates a fine bowler, and, though his arm does not go over as high as the purists wish, he has preferred to retain his action and body swing rather than risk losing natural abilities in trying to bowl with an altered delivery.'
A.L. Hassett   W.A. Johnston   A. Morris   D. Tallon

OBITUARIES INCLUDE

Sir C. Aubrey Smith
'… famous in the world of cricket before making a name on the stage and becoming a universal favourite on the films in comparatively recent years, died on December 20, aged 85,

at Beverly Hills, California … He maintained his love for cricket to the end. Until a few years ago he captained the Hollywood side and visited England for the Test matches … He was knighted in 1944 in recognition of his support of Anglo-American friendship. A very good Association outside-right, he played for Old Carthusians and Corinthians.'

W.E. Astill   E.H. Killick   A.D. Nourse   J. Tunnicliffe

England v Australia, Fifth Test Match, *at Kennington Oval, August 14, 16, 17, 18*
'Everything became different when Australia batted. Barnes and Morris, with controlled assurance and perfect stroke play, made 117, and shortly before six o'clock Bradman walked to the wicket amidst continued applause from the standing crowd. Yardley shook hands with Bradman and called on the England team for three cheers, in which the crowd joined. Evidently deeply touched by the enthusiastic reception, Bradman survived one ball, but, playing forward to the next, was clean bowled by a sharply turning break-back – possibly a googly.'

Sussex v Somerset, *at Eastbourne, August 18, 19, 20*
'An innings of real merit by Gimblett, who hit his highest score in first-class cricket and set up a record for a Somerset batsman with 310 runs, overshadowed all else in a game that yielded 1,097 runs for 19 wickets. Gimblett, who offered difficult chances when 45 and 115, drove with great power on an easy-paced pitch, and in his stay of nearly seven hours and three-quarters he hit two 6's and thirty-seven 4's.'

Glamorgan
'On the afternoon of Tuesday, August 24, 1948, Glamorgan set the seal on a wonderful season by winning the County Championship for the first time. Appropriately, J.C. Clay, a member of the original side which entered the competition in 1921 and whose name has become synonymous with Glamorgan cricket, played a leading part in the victory that day … While strongly supplied with bowlers – six players took more than thirty wickets each – the batting frequently revealed limitations; but, paradoxically though it may seem, this very weakness influenced Glamorgan's triumph. Had the team made bigger totals, they would not have provided their bowlers with sufficient time to dismiss opponents for reasonably low scores.'

'Payments to England professionals in the Test Matches with New Zealand in 1949 were fixed thus: £40 per match; twelfth man, if selected as reserve, £25; reserves £20. Umpires £25. In addition players will receive railway fares and hotel expenses; and umpires get railway fares and hotel accommodation arranged by executive of the grounds concerned.'

1950

WISDEN 1950

87th Edition
Editor: Hubert Preston
Pages: 1011
Price: Limp 9/6d   cloth 12/-

THE WORLD AT LARGE

- India becomes a republic
- Attlee's Labour wins a second term in office
- North Korean troops cross 38th parallel into South Korea, precipitating war
- Deaths of George Orwell and George Bernard Shaw
- *The Archers* is first broadcast, and first publication of *Peanuts* strip cartoon

CRICKET HEADLINES 1949

County Champions: Middlesex and Yorkshire

All four Tests against the visiting New Zealanders were drawn

Hutton scores 1,000 runs in each of two months, June and August

B.B. Nimbalkar scores 443* for Maharashtra v Kathiawar, and is only nine runs behind Bradman's record when Kathiawar concede the match

NOTES BY THE EDITOR

'We constantly hear of overworked players needing rest. Colonel Rait Kerr ... said that "the New Zealanders became a very tired side by July," yet our men are expected to go through the full season without a suggestion of staleness. In order to reduce the risk of spoiling our leading players by too much cricket – and abroad our men have received criticism for slackness, clearly due to want of rest – the arranged dates for tours were amended; but the fixture list at home is more crowded. This is likely to reduce the quality of our cricket.'

FEATURE ARTICLES

Coaching The Schoolboy, by John D. Eggar
'It is not possible to alter faulty technique by intensive personal coaching, such as is available in Alf Gover's school. To do so would be to sacrifice the cricket of the school for the benefit of one individual ... One should remember, too, that the bat lift of most modern Australians, the delivery of Bill O'Reilly, and the action of Clarrie Grimmett would have come in for much harsh criticism if employed by boys in the representative matches at Lord's.'
Warwickshire's Ups and Downs, by M.F.K. Fraser
Tribute to Hutton, by V.G.J. Jenkins
M.P. Donnelly, by R.C. Robertson-Glasgow
West Indies In Test Cricket, by Jack Anderson

FIVE CRICKETERS OF THE YEAR

R.O. Jenkins
'He is eager to learn, ready to take advice, and always thinking of the problems before him. His bowling action is typical of a man of restless, nervous energy. After a short, fidgety roll to the wicket there comes a flailing of arms before Jenkins releases the ball with an almost round-arm action. He tosses the ball higher into the air than most leg-break bowlers, but is swift to adapt his methods against the quicker-footed batsmen.'
T.E. Bailey   John Langridge   R.T. Simpson   B. Sutcliffe

S. Christopherson

'One of ten sons who, with their father, used at various periods in the 'seventies and 'eighties to form a family cricket eleven and play certain matches, mostly against schools in the Blackheath district. A man of great personal charm he was in his young days extremely good looking. During the difficult war years, M.C.C. could not have possessed a better man as President. He was a big figure in the City of London and ... yet despite the calls of business, he went to Lord's on most days and rarely missed a Committee meeting. In all walks of life he always played the game.'

F. Hearne

'He toured South Africa with Major R.G. Wharton's team in 1888-89 and played in two Test Matches for England. Subsequently he settled in South Africa and was engaged by the Western Province Cricket Club. In 1891 he appeared for South Africa when England went to that country and also played in three Tests in the 1895 English tour. In 1894 he was a member of the first South African team to visit England.'

George Cox snr.   A. Fielder   L.H. Gay   E. Humphreys   C.A. Ollivierre   F. Walden

Yorkshire v Minor Counties, *at Lord's, June 11, 13, 14*

'The most satisfactory feature of this interesting match was the successful first appearance at Lord's of two bowlers, Berry, 23-year-old left-arm slow from Lancashire, and Trueman, 18-year-old right-arm fast-medium, of Yorkshire. Berry flighted the ball skilfully and produced genuine leg-spin ... When the Counties were left to make 272, they broke down against Trueman, who took the first five wickets which fell for 44.'

Leicestershire v Nottinghamshire, *at Loughborough, June 11, 13, 14*

'Walsh, with his unorthodox left-arm spin bowling, sorely tried Nottinghamshire, although the pitch favoured batsmen. He achieved a hat-trick by dismissing two men at the close of the Nottinghamshire first innings, and another with his first ball in the second innings ... Hooking strongly, Prentice hit thirty-three 4's during his third century in consecutive matches and made his best score in first-class cricket.'

'For the first time since 1889 the County Championship resulted in a tie, Middlesex and Yorkshire, after a stirring struggle, sharing first place. This was the fifth instance of a tie in the history of the competition, first instituted in 1873.'

Surrey

'There were days when Surrey looked the best team in the County Championship... Instead they fell from second place to fifth. Yet Surrey were the only side to beat each of the Joint-Champions; they overcame Middlesex twice and Yorkshire, once.'

Hubert Preston writes in the Preface: 'This 87th edition of Wisden *differs from its predecessors. For the first time each county section is illustrated with two portraits of leading players and the county badge. With more and more time devoted to radio commentaries, we include diagrams of the chief county grounds, annotated so that broadcast or television descriptions can be followed more easily.'*

Another innovation is John Arlott's review of the previous year's books. He writes: 'One might have expected a small output of cricket books in 1949 after the spate which greeted the Australians in 1948. More than seventy books dated 1949, however, stand before me ...'

1951

WISDEN 1951

88th EDITION
EDITOR: Hubert Preston
PAGES: 1035
PRICE: Limp 10/6d   cloth 12/6

THE WORLD AT LARGE

• Festival of Britain runs from May to September on the South Bank of the Thames
• Treaty of Paris establishes the European Coal and Steel Community, a forerunner of the EU
• Conservative Party wins the General Election
• J.D. Salinger's *The Catcher In The Rye* published

CRICKET HEADLINES 1950

County Champions: Lancashire and Surrey

West Indies beat England by three matches to one, thanks to the spin bowling of Ramadhin and Valentine

Les Ames hits his 100th hundred

Jim Laker takes 8 wickets for 2 runs in the Test Trial match

NOTES BY THE EDITOR

Exuberant Batting by West Indies

'To see their batsmen was an education in the chief purpose of cricket – run-getting – while in bowling and fielding they adopted every means to check speedy scoring by their adversaries in the true sporting spirit of cricket with obvious intent to dismiss the batsmen concerned. To these valedictory remarks I would add the modest bearing of our visitors from the Caribbean, and venture to suggest that Australia will find West Indies difficult to circumvent when they become adversaries.'

FEATURE ARTICLES

John Wisden's New Century, by Lord De L'Isle

'John Wisden, already part-proprietor with George Parr of the Leamington ground, started in 1850 Parr and Wisden's Cricket Club, with which he associated the business of sports outfitter. Five years later he moved to London and opened a Cricket and Cigar depot in Coventry Street off the Haymarket. There, radiant with watch and chain of gold, he became at once the well-to-do, courteous proprietor of a West End cricket emporium.'

Fifty Years of Lancashire Cricket, by Neville Cardus

'It is commonly thought that Lancashire cricket has always expressed North-country dourness and parsimony. This is an error. In 1904 Lancashire won the County Championship without losing a match; and until an August staleness afflicted the team, the rate of scoring by Lancashire averaged 70 to 80 – some days 100 – an hour. No county has boasted three batsmen going in Nos. 1, 2, and 3 possessing more majesty than A. C. MacLaren's, more style and ripple of strokes than R. H. Spooner's, more broadsword attack and brilliance than Johnny Tyldesley's.'

Leslie Ames, A Century of Centuries, by Vivian Jenkins
Ups And Downs On The Veld, by Louis Duffus

FIVE CRICKETERS OF THE YEAR

A.L. Valentine

'Although Valentine bats right-handed, he uses his left for everything else. He did not attempt to model his style on any other bowler, preferring to develop in his own way. Unlike most bowlers, Valentine does not mark the spot where he starts his run. He simply judges the distance to the wicket, takes a few steps, and bowls almost square to the batsman. His action takes little out of him and he can carry on for hours without tiring. Every night he uses surgical spirit to harden the skin of his spinning finger, and this prevents soreness and discomfort.'

S. Ramadhin   T.G. Evans   E.D. Weekes   F.M.M. Worrell

OBITUARIES INCLUDE

R.N.R. Blaker
'His twin daughters, Barbara and Joan, known as the Blaker Twins, were prominent members of the Kent women's cricket team and both played for England. During the last Canterbury Week his tent was the centre of pleasant entertainment, but he showed signs of ill-health and in little more than a month passed away.'

D.W. Carr
'One of the most remarkable cricketers at the start of the century. He was an unknown bowler when, at the age of 37, he entered first-class cricket. Originally an ordinary fast-medium bowler, Carr developed and practised the googly, then almost unknown, and his arrival with this unorthodox type of bowling created consternation among batsmen.'

D. Denton
'Possessed of very flexible wrists, Denton made strokes all round the wicket with considerable hitting power, while he played forward so hard that he always made the ball travel. On fast wickets he seized every opening to score on the off side, cutting in particularly brilliant fashion, and when the ground was slow he employed the pull and the hook with fine effect. The force of his strokes was surprising as he was below medium height and lightly built. He batted in exceptionally good style and never lost any time in getting to work.'

H.K. Foster   A.J.L. Hill   A.J. Holmes   H.S. Squires   S.J. Staples

COUNTY REVIEW

Hampshire
'Hampshire cricket in 1950 was largely experimental, with more opportunities given to youth. For this reason the county's rise from 16th to 12th place in the table was quite satisfactory. Early in June they were third, but the finish was disappointing and only two victories came in the last fourteen matches.'

MATCH REPORTS

England v West Indies, (Second Test Match), *at Lord's, June 24, 26, 27, 28, 29*
'No blame could be attached to the pitch. It gave slow bowlers a little help, but only to those who used real finger spin as did Ramadhin and Valentine. Ramadhin bowled with the guile of a veteran. He pitched a tantalising length, bowled straight at the wicket and spun enough to beat the bat. No English batsman showed evidence of having mastered the problems of deciding which way Ramadhin would spin and he was too quick through the air for any but the most nimble-footed to go down to meet him on the half-volley with any consistency.'

The article by Lord De L'Isle (part quoted above) begins: 'The name of Wisden *is a household word wherever cricket is played, or indeed spoken about. The centenary of the firm which still bears the name of its founder was a notable event in the annals of 1950.' He ends by recounting how at the firm's centenary luncheon, when the principal guest was the President of the Board of Trade, Harold Wilson, a message of congratulations were received from the Australian Prime Minister, Robert Menzies, who said: '*Wisden *and cricket are synonymous.' Lord De L'Isle eulogises: 'Let this message from Australia be the tribute of the whole British Commonwealth at once to a famous cricketer, to the great enterprise which he founded, and to the game of cricket wherever it is played.'*

1952

WISDEN 1952

89th Edition
Editor: Norman Preston
Pages: 1039
Price: Limp 12/6d   cloth 15/-

THE WORLD AT LARGE

- Death of King George VI: Princess Elizabeth becomes Queen
- De Havilland Comet becomes the world's first commercial jet airliner
- *New Musical Express* publishes the first British record sales chart
- *The Mousetrap* opens in London
- Olympic Games held in Helsinki

CRICKET HEADLINES 1951

County Champions: Warwickshire

England beat the touring South Africans by three Tests to one

Australia thrash England by four matches to one during the MCC winter tour of 1950-51

Peter May, still a Cambridge student, announces his arrival by topping the averages with 2,339 runs at 68.79, and nine centuries for four different teams

Len Hutton scores his 100th hundred

NOTES BY THE EDITOR

The editor suggests that the West Indian team returned from their Australian tour 'believing that they cannot meet Australia on level terms until they produce bowlers of like speed and method. That is, men capable of sustained attack of fast short-pitched bowling with the ball repeatedly flying around the batsman's head. In its origin cricket was never meant to be played that way. No matter what the issue involved, the game is greater than the individuals. It is a sad thought that sometimes this truth is submerged in the quest for victory and those with the interests of the game at heart regard the frequent use of the bumper as a menace. Action should be taken before someone is hurt, and hurt seriously.'

FEATURE ARTICLES

How Test Players Are Raised, by Lindsay Hassett
'It is not uncommon for a talented lad of fifteen or sixteen years of age to be selected for his club's first eleven, and then the chances are that he will find himself playing in a match with or against two or three of the current Australian team. Australians generally do not subscribe to the belief that a young player can be spoiled by introducing him into first-class cricket too soon, and I believe that the early contact with inter-state and international players in our Saturday afternoon District cricket does more to improve the young cricketer than any other factor in the organisation of the game in my country.'

Modern County Cricket, by Col. R.S. Rait Kerr

A Call for Culture, by Neville Cardus

F.R. Brown: Leader of Men, by Vivian Jenkins

Twenty Years of Indian Test Cricket, by Vijay M. Merchant

Growth of Hampshire Cricket, by E.D.R. Eagar

Tom Goddard Retires, by David Moore

FIVE CRICKETERS OF THE YEAR

H.E. Dollery
'This is not the place to weigh the arguments for and against professional captains, but no one could disagree that, by his skill and knowledge of the game, his bearing on and off the field, and his ability to summon the best from those under him, Dollery revealed all the finest

qualities of leadership. On personal achievement in runs, 1951 was by no means Dollery's best season, but there could be no doubt that he was one of the personalities of the year.'
R. Appleyard   J.C. Laker   P.B.H. May   E.A.B. Rowan

OBITUARIES INCLUDE

J. Doig
'Born in Victoria, Australia, he went to New Zealand at an early age. As a youth he made a name as a bowler and during his career he was credited with no fewer than fifty hat-tricks. On five occasions he took all ten wickets in an innings, and he would have performed the feat a sixth time but for a dropped catch.'

J.S. Heap
'During his career with Lancashire, Heap took 400 wickets at an average of 23.75 runs each, and scored over 5,000 runs. Unfortunately he was handicapped through periodical attacks of lumbago, otherwise his full county record would have been more imposing.'

R.M. Murray
'... died on April 8 from injuries received when he fell accidentally while visiting a sick friend at Hanmer Springs, Canterbury, New Zealand. Aged 23, he was a right-arm medium-pace bowler and promising batsman who would probably have represented New Zealand but for his tragic death.'

Lord (Lionel) Tennyson
'Under his inspiring leadership, Hampshire accomplished some remarkable performances, the most notable being that in the match with Warwickshire at Birmingham in 1922. Then Hampshire, after being dismissed for 15, followed-on, put together a total of 521 and gained an extraordinary victory by 155 runs. Later in the same season, in a game against Yorkshire on a most difficult pitch at Bradford, where the average score was less than nine, he went in first and knocked up 51 out of 64, a fearless display which decided the issue. His funeral took place during the first Test match between England and South Africa at Trent Bridge, and play was stopped for a brief period as a tribute to his memory.'

W.G. Quaife   H. de Selincourt   F.A. Tarrant

COUNTY REVIEW

Nottinghamshire
'The steady decline of the post-war years reached a climax in 1951 when Nottinghamshire, for so long among the most powerful of cricket counties, found themselves at the foot of the table for the first time in their long history ... As soon as the season was completed the wicket area at Trent Bridge was cleared to the depth of an inch and the subsoil lifted, the top being reseeded. It was hoped that this treatment would bring about a fairer balance between bat and ball.'

MATCH REPORTS

Australia v England, Second Test Match, *at Melbourne, December 22, 23, 26, 27*
'Australia won by 28 runs ... All seemed to depend on Hutton, and he batted correctly for two hours forty minutes for 40 out of 70 until mishitting Johnston to mid wicket. Some of the other batsmen offered an excess of caution which played into Australia's hands. Possibly they were overawed by thoughts of breaking Australia's long run without defeat. Bedser, the number ten batsman, looked so much at ease that the failures of some of his colleagues received greater emphasis. At the end the impression could not be avoided that if England had been left with three or four hours to make the runs instead of three whole days they would have adopted different, and probably more successful, methods.'

Norman Preston takes over as editor, explaining in the Preface: 'After an unbroken association with Wisden *from 1895 my father, Mr. Hubert Preston, on the advice of his doctor, reluctantly retired last June.'*

1953

WISDEN 1953

90th EDITION
EDITOR: Norman Preston
PAGES: 1035
PRICE: Limp 12/6d   cloth 15/-

THE WORLD AT LARGE

- Dwight D Eisenhower inaugurated as President of U.S.
- Death of Stalin
- Coronation of Queen Elizabeth II
- Matthews' Cup Final – Blackpool beat Bolton 4-3 in a thrilling final
- Sir Gordon Richards finally wins the Derby, on Pinza
- Edmund Hillary and Tenzing Norgay climb Mount Everest
- Korean Armistice signed

CRICKET HEADLINES 1952

County Champions: Surrey

England defeat India 3-0 with one match drawn, after sharing the series one match apiece during the winter on the subcontinent

Pakistan play their first Test series, against India, losing the series by two matches to one

Seven players do the double of 1,000 runs and 100 wickets

Denis Compton completes his century of centuries by scoring 107 against Northants at Lord's

NOTES BY THE EDITOR

'The expansion of cricket overseas was emphasised during the past winter when England alone of the Test match countries took a well-earned rest. Pakistan, newly elected to the Imperial Cricket Conference, began their official Test career with a tour of India, and later India went to the West Indies. South Africa visited Australia and New Zealand. In less than eighteen months India took part in no fewer than nineteen Tests... This extension indicates the healthy condition of world cricket, for which M.C.C. as pioneers must be given credit. At the same time I feel sure M.C.C. welcome it from another angle, for with more countries becoming internationally minded they may be able to enjoy more breaks from close-season commitments.'

FEATURE ARTICLES

Australia Throw Down the Gauntlet, by Neville Cardus
'The glory of the game is that its genius, whenever it changes – as change it must if it is to survive and evolve – remains the same creative thing. Spofforth or Barnes or O'Reilly or Tate or Bedser; Grace or Hobbs; Bradman or Fry; Tyldesley or Compton; Hayward or Hammond; Albert Ward or Hutton; Lockwood or Larwood; Richardson or E.A. McDonald; Peel or Briggs; Rhodes or Verity; Oldfield or Evans; J.M. Gregory or Keith Miller; they are not competitors for renown or for our admiration. They are planets in conjunction, equal in distinction and immortality. *Amurath* unto *Amurath*. Eternal sunshine falls on them all.'
A.V. Bedser: A Giant Among Bowlers, by R.C. Robertson-Glasgow
History of Derbyshire Cricket, by W.T. Taylor

FIVE CRICKETERS OF THE YEAR

D.S. Sheppard
'Quiet and unassuming, Sheppard for a long time considered giving up regular cricket to concentrate on the Church … His loss to the game would have been unfortunate, but in September it was announced that he had accepted an invitation to captain Sussex for 1953. Thus, for the moment, Sheppard remains in cricket … Sheppard's captaincy will no doubt be watched closely, for here is a possible future leader of England.'
H. Gimblett   T.W. Graveney   W.S. Surridge   F.S. Trueman

184

H.M. King George VI
'When Prince Albert he performed the hat-trick on the private ground on the slopes below Windsor Castle, where the sons and grandsons of Edward VII used to play regularly. A left-handed batsman and bowler, the King bowled King Edward VII, King George V and the present Duke of Windsor in three consecutive balls, thus proving himself the best Royal cricketer since Frederick, Prince of Wales, in 1751, took a keen interest in the game. The ball is now mounted in the mess-room of the Royal Naval College, Dartmouth.'

C.J. Kortright
'... probably the fastest bowler in the history of the game, died at his Brentwood home on December 12, aged 81 ... A man of splendid physique, standing six feet and possessing abundant stamina, Kortright took a long run and hurled the ball down at a great pace. He was fond of recounting the tale of a club match at Wallingford where, so he declared, he bowled a ball which rose almost straight and went out of the ground without a second bounce. This, he asserted, made him the first man to bowl a six in byes!'

N.B.F. Mann
'The untimely death of this modest and likeable man, known throughout the cricket world as Tufty, was yet another grievous blow to a country which has lost so many fine cricketers in their playing prime. Taken ill soon after the Fourth Test in England in 1951, he underwent an abdominal operation and stayed in England for three months before flying home. He bore his troubles with the steadfastness and patience which characterised him in all things, but another operation became necessary midway through 1952 and he died some six weeks later.'

A. Hearne   A.H. Hornby   H. Makepeace   A.W. 'Bosser' Martin   Nawab of Pataudi

COUNTY REVIEW

Somerset
'Lack of pace bowling and inability to strengthen weak spots in the team by the introduction of fresh talent brought serious repercussions for Somerset. After a disastrous season they finished bottom of the table for the first time ... the only ray of sunshine came from Gimblett, who, like a true cavalier of cricket, produced a galaxy of powerful strokes with more frequency than before and made his benefit year a record one in a personal sense.'

MATCH REPORTS

Australia v West Indies, Fourth Test Match, *at Melbourne, December 31, January 1, 2, 3, 4*
'No more exciting finish could be imagined than that in which Australia made sure of winning the series and West Indies lost the chance of drawing level at two games each, with the rubber depending upon the final game. Hard though they had fought, the Australians seemed doomed to defeat when their ninth wicket fell in the final innings with 38 runs still needed for victory. Then the two bowlers, Ring and Johnston, defied all the efforts of the West Indies to dislodge them and hit off the runs amid mounting tension. Johnston played a comparatively passive role while Ring hit vigorously, gaining a series of boundaries by lofty drives which may have resulted in catches had the field been set deep enough for this known hitter.'

'Dates in Cricket History' which first appeared in the 1941 Wisden is greatly expanded by H.S. Altham.

1954

WISDEN 1954

91st EDITION
EDITOR: Norman Preston
PAGES: 1019
PRICE: Limp 12/6d   cloth 15/-

THE WORLD AT LARGE

• Roger Bannister becomes the first man to break the four-minute barrier for the mile
• Queen Elizabeth and the Duke of Edinburgh return to UK in May after a six-month tour of the Commonwealth
• Food rationing finally ends in Britain
• Winston Churchill celebrates his 80th birthday while still Prime Minister: his fellow parliamentarians give him a portrait of himself by Graham Sutherland – he hates it and eventually his wife destroys it
• First broadcast of *Hancock's Half Hour*

CRICKET HEADLINES 1953

County Champions: Surrey

England win back the Ashes after 19 years, with victory in the final Test, after four drawn games

Alec Bedser takes a record 39 wickets in the Test series

Surrey beat Warwickshire by an innings in one day: only 243 runs are scored as 29 wickets fall – 12 of them to Alec Bedser for 35 runs

Lancashire spoil Bertie Buse's benefit by beating Somerset in one day at Bath; Roy Tattersall takes 13 for 69

NOTES BY THE EDITOR

'When ninety years ago the cricketers of England and Australia began to visit each other they did so mainly for pleasure. The reverse is now often the case in first-class cricket. Watching some modern batsmen at the wicket one gains the impression they are shouldering the burdens and troubles of the whole world. They certainly give little indication of enjoyment. A horrible new term has crept into cricket – "Occupation of the Crease". It means the time has arrived in the day's proceedings when the batsmen shuts out of his mind all ideas about runs and goes back entirely on the defensive.'

FEATURE ARTICLES

Growth of Pakistan Cricket, by Abdul Hafeez Kardar
'In the summer of 1948, with characteristic national optimism, the Board of Control for Cricket in Pakistan was formed. It had to start from scratch, for the undivided assets were retained by the India Board. The four provincial associations – Punjab, North West Frontier Province, Sind and Bhawalpur in Pakistan, had to reintroduce cricket. The response was slow. The name of Mr. Justice A.R. Cornelius will continue to be associated with Pakistan cricket for the services he rendered to the game at this critical time. Almost single-handed he established the Board and succeeded in popularising cricket. It is not an over-estimation to say that cricket has now become the national sport of Pakistan.'
Thirty Years an Umpire, by Vivian Jenkins
Sussex through the Years, by A.E.R. Gilligan
Batsmen must be Bold, by F.R. Brown
A.L. Hassett: A Born Cricketer, by Neville Cardus

186

K.R. Miller
'The place and circumstance of Miller's birth were not without coincidence. He, the youngest of four children, was born at Sunshine, Melbourne, on November 28, 1919, at a time when Sir Keith Smith and Sir Ross Smith were creating world history with the first flight from England to Australia. It took 27 days 20 hours. His parents gave him the Christian names of the two famous airmen. Years later his own exploits in the air, as a night fighter pilot, earned for him a reputation as a dashing, devil-may-care fellow which his subsequent approach to big cricket confirmed.'
R.N. Harvey   G.A.R. Lock   J.H. Wardle   W. Watson

OBITUARIES INCLUDE

Rev. E.T. Killick
'Perhaps it was not altogether surprising that he showed a natural aptitude for games, for he came from a sporting family. A brother, G.S. Killick, represented Great Britain at rowing in the Olympic Games. Another brother was a wing three-quarter, and Stanley, the youngest, also played Rugby and cricket. E.T. Killick was for a time chaplain at Harrow School... He had been Vicar of Bishop's Stortford since 1946.'

J.R.M. Mackay
'*Wisden* of 1907 stated … The sensation of the season was the wonderful batting of J.R.M. Mackay … In face of such form it would seem that a great mistake was committed in not bringing him to England in 1905... Shortly after, Mackay accepted a lucrative position in Johannesburg and was very successful in South African cricket. The question arose as to whether he should be a candidate for selection in the 1907 South African team to tour England, but it was felt that he had not lived lone enough in the Union to qualify. This was a great disappointment to him, for he thus had the hard luck of just missing two visits to the Mother Country.'

L.G. Wright
'Of his fielding, E.M. Grace used to relate how on one occasion when a batsman kept poking at the ball and cocking it up, Wright crept in closer and closer till he was only a yard or so away from the striker. Soon the fieldsman thought he saw his chance of a catch. He made a grab and the crowd cheered, but it was the bat he held, not the ball!'
W. Findlay   Canon F.H. Gillingham   E.G. Hayes   T. Wass   D.R. Wilcox

COUNTY REVIEW

Leicestershire
'Surpassing even their excellent record of 1952, Leicestershire, under the inspiring captaincy of C.H. Palmer, achieved their highest position in the County Championship since entering the competition in 1895. During August, indeed, they succeeded in heading the table for the first time in their history, and eventually they finished level third with Lancashire, only 28 points behind the champions, Surrey.'

MATCH REPORTS

England v Australia, Fifth Test Match, *at the Oval, August 15, 17, 18, 19*
'England won by eight wickets … Edrich magnificently hooked two successive bumpers from Lindwall. Now he was joined by his Middlesex colleague, Compton, and they took England to victory. Compton made the winning hit at seven minutes to three when he swept Morris to the boundary. At once the crowd swarmed across the ground while Edrich, who batted three and a half hours and hit six 4's, fought his way to the pavilion with Compton and the Australian team. In a memorable scene both captains addressed the crowd, stressing the excellent spirit in which all the matches had been contested both on and off the field. The attendance for the Test reached 115,000 and the receipts amounted to £37,000.'

1955

WISDEN 1955

92nd EDITION
EDITOR: Norman Preston
PAGES: 1031
PRICE: Limp 12/6d   cloth 15/-

THE WORLD AT LARGE

- Winston Churchill resigns as Prime Minister; Sir Anthony Eden takes over and holds a General Election, which the Tories win
- Death of Albert Einstein
- ITV service begins
- President Peron of Argentina forced to resign
- Clement Attlee resigns as leader of the Labour Party: Hugh Gaitskell succeeds him
- Ruth Ellis is the last woman to be hanged in Britain

CRICKET HEADLINES 1954

County Champions: Surrey

Pakistan win a Test match on their first tour of England, and halve the four-Test series

England and West Indies win two matches each in the Caribbean, but the tour is marred by bottle-throwing in Georgetown

Surrey dismiss Worcestershire for 25 and 40, and despite declaring at 92 for 3, win by an innings and 27 runs. Only 157 runs are scored – the lowest-ever aggregate for a completed championship match

NOTES BY THE EDITOR

'After the 1954 County Championship final table was published, Mr J.C. Masterman, Worcester College, Oxford, wrote to *The Times:* "Is it not worth noting that the seventeen counties would finish in precisely the same order if the number of matches won was the only figure which was taken into account? Is it just possible that a simple tally of wins is as good a criterion as any one of some seventeen more elaborate systems of scoring points, and that the county which has won the most matches outright is the most worthy to hold the Championship?" Already M.C.C. have made a move towards checking defensive bowling wide of the leg-stump. They resolved that such bowling was neither in the spirit nor in the interests of the game, and that all county clubs should point out to their respective captains the undesirability of such tactics being employed *in any circumstances* in English first-class cricket. M.C.C. also have stated their concern at the tempo at which on occasions the first-class game has been played. Throughout 1954 a record was kept of the number of overs bowled an hour in each innings in each county match. These problems are not confined to county or English cricket as a whole. Time wasting has for too long been a feature of Test cricket. Hutton came in for much criticism from Australian officials and the local newspapers for the stalling which went on when England were in the field, particularly at Melbourne, but Hutton retorted that he learned these tactics in his younger days from the Australians themselves. It is useless attaching the blame to anyone. More important is it to stamp out all negative methods and make cricket the spectacle the public pay so generously to watch.'

FEATURE ARTICLES

The Story of Yorkshire, by J.M. Kilburn
'In the nine seasons between 1931 and 1939 Yorkshire were County Champions seven times and there is no knowing how long their dominance would have continued but for the interruption of the Second World War. When cricket came again the greatness had gone. Sutcliffe and Wood passed into retirement; Bowes was no longer a fast bowler after four years in prison camps; Verity died of wounds in Italy. In 1946 the remainder of the old guard reassembled to win yet another Championship but their success contained the sunset gleam.'
South Africa Offer Serious Challenge, by Neville Cardus
Twilight Reflections, by Sir Pelham Warner

Fazal Mahmood
'Many of Fazal's successes were gained on matting pitches and the Pakistan authorities, realising that their cricketers might be at a disadvantage when touring England, sent a party of young players … here in 1953. Fazal was among them and, besides learning about English conditions, he benefited from the coaching of A.R. Gover, the former Surrey fast bowler. A special feature of Fazal's bowling is his astonishing stamina. For this he owes much to his father, who insisted on a rigid training schedule. From 1940 to 1947 Fazal went to bed no later than 10 p.m. He rose each morning at 4.30 a.m., and whatever the weather, walked five miles and ran five miles."
B. Dooland   W.E. Hollies   J.B. Statham   G.E. Tribe

G.H. Hirst
'Such was his prowess with bat and ball for Yorkshire in a career spanning forty years that Lord Hawke described him as the greatest county cricketer of all time. Certainly this blunt, outspoken man of extreme buoyancy and cheerfulness brought such a tenacity to the game that no match in which he figured was won or lost till the last ball was bowled. Small wonder, therefore, that in Yorkshire he was an unchallenged hero, and throughout the length and breadth of England his popularity stood unrivalled.'
Sir Henry Leveson Gower
'Known wherever cricket is played as Shrimp, a nickname given him, presumably because of his slight physique, during his schooldays, he was born at Limpsfield, Surrey, on May 8, 1873, the seventh of twelve sons of Mr. G.W.G. Leveson Gower … Aside from his playing ability, probably his best service to cricket, for which he was knighted in 1953, was rendered as a legislator and Test Selector.'
W. Bardsley   H.R. Bromley-Davenport   C.B. Harris   W. Mead   C.F. Root

Worcestershire
'The reasons for so many disappointing displays were not difficult to find. Apart from Kenyon, Richardson and Outschoorn, the batsmen lacked resolution and the attack, with an abundance of medium pace, never looked balanced. At the same time the bowlers would have reaped far greater reward had the fielding reached a better standard.'

West Indies v England, Third Test Match, *at Georgetown, British Guiana, February 24, 25, 26, 27, March 1, 2*
'Apparently disagreeing with the decision … sections of the crowd hurled bottles and wooden packing-cases on to the field and some of the players were fortunate to escape injury. The President of the British Guiana Cricket Association went out and suggested to Hutton that the players should leave but Hutton preferred to remain. He wanted more wickets. His was a courageous action for which he deserved much praise.'
England v Pakistan, Second Test Match, *at Nottingham, July 1, 2, 3, 5*
'Compton sent the bowling to all parts of the field with a torrent of strokes, orthodox and improvised, crashing and delicate, against which Kardar could not set a field and the bowlers knew not where to pitch. By methods reminiscent of his former glories, Compton raced through his second hundred in eighty minutes and he made his highest score in his 100 innings for England in four hours fifty minutes before missing a leg-break from Khalid Hassan who, at 16, was the youngest cricketer to be chosen for a Test match.'

Norman Preston warns in the Preface: 'The continuous rise in printing prices coupled with the growth of first-class cricket may compel us either to make drastic cuts in the size of the book or to increase the price which has remained the same since 1952.'

1956

WISDEN 1956

93rd Edition
Editor: Norman Preston
Pages: 1075
Price: Limp 15/-   cloth 17/6d

THE WORLD AT LARGE

- Elvis Presley records *Heartbreak Hotel*
- First performance of John Osborne's play, *Look Back In Anger*
- Olympic Games in Melbourne – Britain wins six gold medals
- Suez Crisis: Anglo-French attacks launched against military targets in Egypt, but US/UN pressure brings quick ceasefire
- Soviet Union crushes revolt in Budapest
- Grace Kelly marries Prince Rainier of Monaco
- President Eisenhower wins a second term in office

CRICKET HEADLINES 1955

County Champions: Surrey

England retain the Ashes in Australia thanks largely to the fast bowling of Statham and Tyson

New Zealand dismissed for 26 by England at Auckland – the lowest-ever Test total

India tour Pakistan and play out the first ever series of five drawn games

South Africa tour England, narrowly losing the Test series by three matches to two

Clyde Walcott scores five centuries in West Indies' home series against Australia, including two hundreds in a match twice

NOTES BY THE EDITOR

'The part cricket plays in cementing good relations between the various members of the British Commonwealth of Nations has yet again been recognised in the Queen's Honours. In the Birthday Honours of June 1955 the award of the M.B.E. to George Headley, the West Indies batsman, was announced, and in the last New Year's Honours Ian Johnson, the Australian captain, and Keith Miller, the Australian vice-captain, received similar recognition for their services to sport.'

FEATURE ARTICLES

Two Eras of Australian Pace, by I.A.R. Peebles
'Gregory and McDonald have one very special niche in all cricket history. At least so far as international cricket is concerned they were the pioneers of all fast opening attack. Since then it has been regarded as the most effective use that can be made of the new ball, and it can well be argued that two fast bowlers, provided they are of quality, have had more influence on the result of a given series than any other factor, with the possible exception of the phenomenal Bradman. In support of this view I would cite Larwood and Voce; Martindale and Constantine in their own country, Lindwall and Miller and finally Statham and Tyson. There have been many fine individual performers during the same time, but it seems that the combined effort is necessary to derive the fullest service from the individual.'
Growing Pains of Cricket, by W.E. Bowes
Len Hutton: The Master, by Neville Cardus
Centenary of The Free Foresters, by Col. K.B. Stanley

FIVE CRICKETERS OF THE YEAR

F.H. Tyson
'In the first Test match in Australia, Tyson took only one wicket and that at a cost of 160 runs, and it looked as though the selectors had made a mistake in choosing him. Then he shortened

his run by three or four yards with remarkable results. In the second Test at Sydney he took four wickets for 45 and six for 85, and in the third at Melbourne achieved his best performance by dismissing seven men for 27 runs in the second innings … Such was his pace that Australian journalists gave him the pseudonym of Typhoon Tyson.'

M.C. Cowdrey   D.J. Insole   D.J. McGlew   H.J. Tayfield

OBITUARIES INCLUDE

L.C. Braund
'His slip-catching was phenomenal. In the 1901 Gentlemen v. Players match at Lord's he dismissed C. B. Fry with the catch of the season and in the 1902 Test match at Birmingham he disposed of Clem Hill with a long talked-about effort which helped Rhodes and George Hirst dispose of Australia for 36 – the smallest total for which they have been dismissed in a Test. Anticipating a leg-glance by the left-handed Hill off Hirst, the fast left-arm bowler, Braund darted across from slip to the leg-side and held an amazing catch.'

W.H. Brookes
'… was Editor of *Wisden* from 1936 to 1939, and for several years until the outbreak of the Second World War a partner in the Cricket Reporting Agency.'

F.L. Fane
In Wisden 1957, this apology appeared: 'Owing to an unfortunate error, the 1956 *Wisden* reported the death of Mr. F.L. Fane, the former Essex and England cricketer. The error occurred because of a similarity of initials. The Mr. F.L. Fane who died in December 1954, was Mr. Francis L. Fane, a cousin of the cricketer, Mr. Frederick L. Fane. By a coincidence, Mr. Fane informs us, his father also once read his own obituary!'

G.L. Jessop
'There have been batsmen who hit the ball even harder than Jessop … but no one who did so more often or who, in match after match, scored as rapidly. Where Jessop surpassed all other hitters was in the all-round nature of his scoring. At his best, he could make runs from any ball, however good it might be. Although only 5 ft. 7 ins. in height, he bent low as he shaped to play, a method which earned him the sobriquet of The Croucher.'

A.G. Fairfax   R.C.N. Palairet   S.G. Shinde

COUNTY REVIEW

Lancashire
'Lancashire in 1955 were still in the process of transition and while their performances again proved only mediocre some encouraging signs for the future were to be found. The development of youth, however, takes time without producing immediate results, and for the second successive season the county finished in the middle of the Championship table.'

MATCH REPORTS

Australia v England, Third Test Match, *at Melbourne, December 31, January 1, 3, 4, 5*
'England won by 128 runs at nineteen minutes past one on the fifth day with a day to spare … Australia still required 165, a task that seemed far from impossible. The pitch was worn and the experts predicted that England must look to Appleyard, pointing out that the conditions were made for his off spin, and probably they were right, but Tyson and Statham saw England home without Hutton having to look elsewhere for any bowling. Sheer speed through the air coupled with the chance of a shooter at any moment left the Australian batsmen nonplussed. Tyson blazed through them like a bush fire. In seventy-nine minutes the match was all over, the eight remaining wickets crashing for 36 runs.'

There is a price increase of half a crown to fifteen shillings – but the editor, although he had warned of the possibility a year earlier, does not mention it in his Preface or his Notes.

1957

WISDEN 1957

94th EDITION
EDITOR: Norman Preston
PAGES: 1051
PRICE: Limp 16/-   cloth 18/6d

THE WORLD AT LARGE

- Harold Macmillan succeeds Anthony Eden as Prime Minister
- The Gold Coast becomes the first of Britain's African colonies to become independent, as Ghana
- The first Premium Bond prizes are distributed
- Juan Manuel Fangio wins his fourth consecutive Formula One World Championship
- Death of Humphrey Bogart
- Lewisham train disaster: 90 die

CRICKET HEADLINES 1956

County Champions: Surrey, for a record fifth successive year

Jim Laker takes 19 wickets for 90 runs in the Fourth Test at Old Trafford, the greatest match bowling performance of all time

England retain the Ashes

Lancashire beat Leicestershire by ten wickets to become the first team in first-class history to win a match without losing a wicket in either innings

Everton Weekes scores five hundreds in successive innings as West Indies tour New Zealand

West Indies win the series, but New Zealand record their first Test victory in their 45th Test over 26 years

NOTES BY THE EDITOR

'The advocates who would confine county cricket to the weekend had a shock during the winter when, by a large majority, the counties directed the Special Committee not to consider the possibility of playing on Sundays. The whole of English first-class cricket is built on the membership of the County Clubs. The members are the backbone of county cricket and no doubt thousands would withdraw their support if they were deprived of mid-week cricket.'

FEATURE ARTICLES

Stuart Surridge: Surrey's Inspiration, by D.R. Jardine
'To borrow a metaphor from the hunting field, Surridge would have been as popular a Master as he proved himself a successful captain. He showed great sport; he went for and achieved definite results, and the number of his kills was satisfactory to a degree. In the course of doing this he undoubtedly entertained the public – but only incidentally. One knew that, had the fortunes of Surrey required it, entertainment would have been relegated to limbo.'

How West Indies Cricket Grew Up, by L.N. Constantine
'In the first games in England most of us youngsters found that we could not tell one white player from another. It was bewildering and annoying, especially when, as it seemed to us, people like Jack Hobbs, Andy Sandham, Ernest Tyldesley and Harry Makepeace, having been dismissed and sent back to the pavilion, immediately came walking out to bat again! It was many years after that I learnt that some English players shared the same thoughts and anguish about us.'

Reviving First-Class Cricket: M.C.C. Special Committee Report
Don't Tamper with The Laws, by W.E. Bowes
The Great Men of Gloucestershire, by H.F. Hutt
Laker's Wonderful Year, by Neville Cardus
Old Trafford Centenary, by A.W. Ledbrooke

D. Brookes

'At 41, Brookes feels he still has a few more years of cricket ahead of him, time in which to make Northamptonshire serious contenders for the Championship and, perhaps, to score the hundred against Surrey which will complete his tally of a century against every county. He may also be able to please the enthusiast who is anxious to see him out for 89, 94, 96 and 99 – the only totals between nought and one hundred for which Brookes, he states, has so far not been dismissed.'

J.W. Burke   M.J. Hilton   G.R.A. Langley   P.E. Richardson

K.E. Burn

'The oldest living Test cricketer. He took part in two Test matches for Australia during the 1890 tour of England, scoring 41 runs in four innings. *Wisden* of the time termed his selection as wicket-keeper the one serious mistake in making up the side, and described how only when he had accepted the terms offered him and joined the ship at Adelaide was the discovery made that he had never kept wicket in his life.'

C.B. Fry

'Fry must be counted among the most fully developed and representative Englishmen of his period; and the question arises whether, had fortune allowed him to concentrate on the things of the mind, not distracted by the lure of cricket, a lure intensified by his increasing mastery over the game, he would not have reached a high altitude in politics or critical literature. But he belonged – and it was his glory – to an age not obsessed by specialism; he was one of the last of the English tradition of the amateur, the connoisseur, and, in the most delightful sense of the word, the dilettante.' – Neville Cardus

Sir Home Gordon

'His memory of the game went back to 1878 when, not seven years old, he was taken to the Gentlemen of England v. Australians match at Prince's. He first went to Lord's on Whit Monday, 1880, being presented to W.G. Grace. In that season he watched the first England v. Australia Test match at The Oval and saw Alfred Lyttelton keep wicket for Middlesex against Gloucestershire at Clifton in a hard straw hat. During his long life he attended no fewer than seventy Oxford v. Cambridge games.'

J. Iremonger   M.W. Tate   M. Tompkin

Sussex

'Sussex had a disappointing season although, as they were in the process of rebuilding through the retirement of John Langridge and George Cox, too much could not be expected of them. They began in encouraging fashion, playing attractive and match-winning cricket, but it soon became evident that the attack possessed limitations … Despite the wet summer, Sussex were extremely fortunate with their home matches, and the season turned out better than that of 1955.'

England v Australia, Fourth Test Match. *At Manchester, July 26, 27, 28, 30, 31*

'At twenty-seven minutes past five a great cheer went up as Laker successfully appealed to the umpire, Lee, for lbw against Maddocks. The match was over and Laker had taken all ten wickets. He earned his triumph by remarkable control of length and spin and it is doubtful whether he bowled more than six bad length balls throughout the match. As Johnson said afterwards: "When the controversy and side issues of the match are forgotten, Laker's wonderful bowling will remain." That night the rain returned and the following day not a ball could be bowled in any of the first-class matches, so it can be seen how close was England's time margin, and how the greatest bowling feat of all time nearly did not happen.'

1958

WISDEN 1958

95th EDITION
EDITOR: Norman Preston
PAGES: 1071
PRICE: Limp 16/-   cloth 18/6d

THE WORLD AT LARGE

- Munich air crash: Manchester United players, officials and reporters among the dead
- Charles de Gaulle comes out of retirement to lead France
- Life peerages, the Duke of Edinburgh's Award Scheme, the London Planetarium and the Campaign for Nuclear Disarmament (CND) all begin this year
- The Preston By-Pass, Britain's first motorway, opens for traffic
- The European Economic Community (Common Market) established
- Death of Pope Pius XII: Cardinal Angelo Roncalli elected as John XXIII

CRICKET HEADLINES 1957

County Champions: Surrey, by a record margin of 94 points

England beat West Indies 3-0 in the home Test series

Peter Loader performs the first Test hat-trick by an England bowler in England since 1899

May and Cowdrey put on 411 for England's fourth wicket at Edgbaston, and Ramadhin bowls 98 overs in the innings

England and South Africa halve the series in South Africa, two matches apiece

John Murray does the wicket-keeper's double, only the second player to achieve this

Mickey Stewart catches seven Northamptonshire players in one innings – a record for an outfielder

NOTES BY THE EDITOR

'Since that notable day at Melbourne in February 1951 when England under F.R. Brown rose from the depths of despondency and beat Australia for the first time since 1938, the old country has not lost a single Test series. Clearly England stand at the top of the cricket world. Rarely has our prestige been so high. There are some who aver that England never possessed a better side.'

FEATURE ARTICLES

The Love of Cricket, by Lord Birkett
'But to all lovers of cricket there is a kind of music in the sound of the great names, the sound of Grace and Hobbs, the sound of Trent Bridge and Old Trafford; but the greatest music of all is the sound of the bat against the ball.'
Denis Compton: The Cavalier, by Neville Cardus
Googly Bowlers and Captains Retire, by E.M. Wellings
Story of New Zealand Cricket, by Charles Bray
Ups and Downs of Northamptonshire, by J.D. Coldham
M.C.C. Examine Amateur Status

FIVE CRICKETERS OF THE YEAR

O.G. Smith
'There is no finer sight than that of a player thoroughly enjoying his cricket. Such a man is O'Neill Gordon Smith, whose infectious enthusiasm and huge grin make him such an outstanding personality. With players like Walcott, Worrell, Weekes and Ramadhin in the West Indies side which toured England in 1957 it might not have been easy for a newcomer

to capture the lime-light, yet Smith did just that and more … Everywhere he went Smith won hosts of admirers by his approach to the game and there was no more popular player anywhere during the season.'

P.J. Loader   A.J. McIntyre   M.J. Stewart   C.L. Walcott

F. Chester
'In 1914 he put together an aggregate of 924 runs, average 27.17, with an innings of 178 not out – including four 6's from the bowling of J.W.H.T. Douglas – against Essex at Worcester, his highest. Then came the war and, in the course of service with the Army in Salonika, he lost his right arm just below the elbow. That, of course, meant no more cricket as a player for Chester; but in 1922 he became a first-class umpire and, with the advantage of youth … he swiftly gained a big reputation.'

H. Dean
'The performance which afforded Dean most satisfaction, however, was against Yorkshire at Aigburth in 1913 in an extra match arranged to mark the visit to Liverpool of King George V. He took nine wickets for 62 in the first innings and eight for 29 in the second, bringing his match figures to 17 for 91. There is no recorded instance of greater success by a bowler in a Roses match.'

E.R. Wilson
'He met with such success in 1920 that he took 64 wickets for 13.84 runs apiece, being fourth in the English averages. This brought him a place in J.W.H.T. Douglas's M.C.C. team who, the following winter, toured Australia. Wilson played in his only Test match during that tour, of which *Wisden* of the time reported: A good deal of friction was caused by cable messages sent home to the *Daily Express* by Mr. E.R. Wilson. This led to a resolution passed at the annual meeting of the Marylebone Club in May deprecating the reporting of matches by players concerned in them.'

W.H. Ferguson   G.V. Gunn   F.H. Huish   S. Santall

COUNTY REVIEW

Northamptonshire
'Northamptonshire's astute team building and steady improvement over the three previous years were amply rewarded in 1957. They enjoyed the most successful season in their history, finishing second in the county Championship, and although 94 points behind Surrey, were the only side who offered any challenge to the leaders in the last month … The fifteen Championship victories in 1957 constituted a new record for the county, and they suffered only two defeats – fewer than any other contestant.'

MATCH REPORTS

Nottinghamshire v West Indies, *at Nottingham, May 25, 27, 28*
'Played on a typically easy-paced Trent Bridge pitch, this game never looked like providing a definite result … Sobers batted throughout the first day for the first double-century of his career. He hit thirty-six 4's, eleven of them in his second 50.'

1959

WISDEN 1959

96th EDITION
EDITOR: Norman Preston
PAGES: 1059
PRICE: Limp 16/-   cloth 18/6d

THE WORLD AT LARGE

- World champion racing driver Mike Hawthorn killed in a road accident
- Buddy Holly dies in an air crash
- Barbie Doll launched
- Dalai Lama flees Tibet and seeks refuge in India
- Alaska becomes the 49th state of USA, and soon after Hawaii becomes the 50th
- Queen Elizabeth II and President Eisenhower open the St. Lawrence Seaway
- The Morris Mini-Minor is launched

CRICKET HEADLINES 1958

County Champions: Surrey, for the seventh time in a row

England beat New Zealand 4-0 in the Test Series

Hanif Mohammad is run out for 499 for Karachi v Bahawalpur, the new world record score

Hanif also hits 337 for Pakistan v West Indies at Barbados, but a month later Garfield Sobers hits 365* for West Indies to beat Len Hutton's record Test score

NOTES BY THE EDITOR

'It would seem that the time is ripe for a complete overhaul of our ideas in regard to pitches, batsmanship and the general conduct of the game. Indeed, after all the reports from Australia of suspect bowling actions and the continued slowing down of the game, so that as far as Tests are concerned run-making has come almost to a standstill, it would surely benefit cricket if all the members of the Imperial Conference would tackle the various problems which confront the game.'

FEATURE ARTICLES

The Story of Somerset, by Eric Hill
'Somerset were involved in an extraordinary finish with Sussex at Taunton in their very first home match after the war... Sussex needed a single to win when their ninth wicket fell. Some of the Somerset fielders thought the match was over as H.J. Heygate, the number eleven, was suffering from rheumatism and the effects of a war wound. He had not fielded and was not expected to bat. Indeed, he had not changed, wickets having gone down so suddenly, but wearing a blue lounge suit he limped out to bat. There was a friendly consultation between the captains … but so slow had been his progress that the umpires, A.E. Street and F.G. Roberts, decided he had exceeded his two minutes and pulled up the stumps, declaring the result a tie. This decision was upheld by M.C.C.'
From Dr. Grace to Peter May, by Herbert Strudwick
India, Be Bold, by Vijay Merchant
Charles Macartney and George Gunn, by Neville Cardus
The Early County Champions, by Rowland Bowen
The Wardle Case

FIVE CRICKETERS OF THE YEAR

J.R. Reid
'It would not be an exaggeration to say that Reid was the mainstay of the team and it came as no surprise when in February, in the second match against West Indies at Christchurch, he

was given the captaincy. Few captains have undertaken such an unenviable task. In 26 years of Test cricket, victory had always eluded New Zealand, but at his third attempt as leader Reid broke the ice in the final Test of the series at Eden Park, Auckland. It was the 45th Test undertaken by his country and Reid, by his masterly batting ... and eventually saw his men triumph by 190 runs.'

H.L. Jackson   R.E. Marshall   C.A. Milton   D. Shackleton

OBITUARIES INCLUDE

F.R. Foster
'The summer of 1911, however, found him by general consent the best all-rounder of the year ... Such wonderful cricket did he play, making 1,383 runs, average 44, and taking 116 wickets for just over 19 runs apiece, that his individual efforts constituted the chief factor in gaining the County Championship for Warwickshire for the first time in their history.'

A. Iremonger
'He was a younger brother of the more celebrated Nottinghamshire batsman, James Iremonger. Albert Iremonger's chief claim to fame was as an Association footballer. He stood nearly 6 ft. 6 in. and, as goalkeeper for Notts County, with whom he was associated for twenty-four years, and later for Lincoln City, could throw the ball as far as most men could kick it.'

G. Gunn   D.R. Jardine   C.G. Macartney   C.P. Mead   C.L. Townsend

COUNTY REVIEW

Essex
'The batting did not afford entire satisfaction, even when Williams, the former Oxford captain, came in late in the summer and gave it extra stability. For one thing, Trevor Bailey did not meet with as much success as usual. Not once did he reach three figures ... Barker... Insole and Dodds each attained 1,000 runs, but none of the other batsmen maintained consistency.'

MATCH REPORTS

England v New Zealand, *at Lord's, June 19, 20, 21*
'The honours of the first day went to New Zealand. They restricted England to less than 40 runs an hour, taking seven wickets for 237 runs. While full credit must be given to Hayes, MacGibbon, Blair and Reid for their steadiness on an easy-paced pitch, some of the England batsmen showed little imagination in dealing with bowling generally short in length ... So much rain fell in London after the close of play that next day the match could not be resumed until 3.20 p.m. and then wickets went down in a heap, thirteen in all in the space of two hours twenty minutes ... New Zealand's fate had been virtually settled on Friday and more rain left the pitch and outfield in a sodden state. The players needed plenty of sawdust to maintain their footholds when the match was resumed in sunshine after a delay of half an hour ... It was one of the shortest Tests for many years, being completed in eleven and a half hours... With 25,000 people present, the captains arranged an exhibition match of 20 overs each which, played in a light-hearted way, caused plenty of fun. Richardson kept wicket for England while Evans bowled.'

1960

WISDEN 1960

97th Edition
Editor: Norman Preston
Pages: 1027
Price: Limp 18/6d   cloth £1.1s

THE WORLD AT LARGE

• Harold Macmillan makes his 'winds of change' speech to the South African parliament
• Princess Margaret marries Anthony Armstrong-Jones
• The obscenity case against Penguin, publishers of *Lady Chatterley's Lover* fails: the book sells 200,000 copies on its first day of sale
• John F Kennedy wins the race for the U.S. presidency, narrowly beating Richard M Nixon
• The Sharpeville Massacre in South Africa – about 70 die
• Russians shoot down a U2 spy place and capture the U.S. pilot, Gary Powers
• Cassius Clay wins a gold medal at the Rome Olympics

CRICKET HEADLINES 1959

County Champions: Yorkshire

England lose the Ashes to Australia by four matches to nil, despite sending what many believed was the best team ever to leave England: it wasn't

Back home, England beat India 5-0, the first home whitewash in a five-match series

M.J.K. Smith scores 3,245 runs in the season, the highest tally for ten years

Trevor Bailey scores over 2,000 runs and takes 100 wickets, the only time this feat has been achieved since the war

NOTES BY THE EDITOR

English Cricket Thrives Again
'I wonder what Lord Hawke's reaction would have been to recent suggestions that the present time may be the twilight of the amateur. It is seriously suggested that all players should be termed "Cricketers" and that there should be no distinction between amateur and professional. In the past I may have thought along these lines, but when one remembers the great work done by B.H. Lyon for Gloucestershire, R.W.V. Robins for Middlesex, A.B. Sellers and J.R. Burnet for Yorkshire, and W.S. Surridge and P.B.H. May for Surrey, surely, no matter what the financial set-up, English cricket, and particularly county cricket, cannot afford to lose the amateur.'

FEATURE ARTICLES

Five Stalwarts Retire, by Neville Cardus
'Evans was not a 'keeper in the classic style, not all quiet balanced outlines, like Bertie Oldfield, who used to catch or stump in a flash and yet appear the embodiment of politeness and almost obsequious deportment, as though saying to his victim: "Awfully sorry, but it is my painful duty – Law 42, you know." Evans was modern in the almost surrealistic patterns achieved by his motions. He seemed to get to the ball by leaving out physical shapings and adjustments which ordinary human anatomies have to observe. He was a boneless wonder.'
Throw and Drag, by Harry Gee
Umpiring, by Tom Smith
Essex, 1876 – 1960, by Charles Bray

198

R. Illingworth

'The wonderful summer of 1959, with firm, true pitches, gave Illingworth the opportunity to blossom. He showed an ability to fashion an innings for the occasion. He could defend hard or hit hard. He lofted the ball with certainty high and wide of mid-on. He punched powerfully from the back foot to the covers. It was the same with his bowling. On helpful wickets he spun the ball. On good wickets he was miserly or prepared to buy at any price as the situation demanded. Again he did the double, scoring 1,726 runs and taking 110 wickets... Reliable in the field, a safe catcher and a good thrower, pleasant in looks, manners and dress, Illingworth thoroughly deserved the honour of representing England in West Indies.'

K.F. Barrington   D.B. Carr   G. Pullar   M.J.K. Smith

K.A. Auty

'Auty, Mr. Karl Andre, who died in Chicago on November 30, aged 81, was the owner of an outstanding cricket book collection.' *[Including a set of* Wisden.*]*

A.S. Kennedy

'Prominent as an all-rounder for Hampshire between 1907 and 1936, in which time he took 2,874 wickets – 2,549 for his county, a record – for 21.24 runs each, scored 16,496 runs, including ten centuries, average 18.54, and held 500 catches... Sturdily built, he bowled at medium pace with a high delivery and in-swing which, combined with spin and a marked accuracy of length, made him difficult to master.'

O.G. Smith

'… died in hospital at Stoke-on-Trent on September 9, aged 26, following injuries received in a motor-car accident in which two other West Indies players, G. Sobers and T. Dewdney, were also involved... His death came as a heavy blow to the West Indies, for much had been hoped from him against P.B.H. May's M.C.C. team last winter.'

K.S. Duleepsinhji   C.W.L. Parker

Worcestershire

'The cloud hanging over Worcestershire cricket in the late winter while the position of P.E. Richardson was being clarified did not lift entirely during the season and the results were poor. The position of fourteenth in the table was five places lower than in the previous year. This should not be taken as an adverse reflection on the efforts of Kenyon, who on the resignation of Richardson took over the task of leading a team which never looked above average standard.'

Sussex v Yorkshire, *at Hove, August 29, 30, September 1*

'Yorkshire won by five wickets, taking 12 points, and so became the new County Champions. They made sure of the title in one of the most exciting finishes seen on the ground after being left to get 215 in 105 minutes. With their batsmen playing strokes at practically every delivery, the winning hit came with seven minutes to spare. Few of the crowd had given Yorkshire any chance of getting the runs …'

The cover price passes the £1 mark for the cloth-board edition. To save space, the pages devoted to overseas domestic cricket are reduced, and bowling analyses are printed in a more space-saving format.

1961

WISDEN 1961

98th EDITION
EDITOR: Norman Preston
PAGES: 1027
PRICE: Limp 18/6d   cloth £1.1s

THE WORLD AT LARGE

- Soviet cosmonaut Yuri Gagarin becomes the first man in space
- Adolf Eichmann is captured in South America and put on trial in Israel. He is found guilty of war crimes
- The Bay of Pigs invasion by U.S. forces into Cuba fails
- Birth control pills are available on the National Health for the first time
- Rudolf Nureyev defects to the West

CRICKET HEADLINES 1960

County Champions: Yorkshire

England beat South Africa 3-0 in the home Test series

England beat West Indies 1-0 with four matches drawn during the winter

Geoff Griffin takes a hat-trick for South Africa at Lord's but later is no-balled for throwing and does not bowl again on tour

Australia and West Indies tie a Test match

Wicketkeepers Binks, Murray and Booth all snare 100 victims during the summer

NOTES BY THE EDITOR

'Most lovers of cricket will look back on 1960 as "The Sad Season". It will be remembered for the rain which spoiled so many matches, for the alarming fall in attendances and for its bitter controversies – the throwing of Griffin, the sacking of Buller as a Test umpire, the withdrawal by M.C.C. and Surrey of privileges to Laker following the publication of his book, *Over to Me*, and the Graveney dispute over the Gloucestershire captaincy. There was also the disappointing South African tour. For the fourth consecutive summer a visiting team failed to extend England in the Test matches.'

FEATURE ARTICLES

The Greatest Test Match, by E.M. Wellings
  'I was there. I saw it all.'
Bowling for Surrey and England, by Alec Bedser
  'Some people argue that there are too many first-class counties. My view is that, if the clubs can produce top-class sides, there are not too many first-class counties. If they cannot, it might be sensible for the smaller counties to amalgamate. Because of the financial question, I cannot conceive two divisions with promotion and relegation. Already attendances are low enough with only one group, so who would go to watch a second division match?'
Cricket Thrives Here, by H.S. Altham
The Throwing Controversy, by Leslie Smith
Cricket Alive Again, by Jack Fingleton

FIVE CRICKETERS OF THE YEAR

J.V. Wilson
  'When in 1960 Yorkshire appointed John Victor Wilson, their 39-year-old left-handed batsman, to be professional captain – their first professional captain since Tom Emmett in 1882 – the attention of the whole cricket world was centred upon him and the doings of his team … And how splendidly Wilson rose to the occasion. Authority fitted him well. Almost overnight a quiet firmness crept into his voice and there was purpose about his actions.'
N.A.T. Adcock   E.R. Dexter   R.A. McLean   R. Subba Row

E.R.T. Holmes
'A marked characteristic about his batting was the ease and certainty of his strokes; a very strong forward player he drove really hard, especially to the off and so good was his footwork and power of wrist that he had no need to exploit the modern method of leg-side play, but even so he was no mean exponent of such strokes. With left shoulder forward and firm right knee, Holmes convinced one directly he went in that he was there to make runs. And never did he change his methods.'

H. Preston
'Hubert Preston was, with [Sydney] Pardon and Stewart Caine, the most courteous and best-mannered man ever to be seen in a Press Box on a cricket ground.' – Neville Cardus.

'His work for cricket with *Wisden* will live for all time and was a great contribution to the game.' – Ronald Aird, secretary of MCC.

A. Skelding
'One of his most cherished umpiring memories was the giving of three leg-before decisions which enabled H. Fisher of Yorkshire to perform a unique hat-trick against Somerset at Sheffield in 1932. "I was never more sure that I was right in each case," he said afterwards, "and each of the batsmen agreed that he was dead in front."'

C.J. Burnup   F.W. Gilligan   V.W.C. Jupp   D.J. Knight

Middlesex
'J.J. Warr ended his spell of captaincy of Middlesex by guiding them to third place in the Championship, the highest for the county since they shared first position in 1949. For their rise of seven places Middlesex owed as much to their fine fielding as anything else. They set and maintained a high standard and were generally acknowledged to be the best fielding side in the country.'

England v South Africa, *at Lord's, June 23, 24, 25, 27*
'Griffin was called eleven times during the course of the England innings, all by F.S. Lee at square-leg. Then, when the match ended at 2.25 p.m. on the fourth day, an exhibition game took place and Griffin's only over consisted of eleven balls. S. Buller no-balled him for throwing four times out of five. On the advice of his captain, McGlew, who had spoken to Buller, Griffin changed to underarm bowling, but was promptly no-balled again by Lee for forgetting to notify the batsman of his change to action.'

Kent v Worcestershire, *at Tunbridge Wells, June 15*
'Kent won by an innings and 101 runs, taking 14 points from the first match to be completed in a day since 1953. The pitch, grassless and soft at first, dried under a hot sun, leaving crusty edges on the indentations made when the ball dug in earlier. No two deliveries behaved alike; many rising sharply, some keeping low and nearly all deviating to an unaccustomed degree. Worcestershire, not the strongest of batting sides, floundered against Brown and Halfyard, both of whom needed to do little more than turn over their arms. The pitch did the rest.'

Norman Preston refers in his Preface to the fact that full scores of Sheffield Shield matches in Australia are again given after the cutback in the previous year: '… we intend to retain the feature permanently.' Also: 'An innovation, in response to many requests, is the use in the scores of all matches of an asterisk to denote the captain and a dagger for the wicket-keeper.'

In this year Wisden *published a limited facsimile edition of the first fifteen volumes, 1864 to 1878, which is advertised on page 1003.*

1962

WISDEN 1962

99th Edition
EDITOR: Norman Preston
PAGES: 1067
PRICE: Limp £1   cloth £1.2s.6d

THE WORLD AT LARGE

- James Hanratty tried and executed for the A6 murder
- Death of Marilyn Monroe
- President Kennedy delivers his "Ich bin ein Berliner" speech at the Berlin Wall
- The Cuban Missile Crisis: for a few days it seems nuclear war is inevitable
- John Glenn becomes the first American in space
- The first James Bond film, *Dr. No* is released
- The Beatles release their first single, *Love Me Do*

CRICKET HEADLINES 1961

County Champions: Hampshire

Australia retain the Ashes by winning the series 2-1

In Australia, one of the most exciting series ever, against West Indies, reignites interest in Test cricket

Australian Bill Alley, aged 42, playing for Somerset, scores 3,019 runs: nobody has scored 3,000 in a season since then

NOTES BY THE EDITOR

'One of the most improved counties in 1961 was Leicestershire. In recent years they have cast their net far and wide for experienced talent and an ambitious season-ticket scheme has lightened their financial troubles. To emphasise the importance of the outright win, which should always be the first objective, the players were given a substantial bonus for each victory – I understand it was £20 apiece – with more for two in succession. Nottinghamshire tried a different method. Doing their best to see that the spectators received value for money, they gave £3 a man when the team scored 280 runs in 80 overs.'

FEATURE ARTICLES

Happy Hampshire, by H.L.V. Day
'Cricket is a glorious game chiefly because such a vast amount of fun can be derived from it by all and sundry, except apparently by that tiny fraction of the playing fraternity who engage in county cricket. The fun seems to have gone out of that ... Much of the blame can be laid at the door of the captains. The difference a lively, gay, adventurous captain can make has been well and truly underlined by A.C.D. Ingleby-Mackenzie. He accepted the challenge between bat and ball which is the essence of cricket, and was rewarded by leading Hampshire to their first championship.'

Cricket Inquiry – Interim Report
'3(h) The views of previous Inquiry Committees that it is impracticable to superimpose a Knock-Out Competition onto the *existing* structure of the County Championship are confirmed.'

My Seven Year 'Stretch', by G.O. Allen
An Enjoyable Visit to Britain, by Jack Fingleton
Statham and Trueman, by J.M. Kilburn

[All are Australian, although Bill Alley was playing for Somerset, not the touring team]
N.C. O'Neill

'If he can conquer himself for a start – his rashness, his uneasiness – O'Neill will not only have many more very big and thrilling scores (he's bound to have them) but he will have them more consistently. His rashness, too, often comes into his running between the wickets. For all that, he has given us some of the most glittering post-war innings. A glorious fieldsman, he has the dream throw.'

W.E. Alley   R. Benaud   A.K. Davidson   W.M. Lawry

OBITUARIES INCLUDE

A.P.F. Chapman

'A defensive policy was abhorrent to his nature, whether batting or fielding, and besides being a punishing though never reckless hitter, he made a name as a silly point, cover or slip of amazing speed and brilliancy.'

A. Jeacocke

'His first-class cricket in 1922 came to an abrupt end when *Wisden* records: "Jeacocke ... dropped out of the team in August under circumstances that gave rise to some friction and discussion, the M.C.C. ruling, after an enquiry asked for by Kent, that his qualification was not valid." The reason was that the house where he lived came within the boundary of Kent; the other side of the road was in the county of Surrey!'

A.C. Russell

'The first English batsman to hit a century in each innings of a Test match.'

M.S. Nichols   H.A. Peach   Col. R.S. Rait Kerr   J.C. White

COUNTY REVIEW

Glamorgan

'Although Glamorgan finished the season in a blaze of glory by defeating Surrey and achieving their first double over that county, 1961 was another disappointing year ... Yet the bare figures do not tell the full story. The team, captained for the first time by O.S. Wheatley, were dreadfully unlucky with injuries. All three fast bowlers, Wheatley, J.B. Evans and I.J. Jones, missed matches, the off-spinner, McConnon, was plagued by injuries ... and the all-rounder, Watkins, who announced his retirement during the season, was troubled by both injury and illness.'

MATCH REPORTS

Australia v West Indies, First Test, *at Brisbane, December 9, 10, 12, 13, 14*

'Kline came in to face the last two balls with the scores level. He played the seventh ball of the over towards square leg and Meckiff, backing up well, raced down the wicket, only to be out when Solomon again threw down the wicket with only the width of his stump as his target. So ended a match in which both sides had striven throughout for victory with no thought of safety first.'

North v South, *at Blackpool, September 6, 7, 8*

'The highlight of the match was a century in fifty-two minutes by Prideaux – the fastest in first-class cricket since 1937 ... After rain had restricted the first day's play to forty minutes, batsmen attacked the bowling and there was a glut of boundaries. On the second day 685 runs were scored for the loss of twenty-three wickets.'

The price of the limp cover version reaches £1.

1963

WISDEN 1963

100th EDITION
EDITOR: Norman Preston
PAGES: 1179
PRICE: Limp £1.2s.6d   cloth £1.5s

THE WORLD AT LARGE

• President de Gaulle vetoes Britain's entry into the Common Market
• The Profumo Affair: War Minister John Profumo admits an affair with Christine Keeler, who was also involved with a Russian spy
• Pope John XXIII dies: Cardinal Montini succeeds as Paul VI
• Assassination of President John F. Kennedy, in Dallas

CRICKET HEADLINES 1962

County Champions: Yorkshire

England beat Pakistan 4-0 in the home Test series

During the winter England lose to India 2-0 in a five-Test series, but beat Pakistan 1-0 in a three-Test series

Kenyon and Simpson score their 30,000th runs, and Shackleton and Lock both pass the 2,000 wicket mark

NOTES BY THE EDITOR

'We have inherited the game of cricket. The story of its development during the last hundred years is appropriately given full treatment in this edition of *Wisden*. Right through these hundred years the amateur has played a very important part. In the time of Dr. W.G. Grace there was talk that the amateur received liberal expenses. Whether this was true or not, I do not believe cricket, as we know it today, would be such a popular attraction, or so remunerative to the professional, without the contribution which Dr. Grace and his contemporaries made as amateurs. By doing away with the amateur, cricket is in danger of losing the spirit of freedom and gaiety which the best amateur players brought to the game.'

FEATURE ARTICLES

Six Giants of The Wisden Century, by Neville Cardus
'I have been asked by the Editor of *Wisden* to write "appreciations" of six great cricketers of the past hundred years. I am honoured by this invitation, but it puts me in an invidious position. Which ever player I choose for this representative little gallery I am bound to leave out an important name. My selection of immortal centenarians is as follows: W.G. Grace, Sir Jack Hobbs, Sir Donald Bradman, Tom Richardson, S.F. Barnes and Victor Trumper.'

Through the Crystal Ball, by John Solan
'A county cricket ground used solely for cricket will soon be an insupportable luxury, but that is no reason why cricket itself should take a seat too far back. To believe that this could happen would be to ignore the indications of the flourishing state of club and village green cricket throughout the land … The county cricket ground of the future, therefore, can be expected to be a comprehensive sports centre, the extent of whose activities will be limited only by the space and facilities available. Members will make it their club, not merely their cricket club, and, by paying a fatter subscription, will be able to enjoy amenities in and out of doors.'

A History of Wisden, by L.E.S. Gutteridge
Cricket Literature of the Wisden Century, by John Arlott
The Wisden Trophy
Cricket – An Enduring Art, by Rt. Hon. Sir Robert Menzies
Stars of The Tests, by E.M. Wellings
The Rise of Worcestershire, by Noel Stone

P.H. Parfitt

'Now an almost automatic choice for his country, Parfitt took centuries off Pakistan in the First, Third and Fourth Tests, and one in each innings for Middlesex at Lord's ... It can truthfully be written that his only real failure was at Lord's in the Second Test, an astonishing record. His success was achieved with an almost impertinent fluency of stroke play, and one of the joys of the 1962 season was the sight of Parfitt destroying every type of bowling with cheerful abandon.'

D. Kenyon   Mushtaq Mohammad   P.J. Sharpe   F.J. Titmus

OBITUARIES INCLUDE

R. Webber

'An accountant before serving with the Royal Air Force in the Second World War, he afterwards decided to turn a long-standing hobby into a profession. Besides acting for many years as official cricket scorer for the B.B.C., he was joint editor of the *Playfair Cricket Monthly* and the author of a number of books.'

E. Hendren   W. Huddleston   E.R. Mayne   T. Rushby   E. Tyldesley

---

COUNTY REVIEW

Lancashire

'By general consent within the county, Lancashire experienced the worst season in the club's history. Throughout the summer they laboured in the lower reaches of the table, and eventually last but one with a record only fractionally better than that of Leicestershire, the bottom county ... As the season progressed, far from showing any sign of recovery, they seemed to become more and more dispirited.'

MATCH REPORTS

India v Pakistan, 2nd Test, *at Kanpur, December, 16, 17, 18, 20, 21*
'Slow-scoring, plodding cricket brought an inevitable draw, and indeed, not until well into the fifth and final day was the first innings of both sides completed. Though the Modi Stadium pitch has the reputation of being helpful to spin bowlers, the batsmen exaggerated the dangers, showing extreme caution almost throughout.'
[Every match in the series was drawn, and every game featured very slow cricket.]

The one hundredth edition of Wisden *was the largest and the most expensive so far. To commemorate the milestone, the publishers presented the Wisden Trophy, to be competed for between England and West Indies 'on the same lines as England and Australia contest the Ashes'. It coincided with the remarkable rise of West Indies cricket in the latter part of the 20th century.*

A 'Calendar 1963', similar in style to the Calendars printed in the early Wisdens, *was included.*

John Arlott, in addition to his regular book reviews, provides a magisterial overview of the game's literature: 'Cricket writing has grown up side by side with Wisden.'

Leslie Gutteridge writes the definitive history of Wisden, *ensuring that this edition is one that collectors most often turn to for information about all facets of the first 100 volumes.*

1964

WISDEN 1964

101st EDITION
EDITOR: Norman Preston
PAGES: 1055
PRICE: Limp £1.2s.6d   cloth £1.5s

THE WORLD AT LARGE

• Beatlemania takes hold in the United States
• In the General Election, Labour, under Harold Wilson, put an end to 13 years of Conservative rule
• Nelson Mandela sentenced to life imprisonment
• Vietnam War escalates: there are now over 20,000 U.S. troops there
• President Johnson defeats Senator Goldwater in the U.S.presidential elections

CRICKET HEADLINES 1963

County Champions: Yorkshire

West Indies beat England 3-1 to take the Wisden Trophy

The Second Test at Lord's is a thriller: Cowdrey with a broken arm helps Allen claim a draw

England and Australia draw the series in Australia, who thus retain the Ashes

Sussex win the inaugural 65-over Knock-Out Competition

Death of Sir Jack Hobbs and Sir Pelham Warner

NOTES BY THE EDITOR

'From almost every point of view, except the weather, one can look back on the season of 1963 with satisfaction. True, England did not win the rubber with the West Indies, but victory should never be put above everything else. The honours went to the West Indies. Their players and supporters enriched the game with their exuberant cricket on the field and their infectious enthusiasm and incessant banter in the background. Approximately half a million spectators were present at the five Test Matches and receipts came to nearly £200,000.

The year was also notable for the successful introduction of the Knock-Out Competition, which in future will be called The Gillette Cup.'

FEATURE ARTICLES

Following Leicestershire, by Brian Chapman
'What is the rarest and maybe least known double? Well, in 1888, Leicestershire won the Second Class Championship and beat Australia. There's unexpected glory for you! It was with much quiet pride that local enthusiasts noted in last year's Centenary *Wisden* that they shared with Northamptonshire (among Counties now rated first-class) the honour of first forming a county organisation in 1820.'
The Gift of Captaincy, by Neville Cardus

FIVE CRICKETERS OF THE YEAR

C.C. Griffith

'He began the tour as a bowler of whom English followers knew comparatively little. Hall was rated the No. 1 attacker and King, with whom Griffith shared hotel rooms throughout the tour, was considered his likely opening partner. But Griffith was an early success with eight for 23 and five for 35 against Gloucestershire at Bristol and five for 37 against the Champions at Middlesbrough and became an automatic choice for the Tests. His deadly yorker – "I can produce it at will' – proved virtually unplayable and he finished the tour with 37 more wickets than Sobers, the next most successful West Indian bowler.'

D.B. Close   C.C. Hunte   R.B. Kanhai   G.S. Sobers

Sir Jack Hobbs
'I never saw him make a bad or a hasty stroke. Sometimes, of course, he made the wrong good stroke, technically right but applied to the wrong ball. An error of judgment, not of technique. He extended the scope of batsmanship, added to the store of cricket that will be cherished, played the game with modesty, for all his mastery and produce, and so won fame and affection, here and at the other side of the world. A famous fast bowler once paid the best of all compliments to him – "It wer 'ard work bowlin' at 'im, but it wer something you wouldn't 'ave missed for nothing." Let Sir Jack go at that.' – Neville Cardus

Sir Pelham Warner
'When Lord Hawke took a team to the West Indies in 1897 he was asked by H.V.L. Stanton (Wanderer of The Sportsman) if he could arrange for somebody to send back accounts of the matches to be played by his team. Lord Hawke turned to Sir Pelham and said "Plummy, you're last from school. Why shouldn't you do it?" He did and that began his career as one of the outstanding writers on the game. Sir Pelham in fact provided the account of that tour for the *Wisden* of 1898 and in 1911 he contributed a short article for the Almanack entitled *Our Young Cricketers.* His *Twilight Reflections,* which appeared in the 1955 *Wisden,* was an extensive survey of the game as well as a critical analysis which contained much advice on problems which still confront us.' – A.W.T. Langford

E.B. Alletson   A.W. Carr   J.N. Crawford   J. Gunn   A.G. Moyes   S.G. Smith

Derbyshire
'Derbyshire suffered a disastrous season, finishing bottom of the championship for the first time since 1924 … The main cause of Derbyshire's decline was a serious deterioration in the batting. Only Lee scored 1,000 runs in championship matches, whereas six players reached four figures in 1962. Carr's skill was sadly missed; when he played during a fortnight's holiday he made 358 runs and headed the batting averages.'

England v West Indies, Second Test, *at Lord's, June 20, 21, 22, 24 ,25*
'One of the most dramatic Test matches ever to be played in England attracted large crowds and aroused tremendous interest throughout the country … When the final over arrived any one of four results could have occurred – a win for England, victory for West Indies, a tie or a draw. The match was drawn with England six runs short of success and West Indies needing one more wicket. Most people felt happy about the result, for it would have been a pity if either side had lost after playing so well.'

'Only two members of the Middlesex team plus the twelfth man were at the ground for the start of the second day of the match with Kent at Tunbridge Wells. In order for the game to continue, the Middlesex innings was closed at the Saturday night total of 121 for three. Kent lent substitutes until the other Middlesex players, who had been delayed by traffic jams, arrived.'

The editor tells in his Notes what a success the 1963 edition proved to be: 'Wisden *itself made an indelible contribution to the summer by the appearance on April 19 of the 100th edition of "The Cricketers' Bible". The newspapers, television and sound radio were lavish in their praise and they treated it as a national event. I don't think I am giving away any secrets when I say that even the publisher was surprised by the public demand for the Almanack. It ran into three impressions by the printers before everyone was satisfied. Naturally,* Wisden, *which specialises in cricket facts and records, established its own record of sales.'*

1965

WISDEN 1965

102nd Edition
Editor: Norman Preston
Pages: 1067
Price: Limp £1.2s.6d   Cloth £1.5s

THE WORLD AT LARGE

• Death of Winston Churchill, aged 90
• Train robber Ronnie Biggs escapes from Wandsworth Prison
• Alec Douglas-Home resigns as leader of the Conservative Party and is replaced by Edward Heath
• Southern Rhodesia, led by Ian Smith, makes its unilateral declaration of independence
• Assassination of Malcolm X
• The first Australian troops arrive in Vietnam: there are now 125,000 U.S. troops there
• Singapore separates from Malaysia

CRICKET HEADLINES 1964

County Champions: Worcestershire

Australia retain the Ashes by winning the only Test to be decided in the series

Australian captain Bobby Simpson scores 311 at Old Trafford, his first Test century in 30 Tests, but his second triple-century in nine months

MCC visits India and tourists are ravaged by illness, but all five Tests are drawn

Tom Graveney hits his 100th hundred

Sussex retain the now sponsored Gillette Cup

Fred Trueman becomes the first man to take 300 Test wickets

NOTES BY THE EDITOR

'To me, the season was one of missed opportunities by both England and Australia. It fell flat by comparison with the exhilarating displays of West Indies under Sir Frank Worrell in 1963. For the most part West Indies did not score their runs any faster, but they certainly conveyed the impression of enjoying themselves. In contrast, too many England and Australian cricketers appeared to be governed first by commercial interests and cricket suffered accordingly.'

FEATURE ARTICLES

The Pleasures of Reading Wisden, by Rowland Ryder
'If I were permitted to take eight editions of the Almanack with me to some remote desert island, I would find the task of selection an extremely difficult one ... *Wisden* is indeed better than rubies. *Wisden* is an inexhaustible gold mine in which lies embedded the golden glory of a century of cricketing summers.'

Neville Cardus, by John Arlott
'The Birthday Honours List of 1964 included the award of the C.B.E. to Mr. Neville Cardus for services to music and cricket. It was the first – and, some may feel, belated – official recognition of the modest man who, for almost fifty years, has written with sympathy and integrity about the two chief interests – indeed, enthusiasms – of his life. Throughout that time his work has never become jaded, but has unfailingly reflected the happiness of one who always felt privileged, even grateful, to earn his living from his pleasures.'

Tom Graveney – A Century of Centuries, by Neville Cardus
Cricket An Art Not A Science, by Sir Learie Constantine
Cricket in the 17th and 18th Centuries, by Rowland Bowen
A Middlesex Century, by I.A.R. Peebles

G.D. McKenzie

'McKenzie, at the age of 23 and 162 days, is the youngest bowler to take 100 wickets in Test cricket, beating A.L. Valentine by 139 days, but Valentine performed his feat in nineteen Tests. The lowest number of Tests for 100 wickets is sixteen by G.A. Lohmann before the turn of the century.'

G. Boycott   P.J. Burge   J.A. Flavell R.B. Simpson

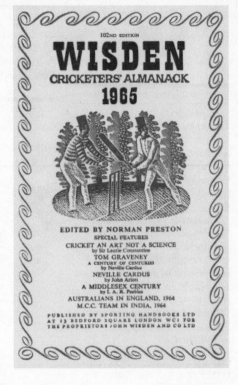

102ND EDITION

WISDEN

CRICKETERS' ALMANACK

1965

EDITED BY NORMAN PRESTON

SPECIAL FEATURES

CRICKET AN ART NOT A SCIENCE
by Sir Learie Constantine

TOM GRAVENEY
A CENTURY OF CENTURIES
by Neville Cardus

NEVILLE CARDUS
by John Arlott

A MIDDLESEX CENTURY
by I. A. R. Peebles

AUSTRALIANS IN ENGLAND, 1964

M.C.C. TEAM IN INDIA, 1964

PUBLISHED BY SPORTING HANDBOOKS LTD
AT 13 BEDFORD SQUARE LONDON WC1 FOR
THE PROPRIETORS JOHN WISDEN AND CO LTD

G. Brown

'The display for which he will always be remembered was that at Edgbaston in 1922. Dismissed for 15, the smallest total in their first-class history, Hampshire followed-on 208 behind and seemed destined to humiliating defeat when they lost six men for 186. Then Brown played magnificently for 172 and a maiden century by W. H. Livsey helped the total to 521. Kennedy and Newman followed by dismissing War-wickshire for 158, carrying their side to a famous victory by 155 runs – a feat which brought considerable financial benefit to that intrepid Hampshire captain, the Hon. L.H. Tennyson, who, after the first-innings debacle, had accepted numerous bets at long odds!"

J.W. Filliston

'... died in hospital on October 25, aged 102, five days after being knocked down by a motor-scooter, acted as umpire to the B.C.C. Cricket Club for many years. Old Joe stood in the Old England v. Lord's Taverners match at Lord's when over 100 ... He liked to tell of the occasion when he gave W.G. out leg-before in a London County game at the Crystal Palace. The Doctor, he said, refused to leave the crease and, as nobody had the courage to contradict him, he continued his innings.'

Cat, Peter

'... whose ninth life ended on November 5, 1964, was a well-known cricket watcher at Lord's, where he spent 12 of his 14 years ... Mr. S.C. Griffith, Secretary of M.C.C., said of him: "He was a cat of great character and loved publicity."'

S.T. Jagger   C.B. Llewellyn   M.D. Lyon   F.T. Mann   R.T. Stanyforth

Middlesex v Yorkshire, Gillette Cup Second Round, *at Lord's. May 27*

'Yorkshire were handicapped through John Hampshire being taken ill with serum fever following an anti-tetanus injection necessitated by a cut eye when fielding a fortnight earlier. They had no twelfth man and E. Lester, the scorer, who had not held a bat for three years nor played for the first team for nine years, was pressed into service. Yorkshire seemed to have done well in dismissing Middlesex for 150 runs, but they gave a woeful display of batting.' *[E. Lester b Price 0]*

For the first time, Wisden *produces a yellow dust jacket for the cloth-bound version (pictured). The edition sold out, we are informed by the editor in his 1966 Preface.*

1966

WISDEN 1966

103rd Edition
Editor: Norman Preston
Pages: 1083
Price: Limp £1.3s   Cloth £1.7s.6d

THE WORLD AT LARGE

- Indira Gandhi becomes Prime Minister of India
- Moors murderers Ian Brady and Myra Hindley sentenced to life imprisonment
- England win the World Cup, beating West Germany 4-2 in the final
- The Beatles play their last live concert, at Candlestick Park in San Francisco
- The Aberfan disaster: a coal tip collapses on to a school, killing 144 people, including 116 children
- Prime Minister Hendrik Verwoerd of South Africa is assassinated

CRICKET HEADLINES 1965

County Champions: Worcestershire

Yorkshire win Gillette Cup

England beat South Africa 1-0 during the winter

The first summer of double Test tours – South Africa and New Zealand each play three Tests in England: New Zealand lose all three, but South Africa win the series 1-0

John Edrich hits 310* against New Zealand, his ninth successive innings of over 50 and the highest score by an Englishman at Headingley

NOTES BY THE EDITOR

'Looking back on cricket in England last season, one can only describe it as mainly disappointing. The sun rarely shone and one remembers mostly the cold, wet and windy conditions that prevailed ... The New Zealanders ... experienced a most unpleasant time in such unfavourable weather. They were a stronger combination than on their last visit in 1958, but clearly inferior to England and went down heavily in the three Test Matches. Due to the wintry conditions, attendances were small at the majority of their matches and they finished £4,000 on the wrong side, but thanks to their foresight in arranging to visit India and Pakistan, where they took part in seven Tests on the way to England, they returned home with a small profit.'

FEATURE ARTICLES

Cricket a Game – Not a Subject, by A.D.G. Matthews
'As a young professional I was fortunate enough to spend a fortnight with G.A. Faulkner, the famous South African all-rounder, at his school in Walham Green ... It was here I heard this superb coach make this noteworthy remark, "The way to coach is to look for the natural, hold on to it, and coach orthodoxy around it." This sort of thing cannot be taught, although it can be learned from experience – there is a subtle but real difference here.'
Welcome West Indies – World Cricket Champions, by Sir Learie Constantine
Walter Reginald Hammond, by Neville Cardus
The Great Years and Great Players of Kent, by R.L. Arrowsmith

FIVE CRICKETERS OF THE YEAR

K.C. Bland
'England were 240 for four wickets and heading for a match-winning lead against South Africa at Lord's when K.F. Barrington, who was 91, played perhaps the most fateful stroke in

the 1965 Test series. He pushed the ball to mid-wicket and scampered down the pitch. Colin Bland ran towards the square-leg umpire. In one thrilling movement he scooped up the ball, swung round his body and threw down the stumps at the bowler's end. The run-out of Barrington, which was followed by Bland's performing a similar feat against J.M. Parks, was the turning point in the 1965 Test matches.'

J.H. Edrich   R.C. Motz   P.M. Pollock   R.G. Pollock

J.C. Hubble

'One of a trio of great wicket-keepers who, playing in succession for Kent, spanned well over half a century. He succeeded F.H. Huish and was succeeded by L.E.G. Ames. Hubble served his county as a professional from 1904 to 1929, helping them on the last occasion they carried off the County Championship in 1913. In that time he scored over 10,000 runs and helped in the dismissal of more than 500 batsmen.'

J.B. King

'… beyond question the greatest all-round cricketer produced by America. When he toured England with The Philadelphians in 1897, 1903 and 1908, Sir Pelham Warner described him as one of the finest bowlers of all time. Very fast and powerfully built, King made the ball swerve late from leg, demonstrating that what could be done with the ball by a pitcher at baseball, at which he was expert, could also be achieved with a ball half an ounce heavier.'

**H.S. Altham   A.P. Freeman   W.R. Hammond   J.W. Hearne   J.W. Hitch
R.C. Robertson-Glasgow   W.M. Woodfull**

COUNTY REVIEW

Northamptonshire

'Northamptonshire did their very best to mark their diamond jubilee by winning the County Championship for the first time, only to be beaten at the post by Worcestershire, for whom this was their 100th year of existence. There could scarcely have been a more exciting finish, with Northamptonshire, having completed their programme on August 24th, fidgeting through three series as Worcestershire … and Glamorgan … fought to oust them from top place. The Welsh county faltered, but Worcestershire did not, beating Hampshire and Sussex to climb to the summit by a mere four points.'

MATCH REPORTS

England v South Africa, *at Nottingham, August 5, 6, 7, 9*

'South Africa won by 94 runs with a day to spare. It was South Africa's first Test victory in England for ten years and a personal triumph for the brothers Graeme and Peter Pollock. Their fraternal effort has no parallel in Test cricket. Graeme, the batsman, made 184 runs, held a fine slip catch and took a vital wicket on the last day. Peter, the bowler, with five wickets in each England innings, finished with an analysis of 10 wickets for 87 runs in 48 overs.'

MISCELLANEOUS

'C. Inman, Leicestershire v. Nottingham at Nottingham, hit 51 in eight minutes, including 32 off one over from N. Hill who presented him with full tosses to hurry a declaration.'

The editor explains in his Preface that the Cricket Reporting Agency, which since the 1887 edition had been responsible for the editorial production of Wisden, *merged with the Press Association on April 1, 1965. The three partners and all the full-time staff move over to the P.A. so there is continuity in* Wisden's *editorial team.*

1967

WISDEN 1967

104th Edition
Editor: Norman Preston
Pages: 1075
Price: Limp £1.3s.6d   cloth £1.7s.6d

THE WORLD AT LARGE

- Francis Chichester completes his solo single-handed circumnavigation of the globe, and is knighted by the Queen as he steps ashore at Plymouth
- King Constantine flees Greece after an unsuccessful counter-coup attempt
- World's first heart transplant, by Dr. Christiaan Barnard, at Groote Schuur Hospital in Cape Town
- Brian Epstein, manager of the Beatles, found dead
- Harold Wilson devalues the pound from $2.80 to $2.40
- Six Day War: Israel occupies the West Bank, Sinai and the Gaza Strip

CRICKET HEADLINES 1966

County Champions: Yorkshire

Warwickshire win the Gillette Cup

West Indies beat England 3-1 in the summer Tests

England draw the series in Australia, one all, so Australia retain the Ashes

Bob Cowper hits 307 for Australia in the Fifth Test, the highest Test score yet made in Australia

The Counties reject the Clark Report on the future of county cricket. Much of what it proposed has since come about.

NOTES BY THE EDITOR

English Cricket at the Crossroads

'The prevalence of medium-fast bowling has brought about the almost complete disappearance of the genuine leg-spin bowler and the left-arm slow bowler. Hence, the authorities rightly complain that the over-rate – 20 an hour is considered acceptable – has fallen. Bring back the slow bowlers with the shorter run-up and the overrate must rise. Much as I dislike any restraint on captains as to their field placings and general conduct of the game, variety would be lent if there were a limitation on the number of overs permitted to seam bowlers during an innings."

FEATURE ARTICLES

My Favourite Summer, by A.A. Thomson
'If the B.B.C. were to maroon me on a desert island and, according to their pleasant custom, demand to know what book I should like to take with me, there would be no difficulty. *Pickwick* I know by heart and, though I revere Tolstoi, to read *War and Peace* under the breadfruit trees would be too much like starting to watch an innings by J.W.H.T. Douglas and waking up to find that Trevor Bailey was still batting. But *Wisden* for 1903 is the perfect companion. It has almost everything the heart of man could desire.'

Counties Reject the Clark Plan, by Charles Bray
The Two David Clark Reports
The Throwing Report
Sobers – The Lion of Cricket, by Sir Neville Cardus
Nottinghamshire's Notable Part in the Growth Of Cricket, by R.T. Simpson
Indian Cricket – Its Problems and Players, by Dicky Rutnagur
The Rise of Cricket In Pakistan, by Ghulam Mustafa Khan

'*For the Five Cricketers of the Year, I looked at those whose performances in these times of so much mediocrity do most to draw the crowds.' [Editor in Preface.]*

B.L. D'Oliveira

'That he did not fall by the wayside of the stony path he was compelled to tread is a tribute to the courage and skill of this player from the land of apartheid. To say that he never contemplated giving up the game before reaching the hour of glory was hardly the case. The hazards he encountered were very nearly too great even for the stout-hearted D'Oliveira. Suffice to say that of the 25,000 South African coloured cricketers who would dearly love to make county grade over here D'Oliveira is the first to have done so.'

R.W. Barber   C. Milburn   J.T. Murray   S.M. Nurse

OBITUARIES INCLUDE

G.F. Cresswell

'... found dead with a shot-gun at his side on January 10, aged 50, did not play in first-class cricket till he was 34. After only one trial match, he was chosen for the 1949 tour of England by New Zealand, and he did so well with slow-medium leg-theory bowling that he took 62 wickets in the first-class fixtures of the tour for 26.09 runs apiece. He played in one Test match that season, the fourth, disposing of six batsmen for 168 runs in an England total of 482.'

N.E. Haig

'Seemingly built of whipcord, Haig, a nephew of Lord Harris, bowled for long spells without apparent signs of fatigue. Among his best performances with the ball was the taking of seven wickets for 33 runs in the Kent first innings at Canterbury in 1920. This was another eventful match for Haig, for he scored 57 in the Middlesex first innings and became the second leg of a hat-trick by A. P. Freeman in the second.'

G. Duckworth   T.W.J. Goddard   James Langridge   C.S. Marriott   C.H. Taylor

COUNTY REVIEW

Somerset

'Somerset enjoyed their most successful season since joining the Championship in 1891. They equalled the previous position attained, third, and by winning thirteen Championship matches established a new record ... Somerset also enjoyed a fine run in the Gillette Cup before they went down in the semi-final to the new holders, Warwickshire. The Cup successes helped to adjust some disturbing losses in membership and gate receipts.'

MATCH REPORTS

England v West Indies, *at the Oval, August 18, 19, 20, 22*

'On Saturday the ... batsmen continued serenely until Gibbs smartly ran out Graveney, who had spent six hours hitting his 165... Murray went on to 112, more than double his previous best Test score, before he was leg before to Sobers at 399 ... The West Indies bowlers must have looked forward to an early rest, but the England opening bowlers, Higgs and Snow, displayed their talent for batting in a highly diverting partnership of 128 in two hours ... Before Higgs left to a return catch this plucky pair came within two runs of the world test record last wicket stand... Neither Higgs nor Snow had previously completed fifty in first-class cricket.'

MISCELLANEOUS

'Northamptonshire hit 355 for seven wickets against Nottinghamshire, at Nottingham, the highest in the first innings under the 65-over regulations and the only total over 300.'

1968

WISDEN 1968

105th Edition
Editor: Norman Preston
Pages: 1111
Price: Limp £1.5s   cloth £1.10s

THE WORLD AT LARGE

• Assassinations of Martin Luther King Jr in Memphis, and of Robert F. Kennedy in Los Angeles
• The first Race Relations Act comes into force in U.K.
• President Johnson announces he will not seek re-election: eventually the race to the White House is won by Republican Richard Nixon
• Student strikes in May, with support from many unions, almost topple the French government

CRICKET HEADLINES 1967

County Champions: Yorkshire

Kent win the Gillette Cup

India and Pakistan both play three Test series in England: India lost 3-0, Pakistan lost 2-0

South Africa, now probably the strongest team in the world, beat Australia 3-1 at home

An MCC Under 25 team tours Pakistan: captain Mike Brearley scores 312* in a day against North Zone

NOTES BY THE EDITOR

'When one takes into account all the publicity and the interest that League football gains from the exchange of players is the time so very far distant when cricket will be conducted in similar fashion? While Yorkshire with their broad acres and vast resources must be admired for their adherence to local talent, the imported player from outside the county border and from overseas is no stranger among the other sixteen counties. Did not Warwickshire win the Championship in 1951 with only C.W. Grove and F.C. Gardner of the regular side born within the county? When Nottinghamshire met Leicestershire at Newark last season half the players who took part in the match were former players of other counties.'

FEATURE ARTICLES

Batsmen Must Hit The Ball Again, by Denis Compton
'Last summer I was surprised when one of our leading batsmen, with many overseas tours behind him, told me he was not happy with the way he was holding the bat. He asked how I held mine. "I've not the slightest idea," I replied. "I never paid any attention to any special grip. I held it the way it felt most comfortable." So I should have thought, would any batsman.'
The Googly Summer, by A.A. Thomson
Warwickshire the Unpredictable, by Rowland Ryder
The Modern Golden Age, by Sir Neville Cardus
Notable Dates in Australian Cricket History, by Rowland Bowen

FIVE CRICKETERS OF THE YEAR

Hanif Mohammad
'Few major innings since the war have provoked such contradictory critical appraisal as that played by Pakistan's captain in the Lord's Test of 1967. It began at 4.40 p.m. on Friday, July 27, and ended only when he ran out of partners at 3.24 p.m. the following Monday. His actual entrenchment at the crease, after deductions for rain, meals, sleep and an interminable English sabbath, lasted nine hours two minutes and his eventual score was 187 not out. Press

comment along the way embraced the full spectrum of colourful opinion: from the outraged puce of those writers who regard themselves as the guardians of sporting entertainment to the purplest prose that could be mustered by others who acclaimed it one of the batting masterpieces of their time. If the reading public were bemused, one man remained totally unconcerned. This was the author of the innings, Hanif Mohammad.'

Asif Iqbal   K. Higgs   J.M. Parks   Nawab of Pataudi junior

OBITUARIES INCLUDE

S.F. Barnes
'Barnes had a splendid upright action, right arm straight over. He ran on easy strides, not a penn'orth of energy wasted. He fingered a cricket ball sensitively, like a violinist his fiddle. He always attacked. "Why do these bowlers today send down so many balls the batsman needn't play?" he asked while watching a Test match many years ago. "I didn't. I never gave 'em any rest."' – Sir Neville Cardus

M. Leyland
'A squat, solid figure, his cap slightly a-tilt, Leyland was a great character on and off the field. Yorkshire did not let him go when his playing days were over. They made him their coach from 1951 until 1963 when his long illness laid him low. Some want to change the structure of county cricket. It would not be necessary if there were a few Leylands about today. He breathed the true spirit of cricket and companionship.'

T.P.B. Smith
'In 1933, Peter Smith arrived at The Oval prepared to play for England against the West Indies, only to learn that the telegram informing him of his choice had been sent by a hoaxer. Thirteen years later he did play for his country, against India on the Surrey ground.'

Sir Frank Worrell
'Sir Frank Worrell once wrote that the island of Barbados, his birthplace, lacked a hero. As usual, he was under-playing himself. Frank Maglinne Worrell was the first hero of the new nation of Barbados and anyone who doubted that had only to be in the island when his body was brought home in mid March of 1967.' – Sir Learie Constantine

COUNTY REVIEW

Worcestershire
'In an excessively dull season after three exciting years some of the matches in which the County were concerned were, in all conscience, not worth watching. Home fixtures, in particular, bore little comparison to the dynamic cricket of the recent champagne summers.'

MATCH REPORTS

South Africa v Australia, First Test, *at Johannesburg, December 23, 24, 26, 27, 28*
'The match will go down as one of the most memorable in the history of South African cricket. Australia's proud record of 64 years without defeat in Test matches in South Africa was smashed after even the most sanguine supporter had written off the Springboks' chances within an hour of play commencing. On a ground saturated by days of rain, which only ceased 48 hours before the start, the margin and quality of victory were unbelievable.'

Prices rise again. Norman Preston writes in his Preface: 'There is an increase of 36 pages compared with last year. Inevitably, more pages mean higher costs, and this, combined with the effect of devaluation on the price of paper, and greater printing and binding costs, makes it necessary to increase the prices of each edition, which have remained unchanged for the past two years.'

1969

WISDEN 1969

106th EDITION
EDITOR: Norman Preston
PAGES: 1095
PRICE: Limp £1.5s   cloth £1.10s

THE WORLD AT LARGE

- Maiden flight of Concorde
- Prince Charles invested as Prince of Wales at Caernarvon Castle
- Charles de Gaulle resigns as President of France: Georges Pompidou replaces him
- Neil Armstrong becomes the first man on the moon
- U.S. and North Vietnam begin peace negotiations, in secret
- Mary Jo Kopechne drowns at Chappaquiddick after Senator Edward Kennedy crashes the car in which they are travelling
- Colonel Gaddafi ousts King Idris of Libya in a coup

CRICKET HEADLINES 1968

County Champions: Yorkshire

Warwickshire win the Gillette Cup

The touring Australians halve the series one game all, and so retain the Ashes

The D'Oliveira Affair: the MCC tour to South Africa is cancelled, signalling the start of South Africa's exclusion from international cricket

Overseas players allowed immediate registration into county cricket

Gary Sobers hits six sixes in an over off Malcolm Nash at Swansea

NOTES BY THE EDITOR

'Looking back on the cricket scene of 1968 one can only call it tumultuous. It began with the riot in Jamaica; later came the D'Oliveira uproar that led to the cancellation of the M.C.C. tour of South Africa, and finally the threat to M.C.C. itself and the memorable meeting in December at Church House, Westminster, where the rebels were defeated after a discussion lasting four hours. To those not acquainted with the game, cricket must appear to be in a sorry state, but that is far from the truth. Apart from the almost incessant rain, I enjoyed most of the first-class cricket I saw last season.'

FEATURE ARTICLES

Watery Reflections From Australia, by Jack Fingleton
'Yorkshire, under the brilliant captaincy of Fred Trueman – and I saw no better leadership in England during the summer – diddled the Australians completely, beating them by an innings and 69 at Sheffield, an ignominious defeat for a touring side against a county ... I must pay tribute, too, to the second successive win of Glamorgan over the Australians on a good pitch in one of the best games of the tour. And in Alan Jones I saw one of the very best batsmen in Britain.'
The D'Oliveira Case, by Michael Melford
M.C. Cowdrey – Centurion and Captain Courteous, by John Arlott
J.B. Statham – Gentleman George, by Sir Neville Cardus
T.E. Bailey – Resolute and Impenitent, by John Woodcock
Yorkshire the Top County, by John Bapty
The Heritage of our Cricket Grounds, by Basil Easterbrook
Notable Dates in West Indies Cricket History, by Rowland Bowen

FIVE CRICKETERS OF THE YEAR

D.M. Green
'In Lancashire there is general regret that yet another fine cricketer got away. Certainly the powers that be at Old Trafford gave a fine stroke-player little opportunity to make a lasting

216

recovery from a leg injury that specialists said required surgery. Green did not think this necessary, believing that time and a winter's rest would restore him to complete fitness. He has been proved right and Gloucestershire have gained a tremendous asset in the signing of a cricketer whose zest for life is embodied in his cricket. David Green is undoubtedly the sort of player the game demands – aggressive, talented and entertaining.'

B.A. Richards

'Richards' horizons seem limitless, and it will be fascinating to see how far his talents will take him. Few, anywhere in the world, have his possibilities.'

J.G. Binks   D.L. Underwood   O.S. Wheatley

OBITUARIES INCLUDE

A.W.T. Grout

'A Brisbane doctor was afterwards reported as saying that Grout knew that he might collapse at any time during the last four years of his Test career and that he took part in the Australian tour of the West Indies only a few months after a heart attack in 1964. Yet Wally's unfailingly cheerful demeanour gave no inkling that there might be anything amiss with him.'

S.J. McCabe

'Perhaps McCabe's most famous innings was his 232 not out in the opening Test against England at Trent Bridge in 1938 which, scored at the rate of one a minute, prompted Sir Donald Bradman, his captain, to greet him on his return to the pavilion with the words: "If I could play an innings like that, I'd be a proud man, Stan."'

A.A. Thomson

'His early boyhood in Yorkshire had formed the subject of his brilliant autobiographical novel, *The Exquisite Burden* (1935), re-issued in 1963. He wrote nearly 60 books in all, including plays, novels, verse, humour and travel books, and in 1953, with *Cricket My Pleasure*, there began his long series of cricket books in which his buoyant philosophy of the game, with all its comedy and character, shone through in rich prose and mellow phrases … He also contributed some delightful articles to *Wisden*. Probably no cricket author since Sir Neville Cardus was in his prime had a closer following.'

R.A. Young

'One of the few spectacled players to represent England at both cricket and Association football.'

COUNTY REVIEW

Nottinghamshire

'Nottinghamshire county cricket gained a tremendous boost from the introduction of Garfield Sobers, the West Indies captain, to lead the side. From the struggling team of recent seasons they were rejuvenated and it was no more than they deserved to finish fourth in the County Championship.'

MATCH REPORTS

England v Australia, Fifth Test Match, *at The Oval, August 22, 23, 24, 26, 27*

'England won by 226 runs with six minutes to spare and squared the rubber with one victory to each country and three matches drawn, but The Ashes stayed with Australia. Down the years Kennington has generally proved a good place for England and now, after rain had robbed Cowdrey's men at Lord's and Edgbaston, even a storm that flooded the ground at lunch time on the last day could not save Australia. Just before the interval England's final task appeared to be a mere formality with Australia toiling at 85 for five. In half an hour the ground was under water, but the sun reappeared at 2.15 p.m. and the groundsman, Ted Warn, ably assisted by volunteers from the crowd, armed with brooms and blankets, mopped up to such purpose that by 4.45 p.m. the struggle was resumed.'

1970

WISDEN 1970

107th EDITION
EDITOR: Norman Preston
PAGES: 1127
PRICE: Limp £1.10s   cloth £1.15s

THE WORLD AT LARGE

- Edward Heath's Conservative Party defeats Labour, led by Harold Wilson, in the June general election, the first in which 18-year-olds could vote
- Tony Jacklin becomes the first British golfer to win the U.S. Open since 1925
- First Boeing 747 Jumbo enters passenger service
- Brazil wins the 1970 World Cup, held in Mexico
- Salvador Allende elected President of Chile
- Japanese author Yukio Mishima commits ritual suicide

CRICKET HEADLINES 1969

County Champions: Glamorgan

John Player 40-over League inaugurated: Lancashire are the first champions

Yorkshire win the Gillette Cup, defeating Derbyshire in the final

England beat the visiting West Indians 2-0 to win the Wisden Trophy

They also beat the New Zealanders 2-0

Ireland dismiss West Indies for 25 and win by nine wickets in a one-day game at Sion Mills

England draw all three Tests against Pakistan in Pakistan, the final Test being ended by a riot

NOTES BY THE EDITOR

'As we move into the seventies cricket in England tries to keep pace with the times. Among the recent better innovations were the introduction in 1968 of bonus points in place of the former award for first-innings lead and the restricted immediate registration of overseas players, and in 1969 the new John Player's Sunday County League. Now for 1970 we have an important change in the lbw law which it is hoped will curb pad play even if it does not eradicate it completely. Behind all this we have been compelled to endure the repercussions of the wretched d'Oliveira affair and the antiapartheid demonstrations against the South African Rugby team which threaten to continue if the South African cricketers manage to fulfil their scheduled tour here this summer.'

FEATURE ARTICLES

A History of Wicket-Covering in England, by Irving Rosenwater
'At the annual meeting of the county secretaries at Lord's on December 7, 1909, it was resolved that the county committees ask M.C.C. to empower the executive of each county ground to adopt any covering to protect the ground, before or during a match, against rain, provided that the said covering does not cover a larger area than 18 ft. by 12 ft. and does not exceed more than 3 ft. 6 in. in front of the popping crease.'
And Gilligan Led Them Out, by Rowland Ryder
Enid Bakewell – Champion Woman Cricketer, by Netta Rheinberg
Emmott Robinson – The personification of Yorkshire cricket, by Sir Neville Cardus
Fiery Fred – The Greatest Bowler of all Time?, by W.E. Bowes
Glamorgan – A Peep Into The Past, by J.H. Morgan
Ken Barrington – The Accumulator, by John Woodcock
Ups and Downs of the Springboks, by Michael Melford

D.J. Shepherd

'Summer after summer he has wheeled down well over 1,000 overs, the cheerful, uncomplaining bed rock of the Glamorgan attack. Many will regard it as equally important that he is one of the best competitors and sportsmen to emerge in the past twenty years. Quick witted, good tempered but never less than a great fighter, an unfailing sense of humour and no tantrums – any captain's *beau ideal*.'

B.F. Butcher   Majid Khan   A.P.E. Knott   M.J. Procter

OBITUARIES INCLUDE

Earl Alexander of Tunis

'… was in the Harrow XI of 1910, taking part in Fowler's Match, which Eton won at Lord's by nine runs … In 1956, he was President of M.C.C. He earned great military distinction in both World Wars, and was later Governor General of Canada and Minister of Defence.'

Dr. R.H.B. Bettington

'In 1923, when he became the first Australian to captain Oxford … he reaped a rich harvest of Cambridge victims. Helped by the effects of what *Wisden* described as the worst thunderstorm for twelve years, he took three wickets for 19 runs in the first innings and eight for 66 in the second, thus playing a leading part in victory for Oxford by an innings and 227 runs – the most substantial in the series between the Universities.'

G.E.V. Crutchley

'Going up to Oxford, he did not gain a Blue till 1912 and in that year against Cambridge he set up a curious record. Having scored 99 not out, he was found at the end of the day to be suffering from measles and had to withdraw from the match … He held another distinction, for he was the last man to play cricket during the Canterbury Week and to act at night for the Old Stagers.'

V.Y. Richardson

'Besides taking part in 19 Test matches between 1924 and 1935, he represented his county at baseball and played for South Australia at Cricket, baseball and golf. He also won a State tennis title, was prominent at lacrosse and basketball and was a first-rate swimmer.'

COUNTY REVIEW

Glamorgan

'Watching Glamorgan's last-wicket pair engaged in a tense struggle to avoid defeat in their first match of the season against Yorkshire at Swansea, not even the most optimistic Welshman would have prophesied that Glamorgan would not only win the County Championship but complete a memorable summer unbeaten – a notable double which had not been achieved since Lancashire's record in 1930.'

MATCH REPORTS

Pakistan v England, Third Test Match, *at Karachi, March 6, 7, 8*

'Drawn. Rioting stopped the final match of the tour early on the third day, when Knott needed only four for a first Test century. He had batted three hours, thirty-five minutes and hit one 6 and ten 4's. Milburn, who had joined the side two days before the second Test, played a storming innings to launch England on their high scoring spree. Altogether he hit one 6 and seventeen 4's and reached his 100 off 163 balls in three and a quarter hours. Graveney was more subdued during a stay of almost five hours, during which he hit nine 4's.'

MISCELLANEOUS

'In the 1969 edition, Obituary, 1967, wrongly described John Seymour as a medium-pace right-arm bowler. He did, in fact, bowl slow left-arm.'

1971

WISDEN 1971

108th Edition
Editor: Norman Preston
Pages: 1127
Price: Limp £1.65   cloth £1.95

THE WORLD AT LARGE

- Ibrox Stadium disaster: 66 killed
- Britain switches to decimal currency on 15 February
- Parliament votes in favour of joining the EEC
- Idi Amin overthrows Milton Obote to become President of Uganda
- Bangladesh secedes from Pakistan

CRICKET HEADLINES 1970

County Champions: Kent

With the cancellation of the South African tour, England play the Rest of the World, and lose 4-1

Australia tour South Africa, the last Test cricket played by South Africa for two decades, and are trounced 4-0 by what is now considered South Africa's greatest ever side

Lancashire win the Gillette Cup and the John Player League

NOTES BY THE EDITOR

'With the continuous weeks of sunshine came also the long awaited improvement of pitches – the two main factors which govern the standard of cricket and the way it is played. In addition, we had the new experimental l.b.w. law which in my opinion gave the batsmen more freedom and consequently led to more attractive cricket, though whether it will become permanent remains to be seen. I am pleased that it will be continued in 1971; it must be given a reasonable trial to see the general trend for better or worse.'

FEATURE ARTICLES

Peter May – The Complete Master, by John Woodcock
'Cricket followers bestowed the same peculiar favour upon May as they had upon Denis Charles Scott Compton and John Berry Hobbs. They knew him by his full name. Ask those who played with or against him between 1955 and 1960, or who watched him play, and they will tell you that Peter Barker Howard May was England's finest post-war batsman.'
Reshaping Lancashire Cricket, by John Kay
Thrills of Sunday Cricket, by Jim Laker
The South African Tour Dispute, by Irving Rosenwater
The Midwinter File, by Grahame Parker
The Dreaded Cypher, by Basil Easterbrook

FIVE CRICKETERS OF THE YEAR

B.W. Luckhurst
'Luckhurst, always immaculately turned out and correctly behaved both on and off the field, is the personification of all that is best in the professional cricketer. He is a fighter by temperament, instinctively serving the needs of his side... His fielding is worth many runs a season to Kent. His understanding with Denness has not only made them a successful opening pair, but has played an important part in the county's revival. Never is Luckhurst anything but a credit to the game.'
J.D. Bond   C.H. Lloyd   G.M. Turner   R.T. Virgin

OBITUARIES INCLUDE

Canon F.B.R. Browne
'His action was extraordinary and was once described by *Wisden* as "a weird delivery that defies description". In the act of bowling, he appeared to cross his legs and deliver the ball off

the wrong foot. This earned him the soubriquet of 'Tishy' – the name of a race-horse of the time who once crossed his legs in running.'

J.S. Buller
'Syd was one of the central figures in what developed into a big controversy at Lord's in 1960, when I was his partner as umpire … I felt at that time, and still do: why should a man be pilloried for conscientiously fulfilling his duty?' – Frank Lee

G.A. Smithson
'Conscripted as a "Bevin Boy" in the mines after the war, he received special permission, after his case had been debated in the House of Commons, to tour the West Indies with the M.C.C. team of 1947-48, taking part in two Test matches. His picture appeared in *Wisden* 1948, page 38. In 1951 he joined Leicestershire, with whom he remained for six seasons.'

H. Strudwick
'In an article, "From Dr. Grace to Peter May", in the 1959 *Wisden,* hailed by the critics as one of the best published by "The Cricketers' Bible" for many years, "Struddy", as he was affectionately known throughout the cricket world, described how hard was life as a professional cricketer in his young days. Then, one dare not stand down because of injury for fear of losing a place in the side and consequent loss of pay. Compared with that of today, the equipment of wicket-keepers was flimsy and the men behind the stumps took a lot of punishment.'

B.H. Lyon   T.F. Smailes   G.T.S. Stevens   A.F. Wensley

COUNTY REVIEW

Essex
'The county gained two fewer victories than in 1969, which meant that they dropped from sixth place in the Championship to twelfth. Yet these two wins could have been achieved but for rain which, in home matches with Lancashire and Middlesex, intervened when success for Essex appeared to be within reasonable range. An additional 20 points would have kept Essex in much the same position as in the year before.'

MATCH REPORTS

South Africa v Australia, Second Test Match, *at Kingsmead, Durban, February 5, 6, 7, 9, 10*
'South Africa won by an innings and 129 runs … The match produced a host of new records, pride of place going to Graeme Pollock for his mammoth 274 which gave him the individual record for a South African in Test matches … His concentration never wavered and he attacked continuously and with merciless efficiency … Another highlight of the match was Richards' maiden Test hundred in only his second Test. In an exhibition of technical perfection the 24-year-old Natal and Hampshire batsman scored 140 of the 229 runs on the board. He reached his hundred off 116 deliveries and his only false stroke in a three-hour innings was his last one. He had Pollock as a partner for the last hour and the spectators were treated to a superb display as the pair added 103 runs for the third wicket. Between them they scored 414 runs of South Africa's gigantic total.'

Warwickshire v Derbyshire, *at Coventry, August 8, 10, 11*
'Kanhai dominated the Warwickshire first innings with a remarkable century – the fiftieth of his career. Ward's hostile pace upset his colleagues and Kanhai scored all but six (singles by Brown and Tidy and four extras) of Warwickshire's last 126. Gibbs failed to contribute to a ninth wicket stand of 53.'

MISCELLANEOUS

'No bowler took nine wickets in an innings – the first time that this has happened since 1887. The best analysis was eight for 37 by L.R. Gibbs for Warwickshire v Glamorgan, at Birmingham.'

Norman Preston completes twenty years as editor, and has been involved with Wisden *since 1933. With decimalisation comes a substantial price rise. Today, this edition is one of the more expensive post-war issues for collectors.*

1972

WISDEN 1972

109th Edition
Editor: Norman Preston
Pages: 1155
Price: Limp £2.00   cloth £2.25

THE WORLD AT LARGE

- The Miners' Strike lasts seven weeks
- Bloody Sunday: 14 killed when troops open fire on demonstrators in Londonderry
- Olympic Games in Munich disrupted by Palestinian terrorists who capture and kill Israeli athletes
- 118 people die in air crash at Staines
- Thousands of Indians expelled by Idi Amin from Uganda arrive in Britain
- Republican party activists break in to the Democratic election headquarters in the Watergate building in Washington D.C.

CRICKET HEADLINES 1971

County Champions: Surrey

Lancashire retain the Gillette Cup, and Worcestershire claim the Sunday league title

England recapture the Ashes in Australia under Ray Illingworth, by 2 matches to nil

Pakistan and India tour England – Pakistan lose the series by one match to nil, but India beat England by one match to nil.

Barry Richards hits 356 (including 325 in a day) for South Australia v Western Australia at Perth

Geoff Boycott averages over 100 for the season, the first Englishman ever to do so

NOTES BY THE EDITOR

'For something like sixty-five years M.C.C. were responsible for organising and sending official Test teams from this country to play overseas. Now we have the Cricket Council ... M.C.C. had no hand in choosing the players who went to Australia. The Test and County Cricket Board selectors, namely A.V. Bedser, D. Kenyon, A.C. Smith and C. Washbrook, were responsible for appointing the captain – the manager having already been named by M.C.C. Surely it would be preferable for the side to be called England in the Tests and England XI in other engagements.'

FEATURE ARTICLES

The Great Wicket-Keepers, by Rowland Ryder
'In 1835 round-arm bowling was legalised, and Alfred Mynn, The Lion of Kent, bowled, says G.D. Martineau, in his incomparable book *The Valiant Stumper*, with a terrifying hum on murderous turf. Ned Wenman (1803-1879) kept wicket to his bowling — barehanded and without pads. Wenman was the first of the great Kent wicket-keepers. He was not expected to take every ball the batsman missed, especially those on the leg side: the position of longstop was no sinecure.'
Compton's Record Season, by Basil Easterbrook
Welcome Australia, by E.R. Dexter
Sir Donald Bradman – Selector, by Irving Rosenwater
A Lifetime With Surrey, by Andrew Sandham

FIVE CRICKETERS OF THE YEAR

B.S. Chandrasekhar

'Chandrasekhar must be unique in that he has turned his deformity, a withered arm, into an instrument of success. The belief is that the thinness of his arm gives it the flexibility of whipcord, enabling him to produce the extra bite in his top-spinner. Indeed, Chandrasekhar is not a wrist-spinner in the classical mould. He is, in fact, medium-paced. Top-spinners and googlies are his stock-in-trade, although it is not that he never delivers a leg-break. In fact, several Indian batsmen have said that he now turns his leg-break more sharply than ever before.'

G.G. Arnold   L.R. Gibbs   B. Taylor   Zaheer Abbas

OBITUARIES INCLUDE

L.A. Bates
'… was born in the pavilion at the Warwickshire ground at Edgbaston, where his father was head groundsman.'

Lord Constantine
'He made his mark in the only way a poor West Indian boy of his time could do, by playing cricket of ability and character. He went on to argue the rights of the coloured peoples with such an effect as only a man who had won public affection by games-playing could have done in the Britain of that period.' – John Arlott

L. O'B. Fleetwood-Smith
'In England in 1938, he took part in four Tests and at Leeds earned match figures of seven wickets for 107 runs, he and O'Reilly (10 for 122) bearing a major part in the victory which decided the rubber. In the final match of the series at The Oval – his last Test appearance – however, he, in company with the other Australian bowlers, came in for a mauling. It was in that game that Leonard Hutton put together his record-breaking 364 and England won by the overwhelming margin of an innings and 579 runs. Fleetwood-Smith's analysis in a total of 903 was one wicket for 298 runs from 87 overs.'

P. Holmes
'Holmes often appeared to improvise; he could change stroke whenever his first glance at a ball's length had deceived him. He might move forward anticipating a half-volley; if the ball dropped shorter than its first flight advertised, he would, on swift feet, move back and cut late exquisitely' – Sir Neville Cardus

COUNTY REVIEW

Sussex
'The season had its gratifying moments, but they were too rare to make 1971 a year Sussex will look upon with any feeling of pride. Although they tempted Dexter back for 15 of the 16 John Player Sunday League games, Sussex were only a middle-of-the-table team in that competition, and they went out of the Gillette Cup in the first round, well beaten by Gloucestershire.'

MATCH REPORTS

England v India, First Test Match, *at Lord's, July 22, 23, 24, 26, 27*
'Soon after the start of the Indian second innings, Gavaskar, racing up to complete a quick single, was barged to the ground by Snow, as the pair ran up the pitch together. It was an incident for which the fast bowler was requested to apologise by both the chairman of selectors, Mr. A.V. Bedser, and Mr. S.C. Griffith, secretary of the Test and County Cricket Board. After he had done so, the Indians announced that they considered the matter closed. Nevertheless, the England selectors omitted Snow from the second Test as a disciplinary measure.'

MISCELLANEOUS

'Kent achieved a unique record by beating another county five times during the season: Yorkshire were defeated in the Gillette Cup, John Player League, Fenner Trophy and twice during the County Championship.'

A 35p price increase on the limp cover version represents a jump of just over 20%.

1973

WISDEN 1973

110th Edition
Editor: Norman Preston
Pages: 1111
Price: Limp £2.00   cloth £2.25

THE WORLD AT LARGE

- Britain joins the EEC
- Richard Nixon inaugurated for a second term, but the year is dominated by the Watergate hearings
- IRA bomb the Old Bailey and Whitehall
- Vietnam ceasefire agreement signed
- Spiro Agnew forced to resign as Vice-President of USA: he is replaced by Gerald Ford
- Arab-Israeli 'Yom Kippur' War

CRICKET HEADLINES 1972

County Champions: Warwickshire

In the first year of the Benson and Hedges Cup, Leicestershire beat Yorkshire in the final

Kent win the John Player League, and Lancashire complete a hat-trick of Gillette Cup wins

Bob Massie takes sixteen wickets on his Test debut at Lord's as Australia draw the series 2-2, and England keep the Ashes

Pat Pocock takes seven wickets in eleven balls as Surrey gain an unlikely draw against Sussex at Eastbourne

Lawrence Rowe scores 214* and 100 on his Test debut for West Indies

NOTES BY THE EDITOR

'From most points of view the English season of 1972 was the best for some time. The presence of the Australians coupled with generous endowment from sponsorship brought beaming smiles from the county treasurers. In other words county cricket is back on its feet again financially, but many people consider that in its present varying forms of one-to three-day contests, jumbled together, standards are falling, especially where batting is concerned.'

FEATURE ARTICLES

Shillings for W.G., by Sir Compton MacKenzie
'Well do I remember the venerated figure of W.W. Read, the Surrey batsman, in his chocolate coloured cap; we were too much in awe of cricketers eighty years ago to pester them for autographs. I recall dark handsome Tom Richardson, the Surrey fast bowler, and fair handsome Lockwood; I recall the burly figure of Sir Timothy O'Brien making terrific swipes of the redoubtable Yorkshire bowler Peel; I recall F.R. Spofforth, the "demon" bowler, with his heavy drooping moustache.'
Skills and Controversy, by Richie Benaud
Ray Illingworth C.B.E., by Trevor Bailey
The Warwickshire Way, by Rowland Ryder
Norfolk and the Edrich Clan, by Basil Easterbrook

FIVE CRICKETERS OF THE YEAR

D.K. Lillee
'The Haslingden Club in the Lancashire League has a lot to answer for in the emergence of Dennis Lillee as Australia's trump card in the 1972 tour of England. Lillee, who is not yet at his peak, should be in even better bowling form when the England side comes to Australia next year, and he gives full credit to the season he had in Lancashire League cricket. "I think it was probably one of the real turning points in my career. It certainly forced me to become

more accurate and learn a little bit about bowling, rather than merely thump down the ball as fast as possible."'

G.S. Chappell   R.A.L. Massie   J.A. Snow   K.R. Stackpole

OBITUARIES INCLUDE

J.S. Cobbold
'... died on July 15, aged 83, while taking off his pads after opening the innings for Old Ipswichians, of which club he was President, in a Suffolk Alliance match at Hadleigh. An active club cricketer throughout his adult life, he played for Suffolk in 1913.'

C. Hallows
'... the cricketer who refused to grow old, died suddenly at his Bolton home on November 10 and the fact that he was aged 77 must have surprised all but the older generation of Lancashire cricket followers. They remembered Hallows as a stylish left-hander who in 1928 hit a thousand runs *in May* – a feat performed by only two other players, Dr. W.G. Grace and W.R. Hammond – and scored more than 20,000 runs for his county between 1914 and 1932 ... yet played only twice in Test matches for England.'

H.L.V. Day   A.F. Kippax   E.A. Martindale   S.J. Pegler

COUNTY REVIEW

Northamptonshire
'Northamptonshire proved one of the surprise teams in the Championship of 1972. They finished fourth after a lean spell which had seen them in the fourteenth position for the two previous seasons ... This was largely due to the foresight of the Club committee in deciding on the value of top class bowlers, and going out to make the Northamptonshire attack one of the strongest in the country. Northamptonshire secured one of the world's best slow left-arm bowlers, Bishen Bedi. The Hampshire ... pace bowler Bob Cottam joined the club ... [and] another pace bowler, John Dye, released by Kent, was the third bowling capture. When Mushtaq, the Pakistani leg-break bowler, was added, Northamptonshire possessed a most powerful bowling quartette.'

MATCH REPORTS

England v Australia, Second Test Match, *at Lord's, June 22, 23, 24, 26*
'Australia soon avenged their defeat at Manchester in a contest which will be remembered as Massie's match. The 25-year-old fast bowler from Western Australia surpassed all Australian Test bowling records by taking sixteen wickets for 137 runs; in all Tests only J.C. Laker, nineteen for 90 for England against Australia in 1956 and S.F. Barnes, seventeen for 179 for England against South Africa in 1913-14, stand above him. Moreover, Massie performed this wonderful feat on his Test debut, the previous best by a bowler on his first appearance for his country being as far back as 1890 when at The Oval, Frederick Martin, a left-arm slow medium pacer from Kent, took twelve for 102 for England against Australia on a pitch that had been saturated by rain.'

MISCELLANEOUS

'For the first time since 1866, no bowler took 100 wickets in the season.'

Norman Preston writes in his Preface: 'I am pleased that at last the Test Match centres have removed the embargo on photographers and extended the list of those who can now attend.' As a result, the first photographs by Patrick Eagar appear in the 1974 edition, including shots of four of the Five Cricketers of the Year.

1974

WISDEN 1974

111th Edition
Editor: Norman Preston
Pages: 1193
Price: Limp £2.25   cloth £2.50

THE WORLD AT LARGE

- Three-day working week imposed to cut power usage
- General election results in a hung parliament, but eventually Labour takes office: a second general election later in the year gives Labour a slim overall majority
- IRA bombings: the Houses of Parliament, a bus on the M62 and pubs in Birmingham and Guildford are among the targets
- The Watergate scandal brings down President Nixon: Gerald Ford takes over and immediately pardons his predecessor

CRICKET HEADLINES 1973

County Champions: Hampshire

Kent win the Benson and Hedges Cup and retain the John Player League title

Gloucestershire win the Gillette Cup

Glenn Turner scores 1,000 runs before the end of May

Colin Cowdrey scores his 100th century

England beat the touring New Zealanders 2-0, but lose to the West Indies by 2-0.

During the previous winter, England lose 2-1 to India and draw all three Tests in Pakistan

NOTES BY THE EDITOR

'It was regrettable that Kanhai showed such open dissent on the field of Edgbaston when umpire Fagg turned down an appeal against Boycott for a catch at the wicket. Fagg threatened to quit the match, and indeed it took a lot of persuasion behind the scenes before he agreed to resume next morning after missing the first over. The reaction of Fagg while at boiling point met with much criticism … but at least it brought the matter to a head. For too long, and not only in this country, players from junior to senior standing have been reflecting their dislike at umpire's decisions almost with disdain. Now the T.C.C.B. have taken a firm stand.'

FEATURE ARTICLES

A Century in the Fiji Islands, by P.A. Snow
'The larger the crowd, the greater the panache, the radiation of zest. Fijians reserve briskness of tempo for their games as a contrast to their everyday existence. For organising Fijians, European administrators have been essential. Sir Basil Thomson (later Governor of Dartmoor and Head of Scotland Yard) and A. B. Joske (later Brewster) of Polish origin (whose widow survives at 101 in Bath), had to resist Fijian attempts to overlay the game's laws with tribal ideas for improving them, such as the crack bowler after an over resuming promptly at the other end and chiefs' inclinations to leave fielding to commoners.'

Kent's Triumphant Revival, by Dudley Moore
Glenn Turner Joins the Elite, by Basil Easterbrook
The Glorious Uncertainty, by Rowland Ryder
When Three-day Cricket was Worthwhile, by C.T. Bennett
Farewell Bramall Lane, by Keith Farnsworth
Cricket's Strongest Wind of Change, by Gordon Ross

B.E. Congdon

'His innings of 176 at Trent Bridge and 175 at Lord's were all he needed to make his mark indelibly in the story of New Zealand cricket. And he has given much more than those two fine performances. Essentially practical, Congdon at thirty-five took New Zealand to Australia for a first full tour there. It was a demanding job. He, almost alone among the New Zealand cricketers of his generation looked capable of withstanding the pressure of the Australian press, public and players. No Trumper; no Bradman; Congdon is simply a cricketers' cricketer.'

K.D. Boyce   K.W.R. Fletcher   R.C. Fredericks   P.J. Sainsbury

Miss M.B. Duggan

'She toured Australia with the England teams of 1948-49 and 1957-58 before being given the captaincy, retiring after ending her career in 1963 with innings of 101 not out and 32 and bowling figures of seven wickets for 72 runs which helped England to victory by 49 runs over Australia at the Oval and so deciding the Test rubber. She bowled fast-medium left-arm.'

J.M. Gregory

'He was a generous and likeable Australian. He gave himself to cricket with enthusiasm and relish. He enjoyed himself and was the cause of enjoyment in others.' – Sir Neville Cardus

J.B. Iverson

'While on Army service in New Guinea, Big Jack, as he was known, developed a peculiar method of spinning the ball, which he gripped between his thumb and middle finger. This enabled him to bowl a wide variety of deliveries, including off-breaks, leg-breaks and googlies, without any change of action. He first attracted attention in big cricket in 1949-50 when he took 46 wickets for Victoria at an average cost of 16.12.'

W. Rhodes

'In his old age he lost his eyesight and found his tongue. He accepted his affliction philosophically, and consoled himself by a flow of genial chatter never before heard from him. He attended cricket as long as health would permit. With an acquired sense he was able to follow the play.' – Sir Neville Cardus

J.C. Clay   J.A. Newman   J.M. Sims   H.W. Taylor   A. Wood   T.S. Worthington

Leicestershire

'It was ironic during such a glorious summer that Leicestershire should have been involved in the one county game where not a ball was bowled, but even so this hardly affected their championship standing considering they finished just one short of a century of points behind the champions, Hampshire!'

England v New Zealand, Second Test Match, *at Lord's, June 21, 22, 23, 25, 26*

'New Zealand have never been closer to beating England than they were on the final afternoon of this match in which Illingworth's side were outplayed almost throughout. Only a mature, dedicated second innings of 178 by Fletcher enabled England to escape. Fletcher, after a long series of disappointments in home Tests … rose to the occasion and denied New Zealand what would have been a well-deserved triumph.'

From the editor's Preface: 'I trust the new photo-typesetting will meet with general approval.'

1975

WISDEN 1975

112th Edition
Editor: Norman Preston
Pages: 1163
Price: Limp £2.75   cloth £3.00

THE WORLD AT LARGE

- Margaret Thatcher becomes leader of the Conservative Party
- End of the Vietnam War: Saigon falls to the North Vietnamese
- In Australia, the Governor-General dismisses Gough Whitlam as Premier and installs Malcolm Fraser in his place
- Death of Franco: Juan Carlos is proclaimed King of Spain
- Ross McWhirter, co-founder of the Guinness Book Of Records, shot dead by IRA assassins
- Moorgate Tube crash kills 43

CRICKET HEADLINES 1974

County Champions: Worcestershire

Surrey win the Benson and Hedges title, despite Ken Higgs' hat-trick for Leicestershire in the final

Leicestershire win the John Player League, and Kent the Gillette Cup

England halve a high scoring series in West Indies, one-all

Lawrence Rowe hits 302 for West Indies against England in Barbados

England beat the visiting Indians 3-0, but draw all three Tests against Pakistan

Jameson and Kanhai add 465 for the second wicket for Warwickshire v Gloucestershire, a world record

NOTES BY THE EDITOR

'Players have to be found this summer to take part in the Prudential (World) Cup and the four Test Matches that will follow against Australia … Others who come to mind are two tall Somerset youngsters, Ian Botham, a 19-year-old opening bowler and splendid batsman, and Peter Denning, a left-handed bat … I would particularly like to see Botham given a chance while he is young and enthusiastic.'

FEATURE ARTICLES

Buying Back One's Past, by John I. Marder
'The advertising in *Wisden* for the past hundred and eleven years is evocative of the times in which we and our fathers have lived. There is a ticket to buy back one's past implicit in the Almanack. A browse through the advertising pages brings memories of days far different from our own. *Wisden* has seen the transition of cricket from a country pastime to a world wide sport. Amateurs have now disappeared from county cricket and one-day cricket is with us. Test cricket will inevitably widen and include some countries not yet in the charmed circle. I think particularly of Sri Lanka who will no doubt merit Test status shortly.'
The Pleasures of Cricket, by HRH the Duke of Edinburgh
Old Trafford Humiliated, by Sir Neville Cardus
Sir Garfield Sobers in Test Cricket, by John Arlott
Joy of Touring, by Henry Blofeld
200 Years of Laws, by Gordon Ross
Gilbert Jessop – The Most Exciting Cricketer, by Rowland Ryder
Willing Workhorses of Cricket, by Basil Easterbrook
Cricket in Israel, by Hon. Terence Prittie

A.W. Greig

'We must not fail to pay tribute to Tackies, the Greigs' young Bantu gardener. Tackies, so called by the family from the big white plimsolls he invariably wore, had no interest in batting but he loved bowling – a Boycott in reverse, as it were.

"He was fast, he was tireless and he could bowl straight. He used to come at me from one end of our back lawn with a variety of cricket balls, tennis balls, hard rubber balls – anything that was round and approximately the right size. I stood at the other end of the lawn with my bat defending a dustbin. The last I heard of Tackies he was working in a goldmine near Johannesburg. I wonder if he's found someone else to bowl at?"'

D.L. Amiss   M.H. Denness   N. Gifford   A.M.E. Roberts

OBITUARIES INCLUDE

A. Booth

'… had one of the most extraordinary careers of any first-class cricketer. It began in 1931 with two matches, ceased at the end of the summer and did not continue until 1946. Then, having headed both the Yorkshire and the complete county bowling averages at the age of 43 … Booth appeared in only four matches in 1947, disappearing once more into the Bradford League … never to play for Yorkshire again.'

C.S. Dempster

'One of the greatest batsmen produced by New Zealand. He played in 10 Test matches between 1929 and 1932, scoring 732 runs, average 65, and hitting two centuries, both against England... It was difficult to realise that such a stylish, gifted batsman never enjoyed the benefit of coaching.'

L. Kilby

'… physiotherapist and medical attendant to Kent C.C.C. for the last five years, died on July 22, the day set for his second marriage. He was 69 and a widower. His wedding was set two days earlier, but he put it back in case Kent got into the final of the Benson and Hedges Cup.'

Earl of Rosebery

'In 164 innings in first-class cricket he scored 3,551 runs, average 23.05. He left £9,650,986 net.'

E.H. Bowley   G.S. Boyes   W.L.C. Creese   K.G. Viljoen   H. Yarnold

---

COUNTY REVIEW

Hampshire

'Hampshire's defence of the County Championship albeit unsuccessful in the end through no fault of their own, was one of the most admirable features of the season. They led the table from early in the season and were not displaced until the finishing line when rain washed out five days' play in the last three matches, allowing Worcestershire to take the title by two points."'

MATCH REPORTS

Hampshire v Yorkshire, *at Bournemouth, August 31, September 2, 3*

'Abandoned without a ball being bowled. Hampshire went into the match with a two-point lead over Worcestershire, who were able to take four points against Essex and win the title while their rivals were imprisoned in the pavilion by rain. Strenuous efforts were made to make the ground playable on the third day but, after it was agreed to start at 3 p.m., rain predictably returned and Hampshire surrendered the title in a most unsatisfactory manner.'

From the Preface: 'One innovation is in the County Championship section where team pictures of each of the seventeen counties are reproduced.'

1976

WISDEN 1976

113th Edition
Editor: Norman Preston
Pages: 1223
Price: Limp £3.00   cloth £3.50

THE WORLD AT LARGE

- Harold Wilson suddenly resigns as Prime Minister: James Callaghan takes over
- The first commercial flight of Concorde
- UK Ambassador to Ireland killed by a landmine outside Dublin
- Democrat Jimmy Carter defeats incumbent Gerald Ford in the U.S. presidential elections
- Death of Chairman Mao
- The Sex Pistols achieve notoriety by swearing live on BBC television

CRICKET HEADLINES 1975

County Champions: Leicestershire

West Indies win the inaugural Prudential World Cup, beating Australia in the final by 17 runs

Down Under in 1974/75, Mike Denness' England are beaten by the speed and brute force of Lillee and Thomson

Australia win the four-Test series that follows the World Cup by one match to nil, with three drawn

David Steele, the 'bank clerk who went to war', becomes BBC TV Sports Personality of the Year for his fighting innings for England against Australia

NOTES BY THE EDITOR

'Surely the season of 1975 will go down in the annals of English cricket as one of the best of all time. England did not regain The Ashes, but the presence of the Australians, coupled with the tremendous success of the Prudential World Cup during weeks of glorious sunshine, created new interest and brought back the crowds to the best of all games when the right conditions prevail. At the beginning of August when England and Australia were engaged at Lord's in an intriguing contest it was hotter than in North Africa at 93 degrees Fahrenheit … so perhaps there was some excuse for the streaker who filled with Australian liquor, invaded the pitch while England were building up their second innings total of 436.'

FEATURE ARTICLES

Eleven West Indies Men of my Time, by Richie Benaud
'Francis Maglinne Worrell … now there was elegance for you. There was a man for all summers … He moved with the sleepy grace generally associated with the cat family and when he batted he was rarely boorish enough to hit the ball. Occasionally he stroked it but mostly he caressed it through the covers or past mid-on, sometimes there was a flick past square leg as a concession to conventional power. A great player, a great man and a wonderful servant to cricket.'
Welcome West Indies, by Henry Blofeld
The Greatest Centenary of them All, by Gordon Ross
M.J.K. Smith Lays Down His Bat, by John Woodcock
John Murray – Champion Keeper, by J.M. Brearley
The Greatly Praised – Hanif and his Brothers, by Basil Easterbrook
F.R. Foster – A Prince Of The Golden Age, by Rowland Ryder
Bert Lock – King Of Groundsmen, by Alex Bannister

FIVE CRICKETERS OF THE YEAR

R.A. Woolmer

'For Kent he had of course moved from No. 9 to No. 5 in a couple of seasons, but to be talked about as a batsman pure and simple required by England, took him some getting used to. He made only five in the first innings but in the second stayed at the wicket for just over eight hours – 385 balls in fact – to score 149. That was the longest innings he had ever played, in fact the slowest hundred for England against Australia and nearly three times as long as his previous longest stay at the wicket.'

I.M. Chappell   P.G. Lee   R.B. McCosker   D.S. Steele

OBITUARIES INCLUDE

M. Boddey
'Martin Boddey, the well-known singer and actor, who died suddenly on October 24, aged 68, was founder of the Lord's Taverners, who since 1949 have raised more than £250,000 to help youth cricket.'

Sir Neville Cardus
'All cricket writers of the last half century have been influenced by Cardus, whether they admit it or not, whether they have wished to be or not, whether they have tried to copy him or tried to avoid copying him. He was not a model, any more than Macaulay, say, was a model for the aspiring historian. But just as Macaulay changed the course of the writing of history, Cardus changed the course of the writing of cricket. He shewed what could be done. He dignified and illuminated the craft.' – Alan Gibson

16th Duke of Norfolk
'On his lovely ground at Arundel, where he firmly believed, not without some justification, that the wicket was the best in the world, sides from the colonies frequently opened their tour in April with a match in aid of charity against his team.'

P.G. Wodehouse
'… the famous novelist, who died in hospital on Long Island on February 14 at the age of 93, had been a member of the Dulwich College XI in 1899 and 1900.'

COUNTY REVIEW

Warwickshire
'Warwickshire had a truly mournful season and dropped five places to fourteenth in the County Championship – their lowest placing since 1960 when they finished fifteenth … Their fall from grace was illustrated by the fact that at one stage from the end of July Warwickshire went fourteen matches without a victory of any kind. They broke the barren spell by beating Surrey in the John Player League but then had a relapse and returned to their dismal form by losing their final Championship match of the season to Northamptonshire.'

MATCH REPORTS

Australia v West Indies, Prudential Cup Final, *at Lord's, June 21*
'Prince Philip presented the Cup amidst hilarious scenes to West Indies' talented captain, the Man of the Match, Clive Lloyd, just before nine o'clock on a glorious summer's evening. From 11am till 8.43pm the cricketers from the Caribbean had been locked in a succession of thrills with the cricketers from the Southern Cross. It might not be termed first-class cricket, but the game has never produced better entertainment in one day. The deciding factor was the wonderful hundred by Clive Lloyd after Ian Chappell had won the toss and invited the West Indies to bat … Australia gained the initiative when Fredericks hooked a bouncer high over fine leg for 6 only to lose his balance and tread on his wicket … Then came Lloyd, and at once he showed himself master of the situation.'

Norman Preston celebrates 25 years in the editor's chair, and 'the 43rd Wisden I have had a hand in producing, but sad to say two of my colleagues over that long period, Ebenezer Eden and Harry Gee, died between September and January of this year.' Also: 'Cricket and music lost one of the great writers of modern times in the passing of Sir Neville Cardus, who did not consider Wisden complete without an offering from his pen.'

1977

WISDEN 1977

114th EDITION
EDITOR: Norman Preston
PAGES: 1127
PRICE: Limp £3.75   cloth £4.25

THE WORLD AT LARGE

- The Queen's Silver Jubilee
- Red Rum wins his third Grand National
- Two Boeing 747s collide on the runway at Tenerife, killing 583 people
- Deaths of Elvis Presley (Aug 16) and Bing Crosby (Oct 14)
- Steve Biko dies while in police custody in South Africa

CRICKET HEADLINES 1976

County Champions: Middlesex

Kent win the JPL and B&H competitions

Northamptonshire win the Gillette Cup

West Indies once again beat England, 3-0 in England

Viv Richards scores 829 runs in the Tests, at an average of 118.42

NOTES BY THE EDITOR

'Whereas in 1975 the cash distribution to the counties from Test receipts, T.V. and radio, and sponsorship amounted to the satisfactory sum of £661,000, the final surplus in 1976 was expected to come to £950,000. Under the able leadership of Mike Brearley, Middlesex won the County Championship outright for the first time since 1947 and they went to Buckingham Palace to receive the Lord's Taverners Trophy from their Patron, the Duke of Edinburgh. There was a tremendous struggle for the John Player Sunday league prize, which went to Kent, who also lifted the Benson and Hedges Trophy, and Northamptonshire, one of the Cinderellas of the county scene, won the Gillette Cup. This was Northamptonshire's first success in their long history which dates back to 1820 and now only Essex and Somerset, of the seventeen first-class counties, have yet to break the ice.'

FEATURE ARTICLES

From Spofforth to Lillee, by Richie Benaud
'Together Lillee and Thomson are the fastest pair I have ever seen. You can throw in Hall and Griffith, Tyson and Statham, Miller and Lindwall and if I had to choose one pair it would be Lillee and Thomson. What ... just what ... would they have done if they had played in the late forties when administrators gave fast bowlers the chance of having a new ball every 40 overs in Australia and every 55 overs in England?'
G.O. Allen – Mr. Cricket, by Ian Peebles
Tales of W.G. Grace, by Jack Arlidge
The Cricket Rhymester, by Basil Easterbrook
Over 100 Years of Scarborough Festivities, by J.M. Kilburn
Derief Taylor – The Natural Coach, by W.G. Wanklyn
The Gillette Cup Spans the World, by Gordon Ross

FIVE CRICKETERS OF THE YEAR

J.M. Brearley

'The Middlesex players, committee and supporters owe much to their captain, especially when they contrast his term as leader with the dark days. Brearley acknowledges his own debts. "Mike Smith and Clive Radley are tremendously helpful. We have an affinity being around the same age. Also Fred Titmus's tactical guidance has proved valuable, but everyone is entitled to his opinion," a view not shared by all county captains and certainly not one prevalent at Lord's in the recent past.'

C.G. Greenidge   M.A. Holding   I.V.A. Richards   R.W. Taylor

OBITUARIES INCLUDE

Lt. Col. G.H.G.M. Cartwright
'A brave hard-hitting batsman and an excellent fielder and he continued to play in good club cricket until he was well over seventy. Known to his countless friends and to many others as "Buns", he was an accomplished player of many games and for years one of the best-known characters in the games-playing world.'

H.P. Chadwyck-Healey
'As a cricketer his enthusiasm greatly exceeded his skill, but he was quite well known as a composer of church music.'

A.E.R. Gilligan
'... was one of the most popular and inspiring captains that England or Sussex ever had.' – R.L. Arrowsmith

W.A. Oldfield
'Oldfield took the fliers of Gregory and McDonald and the googlies of Mailey, Grimmett, O'Reilly and Fleetwood-Smith. Unlike the "blood and iron" wicket-keepers of the old school, he didn't keep raw meat in his gloves: a more fastidious craftsman, he used two pairs of inners and finger stalls: even so, the expresses of McDonald and Gregory left their mark.' – Rowland Ryder

K.J. Wadsworth
'... died in Nelson, N. Z., on August 19, aged 29. He had been New Zealand's regular keeper since 1969, playing in thirty-three Tests, the last of them against India at Wellington in February 1976: in these he dismissed 95 batsmen and made over a thousand runs. He toured England in 1969 and 1973. As a keeper, he was always brilliant and as time went on became more consistent: perhaps even when he died he had not reached his best.'

F. Watson
'... a batsman whom spectators of fifty years ago will, unless they were fervent Lancashire supporters, remember as one of whom they wished to see as little as possible, but there could be no doubt of his value to the county.'

A.W.T. Langford   G.D. Martineau   A. Mitchell

COUNTY REVIEW

Surrey
'There has never been a cricket season when one county or another has not bemoaned its luck, but Surrey had more reason than most to look back in anguish on the year 1976. The ground development scheme fell through; the form of the players went down; injuries and accidents went up; and finally for the first time since MCC went to India in 1951/52, the touring party, announced early in September, did not contain a Surrey cricketer.'

MATCH REPORTS

England v West Indies, Third Test Match, *at Old Trafford, July 8, 9, 10, 12, 13*
'So England went in needing 552 in thirteen and a quarter hours, a forlorn prospect. The period before the close of the third day brought disquieting cricket as Edrich and Close grimly defended their wickets and themselves against fast bowling, which was frequently too wild and too hostile to be acceptable. Holding was finally warned for intimidation by umpire Alley after an excess of bouncers. Lloyd admitted after the match: "Our fellows got carried away. They knew they had only eighty minutes that night to make an impression and they went flat out, sacrificing accuracy for speed. They knew afterwards they had bowled badly."'

1978

WISDEN 1978

115th EDITION
EDITOR: Norman Preston
PAGES: 1163
PRICE: Limp £4.25   cloth £4.85

THE WORLD AT LARGE

• The first test tube baby, Louise Brown, is born
• Former Italian premier Aldo Moro is kidnapped and killed by the Red Brigade
• Death of Pope Paul VI: he is succeeded by John Paul I, who dies after 33 days. Pope John Paul II, his successor, becomes the first Polish pope in history
• Bulgarian dissident Georgi Markov is killed in London by a poisoned umbrella tip
• In Guyana, Jim Jones leads his People's Temple cult in a mass suicide: over 900 people die from poisoning

CRICKET HEADLINES 1977

County Champions: Middlesex and Kent (tied)

England beat the Packer-riven Australians 3-0 at home

Geoffrey Boycott becomes the first player to reach his 100th hundred in a Test match

John Edrich also hits his 100th hundred

Kerry Packer's World Series Cricket causes a major rift in the cricket world, with Test players from all countries joining his 'circus'

Australia win the Centenary Test match in Australia by the same margin as they won the first-ever Test – 45 runs

NOTES BY THE EDITOR

'Without wishing to detract from the very high status of the best in Pakistan cricket, one cannot help but question the validity of some records set up in that country … During the past four seasons up to 1976-77, 57 individual innings of 200 or over have been played and of these 30 have occurred in Pakistan. In a list of 103 players since 1859 whose maiden century was 200 or more, nine of the last eleven were scored in Pakistan. Since 1964 three totals over 800 have been amassed and all in Pakistan: 910 for six in 1964-65; 824 in 1965-66 and 951 for seven in 1973-74.'

FEATURE ARTICLES

The Packer Case, by Gordon Ross
'At the end of May, Packer arrived in England, and at a Press Conference, said: "It is not a pirate series but a Super-Test Series. I have sent telegrams to all the cricketing bodies but they don't reply. I am willing to compromise but time is running out." He referred to cricket as the easiest sport in the world to take over, as nobody had bothered to pay the players what they were worth.'
Judge Hits Cricket Ban For Six
The Centenary Test, by Reg Hayter
The Centurions of 1977, J.H. Edrich and G. Boycott
Effects of the Bumper, by Richie Benaud
One Hundred Years of Leicestershire Cricket, by E.E. Snow
Three Studies in Greatness, by Basil Easterbrook

FIVE CRICKETERS OF THE YEAR

A. Jones
'The extent to which Alan Jones has dominated the Glamorgan cricket scene is reflected in the number of records he has created. His aggregate of 26,590 runs surpasses that of any other Glamorgan player. His total of 43 centuries, 39 for Glamorgan, is again more than any other batsman.'

R.G.D. Willis

'With his 6 ft 6 ins frame topped by a thatch of unruly hair Bob Willis is a big man in every sense. And he had the good sense to turn down an invitation to join the Packer circus.'

I.T. Botham   M. Hendrick   K.S. McEwan

D. Adams

'… had the distinction, curious though not unique, of obtaining his only wicket in first-class cricket by bowling W.G. Grace.'

A.S. Bensimon

'Alfred Samuel Bensimon … had a short but very interesting first-class career. He played a single match for Western Province in 1931-32, making his début at the advanced age of 45, and he played three more matches for them in 1933-34 when he was over 47... He proved a statistician's nightmare, for his younger brother, Abel, had the identical initials, A.S., and he made his first-class début in 1912-13, twenty years before his elder brother; his career ended in 1923-24. Not surprisingly, it was assumed that they were one and the same person.'

A.E. Fagg

'One record which he holds may well never be equalled. In 1938 against Essex at Colchester, he scored 244 and 202 not out, the second innings taking only 170 minutes. His fielding was never on a par with his batting and after his early years, it was difficult to place him anywhere save in the slips.'

Sir Terence Rattigan

'… the famous play-writer … was an elegant stroke player, but unsound.'

D.K. Carmody   10th Viscount Cobham   E.D.R. Eagar   R.T.D. Perks   J. Ryder

---

COUNTY REVIEW

Kent

'In past years Kent have always begun a new season aware of problems besetting them, mainly from England Test calls. By mid-way through 1977 they were even more aware of problems for 1978 and yet further ahead. Four of their players, their new captain Asif, Knott, Underwood and Julien were in the first batch of players to contract to play in Packer's unofficial series … and by the end of the summer Woolmer had joined those ranks. If they did not continue in county cricket the young men of Kent would have even more chances than in 1977.'

MATCH REPORTS

Australia v England, Centenary Test Match, *at Melbourne, March 12, 13, 14, 16, 17*

'The innings to remember was played by Randall, a jaunty, restless, bubbling character, whose 174 took England to the doorstep of victory. The Australian spectators enjoyed his approach as much as the Indian crowds had done on the tour just finished. Once, when Lillee tested him with a bouncer, he tennis-batted it to the midwicket fence with a speed and power that made many a rheumy eye turn to the master of the stroke, the watching Sir Donald Bradman. Words cannot recapture the joy of that moment.'

An announcement at the front of Wisden *states: 'This 1978 edition of* Wisden *is the last to appear under the imprint of Sporting Handbooks Ltd., who have published it for John Wisden & Co. Ltd., the owners of the copyright, since 1938. From the 1979 edition responsibility for publication is being passed on by Wisden's to a larger organisation, Macdonald & Jane's Publishers Ltd., to appear under their Queen Anne Press imprint.'*

Norman Preston, editor of Wisden, *is awarded the MBE, which is reported in the 1979 issue.*

John Arlott's unbroken stint as book reviewer since 1950 ends with this issue, but after Gordon Ross takes over for two years, Arlott returns in 1981.

1979

WISDEN 1979

116th EDITION
EDITOR: Norman Preston
PAGES: 1179
PRICE: Limp £4.75   cased £5.75

THE WORLD AT LARGE

- The Winter of Discontent
- In May, Labour loses the general election and Margaret Thatcher becomes Britain's first female Prime Minister
- Saddam Hussein becomes President of Iraq
- Lord Mountbatten assassinated by the Provisional IRA
- The Shah of Iran is overthrown and Ayatollah Khomeini becomes Supreme Leader

CRICKET HEADLINES 1978

County Champions: Kent, who also win the B&H Trophy

Sussex win the Gillette Cup

The Packer Affair overshadows all cricket, as players are recruited by Australian media magnate Kerry Packer for his World Series Cricket

England beat the touring Pakistanis 2-0 and the New Zealanders 3-0

The batting helmet comes into common use in first-class cricket

NOTES BY THE EDITOR

England Rich In Young Talent
'In addition to … Chris Tavaré (Kent), Mike Gatting (Middlesex), Wayne Larkins (Northamptonshire) and Jon Agnew (Leicestershire) … there are many other young men waiting to prove their worth. Among the batsmen are the left-handed Kevin Sharp and right-handed Bill Athey (Yorkshire), David Smith (Warwickshire) … Joining Agnew as fast bowlers are Graham Dilley (Kent) and Hugh Wilson (Surrey), and there are several wicket-keepers, Bruce French (Nottinghamshire), Jack Richards (Surrey), and Andy Brassington (Gloucestershire), not forgetting Paul Downton (Kent) who went to Pakistan and New Zealand with the England side two winters ago and is now back at Exeter University.'

FEATURE ARTICLES

A Wisden Occasion
'The directors of Wisden gave a luncheon in the Committee During Room at Lord's on Tuesday, December 6, 1977, in celebration of Norman Preston receiving from HM The Queen that morning at Buckingham Palace the MBE awarded in The Queen's Silver Jubilee and Birthday Honours in his 27th year as Editor of *Wisden*.
William Gray, Managing Director of John Wisden and Co. was in the chair and offered his personal congratulations; David Chipp, Editor-Chief of The Press Association, looked back on Norman Preston's long connection with that agency, and Denis Compton CBE, in happy vein, spoke of the high respect cricketers held for Preston's faithful reporting and comments of their deeds on the field.'
Captaincy, by Tony Lewis
The Packer Case, by Gordon Ross
John Langridge – Golden Jubilee, by Jack Arlidge
Three More Studies in Greatness, by Basil Easterbrook
The Cricket Society Movement, by Ron Yeomans

FIVE CRICKETERS OF THE YEAR

J.N. Shepherd
'As Kent cricket followers honour the West Indian all-rounder John Shepherd in his benefit year of 1979, against the usual background of career statistics the question will doubtless be

asked again: why did he play only five times for his country? With nearly 10,000 runs and 1,000 wickets to his credit, Shepherd has reigned comfortably as one of the most successful all-rounders in the world, so there is no ready answer.'

D.I. Gower   J.K. Lever   C.M. Old   C.T. Radley

OBITUARIES INCLUDE

C.A. 'Jack' Anderson
'… shot to death by assailants at his home in Kingston, Jamaica, on April 30, was one of the most experienced and respected of cricket writers in the West Indies. His untimely death two days after his 68th birthday caused shock throughout the Caribbean. The incident occurred shortly after he had returned home after watching the third day of the Test Match between West Indies and Australia at Sabina Park.'

F.E. Woolley
'Even more impressive than the number of runs Woolley amassed was the manner in which he made them. Standing well over six feet, he was a joy to watch. He played an eminently straight bat, employed his long reach to full advantage, and used his feet in a manner nowadays rarely seen. His timing of the ball approached perfection and he generally dealt surely with all types of bowling. Master of all the strokes, he was at his best driving, cutting, and turning the ball off his legs.' – Norman Preston

**Major R. Bowen   P.A. Gibb   A.H.H. Gilligan   H. Gimblett   V.M. Mankad
Sir Robert Menzies   H. Sutcliffe**

COUNTY REVIEW

Yorkshire
'Yorkshire, overcoming the handicaps of Test calls, crippling injury problems, and the constant crossfire of politics, had the satisfaction of climbing from twelfth to fourth in the Championship, establishing an impressive platform on which new team manager Ray Illingworth will be expected to build … The manoeuvring behind the scenes involved a rearguard action by the anti-Boycott lobby, who seized on a welcome run of good results under Hampshire and devalued it by using it as a weapon in the captaincy argument.'

MATCH REPORTS

England v Pakistan, First Cornhill Test, *played at Birmingham, June 1, 2, 3, 5. England won by an innings and 57 runs*
'This convincing victory was accomplished in only twenty hours, four minutes playing time … The satisfaction … was overshadowed, though, by a distressing incident on the fourth and last morning. Pakistan had used Iqbal Qasim as a nightwatchman on Saturday evening after following on, and when play resumed on the Monday, Willis, with a stiff breeze behind him, gave Qasim at least three lifting balls … and, at 12.10, Willis went round the wicket. From this new angle he immediately hurled in another bumper which leapt from the pitch, forced its way between Qasim's hands, and struck him in the mouth. Fortunately he was not severely hurt, but he was led from the pitch bleeding freely and needed two stitches in his lip. The ramifications of this ball continued into the second Test.'

Wisden is published by Macdonald and Jane's for the first time. Norman Preston writes that 'many people feared the change would cause an upheaval in the contents' but he is reassuring: 'Regular readers will find everything in the same place as usual.' He is helped by the new publishers' appointment of Gordon Ross as Associate Editor, 'and I cannot praise too highly the work of their House Editor Graeme Wright' – who will become editor in 1987. The cloth boards edition is now referred to as 'cased'.

1980

WISDEN 1980

117th Edition
Editor: Norman Preston
Pages: 1263
Price: Limp £5.75   cased £6.75

THE WORLD AT LARGE

- Zimbabwe achieves independence
- Great Britain competes in the Moscow Olympic Games, despite boycotts by several countries, and wins 5 gold medals
- John Lennon shot dead in New York
- Peter Sellers dies in hospital after a heart attack
- Ronald Reagan defeats incumbent Jimmy Carter to become President of the USA

CRICKET HEADLINES 1979

County Champions: Essex, for the first time

Essex also win the B&H Cup

Somerset take their first-ever titles – the Gillette Cup and the John Player League

West Indies beat England at Lord's to retain the Prudential World Cup

England retain the Ashes in Australia, thrashing the Packer-weakened Aussies 5-1

England beat India 1-0 in a four-Test series at home

NOTES BY THE EDITOR

'For only the fifth time in over 200 years the Laws of Cricket have been rewritten. The new code came into operation on April 1, this year. The earliest known code was drawn up in 1744 by Noblemen and Gentlemen who used the Artillery Ground in London. It was in 1788 that the first MCC code was adopted, and the Club now holds the world copyright. This latest addition tidies up issues since the 1947 revision was published, and gives particular attention to modern trends in the realms of unfair play.'

FEATURE ARTICLES

Lower Standards, by E.M. Wellings
'Gower most obviously has flair, a gift for stroke-making, a fine sense of timing, and certainly a quick eye... He has been compared to Frank Woolley, but any resemblance does not extend to footwork. It seemed well nigh impossible to bowl a length when Woolley was on the rampage, reaching far forward or going right back to attack. That is what footwork is about. If footwork was better, there would be no call for those ridiculous helmets.'
How Essex Rose to Glory, by Tony Lewis
The Man Who Made All Seasons, by Basil Easterbrook
My Life Reporting Cricket, by Alex Bannister
The Packer Case, by Gordon Ross

FIVE CRICKETERS OF THE YEAR

D.W. Randall
'He was the perky, immortal figure scoring 174 in defiance of the fire-eating Australian fast bowlers in the Centenary Test at Melbourne, and the irrepressible fielder celebrating England's Ashes-winning victory at Headingley in 1977 with a joyous handspring. His batting technique, with its famous shuffle, can be said to be all his own, and as a fielder in the covers he is spoken of in the same breath as Colin Bland and Neil Harvey. No higher praise can be offered.'
J. Garner   S.M. Gavaskar   G.A. Gooch   B.C. Rose

I. Barrow

'... has a place in cricket history as the first West Indian to score a hundred in a Test in England. This was at Old Trafford in 1933, and when he achieved the feat George Headley was on 99 – together they added 200 for the second wicket, Barrow making 105.'

E. Paynter

'A small man, Paynter was by instinct an attacking batsman, particularly effective against slow spin, but also a fine hooker and cutter who did not spare the fast bowler if he pitched short. He was one of the great outfields of his day and almost equally good at cover – a beautiful thrower with a safe pair of hands. This was the more remarkable as early in life he had lost the top joints of two fingers in an accident.'

E.J. Smith

'He was a big, robust man, tall for a wicket-keeper, with wonderful agility in his prime. He had more than a little in common with that kind and manly Alfred Mynn of a former generation. Always a fighter, he had a razor-sharp sense of humour and loved the rigour of the game. It was 'Good morning!' before we started and 'How's that!' for the rest of the day, he said of one hard-fought contest ... He loved thinking about the cricket, and in particular about the craft of wicket-keeping. In assessing Bert Oldfield and Dick Lilley as the greatest wicket-keepers who have ever played, he referred to an enthusiasm greater even than dedication. He was too modest to claim that attribute for himself, but others would claim it for him.' – Rowland Ryder

W.H. Ashdown   Sir Hubert Ashton   B.A. Barnett   J.W. Burke   N. Kilner   W.H. Livsey

COUNTY REVIEW

Gloucestershire

'Gloucestershire, who began the 1970s with a fine bowling side but unreliable batting, finished the decade with the position almost reversed. Their batting was a match for any in the Championship, but their attack was over-dependent on Procter and Brain ... There seems no reason why Gloucestershire should not be challengers for at least one of the four competition trophies in 1980. They will be untroubled by calls for representative cricket and given one more strike bowler they could overcome the best.'

MATCH REPORTS

England v India, Fourth Test Match, *at The Oval, Aug 30, 31, Sep 1, 3, 4*

'The match was drawn after the most gripping closing overs in a home Test since the draw at Lord's against West Indies in 1963, a match it closely resembled as all four results were possible with three balls left. Gavaskar's inspiring and technically flawless 221 earned him the Man of the Match award and brought that rarity in recent Tests in England – a final day charged with interest ... At 76 for no wicket on the fifth morning, India wanted roughly a run a minute ... Botham returned with eight overs left. It was a gamble by Brearley, for Botham had looked innocuous during the day. But he struck with the key wicket, Gavaskar drilling a catch to mid-on shortly after England had taken a drinks break – a rare move, tactically based, with the end so near ... Then Botham firmly ended India's hopes by having Yajurvindra Singh and Yashpal Sharma lbw in successive overs and, in between, making a slick stop to run out Venkataraghavan. Botham's final four overs brought him an absolutely crucial three for 17. A target of 15 from the last over was too much, and the climax came with fielders encircling the bat.'

This is editor Norman Preston's 29th and final Wisden. *He died on March 6, 1980, shortly after this edition was published.*

1981

WISDEN 1981

118th EDITION
EDITOR: John Woodcock
PAGES: 1235
PRICE: Limp £6.95   cased £7.95

THE WORLD AT LARGE

- Prince Charles marries Lady Diana Spencer
- Social Democratic Party formed by the 'Gang of Four' defectors from the Labour Party
- Iran releases its 52 American hostages, who have been held for almost 15 months
- Pope John Paul II shot and almost killed in St. Peter's Square
- Assassination of President Sadat of Egypt

CRICKET HEADLINES 1980

County Champions: Middlesex, who also win the Gillette Cup

The touring West Indians beat England by one match to nil in a very wet summer: the other four matches are drawn

Australia beat England 3-0 in the winter Test series to regain the Ashes, and the Centenary Test at Lord's ends in a dull draw

Warwickshire win the John Player League, and Northamptonshire the Benson and Hedges Cup

NOTES BY THE EDITOR

'There can never have been a side more heavily reliant on their fast bowlers than these West Indians, or better served by them. When the fifth Test match ended in August, West Indies had played ten Tests in 1980 and included a spin bowler in only one of them – that when, against all the odds, they lost to New Zealand in Dunedin. It is a pity, none the less, to see them so committed to speed. A balanced attack adds to the joys of watching cricket; to sit through a day's play in which only 74 overs are bowled, as happened in the Oval Test match, does not.'

FEATURE ARTICLES

Cricketana – A Bull Market, by David Frith
'Whatever the oscillations in price in the areas of silver, art and ephemera, books held steady, with *Wisden Cricketers' Almanacks* the gold bullion. A run of 97 *Wisdens* from 1864 to 1969, lacking nine pre-1900, took bidding to £4,200. This transaction was topped a year later [in 1980] when Sir Pelham Warner's *Wisdens* (1864-1963) were bought for £7,800. Even the auctioneer gulped as bidding reached this unexpected peak.'

Cricket in the Pacific, by Scyld Berry
'Today the clergy maintains as strong a hold on the game in Papua villages as ever it did in the rural England of Cardus's imagination.'

Radio reflections, by E.W. Swanton
'Though others have made acceptable contributions – and Henry Blofeld chalked up a marked success in Australia – the only other notable addition among the younger generation who comes across as combining close knowledge of the game with facility of expression is Christopher Martin-Jenkins.'

Fifty Years On, by G.O. Allen

The Helmet, by Trevor Bailey

FIVE CRICKETERS OF THE YEAR

K.J. Hughes
'The true entertainers of the sporting arena are few and far between. In cricket, rigid coaching routines sometimes take their toll, stifling the glorious individuality that makes it worth paying twice the entrance fee to watch some players in action. Thank goodness nobody bent

to curb the natural brilliance of Kim Hughes. Des Hoare, a tearaway fast bowler for Western Australia who played one Test match … immediately recognised a rare talent, and has closely watched Hughes's progress ever since. "I have most admired him," said Hoare, "because he has had the courage and ability not to become ordinary".

R.D. Jackman   **A.J. Lamb**   **C.E.B. Rice**   **V.A.P. van der Bijl**

OBITUARIES INCLUDE

C.V. Grimmett

'Unlike Arthur Mailey, the first of the Australian spin trilogy of the inter-wars era, Grimmett never insisted on spin as his chief means of destruction. To him it was no more than an important adjunct to unerring length and tantalising direction. Grimmett seldom beat a batsman by spin alone. Mailey often did. I cannot remember Grimmett bowling a long-hop, whereas Mailey averaged one an over … Such wantonness was anathema to Grimmett, who believed that a bowler should bowl as well as he possibly could every time he turned his arm over.' – W.J. O'Reilly

I.A.R. Peebles

'When, after several seasons of intermittent appearances, he returned to regular county cricket in 1939 to captain Middlesex, Peebles was really no more than a change bowler, and though he played occasionally until 1948, the loss of an eye in a war-time air-raid had, to all intents and purposes, ended his serious cricket career. After his playing days were over he entered the wine trade and also became a notable cricket writer and journalist. When writing of players he had played with or seen, he was in the top class; to a deep knowledge of the game he added rare charm and humour. For any student of cricket history over the last 60 years, his many books are compulsory and delightful reading.'

N. Preston MBE

'The 28 [*sic: it was 29*] editions of *Wisden Cricketers' Almanack* published under his editorship … cover a period which saw more changes and innovations than any other in the history of the game. Norman saw to it that *Wisden* faithfully recorded events as they occurred and never forebore to comment forthrightly whenever he thought such comment was called for.' – Denis Compton

J.E. Cheetham   **B. Dooland**   **J.H. Parks**   **J.E. Timms**   **J.E. Walsh**

COUNTY REVIEW

Middlesex

'Observers who believed that Middlesex's fourteenth place was a freakishly false one were vindicated when Brearley's team clinched the County Championship on September 2, four years to the day after their 1976 triumph … It is no coincidence that Middlesex's outright Championship titles have come either side of [Brearley's] spell as England's captain. Both as captain and batsman he is vital to the side.'

MATCH REPORTS

India v England, *played at Bombay, February 15, 17, 18, 19*

'The Test match to celebrate the Golden Jubilee of the Board of Control for Cricket in India produced poor cricket. But it was redeemed by an extraordinary all-round performance by Botham, performing the unprecedented feat of scoring a century and capturing thirteen wickets in a Test.'

John Woodcock takes over as editor from Norman Preston: 'Anyone expecting the end of such an era to be marked by sweeping changes will be disappointed. Since, as a small boy, I was admonished for reading Wisden *in form, I have had a deep affection for it as it is.' But Woodcock makes some shrewd signings: David Frith, founder of* Wisden Cricket Monthly, *writes on cricketana, E.W. Swanton marks the retirement from broadcasting of John Arlott, who is recalled to review books once again. Scyld Berry, a future editor, writes about cricket in the islands of the Pacific for his* Wisden *debut.*

1982

WISDEN 1982

119th EDITION
EDITOR: John Woodcock
PAGES: 1311
PRICE: Limp £7.95   cloth bound £8.95

THE WORLD AT LARGE

• Falklands War: Britain recaptures the islands from Argentina after two and a half months
• Michael Fagan breaks into the Queen's bedroom in Buckingham Palace, and talks to her for some time before being arrested
• The *Mary Rose*, Henry VIII's flagship, is raised
• Death of Soviet leader Leonid Brezhnev: his successor is Yuri Andropov
• Michael Jackson's album *Thriller* released

CRICKET HEADLINES 1981

County Champions: Nottinghamshire

England regain the Ashes, 3-1, thanks mainly to Ian Botham's extraordinary efforts after losing the captaincy

Ken Barrington dies on England's tour of West Indies. England lose by two matches to nil, with one abandoned when Robin Jackman is refused entry into Guyana because of his South African connections

Zaheer Abbas, playing for Gloucestershire, is the first man to 1,000 runs, reaching the target on June 30 despite not having batted at all until June 1

Trevor Chappell bowls an underarm delivery when New Zealand need six to tie off the final ball of an ODI at Melbourne

NOTES BY THE EDITOR

'The tide of commercialism maintains its inevitable advance. Like every other major sport, cricket in its present shape would be unable to survive without the generous help of its many sponsors. Of these, the National Westminster Bank had a successful first season as successors to Gillette in promoting the one-day knockout competition. Less happily, following a match at Hove in which Sussex fielded a discourteously weak side against the Australians, Holt Products, whose sponsorship had been aimed at making these games between counties and touring teams more competitive, withdrew their support. If Sussex's action was only partly responsible for Holt's decision, it was still a pity, in what was a fine season for them, that on this occasion they misjudged their obligations.'

FEATURE ARTICLES

The Escalating Effects of Politics on Cricket, by W.A. Hadlee
'The major area of concern centres around boycotts, blacklists, and who will or will not play one another. In 1981, a Test match was cancelled in the West Indies because Guyana refused entry to Robin Jackman. Worse still, the West Indies Board of Control advised the New Zealand Cricket Council that their team would not be welcome in 1982 – not for cricket reasons, but because a rugby tour by a multi-racial team of South Africans was taking place in New Zealand.'
Mike Procter – A Great All-Rounder, by Alan Gibson
Some Thoughts about Modern Captaincy, by J.M. Brearley
India 1932-1982, by Michael Melford
Cyril Coote – A Cambridge Legend, by J.G.W. Davies
The Career Figures of W.G. Grace, by Michael Fordham

FIVE CRICKETERS OF THE YEAR

Javed Miandad
'It is evident after watching Javed Miandad face no more than a ball or two that he is a natural sportsman of rare talent. His relaxed but commanding attitude is immediately convincing.

Extraordinarily nimble on his feet and with a superb eye, Javed in 1981 gave the Welsh cricketing public something to cheer about in what, for Glamorgan, was a moderate season.'
T.M. Alderman   A.R. Border   R.J. Hadlee   R.W. Marsh

OBITUARIES INCLUDE

K.F. Barrington
'Now that he is gone, it is possible that the rôle he created and played may be forgotten through want of a successor. But Ken gave so much to cricket in the 1970s that he had left a few campaigners for the cause for the remainder of the 1980s. Even now as Gooch starts or finishes a drive or Gatting hooks, a memory of Barrington the batsman is stirred. For a coach there is no finer memorial than that.' – Robin Marlar

J.H.W. Fingleton
'The first of his ten books, *Cricket Crisis,* published thirteen years afterwards in 1946, is far the best story of the Body-line tour of 1932-33, in which he was a participant and victim. There were five tour books, all lively, entertaining, wherein cricket is often merely the continuing narrative thread. It was sad that he died of a heart attack immediately upon publication of his autobiographical *Batting from Memory* – though not before he had read a highly appreciative review of it in the *Melbourne Age,* the paper whose opinion he would have valued most. – E.W. Swanton

A.B. Sellers
'Sellers was captain from 1933 to 1947 and in those nine seasons led Yorkshire six times to the Championship. Had he been a better player, he would have made a captain of England in this country: whether he had the tact necessary to captain a touring side is more doubtful. His career figures of 9,273 runs with an average of 23 do not look much, but it needed a crisis to bring the best out of him and crises in his Yorkshire sides were rare.'
J.F. Crapp   L.G. Crawley   G. Geary   W.E. Hollies   H.W. Lee   A.D. Nourse   A.W. Wellard

COUNTY REVIEW

Lancashire
'The captaincy of Clive Lloyd and the part-time assistance of Michael Holding did little to lift the gloom over Old Trafford in the summer of 1981 … Manager Jack Bond insists he can now "see the light at the end of the tunnel" after two years of sorting things out at Old Trafford, but sixteenth position in the Schweppes County Championship and joint tenth in the John Player League, plus failure to qualify for the knockout stages of the Benson and Hedges Cup leaves something of a mountain to climb.'

MATCH REPORTS

Australia v New Zealand, Third Final Match, Benson and Hedges World Series Cup, *at Melbourne, February 1. Australia won by six runs*
'With New Zealand needing 6 runs to tie the match off the last ball, Trevor Chappell, instructed to do so by his brother and captain, Greg, bowled McKechnie an underarm ball, which caused a furore that could haunt Australian-New Zealand cricket for a long time. Earlier in the day Greg Chappell, when 52, had refused to walk when Snedden, at deep midwicket, claimed what appeared to be a low but fair catch off Cairns; as neither umpire was watching the incident – they said they were looking for short runs – New Zealand's impassioned appeals for a catch were in vain.'

From Woodcock's Preface: 'For the first time, full scores are to be found of such competitions as South Africa's Currie Cup and the Shell Shield in the West Indies … John Arlott remains as a distinguished member of the team, his book reviews being, as usual, kindly yet comprehensive.' Woodcock thanks his assistant editor, Graeme Wright, and his 'admirable assistant', Christine Forrest.

It was at the dinner to launch this edition that Robert Maxwell, the owner of the publishers, Macdonald and Co, suggested the book should switch to a larger format.

1983

WISDEN 1983

120th EDITION
EDITOR: John Woodcock
PAGES: 1347
PRICE: Limp £8.95   cased £9.95

THE WORLD AT LARGE

- General election: Margaret Thatcher's Tory party wins a landslide majority over the Labour Party, led by Michael Foot
- Brinks Mat robbery: gold bars worth £26m stolen
- A bomb at the U.S. Embassy in Beirut kills 63 people: another suicide bomb six months later kills over 300 American, French and Lebanese
- United States invades Grenada
- Cruise missiles arrive at Greenham Common
- Lester Piggott wins his ninth Derby, riding Teenoso

CRICKET HEADLINES 1982

County Champions: Middlesex

Glenn Turner becomes the first New Zealander to score 100 hundreds, his hundredth being a Worcestershire record 311*

England beat the visiting Indians 1-0, and the Pakistanis 2-1

The previous winter England lost to India 1-0, with five matches drawn, but beat Sri Lanka by seven wickets in Colombo, in Sri Lanka's first-ever Test

Surrey, Somerset and Sussex win respectively the NatWest Trophy, the Benson and Hedges Cup and the John Player League

NOTES BY THE EDITOR

'Expressing a modern misconception, Bob Willis, the England captain, wrote: "As for the way everyone's been going into raptures over leg-spin bowling, it doesn't win Test matches." Within a few weeks of his having said this, Qadir had tied Australia's batsmen into all manner of knots, and been, without the slightest doubt, the cause of an Australian defeat. To imply that leg-spin is archaic is to disparage one of the great traditions of the game.'

FEATURE ARTICLES

South Africa: Progress Towards Non-Racial Cricket, by Graham Johnson
'Almost certainly it will be some time before an African cricketer wears a Springbok cap. Nevertheless, given time, I can see no reason why the development of African cricket should not be along the lines of South African football, which has become an African-dominated sport. It is important that the public overseas accepts this perspective and appreciates that a lot of good is being done within South African cricket and South African sport in general, even if the whole South African XI does not come from Soweto.'
J.M. Brearley – Success Through Perceptiveness, by John Arlott
Turner Marches On, by Norman Harris
The Continuing Struggle for Survival, by P.G. Carling
The Fastest Hundreds in Test Cricket, by Gerald Brodribb
The Yorkshire Connection, by C.R. Williamson

FIVE CRICKETERS OF THE YEAR

T.E. Jesty
'When Trevor Edward Jesty mauled the bowling of Bob Willis and his Warwickshire side on the penultimate day of the first-class season, it was a vivid, silent expression of his frustration at being overlooked yet again for international recognition... Just 48 hours earlier, the squad

to tour Australia under Willis had been announced. There was no place for Jesty and now, at the age of 34 and with comfortably his best season drawing to a close, he wondered in vain just what he was expected to do before being selected for England. That the England captain was present, indeed on the receiving end, as Jesty concluded his 1982 business with a 64-minute century almost murderous in its intent, was an appropriate irony.'

Imran Khan   A.I. Kallicharran   Kapil Dev   M.D. Marshall

OBITUARIES INCLUDE

Sir Douglas Bader
'A good attacking bat and a useful fast-medium bowler, he later played for the RAF and in 1931 made 65, the top score, for them against the Army, a fixture which in those days had first-class status.'

M. Fordham
'... had just delivered the copy and corrected the proofs for his statistical contributions to *Wisden*, *Playfair Cricket Annual* and *The Cricketer Quarterly*. A local government officer, his early involvement in statistics was in association with the late Roy Webber, on whose death in 1962 he took over as chief statistician for the Playfair publications.'

C. Jordan
'He was the only man to no-ball Charlie Griffith for throwing in a first-class match.'

N.E. Partridge
Bowling fast-medium in-swingers, he had, like many of his type, a rather ugly action which, though he was never no-balled, was regarded by some as slightly suspect. It is said that a batsman whom he had comprehensively bowled said indignantly to 'Tiger' Smith behind the wicket, "He threw that". "Yes", said 'Tiger'. "And bloody well too."'

E.W. 'Nobby' Clark   Lord Cornwallis   F.S. Lee   K.D. Mackay   A. Sandham Lt. Col. J.W.A. Stephenson

COUNTY REVIEW

Derbyshire
'During May, the new pavilion at Derby was opened by the Duke of Devonshire, there was a comfortable Championship victory over Somerset, and Derbyshire were going well in the one-day competitions. By September, there was considerable unrest within the club.'

MATCH REPORTS

England v Pakistan, Third Cornhill Test, *at Leeds, August 26, 27, 28, 30, 31*
'England's eventual victory to take the series 2-1 was accompanied, as at Edgbaston, by claims from Pakistan's captain, Imran Khan, that umpiring errors, one of which, he said, allowed Gower to survive a catch behind in the early stages of his first-innings 74, cost his side the match and the series. If errors were made, the main reason why Pakistan failed to take an exciting and fascinating series was their own reckless batting, particularly in their second innings when conditions were at their least difficult on a wicket which encouraged seam bowling throughout the five days.'

Somerset v Warwickshire, *at Taunton, September 1, 2, 3*
'Needing 309 in 270 minutes, Somerset faltered to 57 for three before Richards, with two 6s and twelve 4s in 31 overs, and Slocombe, through 41 overs, set the scene for the astonishing finale. Botham arrived with 160 needed in 145 minutes, and in 65 minutes he scored 131 by way of ten 6s and twelve 4s, getting Somerset home with 80 minutes to spare.'

1984

WISDEN 1984

121st EDITION
EDITOR: John Woodcock
PAGES: 1307
PRICE: Limp £9.95   cased £11.95

THE WORLD AT LARGE

- The Miners' Strike: one of the longest and most violent strikes in recent years
- WPC Yvonne Fletcher is shot by somebody inside the Libyan Embassy in London
- The famine in Ethiopia prompts Bob Geldof to raise money by producing a single, *Do they know it's Christmas?*, which tops the charts and becomes the U.K.'s biggest-selling single to date
- Brighton bombing: Irish Republicans attempt to assassinate the entire British cabinet
- Assassination of Indira Gandhi

CRICKET HEADLINES 1983

India win the Prudential World Cup

County Champions: Essex

England beat the touring New Zealanders 3-1, but the Kiwis win a Test in England for the first time.

Zaheer Abbas scores his 100th hundred

Australia regain the Ashes at home, by two wins to one

Surrey dismissed for 14 by Essex at Chelmsford

Somerset win the NatWest Trophy, Middlesex the Benson and Hedges Cup and Yorkshire the John Player League

NOTES BY THE EDITOR

'In the early years of limited-overs cricket no-one, themselves included, took India seriously. Their strength lay much more in waging battles of attrition. Now, on pitches which had had no time to quicken up after all the rain, their lack of fast bowling was not the hindrance it might have been. Three of their batsmen could also bowl, which was vital for the way it shortened their tail. When, after beating West Indies in the final at Lord's, they flew home, it was to be fêted through the length and breadth of India. Not six months later they were being pilloried for having capitulated to the same West Indian side. Indian crowds, like the game itself, can be unmercifully fickle.'

FEATURE ARTICLES

1884 – A Year To Remember, by Stephen Green
'The only President of MCC ever to die during his period of office, the Hon. Robert Grimston, passed away on April 7, 1884. Two days earlier John Wisden had also died, of cancer, at the age of 57. He was a splendid all-round cricketer who seems to have been universally respected … In 1857 he was appointed Secretary of the Cricketers' Fund Friendly Society, an office he held until his death. In 1859 he went with George Parr's pioneering team to Canada and the United States, and in 1864 he set the seal on his distinguished career by issuing the first number of *Wisden,* called then simply *The Cricketer's Almanack.* Though a pale shadow of its later self, it proved to be the Book of Genesis in the Cricketers' Bible.'

Philatelic Cricket, by Marcus Williams
'In view of the antiquity of cricket and stamps it was for long a disappointment to those interested in both fields that, while Olympic Games, football and other sporting issues abounded from the world's post offices, stamps depicting cricket were absent... Honour was eventually satisfied on January 18, 1962, from an unlikely source – the Cape Verde Islands, a Portuguese colony 500 miles off the west African coast whose cricket activity is largely confined to chirping in the hearth. Later the same year Pakistan issued two more stamps with cricketing links and some 30 other countries have followed suit, to the point where stamps are probably as popular as any branch of cricketana.'

MCC and South Africa, by Matthew Engel
Australia – A New Era, by R.J. Parish
Zaheer Abbas – A Flourishing Talent, by David Green

FIVE CRICKETERS OF THE YEAR

M.W. Gatting

'In 1983, for the third consecutive year, he became the highest qualified Englishman in the batting averages. Since the selectors constantly ask: "Where are the batsmen? They are all from overseas," Gatting may have been hard done by recently ... In terms of ability he should have been competing consistently with David Gower, Derek Randall and Allan Lamb for the positions from three to five. His strokeplay is in their class, but the Nottingham Test was his 24th, compared with Gower's 53rd and Randall's 40th. However, the others have made centuries and, as yet, Gatting has not.'

M. Amarnath   J.V. Coney   J.E. Emburey   C.L. Smith

OBITUARIES INCLUDE

L.H. Gray

'Against Essex at Lord's in 1939 he helped Denis Compton to put on 83 in three-quarters of an hour for the last wicket, his own share being 1 not out. To Compton he later owed a great debt. As the senior of the two, Compton was due for his benefit in 1948, but waived his claim in Gray's favour. Gray's benefit raised over £6,000, a sum which, low though it may seem by modern standards, had then only once been exceeded.'

J.C.W. MacBryan

'... who died on July 14, 1983, a few days before his 91st birthday, was England's oldest surviving Test cricketer.'

A.H. McKinnon

'As portly as he was affable, he belonged to the classical school of slow orthodox left-arm bowlers, length, line and flight playing at least as much a part as spin.'

G.A. Headley   V.L. Manjrekar   A. Melville   A.E.G. Rhodes   B.A. Valentine

COUNTY REVIEW

Somerset

'Despite many difficulties, both expected and unforeseen, Somerset enjoyed another in their heartening sequence of successful seasons. Besides achieving record membership subscriptions and a healthy trading position, they won the NatWest Bank Trophy without the advantage of a single home tie, and again finished second in the John Player League.'

MATCH REPORTS

India v West Indies, Prudential World Cup Final, *at Lord's, June 25*

'India defeated on merit the firm favourites, winning a low-scoring match by 43 runs. It was an absorbing game of increasing drama and finally of much emotion. The result, as surprising as, on the day, it was convincing, had much to do with the mental pressures of containment in limited-overs cricket ... Lord's, groomed like a high-born lady, bathed in sunshine and packed to capacity, was at its best when Lloyd won the toss and invited India to bat: a distinct advantage, it seemed, for his battery of fast bowlers. The Lord's wicket often inclines to extravagant morning life.'

The editor writes in his Preface: 'Some pruning has been necessary ... Only the later rounds of the Benson and Hedges Cup and the NatWest Bank Trophy are accompanied by match reports. University Blues before 1947 have gone ... The Index has also been rearranged.' There is an announcement about the publishers: 'From the 1985 edition, Wisden *will be published by John Wisden and Co. Ltd., the owners of the copyright.' So 1984 sees the sixth and last of the Maxwell years.*

1985

WISDEN 1985

122nd Edition
Editor: John Woodcock
Pages: 1298
Price: Limp £9.95   cased £11.95

THE WORLD AT LARGE

- Death of Konstantin Chernenko, Soviet leader: he is succeeded by Mikhail Gorbachev
- Two football crowd disasters – at Bradford where a stand catches fire, and at the Heysel Stadium during the European Cup Final
- The Sinclair C5 is launched: the electric vehicle is not a success
- New Coke, launched by Coca-Cola, is equally unpopular
- Tetris, the first computer game to sweep the world, is released

CRICKET HEADLINES 1984

County Champions: Essex, who also win the John Player League

West Indies win all five Tests in England

During the winter, England lose Test series to New Zealand, and Pakistan, both for the first time

They even concede first innings lead to Sri Lanka in a one-off Test in England

Richard Hadlee completes the double – the first since 1967, before the reduction of Championship matches in 1969

Middlesex win the NatWest Bank Trophy, and Lancashire the Benson and Hedges Cup

NOTES BY THE EDITOR

'It was hard to watch the West Indian, Marshall bowling at Pocock in last season's fifth Test match at The Oval without recoiling. Pocock was the night-watchman from the previous day. As such, he could expect few favours. However, the Laws of Cricket make it abundantly clear that the relative skill of the striker must be taken into consideration by an umpire when deciding whether the bowling of fast, short-pitched balls amounts to intimidation and is therefore unfair. That Marshall, a superb bowler, should have kept bouncing the ball at so inept a batsman as Pocock was unwarrantable; that Lloyd should have condoned his doing so was disconcerting; that Constant, the umpire at Marshall's end, should have stood passively by was unaccountable. It was a woeful piece of cricket, entirely lacking in chivalry.'

FEATURE ARTICLES

The Equipment Revolution, by Norman Harris
'The bat is the item on which most attention will be focused. The innovators will keep experimenting. Some may even follow the example of protective equipment and try to find alternative materials. If non-wood bats are banned, then perhaps an equally resilient but cheaper wood could be found to challenge the hitherto unique willow. Most cricketers, though, will probably go on paying what they are asked to pay for a new, gleaming, white sword which promises to fulfil all their dreams. The top bat in the shops in 1985 is expected to cost £75.'
Forty Years On, by Murray Hedgcock
How Headley's Genius Paved The Way, by E.W. Swanton
Chappell, Lillee and Marsh, by Paul Sheahan
Bob Willis – An Assessment, by David Frith

FIVE CRICKETERS OF THE YEAR

J. Simmons
'Jack Simmons's best years for Lancashire have come since he turned 40, and 1984's all-round performance of 748 runs and 63 wickets at the age of 43 arguably represented his best in sixteen years with the county. He had never before scored as many runs and only once, in the

previous season, had he taken more Championship wickets. He believes he is getting better with the years, and those figures support that contention.'

M.D. Crowe   H.A. Gomes   G.W. Humpage   S. Wettimuny

R.S. Bestwick
'… will be remembered for an incident which one can safely say is unique in first-class cricket. For Derbyshire against Warwickshire at Derby in 1922, for some ten minutes he bowled at one end while his father, the much better known Bill Bestwick, bowled at the other, against W.G. Quaife and his son, B.W.'

J. Fairbrother
'With his gentle smile and love of his job, he became a popular figure at headquarters, twice winning the award as Groundsman of the Year (1981 and 1982) and rarely taking offence, whatever might be said about his pitches.'

W. Pearson
'A prisoner of the Japanese during the war, he owed his survival to the atom bomb, which exploded a week before he was due to be executed.'

J. Arnold   L.H. Compton   J.T. Ikin   H.W. Parks   B.W. Quaife   D. Tallon   M.F. Tremlett W. Voce

---

COUNTY REVIEW

Worcestershire
'Worcestershire re-emerged in 1984 as a force to be reckoned with, if not yet to be feared. Results showed a marked improvement on the previous season, culminating in a rare sequence of seven successive victories … One name to watch out fro in 1985, if Worcestershire can find ways of getting him into the side, is the Zimbabwean batsman, Graeme Hick. He emerged as a prolific scorer for the Second XI and for Kidderminster in the Birmingham League, and marked his Championship debut with an unbeaten 82 after going in at No. 9 in the last game against Surrey.'

MATCH REPORTS

New Zealand v England, Second Test Match, *at Christchurch, February 3, 4, 5*
'Outplaying England in every department, especially in the way their faster bowlers used a suspect pitch, New Zealand achieved their largest-ever victory in twelve hours' playing time. On the first day, abysmal England bowling, later condemned by Willis as some of the worst he had seen in Tests, enabled New Zealand to score 307 at 4.2 per over after winning the toss. Hadlee, coming in with the innings in the balance, struck 99 in 111 minutes (81 balls) … England's hopes of saving the embarrassment of having to follow on for the first time against New Zealand vanished on the third morning … and 40 minutes before lunch their second innings started. They were 225 runs behind. Tavaré and Fowler hung on till the interval, but 65 minutes afterwards the score was 33 for six.'

John Woodcock explains the change of publisher: 'This and future editions will be published under the imprint of John Wisden & Co., the owner of the Wisden *copyright. Thus ends an agreeable association, which lasted for five years, with Queen Anne Press … The change of publishers coincides with a return to the printing firm of Spottiswoode Ballantyne.' The cover and title page explains that John Wisden and Co. Ltd. is 'a member of the McCorquodale Group of Companies'.*

'An Index To Wisden Cricketers' Almanack 1864-1984', compiled by Derek Barnard, is published by Queen Anne Press at £17.50. Barnard writes in the Preface: 'This Index was conceived as a hobby. It became an obsession. Its aim is to help the serious and not so serious students of the game to understand the wealth of material inside the covers of the world's finest cricket reference book.'

1986

WISDEN 1986

123rd EDITION
EDITOR: John Woodcock
PAGES: 1314
PRICE: Limp £12.50   cased £14.50

THE WORLD AT LARGE

- Plans to build a Channel tunnel are announced
- Michael Heseltine and Leon Brittan both resign from the Thatcher Cabinet over the Westland affair
- M25 London Orbital motorway completed
- Space Shuttle Challenger blows up within seconds of launch, killing all on board
- The Big Bang at the London Stock Exchange: electronic trading begins
- Chernobyl: a nuclear accident at the plant in Ukraine causes an environmental and human disaster

CRICKET HEADLINES 1985

County Champions: Middlesex

England beat the touring Australians 3-1, to regain the Ashes

Viv Richards scores 322 for Somerset v Warwickshire, on 1 June

Despite the trauma of two political assassinations during their stay, England beat India 2-1 in India

In the Fourth Test at Madras, Gatting and Fowler both score double-centuries, the first time this feat has been achieved in an England innings.

Ian Botham hits a record eighty 6s during the season

NOTES BY THE EDITOR

'It was not only because of full covering and foul weather that there was a higher percentage (62.7) of drawn games in 1985 than at any time in the history of the competition. It must have been partly because of the exaggerated significance of bonus points, which reduces the incentive to aim for outright victory. Something is surely wrong when 2,034 bonus points are awarded, as in 1985, and only 1,216 points for actually winning games.'

FEATURE ARTICLES

Whither Cricket Now? by Sir Donald Bradman
'Umpires are put under enormous pressure, having to adjudicate frequently on split-second issues: to their credit, I believe they have responded in a very positive manner and improved their standards. Inevitably one sees the odd umpiring mistake, graphically portrayed by the modern marvel of the instant replay on television. With this new aid available, I should see no loss of face or pride if umpires were to agree, when in doubt about a decision, to seek arbitration from the box. This could never apply to LBW, but for run-outs, and on odd occasions, for stumpings or a disputed catch, it would seem logical.'
Alan Knott – A Thorough Genius, by J.M. Brearley
A Financial Revolution, by Jack Bannister
1903 – The Wettest Summer of Them All? by John Kitchin
Covering by Degrees, by E.M. Wellings

FIVE CRICKETERS OF THE YEAR

R.M. Ellison
'Family opinions are divided on the age at which Richard Ellison developed the ability to bowl the out-swinger that devastated Australia in the final two Tests of the 1985 Ashes series

... He gives the credit for his development into a swing bowler to Alan Dixon, his coach at Tonbridge School ... Richard's mother, however, is not a lady to be argued with. Her records of family cricketing achievements show that his great-grandfather played against the Grace brothers in the nineteenth century and that his grandfather captained Derbyshire Second XI at the age of 60.'

P. Bainbridge   C.J. McDermott   N.V. Radford   R.T. Robinson

A.T. Barber
'In 1930 came the captaincy of Yorkshire. He was perhaps the first captain since Lord Hawke was in his prime some 30 years before who was worth his place as a player. Though he was not a heavy scorer, his defence was useful at a crisis and in the field he was fully up to the county's high standard.'

G. Cox
'A player who will be remembered with affection long after some who occupy a bigger space in the records have been forgotten. Though cricket was his profession, to him it was always a game, a game to be won certainly and, if not won, at least saved, but it was a game to be enjoyed: he enjoyed it himself and he did his best to make it enjoyable for the other players and the spectators.'

A.G. Nicholson
'More than once Nicholson was close to playing for England. He was picked for the 1964-65 tour of South Africa but had to drop out through injury. Later, when he was a still better bowler, there were more good bowlers of his type available, and being a modest batsman with a build which made him less than agile in the field – he did not have the all-round qualifications of others.'

G.J. Ross
'... who died at Lord's ... was closely connected with numerous cricket publications ... From 1978-80 he was Associate Editor, under Norman Preston, of *Wisden Cricketers' Almanack*, for whom he reviewed books (1979 to 1980) and wrote articles ... He had just been watching a day's cricket when, having reached his car, he died.'

L.G. Berry   J.L. Bryan   P.G.H. Fender   J.H. Wardle

Nottinghamshire
'In Tim Robinson and Chris Broad they possess an opening partnership that has emerged as one of the country's best – if not the best ... Rice, in his benefit season, also had a healthy average, but the most pleasing aspect of Nottinghamshire's batting were the displays of Randall, who had his most successful season on the county circuit. Considering that at the end of 1984 he had been considering retirement, Randall's consistency, which brought him 2,151 first-class runs, was all the more remarkable.'

Oxford University v Cambridge University, *at Lord's July 3, 4, 5*
'Match Drawn ... Proceedings were dominated to an extraordinary extent by Toogood, playing in the match for a fourth year. Intervening for the first time when Cambridge ... had been given a steady start, and bowling at medium pace, he bowled for most of the rest of Cambridge's first innings, finishing with eight for 52. Next day his 149 ... spanned most of the Oxford innings, and when Miller declared, Toogood took the two wickets to fall. In the whole history of the fixture, the only all-round feat superior to this was P.R. Le Couteur's in 1910.'

This is the last edition edited by John Woodcock.

1987

WISDEN 1987

124th EDITION
EDITOR: Graeme Wright
PAGES: 1311
PRICE: Limp £13.95   cased £15.95

THE WORLD AT LARGE

- Terry Waite is kidnapped in Beirut while trying to negotiate the release of other hostages
- Cross-Channel ferry *Herald of Free Enterprise* capsizes in Zeebrugge harbour: 193 die
- Margaret Thatcher wins her third general election
- 'Don't worry, there's no hurricane' – but there was, causing havoc across southern England
- *The Simpsons* cartoon first appears on American television

CRICKET HEADLINES 1986

County Champions: Essex

David Gower's England are beaten 5-0 by West Indies in West Indies

England lose 1-0 at home to New Zealand, and 2-0 at home to India, using three captains in the process

Dennis Amiss scores his 100th hundred

Sussex win the NatWest Trophy, Middlesex the Benson and Hedges Cup, and Hampshire the John Player League

Two England greats, Jim Laker and Bill Edrich, die on St. George's Day, April 23.

NOTES BY THE EDITOR

'If these Notes seem a catalogue of concerns, they are so because I am concerned about cricket: for the quality of cricket as I am for the quality of life. I do not see the game in isolation but in relation to what is happening in our society. That is, for me, a great part of cricket's attraction. Therefore it does concern me when, for example, I perceive a drift towards more limited-overs cricket, not just in England but internationally; because if cricket does indeed reflect stages of social history, our lives too must become more and more restricted to a set number of permutations. When the American short-story and baseball writer, Ring Lardner, died, Scott Fitzgerald wrote that "Ring moved in the company of a few dozen illiterates playing a boy's game. A boy's game with no more possibilities than a boy could master. A game bounded by walls which kept out danger, change or adventure." Cricket must always be more than that. So must life.'

FEATURE ARTICLES

MCC – 200 Years, by E.W. Swanton
'In those first days, two men of a very different temper held the stage; the Rev. Lord Frederick Beauclerk, reputedly the best cricketer in England around the turn of the nineteenth century, and the first Secretary of M.C.C., Benjamin Aislabie, who doted on the game though much too fat to be any good at it … Aislabie cast on the scene a benevolence which held the club together, a necessary antidote no doubt to Beauclerk (descended from the union of Charles II and Nell Gwynne), who as a dictator of affairs on the field and off, and a sharp betting man to boot, comes across almost as a villain of old-style melodrama.'
Sir George Allen, by J.J. Warr
Time Present and Time Past, by Vic Marks
How Amiss Won His Entry Card, by Jack Bannister

FIVE CRICKETERS OF THE YEAR

C.A. Walsh
'Even his teammates could not anticipate the speed at which the ball would emerge from his hand, so adept had he become at disguising his intentions. Informed opinion in the

Gloucestershire dressing-room is that he has three distinct speeds, all delivered with the same action. There are also minute variations within these, so it is not surprising that Walsh hit batsmen's stumps at some times when they had completed their stroke and at others when they had scarcely started it.'

J.H. Childs   G.A. Hick   D.B. Vengsarkar   J.J. Whitaker

OBITUARIES INCLUDE

A.D. Baxter
'He was a bowler pure and simple, and the generally accepted view was that, had he not overlapped with C.S. Marriott, he would have been the worst bat and field of his time in first-class cricket. None the less everyone loved to have him on a side. He was so cheerful and friendly, enjoyed his cricket so much, and helped others to enjoy theirs.

H.D. Smith
'One of the ten bowlers who have taken a wicket with their first ball in Test cricket. Moreover it was his only wicket in his only Test match.'

J.C. Laker
'No cricketer could have made an impression on the game as vividly as Laker without having the personality to deploy his talent. He might have gone to Surrey from Catford, but Jim Laker was the archetypal dry Yorkshireman. If his tongue could cut, his eye was keen. His humour depended on the detached observance of the passing scene, never better illustrated than in his story of the journey home after that Test, *[Old Trafford 1956]* when he sat in a Lichfield pub alone and unrecognised whilst others celebrated what he had done.' – Robin Marlar

C.L. McCool   R. Aird   W.J. Edrich   L.B. Fishlock   E.L.G. Hoad

COUNTY REVIEW

Glamorgan
'A ... significant feature was the establishment of the club's headquarters at Sophia Gardens, the first time the office had been sited at a playing venue. The Wilfred Wooller Room was opened as part of the complex, and electrically operated scoreboards were installed at Cardiff and Swansea. Significant improvements are being made, and it is hoped that these will be reflected soon in improvements on the field.'

MATCH REPORTS

D.B. Close's XI v New Zealanders, *at Scarborough, August 31, September 1, 2*
'Rutherford rewrote the record books on the second day when he amassed 317 runs in 230 minutes off 245 balls, his eight 6s and 45 4s being the most boundaries in an innings by a New Zealander. His 317 was the highest score by a New Zealander abroad; the most runs by a New Zealander in one day and the sixth highest number in a day by any batsman in England ... Rutherford made 101 before lunch and 199 between lunch and tea, during which session he hit Doshi for four successive sixes, reaching 200 in 186 minutes and scoring his third hundred off 33 balls in 35 minutes ... On the first day Boycott ... took an hour over his first nine runs.'

Graeme Wright, in his first year as editor, left out the Laws of Cricket for space reasons. But he promised they would return in 1988. Wright says that John Woodcock's decision to retire 'filled me with sadness'– but happily he stays on as associate editor. John Arlott continues to review books. 'These two Hampshiremen have provided much encouragement,' writes the new editor. He thanks three people especially: 'Mike Smith and Peter Bather, of the typesetters, SB Datagraphics, and Christine Forrest, who has worked with me on Wisden *since 1979. We are a small team: one that has been together for some years now. That our various tasks never seem a chore, that we approach each edition with a new enthusiasm, says everything for the magic of* Wisden *and of cricket.'*

1988

WISDEN 1988

125th Edition
Editor: Graeme Wright
Pages: 1314
Price: Limp £14.50   cased £16.50

THE WORLD AT LARGE

• Piper Alpha disaster: the North Sea oil rig explodes, killing 167 people
• 270 people die when Pan Am flight 103 is blown up over Lockerbie in Scotland
• Pakistan President Zia Ul Haq killed in a plane crash
• Vice-President George Bush wins the presidential election over his Democrat opponent, Michael Dukakis
• More than eight years after they invaded, Soviet troops begin withdrawing from Afghanistan

CRICKET HEADLINES 1987

County Champions: Nottinghamshire, who also win the NatWest Bank Trophy

Australia beat England by seven runs in the World Cup final in Calcutta

Pakistan beat England in England by one match to nil, with four draws

England, under Mike Gatting, regain the Ashes by two matches to one in Australia

The Deloittes Rankings, the brainchild of Ted Dexter, are introduced. The top batsman as at August 15 is Dilip Vengsarkar, the top bowler Richard Hadlee

Yorkshire win the Benson and Hedges Cup and Worcestershire the inaugural Refuge Assurance League

NOTES BY THE EDITOR

'Given that three, perhaps four, umpires would have to be allocated to each series, the opportunity to use one as a third umpire would present itself. He – or she, now that New Zealand has a female first-class umpire – would have reference to television playback facilities to give an opinion on appeals for certain dismissals. But which ones? I appreciate the arguments in favour of an umpire with a monitor, but I would be a most reluctant supporter. The flow of a match would be greatly interrupted, and it would be only a matter of time before batsmen and bowlers considered it an injustice unless every appeal was referred for appraisal.'

FEATURE ARTICLES

Graeme Pollock – A Retrospective, by Charles Fortune
'If it is permissible to attach the word genius to the artistry of a batsman, then Graeme Pollock is such among cricketers. Like others so acknowledged he was ever the master craftsman. Perhaps the all-important factor was that from the start, the bowling he faced was more skilled and demanding than will have come the way of many others. Only Colin Cowdrey among the cricketers I have known has moved so easily up the rungs that take cricket toddlers to a Test match début. Pollock never underestimated the opposition, nor hesitated to meet a challenge.'
A Coach's Viewpoint, by Don Wilson
The Master Craftsman – A Study of Geoffrey Boycott, by Derek Hodgson
Derek Underwood – An Appreciation, by Doug Ibbotson
150 years at Trent Bridge, by John Lawson

FIVE CRICKETERS OF THE YEAR

J.P. Agnew
'After four or five seasons of injury problems, probably the result of trying to bowl too fast, Agnew had by and large remained fit since 1983. But the injury-prone image had unfortunately

stuck. He has never, for example, had back problems, although one annual cricket publication last year described that as the reason for long absences in his second season. He has had the occasional pulled muscle, which is a difficult achievement for someone with scarcely a muscle about his person. At almost 6ft 4in, he barely tips the scales at twelve stone, and this despite a gargantuan appetite which involves anything between three and six cooked meals a day.'

N.A. Foster   D.P. Hughes   P.M. Roebuck   Salim Malik

OBITUARIES INCLUDE

W.E. Bowes
'There has probably never been a great cricketer who looked less like one than Bowes. Standing 6ft 4in, he was clumsily built and a poor mover. Wearing strong spectacles, he looked far more like a university professor, and indeed batted and fielded like one. However, no side has been so closely welded as Yorkshire in the 1920s and 1930s: every man knew just what he was expected to do and did it without being told.'

L.E. Favell
'It was for his dashing style and fearless strokeplay as an opening batsman that the crowds loved him. From a crouching stance, with his grip low on the handle, he was especially strong on the square-cut and hook, while never averse to driving the fast bowlers straight back down the ground. When facing bowling he particularly fancied, he would allegedly sing "Happy Birthday" as a sign of his confidence. In the field, his throwing, as with so many Australians of his generation, was outstanding, even thrilling.'

A.G. Kripal Singh
'Recalled in 1961-62 for the series against England … he appeared in the First Test alongside his brother, Milkha Singh. Their father, Ram Singh, had represented India in two unofficial tests against Ryder's Australian team in 1935-36 and against Lord Tennyson's 1937-38 team, and two other brothers, Satwender and Harjinder, also played first-class cricket.'

T.C. Dollery   O.W. 'Lofty' Herman   V.M. Merchant

COUNTY REVIEW

Essex
'After scaling the heights in recent years, Essex found the 1987 season was one of disappointments … It can be argued that their cause was not helped by a long list of injuries … however, to put forward injuries as the major excuse for the county's decline would be to ignore the fundamental reason. In short, too many players failed to display consistency of form or application.'

MATCH REPORTS

MCC v Rest Of The World, MCC Bicentenary Match, *at Lord's, August 20, 21, 22, 24, 25*
'Hadlee to Gavaskar was a duel between two masters, the bowler probing with all his skills for an opening, the batsman correct and studious in defence, awaiting the chance to counter-attack. Gavaskar won the bout. But if Hadlee's weapon was the epée, Marshall's was the sabre. From round the wicket, on so placid a pitch, he removed Vengsarkar with a ball that kicked, took the shoulder of the bat, and flew to Gooch, the finer of the two gullies.'

The editor explains in the Preface: 'With the help of Bill Frindall, Philip Bailey and Peter Wynne-Thomas, I have made a study of the career records which appear in Wisden *… Where the research of statisticians has revealed errors in compilation, or shown a difference between scorebooks and published scores, the figures in* Wisden *have been amended … There are, in addition, some career records which may be affected by an interpretation of which matches, prior to 1947, were first-class. In such instances the policy of previous* Wisden *editors has been adhered to. It has been said that history is a hard core of interpretation surrounded by a soft pulp of disputable facts, and that is certainly so here.'*

Colour photographs appear for the first time.

1989

WISDEN 1989

126th EDITION
EDITOR: Graeme Wright
PAGES: 1283
PRICE: Limp £14.95   cased £16.95

THE WORLD AT LARGE

- Death of Emperor Hirohito of Japan
- Ayatollah Khomeini issues his fatwa on Salman Rushdie, who wrote *The Satanic Verses*
- Hillsborough Stadium disaster: 96 die at FA Cup semi-final between Notts Forest and Liverpool
- Tiananmen Square protests in Beijing end in massacre by Red Army
- Fall of the Berlin Wall: communist regimes collapse across eastern Europe

CRICKET HEADLINES 1988

County Champions: Worcestershire, who also take the Refuge Assurance League title

The visiting West Indians score another huge victory over England, this time by four matches to nil with one drawn; England use four captains during the series

After eighteen Tests without a win, England beat Sri Lanka by seven wickets at Lord's at the end of August

Graeme Hick scores 1,000 runs before the end of May, including 405* for Worcestershire v Somerset at Taunton

Franklyn Stephenson does the double, and becomes only the second player ever to score two separate hundreds in a match and take ten wickets

Middlesex win the NatWest Trophy and Hampshire the Benson and Hedges Cup

NOTES BY THE EDITOR

'There is a developing argument in favour of a sixteen-match, four-day County Championship. If the standard of English cricket is to be improved, it should be supported. Not all the county secretaries and treasurers will agree. If such a programme were implemented, it would mean eight fewer days of cricket per county. What will need to be resisted is any attempt to fill those eight days with more one-day cricket; indeed, cricket of any kind except net practice.'

FEATURE ARTICLES

Wisden's Cricketers of the Year, by Anthony Bradbury
'In his preface to the 1889 *Wisden,* the editor, Charles Pardon, wrote that to signalise the extraordinary success that bowlers had achieved in 1888, the Almanack was including six portraits specially taken by Messrs Hawkins of Brighton. Thus marked the start of the Cricketers of the Year feature in *Wisden,* which in 1989 now embarks on its second century. The articles have shown a consistency in two respects throughout the last hundred years. A player can be a Cricketer of the Year only once, and those selected are primarily chosen for their prowess during the English cricketing season. Success in other parts of the world may be only a marker for future consideration.'

England v Australia – The Brand Leader? by Matthew Engel
'It happens that in the 1980s there has been a great deal of personal friendship between the dressing-rooms. This is partly a reaction to the sledging 1970s, and partly due to the personal qualities of the leading players of the era, Allan Border in particular. We have grown used to the sight of Australia's captain playing for Essex, though it would have been inconceivable for his predecessors. On the whole, I am inclined to think that it is a precedent which ought not be encouraged.'

The Problem of Pitches, by Mike Selvey
We Already Knew He Could Bat, by Peter Roebuck
Sunil Gavaskar – The Little Master, by Tony Lewis

P.A. Neale
'With ten O and two A levels, he gained a place at Leeds University to read Russian Studies. "I thought of cricket as something to do, and a university education as something to go along with it," he says. "I chose Russian because, if at some stage I was to go into commerce, there could be huge opportunities if Russia ever opened up its massive markets to the West.""
K.J. Barnett   P.J.L. Dujon   F.D. Stephenson   S.R. Waugh

OBITUARIES INCLUDE

R.L. Arrowsmith
'... made a significant contribution to *Wisden Cricketers' Almanack* as its principal obituary writer from the 1976 edition until the 1988 edition. For at least ten years before that he was a regular contributor, and he wrote also for various journals and books. His writing was marked by his language, his wit and a sense of fun; no-one reading him, or meeting him, could describe him as dull. He was, moreover, concerned about the accuracy of what he wrote, not because he was a pedant about accuracy but because he desired it as a virtue.'

J. Bailey
'He normally went in first with Arnold, and five times they put up more than 100 together. Arnold was a brilliant right-hander and it might seem that Bailey, an essentially defensive left-hander, was an ideal partner. But, with Mead to follow, the tax on the patience of spectators must have been intolerable. Mead, however slowly he scored, was a great player, a genius, but there was no trace of greatness about Bailey, though one might admire his determination. '

M. Jahangir Khan
'Played four Test matches for India in the 1930s and, after Partition, made an important contribution as a player, administrator and selector to the development of cricket in Pakistan. His son, Majid, captained Pakistan, as did his nephews, Javed Burki and Imran Khan. All three emulated him in gaining Blues; Majid like his father at Cambridge, his cousins at Oxford. An elder son, Asad, won his Blue at Oxford.'

R.A. Sinfield
'At the time of his death he was England's oldest surviving Test cricketer, a distinction which then fell to R.E.S. Wyatt. His single appearance for England at Trent Bridge in the First Test of 1938 was the climax to a career which extended from 1921 to 1939 and was a fitting reward for years of loyal service to Gloucestershire.'
H.T. Bartlett   S.M. Brown   C. Gladwin   H.S.T.L. Hendry   S.E. Leary   D.A. Livingstone

COUNTY REVIEW

Sussex
'Although Sussex managed only three wins in the Britannic Assurance Championship, and infrequent limited-overs successes, there was considerable encouragement for the new administration and management team at Hove ... Despite their final position of sixteenth, they were capable of entertaining and effective cricket. By the end of the 1988 season, there was a genuine belief that Sussex were on the way up.'

MATCH REPORTS

Pakistan v England, Second Test Match, *at Faisalabad, December 7, 8, 9, 11, 12*
'The incident occurred when Gatting moved Capel up from deep square leg to prevent a single ... As Hemmings came in to bowl, Gatting signalled to Capel that he had come close enough, whereupon Shakoor Rana, standing at square leg, stopped play to inform Malik of Capel's position. Shakoor claimed that Gatting had been unfairly moving the fielder behind the batsman's back. Gatting informed the umpire that he was, in his opinion, overstepping his bounds. The language employed throughout the discourse was basic.'

257

1990

WISDEN 1990

127th Edition
Editor: Graeme Wright
Pages: 1318
Price: Limp £15.50   cased £18.50

THE WORLD AT LARGE

- Nelson Mandela freed after 27 years in jail
- Anti-poll tax demonstration in Trafalgar Square degenerates into a riot: almost 500 people injured
- Reunification of East and West Germany
- Margaret Thatcher fails to win the support of her party to continue as leader: she steps down and John Major becomes Prime Minister
- Iraq invades Kuwait
- Agriculture Minister John Selwyn Gummer feeds a hamburger to his young daughter, to show that BSE is not a danger to humans

CRICKET HEADLINES 1989

County Champions: Worcestershire, after Essex, second six points behind the champions, had been docked 25 points for a substandard pitch

Australia regain the Ashes by four Tests to two

Viv Richards scores his 100th hundred, for West Indians v New South Wales at Sydney

W.V. Raman (313) and Arjan Kripal Singh (302*), playing for Tamil Nadu v Goa, become the first batsmen to score triple-centuries in the same innings; they added 356 for the sixth wicket as Tamil Nadu finished on 912 for 6

Warwickshire win the NatWest Trophy, Lancashire the Refuge Assurance League and Nottinghamshire the Benson and Hedges Cup

NOTES BY THE EDITOR

'Maybe this is an old-fashioned, not to say unfashionable, concept, but it seems to me that playing for one's country should be an honour – every time. Border spoke of national pride, and it was there for all to see in his team last year. They were playing for themselves, for each other and for their country. Watching some of the professional cricketers who have represented England in recent years, I can't help thinking that they regard a Test match as just another working day.'

FEATURE ARTICLES

Out of Africa Will Come Something New, by Dr. Ali Bacher
"We are not ... being defiant and claiming we can go it alone. We want to be part of world cricket. We want world cricket to be part of what we are doing in South Africa in making cricket a force for change. We do not want to hurt world cricket with unofficial tours, and we do not want to be the catalyst that might force a split in world cricket. But it must be understood that we need outside contact."
ICC and South Africa, by Jack Bailey
The Lawrence Awards, by E.W. Swanton
The County Championship – Relic or Relevant, by Trevor Bailey
The Pride Of His People, by David Foot

FIVE CRICKETERS OF THE YEAR

R.C. Russell

'Like Knott, Russell, in his floppy white hat and taped-up pads, looks as dishevelled as a truant schoolboy behind the stumps, but he is immaculate in his preparation and work. He has the fitness of a jump jockey and the finesse of a fencer. And like most wicket-keepers – as with goalkeepers in soccer – he is cheerfully self-contained: an independent spirit in a team game. He eats nothing but steak and chips on tour – not always easy in the likes of Nagpur and Gwalior.'

S.J. Cook   D.M. Jones   R.A. Smith   M.A. Taylor

OBITUARIES INCLUDE

W.H.R. Andrews
'… welcomed strangers with the cheery greeting, "Shake the hand that bowled Bradman", after he performed the feat at Taunton in 1938. Andrews was always honest enough to record that this happened only after the Australian captain had helped himself to 202 against Somerset.'

S.B. Beckett
'… had two first-class games for Dublin University against Northamptonshire in 1925 and 1926, scoring 35 runs in his four innings and conceding 64 runs without taking a wicket … Beckett, whose novels and plays established him as one of the important literary figures of the twentieth century, bringing him the Nobel Prize for literature in 1969, never lost his affection for and interest in cricket.'

F.G.H. Chalk
'… was shot down over the English Channel on February 17, 1943, while serving with the RAF as a flight lieutenant. He was posted missing, presumed dead, and it was not until early in 1989 that his body was found, still in the cockpit of his Spitfire, when excavations were made twelve miles inland from Calais.'

C.L.R. James
'James was a close friend of the great all-rounder, Learie Constantine, who invited him to Lancashire in 1932 when he was playing league cricket with Nelson. Neville Cardus helped make it possible for James to contribute to the *Manchester Guardian,* and his writing flourished; in addition to his own books on black radicalism, he helped Constantine to produce *Cricket and I.*'

J. Lawrence
'A professional sportsman who did not drink, smoke, swear or play cricket on Sundays because of his strong Methodist faith. But the diminutive Lawrence was a delightful companion, an extrovert with a bubbling sense of fun and a yen for practical jokes who was much loved by colleagues and crowds. Lawrence, perhaps because he bowled mistrusted wrist-spin, could get no further than the Second XI with Yorkshire, so he qualified for Somerset.'

Sir George 'Gubby' Allen   W.N. Slack   E.A. 'Betty' Snowball   J.B. Stollmeyer   N.W.D. Yardley

COUNTY REVIEW

Northamptonshire
'With a new, enthusiastic captain in Allan Lamb, an experienced batting line-up of proven ability, and the fast bowling strengthened by the arrival of Greg Thomas and Curtly Ambrose, Northamptonshire began 1989 full of confidence … It soon became clear that this 'new dawn' was a false one … The summer became a patchwork of heartening individual efforts, less distinguished team performances and too many dropped catches. It all added up to a ninth successive year without a major title.'

MATCH REPORTS

India v New Zealand, First Test, *at Bangalore, September 12, 13, 14, 16, 17*
'The world Test bowling record became Hadlee's alone when he had Arun Lal edging the first ball of his third over to Kuggeleijn at third slip. Thus the series began on a celebratory note for New Zealand and that country's outstanding cricketer. However, trouble was just round the corner for the New Zealanders, with almost the entire touring side being affected by a mystery ailment on the rest day. Some of the players, especially Hadlee, were violently ill, suffering stomach upsets, bouts of vomiting and shivering from what was assumed to be a virus … The series had begun on a note of controversy for India, with Mohinder Amarnath, omitted from the side for inexplicable reasons, calling the selectors a bunch of jokers at a press conference on the eve of the Test.'

For the first time, Wisden *has advertisements in colour.*

1991

WISDEN 1991

128th EDITION
EDITOR: Graeme Wright
PAGES: 1382
PRICE: Limp £16.75   cased £20.00

THE WORLD AT LARGE

- The first Gulf War: it takes six weeks to remove all Iraqi forces from Kuwait
- Provisional IRA launches a mortar attack on Downing Street during a cabinet meeting; no-one hurt
- Birmingham Six freed after it is considered their convictions concerning the bombings in 1974 are unsafe
- Beirut hostages Terry Waite and John McCarthy released
- Robert Maxwell drowns after falling from his yacht, the *Lady Ghislaine*
- Collapse of the Soviet Union: most republics within the Union declare independence, as do the Balkan states of Yugoslavia

CRICKET HEADLINES 1990

County Champions: Middlesex

Graham Gooch hits a triple-century and a hundred in the Lord's Test against India, recording the highest score at Lord's

Sir Richard Hadlee becomes the first man to play Test cricket after having been knighted for services to cricket

England win both three-Test home series, against New Zealand and India, by one match to nil

Lancashire become the first team to win both Lord's finals (NatWest and B&H) in one year: Derbyshire win the Refuge Assurance League

NOTES BY THE EDITOR

'When I first wrote the editor's Notes for *Wisden*, in the 1987 edition, I advocated an international panel of umpires. It would, I wrote then, cost money, but Test matches are cricket's money-spinner. They are also the world's window on the sport. Just how little money is spun by Test cricket, and how much an international panel of umpires would cost, has become apparent in recent months. A sum of around half a million pounds a year has been estimated (less than £75,000 per country), but without sponsorship that is beyond the budget of world cricket. Sponsorship not being forthcoming, nor for the present is the panel of umpires, even though the International Cricket Council voted six to one in favour of its mandatory use in Test cricket.'

FEATURE ARTICLES

A Genuinely Great Cricketer, by Simon Barnes
'There is a case for saying that Headingley 1981 is one of the greatest disasters to have hit England's cricket. Certainly, it lunged into a pattern of self-destructiveness as the echoes of that extraordinary year died away. The England team became based around an Inner Ring, with Botham at its heart: Botham, self-justified by his prodigious feats during that unforgettable summer. To be accepted, you had to hate the press, hate practice, enjoy a few beers and what have you, and generally be one hell of a good ol' boy. Like all cliques, the England clique was defined by exclusion. Nothing could be more destructive to team spirit than a team within a team, but that was the situation in the England camp for years.'

Don't Blame the Ball, by Jack Bannister
Sir Richard Hadlee, by Don Mosey
Lancashire's Revival – Is It Enough? by Michael Kennedy

M. Azharuddin

'Since childhood, Azharuddin has believed in turning out neatly at a cricket match, be it a hit in the park or a Test. Notice how he always goes out to toss in a blazer. By his manner, he also promises to re-establish sporting standards in the game as well as sartorial ones. Certainly, if India's tour of England was a resounding success for the game, Azharuddin can take pride in being a leading contributor to it.'

M.A. Atherton   A.R. Butcher   D.L. Haynes   M.E. Waugh

OBITUARIES INCLUDE

Haseeb-Ul-Hasan

'... who was murdered by an unknown gunman at Joharabad, Pakistan, on April 18, 1990, aged 25, had played in 32 first-class matches for Karachi and Karachi Blues since 1984-85. Only a month earlier, bowling left-arm medium-pace, he had taken five for 66, career-best figures, against Karachi Whites in the final of the Patron's Trophy.'

G.B. Hole

'Played in eighteen Tests for Australia from 1951 to 1955 and toured England under A.L. Hassett in the summer of 1953. The verdict on his Test career must be that it was deeply disappointing both to the player and the selectors, who kept faith with him for as long as they reasonably could. When he was summoned to the colours against England in February 1951, he ... seemed to possess all the qualities needed for the captaincy of Australia.'

Sir Leonard Hutton

'Hutton retained until the end the unassuming manner which marked his apprenticeship. Sir Jack Hobbs had been the same; as disarmingly unboastful after being knighted as before.' — John Woodcock

L.E.G. Ames   J. Hardstaff, jnr   M.J. Hilton   C. Milburn   H.G. 'Tuppy' Owen-Smith

---

COUNTY REVIEW

Leicestershire

'After the disappointments of 1989 ... they decided to appoint a manager: someone with both an unquestionable pedigree and a high media profile ... The county ... were successful in tempting Bobby Simpson, the Australian national coach, to try his hand in the English domestic game ... The Australian's arrival was not treated without scepticism among the players, some of whom held the view that a strong captain was as much leadership as a team required. None the less, within a few days of taking up his duties, Simpson had produced a more organised, professional approach to pre-season preparations than had been customary. Once the new campaign began, however, it was difficult to distinguish the new Leicestershire from the old model.'

MATCH REPORTS

Pakistan v India, First Test Match, *at Karachi, November 15, 16, 17, 19, 20*

'This was Kapil Dev's 100th Test, and with his third wicket he became the fourth bowler to take 350 Test wickets. He also became the first bowler to play in 100 Tests, a singular achievement in a career in which he had missed only one Test match – and that through a controversial disciplinary action by selectors. At the other end of the spectrum, Tendulkar made his début at the age of 16 years 205 days.'

Graeme Wright extends a welcome to Harriet Monkhouse, 'who has joined John Wisden as an editor and whose assistance has already altered the work-pattern of more than a decade'.

1992

WISDEN 1992

129th Edition
Editor: Graeme Wright
Pages: 1362
Price: Limp £18.50   cased £21.50

THE WORLD AT LARGE

• The Conservatives under John Major win a fourth consecutive General Election
• The Maastricht Treaty is signed, paving the way for the European Union
• The Royal family's *annus horribilis*, as the Prince and Princess of Wales separate, as do the Duke and Duchess of York, and Windsor Castle suffers a major fire
• Democrat Bill Clinton defeats incumbent George Bush in the U.S. presidential election

CRICKET HEADLINES 1991

County Champions: Essex

South Africa return to international cricket

England and the touring West Indians draw the Test series 2-2

England beat Sri Lanka in the only Test of the series

Australia retain the Ashes 3-0 as England under Gooch prove far too weak for a rapidly improving Australian side

Hampshire win the NatWest Bank Trophy, Worcestershire the Benson and Hedges Cup and Nottinghamshire the Refuge Assurance League

NOTES BY THE EDITOR

'Money should not be the only determining factor when it comes to broadcasting rights. Cricket is not such a popular sport that audience figures can afford to be ignored, especially with cricket being played at fewer schools and young people being offered a whole range of alternative leisure activities. Cricket needs maximum exposure more than ever. Thousands of viewers in Britain will have watched the World Cup, perhaps hundreds of thousands. The fact that it would have been millions had the World Cup been shown on the BBC or ITV should be of concern to the TCCB. One feels it is not.'

FEATURE ARTICLES

The Lancashire League Celebrates its Centenary, by Chris Aspin
'There have been many times when I have wondered why cricket ever took root in these parts. Snow has more than once prevented play, and the sight and feel of cold Lancashire rain falling from a pewter sky is almost enough to put people off the game for ever. But on a sunny afternoon, with noble hills providing the backcloth to a keenly contested game involving two world-class professionals, there are few better cricketing occasions.'
John Arlott – A Lover of Cricket, by Mike Brearley
Beginnings Are Everything, by Peter Roebuck
The MCC Schools Festival, by Gerald Howat
Women in Cricket, by Teresa McLean
Pushing the Product, by Benny Green

FIVE CRICKETERS OF THE YEAR

P.A.J. DeFreitas
'The fact that his greatest success came in limited-overs cricket, for which he was usually an automatic choice, served only to prove that he was at his most effective when bowling within himself ... He moved the ball both ways off the seam, he recaptured his ability to make the ball bounce from that whippy action of his, and he reaped the reward.'
C.E.L. Ambrose   A.A. Donald   R.B. Richardson   Waqar Younis

L.T.J. Arlott
'When he was doing commentary, or composing a portrait of a Tate or a Trueman, or writing a match report for the *Guardian*, he was at or near the centre of affairs. But he was equally an expert on interests connected with the game: its vast literature, extensive history and collection of artefacts were all within his purview. To fuel his activities he had great energy, the ability to work at speed, and the charm to elicit information from whatever source he was investigating. Add in the fact that he was a poet of some stature and that he enjoyed the laughter and company of friends, whom he loved to entertain in the most civilised way, and you have a man of deep humanity.'

J.L. Guise
'... belonged to the select few who have achieved fame through one big performance. In Guise's case it was his innings of 278 for Winchester against Eton on Agar's Plough in 1921, the largest score in a public schools match.'

F.M. King
'... possibly the best fast bowler produced by the West Indies during the long period between the enforced retirement of Constantine in 1939 and the advent in 1959 of Wesley Hall. In his account of the Fifth Test between West Indies and England at Kingston, Jamaica, in 1953-54, E.W. Swanton commented: "King has real pace and he brings down the ball from the very top. He is 6ft 2in, slender in build and with long arms. His spell this morning was the fastest I have seen in West Indies."'

W. Walker
'... who died on December 3, 1991, in a nursing-home at Keighley, Yorkshire, having just embarked on his 100th year, had for some years been recognised as the oldest living county cricketer. A right-handed batsman and an elegant strokeplayer, he was for much of the time between 1913 and 1937 Nottinghamshire's No. 3.'

C.R.M. Atkinson   F.R. Brown   R.J.O. Meyer   W.H. Ponsford

Hampshire
'Winning the NatWest Bank Trophy made the summer of 1991 one of fond memories for Hampshire supporters ... [Mark] Nicholas's disappointment at having to sit out the match as a spectator was softened by the knowledge that Hampshire had established an enviable record: victory in both their Lord's finals ... Yet the triumph for teamwork perhaps clouded assessment of the overall tenor of the summer. Did it constitute success or was it a smokescreen hiding a season of under-achievement? A dispassionate assessment suggested the latter.'

England in Australia and New Zealand, 1990-91
'John Morris had the misfortune to make his only hundred against Queensland in the final state game, when ... it was too late to challenge for a Test role. It added to Morris's chagrin that Carrara was the scene of his escapade with Gower in a pair of 1938 Tiger Moths. To greet Smith's century they prevailed upon the pilots of their hired planes to buzz the ground at low altitude, for which each was fined £1,000. For all their dereliction of duty in leaving without permission a game in which they were playing, it was a harsh penalty for an essentially light-hearted prank, reflecting all too accurately the joyless nature of the tour. Impressive as Gooch's captaincy was, a hair shirt was usually to be found hanging in his wardrobe.'

John Arlott's book reviews appear for the last time. He had filed his copy just weeks before his death in December 1991, having held sway since 1950 with the exception of 1979 and 1980.

Denstone College and Roedean become the first girls' schools to have their averages included in the Schools Cricket section.

1993

WISDEN 1993

130th Edition
Editor: Matthew Engel
Pages: 1394
Price: Limp £19.50   cased £22.50

THE WORLD AT LARGE

• War in Bosnia: despite the presence of UN peacekeepers, the war escalates
• PLO leader Yasser Arafat and Israeli Prime minister Yitzhak Rabin sign a peace agreement in Washington
• Death of England World Cup winning captain Bobby Moore, from cancer
• Czechoslovakia splits into the Czech Republic and Slovakia
• After two false starts, the Grand National is declared null and void

CRICKET HEADLINES 1992

County Champions: Essex

Durham make their debut as a first-class county, and come last

Pakistan beat England in the World Cup final in Australia

Pakistan also beat England in the five match series in England, 2-1

England beat New Zealand in New Zealand, 2-0

Northamptonshire win the NatWest Trophy, Hampshire the Benson and Hedges Cup and Middlesex the Sunday League

NOTES BY THE EDITOR

'Cricket, at the highest level, has acquired a unique and insoluble problem by turning itself into two separate sports. There is traditional cricket, a game that has stood the test of time as a satisfying pastime and way of life, but which finds it increasingly hard to get an audience. And there is one-day cricket, which is popular among spectators but is regarded with varying degrees of contempt by the professionals forced to play it, administrators forced to stage it, and journalists forced to report it. It distorts cricket's skills and produces a mutant game which, while it might on occasion be tense, is essentially shallow.'

FEATURE ARTICLES

The Roar of the Greasepaint – The Smell of the Linseed, by David Rayvern Allen
'Sir Laurence Olivier once said: "I have often thought how much better a life I would have had, what a better man I would have been, how much healthier an existence I would have led, if I had been a cricketer instead of an actor." On the other hand, Ian Botham gave up the chance of a Test match in New Zealand because he was playing the king in *Jack and the Beanstalk* in Bournemouth. The grass is always greener.'
Pakistani Bowling, Fair or Foul? by Jack Bannister
African Sunrise, by Donald Woods
A Canny First Season, by Simon Hughes
From Gravesend to the Grave, by John Thicknesse
The Murray Report
    The Case In Favour, by Alan Lee
    The Case Against, by E.W. Swanton

FIVE CRICKETERS OF THE YEAR:

N.E. Briers

'A cliché it may be, but he is the model pro; first into the nets, a stickler for practice, and almost irritatingly neat, tidy, and well-ordered with his kit. Furthermore, he has not missed a Leicestershire game since 1987, and has played some of his best cricket for the club since inheriting the captaincy in his mid-30s. An elegant, predominantly front-foot batsman, Briers remains a very fine fielder in the covers, but perhaps his greatest quality is his undiminished enthusiasm for the game.'

M.D. Moxon   I.D.K. Salisbury   A.J. Stewart   Wasim Akram

K.J. Grieves

'For many years after the war Ken Grieves represented to English cricket followers the epitome of the Australian professional, ferociously hard on the field, delightfully charming off it. He played 452 matches for Lancashire between 1949 and 1964, scoring runs, taking wickets and – above all – snapping up close-to-the-wicket catches. Unusually for an Australian, he also played soccer and made 147 Football League appearances as a goalkeeper for Bury, Bolton and Stockport.'

P.F. Judge

'… had the bizarre experience of being dismissed for nought twice inside a minute. In the game against the Indians at Cardiff, he was bowled by C.T. Sarwate at the end of the first innings, at which point Glamorgan followed on. But with little time left, the captain Johnnie Clay decided to give the crowd some entertainment, so he waived the ten minutes between innings, and reversed his batting order. The batsmen then at the crease stayed out there and Sarwate bowled Judge again, first ball.'

E.M. Wellings

'Wellings reported more than 200 Tests with a trenchancy that has never been matched. He attacked inefficiency on or off the field in indignant terms. He hated one-day cricket, overseas players in county teams, South Africa's isolation, faulty technique and, in later years, everything to do with the Test and County Cricket Board. From 1945 to 1972 he also wrote on Public Schools cricket for *Wisden*, which he did with a magisterial sweep that no one else can ever have brought to the subject.'

H.F.T. Buse   R.E. Marshall   W.J. O'Reilly   W.S. Surridge   C.F. Walters

---

Durham

'It was the best of times and the worst of times for Durham in their first season in the County Championship. First-class cricket was rapturously received by a membership of over 6,000, and the team made a highly encouraging start. But once the impetus provided by the successful launch was lost, they began to struggle.'

England v South Africa, Benson and Hedges World Cup Semi-Final, *at Sydney, March 22 (day/night)*
'This game's closing minutes buried South Africa's World Cup hopes, and whatever credibility the rain rule had retained. By putting pressure on the team batting second, the rule supposedly created exciting finishes; on this occasion 12 minutes' heavy rain, when South Africa needed 22 from 13 balls, adjusted their target first to 22 from seven, and then to 21 from one. McMillan could only take a single off Lewis. The losers were disconsolate, the winners embarrassed, and the crowd furious. Why, they asked, were the two overs not played out under the floodlights?'

Graeme Wright, after six years as editor and eight years before that as assistant editor, stepped down, although he was to return for the 2001 and 2002 editions. Matthew Engel reorganises the Almanack into six parts – Comment, Records, English Cricket, Overseas Cricket, Administration and Laws, and Miscellaneous. 'What I have tried to do is to make the book clearer and more accessible to new readers without disturbing the rhythm understood by those who already know and love it.' Engel decides that the book reviews should now be written by someone different each year: 'a reviewer with a literary reputation first and a separate enthusiasm for cricket.' The novelist J.L. Carr is his first choice.

1994

WISDEN 1994

131st Edition
Editor: Matthew Engel
Pages: 1446
Price: Limp £20   cased £22.50

THE WORLD AT LARGE

- The Channel Tunnel is officially opened
- John Smith, leader of the Labour Party, dies from a heart attack. Tony Blair becomes the new leader
- The Provisional IRA declares a ceasefire
- South Africa holds its first multi-racial elections: the ANC wins and Nelson Mandela becomes President
- Racing driver Ayrton Senna is killed during the San Marino Grand Prix

CRICKET HEADLINES 1993

County Champions: Middlesex

Australia defeat England as Shane Warne makes his debut with the 'ball of the century' to bowl Mike Gatting: Australia win the series 4-1

Graham Gooch hits his 100th hundred

Warwickshire beat Sussex in a thrilling and high-scoring NatWest final, and Derbyshire win the B&H Cup

Glamorgan win the Sunday League, now the Axa Equity & Law League

NOTES BY THE EDITOR

'1993 was … the year when the system of umpiring by video spread to engulf the Test-playing world. I may be in a minority; I remain utterly convinced that this is a disaster … Remember that it was a couple of outrageously wrong decisions that led to the demand for this system, not a lot of marginal ones. We saw players starting to pressurise umpires if they did not call for a replay. And we saw increasing demands (sometimes on the field) for the system to be extended to close catches as well. The heart of the game, the finality of the umpire's verdict, is being eaten away.'

FEATURE ARTICLES

Why We Beat The Poms, by Ian Chappell
'England's ability to over-theorise and complicate the game of cricket is legendary. Ever since I became involved in Ashes battles, I've felt that Australia could rely on some assistance from the England selectors. In 1993 they ran truer to form than many of the players they picked. Their magnanimity gave Australia a four-game start before the penny dropped. They then promoted Mike Atherton to the captaincy and, in no time, England picked a reasonably well-balanced side with an attack that bore some semblance of hostility.'
A Whole New World, by Jack Bailey
The Giants Depart: Botham and Richards, by John Woodcock
　　　　　　　: David Gower, by Martin Johnson
Before the Interruption, by E.W. Swanton
Computerised Scoring: An Enthusiast's View, by Ken Lawrence
　　　　　　　: A Scorer's View, by Bill Frindall
How the Welsh Were Won Over, by Edward Bevan
Sri Lanka's Great Game, by Christopher Martin-Jenkins

FIVE CRICKETERS OF THE YEAR

S.K. Warne
'Warne, born in a smart bayside suburb of Melbourne on September 13, 1969, did not display many of the hallmarks of his predecessors – Grimmett, O'Reilly and Benaud – in his youth.

Bleached blond hair, a stud in his ear plus a fondness for good life, which caused his waistline to expand with alarming speed, and an aversion to discipline.'
D.C. Boon   I.A. Healy   M.G. Hughes   S.L. Watkin

D.B. Deodhar
'... who died at Pune on August 24, 1993, aged 101, was the world's oldest living first-class cricketer. He not merely became a real-life centurion, he was the first Indian to score a hundred for a representative side against a visiting team: 148 for All India against A.E.R. Gilligan's MCC team in 1926-27.'

B.A. Johnston
'Along with John Arlott, who died in 1991, he was the central figure of BBC's *Test Match Special* and responsible for its unique style.'

C.G. Pepper
'... often described as the best Australian player never to win a Test cap. He was, without any doubt, one of the greatest characters ever to come near the game, to whom anecdotes clung, as with Fred Trueman, some of them actually true.'

S.C. Griffith   A.L. Hassett   E.A.B. Rowan

COUNTY REVIEW

Warwickshire
'Warwickshire's magnificent last-ball win against Sussex in the NatWest Trophy final redeemed an otherwise poor season, in which they fell from sixth to sixteenth place in the Championship, and failed to survive their first Benson and Hedges match ... Without Donald in 1994, much depends on the fitness of Munton and Small and the form of Prabhakar. Only if they do well, and at least one batsman has an outstanding season, can Warwickshire hope to do better in the Championship.'

MATCH REPORTS

Sri Lanka v England, Test Match, *at Sinhalese Sports Club, Colombo, March 13, 14, 15, 17, 18*
'Sri Lanka won by five wickets ... Sri Lanka comprehensively outplayed England and thoroughly deserved their first win against them ... Although there were individual performances of some merit from England, collectively this was another bad display. The tourists once again failed to produce the standard of performance required to compete with technically skilled and highly motivated opposition in a hostile environment ... The shirts of the England players were soaked in perspiration throughout the match as temperatures soared into the high 90s and the humidity became quite exhausting ... There were also further murmurings regarding the impartiality of Sri Lankan umpiring and the bowling action of Sri Lankan off-spinners Warnaweera and Muralitharan. But, overall, England had nothing and no one to blame but themselves.'

Matthew Engel explains: 'This Wisden *contains a supplementary obituary. Since the Almanack began including an obituary in 1892, inevitably some important and interesting people have been missed ... The tireless work of Robert Brooke has enabled us to fill in a good many of the gaps ... The 1994 Almanack also contains a selection of the more remarkable and eccentric cricketing happenings of 1993 outside first-class cricket. Some people think* Wisden *has always reported such things. That is unfortunately not true, but I see no reason why it should not be true henceforth.* Wisden *remains, above all, a serious volume recording a serious game, but much of cricket's richness derives from its curiosities and its humour and it is proper that we should record them too.'*

This was the first edition produced after John Paul Getty purchased the company and thus assured Wisden's *medium-term future.*

1995

WISDEN 1995

132nd Edition
Editor: Matthew Engel
Pages: 1444
Price: Limp and cased £23.50
Leather-bound £200 (limited edition of 100 copies)

THE WORLD AT LARGE

• Balkan War: Srebrenica massacre by Bosnian Serbs after UN peacekeepers leave the city
• By the end of the year, a peace agreement is signed in Paris
• Earthquake in Kobe, Japan: over 6,000 people die
• Rogue trader Nick Leeson's losses bring down Barings Bank
• O.J. Simpson murder trial: the football and film star is acquitted of murdering his ex-wife and a friend

CRICKET HEADLINES 1994

County Champions: Warwickshire, who also win the B&H Cup and the Sunday League and lose in the final of the NatWest Trophy to Worcestershire

Brian Lara scores 375 for West Indies against England to set a new Test scoring record, and a few weeks later scores 501* for Warwickshire against Durham, the highest first-class innings ever played

England lose 3-1 in the West Indies

England and South Africa share the series 1-1 after Devon Malcolm takes 9 for 57 at The Oval

England beat New Zealand 1-0

NOTES BY THE EDITOR

'England are never boring: each time they plummet to a previously uncharted depth, they stage an improbable leap upwards; they were bowled out under 100 three times in 1994, but invariably came back to score a startling victory a Test or two later. Nonetheless, each depth does seem to be lower than the last. I have never seen a team as dismal and demoralised as the England side that slouched around the field on the fourth day of the Melbourne Test.'

FEATURE ARTICLES

Cheating: The Secret History, by Derek Pringle
'So was Atherton cheating? To my eyes, there was no evidence that he was taking any action to alter the state of the ball and there is no regulation to stop a player having a pocketful of soil. There is a danger now that the authorities will be panicked into rewriting the Laws yet again. The contest between bat and ball will work best with a minimum of fuss and a maximum of self-regulation.'
Looking at Lara: Six views of his two record-breaking innings
Year of Grace 1895
The Record Breakers Retire: Allan Border, by Mike Coward
The Record Breakers Retire: Kapil Dev, by Mike Selvey
Talking A Good Game: 50 Years Of Cricket Societies, by Murray Hedgcock
The Vagrant Gypsy Life: 150 Years Of I Zingari, by John Woodcock
An Alternative Five, by David Hopps

FIVE CRICKETERS OF THE YEAR

B.C. Lara
'It was his 277 in Sydney in January 1993, in his fifth Test, that confirmed what Trinidadians had long since taken for granted, that here was the newest in the long line of great West Indian batsmen ... Rohan Kanhai called it "one of the greatest innings I have ever seen". Its immediate value was that it inspired a revival of West Indian spirits that led to the conversion of a 1-0 series deficit at the time to an eventual 2-1 triumph; its long-term significance was that it

established Lara as batting leader of a team still searching for a central figure in the absence of Richards.'
D.E. Malcolm   T.A. Munton   S.J. Rhodes   K.C. Wessels

A.R. Alston
'His broadcasting style was described as 'pleasant and courteous' in an obituary in *The Times* in 1985. This was accurate; however, Alston was not dead ... The following year he proved his fitness by remarrying and became perhaps the first man to have his death and marriage reported in *The Times* in that order.'

H.R. Carter
'"Raich" Carter was a lower-order batsman and medium-pace bowler who played three away matches for Derbyshire in June 1946 ... He was, though, almost certainly the only man in history to be out for a duck in a county match at Stourbridge six weeks after receiving an FA Cup winner's medal.'

R.J. Crisp
'... was one of the most extraordinary men ever to play Test cricket. His cricket, which is only a fraction of the story, was explosive enough: he is the only bowler to have taken four wickets in four balls twice.'

R.J. Hayter
'Hayter started as a junior with Pardon's, the agency that then produced *Wisden,* in 1933; the editor's notes on the Bodyline tour were dictated to him for transcription. He was associated with the Almanack for many years, covering a number of tours, and also edited *The Cricketer* between 1978 and 1981.'

P.B.H. May
'He was never a soft touch: he was loyal to his players and they were aware of it, but he could be distinctly uncharitable if that loyalty was not returned and he was quick to punish lack of effort, or stupidity, as distinct from naïveté.' – Doug Insole

T.N. Pearce   H.J. Tayfield

Surrey
'To lose one's way halfway through a season may be regarded as a misfortune: to lose one's way twice in as many seasons, and on all fronts, looks like carelessness ... April brought a management reshuffle, which led to the appointment of two non-executive directors ... on an executive board replacing the old management board; the unwieldy sub-committee structure was dismantled. Then came a season not much different from the last.'

Warwickshire v Durham, *at Birmingham, June 2, 3, 4, 6*
'The astonishing record-strewn Monday, including Lara's 501 not out – the highest score in the history of first-class cricket – that concluded this game was possible only because the third day was lost to rain. Having narrowly missed joining Bradman, Fry and Procter in scoring six successive first-class hundreds, Lara became the first man to score seven in eight innings.'

Cricket and the Law in 1994
'Carl Fraser, a 57-year-old former bus conductor, was awarded £113,094 damages in the High Court after a fire engine on an emergency call ran over his foot, causing him to have all his toes amputated and forcing him to give up playing cricket ... Mr Fraser, who played for the North Middlesex club, was reported as saying, "I have lost the passion of my life. No amount of money can ever replace cricket".'

1996

WISDEN 1996

133rd EDITION
EDITOR: Matthew Engel
PAGES: 1460
PRICE: Limp and cased £24.50
Leather-bound £200 (150 limit)

THE WORLD AT LARGE

• Dunblane massacre: a gunman kills 16 children and a teacher at a primary school, before killing himself
• Dolly the sheep, the world's first cloned mammal, is born
• IRA ceasefire ends with a bomb at Canary Wharf in London's docklands
• President Clinton wins re-election for a second term
• Iraq refuses UN inspection teams access to check weapons manufacturing sites

CRICKET HEADLINES 1995

County Champions: Warwickshire, who also take the NatWest Trophy

England and West Indies share the Test series, two matches apiece

Dominic Cork takes the first hat-trick for England in a home Test since 1957

England lose 3-1 to Australia down under

Lancashire win the B&H Cup, while Kent win the Axa Equity & Law Sunday League

NOTES BY THE EDITOR

'The English season of 1995 cannot be ranked with the greatest summers, like 1947 and 1981. It may not be recalled in future quite as often as 1948, 1956 or 1975. But it was a wonderfully rich and satisfying summer as it occurred, and perhaps the memories still need more time to mature before we can decide how long they will last. At the heart of it all was a classic Test series between England and West Indies, who traded punches like battered heavyweights (an analogy which sums up the state of both teams) before collapsing in a heap at 2-2.'

FEATURE ARTICLES

Bat, Ball and Bitter: Cricket and Pubs
'For every cricketing pub that vanishes or changes its name, another one seems to pop up. The drearily named New Inn in West Meon, Hampshire, became the Thomas Lord in 1952 to commemorate the founder of Lord's, who is buried in the village. And in Dewsbury, Yorkshire, there is now the Sir Geoffrey Boycott OBE. It was originally called The Park, then reopened in 1995 under its new name, with a sign depicting Boycott taking strike in his England gear.'
The Bribes Crisis, by David Hopps
Has The Game Got Worse? Interviews, by Pat Murphy
Fifty Years Of Post-War Cricket, by Matthew Engel and Philip Bailey
The Last of the Line, by David Frith
Miracle In Queensland (Somewhat Belated), by Gideon Haigh
Next – Schoolboys In Pyjamas? by Andrew Longmore
Fifty Years of the Cricket Writers' Club, by Derek Hodgson
Tragedy at Nagpur

FIVE CRICKETERS OF THE YEAR

A.R.C. Fraser
'Fraser deals in parsimony and red-faced effort. He is perennially grumpy, kicks savage lumps from the turf at a conceded leg-bye, and could murder a misfielder: the opposite to the millionaire spendthrifts who buy their wickets with boundaries. Somewhere, he believes, he

can always get a cheaper deal. Runs are a commodity to be hoarded, not frittered away on the undeserving. This is Scrooge in flannels. Batsmen? Bah! Humbug!'

D.G. Cork   P.A. de Silva   A. Kumble   D.A. Reeve

OBITUARIES INCLUDE

H.L. Calder

'... was both the youngest ever and the oldest surviving *Wisden* Cricketer of the Year. Calder was chosen as one of the School Bowlers of the Year in 1918 when there was no regular selection because of the war. He was in the Cranleigh XI for five years as a bowler of varied medium-paced spinners. But he ... did not know he had ever been a Cricketer of the Year until he was tracked down in 1994.'

A.H.S. Clark

'... was an engine driver from Weston-super-Mare and one of the most improbable of all county cricketers ... He kept magnificently; however, he is mainly remembered for his batting, which was hopeless. Clark thought his highest score in club cricket was three, and two of them came from overthrows.'

B.V. Easterbrook

'He was a regular writer for *Wisden* and contributed an article every year from 1971 to 1980. Easterbrook was a much loved member of the press corps with a puckish humour. He claimed that while covering a match from the old Lord's press box, he leaned out of the window to throw away his pencil shavings and the Nottinghamshire batsmen walked in, thinking it was the signal to declare.'

H. Larwood

'Bodyline, or leg-theory bowling, with bowlers aiming at the body with a ring of predatory leg-side fielders, was not unknown at this stage; Arthur Carr, the Nottinghamshire captain, would sometimes unleash Larwood in that manner in county matches. Several batsmen were carried off unconscious after being hit by Larwood even when he was bowling normally.'

R.O. Jenkins   G.A.R. Lock   R.E.S. Wyatt

COUNTY REVIEW

Kent

'Kent's recent history has been full off near misses. They have finished as beaten finalists or runners-up nine times in the 17 seasons since their days of regular trophy-collecting came to an end in 1978. When they lost their fifth successive Lord's final, to Lancashire in the Benson and Hedges in July, the sequence looked set to continue indefinitely. September 17, 1995 was the day they finally came good, becoming Sunday League champions and bringing home a piece of silverware at last. It may be a turning point.'

MATCH REPORTS

Australia v England, Third Test Match, *at Sydney, January 1, 2, 3, 4, 5*

'An eighth-wicket stand between Warne and May, lasting 77 minutes, saved Australia from an astonishing defeat in a game that had seemed dead two and a half hours earlier. Australia, who abandoned a bold pursuit of 449 only when rain intervened, were then 239 for two. An hour and a quarter later, however, they were 292 for seven; in three overs Fraser scythed down their middle order with a spell of four for four.'

Matthew Engel writes in the Preface: 'Nothing in four years of editing Wisden *has given me quite as much job satisfaction as the establishment of the Cricket Round The World feature, which has now become an established part of the Almanack. Forty-six different countries, or territories, or dots on the ocean, have now appeared in this section ... We still await news from, for instance, North Korea and Albania. I did go to Albania myself two years ago but, alas, could find no trace of cricket; how different it would have been if C.B. Fry ever had taken up the famous offer of kingship.'*

1997

THE WORLD AT LARGE

- At the General Election, the Labour Party under Tony Blair secures a huge majority
- Sovereignty over Hong Kong is handed to the People's Republic of China
- Death of Princess Diana in a car crash in Paris
- The first *Harry Potter* novel is published
- The Kyoto Protocol on climate change adopted

WISDEN 1997

134th EDITION
EDITOR: Matthew Engel
PAGES: 1460
PRICE: Limp and cased £26.00
Leather-bound £200 (150 limit)

CRICKET HEADLINES 1996

Sri Lanka win the World Cup

County Champions: Leicestershire

England beat the visiting Indians 1-0, but lose to the Pakistanis 2-0

Kevan James scores a century and takes four wickets in four balls for Hampshire v Indians, a unique achievement

Wayne James catches seven and stumps two batsmen in Mashonaland's first innings against Matabeleland in the Logan Cup Final, and catches four more in the second innings, and scores 99 and 99* in the match – the former a world record, the latter only the second instance in a first-class match

NOTES BY THE EDITOR

'The 1996 cricket season in England was in some respects the most depressing in memory, almost entirely due to the continual disasters that afflicted the national team. A calendar year which began with the dreadful conclusion to the tour of South Africa, and a wretched performance in the World Cup, ended with England's glum failures in Zimbabwe. An indifferent summer was sandwiched in between; and a pall of gloom descended on the game. But every time I went to a county match I enjoyed myself hugely, no matter how few people might have been around to share that enjoyment.'

FEATURE ARTICLES

A Wind Blows From The East, by Mihir Bose
'Unlike the Olympic Games, or soccer's World Cup and European Championships, the cricket World Cup is not an event owned by the international authority that runs the game. The country staging it, in effect, owns the competition. In five previous World Cups this had made little difference: the host country had made money, but not so much as to raise eyebrows. The 1996 World Cup changed everything.'
The Wisden World Championship
English Cricket: A Manifesto, by Lord MacLaurin
If You Can Meet With Triumph And Disaster
Sri Lanka: Years of Preparation …, by Gerry Vaidyasekera
… A Night to Remember, by David Hopps
The Man Who Stole The Show, by Tony Lewis
A Spin-Doctor Writes, by Ashley Mallett
Fifty Sheffield Shield Years, by David Frith and Philip Bailey
Years of the Fox, by Martin Johnson

For the first time a player – Sanath Jayasuriya – who did not play in the English cricket season was chosen

S.R. Tendulkar

'He has, it seems, been around for ever. In the Third Test at Trent Bridge last summer, he scored 177, the tenth century of his Test career and his second of the series: yet remarkably, at 23, Tendulkar was younger than any member of the England team, with only Dominic Cork and Min Patel born even in the same decade … With time on his side and a return to a full Test programme, he could prove Sunil Gavaskar right and rewrite the records.'

S.T. Jayasuriya   Mushtaq Ahmed   Saeed Anwar   P.V. Simmons

OBITUARIES INCLUDE

C. Cook

'Sam Cook epitomised everything that has traditionally been considered best about county cricketers in general, and West Country cricketers in particular. He was a phlegmatic, humorous, locally-rooted man who loved a wry laugh, a pint and the lift he led, and made friends everywhere he played. He was also a naturally gifted, slow left-arm bowler who could drop the ball on a length, without bothering to practise, and keep it there all season, with enough flight and variation to outwit the best batsmen in the game.'

D.J. Halfyard

'Perhaps the only umpire to retire and return to playing … His pride and joy was a camper van with almost 400,000 miles on the clock; his cricket had the same improbable durability.'

R. Ryder

'Ryder's final book, *Cricket Calling,* an evocation of the game and his connection with it, was published to widespread acclaim a year before his death. Cricket is not so much a game, he wrote, as an extension of being English: a gallimaufry of paradoxes, contradictions, frightening logic and sheer impossibilities, of gentle courtesy and rough violence.'

K.D. Boyce   L.J. Coldwell   A.H. Kardar   D. Kenyon   R.R. Lindwall   J.D.B. Robertson

---

COUNTY REVIEW

Yorkshire

'In one sense, Yorkshire enjoyed their best season since 1972, when the county game was expanded to take in a fourth major competition, for they challenged strongly on all fronts. They failed, however, to win any of them, and seemed to have the makings of a good side while remaining no more than a useful one … In the final analysis, however, the improvement on 1995 was marginal.'

MATCH REPORTS

South Africa v England, Fifth Test Match, *at Cape Town, January 2, 3, 4*

'The main resistance came from Thorpe, whose innings ended in extraordinary circumstances. He attempted a single off Adams but Hudson hit the stumps with a direct throw from backward square leg. Umpire Dave Orchard turned down the appeal. But the spectators in the hospitality boxes, who all had access to TV sets, watched the replay, which suggested Thorpe should have been given out, and began baying for Orchard to change his mind. The South African captain Cronje approached Orchard, who consulted his colleague Steve Randell and then called for the TV replay, which confirmed the majority view. In a narrow, technical sense, justice was done, but this was perilously close to mob rule.'

'There is one important innovation in the 1997 Wisden,' *writes Matthew Engel in the Preface. 'For the first time the Almanack includes a Register of Players, giving biographical information for almost a thousand of the world's leading cricketers.'*

1998

WISDEN 1998

135th Edition
Editor: Matthew Engel
Pages: 1492
Price: Limp and cased £27.50
Leather-bound £200 (150 limit)

THE WORLD AT LARGE

• The Good Friday agreement between the British, Irish and Northern Irish political leaders is signed
• President Clinton denies on television that he had sexual relations with Monica Lewinsky: the scandal leads to his impeachment
• *Titanic* wins a record 11 Oscars
• In Omagh, a bomb kills 29 people, the most destructive single bomb of the Troubles
• Iraq stops co-operating with UN inspectors

CRICKET HEADLINES 1997

County Champions: Glamorgan

Australia win the home Test series 3-2

Adam and Ben Hollioake become the first brothers to play together for England for forty years

During the winter, England draw their two Tests in Zimbabwe, but beat New Zealand by 2 matches to nil

Essex win the NatWest Trophy, Surrey the B&H Cup and Warwickshire the Axa Life Sunday League

Duckworth–Lewis method for deciding incomplete limited overs matches adopted

NOTES BY THE EDITOR

'Whereas cricket was in crisis in England, West Indies, Zimbabwe, and perhaps New Zealand, it flourished in the countries where people had more cause to cheer their national teams. In Sri Lanka, in particular, the boom kept reverberating: when TV showed an interview with Sanath Jayasuriya, the country's electricity demand broke 1,000 megawatts for the first time. In Australia, the traditional Boxing Day start of the Melbourne Test attracted its largest crowd in 22 years, 73,812, and a CD making fun of Bill Lawry's commentaries sold 100,000 copies in no time. Across the globe and into cyberspace, cricketing Internet sites were consistently among the busiest on the entire web.'

FEATURE ARTICLES

Court on the Boundary, by Richard Colley
  'Reed *v* Seymour 1927: James Seymour was a Kent professional. In the words of the Law Lord, Viscount Cave, he played fine cricket, and in 1920 was given a benefit match which raised £939. The tax inspector assessed Seymour on that amount. He would be liable if it had been paid to him by way of salary of remuneration but not if it were a personal gift. In a decision that set a precedent for which countless cricketers have been grateful, the House of Lords held Seymour's benefit was an expression of gratitude from the public for the services he had already rendered, and was not intended to spur him on to further successes. Accordingly, it was purely a gift and he did not have to pay tax on it.'
Gooch: Cricket's No. 1 Run Machine, by Christopher Martin-Jenkins
Woodcock's Hundred, by John Woodcock
W.G. Grace: 150 Years On, by Geoffrey Moorhouse
And Lord's Said: 'Let There Be Lights', by Rob Steen
The End of Chivalry, by Andrew Longmore
The Appliance of Science, by John Illman and Derek Pringle

S.G. Law

'Law cherishes his one Test appearance, against Sri Lanka in Perth in December 1995, in which he made an unbeaten and effortless half-century in Australia's only innings (and so, of course, he does not have a Test average). "To actually don the baggy green cap... I can take that to the grave with me," he said. By the next Test, Steve Waugh was fit again, Australia were not quite ready to drop David Boon, and Law was jettisoned. Sometimes he dwelt on the injustice, believing that he should have had three Tests to prove or disprove himself. He contests the idea that he is a one-day specialist, yet has to live with it.'

M.T.G. Elliott   G.D. McGrath   M.P. Maynard   G.P. Thorpe

D.C.S. Compton

'The timing, impeccable to the last, was poignant. The news came on the morning the cricketers of England were preparing to call "Play!" on the first day of 1997's County Championship. Then, one by one, the pavilion flags were lowered to half-mast and young men in cream flannels, who knew him not, stood to attention for a minute because they knew who he was all right, and what he had contributed everlastingly to the innate goodness as well as the grandeur of their game. Compton was an all-time great and, as those standards dipped at Canterbury, Chelmsford, Old Trafford, Trent Bridge and Hove – which in his bonny prime he had sunnily beguiled – bells metaphorically tolled the world over at places happy to accept that team-game players can lift spirits by their skill and chivalry. Because of the drab days he so illuminated, Denis was almost a cultural icon to Britain of the immediate post-war, a valorous talisman of gaiety and of hope.' – Frank Keating

N.A.S. Gibson

'Alan Gibson was one of the most remarkable men ever to broadcast or write about cricket. He was president of the Oxford Union and gained a first in history. Perhaps no one has brought more literacy or classical knowledge to the reporting of any game. Men with his background expect to become cabinet ministers at least, and Gibson often seemed conscious of this; a sense of failure may explain the demons that regularly afflicted him.'

J.R. Sheffield

'Roy Sheffield was probably the only Essex wicket-keeper ever to be arrested on suspicion of being a Bolivian spy. He was a small, agile man who kept wicket in 177 games for Essex between 1929 and 1936.'

D.L. Bairstow   B. Constable   A.J. Harvey-Walker   W. Wooller

---

Gloucestershire

'It is rather too facile just to offer a Gloucestershire groan at the county's final seventh position in the table, the lowest place they occupied all season, and share Nevil Road angst over the way the team had trifled with local emotions. The fact was that Gloucestershire intermittently headed an exciting, open race for the pennant. This they did without their best batsman and bowler from the previous year, Andrew Symonds and Courtney Walsh. It was a thoroughly unlikely accomplishment by a side that, at least theoretically, possessed modest skills and suspect balance.'

England v Australia, Third One-Day International, *at Lord's May 25*

'England made a clean sweep of the series with their third consecutive six-wicket victory. Every match began with Atherton winning the toss and ended with a stroke from Adam Hollioake. But it was Adam's 19-year-old brother Ben who stole the show here, on his debut, as he thrilled Lord's with an audacious half-century.'

1999

WISDEN 1999

136th EDITION
EDITOR: Matthew Engel
PAGES: 1550
PRICE: Limp and cased £28.00
Leather-bound £200 (150 limit)

THE WORLD AT LARGE

• The first elections to the Scottish and Welsh Assemblies
• War in Kosovo: NATO makes air strikes against Yugoslav Serb forces
• Boris Yeltsin resigns as President of Russia
• Solar eclipse visible over much of Europe
• The Open Golf Championship at Carnoustie is won by Paul Lawrie after Jean van de Velde throws away a 3-shot lead on the final hole

CRICKET HEADLINES 1998

County Champions: Leicestershire

Graeme Hick scores his 100th hundred, the second youngest player to reach this landmark (two weeks older than Walter Hammond)

England beat the visiting South Africans 2-1

Sri Lanka win their solitary Test in England, by ten wickets as Muralitharan takes 16 wickets for 220 runs

In the West Indies, one Test is abandoned because of an unfit pitch, but West indies win 3-1

MCC members vote to admit women

NOTES BY THE EDITOR

'The Australian Cricket Board was finally forced to admit something it had known, and covered up, since February 1995. Mark Waugh and Shane Warne, who had made the original allegations of attempted match-fixing against the former Pakistan captain Salim Malik, had themselves accepted thousands of dollars from an Indian bookmaker for providing apparently innocuous information … The Waugh-Warne case is just a small but rocky outcrop of the mountain range of corruption that almost certainly still lies shrouded in the mists elsewhere.'

FEATURE ARTICLES

The Year The Citadel Fell, by Peter Hayter
'For the lot of the English woman cricketer to be significantly improved, it will not be enough for a few token members to be admitted to MCC … To some, Vodafone's publicity gimmick to drum up media interest in the women's 'Ashes' might have been considered retrograde in tone: journalists were sent a bunch of red roses with a card reading "Eleven English roses playing cricket – watch this space". And even Rachael Heyhoe Flint's comments in celebrating women's admission to MCC sounded peculiar: "Perhaps now," she suggested, "you will be able to buy MCC nighties and fluffy slippers as well as pyjamas."'
The Corruption of Cricket, by Mihir Bose
The Light That Flickered, by Peter Roebuck
The History of Mystery, by Simon Wilde
The Speedometer Summer, by Paul Allott
And Now For Something Completely Different, by Scyld Berry
Slow, Slow, Quick, Quick, Slowie by Micky Stewart
The Scottish Connection, by Alan Massie

FIVE CRICKETERS OF THE YEAR

I.D. Austin

'Cricketers are not supposed to look like Ian Austin any more. He is a burly man and, though he is fit, still has the air of an old-fashioned pie-and-chips player. Mike Selvey once compared him to a stoker on a merchant steamer … He proved that, in a game trying desperately hard to sell itself as something young and trendy in readiness for the World Cup, there is still room for the old-fashioned county stalwart who looks as if he has stepped off the village green. If cricketers can be divided into occupants of the lounge bar or the tap-room, there isn't much doubt which door Austin emerged from.'

D. Gough   M. Muralitharan   A. Ranatunga   J.N. Rhodes

G.A. Copinger

'… owned the world's largest private collection of cricket books: about 12,000 … He also had thousands of items of cricketana. E.W. Padwick, compiler of *A Bibliography of Cricket*, made 23 visits to Copinger's house for his first edition. The collection was sold to an anonymous buyer in a deal arranged just before his death. A figure of £250,000 was reported, but is understood to be exaggerated. Copinger was a fount of knowledge on cricket from his prep school days, and in his spare time while working as a banker he was chief statistician for *Wisden* from 1947 to 1963.'

B. Green

'Benny Green … reviewed the Almanack one year in *The Spectator*, and suggested there ought to be an anthology. There was only one candidate for the job. In 1979 he began work, reading the entire canon cover-to-cover before slimming down the first 119 editions into four (chunky) volumes, brought alive by Green's eye for telling and quirky detail. This turned into a cottage industry: spin-offs included *The Wisden Book of Obituaries* (1986), *The Wisden Papers* (1989) and *The Concise Wisden* (1990), originally published two years earlier especially for Marks & Spencer, a very Greenish connection itself. His various introductions are mini-classics.'

A.C. Revill

'Hardly the best-known cricketer of the post-war era, but many of his contemporaries considered him the most charismatic. He epitomised county cricket as a way of life – and a wonderful one at that – rather than just a profession.'

H. Horton   I.W. Johnson   D.J. McGlew   C.G.A. Paris   A.H. Phebey   D.V.P. Wright

Middlesex

'Middlesex had a dreadful season, culminating in five consecutive defeats and their worst ever Championship placing – 17th. Nor was there much consolation on the one-day front, where an inept performance in the NatWest quarter-final was the abiding memory. Even veteran Middlesex watchers, who remember the barren period before the Brearley era, could not recall so many embarrassing displays.'

West Indies v England, First Test Match, *at Kingston, January 29*

'After the third ball of the match flew off a length past the England captain's nose, one alleged sage turned to his neighbour in the press box and whispered: 'Well, we can rule out a draw, that's for sure.' This was proved wrong with astonishing rapidity. After just 56 minutes' cricket, the contest … was called off in sensational and, at this level, unprecedented circumstances because the umpires considered the pitch to be dangerous. Sixty-one balls (and a no-ball) were bowled in that time, and the England physio Wayne Morton came on to the field six times to attend batsmen who had suffered direct hits from Ambrose and Walsh.'

Matthew Engel writes in his Preface: 'In November 1998 came the first edition of Wisden Cricketers' Almanack Australia, *sporting a natty green cover and already over 800 pages … Readers aware of the current value of our own 1864 edition might think it worthwhile to be in on the start of our Aussie counterpart.' Sadly, this excellent Antipodean version of* Wisden *lasted just eight years. Engel welcomes* Wisden's *new managing editor, Hugh Chevallier, who has overseen every edition since.*

2000

WISDEN 2000

137th EDITION
EDITOR: Matthew Engel
PAGES: 1638
PRICE: Limp and cased £29.99
Leather-bound £225 (150 limit)

THE WORLD AT LARGE

- Ken Livingstone is elected the first Mayor of London
- At the Sydney Olympic Games, Steve Redgrave wins his fifth gold medal
- Wembley stadium closes, to be rebuilt and reopened in 2003
- Vladimir Putin elected President of Russia
- After the closest election in decades, George W Bush is elected President of the United States

CRICKET HEADLINES 1999

Australia win the World Cup, beating Pakistan by eight wickets in the final

County Champions: Surrey

New Zealand beat England 2-1 in England

Mark Taylor scores 334* for Australia v Pakistan at Peshawar, and then declares overnight so that Bradman's Australian Test record score remains unbeaten

Anil Kumble takes 10-74 for India v Pakistan, the second man to take all ten in a Test

England under Alec Stewart lose 3-1 in Australia

Gloucestershire win the NatWest Trophy and the Benson & Hedges SuperCup, and Lancashire win the new CGU National League

NOTES BY THE EDITOR

'With the match-fixing scandal temporarily swept under various carpets, the English crisis is now the greatest crisis in world cricket. It is currently difficult to imagine any circumstances in which England (male version) could face Australia over at least the next three series and have a cat in hell's chance of the Ashes. That's not even good for Australian cricket. It is particularly bad for the future of traditional Test cricket, which depends greatly on English influence wherever it is played.'

FEATURE ARTICLES

Five Cricketers of the Century
'The major problem with this exercise is, of course, that no one watched all the cricket of the century. Some, however, came close, led by E.W. Swanton, whose first-hand knowledge of all cricket since the First World War was unsurpassable. We were fortunate that he was able to take part before he died in January 2000.'
[The Five Cricketers of the Century were Jack Hobbs, Don Bradman, Garry Sobers, Viv Richards and Shane Warne (all pictured in a mock team on the cover of A Century of Wisden). The five were chosen by a panel of 100 respected cricket people, a mixture of writers, commentators and former players.]

A Century of Notes, by Sir Tim Rice
'This edition of *Wisden* is the 100th since Sydney H. Pardon, the Almanack's fourth and longest-serving editor, initiated "Notes by the Editor". Ninety-nine years and nine editors later, this has become the most important disinterested pontification of the cricket calendar.'

A Century of Editors, by E.W. Swanton
'No evidence has survived with regard to Sydney Pardon as a player. He wrote with distinction in *The Times* on music, on drama, and on racing. He was a talented, civilised man who, luckily, gave the best of himself to cricket.'

The Great Sage: E.W. Swanton, by John Woodcock

'His writing, like his broadcasting, had clarity and resonance, and was never forced. His reports were informative, his commentaries judicial.'

A Century of Cricket Writing, by Stephen Moss

'The commemoration of the past is dangerous for a sport which must quickly find a role for the future. Cricket writing, like cricket as a whole, must remake itself.

In doing so, the model should perhaps not be the elegance and erudition of Cardus or Alan Ross but the astringency of R.C. Robertson-Glasgow, the cultural breadth of C.L.R. James, the honesty and simplicity of style of Arlott, the perceptive qualities of David Foot, the coolness of Mike Brearley, the bloody-mindedness of Simon Hughes.'

County of the Century, by Philip Bailey

'To prove that the methods of the hare occasionally prevail, Yorkshire have clearly emerged as the county side of the 20th century. They dominated the first seven decades, winning 26 Championships out of 60, and shared one of the others. Then they went to sleep, but still clearly emerged as the most successful county throughout.

Yorkshire achieved their 1,000th victory since 1900 at Trent Bridge in August 1999. No one else came close to reaching that target.'

Summers of the Century (1), by Philip Eden
Summers of the Century (2), by Frank Keating
John Wisden – 150 Years On, by Murray Hedgcock
Images of the century, by Patrick Eagar
A Hundred Matches of the Century, by Steven Lynch
County of the Century, by Philip Bailey
Taylor: his Place in the Pantheon, by Scyld Berry
A Lovely Day, Everything Right, by Patrick Collins
Rich Game, Poor Game, by Stephen Fay
Fifty Years of The Lord's Taverners, by Pat Gibson
The Great Fast Bowler: Malcolm Marshall, by Mark Nicholas
The Great Wicket-Keeper: Godfrey Evans, by Lord Cowdrey

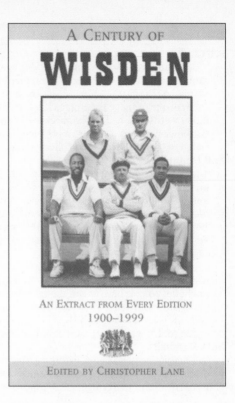

A CENTURY OF

WISDEN

AN EXTRACT FROM EVERY EDITION
1900–1999

EDITED BY CHRISTOPHER LANE

FIVE CRICKETERS OF THE YEAR

[All five are overseas players, only the fifth time this has happened.]

L. Klusener

'He grew up on his parents' sugar-cane farm, and would retain the independence and shyness of a country boy. His companions were largely the children of black farm workers, with whom he talked in Zulu and played garden games of football and cricket. His team-mates still call him "Zulu". Though his father played polo, sport did not feature large in the family. As a boarder at Durban High School, he made the first team, as a batsman, only in his final year. It was not until his military service – which he extended from one to three years for want of anything else to do – that he attracted attention.'

C.L. Cairns   R. Dravid   T.M. Moody   Saqlain Mushtaq

S.T. Clarke

'... died suddenly on December 4, 1999, aged 44. He died the day after Sir Conrad Hunte and a month after Malcolm Marshall, completing a terrible treble for Barbadian cricket. Yet it was estimated that Clarke's funeral was the best-attended of the three. "You see," said one Bajan, "he was one of us." Clarke played in only 11 Test matches, and six of those were when West Indies were weakened by the absence of their World Series players. But he was an exceptional fast bowler, and in ten years with Surrey rapidly acquired a reputation as perhaps the most feared of them all. He bowled chest-on, and he had a very big chest.'

M.P. Donnelly

"... who died on October 22, 1999, aged 82, left an indelible impression on cricket despite the brevity of his career. As a New Zealander at Oxford, he entranced cricket-followers in the immediate post-war years in a manner surpassed only by Compton. He proved that reality matched appearance with a magnificent double-century against England in the Lord's Test of 1949. C.B. Fry said he was as good a left-hander as any he had seen, including Clem Hill and Frank Woolley. Then Donnelly retired and became a businessman in Sydney.'

T.G. Evans

'Godfrey Evans was arguably the best wicket-keeper the game has ever seen. Debates about wicket-keepers cannot be stilled by statistics in the way that a challenge to Don Bradman might be. What is beyond question is that Evans was the game's most charismatic keeper: the man who made the game's least obtrusive specialism a spectator sport in itself. His energy and enthusiasm brought the best out of other fielders, whatever the state of the game. But he added to that a technical excellence that has probably never been surpassed.'

M.D. Marshall

'He maintained excellence without arrogance, earned respect without ever assuming it, and displayed confidence and self-assurance within his immense humility.' – Mark Nicholas

C.C. Hunte   John Langridge   C. Washbrook

Lancashire

'Lancashire's 1999 season will always be associated with Muttiah Muralitharan. His dazzling performances were the spark that lit a winning streak that eventually earned them runners-up honours in the Championship, for the second year in succession, and the inaugural National League title to follow one the previous year in the final Sunday League... Muralitharan finished with 66 wickets from the six Championship games in which he bowled. Around the county circuit, there were still occasional murmurs about his action, but the general impression was of a unique spin bowler who could transfix spectators as well as opponents.'

The Mini World Cup, *in Bangladesh, October/November 1998*

'Dhaka was only the third-choice venue for the competition... and it was nearly moved to Calcutta when Bangladesh was ravaged by one of its worst ever floods only weeks before the tournament. Yet it turned out to be the perfect site. Though the Bangladeshi team was not allowed to take part, the population reacted with enormous enthusiasm to the biggest sporting event - some said the most positive event of any kind - in the country's short, fraught, history.... Hansie Cronje gained most in stature during the week, as both leader and player. When he held the trophy aloft, South Africa had firmly established themselves as long-range World Cup favourites. The real stars, though, were the population of Bangladesh. In villages without electricity, people huddled round radios listening to commentary, and kids began playing, Sri Lanka-style, with makeshift kit wherever there was a space. The moment Bangladesh gets a national team which does them credit, it will be cricket's boom country.'

280

England v New Zealand 1999

'For England, misery, was unconfined. Losing to New Zealand, one of the two teams - with India - that they have regularly beaten in recent years, was bad enough. Losing after going one up, something that has only happened on eight other occasions in three or four-Test series, was worse still. But what really started the media circling like vultures over the body of English cricket was the news that they were now the worst Test team in the world, according to the *Wisden* World Championship at least. This result toppled England from seventh to ninth place. New Zealand, who had been bottom since the table was launched in November 1996, climbed one place to eighth, just behind Zimbabwe. Echoing the Ashes announcement of 1882, *The Sun* turned its front page to its obituary for the English game.'

The Millennium Edition contains a number of articles about the history of Wisden *itself. Each copy was sold with a free paperback,* A Century of Wisden, *(pictured on page 279) edited by Christopher Lane, which contained an extract from every edition from 1900 to 1999.*

George Beldam's shot of Victor Trumper jumping out to drive in the 1900s.
One of cricket photographer Patrick Eagar's 'Images of the Century'
and a picture that has become an Australian icon.

2001

WISDEN 2001

138th Edition
Editor: Graeme Wright
Pages: 1670
Price: Limp and cased £29.99
Leather-bound £225 (150 limit)

THE WORLD AT LARGE

- An outbreak of foot and mouth disease brings more problems for farmers
- Labour easily win the general election: William Hague resigns as leader of the Conservatives
- Jeffrey Archer imprisoned for perjury
- On September 11, two hijacked aircraft fly into the Twin Towers in New York, and another crashes into the Pentagon
- The Crown Prince of Nepal kills his father King Birendra and several members of his family before shooting himself
- The United States invades Afghanistan

CRICKET HEADLINES 2000

County Champions: Surrey, in the first season of the two-division Championship

England beat the touring Zimbabweans 1-0 in a two-match series

They then beat West Indies 3-1 to regain the Wisden Trophy which West Indies had held for 27 years

South Africa beat England 2-1, England's one victory coming when Cronje deliberately sets up a result to satisfy his match-fixing contacts

Gloucestershire retain the NatWest Trophy, becoming the first side to win a Lord's final by the Duckworth-Lewis method. They also win the B&H Cup and the National League, the first team to achieve this treble

NOTES BY THE EDITOR

'On December 31, 1999, the ICC banned the Pakistan fast bowler, Shoaib Akhtar, because of a suspect bowling action. Pakistan alleged racial bias, a card that's beginning to fray at the edges, and appealed directly to ICC president Jagmohan Dalmiya and cricket chairman Sir Clyde Walcott. In little more than a week, the Rawalpindi Express was steaming in again, though only in one-day internationals. The thinking behind his reprieve had touches of Alice: Shoaib's bouncer was the delivery that concerned the ICC bowling panel; bouncers are not legitimate deliveries in one-day cricket; ergo, Shoaib won't bowl bouncers and his bowling won't be suspect.'

FEATURE ARTICLES

A Wisden's War, by David Rayvern Allen
[Details, and a photograph, of E.W. Swanton's cherished 1939 Wisden that accompanied him in the war and was 'thumbed by thousands' in prisoner-of-war camps; now in the museum at Lord's.]
Never a Famous Cricketer, by Jonathan Rice
Into the Dark, Cold Night, by Frank Keating
A Game in Shame, by Mihir Bose

FIVE CRICKETERS OF THE YEAR

M.P.Bicknell
'On a beautiful pitch, after his batsmen had conceded a lead, he annihilated Leicestershire with bowling that was hostile, quick and accurate. His seven for 72 in the first innings, which he considers his best bowling of all, became 16 for 119 by the end of the match. A headline-making sensation.'
M.W.Alleyne   A.R.Caddick   J.L.Langer   D.S.Lehmann

M.C. Cowdrey

'The initials MCC, given his young son by his cricket-loving father, could well have been a Sword of Damocles over a lesser person. In fact, they proved an inspiration to one who would come to adorn cricket as a batsman and slip-catcher of the highest calibre, a person who displayed those images of clean-cut sportsmanship, even chivalry, to be found in a tale by John Buchan, and an administrator who constantly fought for The Spirit of Cricket against shabby behaviour on and off the field.' – Hubert Doggart

L.E.S. Gutteridge

'While running Epworth Books, primarily an arm of the Methodist Church, he started a sideline in cricket books at their shop in north London and turned it into an unrivalled centre of cricketana in the two decades after World War II. *[His 1955 catalogue listed a complete run of* Wisdens *at £150, an investment which would have multiplied almost 200 times by now.]* Gutteridge was an enthusiastic cricket historian and wrote the well-researched history of *Wisden* in the 100th edition in 1963. He emigrated to Canada in 1967 and, having been born in Edmonton, London, died in Edmonton, Alberta.'

J.B. Statham

'His methods remain a matter of some debate. His action was certainly too chest-on to be accepted as classical. He swung the ball only rarely, and perhaps never by design. Part of the secret seems to have been that Statham was not merely supple but doublejointed.'

E.W. Swanton

'His first nationally published article, in *All Sports Weekly* (under the byline Ernest Swanton, which he never used again), was an appreciation of Frank Woolley. He voted for Woolley – along with Constantine, Bradman, Sobers and Worrell – when asked to name his Five Cricketers of the Century for *Wisden* 2000, making the point that Woolley had scored his runs at 50 an hour. He applauded good, joyous, sporting cricket.'

COUNTY REVIEW

Derbyshire

'It was one of Derbyshire's disputes with the ECB that they received compensation only when [Cork] was playing in a Test match. The new system of centrally contracted players was exposed as flawed when, prior to the Old Trafford Test, the England management asked that Cork, who was not contracted, be rested from the Championship match at Canterbury. Derbyshire complied and received nothing, while Kent had Dean Headley sitting on the treatment table with a central contract.'

MATCH REPORTS

South Africa v England, Fifth Test, at Centurion, January 14, 15, 16, 17, 18

'Inevitably, some wondered whether Test cricket had been compromised, even belittled, by the contrived result. Cronje was adamant that, should the game's administrators at the ICC be among those showing disapproval, he "wouldn't want to be a part of cricket any more. What is wrong with trying to make a game of it?" he said afterwards … Hussain, understandably delighted, paid special tribute to Cronje at the time. "It was a very special thing that Hansie did and I hope he gets the credit he deserves. It certainly was a great finish to be a part of." But later, when it emerged that corruption had played its regrettable part in the shaping of the final day, he would write in his newspaper column that England's win had been ruined. "We can't get away from that," he said. "It will always be remembered as a Test that was fixed."'

Matthew Engel is posted to Washington by The Guardian *and Graeme Wright returns as editor.* 'Literally as this Wisden *was being printed, we received news of the death of Sir Donald Bradman':* a last-minute notice of his death replaces the Preface.

2002

WISDEN 2002

139th EDITION
EDITOR: Graeme Wright
PAGES: 1654
PRICE: Limp and cased £35.00
Leather-bound £225 (150 limit)

THE WORLD AT LARGE

- The Euro replaces the currencies of twelve European countries
- Death of Princess Margaret, aged 71, and six weeks later, of her mother, Queen Elizabeth the Queen Mother, aged 101
- The Queen celebrates 50 years on the throne
- UN Security Council Resolution 1441 passed, forcing Saddam Hussein to disarm or face the consequences
- Hu Jintao becomes general secretary of the Communist Party of China

CRICKET HEADLINES 2001

Death of Sir Donald Bradman

County Champions: Yorkshire

Australia retain the Ashes in England, by four matches to one

Pakistan and England share the two match series, one all

In the winter, England beat Pakistan 1-0, and Sri Lanka 2-1

India beat Australia in India by two matches to one, thanks largely to Laxman and Dravid adding 376 for the 5th wicket as India followed on in the Second Test, and go on to win by 171 runs, thus ending Australia's record 16-Test winning streak

Somerset win the Cheltenham & Gloucester Trophy (née Gillette, formerly NatWest), Surrey win the Benson & Hedges Cup, and Kent the Norwich Union League

NOTES BY THE EDITOR

'Dalmiya is a smoking gun or a loose cannon, but he epitomises the progressive, post-imperial, nuclear India … It is … an irony that Dalmiya's business acumen, when ICC president, provided the council with the financial muscle to stand up to India. Through television rights to the World Cup and interim knockout tournaments, he showed how cricket could be enriched beyond previous imagination. He may not always have won friends, but he knew how to influence people. He knew, too, how to nurse a grudge, for he had been sorely hurt by the peremptory way the ICC had dropped their pilot once they were in secure waters. When the opportunity came to rock their boat, he was hardly likely to resist it. Dalmiya aside, old attitudes towards India will have to change.'

FEATURE ARTICLES

To Be Disliked Again: Reflections on Yorkshire Cricket, by Roy Hattersley
'For years, Yorkshire ignored cricketers of the highest quality. Bob Appleyard took 200 wickets in his first full season with the county, 1951, and, as he was a "mature" man at the time, John Arlott … wondered aloud how he had spent his summers during his early twenties. Long after his retirement, I met the overnight sensation and asked him the same question. "Bowling myself silly in the Bradford League," he told me. Nobody has been able to explain why it took the Yorkshire committee so long to discover him.'
Sir Donald Bradman AC, 1908-2001:
  A Personal Recollection, by E.W. Swanton
  Bradman and the British, by Richard Holt
  Beyond the Legend, by Gideon Haigh
Untouched By Fortune, by Peter Roebuck
A Game In Flux: As Viewed From The Boundary, by Simon Heffer
  An Eye To The Future, by Simon Hughes
  Second String, First Choice, by Catherine Hanley

[For the sixth time, all five are overseas players, including Andy Flower and VVS Laxman, who did not play in England during the summer]

A. Flower

'Returning after injury to play South Africa in September 2001, he did not concede a bye in an innings that lasted ten hours. He followed that up by becoming the first keeper to make hundreds in each innings of a Test, batting for almost 15 hours. His 142 and 199 not out took him to No. 1 in the PwC rankings, the first Zimbabwean and the first wicket-keeper/batsman to top the world list. Still Zimbabwe lost. No wonder Andy Flower is thought of as "The Rock" in some circles – and the patron saint of lost causes in others.'

A.C. Gilchrist   J.N. Gillespie   V.V.S. Laxman   D.R. Martyn

Sir Donald Bradman

'The numbers are mightily persuasive. Donald Bradman is assuredly the most efficacious batsman cricket has known. There may be mutterings about this or that batsman emulating him on damp wickets, but they scarcely affect the outcome, and it should be recalled that Bradman played all his first-class cricket in Australia or England and none, for example, on the subcontinent, where he might have found conditions to his especial liking.'

A.R. Gover

'The Mr Chips of cricket teachers, died in south London on October 7, 2001, at the age of 93 … As well as cricketer and coach, he was also a journalist, although whether he would wish to be remembered as the technical adviser to the leaden-footed 1953 film, *The Final Test,* is a moot point. He was president of The Lord's Taverners in 1974 and of Surrey in 1980, and manager of two Commonwealth cricket tours to the subcontinent in the 1960s.'

R. Gilchrist   F.G. Mann   B. Sutcliffe

Somerset

'By general agreement, certainly in every parish across the Mendips and the Quantocks, Somerset's season was the best in their variegated history. Perhaps there were more flash, pulsating days when players of mighty individual talent such as Botham, Richards and Garner were around … but 2001 was better, a more balanced triumph from lesser souls.'

Pakistan v England, Third Test, *at Karachi, December 7, 8, 9, 10, 11*

'With failing light always going to be a factor, Pakistan captain Moin Khan adopted desperate delaying tactics, for which he was fiercely criticised, after his side were bundled out for 158 on the final afternoon, leaving England a target of 176 in a minimum of 44 overs. His bowlers took 40 minutes to send down the first seven of these before tea, and almost three and a half hours to bowl a total of 41.3 intense, nail-biting overs. Moin, who was warned for his go-slow strategy by referee Ranjan Madugalle during the tea interval, made three unsuccessful appeals for bad light to umpire Steve Bucknor as Thorpe and Hussain resolutely stood their ground. With victory in sight, but little else, Thorpe edged the winning runs. Some of the Pakistani players thought he had been bowled, until the ball was spotted by a searching fielder.'

Graeme Wright thanks contributors to the Almanack: 'Wisden is fortunate in its network of correspondents, statisticians and informants.'

2003

WISDEN 2003

140th Edition
EDITOR: Tim de Lisle
PAGES: 1782
PRICE: Limp and cased £35.00
Leather-bound £225 (150 limit)

THE WORLD AT LARGE

- The London Congestion Charge comes into force
- U.S. and British forces invade Iraq in March: Saddam Hussein is soon overthrown, and captured at the end of the year
- England wins the Rugby World Cup, beating Australia in the final
- The first recorded cases of SARS are reported
- China puts a man in space for the first time

CRICKET HEADLINES 2002

County Champions: Surrey

Ben Hollioake and Hansie Cronje both die young – Hollioake in a car smash, Cronje in a plane crash

England beat Sri Lanka 2-0 and draw 1-1 with India during the summer

During the winter, England lose 1-0 in India, and draw the series in New Zealand, one-all

Yorkshire win the C&G Trophy, Warwickshire win the final Benson & Hedges Cup, and Glamorgan the Norwich Union League

NOTES BY THE EDITOR

'For most of the past 126 years, Test cricket was conducted at a leisurely pace. The occasional burst of frenzied activity only emphasised that the standard tempo was sedate. Nowadays, the longest form of the game – of any game – rattles along like a good television drama (which it is).'

FEATURE ARTICLES

Batting for a Billion: Sachin Tendulkar at 30, by Rohit Brijnath
'He is both tyrant and technician, batting with a thug's ferocity and a sculptor's finesse … He will uppercut the ball gleefully for six with muscle, and next ball, in a perfect marriage of feet and bat and judgment of length, slide it softly past the bowler for four.'
The Man Who Changed The Game: Steve Waugh, by Simon Barnes
The 21st Century Coaching Book, by Simon Briggs
Crying Out For Less, by Christopher Martin-Jenkins
Don't Marry A Cricketer, by Derek Pringle
Being There: Who's Seen Most Tests? by Tim de Lisle
On Top Of The World: 1953 Relived, by Steven Lynch
No Anorak Required: Interactive Statistics For All, by Chris Ryan

FIVE CRICKETERS OF THE YEAR

S.M. Pollock
'Shaun Pollock has not had an outstanding year. He has had seven. Sport's holy grail is consistency, and Pollock found it as soon as he entered international cricket. Whatever happens in his thirties, he will go down as one of the game's great allrounders. His bowling is as straight, tight and incisive as Glenn McGrath's, and he is also an elegant, sometimes explosive batsman who averages 59 at No. 9.'
M.L. Hayden   A.J. Hollioake   N. Hussain   M.P. Vaughan

B.C. Hollioake
'... in the game's collective memory, the picture of Ben Hollioake remained fixed on a spring afternoon in 1997 when, making his England debut at 19, this tall, loose-limbed all-rounder set Lord's alight with 63 in 48 balls against Australia to take the Man of the Match award.'

R.H. Moore
'He still held the record for Hampshire's highest individual score, 316, set at Bournemouth one July day in 1937. The Dean Park boundaries were short and the 23-year-old Dick Moore made the most of them, hitting three sixes and 43 fours in an innings that began with play at 11.30, reached three figures off the ball before lunch and continued until almost 7 p.m. when he was last out and the big crowd reluctantly set about going home.'

W.J. Cronje   A.G. Finlayson

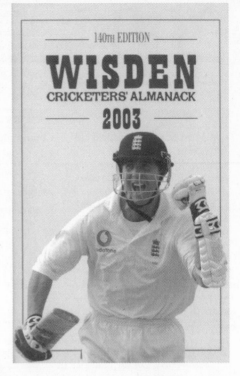

140TH EDITION
WISDEN
CRICKETERS' ALMANACK
2003

Worcestershire
'Two near misses by the narrowest of margins left Worcestershire to reflect on an ultimately disappointing season. The biggest setback came when a late surge from Nottinghamshire edged them out of the third promotion spot in the Championship by one and three-quarter points. And it was the same in Division One of the National League: Worcestershire, fresh from promotion, at one stage led the table by eight points, only for Glamorgan to beat them twice and pip them to the honours.'

New Zealand v England, First Test, *at Christchurch, March 13, 14, 15, 16*
'This was, and will always be, Astle's match. A cricket ball had perhaps never been hit so cleanly, so often. Astle's first hundred had come from a brisk 114 deliveries, but he was merely playing himself in. The carnage began in earnest when Hussain took the second new ball: the next four overs, even though they included a wicket maiden from Caddick, yielded 61 runs. Hoggard, unplayable on the second day, was smashed for 41 in two overs – and out of the attack. So Astle turned his attention to Caddick...'

South Africa v India, Second Test, *at Port Elizabeth, November 16, 17, 18, 19, 20*
'Achievements on the field, even Gibbs's 196, were overshadowed by a furore which snowballed into one of the game's biggest crises. It was triggered by the announcement on the final morning of penalties imposed by the referee, Mike Denness, on six Indian players for alleged breaches of the Code of Conduct. The tourists considered them excessive and, in Tendulkar's case, grossly unfair.'

Tim de Lisle takes on the role of editor for one year only: he accepts he is 'the most fleeting of Wisden *editors'. But nonetheless he makes his mark on the book. He put a photograph (of Michael Vaughan) on the cover (pictured), but in case this might prove a step too far for some, a traditional jacket with the* Wisden *woodcut was made available, as it has been every year since.*

2004

WISDEN 2004

141st EDITION
EDITOR: Matthew Engel
PAGES: 1667
PRICE: Limp and cased £35.00
Leather-bound £230 (150 limit)

THE WORLD AT LARGE

• Ten new member states join the EU
• Terrorist bombs in Madrid kill 190 people
• At the Olympic Games in Athens, Kelly Holmes wins two gold medals for Britain
• Like Vladimir Putin of Russia earlier in the year, President George W Bush is re-elected for a second term
• A tsunami strikes the Indian Ocean on Boxing Day, killing thousands in Indonesia, Thailand, Sri Lanka and elsewhere

CRICKET HEADLINES 2003

County Champions: Sussex

The first Twenty20 Cup in England is a huge commercial success, won by Surrey

Australia thrash India in the World Cup final in South Africa

England beat Zimbabwe 2-0

Chester-le-Street becomes the first new Test ground in England for 101 years

South Africa and England share a dramatic Test series 2-2

During the winter, England lose 4-1 to the Australians

NOTES BY THE EDITOR

'On my very first weekend back in England last summer, I went down to the New Forest for a family party. On the Saturday there was a game – Brockenhurst v Ellingham – being played on a lovely cricket ground on a heavenly afternoon. I settled down to enjoy it but the over after I arrived, a herd of New Forest ponies suddenly galloped out of the woods and on to the outfield around deep extra cover. Wild Horses Stopped Play. I watched a lot of baseball in the US, and loved that too, but somehow only cricket produces stuff like this.'

FEATURE ARTICLES

Would You Rather Be An Oaf Than A Fool? by Glenn Moore
'Phil Neale, of Lincoln City and Worcestershire … found football to be mentally tougher. There is a casual hardness about the game bred, he feels, by the insecurity that comes from having more time between performances and being one bad tackle away from a broken career. The cricketer does still have rewards denied to the muddied millionaires. In their peripatetic careers, footballers … tend to make acquaintants. Cricketers, living cheek-by-jowl with team-mates and drinking with opponents, do still make friends.'
Trying to Melt the Iceman, by Nasser Hussain
Stumpers or Stoppers? by Pat Murphy
Fortifying the Over-Forties, by Nick Mason
Call My Agent, by Paul Kelso
The Year of The Martlet, by Robin Marlar
Temples of Bumblepuppy, by Christopher Douglas

FIVE CRICKETERS OF THE YEAR

A. Flintoff

'Did you see it? That Sunday morning at The Oval when, in late-summer sunshine, a blond Apollo destroyed South Africa with a joyful 95. There always was something about Andrew Flintoff, this amiable giant who carved into the bowling, a farmhand delighting in the coconut shy. His spine-tingling whirl of the bat, exaggerated defensive shot and love of replaying his own strokes in slow-motion made him a crowd favourite and annoyingly impossible for the armchair punter to switch off.'

C.J. Adams   I.J. Harvey   G. Kirsten   G.C. Smith

LEADING CRICKETER IN THE WORLD

R.T. Ponting (Australia)

OBITUARIES INCLUDE

R.P. Davis
'… had been suffering from a brain tumour since 2001, the season he became the first cricketer to play for five first-class counties. At 22, Dickie Davis, born in Margate, succeeded Derek Underwood as Kent's left-arm spinner, daunting enough even without the end of uncovered wickets, which made his task near-impossible. In 1992, he was the leading slow bowler in the country, taking 74 wickets and finishing sixth in the national averages.'

W.R. Endean
'Endean was involved in two of the most bizarre dismissals in Test history: when he kept at The Oval in 1951, umpire Frank Chester ruled that Len Hutton, who instinctively flicked his bat when the ball ran off his arm and looked like dropping on his wicket, had impeded Endean's attempt to catch the ball and gave him out for obstruction. Against England at Cape Town in 1956-57, Endean himself became the first batsman out "handled the ball" in Test cricket when he tried to stop a top-edged paddle hitting his stumps.'

Sir Paul Getty
'His ownership of *Wisden,* sealed in 1993, brought together the two great passions: cricket and books … Those who knew him valued him as a generous spirit, a quality that has nothing to do with money. And cricket repaid him a little by giving him a sense of his own self-worth as a man, not just as a benefactor.'

D.T. Ring
'… one of the spear-carriers for the 1948 Australian Invincibles, cheerfully describing himself as one of the "groundstaff bowlers" as he wheeled round the counties without getting near the Test team until the morning of the final Test, when Bradman asked Ring to sit alongside him in the taxi and told him he was playing.'

COUNTY REVIEW

Nottinghamshire
'Individuals played their parts; the problem was that they played them as individuals. Seldom was a clutch of top-order batsmen in form at the same time, and an inability to forge lengthy, let alone meaningful, partnerships cost Nottinghamshire dear.'

MATCH REPORTS

Surrey v Warwickshire, Twenty20 Cup Final, *at Nottingham, July 19*
'Surrey had around three hours less recovery time than Warwickshire, but no one would have guessed … When Ormond finished his fourth over, the seventh of the game, he had figures of four for 11 and Warwickshire, 33 for 5, were dead in the water.'

Matthew Engel, back in the editor's chair, reorganises the Almanack and introduces a new accolade – Wisden's Leading Cricketer in the World. He writes in the Preface: 'This is a 15-month book. Traditionally, the Almanack reported cricket from September to September. Henceforth the focus will be squarely on each calendar year. To catch up, Wisden 2004 is thus a record of cricket from September 2002 to the end of 2003.'

2005

WISDEN 2005

142nd EDITION
EDITOR: Matthew Engel
PAGES: 1763
PRICE: Limp and cased £36.00
Leather-bound £235 (150 limit)

THE WORLD AT LARGE

• In the general election, the Labour Party wins a third term in office
• Bombs on the London Underground and a double-decker bus kill at least 50 people
• Police shoot and kill Jean Charles de Menezes, mistaking him for a suicide bomber
• Hurricane Katrina devastates New Orleans
• David Cameron elected leader of the Conservative Party
• Death of Pope John Paul II

CRICKET HEADLINES 2004

County Champions: Warwickshire

ECB sells television rights to domestic Test cricket to Sky

England win all seven Tests of the summer – three against New Zealand and four against West Indies

Matthew Hayden scores 380 for Australia v Zimbabwe, but six months later Brian Lara reclaims his record with 400* against England in Antigua

Despite this innings, England beat West Indies 3-0 in West Indies

India beat Pakistan 2-1 in Pakistan, a first for India

Gloucestershire win the C&G Trophy, for the fourth time in six years, Glamorgan win the Sunday league (now the Totesport League) and Leicestershire win the Twenty20 Cup

NOTES BY THE EDITOR:

'It would not be difficult to argue that a majority of the ... governing bodies could, in varying degrees, be categorised as either incompetent, corrupt, government-controlled or racist. The Kenya Cricket Association acquired a reputation so bad even by the standards of its own country – one of the most notoriously corrupt in Africa – that it was disbanded by the government. The USA Cricket Association has been appalling for years, and by the end of 2004 the ICC felt stung into sending it a letter of such vituperative splendour ... that it should stand as a classic of its kind.'

FEATURE ARTICLES:

The Greatest Editor, by Matthew Engel
[A tribute to Sydney Pardon marking the 150th anniversary of his birth.]
    'The Notes by the Editor grew out of his personal crusade against throwing. They turned into an institution he made powerful enough to endure to the present day.'
Hello Sky, Goodbye World, by Steven Barnett
Cricket's Migrant Soul, by Robert Winder
England's Revival:
    The Only Way Was Up, by Mike Selvey
    Goodbye Gin and Tonic: An Insider's View, by Malcolm Ashton
The Man Who Made Cricket Glow, By Richie Benaud
Another Country: Village Cricket Splits In Two, by Alan Lee
Bent: A History of Chucking, by David Frith
Breaking the Silence, by David Rayvern Allen
Hansie: The Making of a Martyr, by Rob Steen
The Tragedy That Brought us Together, by Charlie Austin

[For the first time since 1960, all five are English.]

R.W.T. Key

'He concedes he has played better – he was reprieved twice before making 60 – though 221 in a Lord's Test suggests something has gone right. In fact, most things went right in 2004. He unfurled a majestic hundred in Kent's opening game and in May transmuted his form from gold to platinum, stockpiling runs as though they were going out of circulation. In one sublime seven-innings sequence he passed 100 five times.'

A.F. Giles   S.J. Harmison   A.J. Strauss   M.E. Trescothick

S.K. Warne (Australia)

W.E. Alley

'Bill Alley became a Somerset legend, although he was born in Australia and did not make his county debut until 1957, when he was 38. In 1961 he was the last man ever to score 3,000 first-class runs in a season. He later became a Test umpire, and one of the game's most durable characters.'

V.S. Hazare

'He put together an extraordinary sequence from March 1943 to February 1944 of 264, 81, 97, 248, 59, 309, 101, 223 and 87. That 309, in the Bombay Pentangular final, was an extraordinary innings, made out of a total of only 387 as the Rest followed on against the Hindus. He shared (if that is the word) a stand of 300 with his brother Vivek, who scored just 21.'

K.R. Miller

'He was, Neville Cardus wrote, "Australia in excelsis". Free-spirited, generous, sometimes bloody-minded, altogether bonzer, Miller was the most colourful cricketer of his post-war generation, driving sixes beyond imagination, bowling fearsomely fast and catching with a predatory instinct, playing to and for the crowd.'

C.S. Elliott   J.A. Flavell   A.L. Valentine   W. Watson

Glamorgan

'Glamorgan ticked off their main pre-season objectives by returning to the first division of the Championship, after a three-year absence, and by blazing to the one-day League title with such ease that it was all over with three games left. They also reached the semi-finals of the Twenty20 Cup, where they lost out to Leicestershire – the eventual winners … Robert Croft had a memorable year as captain, and as an imaginative leader he made a significant and bold contribution.'

West Indies v England, Fourth Test, *at St John's, April 10, 11, 12, 13, 14, 2004*

'The Trinidad & Tobago government, which again lavished their most famous citizen with praise and gifts, was certain of the innings' [400*] significance. The prime minister, Patrick Manning, told Lara it was "symbolic of what we are capable of achieving when we harness our strengths and persevere with grit and determination in pursuit of excellence". As it was, a minimum of 240 overs remained at the declaration. Had Lara not dropped a juggled catch at slip off Sarwan when Flintoff was 27 late on the third afternoon, West Indies would have been closer to a satisfying triumph to match that over Australia.'

291

2006

WISDEN 2006

143rd EDITION
EDITOR: Matthew Engel
PAGES: 1627
PRICE: Limp and cased £38.00   Large format £50.00
Leather-bound £240 (150 limit)

THE WORLD AT LARGE

- £53m stolen from a Securitas depot, the biggest robbery in British history
- North Korea claims to have conducted its first-ever nuclear test, while Iran seeks to enrich uranium
- Saddam Hussein executed

CRICKET HEADLINES 2005

County Champions: Nottinghamshire

England win back the Ashes, 2-1, after sixteen years, in the most thrilling series for decades

Before the Ashes series, England beat Bangladesh 2-0

During the winter, England lose 2-0 in Pakistan

Hampshire win the C&G Trophy, Essex the Totesport League and Somerset the Twenty20 Cup

NOTES BY THE EDITOR

'Around the country … there was evidence that the craze did not subside with the England team's sore heads, and that cricket had truly recaptured a slice of the nation's heart … Journalists still tended to write that we had witnessed Probably The Greatest Test (Edgbaston), Probably The Greatest Series, and Probably The Greatest Crowd To Greet A Victorious England Team. There is no need for the nervous adverb. This was The Greatest. The 2005 Ashes surpassed every previous series in cricket history on just about any indicator you choose.'

FEATURE ARTICLES

The Amazing Story of the Runaway Train, by Siddhartha Vaidyanathan
'The left-arm spinner Madan Yadav, did the damage in Mohali that gained Railways first-innings lead; in a drawn game, that was enough to secure the title. Parida, the poor boy from Orissa, was also an established member of the side. But Madan had to spend 2004 undergoing the experience Parida had ten years earlier. For most of the year he was in Bhopal repairing train wheels with massive pliers and monitoring electrical connections – and, between whiles, working on his flight, spin and angle of delivery. When asked about the importance of the title, Jai P. Yadav said, "Class IV employees like Madan will get a promotion and his quality of life will improve".'

Suddenly Everything Went 'Boom!', by Roland Watson
Next Botham: The Quest Ends, by Peter Hayter
No Hard Feelings, Mate: The Beer Is Back, by Derek Pringle
Aye, Aye, Coach, by Gideon Haigh
With Allah On Their Side, by Osman Samiuddin
'We'll Have A Bowl.' And Why Not? by Rahul Bhattacharya
Seeing Twenty20
   A Father's View, by Francis Wheen
   An American View, by Michael Goldfarb
   A View from the Old Dear, by Clement Freud
The World of Flantiff and Vorner, by Ben Wilson
The Commons Blames Lord's, by Steven Barnett
Sixty Years of Post-War Cricket, by Matthew Engel and Philip Bailey
The Members? Oh, Them, by Stephen Fay
Setting The Records Straight, by Matthew Engel and Andrew Samson

S.P. Jones
> 'During the South African tour in 2004-05 his accuracy improved remarkably ... And it all came together to befuddle the Australians in 2005. At Old Trafford, when play began late on the third day, Vaughan even turned to Jones first. His six for 53 there surpassed his father's six for 118 at Adelaide in 1965-66, the previous best by a Glamorgan bowler for England. Jones junior had arrived: now not only trusted, but rightly lauded.'

M. J. Hoggard   B. Lee   K.P. Pietersen   R.T. Ponting

LEADING CRICKETER IN THE WORLD

A. Flintoff (England)

OBITUARIES INCLUDE

Ms A.G. Doyle
> 'Nancy Doyle was the châtelaine of the players' dining-room at Lord's for many years until her retirement in 1996. Her lavish lunches – Mike Brearley once asked, unsuccessfully, if she could limit the number of courses to five – were legendary around a county circuit on which the staple diet in most places at the time was salad, and she was popular with generations of players.'

Mushtaq Ali
> 'Tall and debonair, often with a kerchief knotted jauntily round his neck, Mushtaq Ali – the son of an Indore police inspector – was a prototype for India's modern cricket heroes. In his foreword to Mushtaq's autobiography, *Cricket Delightful*, Keith Miller called him "the Errol Flynn of cricket – dashing, flamboyant, swashbuckling and immensely popular wherever he played".'

Baron Sheppard of Liverpool
> 'Rev. David Sheppard, as he was known for most of his playing career, was one of the most remarkable men ever to play cricket to a high level. His involvement was intermittent but always eventful. He captained England in two Tests in 1954. Had he devoted himself to cricket, Sheppard would have captained more often, and could easily have scored a hundred hundreds. Instead he devoted himself to the Church, where he rose to become a long-serving, distinctive and, by most reckonings, outstanding Bishop of Liverpool. Politics cost him his chance of becoming an archbishop.'

E.J. Barlow   B.W. Luckhurst   K.F.B. Packer   C.H. Palmer   K.G. Suttle

COUNTY REVIEW

Essex
> 'Thoroughbreds in the totesport League, Essex were more like carthorses in the other competitions ... but in the rapid development of two talented 20-year-olds, Essex had cause for satisfaction. The expansive left-hander Alastair Cook gained high praise ... Ravinder Bopara, Essex's second emerging talent ... ending his first full season with nearly 900 first-class runs.'

MATCH REPORTS

England v Australia, Second Test, at Edgbaston, *August 4, 5, 6, 7*
> 'England won by two runs ... After umpteen TV replays, it was possible to conclude that Kasprowicz's left hand was off the bat at the moment of impact and, technically, he was not out. Bowden, however, would have needed superhuman vision to see this, and an armed escort involving several regiments to escape the crowd had he actually refused to give it out. It was also the right decision for cricket: 2-0 to Australia would have been the signal for the football season to begin; 1-1 lit the blue touchpaper. The Greatest Test became the Greatest Series, and the pyrotechnics illuminated the summer.'

For the first time, Wisden *was also published in a large format version, which this year only was limited to 5,000 copies, with each copy individually numbered.*

2007

WISDEN 2007

144th EDITION
EDITOR: Matthew Engel
PAGES: 1691
PRICE: Limp and cased £40.00   Large format £50.00
Leather-bound £245 (150 limit)

THE WORLD AT LARGE

- Power sharing begins in Northern Ireland
- Tony Blair steps down as Leader of the Labour Party and Prime Minister, and Gordon Brown is elected in his place
- Smoking is banned in virtually all public places in England
- Madeleine McCann goes missing in the Algarve
- Former Pakistan Prime Minister Benazir Bhutto is assassinated while campaigning

CRICKET HEADLINES 2006

County Champions: Sussex

England draw with Sri Lanka 1-1 and then beat Pakistan in England, 3-0, with one match forfeited by Pakistan after a ball-tampering row.

A hopelessly awful England lose 5-0 to Australia and thus surrender the Ashes

Five triple-centuries are scored during the English county season, but only one by an England qualified player (Mark Ramprakash)

Ramprakash scores over 2,000 runs and averages over 100

Mushtaq Ahmed takes over 100 wickets in the season: no England qualified player has managed this feat since 1987

NOTES BY THE EDITOR

'Counties need to have some connection with their local heroes, for everyone's sake. Why support Durham if you never, ever see Paul Collingwood? A junior Lancashire player would have more evidence for the existence of Father Christmas than Andrew Flintoff ... No one wants to go back to the days when counties could knacker England fast bowlers with impunity. But it is now way, way out of balance in the other direction.'

FEATURE ARTICLES

Warne: The Mighty Craftsman, by Mike Atherton
Touch Players and Touched Journalists, by Dicky Rutnagur
Wisden's All-Time Greats:
   Picking Players For The Pantheon, by Matthew Engel
   The Leading Cricketer In The World, 1900-2006
Trueman: Bloody Minded, Beautiful, t'Best, by Michael Parkinson
Test Match Special At 50:
   Not So Much A Programme, More A Way Of Life, by Gillian Reynolds
   Setting The Style, by Jim Maxwell
Being There:
   Cold? Windy? Boring? Let's Go, by Simon Lister
   The Real Contest: Barmies v Calmies, by Andrew Miller
Why *Do* They Always Get Injured, by Kamran Abbasi
Captain! The Pitch Is Sinking, by Marcus Berkmann
Reverberations: The Boom Goes On ... by Roland Watson
... But The Ratings Go Bust, by Steven Barnett
Out of the Frying Pan, by Sambit Bal
The Oval and After: Where Do We Go From Hair?
Now Hick Passes Hobbs, by Steven Lynch and Philip Bailey

P.D. Collingwood

'It was generally accepted that, with Andrew Flintoff fit again, Collingwood would be left on the sidelines for the 2006-07 Ashes rematch. The early exit of Marcus Trescothick, however, restored him to the team, and at No. 4 to boot. Over-promoted? His response was a fluent, occasionally exquisite, second-innings 96 in the defeat at Brisbane and an outstandingly resolute (if ultimately equally futile) 206 at Adelaide.'

D.P.M.D. Jayawardene   **M.S. Panesar**   **M.R. Ramprakash**   **Mohammad Yousuf**

A.J. Bannister

'Alex Bannister was cricket correspondent of the Daily Mail from 1947 to 1979, apart from two short breaks when he was displaced by flashier rivals. His journalism was never flashy, but it was the epitome of the old Mail tradition, based on hard graft and top-class contacts, superbly maintained: Bannister got much of his information from Sir Alec Bedser and Sir Donald Bradman, which was hard to match.'

A.C.D. Ingleby-Mackenzie

'Colin Ingleby-Mackenzie was one of the most extraordinary, and best-loved, men ever to play cricket. He gave the impression that his life was a party that lasted 72 years, which was not that far from the truth. Nonetheless, he was a successful captain – leading Hampshire to their first County Championship – and a radical president of MCC.'

I. Rosenwater

'… was a cricket statistician and historian. He pursued these not so much as a career or a hobby, but as an obsession and, often, a form of unarmed combat … His gift for evidence-based cricket writing was subsumed by his prickly obsessiveness.'

F.S. Trueman

'He was at the heart of the England team for more than a decade, during which time it usually beat the world. He was also English cricket's most enduring and best-loved character, representing a certain kind of Yorkshireness – chippy, forceful, sometimes humorous – that spread his fame far beyond the game and maintained it long after his retirement.'

E.A. Bedser   **G.M. Griffin**   **W.A. Hadlee**   **Hanumant Singh**   **N.S. Mitchell-Innes**
Ms N. Rheinberg   **G.R.J. Roope**   **P.R. Umrigar**   **Sir Clyde Walcott**

Sussex

'Their second Championship was harder than the first. Sussex had their best start since 1934, winning six of their first eight matches. But it took three wins from the final four to deny Lancashire, who began the last round only eight points behind.'

England v Sri Lanka, First Test, *at Lord's, May 11, 12, 13, 14, 15*

'Patronised as mere fodder for England's seam bowlers in the damp and dewy pastures of Lord's in early May, Sri Lanka's batsmen pulled off one of the finest acts of escapology since Clint Eastwood bust out of Alcatraz. Asked to follow on, 359 behind, after lunch on the third day, they survived 199 overs and three new balls on a pitch which turned out to be completely moribund.'

Matthew Engel records in the Preface that sales of the 2006 edition topped 50,000 – believed to be unprecedented: 'We can't be certain because the company's books up to 1936 were destroyed in the war. But we do know that the print run in those days was much lower (which is one reason old Wisdens *are valuable), so we think it must be true.' Engel says he is to take a sabbatical and hands over to Scyld Berry.*

2008

WISDEN 2008

145th Edition
Editor: Scyld Berry
Pages: 1699
Price: Limp and cased £40.00   Large format £50.00
Leather-bound £245 (150 limit)

THE WORLD AT LARGE

• Lehman Brothers Bank files for bankruptcy, triggering the worldwide recession and credit crunch
• An earthquake in Sichuan Province in China kills around 80,000 people
• Barack Obama wins the Presidency for the Democrats: he is the first non-white President of the United States

CRICKET HEADLINES 2007

County Champions: Sussex

The World Cup, won by Australia, is overshadowed by the death of Pakistan's coach Bob Woolmer

India win the inaugural Twenty20 World Cup

For the second season in a row, Mark Ramprakash scores over 2,000 runs at an average of over 100

England beat West Indies 3-0 at home, then lose 1-0 to India

Sri Lanka beat the visiting England 1-0 in a three-Test series

NOTES BY THE EDITOR

'Leading cricketers can now earn more by representing an Indian city, whether in Zee TV's Indian Cricket League or the officially sanctioned Indian Premier League. City-based cricket has arrived and will surely spread, annulling the player's traditional relationship with his county, state or province. The day has lurched closer when England's best cricketers, in addition to representing England, will play for an English region in a first-class tournament at the start of each season; for an English city in the 20-over competition in mid-summer; and for an Indian city. County cricket will then become a relic at amateur level, like the county championship of English rugby.'

FEATURE ARTICLES

Never a Cricketer of the Year, by Scyld Berry
'Almost every cricketer of the highest skill since 1889 has been commemorated by *Wisden* for posterity. The traditional criterion has been the player's performance in the English cricket season ... This has led to several cricketers of the highest skill slipping through the net: players who have been great in other lands but who have not excelled on a tour of England, or who have not been engaged in county cricket.'
Salmon at Deep Midwicket, by Andrew Thomas
Bradman Centenary:
  Capitalising on Cricket, by Carl Bridge
  Thin-skinned, Warm-hearted, by Doug Insole
Woolmer: Tragedy at The World Cup, by Paul Newman
What Duncan Did For Us, by Andrew Strauss
Three All-Time Greats:
  Gilly Walks into the Sunset, by Ian Healy
  Brian Lara: The Entertainer Departs, by Mike Atherton
  Glenn McGrath: The Most Unremarkable of Bowlers, by Robert Craddock
The County Cricketers' Year, by Tanya Aldred
The Appeal of Technology, by David Frith
Only in Tassie, by Mark Ray
Gandhi: Did He Spin More Than Khadi? By Ramachandra Guha
Scratching a Living, by Nick Newman

O.D. Gibson
'By common consent, Ottis Gibson was the greatest single force in county cricket in 2007. He was Player of the Year in the estimation of the Professional Cricketers' Association. He propelled Durham to second place in the County Championship with his 80 wickets, a total exceeded only by Mushtaq Ahmed whose average was higher. Against Hampshire he took all ten wickets in one innings, only the third bowler to achieve the feat in the Championship in the last 50 years.'
I.R. Bell   S. Chanderpaul   R.J. Sidebottom   Zaheer Khan

OBITUARIES INCLUDE

B.G. Brocklehurst
'His greatest contribution to cricket came in 1962 when he persuaded his employers Mercury House to buy *The Cricketer* magazine, then in danger of closure. Ten years later he bought it himself and maintained it until 2003.'
T.W. Cartwright
'Tom Cartwright was a cricketer's cricketer. Perhaps no player of his generation had so much respect from his colleagues – for his abilities, his character, which was forceful without being abrasive, and his love and knowledge of the game.'
D. Shackleton
'Of the 159,001 balls he delivered in first-class cricket, the overwhelming majority landed precisely where he intended.'
R.A. Woolmer
'In life, Bob Woolmer had been a gifted player and an innovative, much-admired coach. In death, he became a global celebrity.'
K. Cranston   H.L. Jackson   W.A. Johnston   C.A. Milton   I.E. Wooldridge

COUNTY REVIEW

Northamptonshire
'No fewer than 23 cricketers turned out in the Championship (none born in Northamptonshire) and 11 made their first-class debuts for the county – a figure equalled in 1947 but not surpassed since 1922, when George Thompson made his final appearance and Nobby Clark his first.'

MATCH REPORTS

Australia v India, Second Test, *at Sydney, January 2, 3, 4, 5, 6, 2008*
'Australia won with just nine minutes of the last hour remaining... However, they would never have done so but for a series of umpiring blunders … Australia's victory was overshadowed by the row that erupted over the allegation that Harbhajan Singh had racially abused Andrew Symonds, the only non-white player in the Australian side. The original decision of referee Mike Procter to suspend Harbhajan for three Tests incensed the Indians, and there was talk of the tour being called off if his appeal was unsuccessful.'

Although Matthew Engel's original plan was to hand over for just one edition, he eventually decided not to return to the editorship.

Scyld Berry writes in the Preface: 'As my initial brief was to keep changes to a minimum during a stand-in year, I have made only a few innovations.' One is a new Wisden *award, the Schools Cricketer of the Year, won by Jonathan Bairstow.*

2009

WISDEN 2009

146th Edition
EDITOR: Scyld Berry
PAGES: 1698
PRICE: Limp and cased £45.00   Large format £55.00
Leather-bound £250 (150 limit)

THE WORLD AT LARGE

- Royal Bank of Scotland and Lloyds Bank announce massive losses: the government steps in to prop them up
- Iranian presidential elections provoke riots after claims of vote rigging
- Michael Jackson dies
- MPs expenses: a computer disk leaked to the *Daily Telegraph* triggers months of revelations about financial shenanigans in Parliament

CRICKET HEADLINES 2008

County Champions: Durham

Mark Ramprakash hits his 100th hundred

Kevin Pietersen is appointed England captain when Vaughan steps down, but only lasts a few months

England beat New Zealand 2-0 but lose to South Africa 2-1 during the home summer

Terrorism in Mumbai interrupts but does not cancel England's tour to India

England takes part in the Stanford Super Series in West Indies, and soon regrets it

NOTES BY THE EDITOR

'Any contest is a purer test of skills if not limited by time: Hector v Achilles could not have been a Homeric contest if limited to five minutes, or a Wimbledon final confined to an hour. Yet these values were not reflected in payments. Some Sri Lankans were being paid a few thousand dollars for a Test and a hundred times as much for a six-week IPL season. Predictions were made … that the cricketer of the future would be a mercenary flying from one 20-over tournament to another without ever playing Test matches for his country.'

FEATURE ARTICLES

It's Wednesday, it must be … Dunno, by Matthew Engel
    'There used to be a rhythm to an English cricket season, and nothing was more rhythmic than an Ashes summer: the arrival down the gangplank at Tilbury; the first gentle day out at Arundel; the much-anticipated opening county match at Worcester; the troll east and south; Australian sweaters slowly being discarded and fingers growing less numb, before the MCC match and the First Test in the Midlands.'
The England Captaincy:
    Littered with Sad Captains, by Simon Barnes
    Losing the X-Factor, by Michael Vaughan
    Brief Encounter, by Mike Atherton
The Ashes Masters, by David Frith
You've Never Got Enough, by Nasser Hussain
    Mark Ramprakash In Figures
    Graeme Hick In Figures
Decline of a Proud Tradition, by Dean Wilson
Captain, Kolpak, Colt, by Tanya Aldred
Imperial … International … Independent? by Gideon Haigh
The Wisden Test XI, by Scyld Berry
Flight Twenty20 Takes Off, by Lawrence Booth
A Lyon-hearted Experiment, by David Foot

[For the first time ever, a woman was named as one of the Five Cricketers of the Year.]

S.C. Taylor
'Last summer, as England Women won all nine of the one-day internationals that rain allowed to conclude, Taylor was dismissed only twice by a bowler, and twice run out. In May, she was named England Women's Cricketer of the Year. In October, she was installed at No. 1 when the ICC launched its one-day international rankings for women.'

J.M. Anderson   D.M. Benkenstein   M.V. Boucher   N.D. McKenzie

LEADING CRICKETER IN THE WORLD

V. Sehwag (India)

OBITUARIES INCLUDE

R.W. Harris
'Pending other claims, Reg Harris is thought to be the oldest person ever to have played regular organised cricket. He was still keeping wicket most Sundays (not to mention his Thursday games) for the Northamptonshire village of Bugbrooke in 2001, when he celebrated his 90th birthday by taking a catch. He reluctantly agreed to retire in 2003.'

N.C. O'Neill
'In the helter-skelter of the Tied Test at Brisbane in 1960-61, he disciplined himself for nearly seven hours in making 181, an innings which gave Australia a small but crucial first-innings lead … O'Neill was also at home in English conditions on the 1961 Ashes tour … causing *Wisden* to describe him as "a sheer joy to watch" and name him as one of the Five Cricketers of the Year.'

H. Pinter
'A month before he died, and very ill, he recited Francis Thompson's *At Lord's* to a gathering of friends, as he was wont to do. The circumstances lent the poem ("… the field is full of shades as I near the shadowy coast") the same sense of grim portent he habitually brought to the stage.'

W.A. Brown   B.D. Wells   D.W. White   J.V. Wilson

COUNTY REVIEW

Leicestershire
'On the field … it was largely a season of disappointment … That might suggest a barren year. But though this was true in terms of results, it was not the complete story … True to their word, Leicestershire did give a handful of promising youngsters an opportunity in the second half of the summer – and that is why the year was nowhere near the write-off it might have been.'

MATCH REPORTS

The Stanford Super Series, 2008-09
'In the middle of February 2009, while England were playing the second of their two Test matches in Antigua, Sir Allen Stanford was charged by the Securities and Exchange Commission of the United States with an alleged $9.2 billion investment fraud. The ECB immediately suspended negotiations with Stanford but, by then, they had suffered enormous embarrassment from their close links to the Texan who claimed to be a billionaire.'

This is the first edition published under the new ownership of A&C Black, part of the Bloomsbury Group. As Scyld Berry writes in the Preface: 'We are reunited with Whitaker's, who were the publishers of Wisden from 1938 to 1943.'

2010

WISDEN 2010

147th EDITION
EDITOR: Scyld Berry
PAGES: 1747
PRICE: Limp and cased £45   Large format: £55
Leather-bound £260 (150 limit)

THE WORLD AT LARGE

- Earthquake in Haiti kills about 230,000 people
- An Icelandic volcano erupts: the resulting ash in the atmosphere causes chaos for air travellers in Europe
- General election: a hung parliament results in a Conservative/Liberal coalition, the first in British government since World War II
- A BP oil pipe splits in the Gulf of Mexico, triggering attempts to avert a major environmental disaster
- Spain wins the World Cup
- Prince William and Kate Middleton announce their engagement

CRICKET HEADLINES 2009

County Champions: Durham

England regain the Ashes, beating Australia 2-1 at home, having already beaten the touring West Indians 2-0

Terrorist attack on the Sri Lanka cricket team in Pakistan on 3 March 2009

Murray Goodwin scores a county record 344* for Sussex v Somerset at Taunton: James Hildreth also scores a triple-hundred at Taunton, that most batsman friendly of grounds

Hampshire win the Friends Provident Trophy and Sussex the Twenty20 Cup and the Pro40 League title

Rafatullah Mohmand (302*) and Aamer Sajjad put on 580 for WAPDA's second wicket against Sui Southern Gas at Sheikhupura, a world record for this wicket and the second highest partnership of all time

NOTES BY THE EDITOR

'The natural order over the last century is pretty clear: in Australia, Australia win almost twice as many Tests as England; in England, the sides are well matched; and normally England need a great fast bowler to tip the balance, wherever the series is staged. Strauss had the benefit of two superlative spells of fast bowling, by Andrew Flintoff at Lord's and by Stuart Broad at The Oval. But the most succinct explanation of this conundrum – how on earth did England win when they averaged 34.15 runs per wicket against Australia's 40.64, the biggest disparity that has ever been overturned in any Test series – has to be this: Strauss's batting and captaincy, and the team spirit which he and the new coach Andy Flower created.'

FEATURE ARTICLES INCLUDE

Glazed, Not Gimlet-Eyed ..., by Gideon Haigh
'The wins were conquests. The losses were capitulations. The batting collapses were ruinous and utter. The bowling collapses – see Mitchell Johnson at Lord's, Monty Panesar at Cardiff – were complete. Have teams played more contrasting consecutive Tests than Headingley and The Oval? Have teams struggled as much with putting consecutive deliveries in the same place?'
When Cricket Lost its Innocence, by Nagraf Gollapudi and Scyld Berry
How We Won The Ashes, by Andrew Strauss
The Coach's View, by Andy Flower
A Particularly Australian Mongrel, by Michael Parkinson
Pitching for Change, by Justin Langer
"We Were Prisoners No Longer", by Stephen Chalke
This Little Social Heaven, by Ivo Tennant
From Church to Chappell, by Tanya Aldred
Bizarre and Short-sighted, by Duncan Fletcher

300

G. Onions

'His Test debut at Lord's in early May had inauspicious beginnings. After a golden duck, he had his first ball pulled for four, and conceded 22 runs in his first four overs. But his fifth was a maiden, and in the sixth he had Lendl Simmons caught at first slip, Jerome Taylor by the wicketkeeper and Sulieman Benn at third slip. Denesh Ramdin was lbw in his seventh over, and last man Lionel Baker in his tenth. In a single spell, he had taken five for 38.'

S.C.J. Broad   M.J. Clarke   M.J. Prior   G.P. Swann

LEADING CRICKETER IN THE WORLD

V. Sehwag (India)

OBITUARIES INCLUDE

Sir Derrick Bailey

"... a surprise choice as Gloucestershire's amateur captain in 1951 ... he lasted for two seasons before seven of the senior professionals wrote to the committee complaining about his rather eccentric leadership.'

W.H. Frindall

'... was the most famous of all scorers and statisticians. His reputation and celebrity, which spread to those who knew little of cricket, derived from his 43 seasons (1966-2008) scoring for BBC Radio's Test Match Special ... Sometimes he gave the impression that brain surgery and world peace might be trivialities in comparison to the great issues of leg-byes and first-class status. But he single-handedly elevated an obscure corner of an arcane sport: he made it matter because he insisted that it did matter.'

D.R. Shepherd

'... made his name in two separate cricketing incarnations: first as a highly distinctive if never outstanding county cricketer; and then as an umpire, in which capacity he rose to be, by common consent, the best in the world.'

A.J.W. McIntyre   G.E. Tribe

COUNTY REVIEW

Durham

'Durham have gone from doormats to dominant force, whipping boys to whippers. When they won the Championship for the first time in 2008, it was considered something of a fairytale; suddenly in 2009, they were in a class of their own.

Their winning margin of 47 points was a record since the advent of two divisions in 2000, even though their last two games were drawn with the title already secured.'

MATCH REPORTS

England v West Indies, Second Test, *at Chester-le-Street, May 14, 15, 16, 17, 18*

'There were times before, during and immediately after this match when it felt as if Test cricket in England had reached its nadir. Although the hosts were occasionally as inspired as the tourists were lacklustre, the suspicion was never shaken off that this was a game few wanted to play or to watch. The surrender of the Wisden Trophy by West Indies, who had held it for a mere 69 days – following a gap of nine years – seemed as inevitable as had, once upon a time, their continued possession of it.'

Scyld Berry writes in his Preface: 'I am proud to say I cannot think of any human activity which records itself, and thus perpetuates and strengthens itself, as Wisden *chronicles cricket.'*

WISDEN CRICKETERS' ALMANACK AUSTRALIA

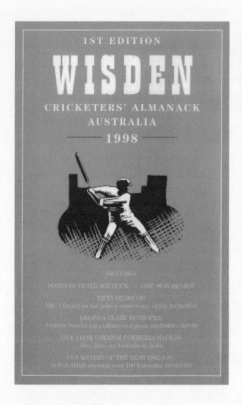

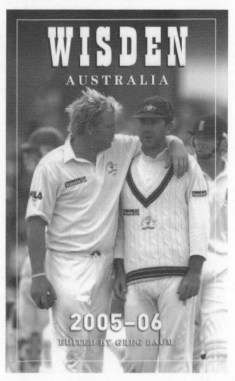

An Australian edition of *Wisden* was published between 1998 and 2005 by Hardie Grant Books with the copyright of John Wisden & Co Ltd.

It was intended that 'Ozden', as it was dubbed, would record Australian cricket as its British counterpart had done for England, and indeed the rest of the cricketing world, since 1864. However, its run ended after just eight editions.

The first six green covers had a stylised impression of the iconic photograph of Victor Trumper jumping out to drive; the last two editions sported colour covers featuring Shane Warne – the final one showing him with a consoling arm around Ricky Ponting's shoulder as the Ashes slipped from the Aussies' grasp in 2005. The eighth edition contained reports of that series in England, but whereas the 143rd edition of *Wisden* in 2006 achieved record sales, *Wisden Australia* 2005-06 proved to be the final one.

A leather-bound version was produced for each year in a limited edition of 100. There were also three editions of a *Pocket Wisden Australia* of 160 pages, covering 2002-03, 2003-04 and 2004-05.

1998

WISDEN AUSTRALIA 1998

1ˢᵗ Edition
Editorial Director: Graeme Wright
Pages: 791
Price: A$ 39.95   £19.99

PREFACE

"'*Wisden* is coming to Australia," proclaimed an article in the *Australian* in March 1981. "The world's most famous and most respected reference book – a description that utterly fails to do it justice – is about to spawn its own Australian edition." Though no less prophetic, but perhaps more appropriate, were the words of the London publisher responsible at that time for the production of *Wisden Cricketers' Almanack*. "We want to get it exactly right, so we are going to hasten slowly." Well, the prophecy has been fulfilled, even if it has taken 17 years.'

NOTES BY PETER ROEBUCK

'At first sight 1997-98 might not seem an auspicious time to launch upon an unsuspecting and, as far as can be told, undemanding public, a tome dedicated to the recording in minute detail of such cricketing events of the previous year as had caught the discerning eye.'

CRICKETER OF THE YEAR

Belinda Clark, by Amanda Weaver
[The new baby steals a march on its English mother by selecting a woman for the first accolade.]

SHEFFIELD SHIELD CRICKETER OF THE YEAR

Colin Miller, by Ashley Mallett

FEATURE ARTICLES

Cricketers of the Year 1892–1997, by Gideon Haigh
'Roving over a century or so of southern summers to choose a single Cricketer of the Year for every season of Australian cricket, I've consciously searched for those cricketers who show the game here in the round. The greats are here, be assured, but so are the not-quite-so-great, as well as a few feats of the forgotten.'
Notes from the Northern Hemisphere, by Matthew Engel
'As the 1998 northern summer turned to autumn, and the focus of the game once more moved southwards, what might be cricket's scandal of the century threatened to erupt... The scandal – the possibility (some would say near-certainty) that cricketers had taken bribes to fix the results of international matches – received the minimum of discussion.'
The players' dispute, by Malcolm Knox, Tim May and Malcolm Speed
One-day cricket: taking the 'limited' out of limited overs, by Malcolm Knox
Fast bowlers and the modern game, by Dennis Lillee
50 years on – the golden anniversary of the Invincibles, by Mike Coward

1999

WISDEN AUSTRALIA 1999

2nd Edition
Editor: Gideon Haigh
Pages: 864
Price: A$ 39.95   UK £22.50

PREFACE

'If you are the sort of person who believes that too much cricket is not enough, season 1998-99 would have been your idea of heaven … At *Wisden Australia,* we often felt like New South Wales at the MCG in 1926-27, watching Victoria pile up 1,107. Every match in Australia from first-grade level up adds a little to our statistical bailiwick. Every journey interstate or overseas must have its appointed scribe. It's not as hard for us as it is for the cricketers, of course, but we don't drive Ferraris or get to pile up a lifetime supply of frequent flier points.'

NOTES BY PETER ROEBUCK

'Notoriously the second year is harder upon the aspiring cricketer than its predecessor. Nothing is easier, it seems, than to appear as a flash Harold cutting a swathe through the crusty ways of yesteryear. Whether this accurately captures the first incarnation of *Wisden Australia* is for others to determine. At any rate, we felt sufficiently encouraged to try what, in the world of music and cinema, would be called a "follow-up", though we prefer to describe it as a second edition.'

CRICKETER OF THE YEAR

Glenn McGrath, by Daniel Williams

SHEFFIELD SHIELD CRICKETER OF THE YEAR

Simon Katich, by John Townsend

FEATURE ARTICLES

Notes from the Northern Hemisphere, by Matthew Engel
    'When one country is supreme at both Test and one-day cricket – a position Australia secured at the World Cup final – it is inevitable that other teams must suffer. No one else suffered like England, though others did so more theatrically. It is in the nature of one-day cricket that one-sided games can be very one-sided. On another day, Australia could have lost the final to Pakistan just as easily as they won it … Pakistan had a shocking day; it could have happened to anyone. The defeat against Bangladesh, in a dead game at the end of the preliminary stages, might have been a different matter. There were certainly rumours. The International Cricket Council, of course, remained useless and impotent, as ever.'
The green and gold – 100 years young, by Philip Derriman
Dumb and dumber, by Mark Ray
Milestones, by Jim Tucker and Tim Lane
Future tense – cricket in the new millennium, by Ross Stevenson
First among equals, by John Benaud
Arjuna Ranatunga: 'More sinned against …'? by Michael Roberts
Run riot, by Peter Roebuck
The Australian rope trick: victory in the World Cup, by Stephen Fay

2000-01

WISDEN AUSTRALIA 2000-01

3rd Edition
EDITOR: Gideon Haigh
PAGES: 839
PRICE: A$ 39.95   UK £22.50

PREFACE

'Perhaps it was the indifferent opposition, perhaps the opportunities they afforded for lavish tributes, but during the 1999-2000 summer we seemed abnormally conscious of the rigmarole of records and record-breaking. There was the obsessive attention paid to Shane Warne's pursuit of Dennis Lillee's Australian Test wicket record, which finally came his way in Auckland. There was the captivation with the Australian team's steady accumulation of a record nine consecutive Test victories, a landmark attained in the following Test at Wellington. Thanks in part no doubt to Channel Nine's computational vigilance, some milestone of sorts always seemed in the offing: fastest ball, slickest fifty, loudest snick, smartest hat. At *Wisden*, of course, we regard this as good for business!'

NOTES BY PETER ROEBUCK

'Only one criticism can be made of the powerful Australian outfit. At times the fast bowlers took aggression too far, spoiling the atmosphere with some excessive attacks on opponents. The sight of McGrath screaming at Sachin Tendulkar in Sydney is not easily forgotten. It did not seem right to treat a visiting captain and a champion batsman with such disrespect. Brett Lee's hysterics in New Zealand were also unacceptable.'

CRICKETER OF THE YEAR

Steve Waugh, by John Birmingham

PURA MILK CUP CRICKETER OF THE YEAR

Paul Reiffel, by Greg Baum

FEATURE ARTICLES

Notes from the Northern Hemisphere, by Matthew Engel
   'To some extent, county cricket did appear more purposeful in 2000 *[the first year of the two-division County Championship]* ... Much of that purpose was generated by Australian players, who continued to dominate the county game. Shane Warne's stay with Hampshire was less than triumphant. His form was ordinary and the team slumped towards the bottom of the First Division. However, people close to the club spoke warmly of his attitude (even if one nurse he supposedly telephoned was more indignant).'
Still the one: how Channel Nine has changed the face of cricket, by Greg Manning
The new paddock that grew, by Greg Baum
A question of legality, by Bob Simpson
Positive spin: the record-breaking Shane Warne, by Richie Benaud
The patient Australian: the record-breaking Jamie Siddons, by Daniel Williams
The greatest tour of all, by Phil Opas QC
Brightly fades the Donn, by Bernard Whimpress
Field of dream teams, by Gideon Haigh

2001-02

WISDEN AUSTRALIA 2001-02

4ᵗʰ Edition
Executive Editor: Warwick Franks
Pages: 876
Price: A$ 39.95   £22.50

PREFACE

'The most significant cricket event of the year was one which was also of national significance: the death of a man who played his last Test match over half a century ago. That man was Sir Donald Bradman, whose absolute dominance with the bat was complemented by his crucial role in shaping modern Australian cricket as an administrator, and whose long life saw him come to be regarded as a national treasure.'

NOTES BY THE EDITOR

'Despite the tragic peaks of men such as Jack Marsh and Eddie Gilbert, cricket has not generally proved congenial to Aboriginal Australians. Historians such as Colin Tatz and Bernard Whimpress have traced the complex reasons for this, but the ACB has made a fresh start in trying to address the issue. After a skilful game between the ATSIC Chairman's XI and the Prime Minister's XI at Manuka Oval, Canberra, in April 2001, an Aboriginal Cricket Working Party was formed.'

CRICKETER OF THE YEAR

Glenn McGrath, by Rick Smith

PURA MILK CUP CRICKETER OF THE YEAR

Jamie Cox, by Ric Finlay

FEATURE ARTICLES

The Don: a eulogy, by Richie Benaud
[Delivered at the memorial service for Sir Donald Bradman on March 25, 2001.]
'It's not quite perfect outside, I guess. Rain coming down. A bit of a dodgy pitch. Wind blowing. But I reckon he would have handled it with all his consummate skill, no matter what it might provide out there. There is a crowd out there filled with memories. The bowling changes here at the Cathedral end have been many and varied. We've now got an ageing leg-spinner, and I think the Don might have welcomed that. He was the most famous of them all at a time when despair ruled Australia because of the Great Depression. Seventy years later 100 selectors from around the world nominated the five greatest players of the century. The Don received 100 votes. Not far away from him was that finest of all-rounders, Garry Sobers, who got 90. But 100 out of 100 is pretty good.'
Cricket's Superman, by Charles Davis
Sir Donald Bradman: obituary, by Philip Derriman
The Australian hero, by Brett Hutchins
The rise and rise of Queensland cricket, by Martin Rogers
Half a century of Test watching: a personal survey, by David Frith
Australia has melted, by Tony Wilson
A stepping stone to first-class cricket, by John Pollack

2002-03

WISDEN AUSTRALIA 2002-03

5th Edition
Executive Editor: Warwick Franks
Pages: 861
Price: A$ 39.95   UK £22.50

PREFACE

'During the 1970s and 1980s, there was a fatally easy acceptance of the new phenomenon of sledging as an orchestrated tool of what the current Australian captain is pleased to call the "mental destabilisation" of the opposition. After all, giving your opponents a spray was part of that aggressive larrikinism which was supposed to be quintessentially Australian, any rough edges of which could be smoothed over by a beer with the opposition after play. Increasingly, it is being seen for the boorish, cretinous blight on the game that it is, and Brian Booth gives a considered analysis of its growth and challenges its continued presence.'

NOTES BY THE EDITOR

'... the rabid conspiracist will quickly point to the fact that only in Australia have umpires been courageous and truthful enough to call Muralitharan, acting in that great Australian tradition of fearless honesty. Rhetoric like this is a reminder that there is still plenty of myopia and insularity in the way we approach the cricket of other nations, particularly those of the subcontinent, and even more particularly Sri Lanka's. Australian cricket needs to be mindful of the fact that while the Australian crawl was a distinctively Australian swimming stroke, the Australian whine is much less productive.'

CRICKETER OF THE YEAR

Adam Gilchrist, by Mark Ray

PURA CUP CRICKETER OF THE YEAR

Jimmy Maher, by Andrew Dawson

FEATURE ARTICLES

Can the Australian Empire last? by Greg Baum
'Australian cricket can be compared with a great empire, like those of the Romans, Moghuls and Ottomans, ruling almost all the known world. The comparison holds down to the detail of a pocket of resistance, India, that heroically refuses to bend to Australian sovereignty.'
The MacGills and the Meulemans, by Bill Reynolds
The curse of sledging, by Brian Booth
Bill Brown – elder statesman of Australian cricket, by Ian Diehm
Grassroots cricket, by Jim Young
The art of cricket fiction, by Steven Carroll

2003-04

WISDEN AUSTRALIA 2003-04

6ᵗʰ Edition
Executive Editor: Warwick Franks
Pages: 928
Price: A$ 39.95   UK £22.50

PREFACE

'There were many times during the past year in which cricket seemed but a distant echo in the apparently endless cycle of war, terror and death. It was a salutary reminder that cricket, like any sport, should not be puffed up with self-importance and delusions of political grandeur. Rather, it is the very ordinariness of cricket which gives it its meaning, and its importance lies in its essential unimportance. To play, to watch and to talk about cricket might never avert war or cure the ills of the world, but it provides a way of remembering our humanity in the whirlwind of coldly impersonal forces which bear down on us.'

NOTES BY THE EDITOR

'In this hard-nosed world of cricketing realpolitik, there was a delightful exception which produced some curious reactions. In the World Cup pool match against Sri Lanka at Port Elizabeth, Adam Gilchrist walked after a ball from Aravinda de Silva ballooned up from his pads to be taken by the wicket-keeper. The batsman departed even as umpire Rudi Koertzen appeared to be mouthing "not out". Although the pragmatic temper of Australian cricket has generally not produced batsmen who walk, Gilchrist's action showed sporting decency of a high and refreshing order. There followed some fascinating responses…'

CRICKETER OF THE YEAR

Ricky Ponting, by Nabila Ahmed

PURA CUP CRICKETER OF THE YEAR

Wade Seccombe, by Martin Rogers

FEATURE ARTICLES

Shane Warne: celebrity in the firing line, by Mark Ray
'The most damaging drug Warne has taken is the drug of fame. His attitude to fame is not as complex as that of the wider society. He was seduced by it long ago. The result is that he seems to have come to believe that he can manipulate it and the public's view of him as easily as he can a cricket ball. But the world beyond the boundary is more complex than that. Warne's fumbled attempts to spin himself out of the drugs scandal confirmed this.'
The best of the best: Australia's World Cup Final teams, by Bernard Whimpress
A cup of the World's best spare parts, by Greg Baum
What is the point of the ICC?, by Gideon Haigh
When will we see c Nguyen b Yunipingu?, by Chris Ryan
The Australian factor in English county cricket, by Catherine Hanley
Mark Waugh – even more than met the eye, by John Benaud

2004-05

WISDEN AUSTRALIA 2004-05

7th EDITION
EDITOR: Christian Ryan
PAGES: 976
PRICE: A$ 49.95   UK £22.50

PREFACE

'Another summer, another 12 months of Australia squashing every opponent in sight, another *Wisden*. Actually, not quite. In the same year that Sourav Ganguly's Indians provided an unexpected hiccup to Steve Waugh's carefully choreographed farewell lap, we have been doing a bit of tinkering with the script ourselves. We started at the very beginning – the first full-colour pictorial cover in the history of *Wisden*.'

NOTES BY THE EDITOR

'Cricket hovers at the cusp of a heavenly, unprecedented trinity: a strong Australia, India and England. Listen to the gibberish of excitable Poms and you'd think the day had arrived already, that the 2005 Ashes are as good as England's. That's what winning seven out of eight Tests against West Indies will do for you. As a book of record, it is our sober duty to point out that Australia have won nine of their past 10 Tests against those same downtrodden opponents. The reaction was not national hysteria but to wonder what the blazes went wrong in Antigua.

'At the risk of stating the bleeding obvious, we confidently assert that when Australia play England in July, Andrew Flintoff and Marcus Trescothick will be pegged flatfooted to the crease. Andrew Strauss will discover that teeing off against Edwards, Collymore and Bravo is no rehearsal for seeing off Gillespie, McGrath and Warne. Michael Vaughan's scudding cover drive will pick out the man at extra cover as unerringly as it evaded him two summers ago. Graham Thorpe, missing from 13 of the past 15 Ashes Tests, will again go AWOL against crunch opponents. Ashley Giles will neither rip nor bounce it enough to bother inventive Australian batsmen. The selectors will get in a muddle over whether to pick a batsman-keeper, a keeper-batsman or scuttle back to Alec Stewart. Steve Harmison will be found to be only human. Heaven will have to wait till 2006-07.'

CRICKETER OF THE YEAR

Darren Lehmann, by Christian Ryan

PURA CUP CRICKETER OF THE YEAR

Matthew Elliott, by Peter Hanlon

FEATURE ARTICLES

The hurricane hundred, by Charles Davis
Forgiven, not forgotten, by John Harms
The mourning after, by David Frith
Premature evacuation, by Malcolm Knox
The Invisibles, by Max Bonnell
Still grappling, still squirreling, by Gideon Haigh
That coil-like wrist: Shane Warne
A tragic case, by Matt Price
The man who averaged infinity, by John Birmingham

2005-06

WISDEN AUSTRALIA 2005-06

8th Edition
Editor: Greg Baum
Pages: 976
Price: A$ 55.00   UK £25.00

PREFACE

'The Editor's Notes were largely written in the blear of several long Ashes nights. It was the single major happening in world cricket in the last 12 months, and so forms the heart of this year's publication. *Wisden's* publishers held its presses for longer than any other publisher would have dared, to make sure that our coverage was up to date, comprehensive and meaningful in the best *Wisden* tradition.'

NOTES BY THE EDITOR

'Before the series, it had been Englishmen doubting England, or Australians full of hubris. Now it was Australians despairing of Australia, or otherwise wiping egg from their faces. The world and the tide had turned. In a series played in Homeric temper, England outdid Australia in all facets, batting, bowling, fielding and, uncharacteristically, thinking.'

CRICKETER OF THE YEAR

Glenn McGrath, by Geoff Lawson
'McGrath, who grew up in Narromine in central NSW, comes from an uncomplicated rural background where hard work and perseverance were essential for survival in a harsh and unforgiving climate. They are conditions similar to elite sport. While the dash and flair of Australia's batsmen are up in neon lights, McGrath has helped haul the side to the top with his simplicity, hard work, adherence to a fundamental yet almost unique bowling discipline and wonderful tactical sense. He is the true colossus of the early 21st century bowlers.'

PURA CUP CRICKETER OF THE YEAR

Michael Bevan, by Martin Blake

FEATURE ARTICLES

Keith Miller, 'The best loved Australian', by Tony Charlton
'We do well to acclaim Keith. He was a free spirit who played for the joy of the game. As he leaves us to fly again among the clouds, those of us who knew him and watched him will forever by uplifted by indelible memories, and by the warmth of his company. Neville Cardus, who he knew well, once described him as "an Australian *in excelsis*"…
'May he of blithe spirit, who fought the good fight – in everything – in his unique way of dash and splendour and decency and good fellowship, dwell among those who follow. Let us all thank him for the marvellous memories captured by the name of Keith Ross Miller. It remains a constant that the best teachers of humanity are the lives of great men.'
Warne and the wrong 'un, by Charles Davis
Short-sighted – or visionary? by Matt Price
The mystery of the missing cycle, by Mike Coward
The trouble with extra cover, by Tim Lane
Grounds for change, by John Harms
Pickers of the crop, by John Benaud
Lunatics' coup in the asylum, by John Townsend
The one that didn't get away, by Belinda Clark

310

PART THREE
A GUIDE FOR COLLECTORS

COLLECTING *WISDEN*

The Wisden collector's ultimate aim is to own a perfect set – original editions from 1864 to 1895 in paper wrappers and from 1896 to the present day in hardback. Achievement of this ambition is simple enough: you register your 'wanted' list with the specialist book-dealers, wait until a set becomes available – and pay £300,000. One such perfect set was sold for more than this sum in January 2011.

For the rest of us, collecting *Wisden* is much more interesting and much less costly.

A full run can be obtained for under £10,000. It would comprise the first 15 editions (1864–78) in a boxed facsimile set, moving on to Willows reprints, and then with originals (either linen bound or hardcloth) from 1946 onwards. The books contain exactly the same information as the originals and will have a pleasingly uniform look on your bookshelf. However, we feel duty bound to issue three warnings.

(a) Health warning: collecting anything is addictive and could seriously damage your health as you are compelled to complete your quest for more *Wisdens*. What may start as an innocent matter of buying a *Wisden* to commemorate a birth year can become a lifetime's enslavement.

(b) Shelf warning: you will need to find around twenty feet of shelf space to house all the editions. If you have a private study, this is fine, but on no account should these books appear in family rooms where pets and children will not appreciate them as much as you do, and where they may become a focus of resentment for a spouse or partner because of (a) or (c).

(c) Wealth warning: your collecting habit will not lessen once you have a full run. You will want to replace those facsimiles with originals. You will discover that Second World War originals are rare and costly (don't mention the Great War) and with each year that you go backwards, the price of the originals will rise. Ultimately, you will justify your purchase as being a sound investment – which at least should be true: although prices may soften in the short term as well as rise, the trend over time is definitely upwards. That will be good news for both your partner and your bank manager.

The information that follows is designed to assist collectors in their quest to acquire *Wisdens*. What it cannot do is explain the endless fascination of the books themselves – their content, not just about cricket but the wider society – and a lifetime's pleasure that comes from the ownership of them.

BUYING *WISDEN*

Long gone are the days when the hunt for *Wisdens* would take you into the secondhand bookshops which existed in almost every town; the ones with a rack of cheap books outside the shop window and shelves in the doorway. An inquiry of the owner – 'Have you any cricket books, especially *Wisdens*?' – would elicit directions, often to a cluttered room up a winding, creaking staircase. There, on a dusty top shelf, or piled in a cardboard box, would be a handful of limp volumes in various degrees of yellow or a run of brown hardbacks. Sometimes the edition you wanted was there, more often not, and occasionally a bargain was unearthed.

Of course, everyone uses the internet today (although you still won't walk past a bookshop without dropping in). The internet is efficient and transparent: you can compare prices in an instant – although you will rarely be comparing like with like, because the condition of every book is different.

Go to one of the online retailers, type 'Wisden 1951', and you will find copies that are for sale in bookshops not only in the UK but throughout the world. In a test run, **www.abebooks.co.uk** listed 29 copies; another similar site, **www.biblio.com**, had 17 copies; and the mighty **www.amazon.co.uk** found 9. With all three sites, you will not need to deal direct with the seller. The same is true of **eBay**.

BOOK DEALERS

The official website of **John Wisden & Co** is www.wisden.com. The site contains information about *Wisden's* history as well as allowing purchasers to obtain the current edition, and there are occasionally special offers on more recent editions. A link on this site at 'Bookshop' takes browsers to the publishers, **Bloomsbury**, where past, present and future publications can be ordered.

The John Wisden & Co site also has a link to 'Buy old Wisdens' where it gives a list of recommended specialist book-dealers who all hold extensive stock.

THE SPECIALISTS

John McKenzie celebrated 40 years of selling cricket books in 2011. During that time, an incalculable number of *Wisdens* of every year and in every condition have passed through his hands. Back in 1971, his valuations caused a stir when he advertised a set at £650; since then, prices have gone in only one direction. John issued his first catalogue in July 1972 after purchasing the stock and mailing list of Roland and Betty Cole of Colchester. He has produced them four times a year ever since, and they have become collectors' items in themselves. The website lists only about a quarter of the stock of over 10,000 cricket books; these are best viewed at his shop in Ewell, Surrey, during normal weekday opening hours of 9am to 5pm. Allow plenty of time, and as with all these specialists, it is advisable to phone first to check they will be open.

● J. W. McKenzie   www.mckenzie-cricket.co.uk   020 8393 7700

Christopher Saunders has details of over 9,000 books on his excellent website and issues comprehensive catalogues: his 2009 catalogue devoted solely to *Wisdens* is a mine of information and lists among its treasures the first 15 years bound in four volumes and priced at £75,000. Assisted by David Wilkinson, Chris maintains a large showroom at his home by the River Severn in Gloucestershire. Almost uniquely among dealers, he takes a selection of his stock to book fairs all around the country; he used to attend 40 events a year, but by 2011 he had greatly reduced his travelling.

- Christopher Saunders   www.cricket-books.com   01594 516030

Sportspages, founded by Giles Lyon in London as Bodyline Books, moved from London to a former oasthouse in Farnham in 2005 when the original business was sold, although Giles remained as a consultant until 2010. The stock encompasses not only a large number of *Wisdens* and cricket books, but literature on all sports, from angling to wrestling. The website displays the comprehensive range of *Wisdens* by period and format, so any edition is easy to find. Sportspages' location in a Surrey market town makes for a pleasant excursion (phone first), accompanied by lunch at a nearby pub or restaurant.

- Sportspages   www.sportspages.com   01252 727222

Bill Furmedge of WisdenWorld is a collector turned dealer. In 2002 he began to enlarge his collection, 25 years after buying his first *Wisden*. As he describes it, he was not over-enthused by the way he was treated, so in due course he set out to offer an alternative level of service. His website is bright and welcoming, and he takes pride in being available seven days a week to assist collectors.

- WisdenWorld   www.wisdenworld.co.uk   01480 819272

Ken Faulkner was introduced to the world of cricket books when he assisted a fellow club cricketer who ran the bookshop at Gloucestershire CCC. He took over the role in 1996 and built up his knowledge of *Wisdens*. In 2009 he handed over the county shop to Tony Sanders and now specialises in Almanacks from his home in Wokingham, Berkshire. Ken's website, named after a favourite tipple, lists copies for most years; as with all dealers, a phone call is vital to get information on the rarer editions or to make an appointment to view his book room. He takes a selection to the annual Cheltenham cricket festival where he has a tent in conjunction with Tony Sanders.

- Ken Faulkner   www.bowmore.demon.co.uk   01189 785255

Ian Dyer, whose son Robin played for Warwickshire, ran the shop at Edgbaston and founded his own business in 1979. When he retired in 1990, he sold it to his nephew, Michael Gauntlett, and his wife, Jennifer. They set up the first specialist website for cricket books in 1997 and it continues to list *Wisdens* among an impressive range of books.

- Ian Dyer Cricket Books   www.cricketbooks.co.uk   01748 822786

St Mary's Books is that increasingly rare outlet – a traditional antiquarian bookshop. Located near the church from which it takes its name in the old coaching town of Stamford, St Mary's sells maps and prints as well as its 50,000 books (and is a leading stockist of taxidermy). *Wisden* has become a speciality; editions are well described and displayed on the website, but a personal visit is recommended.

- St Mary's Books   www.stmarysbooks.com   01780 763033

314

Boundary Books was formed in 1989, and an early coup was the sale of A. D. Taylor's first 15 *Wisdens,* complete with original wrappers, for £23,400. In 2009, to celebrate its twentieth year in business, and having moved operations from Cheshire to Oxfordshire, Boundary Books revamped its website and opened new showrooms. Meanwhile owner Michael Down produces consistently lavish catalogues; in the introduction to No. 38, he wrote: 'I am now able to devote more time to Boundary Books and have welcomed the opportunity to meet far more of the customers who had previously only been voices on the end of a telephone line or names on a mailing list. While the internet and emails have made so many aspects of collecting cricket books easier, many of us regret the gradual passing of the old collector / dealer relationship.' (Our advice to collectors is still to cultivate such a relationship with two or three dealers.)

- Boundary Books   www.boundarybooks.com   01235 751021

Martin Wood, based in Sevenoaks, Kent, has been selling cricket books full-time since 1970. His accumulated knowledge and comprehensive stock mean he can supply most needs. Visitors are welcome by appointment.

- Martin Wood   www.martinwoodcricketbooks.co.uk   01732 457205

William H. Roberts also asks callers to make an appointment to see his stock in Huddersfield, Yorkshire. The website lists a choice of *Wisdens* in various conditions for almost every year from 1880 onwards, including Willows facsimiles. He is a member of the Provincial Booksellers Fairs Association.

- William Roberts   www.williamroberts-cricket.com   01484 654463

Other specialist cricket booksellers:

Aardvark Books: 01522 722671
Acumen Books: www.acumenbooks.co.uk
Grace Books: 0116 271 6363 (weekdays); 0116 271 4267 (evenings and weekends)
John Jeffers: 01296 688543
Parker's Cricket Books: www.parkerscricketbooks.co.uk
Roger Heavens: www.booksoncricket.net
Stuart Topps: 01302 300906
Tim Beddow: 0121 421 7117
In Australia, Roger Page: (+61) 3 9435 6332; email:rpcricketbooks@unite.com.au

See **www.thebookguide.co.uk** for a list of independent bookshops and fairs.

Also recommended is the unofficial *Wisden* collectors' website, **www.wisdens.org**. This site was created by Yorkshire-based IT expert Chris Ridler in 2005. It offers a price guide for old *Almanacks* and furnishes collectors with extensive sales data: there are lists of prices realised at auctions since January 2006 (including eBay sales) and historic valuations going back to 1976. The site also provides an outlet for opinions (many learned, some tendentious, most fascinating) on its discussion forum, has a search service and hosts rolling auctions with books being sold every day. Chris emails newsletters twice a week about auction listings, and e-catalogues can be downloaded.

It is worth popping in to **charity shops**, although Oxfam is well clued up about prices. The first four editions of *Wisden* (1864–67) bound in one volume were handed in to the Hertford shop in 2010: they raised £8,520 at a Bonhams auction after being rebound into the four individual years.

There is always a good selection of *Wisdens* on the bookstalls set up at **county cricket grounds**. Discovering a missing volume during the lunch interval at Arundel or Tunbridge Wells is to be in very heaven. Memo to the ECB: counties that do not cater for bibliophiles should have points deducted; why not employ *Wisden* inspectors?

AUCTIONS

It is natural to think first of **eBay**, and data on prices confirm that the cheapest books are often to be found here. Buyers may certainly get bargains, but *caveat emptor* applies here more than anywhere else in the *Wisden* universe. At any one time, up to half a dozen copies of post-war editions may be listed, and their price is not high. But if you are looking at copies costing more than £100, you should be very certain of what you are buying.

Condition is all-important. How accurately is the book described? Will returns be accepted if the book proves to have flaws that were not mentioned? This should not be a problem with dealers, who do not wish to have an unhappy customer, and there are dealers who sell *Wisdens* through eBay.

Don't get carried away in the chase if the bidding hots up. Willows reprints, for example, have been sold for far more than they would cost if bought direct from Willows themselves, or from many dealers. Do your research and set a realistic limit.

The major auction houses hold 'big name' sales when a whole collection may be sold, although often the editions are lotted separately. In London, **Christie's** (www.christies.com) and **Bonhams** (www.bonhams.com) are the big auction houses that are most likely to stage the major sales. **Graham Budd** (www.grahambuddauctions.co.uk) is a specialist in sporting memorabilia and holds auctions at the **Sotheby's** (www.sothebys.com) saleroom in New Bond Street where, in 2007, the then record price of £120,000 for a set was achieved.

These auctions will be widely advertised in *Wisden* itself, in *The Wisden Cricketer* magazine and in *Antiques Trade Gazette (ATG)*. The owners of the weekly *ATG* also run the auction website **www.the-saleroom.com** through which you can view catalogues and sign up to bid live at sales. Internet bidding saves time hanging around on auction days waiting for the lots in which you are interested, but prospective bidders should still attend a viewing to inspect copies and make notes on their condition.

Outside London, **Tim Knight** holds *Wisden* sales twice a year. Although based in Norfolk, these specialist sales are held at a hotel in a central location near Leicester with good motorway access (www.knightswisden.co.uk). There are also general sporting sales (www.knights.co.uk).

Established in 2000, **Anthemion Auctions** in Cardiff are gaining a reputation as specialists in sporting memorabilia with two sales a year (www.anthemionauction.com).

Trevor Vennett-Smith in Nottinghamshire holds twice-yearly sales of sporting memorabilia that contain some *Wisdens*, although he is best known for cigarette cards, postcards and ephemera (www.vennett-smith.com).

Mullock's includes *Wisdens* in its sporting and cricket memorabilia sales at Ludlow Racecourse. These are open for internet bidding via the-saleroom.com, the site run by *Antiques Trade Gazette* (www.mullocksauctions.co.uk).

Dominic Winter Book Auctions are held at a saleroom near Cirencester in Gloucestershire and sometimes have *Wisdens* in their sporting books sales (www.dominicwinter.co.uk).

Be aware that all these auction houses charge a buyer's premium ranging from 15% to 25%, and there is VAT to pay on the premium.

The rolling online auctions at **Chris Ridler's** collectors' website, www.wisdens.org, do not charge buyers a premium. On their actual auction site (www.wisdenauction.com) there are several photographs of each book being sold, with descriptions of any flaws such as weak hinges or creased covers, so buyers get a good idea of the condition of copies. Books are also given a rating as to condition, from 1 to 10 (the finest).

The **Cricket Memorabilia Society** (www.cricketmemorabilia.org) holds two or three premium-free auctions a year which include *Wisdens*. Society chairman Keith Hayhurst (for whom the word enthusiast might have been specially coined) edits a quarterly magazine in which he records the latest auction prices achieved for *Wisdens* and memorabilia. Commenting on prices in the December 2010 magazine, Keith advises: 'It is a good time to start your *Wisden* collection.'

In Melbourne, Australia, **Charles Leski Auctions**, established in 1973, hold regular sporting memorabilia auctions with a live online bidding facility (www.leski.com.au).

REPRINTS

Facsimiles are the collector's friend. These have all been of the highest quality and enable collectors to build a run of *Wisdens* at a reasonable cost. The initial facsimile reprint of the first 15 editions, 1864–78, produced for the then publishers Sporting Handbooks, was by printers Billings & Sons Ltd of Guildford and London in 1960. These copies in salmon-pink wrappers were mainly sold as a boxed set for £40, although individual copies were available at £3 3s (£3.15). About 150 copies of each year were produced, of which it is thought some 100 were sold as sets.

These first 15 years were reprinted for a second time in 1974, this time by Lowe & Brydone (Printers) Ltd for £50 a set. Again, there were probably about 100 sets of this reprint, which came encased in yellow card, while about a further 50 copies of each year were sold as individual copies at £4 each.

By 1991, these sets were selling for up to £800. John Wisden & Co responded to demand from collectors by producing a handsome boxed set of the same first 15 years, this time giving the books hardback covers with the facsimile paper wrappers inside. The sets were limited to 1,000 numbered copies and cost £450, the price being unchanged until all were sold in 2008.

Meanwhile, the Willows Publishing Company Ltd has reprinted every edition under a licence from John Wisden & Co Ltd from 1879–1936 and 1940–45. The missing years of 1937–39 will be filled by March 2012. Willows was set up in 1983 by David Jenkins, a geography teacher at the time, as an extension of his *Wisden* collecting hobby. Together with his wife, Pauline, he runs Willows from his home in Stone, Staffordshire. His original aims were to gain a full run of *Wisdens* for himself and to help other collectors towards this holy grail. He has now achieved his target with a run that are all originals from 1879, plus the first 15 in John Wisden & Co's boxed set. All are proudly displayed in a purpose-built bookcase, accompanied by a file of letters and emails from collectors expressing their gratitude for being given the opportunity to complete their own runs thanks to his facsimiles.

Willows started by reprinting the 1885 edition in an unnumbered run, with hard covers. The 1885 reprint was quickly followed by 1884 and 1886; and Willows have produced two or more facsimile editions every year since they first embarked on the enterprise. The reprints are produced as numbered limited editions. Most years have been limited to 500 copies, although 1879 and 1916 were each limited to 1,000, and the Second World War editions of 1941–45 to 750. All the reprints from the 19th-century sold out many years ago so a second reprint (limited to 250 copies) was published for the 1880s and 1890–95 editions. There was also a second reprint of the 1896–99 editions in 2011.

The presentation of reprints from 1879 to 1895 is a tan cloth binding with gilt printing on the front cover and spine, encasing end papers and the paper wrapper version of the Almanack. From 1896 onwards, to reflect the introduction of the hardcloth copy of the Almanack and in addition to the paper wrapper edition, Willows also produced an exact facsimile of the hardcloth style: it replicated the gilt embossing on the front binding and spine, and included the advertisement pages that originally appeared on the inside of the front and rear bindings. As the presentation of the softback *Wisdens* changed from paper wrappers to linen in 1938, this has also been reflected in the reprints, with the yellow linen covers encased. Where 500 reprints were produced of copies from 1896 onwards, the split between the two versions is 300 copies of the paper wrapper edition and 200 of the hardback for each year. The split between the two versions of 1941–45 is 450 linen and 300 hardcloth.

Great care has been taken with the look and feel of Willows reprints. They are clearly identified as reprints on the bindings – the number of the copy and the limitation is on the back cover – and on the title page of each edition. The bindings give the books a consistency of style and a robustness that provides the collector with confidence that the book will not fall apart when searching for a match report or obituary from a bygone age.

Reproducing *Wisden* in exact facsimile is no simple process. First, Willows dismantle an original copy so that each page can be scanned and cleaned before being printed. Sometimes more than one original is needed to create a complete copy – for example, if pages are missing or if a previous owner has annotated pages in ink. After collation of all the reprinted pages and any photographs, the books are then bound.

The entire process is something of a cottage industry, involving local printers and bookbinders in north Staffordshire. At the bottom of the title page of all copies there is a reference to the reprint being for the Willows Publishing Company, the date it was produced, and until 2010, the printers: J. H. Brookes Ltd of Hanley, Stoke-on-Trent.

Since 1997, the binding has been meticulously carried out by a company at Keele University now called Bookbinding Direct. From the 1935 facsimile produced in November 2010, they have also been responsible for the printing, using the latest technology that allows print on demand. This will give Willows greater control over their costs as they will not have to tie up money in stock, only printing copies (up to the limit) once orders are received.

It is remarkable that in an era of high inflation, prices of the Willows reprints when issued have only risen from £20 in 1983 for the 1885 edition of just 312 pages to £63 (tan) and £67 (original hardcloth) in 2011 for the bulky 1936 edition of 1,047 pages. In that same period, the cost of *Wisden* each year has increased from £9.95 in 1983 to £45 in 2010. Furthermore, Willows have given regular subscribers a discount as each new facsimile has been published.

Willows still hold stock of many *Wisden* reprints. For details, telephone David or Pauline Jenkins on 01785 814700 or email jenkins.willows@ntlworld.com.

Willows limited editions

1879	1,000
1880–1884	first reprint 500
1880–1884	second reprint 250
1885	un-numbered (not limited)
1886–1895	first reprint 500
1886–1895	second reprint 250
1896–1915	tan (300), original hardcloth (200); combined 500
1896–1899	second reprint, tan (100), original hardcloth (150); combined 250
1916	tan 1,000, original hardcloth 200
1917–1936	tan (300), original hardcloth (200); combined 500
1940	linen (300), original hardcloth (200); combined 500
1941–1945	linen (450), original hardcloth (300); combined 750

DUST JACKETS

Dust jackets were introduced for the hardback book from the 102nd edition (in 1965) onwards. These paper wrappers featured the woodcut, and the typography was in red, blue or green up to 1978, at which point it changed to brown. Dust jackets may be a little harder to find for the years 1965 and 1966; it is thought that some collectors ditched them in those first two years, believing the yellow covers spoilt the look of their run of brown volumes.

From an investment point of view, it is worth buying copies with the dust jacket in good condition. A jacketless *Wisden* of 1965 sells for less than one with a good dust jacket, but the price differential (about £50 with a jacket against £35 without) is nowhere near as great as with, for example, Ian Fleming's *The Man with the Golden Gun*, also published in 1965, where the difference is counted in thousands. The paper jackets generally reflect their age, and it is getting harder to find them in top condition. Nicks, tears, marks and discolouration all have an impact on the price, but the wrapper does protect the book itself and helps to keep the gilt bright.

Buyers should be cautious about imitation photocopied or digitally printed dust jackets masquerading as originals. Genuine dust jackets of the period 1965–81 are printed on thick yellow paper so will not be white on the reverse, which could be a tell-tale sign of a replica; however, the jackets for 1982–84 and 2003 are white on the reverse.

From 1994, the dust jackets were laminated to make them more hard wearing. In order to mitigate the problem of the easily damaged covers on editions from 1965 to 1993, Wisden produced a set of facsimile laminated dust jackets for these years. They were first advertised in the 1998 edition: 'Make your collection of *Wisdens* look like new' – and they do exactly that. First produced in three sets (and now in five, depending on whether you want covers for all the years or for shorter runs), they are advertised in *Wisden* every year. At £1 each if all 29 jackets are purchased, this is a cheap and effective way of rejuvenating a set. Original covers can then be stored away safely or wrapped inside the laminated replacements.

New collectors could buy the 1965 to 1993 editions cheaply without their original covers and then redecorate them with a 'replacement dust jacket' (they are clearly marked as such on the back cover). This provides a relatively cheap entry point for collecting hardbacks from 1965 onwards. The replacement jackets are all printed black on yellow and brighten up any collection.

In 2003, *Wisden* broke new ground for the 140th edition by featuring a player on the cover – Patrick Eagar's photograph of a jubilant Michael Vaughan, one of the Five Cricketers of the Year. This has become the established style, although it was not until 2008 that an action shot (of Kevin Pietersen) was used. Wary of upsetting traditionalists, Wisden also produce an old-style cover which could be claimed free in 2003. The following year, a charge of £2.50 was introduced and this rose to £3 in 2009. Completists will want to collect the alternative covers; details are given at the bottom of the rear flap.

Wisden have also produced special commemorative dust jackets in limited runs. In particular, they have done so for counties such as Yorkshire, Sussex and Durham to celebrate their Championship title of the previous season. Individual players have also ordered special covers for their benefit years, and sponsors and advertisers have commissioned their own bespoke covers.

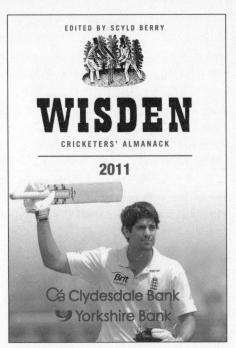

Year	Sponsor	Details
1999	Channel 4	Test match broadcasters for the first time
2000	PPP healthcare	Sponsors of the first two-division County Championship
2000	The Lord's Taverners	Marking the charity's golden anniversary
2000	Gray-Nicolls	Cricket bat manufacturers promoting 'Millennium Range'
2000–02	PricewaterhouseCoopers	Sponsors of cricket ratings
2001–02	Somerset CCC	
2002	Mark Ilott	Essex beneficiary
2002	Martin McCague	Kent beneficiary
2002	Yorkshire CCC	County Champions in 2001
2002	npower	Test match sponsors; a different cover was produced for each Test
2003	David Leatherdale	Worcestershire beneficiary
2004	Tom Moody	Worcestershire testimonial year
2004	Sussex CCC	County Champions for the first time in 2003
2005	Wolf Blass	Official wine of the Test match grounds
2006	St Lucia Tourist board	Hosting England team during 2007 World Cup
2009	Durham CCC	County champions in 2008
2011	Clydesdale Bank	Sponsors of 40-overs competition
2011	Gray-Nicolls	Cricket bat manufacturers

PHOTOGRAPHIC PLATES

The first photographic plate appeared in the 1889 *Wisden*, featuring portraits of 'six great bowlers of the year 1888'. The innovation was so well received that it was repeated the next year with portraits of 'nine great batsmen of the year 1889', and the photographic plate – generally of the Five Cricketers of the Year, which became an established feature from 1897 – appeared in every subsequent edition up to and including 1937. The years 1916 and 1917 were the only exceptions. From the 1938 edition onwards, a variety of photographs and text appear within a section printed on glossy paper.

In 1896, for the first time there is a full-length photograph of a player – W. G. Grace at the wicket, with bat raised. Others to have individual photographs were John Wisden (1913), Pelham Warner (1921), Jack Hobbs (1926) and Lord Harris (1933).

Collectors should always check that the photograph is present and correct. Unfortunately, there was a fashion at one time for the plate to be removed and framed, and the photo of Grace was most likely to receive this treatment. It was forgivable, perhaps, to desecrate a book costing a shilling or two (and because of the binding, the photo page could also fall loose), but the lack of the photograph now can prove very costly, as the price of an incomplete copy is greatly reduced.

The photograph was protected by tissue paper in copies up to 1915. Lack of the tissue paper is not a concern today for all but the most fastidious collector. Foxing on the photograph, which is commonly seen in *Wisdens* of a century or more ago, has to be accepted in books of that vintage.

INSERTS IN *WISDEN*

ERRATUM SLIPS

1920, on page 11 of the second section: 'In the description of the Oxford and Cambridge match – M.C.C. section – there is a mistake. Eight old blues took part in the match. By an oversight the Hon. F.S.G. Calthorpe, of Cambridge, was not included among them.'

1923, on page 221 of the first section: 'Cricket Records – page 220. Below W. Ward, in Largest Individual Scores made at Lord's, read: 277 (not out), Hendren (E.), Middlesex v Kent 1922.'

1926, on the page opposite the portrait of Jack Hobbs is a photo credit: 'The portrait of Hobbs has been reproduced from a photograph by the Central News Agency.' The omission of this credit to the agency could have proved expensive for the publishers.

1933, in the Births and Deaths section on page 77, gives W.R. Hammond's date of birth, plus an entry for the Marquis of Hamilton, later 2nd Duke of Abercorn, who was President of MCC in 1874. A line of type giving the date of Hammond's birth had been transposed into the details of the Marquis of Hamilton in the opposite column.

QUALITY CONTROL

Other small inserts that appear on page 17 in hardbacks between 1927 and 1935 are slips, variously white, blue or yellow, with a number like a raffle ticket and the words: 'Examined by No. 136 [for example]. If any cause for complaint, please quote number above. B & M., W.' These initials referred to the printers, Balding & Mansell of Wisbech. The ticket also appears on page 13 in the 1937 limp edition with the initials S. H. B. Ltd when the printers were S. H. Benson Ltd. These tickets have no bearing on prices.

BOOKMARKS

From 1933 to 1939 the limp editions included a bookmark in the form of a bat which was attached to the spine with a yellow cord. Many are missing because the narrowness of the bat's handle meant they were easily torn. Sale descriptions of limp copies for these years should state whether the bookmark is present or not. For a copy to be described as in 'fine' condition, it must contain this bookmark.

REBINDS

Many paperback copies have been rebound by collectors and retailers over the years. Ideally, the original paper wrappers are to be found incorporated within the new hard covers. However, often they are missing either because it was the practice of the binder to remove the wrappers, or the wrappers were too badly damaged to be preserved: indeed, it may have been due to some damage that the owner decided to have their copy rebound in the first place.

Rebound copies containing both covers and all the advertisement pages – also sometimes omitted at the rebinding stage – command a much higher price than those without the original wrappers and with pages missing. But hardbacks after 1896, if rebound, are worth much less than if left in their original cloth binding, provided they are in good condition.

Binders often trimmed the book, occasionally by so much that the text either comes perilously close to the edge of the page, or worse, is actually affected.

The publishers themselves also did special rebinds, and copies bound by Wisden throw up some interesting examples: they have created 'hardback' copies for years before 1896 when hardback editions were introduced. These have been seen going back to the 1890 edition.

Editions for 1892 to 1895 rebound in the publisher's cloth sold at a Gorringes auction in Lewes, Sussex, in September 2008 for £650 and £750. They looked as good as the real thing, but the following original 1896 and 1897 editions then sold for a hammer price of £17,000 each.

Liverpool Cricket Club had copies rebound by the publishers, and again, these created some pre-1896 hardbacks. We have also seen a 1951 linen edition rebound for Northamptonshire CCC with the gilding on the cover in the style of the pre-1938 hardbacks. Just as bizarre is an 1884 copy rebound with the name of Sydney Pardon on the cover, seven years before he became editor – not so much a fake as an aberration.

One way to detect Wisden's own rebinds is to check whether the endpapers are blank rather than carrying advertisements as in the authentic hardbacks. Because we have no definite information about the early print runs, there may be another explanation for the hardback *Wisdens* that do not carry ads on the endpapers. Book dealer Christopher Saunders (see page 313) suggests the following theory: 'I have always thought that a very small number of hardbacks would be printed for sale, with others produced to order. This is partially backed up by the numbers that appear with plain yellow endpapers. I assumed that Wisden produced a certain number of endpapers for hardbacks, used them as required but did not reprint, so if an order for a hardback came in towards the end of the season when printed endpapers had run out, then they would bind with plain endpapers. I have seen copies with one endpaper plain and one printed.'

Wisden also produced copies in green limp calf covers for the MCC. These have a gilt title on the spine and 'M.C.C.' on the cover. The page edges are also in green to match the boards. Copies were sold on behalf of MCC at a Christie's auction in November 2010.

The multitude of colours and bindings possible means that a collection with rebinds will have a variegated appearance on the bookshelf. On the other hand, collectors who have themselves had their copies rebound have achieved a uniform, and often very handsome, line-up for their library. Although these sets occasionally come on the market, they are most likely to be broken up in order to achieve the best sale price as collectors compete for their individual missing years.

RESTORING *WISDEN*

If John Wisden had known that his shilling booklets would be so coveted a century and a half later, he would surely have made them more durable. Not until the hardback edition was launched in 1896 did the Almanack become sturdy enough to withstand a long life of reading and reference. Consequently, many an older *Wisden* has suffered (not least from visits to damp English cricket grounds in April) and the collector is naturally interested in their preservation and restoration.

Although the art of the bookbinder may seem archaic and even mystical, a surprising amount can be done to renovate a mournful volume, and perhaps even increase its value. Not all remedies involve rebinding: many common faults can be simply corrected, some even on a do-it-yourself basis.

The first thing to remember is that making any alteration to a collectable book will have an effect on its value. Many collectors and dealers frown upon any type of restoration; this is why a pristine original *Wisden* will always command a high price. It is also worth asking whether restoration is strictly necessary. Some editions, particularly 1947 and 1948, used poor-quality materials, and little can be done to restore browned pages and bumped edges. It can be just as pleasing to own a 'rustic' original as to attempt to turn the clock back sixty years.

The traditional way to revive a battered *Wisden* is to have it rebound. The cost varies dramatically with each bindery, and it is recommended to get several quotes before making a decision. It is usually cheaper in the long run to have several books rebound at once, in matching style. Many bookbinders also offer courses in their trade, and with a little time and equipment it is possible to become reasonably proficient in the basics.

Bindings may be of cloth boards or leather. Colours vary: sometimes the brown of the clothboard editions is copied, but red, blue, green and black are all to be found. For leather, goatskin (also known as Morocco) or calf is used: the bindings may be quarter, half or full, with the page edges gilt.

When taking a book to be rebound, it is advisable to have a prepared list of questions and specific requirements:

1. Will the binder trim your book? Thankfully, trimming catastrophes are mostly a thing of the past, but *Wisden* was not immune to production errors which left some text very close to the page edge. Trimming gives the pages a uniform size and a clean, crisp edge, but if any text is cut away, the book can become almost worthless in an instant. A *Wisden* should not be trimmed unless absolutely necessary.

2. Will your binder use a sympathetic brown cloth? A bright-blue *Wisden* may look attractive on the shelf but it could be difficult to sell in the future.

3. What are the options for gilt titles? Again, a choice that is sympathetic to the original hardbacks will be attractive and more desirable to the collector. Be sure to spell out exactly what you want: there would be nothing worse than receiving back a copy of *Wisdom's Cricketing Annual* because this was left to chance. Think about the future of your own collection too. Details such as whether the spine text runs top-to-bottom or bottom-to-top should be confirmed beforehand.

An alternative that has become popular in recent years is having a *Wisden* fitted with exact facsimile paper covers rather than cloth boards. This helps to standardise a bookshelf, particularly when collecting original paperbacks. Facsimile covers are attractive but not as durable as a hardbound copy, and only time will tell what effect this style has on the true value of the book. If the *Wisden* has its paper covers intact and in good condition, it is possible to attach colour-matched facsimile paper to the spine. The benefit here is that the copy can withstand normal handling but has been altered as little as possible. *Wisden* restoration experts have produced facsimile advertisement pages, which is particularly helpful when 'converting' a rebind back into a paperback if the original covers and adverts have all been removed. Care must be taken, though, to ensure that the cost of restoration does not exceed the book's value.

From 1965 the yellow dust jacket gave the Almanack a vibrant new image, yet brought its own problems and solutions to the collector. Dust jackets from 1965 to 1993 are easily damaged and can discolour with age. A pristine dust jacket brings a price premium, but damaged jackets can be repaired, although not by Sellotape which will cause irreparable harm. Professional restorers use colour-matched card and acid-free adhesives to repair nicks and tears from behind the wrapper.

Prevention can be better than cure: use transparent sleeving popular with libraries and specialist bookshops such as Adaptaroll or TrimSleeve. Around 40 dust jackets can be protected with one £20 roll. The sleeving may be removed later without causing any damage.

Dust jackets have a significant bonus in that they protect a book's gilt lettering from fading. Hardbacks until 1932 were blocked in genuine gold leaf, but from 1933 the bronze or imitation gilt is prone to becoming dull or faded. Due to wartime economy, the 1916 and early 1940s editions used cheaper materials and those with bright lettering are now rare. It is possible to restore the lettering: gilt is reapplied by hand to the indentations and sealed with a special coating. This is a job for a highly skilled expert, although the cost is modest at around £15 per book spine.

Regilding work can look very convincing and the collector should be wary when purchasing books which look 'too good to be true' for that particular year. Other than comparing it with a book known to be original, it is somewhat akin to spotting a counterfeit pound coin. The best way to identify regilding is a bright yet uneven *patina* to the gilt, and lettering which looks far too sharp and distinct for the age. Editions after 1949 are rarely regilded as it is cheaper simply to wait for a better original copy.

The photographic plate of Five Cricketers of the Year is a celebrated part of the early editions. *Wisden* were not the first to issue photographs in their books: *James Lillywhite's Cricketers' Annual* had been including portraits and team photographs since 1876, pasted in as a frontispiece. By the time of *Wisden's* first plate in 1889, *Lillywhite's* had already changed to a photomechanical print, similar to that used in the 1918 *Almanack*. But *Wisden's* photographs were so successful that they are sometimes missing from the book, presumably framed or sold on as antique images.

A *Wisden* loses much of its value without the photograph. Facsimile plates can be made, even with the protective tissue. These are fairly obvious facsimiles – it is possible but extremely difficult to replicate a 100-year-old photograph – but the repaired book will be complete, and also easier to sell should the collector be upgrading. Prices start at around £15. It should be noted that an original, however poor, is always preferable to a facsimile.

The photographs themselves can be subject to deterioration. Foxing cannot be restored except at considerable expense, and a faded photograph must be accepted as part of the ageing process. Plates from 1905 to 1915 were made on a fibre-based material, and whilst more stable, sometimes the surface silver can tarnish, but this can be fixed. Occasionally, especially with former public library books, the plate is misbound at the front of the book. Depending on the adhesive used, it can be removed to the correct position. Real photographs gave way to photomechanically printed images from 1918, and there are fewer faults from then on.

An altogether trickier issue is what to do with a valuable early hardback lacking the photograph plate. It is possible to remove an otherwise excellent plate from a cheaper rebind and attach it to the hardback; after all, both items are original and were made at the same time. However, this practice is largely frowned upon by collectors. It may be as well to take advice from a restorer on the best course of action to repair such a hardback.

Other repairs that can be carried out by a restorer include removal of library stamps and labels, improving damaged cloth boards, and correction of the spine curvature common in early linen editions. It is also possible to recreate in exact facsimile the bat bookmarks found in the Almanack from 1933 to 1939, which rarely survive intact.

Some minor repairs such as to the hinges can be carried out by a confident owner, but the most important piece of advice – which we therefore repeat – is to keep Sellotape well away from an ailing *Wisden*. The same applies to glue-sticks and superglue; the correct glue must be acid-free. And it's best to practise first on an unwanted book – definitely not a *Wisden!*

- Peter Taylor at Aardvark Books specialises in restoration work. Tel: 01522 722671; email pete@aardvarkcricketbooks.co.uk
- Syston Bindery offers restoration, repairs and complete bindings. The company is responsible for the binding in full Morocco with gilt finishing of the limited edition leatherbound *Wisden*. Tel: 0116 253 9552; email: paul@systonbindery.co.uk.
- Sangorski & Sutcliffe, established in 1901, is a company name often seen inside early rebound *Wisdens* and is still in business today as part of Shepherds. An informative website covers every aspect of binding, as well as giving an indication of current charges (www.bookbinding.co.uk).

SIGNED COPIES

Leslie Gutteridge wrote in his 1963 history of *Wisden*, 'What a pity it is that all owners of books do not put their signatures on a fly-leaf! It is far more interesting than a bookplate and takes up less room. It is most interesting to learn who have been the previous owners and to trace them through the relevant volumes.' He goes on:

> I have, for example, seen the signatures of Haygarth, C.B. Fry, R. Daft and even Horatio Bottomley (once rightly mis-spelled Hotairio) on *Wisdens,* and perhaps even more rewarding are the signatures of such relatively little-known players as W. Rashleigh. Perseverance produced the information that he played for Oxford University in 1886 and that he made 21 and 107 against Cambridge University. That he made 49 against a strong M.C.C. side which included Studd, Hearne and Webbe and that in seven matches that year, he had 13 innings and made 343 runs.

> Did Rashleigh own only the one copy of *Wisden* in which his name appeared to such advantage, or was he a genuine devotee and are the rest of his volumes with his bold signature still in existence somewhere?

So many of these inscriptions have a story to tell. Take as an example a particular 1924 *Wisden* we have come across, signed by one W.N. McBride who played for Hampshire from 1925–29. In 1923 McBride was at Westminster School, and that year's report of public school cricket contains a glowing mention of him: 'A man who can score three consecutive centuries in school matches must clearly be ranked as one of the personalities of the year.' Reading those words today, in the very copy owned by Walter Nelson McBride, the sense of pride is almost tangible.

The famous signature of W.G. Grace was inscribed in many of the copies he owned, greatly increasing their value when they came to auction in 1996. Pelham Warner and John Arlott also enhanced their copies – and the ultimate sale prices of those copies – by signing the books in their collections.

In more recent times, there has been a trend for the Five Cricketers of the Year to be asked to autograph their portraits, but copies do not have to be signed by cricketers to be of interest. 'Niel' bought a 1912 *Wisden* because it contained a report of his brother's season at Rugby School. He gave it to their father for his birthday: *Wishing Daddy a very happy birthday, and many happy returns of the day from Niel. July 5th 1912*. Below that inscription in different handwriting is the memorial: *Dulce et decorum est pro patria mori. Finis coronat opus. 20 July 1916.* Niel had died of injuries sustained on the first day of the Somme. Another 1912 *Wisden* is signed by Brian Gardiner Whitfield who in 1956 published *A classical handbook for sixth forms*, a Latin and Greek grammar. He would have translated what Wilfred Owen termed the 'old lie': 'It is sweet and right to die for your country. The end crowns the work.'

Many editors signed copies of the books they put together. A 2009 catalogue issued by Christopher Saunders Books (*see* page 313) has an 1873 *Wisden* dedicated by the compiler, W.H. Knight, to umpire R. Thoms and dated Jan 7, 1873. A copy of the 1916 hardback, inscribed by the editor Sydney H. Pardon to future editor Sydney James Southerton, was listed by Sportspages (*see* page 314) at £9,500 in January 2011; at the same time, a 1922 hardback inscribed by Pardon to his immediate successor, C. Stewart Caine, was for sale through wisdenauction.com for the price of £750. The 1936 Preface was signed by Wilfrid Brookes, while Hubert Preston presented a 1941 *Wisden* (nominally edited by Haddon Whitaker) to Reg Hayter *with all good wishes, December 1941*. Norman Preston inscribed a 1959 copy *To Miss Voller: A souvenir of many hours at the typewriter* – Pat Voller being the first woman to work for the company.

Some inscriptions give a clear idea of *Wisden's* publication date. Preston's dedication to Hayter, dated December 1941, marks the latest the Almanack has appeared – a delay that Whitaker blamed on 'the sustained efforts of the enemy to prevent publication'. More often, the dates show how early *Wisden* appeared: a hundred years ago, January or February was the norm; before that, it was 'published every Christmas', as *Wisden's* own advertisements (see, for example, the 1899 edition) announced.

MY UNCLE'S WISDENS

'What *are* all these funny old books?'

That is how *Wisden* headlined an article in 2007 on the subject of an astonishing listing that appeared on eBay in November 2006. 'I have recently inherited my uncle's collection of books,' began the post, 'which includes a large number of *Wisden Almanacks*.'

As it turned out, the *Wisden*-collecting world had never witnessed such an understatement. All told, there were 504 volumes making up one extraordinary lot. As well as complete sets, there were around 240 duplicates.

The seller's uncle, the listing explained, had lived in Church Stretton, Shropshire. But no one, not even the dealers whose livelihoods depend on the tracking and tracing of rare *Wisdens*, seemed to have had an inkling of the treasures he had amassed there. And the wording on eBay suggested that the vendor – a woman in Surrey – certainly had no idea of the value of her inheritance.

'Oddly, some years have no duplicates,' the eBay listing continued, 'whilst other years have up to eight copies! Why he had so many duplicates is a mystery. For instance, there are loads of thin copies from both wars … six for 1916.' The 1916 *Wisden*, which contains the obituaries of both W.G. Grace and Victor Trumper, together with page after page of names of those slain in the war, is the most collectable of all the 20th-century editions and in good condition sells for around £10,000.

The lot had an opening bid of £1. It was no surprise that the seller was inundated with enquiries, to the extent that she was forced to remove the sale from the internet. The fate of the 500-plus volumes became the subject of intense speculation. One dealer was rumoured to have had an offer of £250,000 turned down; another forecast that the collection would surface at a major London auction house.

In fact, the eBay listing was a hoax, perpetrated by a collector who had become disenchanted during his dealings with a *Wisden* bookseller. His identity is known to only two or three people; he confessed to them in confidence. The listing, he explained, was not made in malice: it was more of a practical joke, but it got out of hand the moment the books and their 'provenance' were described on eBay. Inevitably, the 'niece' in Surrey was contacted by several dealers; interestingly, 'she' received widely different offers and advice. To that extent, the hoaxer may have learnt something about each of them. He has since kept a low profile.

MIND THE LANGUAGE

Wisden was again enmeshed in controversy when it reported verbatim in the 2010 edition the words of an England player who had been ranting on twitter. The *Daily Telegraph* was duly enraged, and informed readers that '*Wisden's* hallowed pages turn blue':

> *Wisden* may be an institution, but that doesn't prevent it from engaging with the modern world. The new edition features a section called 'Cricket on twitter', complete with a supposedly unprintable four-letter word – the first, in fact, that has appeared in cricket's bible. However, the 'Cricket on twitter' section does appear on page 1628, so only dedicated readers are likely to stumble across it.

Two days later, the same newspaper returned to the subject in a comment piece headlined 'Swear words in *Wisden*? It's just not cricket.' Max Davidson harrumphed:

It was only a matter of time, I suppose. Four-letter words have become so ubiquitous that to see them printed sans asterisks in *Wisden*, the bible of cricket, is not going to cause many apoplexies, even in the Long Room at Lord's. But as one of the denizens of the Long Room, an MCC member man and boy, a dyed-in-the-wool cricket traditionalist, still shuddering at those pictures of English teams playing in Dubai with pink balls, wearing comedy pyjamas, I cannot help issuing a bleat of protest.

According to the 2010 *Wisden Cricketers' Almanack*, published this week, England fast bowler Tim Bresnan has recently sent a post on twitter, laying into someone who has been rude about him. His post deploys the f-word, which is fine to me. One likes England fast bowlers to have fire in their belly. In fact, if Bresnan wants to deploy the f-word against Australian batsmen, that is also fine by me.

If he takes my advice, he will lay off the f-word when addressing umpires, women and children, but it is a free country, and I would defend to the death his right to swear like a trooper, particularly on flat pitches on hot days.

But why does *Wisden*, which is not compiled on a hot day, and boasts literary standards which no other sporting publication can match, feel obliged to transcribe his words verbatim, as if they were Holy Writ? The genius of *Wisden*, beloved by generations of cricket-lovers, is its ability to move with the times without compromising its core values. Thirty years ago, it was still quite a dry publication: page after page of scorecards and batting averages and bowling analyses and little-known records from the 1920s. But it has entered the 21st century with aplomb, freshening up its act, and throwing wit and humour into the mix.

If a pigeon knocks off the bails while the batsman is distracted by an exploding kettle in the tea tent, *Wisden* will record the incident in scholarly detail, relishing the fact that the batsman is called Partridge, and the bowler Sparrow, and drawing readers' attention to a similar incident at Old Trafford in 1876.

The *Almanack* is an Aladdin's cave of quirky happenings, quintessentially English in character, and described in lapidary prose. And I am not sure that foul-mouthed fast bowlers issuing crudely monosyllabic posts on twitter belong in its pages. They debase the currency.

What had not been noticed is that this was not the first time *Wisden* had published a swear word verbatim. In 2007, it had reported the racial abuse shouted by Australian spectators which led to their removal from the Adelaide Oval. The words may have been buried deep in the book, but remarkably, not one complaint was received in the editorial office.

Nor was that the first instance. The year before, the obituary of Kerry Packer recalled that he had once been clinically dead after suffering a heart attack. He subsequently announced in no uncertain terms that there was '******* nothing' on the other side.

Wisden has never lost its power to surprise – for those who read its pages carefully.

A HISTORY OF *WISDEN*

Leslie Gutteridge's history in the 100ᵗʰ edition of *Wisden* in 1963 contained a vast amount of information which is updated here and extended.

PUBLISHERS

1864–1867	John Wisden & Co Ltd
1868	Wisden and Maynard
1869	Wisden & Co
1870–1937	John Wisden & Co Ltd
1938–43	J. Whitaker & Sons Ltd, for John Wisden & Co Ltd
1944–78	Sporting Handbooks Ltd, for John Wisden & Co Ltd
1979–80	Queen Anne Press, Macdonald and Jane's Publishing Group Ltd, for John Wisden & Co Ltd
1981	Queen Anne Press, Macdonald Futura Ltd, for John Wisden & Co Ltd
1982–1984	Queen Anne Press, Macdonald & Co (Publishers) Ltd, for John Wisden & Co Ltd
1985–2008	John Wisden & Co Ltd
2009–10	John Wisden & Co, an imprint of A & C Black Publishers Ltd
2011 to date	John Wisden & Co, an imprint of Bloomsbury Publishing Ltd

OWNERS SINCE 1985

1985	McCorquodale plc
1986–87	Jointly owned by Grays of Cambridge (International) Ltd and McCorquodale plc
1988	Jointly owned by Grays of Cambridge (International) Ltd and Norton Opax plc
1991–93	Jointly owned by Grays of Cambridge (International) Ltd and Bowater plc
1994–2003	J. Paul Getty
2004–08	Mark H. Getty
2009 to date	Bloomsbury Publishing Ltd

COMPILERS AND EDITORS

1864–69	It is likely that W.H. Crockford and W.H. Knight were concerned. *Scores & Biographies* (XIV-xxviii) refers to a list of mourners at John Wisden's funeral in 1884: 'Also Mr. W.H. Crockford, the compiler of several numbers of *Wisden's Cricketer's Almanack*.'
1870–79	W. H. Knight (16 editions)
1880–86	George H. West (7)

1887–90	Charles F. Pardon (4)
1891–1925	Sydney H. Pardon (35)
1926–33	C. Stewart Caine (8)
1934–35	Sydney J. Southerton (2)
1936–39	Wilfred H. Brookes (4)
1940–43	Haddon Whitaker (4)
1944–51	Hubert Preston (8)
1952–80	Norman Preston (29)
1981–86	John Woodcock (6)
1987–92	Graeme Wright
1993–2000	Matthew Engel
2001–2	Graeme Wright (8)
2003	Tim de Lisle (1)
2004–7	Matthew Engel (12)
2008–11	Scyld Berry (4)
2012–	Lawrence Booth

From 1887 to 1965 the material was compiled by staff of the Cricket Reporting Agency, while the editorial responsibility was undertaken by one of its partners, except for 1940–43, in the uncertainty of the early war years. From 1965 the Cricket Reporting Agency was merged with the Press Association, the last former Agency editor being Norman Preston.

PRINTERS

1864–86	W. H. Crockford
1887–93	Not known
1894–96	Wyman & Sons
1897–35	Balding & Mansell
1936–37	S.H. Benson Ltd
1938–40	Purnell & Sons
1941–63	Unwin Brothers Ltd
1964–78	William Clowes & Sons, Ltd
1979–81	Spottiswoode Ballantyne Ltd
1982–84	Hazell, Watson and Viney Ltd
1985–87	Spottiswoode Ballantyne Ltd
1988–94	William Clowes Ltd
1995–4	Clays Ltd, St Ives plc
2005–8	William Clowes Ltd
2009– *	CPI William Clowes

No name of a printer is stated from 1887–93. However, there appears to be no difference in the typography between the issues of 1889–93 and those printed by Wyman from 1894–96. It is therefore probable that Wyman were the printers from 1889 onwards. There are only minor differences in the 1887 and 1888 issues and it is possible that these were produced by a different printer. It is also quite conceivable that the printers were again Wyman. The publishers lost all their records of this period during the Second World War. The printer's name does not appear in the cloth boards edition from 1938–62, but is given in the limp cloth edition.

PRINT RUNS

'It would be fascinating to know the quantity printed of the early years,' wrote Gutteridge, but he was unable to trace any printing orders earlier than 1936. It is widely acknowledged that he was best placed of anyone to discover this information. The following table shows the number printed in the years from 1936, as given in the 1963 *Wisden*:

	limp	cloth
1936	8,500	total, no separate cloth boards figure known
1937	8,000	total, no separate cloth boards figure known
1938	12,000	not known
1939	12,000	not known
1940	8,000	not known
1941	3,200	800 (war paper restriction)
1942	4,100	900 (war paper restriction)
1943	5,600	1,400 (war paper restriction)
1944	5,600	1,400 (war paper restriction)
1945	6,500	1,500 (war paper restriction)
1946	11,000	5,000 (war paper restriction)
1947	14,000	6,000 (restrictions eased)
1948	14,500	6,500 (restrictions eased)
1949	21,000	10,500 (restriction ended)
1955	15,500	11,000
1962	11,000	10,000 (average sales)

Gutteridge wrote: '1949 was the peak. With other consumer goods in stringently short supply, and sport one of the few outlets, sport and writing about sport boomed as never before. The boom slowly diminished, but even in 1955 the limp edition sold 15,500 copies and the cloth boards edition had increased to 11,000 copies. Today [1963] the sale is steady, averaging 11,000 of the limp edition and 10,000 of the cloth boards edition.' Of the 1963 edition, *The Cricket Quarterly* of January 1964 stated: 'These three printings must have amounted to hardly less than 40,000 copies, though we do not know the exact figure.'

We know that sales of the 2006 Almanack topped 50,000 which, as Matthew Engel wrote in his 2007 Preface, was believed to be unprecedented: 'We can't be certain because the company's books up to 1936 were destroyed in the war. But we do know that the print run in those days was much lower (which is one reason old *Wisdens* are valuable), so we think it must be true.'

Year	Format	Price	Format	Price	Format	Price	Format	Price
1864–95	paper cover	1/-	cloth boards	2/-				
1896–1914	paper cover	1/-	cloth boards	2/6				
1915–17	paper cover	1/6	cloth boards	3/-				
1918	paper cover	2/-	cloth boards	4/-				
1919–20	paper cover	2/6	cloth boards	7/6				
1921–37	paper cover	5/-	cloth boards	7/6				
1938–42	limp linen	5/-	cloth boards	8/6				
1943–46	limp linen	6/-	cloth boards	9/6				
1947	limp linen	7/6	cloth boards	12/-				
1948–50	limp linen	9/6	cloth boards	12/6				
1951	limp linen	10/6	cloth boards	15/-				
1952–55	limp linen	12/6	cloth boards	17/6				
1956	limp linen	15/-	cloth boards	18/6				
1957–59	limp linen	16/-	cloth boards	21/-				
1960–61	limp linen	18/6	cloth boards	22/6				
1962	limp cover	20/-	cloth boards	25/-				
1963–65	limp cover	22/6	cloth boards	27/6				
1966–67	limp cover	23/6	cloth boards	30/-				
1968–69	limp cover	25/-	cloth boards	35/-				
1970	limp cover	30/-	cloth boards	£1.95				
1971	limp cover	£1.65	cloth boards	£2.25				
1972–73	limp cover	£2	cloth boards	£2.50				
1974	limp cover	£2.25	cloth boards	£3				
1975	limp cover	£2.75	cloth boards	£3.50				
1976	limp cover	£3	cloth boards	£4.25				
1977	limp cover	£3.75	cloth boards	£4.85				
1978	limp cover	£4.25	cloth boards	£5.75				
1979	limp cover	£4.75	cased edition.					

1980	limp cover	£5.75	cased edition	£6.75				
1981	limp cover	£6.95	cased edition	£7.95				
1982	limp cover	£7.95	cased edition	£8.95				
1983	limp cover	£8.95	cased edition	£9.95				
1984	limp cover	£9.95	cased edition	£11.95				
1985	soft cover	£9.95	cased edition	£11.95				
1986	soft cover	£12.50	cased edition	£14.50				
1987	soft cover	£13.95	cased edition	£15.95				
1988	soft cover	£14.50	cased edition	£16.50				
1989	soft cover	£14.95	cased edition	£16.95				
1990	soft cover	£15.50	cased edition	£18.50				
1991	soft cover	£16.75	cased edition	£20				
1992	soft cover	£18.50	cased edition	£21.50				
1993	soft cover	£19.50	cased edition	£22.50				
1994	soft cover	£20	cased edition	£22.50				
1995	soft cover	£23.50	cased edition	£23.50	leatherbound	£200		
1996	soft cover	£24.50	cased edition	£24.50	leatherbound	£200		
1997	soft cover	£26	cased edition	£26	leatherbound	£200		
1998	soft cover	£25.50	cased edition	£27.50	leatherbound	£200		
1999	soft cover	£28	cased edition	£28	leatherbound	£200		
2000–1	soft cover	£29.99	cased edition	£29.99	leatherbound	£225		
2002–3	soft cover	£35	cased edition	£35	leatherbound	£225		
2004	soft cover	£35	cased edition	£35	leatherbound	£230		
2005	soft cover	£36	cased edition	£36	leatherbound	£235		
2006	soft cover	£38	cased edition	£38	leatherbound	£240	large format	£50
2007–8	soft cover	£40	cased edition	£40	leatherbound	£245	large format	£50
2009	soft cover	£45	cased edition	£45	leatherbound	£250	large format	£55
2010–11	soft cover	£45	cased edition	£45	leatherbound	£260	large format	£55

No price is given on the title page from 1891–38 and nowhere at all on the 1938 edition except on the rare red paper band originally wrapped around linen copies. From 1939 the price reappears on the title page.

Five Cricketers of the Year appeared in the following issues: 1897, 1898, 1902–08, 1910–11, 1914–15, 1922-1923, 1925, 1927–37. From 1938 many other illustrations have been given together with the Five Cricketers of the Year. No portraits appeared in the war issues for 1916–17 and 1941–46. In other years before 1938 the following illustrations have appeared:

1889	Six Great Bowlers
1890	Nine Great Batsmen
1891	Five Wicket Keepers
1892	Five Great Bowlers
1893	Five Batsmen of the Year
1894	Five All-round Cricketers
1895	Five Young Batsmen of the Year
1896	W.G. Grace
1899	Five Great Players of the Season
1900	Five Cricketers of the Season
1901	Mr. R.E. Foster and 4 Yorkshire Cricketers
1909	Lord Hawke and 4 Cricketers of the Year
1912	Five Members of MCC to Australia
1913	John Wisden
1918	Five School Bowlers of the Year
1919	Five Public School Cricketers of the Year
1920	Five Batsmen of the Year
1921	P.F. Warner
1924	Five Bowlers of the Year
1926	J.B. Hobbs
1933	Lord Harris

SECOND EDITIONS

Second issues appeared from 1889–1901. They are the same as the ordinary issues save only for: (i) The additional words on the front cover 'Second Issue.' (ii) The price 2/- paper (3/- cloth boards from 1898) instead of the normal 1/-, (iii) The price and words 'Second Issue' on the title pages of the 1889 and 1890 issues.

The 1963 edition ran to three impressions: it was published on April 19th, with a second impression dated May and a third June in which several printing errors apparent in the initial run were corrected. However, the contents table was not corrected: it states that the photograph of S.H. Pardon is on page 74 (it is on page 77) and 'A History of Wisden' by L.E.S. Gutteridge is on page 75 (it starts on page 74). The second and third impressions are marked as such at the bottom of page 1127 where the name of the printer (Unwin Brothers Ltd) is given.

The linen edition only of 1999 was reprinted as extra copies were required in conjunction with the International Cricket Captain computer game.

There were second editions in 2006 and 2010, both of which had minor text amendments; the second impression was marked as such on the verso page.

STYLE OF FRONT COVER OF LIMP EDITIONS

1864–69	first style (1865 slightly different from 1864)
1870–77	second style
1878–80	second style – *first variation*
1881–84	second style – *second variation*
1885	third style
1886	third style – *first variation*
1887	fourth style
1888	fourth style – *first variation*
1889–96	fourth style – *second variation*
1897–1935	fifth style
1936–37	fifth style – *first variation*
1938–62	sixth style
1963	seventh style (unique special edition)
1964–71	sixth style
1972–78	sixth style – *first variation* (coloured text)
1979–97	sixth style
1998–2002	eighth style
2003–	ninth style (pictorial covers, different for each year)

STYLE OF LETTERING ON SPINE OF LIMP EDITIONS

Title vertically reading from the bottom:

1887–95	first style
1896–1907	first style – *first variation* (slightly bolder)
1908–35	first style – *second variation* (slightly larger)
1936–37	first style – *third variation* (slightly larger again)
1938–40	second style
1941–46	second style – *first variation* (name and year in smaller size)
1947–48	second style – *second variation* (year only in smaller size)
1949–62	second style

Title horizontally:

1963	Third style (unique special edition)
1964–71	Fourth style
1972–78	Fourth style – *first variation* (coloured text)

1979	Fourth style – *second variation* (change of publisher)
1980	Fourth style – *third variation* (font change, change of publisher)
1981	Fourth style – *fourth variation* (change of publisher)
1982–84	Fourth style – *fifth variation* (change of publisher)
1985–2002	Fourth style – *sixth variation* (change of publisher)
2003–	Fourth style – *seventh variation* (addition of woodcut logo)

Some copies of the 1901 first (but not second) issues had 1900 on the spine, covered over with a label bearing the correct date. The 1904–05 paper spines bore the words 'Almanac' not the usual 'Almanack'. The unusual spelling does not occur on the front cover nor on the spine of the cloth edition.

STYLE OF BRASSES ON FRONT COVER OF CLOTH BOARD EDITIONS

1896	First style
1897–1902	first style – *first variation*
1903–07	second style
1908	dirst style – *first variation*
1909–28	second style
1929–37	second style – *first variation* (change of address)
1938–40	third style
1941–64	third style – *first variation* (year is slightly larger)
1965–75	third style – *second variation* (year is slightly finer)
1976–84	third style – *third variation* (year is slightly bolder)
1985–2000	third style – *fourth variation* (font change to year)
2001–06	fourth style
2007–	fifth style

From 1896 to 1937 the yellow front and back covers appear as end papers and are faced with advertisements on the insides of the front and back cloth boards.

STYLE OF BRASSES ON SPINE OF CLOTH BOARD EDITIONS

1896–1937	first style – title vertically reading from bottom
1938–40	second style – title horizontally; at bottom number of issue
1941–48	third style – title vertically reading from top
1949–62	second style – title horizontally; at bottom publisher's name – *first variation*
1963	fourth style – title larger in bold; addition of number of issue
1964	fourth style – font and minor layout changes – *first variation*

1965–67	fourth style – font change to number of issue – *second variation*
1968–78	fourth style – font change to number of issue – *third variation*
1979	fourth style – variation due to change of publisher – *fourth variation*
1980	fourth style – variation due to change of publisher – *fifth variation*
1981	fourth style – variation due to change of publisher – *sixth variation*
1982–84	fourth style – variation due to change of publisher – *seventh variation*
1985–2000	fourth style – font changes; change of publisher – *eighth variation*
2001–03	fourth style – font and layout changes – *ninth variation*
2004–	fourth style – minor layout changes – *tenth variation*

COVER DESIGNS

1938	Linen covers were introduced which featured the Ravilious woodcut
1963	The 100th edition was celebrated on the linen cover with a one-off design
1998	The size of the woodcut on the linen cover and dust jacket was reduced and the contents typeface increased
2003	Pictorial covers were introduced and featured:
2003	Michael Vaughan
2004	Ricky Ponting and Steve Waugh
2005	The England huddle
2006	Andrew Flintoff and Shane Warne
2007	Shane Warne
2008	Kevin Pietersen
2009	Andrew Flintoff
2010	Andrew Strauss
2011	Alastair Cook

COLOUR OF LIMP COVERS

1864–71	pale buff
1872–77	pale pink/buff
1878–79	glossy paper; pale yellow/buff
1880–82	pale yellow/buff
1883–86	pale pink/buff
1887–1937	bright yellow which can fade to buff
1938–56	limp cloth in bright yellow with little or no fading
1941–46	some war issues rather brown
1957–	cloth-effect soft card covers in bright yellow

1965	limp	black	D/J (name, year, publisher) black (edition) green
1966	limp	black	D/J (name, publisher) black (year, edition) red
1967	limp	black	D/J (name, publisher) black (year, edition) sky blue
1968	limp	black	D/J (name, publisher) red (year, edition) black
1969	limp	black	D/J (name, publisher) sky blue (year, edition) red
1970	limp	black	D/J (name, edition) black (year, publisher) red
1971	limp	black	D/J (name, edition) green (year, publisher) red
1972	limp	red	D/J (name, edition) red (year, publisher) black
1973	limp	sky blue	D/J (name, edition) sky blue (year, publisher) red
1974	limp	green	D/J (name, edition) green (year, publisher) red
1975	limp	brown	D/J (name, edition) red (year, publisher) black
1976	limp	red	D/J (name, edition) black (year, publisher) sky blue
1977	limp	dark blue	D/J (name, edition) green (year, publisher) red
1978	limp	brown	D/J (name#, year, publisher) black (edition) red

Cricketers' Almanack also appears in red

COLOURING OF DUST JACKET COVERS
FROM 1965–78

1965	The woodcut and border follows the described pattern of colours above for 'edition'. Other text is in the alternative colour.
1966–69	The woodcut and border follows the described pattern of colours above for 'year'. Other text is in the alternative colour.
1970, 1974	The woodcut, border and publisher's text follows the described pattern of colours above for 'edition'. Other text is in the alternative colour.
1971–73, 1975–77	The woodcut, border and publisher's text follows the described pattern of colours above for 'year'. Other text is in the alternative colour.
1978	Year and selected lines in red, the remainder in black.

Note: Wisden's official replacement dust wrappers for this period, issued from 1998, are laminated in the style of 1994–date, and have no coloured text. Fakes in the form of colour photocopies have been occasionally sighted. Genuine dust jackets of the period 1965–1981 are printed on thick yellow paper so will not be white on the reverse. However, the jackets for 1982–1984 and 2003 are white on the reverse.

In 1995, a special leatherbound edition was first printed, in a limited run of 100 copies. The quantity was increased to 150 copies in 1996 and has remained the same since. The first five copies are given to each of the Five Cricketers of the Year, Brian Lara being the first recipient in 1995. Each edition is signed by the editor on the title page, and housed in a slipcase. The books are finely bound in red leather with decorative gilt titles and gilt-edged pages.

LARGE FORMAT EDITIONS

In 2006 a large-format octavo edition was published (an idea first mooted twenty years previously) in a limited edition of 5,000 copies. The format is now published each year but unlimited. The volumes for 2006 and 2007 were supplied in a yellow slipcase, but since 2008 the books are sold alone. Each copy contains a ribbon bookmark and is cased in the familiar dust jacket.

FACSIMILE EDITIONS

1961	A facsimile reprint (limited to 150 sets) of the issues from 1864–78 was published by Billings & Son
1974	A facsimile reprint (limited to 150 sets) of the issues from 1864–78 was published by Lowe & Brydone
1991	A numbered hardbound reprint (limited to 1,000 sets) of the issues from 1864–78 was published by John Wisden & Co
Willows	All editions from 1879–1936 and 1940–45 have been reprinted to date (and 1937–39 due by 2012) in varying quantities as both facsimiles of the original hardbacks (from 1896) and facsimiles of the original paperbacks, bound in tan boards; 1940–45 have also been reprinted in limp linen format.

WISDEN ANTHOLOGIES

- Wisden *Anthology* 1864–1900, edited by Benny Green; Queen Anne Press, 1979
- Wisden *Anthology* 1900–40, edited by Benny Green; Queen Anne Press, 1980
- Wisden *Anthology* 1940–63, edited by Benny Green; Queen Anne Press, 1982
- Wisden *Anthology* 1963–82, edited by Benny Green' Queen Anne Press, 1983
- *The Illustrated* Wisden *Anthology* 1864–1988, edited by Benny Green; Macdonald & Co for Marks & Spencer, 1988
- *Endless Summer: 140 Years of Australian Cricket in* Wisden, edited by Gideon Haigh; Hardie Grant Books (Melbourne) 2002
- *Wisden Anthology 1978–2006: Cricket's Age of Revolution*, edited by Stephen Moss; John Wisden & Co Ltd, 2006. Also published in a leatherbound limited edition of 300, signed by Stephen Moss and three Wisden editors: Matthew Engel, Tim de Lisle and Graeme Wright

- *Wisden on the Ashes*, edited by Steven Lynch; A&C Black (Bloomsbury Publishing Ltd), 2009
- *Wisden on India*, edited by Jonathan Rice; A&C Black (Bloomsbury Publishing Ltd), 2011
- *Wisden on Yorkshire*, edited by Duncan Hamilton; A&C Black (Bloomsbury Publishing Ltd), 2011

WISDEN INDEXES

- *An Index to Wisden Cricketers' Almanack 1864–1943*, compiled by Rex Pogson; Sporting Handbooks Ltd, 1944
- *An Index to Wisden Cricketers' Almanack 1864–1984*, compiled by Derek Barnard; Queen Anne Press, 1985

WISDEN AUSTRALIA

A dedicated *Wisden Cricketers' Almanack* for Australia was published between 1998–2006. Eight issues were printed, the first six in distinctive green covers and dust jackets; the last two had pictorial dust jackets. The first issue was edited by Gideon Haigh and covered the season of 1997–98. For the third edition the numbering sequence was altered to reflect the Australian season, and was titled 2000–01. Each issue kept the general format and style of *Wisden*, but concentrated on domestic and first grade cricket, and selected just one *Cricketer of the Year*. All eight issues were also available in special green leatherbound editions limited to 100 copies each.

WISDEN INDIA

The 2004–09 editions were also printed locally in India for the Asian market. All were produced as paperbacks using different paper, and all had the local publisher's imprint on the spine and back cover. Details and variations from the UK edition are:

2004: Macmillan India, price Rs 585

2005: Macmillan India, price Rs 685
Front cover image and back cover wording different

2006: Macmillan India, price Rs 650
Only 12 colour plates, omitting the 12 Ashes colour plates
Front cover image and back cover wording different

2007: Macmillan India, price Rs 765
The two colour plate sections each had only 8 pages rather than 12, thus 8 colour plates were omitted
Back cover wording different

2008: Penguin India, price Rs 799
No colour plates
Back cover wording different from UK version

2009: Penguin India, price Rs 999
No colour plates

WISDEN RUGBY FOOTBALL ALMANACKS

Three editions of the *Rugby Football Almanack* were published, covering 1923–24, 1924–25 and 1925–26. They followed a similar style to the *Cricketers' Almanack*, including the typography on the wrappers, except the paper wrappers were blue. All three were edited by C. Stewart Caine who took over editorship of the 1926 *Wisden* after the death of Sydney Pardon.

CONDITION TIMELINE

Collectors will want to obtain copies in the best condition that their budget allows. Prices are very dependent on condition, and descriptions of books for sale should detail all faults and refer to any restoration such as regilding or repairs to hinges. The purist may prefer an original with all its faults to a smartly restored copy.

The following is a guide to changes in production over the years and some of the problems that may be encountered. For example, if you are looking at a scarce (and therefore expensive) 1916 hardback, do not expect to find bright gilding on the spine, but also do not worry that there is no photoplate, because there wasn't one in this year, nor in 1917. Perfect copies of all editions do exist, but they command a substantial premium.

1864–78	Copies with complete paperback spines are hard to find and the books tend to spot ('foxing'), especially to the early and late pages. These first 15 volumes are by far the scarcest in original condition.
1875	There are three variants: 212 pages, 214 pages and 214 pages with an extra blank page at the end (making 216 pages).
1876	String was used next to the spine to hold this edition together so they are usually more complete and tightly bound than other early years.
1878–79	For two years the covers had a shine to them; this causes the lettering to fade badly and a lot of covers have almost no text remaining, so it is hard to find with near mint covers.
1878	The rear cover is an advertisement for Wisden's *Oxford v Cambridge* book which was published in 1877: the *Wisden* facsimile copy produced in 1991 has the wrong back page.
1879	More common than the first 15 but still scarce.

1880s	This decade (and one assumes from 1864), the binding behind the spine paper is about one centimetre from the top and the bottom of the book; this rubs the spine paper away at the string position, and original paperbacks will be found with the top and bottom of the paper missing due to this sheering.
1887	First edition with lettering on the spine.
1887–88	The spine tends to darken; shows up clearly next to the 1886 and 1889 editions.
1889	First edition to contain a photoplate which was also protected with thin tissue paper. Photoplates and tissue paper tend to have foxing in all early editions; the tissue paper tends to fox more because of the chemical residue of the photoplate. The plate appears up to 1915.
1889–1901	Two editions were produced, which has no effect on their current value, although the second issue (noted as such on the cover and title page) cost more than the first when new.
1896	Hardbacks were introduced and the first four years are very scarce, becoming less so up to 1915. Although 1903 can be difficult to find, 'the earlier, the scarcer' is true.
1896–1915	The early hardbacks have held their condition well considering their age: gilt is usually bright and hinges generally hold up (except 1903–04), but given their value a hinge is worth repairing, and the repair is usually obvious. The yellow pages to the front and back can separate as the glue dries out. The spine cloth sometimes wrinkles in line with the lettering.
1898	It is possible that two versions of the photoplate exist.
1903	The hinges on the hardback edition were not strengthened in the usual way. If you look behind the yellow pages you can usually see a hinge strengthener, but this was missing in 1903, hence broken hinges are very common for this year
1904	The hinges are as per 1903 but only one hinge tends to break.
1904–05	On the paperback the word 'Almanack' is missing the 'k'.
1904 onwards	The publishers claim the photos are 'in a more permanent form' and they certainly fade much less than in earlier copies.
1915	The last year with a protective tissue paper for the photoplate. It did not return in 1918 with the new style of photograph.
1916	If the spine gilt is bright, then take care that it has not been regilded. The letters used on the 1916 spine (and in some cases the front cover) were without the usual gold plating and so seem dulled. Also, there is no full stop after the date on the spine (twice) and cover; restorers have made the mistake of inserting it.
1916–1917	No photoplate was issued with these two editions.
1918	The photograph returns but is no longer a photographic plate.

1919	The yellow pastedowns in 1919 (and 1920) tend to be a little darker than normal. All 1919 copies have two-toned pages: around page 163 the pages switch from lighter page edges to darker, which can be seen by looking at the page block.
1920–22	Paperbacks have browny/orangey covers which have the colour printed on white card rather than the all-yellow card before and after.
1921	The last of the scarce hardbacks from 1916 onwards; the 1916 is the most expensive, but 1919 is the hardest to locate.
1922	The cover of the hardback is rarely seen in immaculate condition; it is usually darker and rougher than 1921 and 1923.
1923	An oddity is that the yellow pastedowns on the hardback have a tendency to fade to white around the edges.
1924	The paperback covers and the pastedowns for the hardback tend to be paler than the rest of the 1920s *Wisdens* due to poorer yellow dye. This has also been seen in 1923.
1928–30	These books are behemoths. As a result, the paperbacks often have broken spines, and even the hardbacks buckle under their own weight; they also tend to have the odd bubble under the spine cloth.
1933–36	The plating of the lettering on the hardback changed from gold to copper, resulting in faded gilt to the cover and spine. A collector needs a sharp eye to spot replacement spine gilt that is not mentioned in the sale description.
1933–39	Within the paperback *Wisdens* there is a bookmark in the shape of a bat which is attached by string to the spine; these can go missing or commonly the handle of the bat is torn or removed. Collectors believe a full bat bookmark holds a premium: in reality, the reason for this may be that a book with a full bookmark has not been so well read and therefore is in better condition, and it is this that drives up the price rather than the bookmark alone – it is rare to see a complete bookmark in a tatty copy. Some hardbacks have been seen with a bookmark, but these have been moved across from a paperback.
1934	The rarest of the 1930s editions, probably because it covers the Bodyline series.
1936	Print runs of the paperback editions are known thanks to Gutteridge, *see* page 333 (and from 1941 for the hardback).
1937	The last of the old-style hardbacks (with gilt usually better than on the 1933–36 editions) and the last year of the paperbacks.
1938	The new-style hardback has blank pages at the front and the rear which at first glance make it look like a rebind. The spine gilt tends to be poor. Paper wrappers are replaced by linen cloth.
1938–40	The linen editions tend to bow to the spine. The 1938 linen was issued with a red paper band around it and it usually perished (the 1939 had

a green band); copies with the band sell for more, but still nowhere near the price of a hardback.

1939 Owners had a terrible urge to colour in the L of the LBW in the whisky ad on page 3. The hinges are weak and show through the mesh; spine gilt is usually poor.

1940 One of the hardest hardbacks to find in reasonable condition, as with 1947 and 1948. Gilt is very poor and is often replaced to front and spine; the hinges are weak and the spine cloth can split.

1941–46 The linen editions brush up well due to fewer pages but can spot on the spine cloth. The hardbacks, especially 1943 and 1944, have faded spine lettering and many have had this replaced; this can be hard to spot unless you have an original to compare it with, so if in doubt, ask the seller. Of these war years, 1941 is the rarest and 1942 is much scarcer than 1943 to 1945. The latter three have a similar value, although 1945 is the hardest to find. For 1941 to 1948 the spine gilt runs parallel to the spine; this has also been seen on 1949 to 1951, but generally from 1949 to date the lettering runs across the top of the spine.

1946 The hardback has two styles – the standard brown hardback, known as the 'red', and also an 'orange' version which is rarer, but values are similar as the 'orange' books appear faded and look out of place.

1947 Paper restrictions were still in place when a cheap acidic newsprint was used. The linen cloth edition comes in two sizes, with good or poor paper, the latter nearly twice as thick. The hardbacks (always in a larger size) have a high percentage of poorly made copies, with hinges that break readily and spine gilt that fades. The spine cloth on the linen edition can fade, and the spine itself tends to be straight. Hardbacks are difficult to find in near mint condition.

1948 These have the same problems as 1947 but with an added defect that a block of pages is much darker (around pages 45 to 556).

1949 The hardback boards are generally of different material to the rest of the 1950s, and the same cloth has been seen for 1950.

1949 onwards Linen editions from 1949 can show bowing to the spine.

1950–57 The spine gilt tends to fade on the early 1950s hardbacks, which often also suffer from broken hinges. Due to their lower prices today, these tend not to be repaired. Also in this era, the pages behind the boards tend to go brown.

1956–57 The hardbacks may have a problem with the spine cloth, which tends to 'bobble' and can cover the whole spine, although you can find copies without the bobbling.

1957 Copies tend to be rarer than others in this decade as a result of the Laker 19-wicket factor. From 1957, linens are technically 'cloth-effect soft card'.

1960	The hardback may have wrinkling to the edge of the spine, as in 1956 and 1957 and other years.
1963	The linen 100th *Wisden* is huge and the spine is almost always bowed. The hardback can buckle under its own weight (also 1964). There were three editions (second and third impressions are stated on page 1127). The hardback was issued with a blue band around it stating '100th edition!'
1965	First year of the dust jacket, which tends to spot, but the bigger problem is that it may not to be present at all: collectors were not so keen on the garish yellow next to their set of brown books, and hence many were discarded.
1968	The spine on the dust jacket tends to be a little dark.
1970–72	These years, and especially 1971, are rarer than others in the 1970s, but print runs are not known.
1975–76	The quality of the dust jackets is poorer than the years around them.
1979	Colour typography used on the dust jackets for the last time. Jackets are black and yellow from 1980 onwards.
Early 1980s	The early years of this decade were made of poor materials, the pages usually brown and the dust jackets prone to tear and fade. For their size they are brittle, especially 1983 and 1984. Watch out for Book Club dust jackets (1984 and 1985). There is bright gilt to the plastic fabric 1982–84 editions. In 50 years' time a mint 1983 will be worth its weight in gold – and it has some weight.
1988	Wisden started using colour photographs and thinner, whiter paper.
1994	onwards The dust jackets were laminated so marks can easily be removed with a damp cloth – but do not try this on 1993 or earlier. Most books are near mint after 1994.
1995	The paper gets even thinner.
2000	Issued free with the Almanack was a copy of *A Century of Wisden* (208 pages) containing an extract from every edition 1900–99, edited by Christopher Lane. It was also sold separately for £5.99.
2002	Issued free with the Almanack was a copy of *The Best: The 40 Leading Cricketers in the World Today* (64 pages), edited by Tim de Lisle. It was marked: 'This book is not to be offered for sale in any circumstances.'
2003	The dust jacket may fade on the spine. This is the first year with a photograph on the front of the dust jacket, but jackets in the original style are available for 2003 and onwards.
2005	There was a circular black sticker on the cover, or if removed, there may be a faded circular mark. It read: 'England's Record-Breaking Year: The Full Story'.

Collectors may wish to form a strategy for purchasing copies dependent on condition. The commentary above shows how difficult (and therefore expensive) it is to buy copies in mint condition. Most collectors will settle for what is best within their budget. Alternatively, you may decide that the quickest way to complete a set is to grab any copy you can, and upgrade later.

You will also have to decide whether to collect hardbacks, paperbacks / linens, rebinds or a mixture. If the decision is to collect hardbacks, finances will probably dictate that at some stage you will have to settle for switching to paperbacks or rebinds; in any case, you have to do this at 1895. Popular choices for making the switch from the last hardback are 1946, 1938, 1920 and 1900.

And when do you accept that you have to settle for a rebind or facsimile copy for that hard-to-find edition? Today, the first 15 editions are out of reach of all but the super-rich or lottery winners. Somewhere from 1879 onwards lies the choice between an expensive original or an attainable rebind or reprint.

PRICES / AUCTIONS TIMELINE

Wisden watchers have been regularly shocked over the years as new sales records have been recorded. As long ago as 1936, John Goldman thought that prices achieved for the first 15 volumes were 'fantastic'. We continue to be shocked today as the bidding takes *Wisden* prices to new peaks – but perhaps not surprised. There are a finite number of sets in circulation, and each new generation brings more collectors to the chase. The investment 'bubble' may from time to time deflate slightly, as economies flourish or fall into recession, but the overall trend heads ever upwards.

The prices below include buyer's premium and VAT, unless the hammer price is given, which is denoted by (h).

1899   Set (1864–98) advertised for £10 in catalogue issued by A.J. Gaston of the library of T. Padwick.

1909   Catalogue of A. Maurice & Co, of Covent Garden, London, lists the rarer editions at 5s. each.

1925   Gaston catalogue has a bound set (1864–1924) at 50 guineas.

1936   Collector J.W. Goldman writes in *The Cricketer*: 'Editions from 1864 to 1878 have realised at auction even fantastic prices, but, in my view, anybody who can get hold of these first 15 volumes for £20 in proper condition could get a bargain. Apart from these, the only two numbers of any real value are 1889 and 1916, which are worth £3 or £5 per piece.'

1937   Sotheby's auction of J.A.H. Catton's library has a set (1864–1936) and 11 duplicate volumes which fetches £33.

1954   Hodgson & Co, of Chancery Lane, London, auctions a set (1864–1953) for £145.

1955	Epworth Books list: '*Wisden* complete 1864–1954. Once the property of A.D. Taylor. Volume One loose in cover, else a good set. £150'
1963	Leslie Gutteridge (of Epworth Books) writes in *Wisden*: 'The present accepted price for a set in good condition and collated as complete is £250.' When Gutteridge emigrated to Canada in 1967, he sold his set to the publishers for about £150.
1973	Set purchased for £750 from J.W. McKenzie by Tim Rice (*see* page ix).
1979	A run of 97 (1864–1969, lacking nine pre-1900) sells at auction for £4,200.
1980	Sir Pelham Warner's set (1864–1963) sells at auction for £7,800. David Frith writes in 1981 *Wisden*: 'Even the auctioneer gulped as bidding reached this unexpected peak. It should be remembered, too, that 11.5 per cent had to be added as buyer's premium plus VAT.'
1985	At Phillips, 1864–1985 make £7,000 (h).
1986	A set sells for £15,565 at the G.B. Buckley sale in Bristol.
1991	John Arlott's set is broken up and sells at Christie's for £22,160 (h); 1864–66 bound together go for £6,800 (h).
1992	At Christie's, 1875 and 1876 bound together (no covers) go for £4,180.
1993	At Phillips sale in April, 1864 fetches £4,000 and 1865 and 1866 over £3,000 each. At Phillips sale in October, set withdrawn at £21,000 against estimate of £25–£30,000. 1864 (with covers detached and some staining) sells for £2,700. The set was later sold in 39 lots for £25,450 (h).
1993	At Christie's, a set based on Sir Pelham Warner's collection is withdrawn at £22,000.
1994	Bonhams sells 1875 for £2,180.
1995	Hal Cohen Collection sold at Phillips: top prices (h) are £2,900 for 1869, £2,800 for 1875, £2,700 for 1864 (lacking front wrapper, torn end wrapper, some pages loose and taped) and £2,500 each for 1866 and 1867. The first fifteen make £24,000.
1996	The 'ultimate combination' of a run (1864–1915) with many copies signed by W.G. Grace goes for £94,100 at Bearne's in Exeter; first 38 editions bound in half calf. David Frith described the set, sold by Grace's descendants, as 'the most desirable *Wisdens* ever offered.'
1998	At Christie's, 1896 original hardback sells for £3,220, 1897 and 1901 for £2,990.
1999	Set goes for £29,500.
2000	At Phillips, 1864 sells for £8,400 and 1866 for £5,400.
2000	At Christie's, 1875 for £4,700.
2002	At Christie's, set sells for £41,125 (some rebound, some lacking adverts); a separate 1864 makes £6,345 and 1875 £4,935.
2002	At Christie's, 1874 and 1875 bound together sell for £5,875.
2002	At Christie's, 1875 sells for £4,935.

2003	Bonhams sale of B.J. Wakley collection: individual copies, highest price of £6,931 for 1869, while 1875 (lacking lower wrappers) goes for £5,019.
2005	At Christie's, run of the first 70 (1864–1933) sell for over £80,000 (h) – almost £100,000 with the buyer's premium.
2005	At Christie's, 1872–75 bound together sell for £20,400.
2006	New York-based internet auctioneers igavel sell Karl Auty library in Canada: rebound 1875 fetches $48,000 (£24,000).
2007	At Graham Budd Auctions in association with Sotheby's: set (1864–1999) goes for £120,000 (h). All rebound in green cloth boards with gilt titling to spine; 1864–1953 with the original wrappers preserved (with some exceptions) and from 1954 without covers; the 1873 and 1875 editions in non-uniform brown bindings.
2007	At Knight's, the first hardback year of 1896 sells for £21,000 (h).
2007	At Christie's, Pelham Warner's 1864–67 rebound in one volume sells for £42,000.
2008	At Bonhams, a set 1864–2007 uniformly bound in half morocco sells for £84,000; included was sufficient goatskin to continue the same binding through to 2030.
2010	At Knight's, rebound 1875 lacking wrappers sells for £10,000, rebound 1864 lacking wrappers £6,500 (h).
2010	At Dreweatts, from Glamorgan CCC collection, 1866–69 bound in one volume, lacking end wrappers, sells for £18,000 (h).
2010	Graham Budd sells rebound set 1864–2009 for £10,000 (h). Only four of first 15 editions were originals; many years without wrappers.
2010	At Christie's, 1872–75 rebound in one volume from MCC collection sells for £30,000 (h).

Sources: *Wisden Cricketers' Almanack* (various), *The Wisden Book of Cricket Memorabilia* (1990) by Marcus Williams and Gordon Phillips, magazines of the Cricket Memorabilia Society edited by Keith Hayhurst, auction catalogues.

PAGINATION GUIDE

The pagination used by *Wisden* has changed over time, and to avoid confusion a consistent approach has been taken where possible. The front cover was first included in the page-count in 1898. The paperback rear cover and endpaper advertisements in pre-1938 hardbacks are not counted. The advertisement on the inside rear cover was not always counted in Gutteridge's 1963 notation, but in 1906 the page was numbered, so for consistency it has been included from 1906 onwards. Some editions have extra pages in the sequence, for example in 1940, page 31, 31a, 31b, 31c,31d; these are noted as '+4' *etc.*

[**Square brackets**] Denotes unnumbered pages – advertisements for example – or occasional blank pages in early editions.

[**pp**] Denotes unnumbered photograph or colour advertisement pages in modern editions.

* Denotes largest issue to date.

Year	Pages	Total
1864	[4]+112	(116)*
1865	[4]+160	(164)*
1866	[4]+195+[1]	(200)*
1867	[4]+159+[1]	(164)
1868	[4]+112	(116)
1869	[4]+120	(124)
1870	152	(152)
1871	152	(152)
1872	172	(172)
1873	208	(208)*
1874	180	(180)
1875	214/214	(212/214)* *see note a*
1876	224	(224)*
1877	248	(248)*
1878	250	(250)*
1879	241+[5]	(246) *see note b*
1880	[2]+216+[18]	(236)
1881	[2]+228+[10]	(240)
1882	[2]+212+[10]	(224)
1883	[2]+284+[18]	(304)*
1884	[2]+268+[18]	(288)
1885	[2]+290+[20]	(312)*
1886	[2]+360+[22]	(384)*
1887	[2]+xx+308+[18]	(348)
1888	[2]+xxviii+362+[20]	(412)*
1889	[2]+xl+356+[22]	(420)*

Year	Pages	Total
1890	[2]+lii+301+[21]	(376)
1891	xlvi+354+[20]	(420)
1892	lxii+330+[20]	(412)
1893	liv+376+[18]	(448)*
1894	lxxiv+390+[24]	(488)*
1895	lxxviii+386+[14]	(478)
1896	lxxviii+418+[28]	(524)*
1897	lxxxii+416+[30]	(528)*
1898	xciv+428+[24]	(546)*
1899	cxiv+438+[26]	(578)*
1900	cxii+506+[28]	(646)*
1901	cxx+477+[35]	(632)
1902	cxxxviii+536+[38]	(702)*
1903	cxl+532+[42]	(714)*
1904	cxl+492+[50]	(682)
1905	clxviii+528+[50]	(746)*
1906	clx+603	(763)*
1907	clxxviii (pt.1)+510 (pt.2)+[37]	(725)
1908	206 (pt.1)+575 (pt.2)	(781)*
1909	208 (pt.1)+563 (pt.2)	(771)
1910	212 (pt.1)+535+[2] (pt.2)	(749) *see note c*
1911	216 (pt.1)+551 (pt.2)	(767)
1912	220 (pt.1)+567 (pt.2)	(787)*
1913	iv+236+2 (pt.1)+607 (pt.2)	(849)*
1914	iv+252 (pt.1)+543 (pt.2)	(799)
1915	iv+252 (pt.1)+535 (pt.2)	(791)
1916	299	(299)
1917	351	(351)
1918	339	(339)
1919	327	(327)
1920	xii+284 (pt.1)+431 (pt.2)	(727)
1921	272 (pt.1)+523 (pt.2)	(795)
1922	3+320 (pt.1)+675 (pt.2)	(998)*
1923	3+360+4 (pt.1)+607 (pt.2)	(974)
1924	328+2 (pt.1)+683+2 (pt.2)	(1015)*
1925	4+336+2 (pt.1)+615 (pt.2)	(957)
1926	12+340 (pt.1)+679 (pt.2)	(1031)*
1927	350 (pt.1)+693 (pt.2)	(1043)*
1928	352 (pt.1)+711 (pt.2)	(1063)*
1929	308 (pt.1)+707 (pt.2)	(1015)
1930	320 (pt.1)+739 (pt.2)	(1059)
1931	336 (pt.1)+731 (pt.2)	(1067)*

Year	Pages	Total
1932	312 (pt.1)+723 (pt.2)	(1035)
1933	12 (pt.1)+719 (pt.2)	(1031)
1934	338 (pt.1)+721 (pt.2)	(1059)
1935	336 (pt.1)+711 (pt.2)	(1047)
1936	356 (pt.1)+679 (pt.2)	(1035)
1937	340 (pt.1)+715 (pt.2)	(1055)
1938	990+8+[1]	(999)
1939	958+8+[1]	(967)
1940	871+4	(875)
1941	426	(426)
1942	391	(391)
1943	03+4	(407)
1944	343	(343)
1945	367	(367)
1946	xvi+463	(479)
1947	xxxii+715	(747)
1948	xxxii+843	(875)
1949	viii+935	(943)
1950	viii+1003	(1011)
1951	xvi+1019	(1035)
1952	viii+1031	(1039)
1953	xx+1015	(1035)
1954	xx+999	(1019)
1955	xx+1011	(1031)
1956	xxxii+1043	(1075)*
1957	xxxii+1019	(1051)
1958	xxxvi+1035	(1071)
1959	xlviii+1011	(1059)
1960	iv+1023	(1027)
1961	viii+1019	(1027)
1962	iv+1063	(1067)
1963	xlviii+1131	(1179)*
1964	xxviii+1027	(1055)
1965	xxiv+1043	(1067)
1966	xl+1043	(1083)
1967	xxxii+1043	(1075)
1968	xxxii+1079	(1111)
1969	xl+1055	(1095)
1970	xxxvi+1091	(1127)
1971	xxiv+1103	(1127)
1972	xxxii+1123	(1155)
1973	xxviii+1083	(1111)

Year	Pages	Total
1974	xlvi+1147	(1193)*
1975	xx+1143	(1163)
1976	lii+1171	(1223)*
1977	iv+1123	(1127)
1978	xii+1151	(1163)
1979	xxiv+1155	(1179)
1980	xxiv+1239	(1263)*
1981	iv+1231	(1235)
1982	xii+1299	(1311)*
1983	iv+[12pp]+1331	(1347)*
1984	iv+[12pp]+1291	(1307)
1985	[3]+[12pp]+1280+[3]	(1298)
1986	[3]+[12pp]+1296+[3]	(1314)
1987	[3]+xii+1296	(1311)
1988	[3]+xii+1296+[3]	(1314)
1989	[3]+xii+1264+[2pp]+[2]	(1283)
1990	[3]+xii+1296+[4pp]+[3]	(1318)
1991	[3]+xii+1360+[4pp]+[3]	(1382)*
1992	[3]+xii+1344+[3]	(1362)
1993	[3]+xii+1376+[3]	(1394)*
1994	[3]+xii+1424+[4pp]+[3]	(1446)*
1995	[3]+xii+1424+[2pp]+[3]	(1444)
1996	[3]+xii+1440+[2pp]+[3]	(1460)*
1997	[3]+xii+1440+[2pp]+[3]	(1460)
1998	[3]+xii+1472+[2pp]+[3]	(1492)*
1999	[3]+xxiv+1520+[3]	(1550)*
2000	[3]+xxxii+1600+[3]	(1638)*
2001	[3]+xvi+1648+[3]	(1670)*
2002	[3]+xvi+1632+[3]	(1654)
2003	[3]+[16pp]+1760+[3]	(1782)*
2004	[16pp]+1648+[3]	(1667)
2005	[16pp]+1744+[3]	(1763)
2006	[24pp]+1600+[3]	(1627)
2007	[24pp]+1664+[3]	(1691)
2008	[16pp]+1680+[3]	(1699)
2009	[16pp]+1680+[2]	(1698)
2010	[16pp]+1728+[3]	(1747)
2011	[24pp]+0000+[3]	(0000)

Notes:
a. The two unnumbered pages in 1875 are blank, and often presumed lost when rebinding.
b. 1879 has a variant edition with the first advertisement unnumbered, making 240+[6].
c. In 1910 the unnumbered page is opposite p142 (pt.2), or placed nearby in some copies.

PRICES

Book and Magazine Collector carried articles about *Wisden Cricketers' Almanacks* in the issues of May 1984 and June 1993. Both included price guides to the then current values of copies listed in 'very good' condition in their original cloth or wrappers. These are given here, together with an indication of values at February 2011 based on prices achieved within the previous year for 'very-good-quality' copies. Buyers should note that these prices are to be taken as estimates only, and that condition is paramount in assessing the value of *Wisdens*.

HC: Hard-cloth covers
SC: Paper or linen wrappers
Rebind: Rebound without original covers, for first 15 editions

Year	1984		1993		2011		
	HC	SC	HC	SC	HC	SC	Rebind
1864	–	900	–	3–5k	–	25k	12k
1865	–	550	–	2.5–3.5k	–	10k	6k
1866	–	n/a	–	2.5–3.5k	–	10k	6k
1867	–	n/a	–	2–2.5k	–	10k	6k
1868	–	n/a	–	1–1.5k	–	10k	6k
1869	–	800	–	1–1.5k	–	15k	10k
1870	–	n/a	–	1–1.5k	–	7k	2.5k
1871	–	n/a	–	400–500	–	7k	2.5k
1872	–	n/a	–	400–500	–	6k	2.5k
1873	–	n/a	–	300–400	–	5k	2.5k
1874	–	n/a	–	350–450	–	5k	3.5k
1875	–	480	–	1.5–2k	–	35k	15k
1876	–	300	–	400–600	–	5k	2k
1877	–	300	–	500–700	–	3k	2k
1878	–	320	–	300–400	–	2.5k	2k
1879	–	250	–	400–500	–	1k	
1880	–	250	–	300–400	–	1k	
1881	–	250	–	200–300	–	1k	
1882	–	250	–	200–300	–	1k	
1883	–	250	–	200–300	–	1k	
1884	–	250	–	200–300	–	1k	
1885	–	250	–	200–300	–	900	
1886	–	250	–	200–300	–	900	
1887	–	240	–	200–300	–	800	
1888	–	220	–	200–300	–	800	
1889	–	200	–	300–400	–	900	
1890	–	160	–	150–200	–	750	

	1984			1993			2011		
Year	HC	SC	HC	SC	HC	SC	Rebind
1891	–	140	–	150–200	–	600	
1892	–	120	–	150–200	–	500	
1893	–	100	–	150–200	–	500	
1894	–	90	–	150–200	–	500	
1895	–	75	–	150–200	–	350	
1896	80	60	300–400	150–200	25k	500	
1897	80	60	300–400	150–200	12k	400	
1898	70	50	300–400	150–200	10k	275	
1899	65	50	300–400	150–200	10k	275	
1900	60	45	200–300	100–150	4k	250	
1901	60	40	200–300	100–150	3k	200	
1902	60	35	200–300	100–150	3k	200	
1903	60	35	200–300	100–150	2.5k	200	
1904	60	35	200–300	100–150	1.5k	200	
1905	60	35	200–300	100–150	1.5k	200	
1906	60	35	200–300	100–150	1.5k	200	
1907	60	32	200–300	100–150	1.5k	200	
1908	55	30	200–300	100–150	1.5k	200	
1909	55	28	200–300	100–150	1.5k	200	
1910	50	27	200–300	100–150	1.5k	150	
1911	50	25	200–300	100–150	1.5k	150	
1912	50	27	200–300	100–150	1k	150	
1913	50	27	200–300	100–150	950	150	
1914	50	25	200–300	100–150	950	150	
1915	50	25	200–300	100v150	950	150	
1916	100	80	500–800+	400–600+	7.5k	900	
1917	70	40	250–350	100–150	4k	400	
1918	70	40	250–350	100–150	4k	400	
1919	70	40	250–350	100–150	4.5k	450	
1920	50	25	100–150	80–100	1.5k	200	
1921	50	27	100–150	80–100	1k	175	
1922	50	25	100–150	80–100	750	150	
1923	50	25	100–150	80–100	750	150	
1924	50	25	100–150	80–100	750	150	
1925	50	25	100–150	80–100	750	150	
1926	50	25	100–150	80–100	750	150	
1927	50	27	100–150	80–100	750	150	
1928	50	25	100–150	80–100	750	200	
1929	50	27	100–150	80–100	750	200	
1930	50	30	150–200	100–120	750	150	

Year	1984		1993		2011		Rebind
	HC	SC	HC	SC	HC	SC	
1931	50	30	150–200	100–120	750	150	
1932	50	28	150–200	100–120	750	150	
1933	50	30	150–200	100–120	750	150	
1934	50	30	150–200	100–120	800	225	
1935	50	28	150–200	100–120	750	150	
1936	45	27	150–200	100–120	750	150	
1937	45	30	150–200	100–120	750	150	
1938	45	30	150–200	100–120	800	125	
1939	45	30	150–200	100–120	800	125	
1940	55	33	150–200	100–120	1400	200	
1941	70	37	300–400	150–200	1500	350	
1942	70	37	150–180	80–100	1250	250	
1943	50	30	200–300	120–160	500	175	
1944	35	30	150–250	100–120	500	175	
1945	30	25	100–120	50–80	500	150	
1946	25	20	50–80	40–60	200	75	
1947	20	18	50–80	40–60	150	40	
1948	16	16	50–80	40–60	150	40	
1949	16	14	50–80	40–60	75	30	
1950	10	8	50–80	40–60	50	20	
1951	10	8	15–25	14–18	50	20	
1952	10	8	15–25	14–18	50	20	
1953	10	8	15–25	14–18	50	20	
1954	10	8	15–25	14–18	50	20	
1955	10	8	15–25	14–18	50	20	
1956	10	8	15–25	14–18	50	20	
1957	10	8	15–25	14–18	55	20	
1958	10	8	15–25	14–18	50	20	
1959	10	8	15–25	14–18	50	20	
1960	11	9	15–25	14–18	50	20	
1961	11	9	15–25	14–18	50	25	
1962	11	9	15–25	14–18	50	25	
1963	11	9	15–25	14–18	40	20	
1964	11	9	15–25	14–18	40	20	
1965	11	9	15–25	14–18	70	20	
1966	11	9	15–25	14–18	55	20	
1967	11	9	15–25	14–18	50	20	
1968	11	9	15–25	14–18	50	20	
1969	11	9	15–25	14–18	50	20	
1970	13	9	20–30	15–20	55	20	

| | 1984 | | 1993 | | 2011 | | |
Year	HC	SC	HC	SC	HC	SC	Rebind
1971	13	9	25–35	15–25	75	25	
1972	10	9	10–15	5–8	50	20	
1973	13	10	10–15	5–8	50	20	
1974	13	10	10–15	5–8	45	20	
1975	12	10	10–15	5–8	40	20	
1976	10	8	10–15	5–8	30	15	
1977	10	8	10–15	5–8	20	15	
1978	8	6	10–15	5--8	15	10	
1979	6	5	10–15	5–8	15	10	
1980	6	5	10–15	5–8	15	10	
1981	6	5	10–15	5–8	15	10	
1982	6	5	10–15	5–8	15	10	
1983	8	7	10–15	5–8	15	10	
1984	-	-	10–15	5–8	15	10	
1985	-	-	10–15	5–8	15	10	
1986	-	-	10–15	5–8	15	10	
1987	-	-	10–15	5–8	15	10	
1988	-	-	10–15	5–8	15	10	
1989	-	-	10–15	5–8	15	10	
1990	-	-	10–15	5–8	12	6	
1991	-	-	10–15	5–8	12	6	
1992	-	-	10–15	5–8	12	6	

Values for more recent years are not given as copies in very good or even mint condition can generally be found at £20 or less.